SOLUTIONS

SOLUTIONS

Lauren Hartman

THE WOMAN'S CRISIS HANDBOOK

Houghton Mifflin Company

Boston New York

1997

For information about permission to reproduce
selections from this book, write to Permissions,
215 Park Avenue South, New York, New York 10003.

Library of Congress Cataloging-in-Publication Data

Hartman, Lauren.
    Solutions : the woman's crisis handbook / Lauren
Hartman.
      p.   cm.
    Includes bibliographical references and index.
    ISBN 0-395-70739-0
    1. Women—United States—Life skills guides.
2. Women—United States—Psychology.
3. Women—Health and hygiene—United States.
I. Title.
HQ1904.H37   1998
646.7'0082—dc21   97-29472   CIP

Book design by Anne Chalmers
Typeface is Linotype-Hell Fairfield Medium

Printed in the United States of America

QUM 10 9 8 7 6 5 4 3 2 1

Contents

Acknowledgments   xi
Introduction   1

CHAPTER ONE: CRISES AT WORK

When You're Fired or Laid Off   4
Discrimination in the Workplace   18

CHAPTER TWO: CHILDREN IN CRISIS

Child Abuse and Neglect   44
When a Child Runs Away from Home   65
If Your Child Is Arrested   72
Loving Your Gay, Lesbian, or Bisexual Teen   82
Teenage Pregnancy: Young Women in Crisis   88

CHAPTER THREE: DIVORCE

How Much Do You Know About Divorce?   98
Divorce   99
Mediation   104
Dividing Property   107
Create a Budget for Future Expenses   111
Alimony   112
Social Security Benefits for Divorced Women   114
Welfare: Applying for Assistance   116
Child Custody   117
Helping Your Children Cope with Divorce   125
Child Support   127

CHAPTER FOUR: VIOLENCE AGAINST WOMEN

Rape   137
Domestic Violence   158
Stalking   183

CHAPTER FIVE: CRISES IN CONCEPTION AND SEXUALITY

Emergency Contraception   186
Facing an Unexpected Pregnancy   189
Abortion   190
Placing Your Infant for Adoption   201
Pregnancy and Infant Loss   222
Special Situations   231
Postpartum Depression   243
Sexually Transmitted Diseases   248

CHAPTER SIX: RESOURCES FOR ADULTS AND CHILDREN WITH DISABILITIES

PART ONE: Resources for Adults with Disabilities
    Finding Information and Assistance   265
    Medical Rehabilitation   267
    Medical Rehabilitation Professionals
            and the Services They Provide   269
    Paying for Rehabilitation   276
    Preparing for Your Return Home: Do You Have the
            Asistance You Need?   278
    Centers for Independent Living   279
    Going Back to Work: Vocational Rehabilitation   283
    Discrimination and Legal Assistance   288
    Protection and Advocacy Systems   293
    Tips on Applying for Benefits   297
    Workers' Compensation   298
PART TWO: Resources for Children with Disabilities
    Services for Newborns and Toddlers: Early
            Intervention   301
    Children Aged Three to Twenty-one: Special
            Education   306
    Head Start   311

EPSDT: Getting Health Services for
          Your Children   312
     Respite Care: Time Off for Caregivers   312

CHAPTER SEVEN: CRISES IN MENTAL HEALTH

Suicide Prevention   314
Getting Mental Health Care   321
Women and Alcohol and Other Drugs   349
Health Facts About Alcohol and Other Drugs   351

CHAPTER EIGHT: LIFE-THREATENING ILLNESS

Stroke   362
Women and Heart Disease   371
Hormone Replacement Therapy   378
Cancer and Resources for Information   380
HIV Infection and AIDS   384

CHAPTER NINE: CRISES IN AGING

Before a Crisis Occurs: Be Prepared   410
Your Keys to Information   411
When You Need Help at Home: Home Health Care   422
Alternative Housing   440
Nursing Homes and Alternative Housing Options   442
Nursing Home Care   449
Elder Abuse and Neglect   464

CHAPTER TEN: DEATH AND DYING

Support for People Who Are Terminally Ill and Their
          Families   471
Putting Paperwork in Order   474
Pain Control   488
Alternatives to Dying in the Hospital   490
Hospice   491
After the Death of a Loved One   495
Grief and Mourning   507

THE SOLUTIONS RESOURCE DIRECTORY

About the *Solutions* Resource Directory   517

CRISES AT WORK

Childcare   521
Environmental Health   521
Government Agencies   522
Job Resources for Women with Disabilities   523
Legal Resources   524
Work-Related Services   526

CHILDREN IN CRISIS

At-Risk Youth/Youth Development   526
Child Abuse and Neglect/Crisis Hotlines   528
Child Abuse and Neglect Services   529
Juvenile Justice Research   530
Legal Help and Advocacy for Children   531
Lesbian, Gay, and Bisexual Youth   531
Missing Children   532
Missing Children, International   533
Religious Organizations Serving Lesbian, Gay, and
              Bisexual People and Their Families   534
Runaway Hotlines and Services   534
Information About Runaways and Homeless Youth   534
Teen-Parent Education   535

DIVORCE

Alternative Dispute Resolution   535
Attorneys   535
Child Custody   536
Children's Grief   536
Child Support and Visitation   537
Office of Child Support Enforcement
              Regional Offices   537
Parents' Organizations   539
Pension Issues   540
Welfare System   540

VIOLENCE AGAINST WOMEN

Family Counseling   541
Hotlines   541

National Domestic Violence Coalition   542
Plastic Surgery for Victims of Violence   542
Research Resources/Publications   542

CRISES IN CONCEPTION

Emergency Contraception   543
Abortion Information/Reproductive Rights   543
Adoption   545
Infertility and Reproductive Health   546
Postpartum Depression   547
Pregnancy and Infant Loss   548
Sexually Transmitted Diseases   551

DISABILITIES

General Information and Referral   551
Caregivers/Families of Adults   552
Children and Students with Disabilities   552
Discrimination/Legal Help and Information   555
Home Adaptation   557
Independent Living   557
Library Program   557
Publications   557
Rehabilitation and Technology Resources   558
Social Security   559
Women with Disabilities   560
Veterans and Their Families   561
Disability-Specific Organizations   561

CRISES IN MENTAL HEALTH

Alcohol and Drug Information   581
Addictions/Recovery Groups   582
Consumer and Family Organizations   584
Family Service Agencies   586
Government Agencies   587
Hospital Accreditation   589
Professional Associations   589
Survivors of Abuse and Incest   591

LIFE-THREATENING ILLNESS

General Resources   592
Government Resources   593
AIDS/HIV Infection   595
Breast Implant Information   597

Cancer   597
Heart Disease and Stroke   601
Professional Organizations   602

CRISES IN AGING

General Information and Referral Services   603
Aging Organizations   603
Caregivers   605
Consumer Information   606
Government Resources   607
Home Care and Visiting Nurses   607
Legal Professionals   608
Nursing Homes and Assisted-Living Facilities   608

DEATH AND DYING

National Organizations   609
Complaints about Funeral Services   610
Grief/Emotional Support   610
Hospice Organizations   612

Recommended Reading   614
Notes   639
Index   646

Acknowledgments

I dedicate this book to the men in my life who have provided me with constant encouragement and inspiration: my father, John Loren Hartman, Esq., my grandfather, Fred A. Nilson, and my friend, Mark Rucker.

I would like to thank those who contributed to *Solutions: The Woman's Crisis Handbook.*

Tracey Alexander, for her vision, her intellectual contributions to this book's development, and her lasting friendship. I am indebted to her.

My agent, Faith Hamlin, for her kindhearted mentoring. She managed to focus a sprawling proposal into a work with direction and purpose.

The editors at Houghton Mifflin Company for their guidance, patience, and professionalism: Marnie Patterson Cochran, Gail Winston, Jane von Mehren, Susanna Brougham, and Dorothy Henderson. I also wish to thank Anne Chalmers for her excellent book design.

Lynn Napoli, M.D., for her assiduous, exacting research into the medical aspects of this book. I am indebted to her for the time that she gave this book from its inception through the final drafts, researching topics, answering my questions, and reviewing book material. It was because of her standards and devotion to the work that I was able to include valuable medical and related topics in this book.

Safini Convey, whose tireless dedication, thorough investigative research, and critical commentary helped to shape the book.

Susan Hartman, who not only developed the Resource Directory, assisted with research, and managed all of the business aspects of this book, but provided me with unflagging emotional support. She was always ready to discuss ways in which this book could assist the individual woman.

I also wish to acknowledge the memory of my grandmother Alvoy Nilson, a vibrant, beautiful woman whose love moves me still, and to thank Thomas Napoli, Lana Griffin, David Brown, Jane Lee, Ruth Rafidi, Laura Picard, Preston Wilson, Leslie Hagen, Jerry Jones, Edward Mickle, Ivan Roth, Paul Sandberg, Esq., Russell Garner, Charlene Suneson, Sumaya Wallace, Dante DiLoreto, Randy Paulos, Tony Enos, Camy, Amanda, and Pepper.

SPECIAL ACKNOWLEDGMENTS

Although as the author I bear the responsibility for the accuracy of the information presented in this book, I wish to acknowledge the professionals who gave their time to review and comment on book material in their field of expertise. Special thanks are due to Virginia Walther and Sloane Elman, who took an interest in this project from the start and who reviewed much of the material, contributing suggestions for its improvement. Without the help of these dedicated women, this book would not be possible.

Sloane Elman is vice president, Faculty Practice at Mount Sinai School of Medicine in New York City, where she is a member of the Women Faculty Group and serves on the steering committee of the Rape Crisis Intervention Program. Ms. Elman has practiced law as Associate General Counsel at the Mount Sinai Medical Center and as an associate at the law firm of Milbank, Tweed, Hadley & McCloy. She is a graduate of Vassar College and New York University School of Law.

Virginia Walther is senior assistant director of Social Work Services at the Mount Sinai Medical Center and assistant professor in the Department of Community Medicine at the Mount Sinai School of Medicine in New York City. Her research and clinical interests, as well as publications, are in the area of reproductive technologies' impact on women's health, the psychosocial consequences of chronic illnesses in families, and the empowerment of women as consumers of health care.

I am also indebted to the following professionals and organizations who have generously given their valuable time to review and comment on book material relevant to their area of expertise:

Nancy C. Aldridge, L.C.S.W., Executive/Clinical Director of the Georgia Center for Children.

Robyn Johnson-Alsop, Coordinator of Information Services and Publications Development for the Children's Division of the American Humane Association (AHA) and editor of *Protecting Children*, the division's quarterly publication. In addition to her information/library services, she serves as managing editor for all divisional publications. She has been with AHA since 1987. Ms. Johnson-Alsop received her master's degree in Librarianship and Information Services from the University of Denver and her bachelor's degree in sociology and English from Lycoming College in Pennsylvania.

Elizabeth C. Baxter, Coordinator, Senior and Chronic Care Services, Legacy Portland Hospitals.

Glen Blix, Dr.P.H., C.N.S., Associate Professor, Health Promotion and Education, School of Public Health, Loma Linda University.

Susan F. Buckley, Technical Assistance Specialist at the National Hospice Organization.

Trish Bukowski, Operations Director of Depression After Delivery, Inc.

Alana Calfee, Director of Home Care Aide Certification, Foundation for Hospice and Homecare.

The Center for Reproductive Law and Policy, founded on June 1, 1992, by a nationally recognized group of expert reproductive rights attorneys and activists. The Center is an independent organization dedicated to ensuring that all women have access to freely chosen reproductive health care. Its primary focus is on young women, low-income women, rural women, and women of color, whose reproductive health needs have been largely neglected.

Charlene Clemens, M.P.A., Division Director, Children, Youth and Families, Teenage Pregnancy and Parenting Project, Family Service Agency of San Francisco. Among her many and varied professional activities, she serves as northern chair of the Adolescent Family Life Providers Association and as an executive committee member of the San Francisco Perinatal Forum.

Dawn Dailey, R.N., M.S.N., has been working as a public health nurse for more than seven years. She is coordinator of the Contra Costa County SIDS Program and serves as consultant for the California SIDS Program. Ms. Dailey has provided support services for SIDS families for more than six years. She is the president of the Northern California Regional SIDS Advisory Council.

Susan Dudley, Ph.D., Access Initiative Director, National Abortion Federation (NAF). Ms. Dudley has been involved with reproductive issues throughout her career, from basic physiological research on reproduction to an NIH appointment in the Department of Ob-Gyn at Pennsylvania State

University Medical School to prochoice political work as a lobbyist and media spokesperson. She is directing NAF's efforts to increase access to legal abortion through a variety of initiatives and has written several of NAF's consumer publications.

Gwen Edelstein, R.N., C.P.N.P., M.P.A., has more than twenty-five years of nursing experience in a variety of public health areas, including maternal and child health. As a professional SIDS advocate, she joined the California SIDS Program nearly four years ago and has served as the program's director since February 1996. Under her leadership, the California SIDS Program strives to serve the needs of the SIDS community and to reduce the emotional suffering of those affected by a SIDS death while promoting education, awareness, training, and SIDS research.

Leslie J. Forbes, Executive Director of Options House, a Hollywood-based shelter for runaway and homeless teens.

Sara S. Hunt, A.C.S.W., a consultant on nursing home topics and consumer advocacy.

Sally Balch Hurme, Senior Legal Programs Specialist, Legal Counsel for the Elderly, AARP.

Geraldine Jensen, President of the Association for Children for Enforcement of Support.

Jean Kirkpatrick, Ph.D., Executive Director and Founder of Women for Sobriety, an organization and program for women alcoholics that has been providing services to women since 1976 and has self-help groups throughout the world.

Frances Kunreuther, Executive Director of the Hetrick-Martin Institute.

Susan Letteney, A.C.S.W., is the principal investigator of the Women's Project and co-director of Families in Transition of Beth Israel Medical Center in New York City. The programs provide education, support, and counseling, including permanency planning, for women faced with the challenges of HIV and AIDS.

Helen Lettlow, M.P.H., Director, Women's Health, American Social Health Association (ASHA). ASHA's mission is to stop sexually transmitted diseases and their harmful consequences to individuals, families, and communities.

Michelle Wilson Lewis, Probation Director, Los Angeles County Probation Department. Ms. Lewis has worked for thirty years in juvenile probation services, including court investigation, field supervision, detention, and residential treatment.

Pat McGinnis, Executive Director of the California Advocates for Nursing Home Reform (CANHR), a nonprofit organization that provides California consumers with nursing home preplacement information, a lawyer referral service for estate planning and elder abuse issues, and advice on Medi-Cal issues.

Lynelle Detzler Morgan, Family Law Project, University of Michigan Law School.

The National Association of Professional Geriatric Care Managers (GCM), an organization of practitioners whose goal is the advancement of dignified care for the elderly and their families. GCM is committed to maximizing the independence and autonomy of elders while striving to ensure that the highest quality and most cost-effective health and human services are used when and where appropriate.

Gail Pendleton is coordinator of the National Immigration Project of the National Lawyers Guild. The National Immigration Project is a network of immigration lawyers, law students, legal workers, and jailhouse lawyers working to recognize the contributions of immigrants in this country, to promote fair immigration practices, and to expand the civil and human rights of all immigrants, regardless of their status in the United States.

The Reproductive Health Technologies Project, whose mission is to advance the right of every woman to achieve full reproductive freedom through increased information and access to a wide range of safe and effective means for controlling fertility and protecting her health.

Fran Rybarik, R.N., M.P.H., Director, Bereavement Services/RTS at Gundersen Lutheran Medical Center.

Janie B. Scott, O.T.R./L., Administrator, Clearinghouse for Rehabilitation and Technology Information, Maryland Department of Health and Mental Hygiene in Baltimore.

Debra Smith, A.C.S.W., Director of the National Adoption Information Clearinghouse in Rockville, Maryland, since 1990. Prior to that, she was a foster care and adoption worker in both public and private child welfare agencies for nine years. She and her husband are the adoptive parents of two children and are active in local adoption organizations.

Melissa Steinmetz, A.C.S.W., C.C.S.W., Director of the Elkhart County Child and Family Advocacy Center since 1991. Prior to this she worked as a therapist, providing individual and group therapy for child and adolescent victims, adult survivors, nonoffending parents, and adolescent and adult perpetrators. Ms. Steinmetz has operated as a contractual child abuse specific child interviewer for the United States Department of State. She has extensively conducted trainings on national, regional, and local levels for professionals and communities. She also serves as trainer for the National Resource Center on Child Sexual Abuse and has served as an expert panelist two times on *Oprah*.

Patricia Aldrich Still, Executive Director, Well Spouse Foundation.

Margaret B. Strand, Executive Secretary of the Los Angeles Funeral Society, Inc.

Paul F. Tschudi, M.A., L.P.C., Executive Director of St. Francis Center, a nonsectarian resource center providing guidance, training, information, and support for individuals and communities living with loss, illness, and grief in Washington, D.C. Mr. Tschudi teaches at George Washington University.

Carolyn Vash, Ph.D.

Vivian Weinblatt, a board-certified genetic counselor primarily working with patients in high-risk pregnancies considering prenatal diagnosis and those with multifetal gestations. She is a graduate of the College of Human Ecology at Cornell University, with a master's degree in genetic counseling from the University of California at Berkeley.

David Westgor, Esq., an associate in the Los Angeles office of Pillsbury, Madison & Sutro, L.L.P.

Rosalie S. Wolf, President of the National Committee for the Prevention of Elder Abuse and editor of the *Journal of Elder Abuse and Neglect*.

Although too numerous to mention individually, I wish to thank the many professionals and volunteers working in legal aid organizations, legal advocacy groups, independent living centers, vocational rehabilitation programs, child support enforcement agencies, law enforcement agencies, support and advocacy groups, rape crisis centers, domestic violence shelters and advocacy programs, runaway and homeless shelters, detention centers, teen parent programs, mental health associations, drug and alcohol departments and recovery programs, adult protective services agencies, child protective services agencies, nursing home advocacy programs, ombudsman programs, home health agencies, hospices, AIDS service organizations and comprehensive treatment programs, and the professionals in private practice and government organizations who patiently answered the questions I and Safini Convey put to them over the course of the book's research. Without their cooperation and willingness to serve the public by providing information, this book would simply be academic in nature. Their insights, admonitions, and reports from "the trenches" have helped to make the information provided as realistic as possible.

SOLUTIONS

Introduction

ALMOST EVERYONE will endure a serious crisis at some point in her life, and often one crisis leads to another. Not knowing how to respond is frightening. When a crisis occurs, time is scarce. Decisions must be made quickly. Fast access to information and support is vital. Without it, a crisis can be overwhelming.

I wrote this book for a very simple reason: to give women information. Because as women we face a distinct set of life challenges and because we are often the source of information and comfort for others, we must learn to become effective self-advocates. The power of information is tangible. When you know what your options are, you can defend yourself against the world. You can make informed choices. You can stand up for yourself.

Crisis situations are often complex. There is much to learn in order to understand your options and to find the best sources of assistance. Most people simply don't have the time or the resources to research the answers to their questions. But the information — and the help — is there. While researching this book, I spoke to hundreds of dedicated people who spend every day helping others. I culled information from an array of sources ranging from academic texts and journals to government publications and popular books and interviewed professionals who were willing to share their expertise to benefit the book's readers. Each chapter has been reviewed by a professional or a group of professionals with expertise in the field discussed.

Because it's common to experience more than one crisis at a time, topics ranging from job discrimination to child sexual abuse are combined into a single volume so that you can address a number of problems simultaneously. But you don't have to be in crisis to use this book. Access to information can often mean the difference between trouble and disaster. With this book you can learn how to recognize and avert a crisis.

Although each topic covered in this book is an emotional and difficult one, this book focuses on providing practical information that you can apply to your own unique circumstances. To be sure, there are seldom easy answers to life's dilemmas. Sometimes there are no answers. Often it is simply necessary to have the sort of information that can help you better understand and cope with your experience. Whenever possible, this book provides that information.

You are never alone in crisis. Across the country, hundreds of organizations offer information and assistance to people with varying needs. The *Solutions* Resource Directory will put you in touch with many of these groups. Help is often a telephone call away.

WHAT'S IN THIS BOOK AND HOW DOES IT WORK?

Solutions: The Woman's Crisis Handbook covers crises in the workplace, divorce, select children's issues, sexual assault, domestic violence, stalking, unexpected pregnancies, pregnancy and infant loss, postpartum depression, sexually transmitted diseases, resources for adults and children with disabilities, mental health resources, alcohol and other drug abuse problems, and life-threatening illnesses, including stroke, heart disease, HIV infection, AIDS, cancer resources, crises in aging, and death and dying.

The information provided is intended to help you take initial steps to manage a crisis. You'll find a basic overview of each issue and referrals to other resources — organizations, books, and low-cost educational materials — to help you continue your search for information.

KEEPING CURRENT

This book was written at a time when dramatic changes in federal law were being proposed. While it's important to realize that all laws change, you should be aware that new changes in federal law may have occurred by the time you read this book. Whenever possible, I've included information to help you keep current.

There are two parts to this book. The first part contains chapters with information; the second is the Resource Directory. Each chapter is divided into sections under topic headings. At the start of each chapter you'll find a box titled "What's in This Chapter?" The box breaks down the chapter's contents, and boxes within chapters highlight information and important resources for quick reference. Questions and checklists are bulleted for clarity. Where relevant, you'll be referred to national helping organizations listed in the Resource Directory.

The Resource Directory contains listings of national organizations that provide information, publications, support, and other types of assistance relevant to the topics discussed in the book. For each book chapter there is a corresponding Resource Directory chapter.

You can use the Resource Directory without reading the book. Use the book index or watch the running feet at the bottom of the directory pages for subject headings. In the front of the directory, you'll find information to help you locate resources in your community and organize your search for further information for the best results.

WHAT'S IN THIS CHAPTER?

✤ When You're Fired or Laid
   Off: The First Steps
✤ Discrimination in the
   Workplace
   ◆ Title VII of the Civil Rights
      Act of 1964
   ◆ Sexual Harassment
   ◆ Pregnancy Discrimination
   ◆ Racial Harassment
   ◆ Discrimination Against
      Older People
   ◆ Discrimination Against
      People with Disabilities
✤ Discrimination Related to
   Sexual Orientation

✤ I ✤

Crises at Work

WHEN YOU'RE FIRED OR LAID OFF:
THE FIRST STEPS

You can, and will, survive job loss. Taking immediate action is the key to recovery. Start by asking your employer for a written statement of the reasons for your dismissal. This information will be extremely valuable should your former employer dispute your eligibility for unemployment compensation or make false statements about your job performance. When approaching your former employer for a statement, be careful to maintain your calm and professional demeanor. Expressions of anger or threats of retaliatory action are extremely unwise, considering that your former employer can provide you with a good reference, help you seek new employment, and possibly give you severance benefits.

Negotiate your severance pay

Most states have laws governing when wages must be paid after termination and what may be counted as part of your wages, but only a few states have laws mandating severance pay in certain situations, such as after a plant closing. (For information on wage collection laws in your state, call the state Department of Labor or Wage Board. These agencies have different names in different states.)

Severance pay is a benefit that may be granted by employers to employees who have lost their jobs except for reasons of misconduct. It is usually part of your employee benefits package, although some employers may offer severance as a matter of custom or policy. Severance can include compensation in addition to earned wages and/or an extension of benefits. It is intended to compensate workers for losses

GET INFORMATION
AND ACT QUICKLY!

The information given in this chapter is not intended as legal advice. It is meant only to give you a basic sense of your rights as an employee. Employment law is always changing, and the laws differ greatly from state to state and place to place. Your situation is unlike any other, and the only person who can give you legal advice is an attorney experienced in employment law. If you have a serious problem regarding your employment, it is most important to get information and to act quickly!

such as unemployment or the loss of seniority status. Acceptance of severance pay may negate or delay your eligibility for unemployment compensation depending on the amount you receive. Call the unemployment office nearest you to find out whether you are eligible.

Negotiating severance can be very difficult both because there is no standard formula for severance payments and because your emotions are likely to be running high at the time of your termination. Asking for severance, let alone negotiating a reasonable agreement, may be the last thing you want to do at the moment, but it is vital that you keep calm, forge ahead, and try to obtain this valuable income.

Severance pay arrangements typically provide either lump-sum payments or continued payments for a limited period of time. The amount is usually determined by the number of years you worked and/or the compensation you received. For example, formulas for severance pay might range from one week to one month of severance pay for every year of service. Naturally, your goal is to extend your compensation, including earned but unused vacation time, and benefits over the longest possible period. You will have to assess what you think is fair as well as remember that you and your family may have to survive on severance pay, unemployment compensation (if available to you), and your savings for some time.

Employers sometimes ask employees to sign an agreement that releases the employer from any employment-related claim or legal action brought by the employee as a condition for handing over severance. The agreement may specifically include a release from discrimination claims. If you are presented with such an agreement, it is wise to have a lawyer review it before signing, especially if you believe that you have a claim based on discriminatory conduct.

Maintain Your Health Insurance

Being able to maintain insurance coverage after a job loss is vital to families' and individuals' routine and critical health care. One option for those who lose their insurance is to enroll in a spouse's (or partner's, if possible) employer-provided health plan. You also have the option of staying on your company's group health insurance plan, if you leave your job voluntarily or lose your job for any reason other than gross misconduct. The Consolidated Omnibus Budget Reconciliation Act of 1986, otherwise known as COBRA, gives an employee who has been terminated or who has had her hours reduced the right to choose continued coverage under her employer's group health plan for up to eighteen months. Coverage also extends to your spouse or dependents, if they would otherwise lose coverage because of your termination or reduction in hours. Your employer must offer you the "core" benefits of the plan and will most likely require you to pay up to 102 percent of the premium. Your coverage under COBRA will end if you fail to pay your premiums on time, when you become covered by another group health plan, when you become entitled to Medicare, or when your employer ceases to offer coverage to any employee. If you or a beneficiary, such as a child, qualify for Social Security disability insurance (SSDI), you may be able to extend your COBRA coverage for eleven additional months.

Spouse and dependents who lose health coverage because of the death of a covered employee, divorce or legal separation, an employee's Medicare entitlement, or a child's attaining the age of majority (eighteen or twenty-one, depending on state law) can elect continued coverage under COBRA for thirty-six months.

COBRA does not apply to employers with less than twenty employees, certain church-related organizations, or to federal government plans.

A new federal law, the Health Insurance Reform Act, allows you to buy an individual policy regardless of your health or claims history if you were covered by your employer for eighteen months, are not eligible for coverage under another group plan, and have exhausted your COBRA benefits. This law generally limits to twelve months the time employer-provided health plans can exclude coverage for preexisting conditions, making it easier for employees to switch jobs without losing health insurance. Workers will also be able to get credit for previous qualifying coverage if they change jobs or lose their jobs without letting their coverage lapse for sixty-three days or more. For example, if you change jobs after three months of coverage and without a lapse in coverage, the preexisting conditions waiting period at your new job would only be nine months. Employers can, however, impose waiting periods before offering insurance. These waiting periods are not considered gaps in coverage for the purpose of portability.

Some state laws also limit waiting periods for coverage for preexisting conditions. You may want to call your state insurance department or the state Department of Corporations, listed in the government section of your white pages, for more information about state laws regarding health insurance. For detailed information about your insurance options, talk to your personnel or human resources department.

Extend Your Disability Insurance

Disability insurance is another important benefit that you will want to maintain. It may be included in your employee benefits package, so find out if your company pays for disability insurance and if you can extend your coverage. If you cannot continue disability insurance with your employer, and you don't have an additional policy, think about buying disability insurance *before* you leave your job. Without disability insurance you risk financial disaster in the event that you become disabled while unemployed. Social Security disability insurance may not protect you. To qualify for SSDI, you must have earned a certain number of Social Security credits and meet the strict criteria for eligibility established by the Social Security Administration. Moreover, you will not receive benefits until the sixth full month of disability.

Discuss Your Pension

The decision to take your pension in a lump-sum payment or in an annuity, once you become eligible, depends on many factors, including your age, your immediate financial needs, and whether you have the option of a lump-sum payment. Discuss this matter with the appropriate company officer.

Finally, you may also be entitled to the use of outplacement services, which may include job/career counseling, the use of a computer, secretarial services and, in some cases, the use of an office. If you drive a company car, its use and other benefits may also be negotiated as part of your severance package.

As with any agreement, it is crucial that you get your severance agreement in writing. Make sure that the terms of the agreement are clearly spelled out, that the agreement is stated to be for severance pay, and, if you were fired for a reason other than misconduct, the reason you were let go.

Funded severance plans and pension plans are covered by the Employee Retirement Income Security Act (ERISA), a federal law, which is administered by the Department of Labor and the IRS. Employee benefits plans are also covered by discrimination laws. If you think that you are being treated unfairly, and you are facing the loss of a considerable amount of money, consider contacting an attorney as a last resort.

If you are presented with an incentive for early retirement, you may be asked to sign a waiver of your right to sue your employer. Under the 1990 amendment to the Age Discrimination in Employment Act called the Older Workers Benefit Protection Act (OWBPA), such waivers are not considered voluntary unless:

- the waiver is part of an agreement between you and your employer that is written in plain language, so that you can understand it
- the waiver specifically refers to the rights you are giving up under the Age Discrimination in Employment Act
- you do not waive any rights or claims arising after the date on which you signed the waiver
- you waive your rights only in exchange for something of value in addition to that to which you are already entitled (for example, severance payments or increased severance payments)
- you are advised in writing to consult an attorney before signing
- you are given at least twenty-one days to consider the agreement before signing or forty-five days, if the waiver is presented to a group of employees as part of an exit incentive or employment termination program
- you are allowed seven days to revoke the waiver after signing it

❖ If the waiver is requested in connection with an exit incentive program, you and the other employees involved must be informed in writing of any group or unit selected for the program, how they were selected, their job titles and ages, the job titles and ages of others in the same job classification who were not selected for the program, and any time limits that apply to the program.

UNEMPLOYMENT COMPENSATION

Unemployment compensation is provided through a state-federal unemployment insurance system. It is paid for by your employer or, in some states, by you and your employer. Its purpose is to help you, the worker, endure hardship caused by job loss through no fault of your own. The amount of unemployment compensation you will receive, if applicable, depends on the amount you earned while you were employed and is controlled by minimum and maximum limits on benefits, which differ from state to state. In most states, you can expect to receive about half of your average weekly income.

To be eligible for unemployment compensation, you must be able to work, as well as be available for and actively seeking suitable employment. Suitable employment is regarded as work that requires the same general level of training, experience, and pay as your previous job. Be aware that a common reason for loss or denial of benefits is the applicant's apparent refusal of suitable work. Thus, you should be as flexible as possible when filling out your application so that the unemployment office does not find a reason to deny your claim right away.

Most people who are fired or laid off are eligible for unemployment compensation, although there are exceptions. But remember, there are always exceptions to exceptions. The laws guiding unemployment compensation differ from state to state and change frequently. Moreover, law is always subject to interpretation. Don't automatically disqualify yourself. You have the right to file a claim and the right to appeal the decision in your case. Not every reason for ineligibility is listed in this book.

Independent contractors and, in most states, self-employed people are usually not eligible for unemployment benefits. The extent to which an employer controls your work typically determines whether you are an independent contractor. If you work for yourself, perform a specific service for a number of companies or people, use your own tools, and are able to determine what services you will provide and how you will perform them, you are probably an independent contractor. However, you must contact the IRS for information.

It is unlikely that you will be eligible for benefits if you are involved in a labor dispute, although some states allow for benefits during a lockout. In many states, workers on small farms are not covered by unemployment insurance. In some states, employees of religious organizations and churches that are exempt from participating in the unemployment system are not covered.

If you were fired for willful misconduct, the likelihood that your benefits will be denied, delayed, or reduced is great. Misconduct is not usually equated with a lack of job skills, incompetence, accidents, or with personality conflicts between an employee and her boss. Some examples of misconduct may include stealing, lying about your work, taking excessive, unjustified absences without notification, insubordination, and violating reasonable rules.

In general, misconduct must be connected to your work. For example, drinking off duty may not be considered misconduct unless your employer can prove an effect on your work. The burden is on your employer to prove that you were fired for misconduct.

Generally, people who quit their jobs voluntarily are ineligible for unemployment compensation unless they quit for good cause. Good cause must usually be work-related. An employee who quit because of racial or sexual harassment, because she was asked to work in unsafe conditions, or because she was asked to work on her Sabbath may qualify for unemployment. However, in most cases, she must have made some attempt to resolve the problem with the employer before quitting.

A significant problem for women arises with the need to quit work in order to assume domestic responsibilities or escape violent abuse. Personal reasons, including pregnancy and domestic violence, do not generally suffice as good cause for quitting. Check with your state unemployment agency, a legal aid organization, or an employment lawyer for information about current law, as there may be an exception in your state.

How to Apply for Unemployment Compensation

Apply as soon as possible. Go to the unemployment office in person. Take your Social Security number, another form of identification, your pay stubs or record of your wages or salary, and the names and addresses of the employers for whom you worked over the last two years. Be truthful on the application, but do not state that you were fired. The unemployment agency may interpret this as an admission that you were fired for misconduct. Instead, write that you were laid off.

After the unemployment office contacts your employer, it will make a determination about your claim. If you are denied benefits, you can, and should, request a hearing. You must act very quickly to appeal. Find out what the deadline is and don't miss it. The more information you bring to the hearing, such as relevant documents and witnesses, the better chance you have of winning your appeal. It is advisable to seek professional help in preparing for your hearing. Legal aid organizations, professional organizations, senior centers, or other community organizations may be able to assist you. You can appeal your hearing, and, if need be, take your case to court.

Unemployment benefits can be federally taxed, but the government will not automatically take taxes from your check. Beginning in 1997, you will be able to elect whether or not you want federal income tax withheld. Ask the unemployment office or contact the IRS for more information.

When money is tight, economic difficulties can quickly become economic disasters. Facing the prospect of eviction and being hounded by creditors are perhaps the most frightening aspects of a loss in income, but you do have rights and there are sources of assistance.

In virtually all states, a landlord cannot evict a tenant without going to court. You are entitled to notice of any proceedings against you, and you have a right to defend yourself at a hearing. But you must respond quickly if you intend to fight an eviction. If you do not respond to notice of proceedings or appear in court, your landlord can get a default judgment against you, in which case the court will issue an order to evict you. Therefore, if you think that an eviction is possible, or if you want to offer your landlord partial rental payments, seek legal advice immediately. Tenants' rights groups, legal aid organizations, and fair housing organizations (where they exist) are good sources of low cost or free information and assistance. Look in the front section of your local telephone directory, the white pages, or call city hall for information about tenant or fair housing organizations in your area. Your state's office of consumer affairs or the consumer protection division of your state attorney general's office may be able to provide you with information or refer you to a helpful organization. If you live near a law school, find out if low-cost legal services are available to the public. Many law schools sponsor law clinics through which students, under the supervision of an attorney or law professor, provide legal assistance to those who cannot afford a private lawyer or whose cases are particularly unique. Private lawyers specializing in landlord-tenant law can also be of service. If you live in an area governed by rent control, contact the rent control board to learn more about your rights and obligations. Lastly, some county bar associations and legal aid organizations sponsor telephone services to provide the public with recorded information about local laws governing a range of issues, including landlord-tenant problems. Check the front pages of your local telephone directory or call your county bar association for information.

If you're unemployed for any length of time, debts are a reality. Do not let your debts get out of control. Write or call the original creditor (the organization or person to whom you owe money) as soon as possible. Inform the creditor of your setback and intent to pay. You may be able to reduce your payments or work out a payment plan. Do what you can to prevent your creditor from turning your debt over to a debt collector. While the original creditor may want to keep your business, a debt collector is not very likely to have this concern.

❖ If you are being harassed by a debt collector, you should know about a federal law called the Fair Debt Collection Practices Act, which forbids debt collectors from engaging in certain unfair, abusive, or deceptive practices. It does not apply to the original creditor (for example, the bank or the doctor) but it does apply to debt collection agencies and attorneys who regularly pursue debt collection. State law may also limit debt collection activities. Call your state department of consumer affairs or your state attorney general's office, listed in the government section of your local white pages, and ask to be sent any available informational pamphlets about federal and state debt collection laws. The Federal Trade Commission, Correspondence Branch, 6th and Pennsylvania Ave. NW, Washington, D.C. 20580, (202) 326-2222 or (202) 326-2502 (TDD), can send you pamphlets on fair debt collection, vehicle repossession, and credit repair scams, among other topics. You might also take a trip to the local library or bookstore for a good book about budgeting and handling debts.

Being fired is not a pleasant experience; thus it's often difficult to characterize a dismissal as being just or fair. Nonetheless, it's important to address the circumstances surrounding
your termination — to think about them realistically and
accept the result as part of your continuing life education.
But sometimes discharge is truly unjust and, perhaps, illegal.
If you think you may have been fired illegally, it's important
to understand your rights as an employee and to weigh the
pros and cons of seeking redress. The following is a very
basic discussion of wrongful termination. Only an attorney
can advise you regarding your unique situation.

Traditionally, private employers have had the right to fire
an employee for any reason and at any time. Likewise, employees have been free to quit at any time and for any reason.
This principle is termed the "at will" doctrine because employees are said to work "at the will" of an employer.

However, there are a few exceptions to this rule. Individual written contracts or collective bargaining agreements
that define the duration of employment or specify the conditions under which the employee may be fired are generally enforceable in court. Employee handbooks or personnel
manuals are often viewed as contracts, although those with
disclaimers attached, such as a statement declaring employees to be "at will" or that the handbook is "not a contract,"
may protect the employer from liability. Job applications may
also contain similar statements.

In some states, judges will find an employee who does not
have a written contract to be protected by an "implied" contract when, in light of the facts and circumstances of the
employment, there is evidence that the employer implicitly
promised not to terminate the employee except for good
cause. In the past, some courts have found a combination of
factors, such as an employee's lengthy period of service,
commendations and promotions, handbook statements or
industry practices that limit termination, and assurances of
job security as evidence of an implied contract. Some courts,
however, do not view such circumstances as altering the "at
will" employer-employee relationship. The success of any as-
sertion based on an implied contract will depend very much
on the attitude of the courts in the state where the claim is
presented as well as the facts surrounding termination.

Many state courts have held that it is illegal for an employer to fire an employee for attempting to exercise a statutory right or duty, such as filing a workers' compensation
claim or serving on a jury. Similarly, many states have come

to view terminating an employee for exercising a legal right or refusing to commit an illegal act, like perjury, to be a violation of the public policy of the state. In other words, it could be considered contrary to the interests of the state to allow an employer to fire someone for obeying her legal duty or for practicing a right guaranteed by law. As well, many states have enacted laws to protect workers who complain to government officials about the illegal practices of an employer. These are often called whistle-blower statutes. However, laws and court decisions differ. Lack of knowledge about what constitutes wrongful discharge in your state and the specific circumstances under which a worker may be protected could jeopardize your case. Employees considering "blowing the whistle" are advised to learn more about the laws in their state before taking any action.

Federal Laws That Prohibit Wrongful Firing

In addition to laws that prohibit discrimination, which will be discussed shortly, there are numerous federal (and state) statutes that define other illegal reasons for firing. The following are federal laws.

The Bankruptcy Act makes it unlawful for an employer to discriminate against a person who has been a debtor or bankrupt or to fire an employee for filing bankruptcy.

The Consumer Credit Protection Act prohibits firing an employee because of a wage garnishment (money withheld from your check to pay a debt); and

The Fair Labor Standards Act forbids an employer to fire an employee for reporting a violation of the FLSA, such as being paid less than the minimum wage or not being paid for overtime, to the Wage and Hour Division of the Department of Labor. The Equal Pay Act, an amendment to the FLSA, requires employers to pay women and men who do work that is substantially the same in the same establishment equally, unless payment is made according to a bona fide seniority or merit system or is based on any other factor besides sex. Although the EPA covers almost every employer, its application is of limited use to women who work in female-dominated jobs where there are few men performing equal work. Title VII of the Civil Rights Act of 1964, discussed below, provides another potential means of combating wage discrimination.

The Employee Retirement Income Security Act prohibits firing an employee in order to interfere with any right to which she may be entitled under an employee benefits plan, including medical and pension plans.

The National Labor Relations Act protects the rights of union members and generally outlaws discrimination because of membership in or lack of membership in a union.

The Occupational Safety and Health Act makes it illegal for an employer to fire an employee who files a complaint with the Occupational Safety and Health Administration.

The Polygraph Protection Act prevents a private employer from requesting or requiring lie detector tests or similar tests, except in very limited circumstances or when an employer has reason to suspect an employee of causing an "economic loss or injury" to the business. An employer may not fire or otherwise discriminate against an employee for refusing to take a polygraph or similar test.

Other federal statutes and state laws may offer other kinds of protection. For example, some states have also passed laws protecting employees from termination for absences due to voting, jury duty, or call to active military duty.

What to Do If You've Been Fired Wrongfully

When an employee is fired in violation of federal or state discrimination laws or other statutes that limit the at-will doctrine, or in violation of an implied contract, she may have the basis for a claim of wrongful termination. Although those employees with individual or union contracts are in a fairly good position to get redress, other kinds of wrongful discharge claims are much more difficult to pursue. Even if you do have a basis for a lawsuit, it may be in progress for many years before any result is achieved, and you may end up spending more money for legal services than you receive in compensation.

However, if you believe that you have been wrongfully terminated — for example, because you refused to commit a patently illegal act or because you filed a workers' compensation claim — you should consider contacting an attorney to assess your case, particularly if the wrong done to you was severe. In most cases, the lawyer will be able to tell you quickly whether your case has any potential. But it's a good idea to do some research on your own before seeing an attorney.

If you have suffered discrimination, contact your state or local human rights commission for information about state and local discrimination laws as well as federal discrimination laws, which will be discussed shortly. These laws are fairly comprehensive and may offer you the best means of redress.

It is important to look for another job as soon as you are

able — even if you stand to win your old job back. By not seeking a new job, you risk presenting yourself as someone who is unwilling to work, thus potentially weakening your case. You may also have a legal duty to "mitigate damages" by looking for new employment. Otherwise, any compensation on your claim may be reduced by the amount the court determines you could have earned had you made reasonable efforts to seek employment. Your former employer may also be able to defend against the award of damages by showing that you didn't try to find work.

Most importantly, landing a new job will start you on the path toward emotional recovery. Your injury may be profound and the legal process grueling, but you risk suffering even greater harm to your spirit by letting your loss define and consume you. If you have been maltreated by an employer or are involved in a lawsuit, there are many people to whom you can speak about your difficulties. Professional therapy or counseling is often appropriate and helpful.

JOB LOSS AND YOUR EMOTIONS

Regardless of the circumstances under which you have been let go, losing a job can be a psychologically and financially trying experience. As adults, we often define ourselves by what we do for a living. When we lose a job, we may suddenly feel as if we've lost a portion of our identity. We may even begin to see ourselves as somehow less valuable because of the loss. But it is important to separate your professional identity from your life as a whole and from your identity as a multi-faceted person. Your worth cannot be measured in terms of the services you perform, no matter how significant, nor even in terms of the income that you provide for yourself or your family.

The feelings that accompany job loss — shock, anger, a sense of betrayal, grief, and depression — are very much akin to those felt at the death of a loved one. You may blame yourself. If you have made mistakes, admit them and learn from them. Many successful people have been fired from a job and have used the experience as an opportunity to re-evaluate their direction. This may be the first chance you have had to look for more meaningful employment.

There are several steps that you can take to help manage the pain of job loss. First, keep an open line of communication with your family. If they know what has happened and how you are feeling, they can offer you a great deal of support. Talking with other unemployed people in support groups offered by community programs, places of worship, and schools may be helpful. If you become depressed, or if you're having a hard time beginning a job search, try speaking to a career counselor. Good career counselors are familiar with the emotions experienced by people who have lost their jobs and can help you with practical advice.

Being unemployed can be more stressful than being employed. Although you may feel that you don't deserve time for enjoyment, it is necessary to socialize, exercise, eat right, and to get rest. Talking with friends, walking, playing sports, preparing a meal, or pursuing your other interests can refresh your spirit and add to your sense of purpose as you look for new employment.

FINDING A NEW JOB

Most jobs are found through informal networking. So before you leave your job, make sure that you have the names and addresses of your business contacts (if they are legitimately your property and not confidential documents) and your co-workers. They and your previous employers, family, friends, neighbors, members of your religious organization, or any club or professional organization to which you belong, will become part of your networking list. Tell anyone who might be interested that you are looking for a job. If your company offers job counseling or outplacement services, ask to use them.

Give yourself the job of finding a job. Start looking right away. Don't take time off to go on a vacation or make plans that are not directly related to your economic survival. Expect to spend at least twenty to forty hours a week looking for a new situation. Get organized and stay on a schedule. If you haven't conducted a job search or created a resume in some time, you will benefit from reading one of the many good books on job loss, job searching, or resume writing available at your public library or local bookstore. A few titles are listed in the Recommended Reading section at the end of this book.

Be prepared for a long search. It's not unusual for unemployment to last several months to a year. It is crucial to create a financial plan to carry you through this time, even if you are optimistic about new opportunities. You can always revise your budget later. Talk with your spouse or partner. Decide what you can and cannot do without. This does not mean that you have to cut out every entertainment or luxury, simply that you must decide what is vital to your well-being and what is not.

Set a goal for new employment, but be realistic about the

kind of work you can do. Be honest about the kind of work you are willing to do to make ends meet. Clarify your alternative choices now. You need not view an alternative job as anything more than a temporary stop on the way to more rewarding work and a means of keeping yourself and your family financially afloat.

Contingent or part-time employment can provide you with the advantage of staying actively attached to the workforce while earning income. Nonetheless, there are definite disadvantages to part-time work: advancement is often limited, the wages are lower, and the benefits fewer. You may be able to work part-time and still collect some unemployment compensation. Contact your local unemployment office to find out what you can earn without reducing your benefits.

The only time it's wise to delay a job search is when you are very angry or depressed. You may need time to cool off and work through your feelings before interviewing so that you can present yourself to a prospective employer in the best light. As much as you try to hide them, negative feelings are often very apparent to others. Even if you were treated unfairly by your former employer, don't criticize the company in an interview; it's not professional and it will not make you seem an attractive prospective employee. Instead,

---

TROUBLE SPOTS: EMPLOYMENT AGENCIES AND WANT ADS

While looking for work you may think about using the services of an employment agency. Although employment agencies can offer people with specific skills an expeditious means of finding new work, they are not for everyone. Keep in mind that employment agencies may charge fees to you or the employer. Their staff members are salespeople, not career counselors. Some unscrupulous employment agencies offer listings for jobs that are nonexistent or they refer you to 900-number job information lines that charge by the minute. Others may advertise stale or nonexistent jobs in the newspapers. Never sign a contract with an employment agency until you have had time to read and evaluate it thoroughly. If you feel pressured to sign, leave.

Looking for jobs through the want ads is a relatively ineffective way to find new work. The competition is extremely fierce. If you are thinking about responding to advertisements for work at home, such as those offering jobs stuffing envelopes, reading books, or assembling toys, you should know that these ads are rarely legitimate. They are schemes to take your money. Do not send any money for materials, supplies or parts, or for any other items the advertiser asks you to buy in order to start work. If you have responded to a work-at-home ad and lost money, don't blame yourself. It happens to many, many people who are out of work and in need of income. Call the postal service, your local better business bureau or consumer protection agency, and the Federal Trade Commission to report the fraud. (Check the government listings in your white pages.) You may keep another person from experiencing the same disappointment.

You can find job or career counseling without paying a lot of money. City or community colleges may offer low-cost counseling to nonstudents, although this is not always the case. Contact schools in your area to find out what is available. Local schools may also be able to provide referrals to low-cost career planning centers.

If you have a college degree, try calling the college or university from which you graduated. Your school may offer services to alumni. If you graduated from a university out of state, contact the career development center or placement center of your alma mater and explain that you are an alumnus who would like to know if the university has a reciprocal arrangement for career counseling with another university in your area. The career development center can then write a letter to a local university requesting services. The services you receive will depend on the university's policy. You may gain access to the job board or receive complete career counseling services.

❖ The YWCA often provides job and career assistance, including programs for displaced homemakers, but services vary widely across organizations. Again, call around to learn what's available.

concentrate on the talents, skills, and experience you have to lend to a new employer in a more productive environment.

DISCRIMINATION IN THE WORKPLACE

Discrimination continues to pervade the American workplace, and although its practice is often subtle, its effect can be devastating. There are many ways to address discrimination, and each woman who experiences it is entitled to her own response. But every woman should know that discrimination in the workplace is against the law.

This section will discuss major federal laws directed against discrimination in employment. If you believe that you have been the victim of discrimination, you'll need a basic understanding of the laws that may apply to your situation and the facts to help you make an informed decision about pursuing a claim. Learn as much as you can from as many sources as possible. The Resource Directory contains listings of a few national law groups that focus on employment discrimination. Although these organizations may not offer representation, they can be good sources of information. You will also find books that include discussions of discrimination laws in the reading list at the end of this book. Remember, your experience is unique; you are your own best advocate; and you are entitled to the information you need in order to make a decision that best suits you.

FEDERAL DISCRIMINATION LAWS: A BRIEF OVERVIEW

Title VII of the Civil Rights Act of 1964
(42 U.S.C. 2000e *et seq.*)

Title VII of the Civil Rights Act of 1964 is the broadest federal law prohibiting discrimination in the workplace. It forbids discrimination by employers (including state and local governments), employment agencies, and labor unions on the basis of race, color, religion, sex, or national origin. Federal employees are also covered by Title VII but must use different procedures for complaints. It protects full- and part-time workers, citizens of the U.S., as well as permanent residents and undocumented aliens,[1] but does not protect against discrimination solely on the basis of citizenship.[2] The law protects people of color and women as well as men and white people.

Title VII applies only to employers with fifteen or more

employees. However, many states have fair employment practice laws similar to Title VII that apply to businesses with fewer workers. Religious organizations with the required number of employees are also covered by Title VII. They are allowed to discriminate on the basis of religion or religious belief but for no other protected reason. Lastly, Title VII does not cover independent contractors. (Section 1981 of the Civil Rights Acts of 1866, discussed below, does protect independent contractors who are victims of intentional race discrimination.)

Under Title VII, it is illegal for an employer to "fail or refuse to hire or to discharge any individual, or otherwise to discriminate against any individual with respect to his compensation, terms, conditions, or privileges of employment because of such individual's race, color, religion, sex, or national origin."[3] The statute also forbids an employer to "limit, segregate, or classify his employees or applicants for employment in any way which would deprive or tend to deprive any individual of employment opportunities or otherwise adversely affect his status as an employee, because of such individual's race, color, religion, sex, or national origin."[4]

The law covers almost every area of employment, including decisions about recruitment, testing, hiring, training, firing and layoff, compensation, promotion, assignment and classification, benefits, retirement plans, and disability leave, as well as other terms and conditions of employment.

Acts of intentional and overt discrimination as well as unintentionally discriminatory practices are prohibited by Title VII. One type of overt discrimination, which is referred to as *sex-* or *race-plus discrimination,* occurs when an employer places a requirement on members of one sex or race that is not imposed on members of the opposite sex or people of another race. For example, it is discriminatory to refuse to hire or accept job applications from women with children but not to disqualify men with children.[5]

Other examples of obvious discrimination include firing an employee of one race but not an employee of another race though they were both engaged in misconduct, or harassing an employee because of her national origin or race so severely that she is forced to quit. Constructive discharge is the term used when an employer makes working conditions so bad that an employee is compelled to leave. It is the equivalent of being fired illegally. If you left your job under such circumstances, you will generally be entitled to unemployment compensation and may have a cause of legal action.

It is not always illegal to discriminate against an employee or job applicant. In very rare instances, employers may be able to show that a certain requirement, such as being male or not being pregnant, is a *bona fide occupational qualification* (BFOQ) "reasonably necessary to the normal operation of that particular business or enterprise."[6] In order to prove a BFOQ, employers must show that all or substantially all members of the excluded group cannot safely perform the *essential* duties of the job. Generally, a BFOQ cannot be based on customer or employer preference, because such expectations do not affect the employee's ability to perform the essential tasks of the job. For example, customers' desire not to be served by a pregnant waitress has no bearing on whether she is qualified to do the job. Narrow exceptions to this rule might occur in some situations where "authenticity" is required, such as with acting jobs, or, in some circumstances, when it is necessary to respect customers' or patients' privacy. Discrimination that results from the use of a bona fide merit or seniority system is likewise permissible under Title VII.

An employment practice that appears to be fair on the surface and is not intentionally designed to discriminate can also be illegal. Making a requirement of job applicants that is not job-related and for which there is no business necessity may be illegal when it has a *disparate impact* (or adverse effect) upon the employment opportunities of a protected group. The landmark case in this area is *Griggs v. Duke Power Co.*, in which the Supreme Court held as discriminatory against African-Americans an employer's policy of requiring job applicants to have a high school education and a passing score on two standardized intelligence tests where neither standard was shown to be significantly related to job performance.[7] Legal theories developed under Title VII have been used to attack wage discrimination issues that the Equal Pay Act cannot effectively reach. For information about wage discrimination, contact:

> National Committee on Pay Equity
> 1126 16th St. NW, Suite 411
> Washington, D.C. 20036
> (202) 331-7343

The National Committee on Pay Equity can answer basic questions about wage discrimination and offer publications on wage discrimination issues, but it does not offer legal advice or referrals to attorneys.

What Is Sexual Harassment?

Harassment is not something that occurs in the course of seduction or romance. It is a deliberate abuse of power and a means of gaining control over another person. It happens in the workforce, on the street, in the context of the landlord-tenant relationship, and in the classroom. In career fields traditionally dominated by men, where women are often unwelcome, or in jobs where men have authority over a number of women workers, incidents of sexual harassment are high. The sexism implicit in sexual harassment is often mixed with racism or bias on the basis of national origin, ethnic background, or sexual orientation. Sexual harassment is an experience shared by women of all ages and walks of life. It is sex discrimination and, under Title VII of the Civil Rights Act of 1964, it is illegal.

According to the Equal Employment Opportunity Commission, the federal enforcement agency that investigates complaints of discrimination, sexual harassment is constituted by "unwelcome advances, requests for sexual favors, and other verbal or physical conduct of a sexual nature."[8] This includes (but is not limited to) leering, ogling, unwanted touching, suggestive remarks about your clothing or body, remarks about your sex life, being asked for sex in return for a job or promotion, being made to wear revealing uniforms, being exposed to pornography in the workplace, and being assaulted or raped. If you have been assaulted or raped, consider calling the police and filing a criminal charge.

Harassment that is based on sex is not always overtly sexual in nature. Sexist remarks, practical jokes, insults and comments used to demean women or make women feel unwanted in the workplace are all potentially illegal forms of sex discrimination.

Are You Being Sexually Harassed?

Who defines sexual harassment? Sexual harassment can be viewed from the perspective of a reasonable person of the victim's gender and from the point of view of the person being harassed. Because we all have different feelings about what we think is acceptable behavior, it is fair to say that if you are not bothered by another's actions, you are not being harassed. However, the intent of harassment *is* to bother,

FEDERAL CONTRACTORS AND FEDERALLY FUNDED EMPLOYERS: EXECUTIVE ORDER 11246

Executive Order 11246, as amended by Executive Order 11375, prohibits federal contractors, subcontractors, and employers with federally financed construction contracts of more than $10,000 from discriminating on the basis of race, color, sex, religion, or national origin. E.O. 11246 also requires such employers to take *affirmative action* in the areas of hiring, employment, upgrading, promotion, transfer, layoff or termination, pay, training, selection, and apprenticeship. Further, the law requires employers with fifty or more employees and at least $50,000 in federal contracts to set goals and timetables for hiring qualified women and minorities. Although you cannot generally take private action against an employer, you can file a complaint within 180 days of a discriminatory act with the Office of Federal Contract Compliance Programs (OFCCP). The main office of the OFCCP is located at the U.S Department of Labor, 300 7th Street SW, Room 203, Reporters Building, Washington, D.C. 20407, (202) 401-8818. Operators can give you information or refer you to your regional office. Individual complaints may thereafter be referred to the Equal Employment Opportunity Commission.

distress, abuse, intimidate, coerce, humiliate, or alarm another. Trust your instincts. If you feel bothered by something someone is saying or doing to you, and you have told that person to stop, but he or she is continuing the action, the conduct is probably harassment.

It is important to make a distinction between behavior that is unacceptable and behavior that may be viewed as harassment under the law. An isolated remark, an off-color joke, or a single expression of bias will not typically constitute harassment in the legal sense. This does not mean that this sort of talk ought to be silently condoned. A remark that offends your dignity, language that makes you feel uncomfortable, any derogatory speech or action should be firmly and clearly addressed at the time of the incident. When someone makes a comment that upsets you, tell that person how you feel. Don't make light of it, and don't wait for another time. Most people don't want to embarrass themselves or offend others and will usually refrain from making such remarks in the future.

If you are being harassed, it may be difficult for you to define what is happening. However, there are organizations you can call for information and support. Local rape crisis centers can often answer questions about sexual harassment. In many states, organizations called commissions on the status of women, or women's commissions, can either provide you with information about sexual harassment or offer you referrals to helpful organizations. You can locate women's commissions by looking in the government section of your local telephone directory. Also see the Resource Directory for information about organizations addressing sexual harassment.

Because harassment often occurs over a long period of time, its effect can be cumulative. Common reactions to harassment include shock, denial, low self-esteem, trouble sleeping, physical illness, depression, anxiety, and fatigue. The problems caused by harassment can interfere with your sense of freedom and your ability to do your job. If you are experiencing these or other problems, consider seeking the services of a therapist or counselor experienced in helping victims of sexual harassment.

Taking steps to stop harassment before it escalates is the best way to avoid impairment of your health and happiness. Even if you have kept silent and have endured the harassment for many years, you can still speak up and end the abuse.

Very often, you can end harassment without risk to your job and without going through formal channels for relief. Start by plainly and firmly telling the harasser to stop. Characterize the behavior as harassment, and remind the harasser that his or her behavior is against the law. Try to get witnesses, and tell the harasser that there are witnesses. If a verbal response does not work, or you feel that you cannot confront the harasser verbally, write the harasser a letter describing the conduct that you find objectionable, state that it is unwelcome, and articulate the ways in which you would like the matter resolved. Be sure to make copies of the letter.[9] By having a written document that describes the harassment and your objections to it, you create a valuable piece of evidence to bring to management or to an enforcement agency in the future.

Keep a record of every incident of harassment, including the date, time, and place at which the harassment occurred. Describe the incident in detail. Note what was said or done by the harasser and others. Write down what you said or did and include the names of any witnesses. This sort of documentation will help protect you from assertions that you fabricated the harassment and complained in order get back at your employer for some unfavorable decision, such as being denied a promotion.

Document your work performance. Although it is illegal for your employer to fire you for making a complaint of sexual harassment, if you are fired, your employer may try to prove that you were dismissed for poor job performance or another legitimate reason. Documentation of your performance, discussed later in this chapter, will help counter such allegations. Find allies. Coworkers whom you trust can verify that what you're experiencing is harassment. They can also corroborate your story. If they are willing, take their names and telephone numbers. It is possible that some of your coworkers have also been harassed. Confronting the harasser as a group can be an extremely effective way of stopping the abuse. As well, a class action lawsuit may be brought on behalf of a group of workers against an employer who discriminates. But don't be surprised if you receive no support. There may be many reasons for this, such as fear of losing one's job.

If verbal and written confrontations do not work, the next step is to go through your company's grievance procedure. Ask the personnel or human resources department for information about your company's discrimination and harassment policy. If there is no specific policy and no one designated to handle complaints, talk to your supervisor. If your supervisor is harassing you, go to the next level of management. Evidence that your employer knew about the harassment but did nothing to stop it can greatly strengthen your case, because an employer may be liable for harassment if it knew or should have known about the harassment but took no action or inadequate action in response.

There are times when a woman who is being harassed by her supervisor in a company without an antiharassment policy feels that she cannot go to the next level of management without substantial risk to her job. If this is true for you, try calling one of the advocacy groups listed in the Resource Directory. A counselor or staff lawyer may be able to help you make a decision about going directly to a government agency.

If the harassment continues after you have followed your company's internal procedure, consider filing a charge with the EEOC. In fact, it is a good idea to file with the EEOC as soon as it becomes apparent that the in-house procedure will be ineffective, because there are strict deadlines for filing.

Are You to Blame? Fears About Reporting Harassment

Victims of harassment are often made to feel that they did something to warrant the abuse they experience. But you are not to blame. It is vital that you understand this. The clothing a woman wears, her appearance, her attitude, the way she chooses to live her life are not causes of harassment. You are not responsible for other people's behavior. Don't believe anyone who tells you that you are.

Feelings of shame or embarrassment, fear of being thought of as a troublemaker, too sensitive, or "not tough enough" to endure what others might term as harmless play, fearing for your job, thinking that you will not be believed, even fears about doing harm to the harasser can cause you to delay taking action against discrimination.

If you are an undocumented worker, it is best to get information and advice from an advocacy group, such as those listed in the Resource Directory, before pursuing a discrimination claim. If you do not see a listing of an organization that meets your needs, try asking the listed advocacy organizations for referrals or calling local legal aid and immigrants' rights organizations. Even if you decide not to take legal action, you can use ordinary measures to stop harassment.

The law recognizes two distinct forms of sexual harassment, although they often overlap. Harassment that has come to be termed *quid pro quo* ("this for that") harassment occurs when an employer conditions economic or job benefits upon the receipt of sexual favors or punishes an employee for rejecting sexual advances. A supervisor who seeks sex in return for a job or promotion — whether the demand is clearly stated or implied — is committing quid pro quo harassment. Likewise an employee who was fired or demoted because of a refusal to comply with requests for sexual favors is a victim of this type of harassment.

When harassment is extremely severe or pervasive, it is viewed as creating a *hostile environment*. This is the second theory of harassment, and it also applies to cases of racial or ethnic harassment. Under this theory, unwanted sexual advances, offensive remarks or physical conduct, and behavior intended to intimidate or humiliate an employee occur so frequently or are so severe that working in such an atmosphere becomes, in effect, a condition of employment. Sometimes, a woman is forced to quit her job in order to escape intolerable conditions that her employer has done little or nothing to remedy. This may be viewed as constructive discharge and as such is equated with being wrongly fired.

However, it is not necessary to quit your job or to have suffered economic loss to show that your employer created a hostile environment. Further, in 1993 the Supreme Court ruled that an employee need not prove that she suffered psychological injury or that her job performance was affected in order to win a case under the hostile environment theory. However, harassment in this context must still be "severe or pervasive enough to create an objectively hostile or abusive work environment — an environment that a reasonable person would find hostile or abusive"[10] and must be perceived by the victim as such.

Although harassment is illegal regardless of who is doing it, you cannot sue coworkers, clients, or customers directly under Title VII. You can sue your employer. A company will typically be held liable for harassment when it is committed by a supervisor. The company may also be liable when it knew or should have known about the harassment. This might happen when a complaint is received but no action is taken or when an employer has no antiharassment policy or grievance procedure.

You do not have to have evidence of harassment to file a charge with the EEOC. It's the government agency's job to investigate the matter. But if you are wondering whether you have a good case, you are wise to get an evaluation of your situation from a trained professional knowledgeable in the field of employment discrimination. Law groups focusing on discrimination and harassment may be able to assess your situation.

$\mathcal{P}$REGNANCY DISCRIMINATION

In 1978, Congress passed the Pregnancy Discrimination Act as an amendment to Title VII of the Civil Rights Act of 1964 in order to make clear that discrimination against women because of pregnancy is illegal sex discrimination. Very basically, the act requires employers to treat pregnant women and women affected by pregnancy-related conditions the same as other applicants and employees on the "basis of their ability or inability to work."[11] An employer with fifteen or more employees cannot fire, refuse to hire, or deny a promotion to a woman solely because she is pregnant or has had an abortion.

If a pregnant woman is willing and able to do her job during pregnancy, her employer cannot force her to take maternity leave. Similarly, under the Pregnancy Discrimination Act, an employer may not make a rule that prohibits women on maternity leave from returning to work until after a specific period of time has elapsed.

Maternity or disability leave is very important to pregnant women. However, the PDA does not *require* employers to provide disability leave to any worker. It only requires that the practice of providing leave not be discriminatory. A woman who is disabled by pregnancy must be treated in the same way as other workers who are temporarily disabled. If other temporarily disabled workers are allowed to be transferred, pregnant women also have the right to be transferred. Likewise, women who are disabled by pregnancy-related conditions must be allowed sick leave benefits on the same basis as other employees who are unable to work.

If you work for an employer with fifty or more employees, you will want to know about the Family and Medical Leave Act, which does mandate unpaid leave and reinstatement for employees of large companies.

Unless she informs her employer that she does not intend to return to work, a woman taking leave for a pregnancy-related condition is entitled to have her job back when it is the employer's policy to reinstate other employees returning from sick or disability leave. Being reinstated to a job with lower pay or fewer responsibilities is not permissible unless other employees who return from sick or disability leave are similarly treated.

Employers are not allowed to discriminate between men and women in the offering of health insurance benefits. Thus, a health insurance plan offered by an employer cannot exclude pregnancy and childbirth and must cover expenses for pregnancy-related conditions on the same basis as other medical conditions. For example, employers cannot impose a different deductible for pregnancy-related conditions than for other medical conditions. Coverage for pregnancy-related conditions cannot be restricted to married employees unless coverage for all medical conditions is limited only to married people. Further, the spouses of men and women employees must be treated similarly. If an employer provides coverage for the medical conditions of spouses of employees, then the level of coverage for pregnancy-related conditions of the spouses of male employees must be the same as the level of coverage for other medical conditions of the spouses of female employees.[12]

The PDA does not prevent employers from providing health insurance benefits for abortion, yet it does not require employers to pay for abortions, except when the life of the mother is endangered. However, employers must pay for complications arising from an abortion, providing, of course, that the employer offers health insurance benefits to employees.

The issue of whether an employer can justly bar fertile or pregnant women from a workplace where toxic substances are in use was decided in 1991, when the Supreme Court ruled that a company's policy of excluding fertile or pregnant women, but not fertile men, from jobs in which employees were exposed to lead was an illegal form of sex discrimination.[13]

This decision does not dissuade employers from creating safer workplaces, only from discriminating. Because lead can impair both female and male reproductive health, employers and employees should take precautions to limit exposure.

If you are concerned about toxic substances in the workplace, ask your employer for information about the chemical hazards of your job. Get a copy of the Material Safety Data Sheet (MSDS) for the products you use at work. (Call CHEMTREC Non-Emergency Services at 1-800-262-8200 for information about specific chemical products. Have the product manufacturer's name and product number at hand.) You can also call the manufacturer of the product directly and ask for a copy of the MSDS. You will want to learn how the chemical will affect you and what measures you can take to limit your exposure. With this knowledge you can begin to make informed decisions about your health.

The only time it may be permissible to discriminate against pregnant women is when an employer can establish nonpregnancy as a bona fide occupational qualification which is "reasonably necessary to the normal operation of that particular business or enterprise."[14] This very narrow exception may allow an employer to exclude a pregnant woman from the workplace when pregnancy actually interferes with her ability to do the essential tasks of the job or puts others, whose safety is necessary to the normal operation of business, at great risk. However, the employer cannot make decisions based on presumptions about pregnant women: each woman's ability must be evaluated individually. If this cannot be done, the employer must prove that all or almost all pregnant women cannot perform the job safely and effectively, and if a reasonable alternative to excluding all pregnant women exists, the employer must use it.

State Laws on Maternity and Parenting Leave

State laws regarding maternity and parenting leave vary considerably, with some states offering greater protection than others. Your state fair employment practice agency or civil/human rights commission should be able to furnish you with more information about the laws in your area. (Check the state and local government listings in your white pages for the telephone numbers.)

What to Do If You Think You Have Been Treated Unfairly

Because the PDA requires employers to treat pregnant women like other workers, your first course of action should be to talk to others who have taken leave for reasons related to pregnancy and for reasons unrelated to pregnancy to find out what their experiences have been. Also, be aware that employers may use certain defenses, such as poor job performance, as a pretext for discriminating against pregnant employees. Therefore, you should carefully document your work performance and all evidence that supports your claim of unfair treatment.

If you are fired or otherwise punished because of your pregnancy, consider talking to a professional advocate or lawyer and filing a charge of discrimination. The Resource Directory contains listings that may offer you more informa-

The Family and Medical Leave Act requires that employers of fifty or more allow employees who have worked at least a year to take up to twelve weeks of unpaid leave annually for the birth, adoption, or foster care placement of a child, for the care of a relative with a serious health condition, or because of the employee's own serious (mental or physical) health condition. An employer is not required to, but can, ask that you exhaust your paid leave before taking your FMLA leave. You must give your employer at least thirty days notice before taking leave and, if this is not possible, as much notice as you can. If you are taking leave because of a serious health problem or a relative's serious condition, you have the option of taking leave on an intermittent basis or working on a reduced schedule. The law requires your employer to reinstate you to the same position that you occupied before your leave or to an equivalent position, with the same pay, benefits, terms, and conditions of employment. One possible exception to this rule is for high-salaried employees whose leave might cause a substantial and grievous injury to the employer; and in these cases, the employer must notify the employee of its intent not to reinstate.

The FMLA does not replace any state or local law that gives employees greater leave rights. In addition, if your state law provides greater rights in one way, such as mandating paid leave or allowing earlier eligibility or longer periods of unpaid leave than the FMLA, your employer must follow the requirements of the more generous law in that respect.

tion. Also see the section in this chapter on page 37 titled The EEOC Process: Taking Legal Action Against Discrimination.

In addition to the Pregnancy Discrimination Act, your state may have a law that forbids pregnancy discrimination. It will be important to learn as much as you can about the federal and state laws prohibiting sex or pregnancy discrimination before taking action.

Racial harassment

Harassment based on race or ethnicity, including repeated crude or practical jokes, insults, ethnic slurs, ridicule, or racist graffiti is illegal under Title VII of the Civil Rights Act of 1964. But there is another federal law that addresses this kind of discrimination.

Section 1981 of the Civil Rights Acts of 1866 (42 U.S.C. 1981) prohibits *intentional* racial or national origin discrimination in the making and enforcement of contracts. This definition encompasses "the making, performance, modification, and termination of contracts, and the enjoyment of all benefits, privileges, terms, and conditions of the contrac-

The Immigration Reform and Control Act of 1986, which makes it illegal for an employer to knowingly hire employees who are not legally authorized to work in the United States, also forbids intentional discrimination on the basis of citizenship or national origin. IRCA covers employers of four or more employees and protects U.S. citizens, U.S. nationals, permanent residents, temporary residents who have gone through the legalization program, and refugees. Under IRCA, it is illegal for an employer to refuse to hire a worker only because she "looks" or "sounds" foreign. Employees have a choice of documents they may present to prove eligibility for employment after they have been hired. Acceptable documents are listed on the I-9 Form, which employers must complete when hiring new employees. Under IRCA, an employer may not ask that you give more or different documentation than legally required or refuse to accept documents that reasonably appear to be genuine in order to discriminate on the basis of citizenship or national origin.

If you would like more information about IRCA, call the Office of Special Counsel for Immigration-Related Unfair Employment Practices at 1-800-255-7688 (voice) or 1-800-237-2515 (TDD). Operators can answer your questions or refer you to a staff attorney. There is no charge for calling. You will have 180 days from the date of the alleged discrimination to file a complaint. It is also against the law for an employer to retaliate against an employee for filing a complaint of discrimination or for participating in an IRCA investigation.

tual relationship."[15] The act prohibits racial harassment, discrimination in pay, firing, transfers, and promotions. It covers private and government employers and protects both employees and independent contractors. Remedies under Section 1981 are greater than under Title VII. There is no requirement to file a charge with a government agency. Alternatively, filing a charge with the EEOC under Title VII does not usually prevent you from filing a private lawsuit under Section 1981. If you have been the victim of discrimination applicable to this law, you should discuss all your options for redress, including Title VII and your state discrimination laws, with an attorney experienced in cases of racial harassment.

DISCRIMINATION AGAINST OLDER PEOPLE

The Age Discrimination in Employment Act of 1967 (ADEA) (29 U.S.C. 621 et seq.) is the federal law that prohibits discrimination against people over forty years of age by both private and government employers. It affects all areas of employment including hiring, firing, promotions, assignments, wages, and the working environment. Employee benefits and benefits plans are also subject to the ADEA. There is no age limit on this law; it was removed in 1987.

Like Title VII, the law covers employers, employment agencies, and labor unions. However, the ADEA only affects those employers with twenty or more employees and labor unions with twenty-five or more members. State statutes may cover employers with fewer employees and some state age discrimination laws protect people younger than forty.

Stereotypical notions about older people may lead to unlawful employment practices, such as requiring tests of older people that are not required of younger people or failing to train older workers as well as younger workers. Older workers often experience subtle discrimination when interviewing for jobs, such as when a prospective employer rejects an older worker for a position saying that she has too much experience or is overqualified and fails to give any specific justification for these comments. An employer may wrongly assume that all older people cannot do certain types of work. However, under the ADEA, you as an individual must be given the chance to prove that you are capable of doing the essential tasks of the job.

On the other hand, the ADEA, like Title VII, does permit discrimination in instances where age might be a bona fide occupational qualification (BFOQ) reasonably necessary to the normal operation of business. In this case, an employer must be able to show that all or substantially all older workers cannot perform the job in question safely and efficiently and that it is not possible to make these determinations individually. The ADEA also permits discrimination based on a bona fide seniority system that is not meant to evade the purposes of the act[16] or reasonable factors other than age, such as prior experience or the quality of performance.[17]

With few exceptions, the ADEA and a number of state laws prohibit employers from forcing workers to retire because of age. For example, an employer may not make a reduction in force simply to eliminate older workers. An employer, however, may be able to justify a decision that adversely affects older workers by showing that it was motivated by factors unrelated to age. Also, under the ADEA certain high-level policymakers or executives who are over the age of sixty-five and immediately entitled to a nonforfeitable pension of at least $44,000 a year can be involuntarily retired.

It is illegal for an employer to establish different ages for voluntary retirement based on race or sex. As well, it is illegal for an employer to try to force an employee into accepting a retirement incentive. For example, if you are asked to choose between voluntarily retiring and being fired and losing your benefits, your choice may not be seen as voluntary and could be illegal.

If you feel that you have been discriminated against and want to find out whether you have a legitimate complaint, consider contacting an attorney or a legal aid organization in your area. The EEOC can advise you as to whether your complaint is current enough to merit a charge. Discrimination claims are discussed later in this chapter. As with other prohibitions against discrimination, state law may offer more or less protection than the federal law.

DISCRIMINATION AGAINST PEOPLE WITH DISABILITIES

There are two major federal laws that prohibit discrimination against people with disabilities: the federal Rehabilitation Act of 1973, which prohibits discrimination by federal agencies, federal contractors and subcontractors, and agencies receiving federal funds, and the Americans with Disabilities Act of 1990 (ADA) (42 U.S.C. 12101 et seq.), which applies to private employers, state and local governments, labor unions, and employment agencies. Like Title VII, the act only applies to employers with fifteen or more employees. State and local government employers of all sizes are covered.

Title I of the ADA is the section concerning employment issues. The ADA also addresses discrimination in public services, transportation, public accommodations, and telecommunications.

The ADA forbids an employer to discriminate against a qualified person with a disability in any aspect of employment, including medical benefits and examinations. It is also illegal for an employer to discriminate against a person who has a relationship or association with someone with a disability.

The ADA prohibits a range of discriminatory practices, including limiting, segregating, or classifying a job applicant in a way that hurts her employment opportunities because of her disability. For example, it is illegal to use qualification standards, tests, or other criteria "that screen out or tend to screen out" people with disabilities unless the standards are related to the job and are necessary for business.[18] It is also unlawful for an employer to refuse to make reasonable accommodations for the qualified person's disability, unless it would cause the employer undue hardship. The means of reasonable accommodations are discussed below.

The ADA's definition of disability, derived from the definition of disability under the Rehabilitation Act, is specific. According to the ADA's definition, a person with a disability is someone who

- has a physical or mental impairment that substantially limits one or more major life activities;
- has a record of such impairment; or
- is regarded as having such an impairment

Many disabilities are addressed by the act, including physiological disorders or conditions, mental or psychological disorders such as emotional or mental illness, and learning disabilities. HIV infection and AIDS are covered. Pregnancy, which is considered to be a temporary disability, is not.

The extent to which the ADA protects a person with a disability depends on the extent to which the disability limits the person's ability to perform major life activities, such as walking, breathing, speaking, seeing, hearing, sitting, standing, caring for oneself, or in some cases working. The severity and longevity of the disability are also considered when determining whether a person qualifies as disabled under this definition. For example, a back injury that causes you pain and temporarily restricts your activities probably does not qualify as a disability; but a back injury that causes you to be permanently unable to sit or stand without pain or to care for yourself without help does qualify as a disability.[19] However, it's important to remember that assessments of one's qualification for protection under the ADA are made on an individual basis.

The law may also protect people who have a history or record of a greatly limiting condition (such as cancer, heart disease, or mental illness), a misdiagnosis of disability, and those who are perceived as having a disability, as might happen due to others' fearful misunderstanding of disfigurements such as scars. People who are currently using illegal drugs are not protected by the ADA. However, persons who have a history of addiction but who are recovered and people who are in the process of completing a rehabilitation program are protected.

An important feature of the ADA is its requirement that the job applicant or employee be able to perform the essential tasks of the job (with reasonable accommodation, if necessary, or without) in order to be protected from discrimination in employment. In other words, an employer does not have to hire someone who does not have the necessary skills and background to perform the essential duties of the job. However, if you are qualified, you must be given the same opportunity as other job applicants. This is where the principle of reasonable accommodation comes into play.

Employers must make the interview process accessible to all applicants. If you are deaf, for example, a sign interpreter may be requested for the interview, if needed. Until a job offer is made, an employer may not ask you questions about any prior workers' compensation claims or about your medical status or history. Nor can an employer ask you to take a medical examination. A medical examination may be required after a job offer is made, providing it is required of all employees in the same job category and the examination is both job-related and a business necessity. The results must be maintained in a separate, confidential file. An employer may test an employee for illegal drugs and alcohol without violating the ADA. (Testing for drugs and alcohol may give rise to other legal questions that are not within the scope of this discussion.)

Additionally, if you have a disability that hinders your performance in a job for which you are otherwise qualified, the employer must offer to reasonably accommodate your individual limitation so that you can enjoy the same benefits of employment as a nondisabled person. To accomplish this, you must make the employer aware of your needs. The employer can then make the facility more accessible, change the work schedule to provide more flexible hours, provide equipment or devices that enable you to perform the job, or change when and how the essential functions of the job are done, among other measures. A legitimate defense for not making such accommodations may be raised when the accommodation would impose "undue hardship" on the employer, for example, if the necessary accommodation is very costly, extensive, or disruptive. Determinations of whether the accommodation imposes undue hardship are made on a case-by-case basis, with factors such as the size and resources of the business taken into account. Still, employers must consider alternative accommodations that would not impose undue hardship on the business.[20]

If you have experienced discrimination because of a disability and attempts to reach an understanding with your employer have failed, further action may be in order. To get information about your rights under this law, you may contact the U.S. Department of Justice, Disability Rights Section, listed in the Resource Directory, or the nearest Disability Business and Technical Assistance Center by calling 1-800-949-4232. There is no charge for calling. You can also contact the Equal Employment Opportunity Commission and private disability law groups for information.

DOES YOUR STATE HAVE A DISCRIMINATION LAW?

Most states, and many cities, have enacted state fair employment practice laws that parallel federal discrimination laws or offer broader protection by reaching smaller businesses that are not covered by federal statutes. In addition, some state laws protect employees from discrimination on the basis of marital status, sexual orientation, parenthood, personal appearance, or political affiliation. Your state or local human/civil rights commission or fair employment practice agency will be able to give you information on the laws in your area. Look in the government section of the white pages of your local telephone directory for the number and address.

DISCRIMINATION RELATED TO SEXUAL ORIENTATION

As of yet, there is no federal law that forbids discrimination in employment on the basis of sexual orientation, although the Employment Non-Discrimination Act (ENDA), which would protect lesbians, gay men, and bisexual people from employment discrimination, has been introduced in Congress in the past, and efforts to secure federal protection from employment discrimination will most likely continue. At present only a few states have laws that prohibit discrimination on the basis of sexual orientation. At the time of this writing, these states include California, Connecticut, Hawaii, Massachusetts, Minnesota, Wisconsin, New Jersey, Vermont, and Rhode Island.[21] Many large cities and counties have passed laws that forbid discrimination against lesbians, bisexuals, and gay men. If you live in an area with antidiscrimination laws protecting sexual orientation, contact your state or local human/civil rights commission or fair employment agency for more information.

If you live in an area where there is no antidiscrimination law to protect you, it is more difficult to find redress. Depending on your situation, however, there are a few avenues that you and an attorney experienced in discrimination cases based on sexual orientation may be able to explore.

If you are covered by a written contract or collective bar-

THE CONGRESSIONAL ACCOUNTABILITY ACT

The Congressional Accountability Act extends the protections of several federal workplace statutes, including Title VII of the Civil Rights Act of 1964, the Age Discrimination in Employment Act, the Americans with Disabilities Act, and the Family and Medical Leave Act, among others, to employees of the legislative branch of the federal government. However, the means of resolving disputes are different from those discussed in this chapter. For more information, contact the Office of Compliance, Room LA 200, John Adams Building, 110 Second Street SE, Washington, D.C. 20540-1999, or call (202) 724-9250 or (202) 426-1912 (TDD).

---

gaining agreement which states that you will not be fired except for just cause, you may be in a very good position for action. Being a lesbian or bisexual woman, it can be argued, is not good cause for being fired. This type of action is also available in states with sexual orientation discrimination laws.

You should have a copy of your personnel manual or employee handbook. In states where the courts have viewed the language of employee handbooks as contractual, you may be able to seek relief, providing that your handbook contains a statement that you won't be fired without good cause. Again, this possibility depends very much upon your situation and the state in which the discrimination took place.

Public employees, whose employers are governed by the U.S. Constitution, often have rights unavailable to private employees, such as the right of due process. If you are a public employee, you may have the right to a hearing on the grounds for your dismissal. In addition, public employees are protected by the right to freedom of speech in many circumstances. Coming out may be viewed as politically protected speech in the public workplace and in states with laws protecting against discrimination on the basis of political affiliation. However, public employees are also limited in their political activities by the Hatch Acts, which forbid partisan politicking.

Lesbians and bisexual women who are sexually harassed in the workplace may also have a course of action under Title VII of the Civil Rights Act of 1964, discussed earlier. For example, an employer or supervisor who continually harasses you by pressuring you for sex or dates may be guilty of sex discrimination.

By finding other employees who have been subjected to the same unfair treatment or who are willing to fight with you for an end to discrimination, you can form a grassroots movement to expose the employer's practices. If efforts to solve the matter with your employer have failed, this may be a useful tactic. You must, however, consider the possibility of repercussions. If you feel the risk of losing your job is too great, or if you do not feel comfortable with the idea of having your orientation known by many, this avenue may not work for you.

Whatever your situation, wherever you live, you will be able to build your case by documenting what is happening to you. If you are wondering whether your employer's actions are discriminatory or illegal, try calling one of the advocacy groups listed in the Resource Directory for information. If you are considering taking legal action, it is advisable to see an attorney as soon as possible.

THE EEOC PROCESS: TAKING LEGAL ACTION AGAINST DISCRIMINATION

When considering whether to take legal action against an employer who discriminates, it's necessary to gain a basic understanding of the ways in which claims can be pursued and to weigh the advantages and disadvantages of civil action. This section and the following will tell you how to file a charge and help you decide whether you want to pursue your claim.

What Is the Equal Employment Opportunity Commission?

The Equal Employment Opportunity Commission (EEOC) is the agency established by the Civil Rights Act of 1964 to investigate charges of discrimination in employment and to enforce Title VII (and its amendment, the Civil Rights Act of 1991), the Age Discrimination in Employment Act (ADEA), the Americans with Disabilities Act (ADA), and the Equal Pay Act (EPA). Section 1981 of the Civil Rights Acts of 1866 is not enforced by the EEOC; rather, cases are filed privately.

The following section will give you a general idea of how to file a charge with EEOC and what will happen if you do.

How to File a Charge Under Title VII or the Americans with Disabilities Act

If you believe that your employer has discriminated against you in violation of Title VII or the ADA, you can file a charge with the Equal Employment Opportunity Commission. The EEOC will investigate the charge and attempt to resolve the problem between you and your employer. If no resolution can be achieved, the EEOC will either bring a lawsuit on your behalf, although this is very rare, or issue you a "right-to-sue" letter, which allows you to sue in court on your own. You cannot sue under Title VII without going through this process. However, if you fail to file your charge with EEOC within the time limits discussed below, or if your employer is not covered by Title VII because there are too few employees, you may still be able to use state fair employment practice laws or, in cases of intentional racial discrimination, the Civil Rights Acts of 1866, to gain redress.

State fair employment practice agencies, human rights

commissions or civil rights commissions (the agencies have different names in different states) work together with EEOC. If your state has an antidiscrimination law and a fair employment practice agency (most states do), your case will initially be referred to the state or local agency.

Even if you are pursuing your charge through the grievance procedures of your company or union, you might consider filing with the EEOC as well, in order to avoid an untimely charge.

To file a charge, contact the EEOC office nearest you. For the telephone number, call the national office of the EEOC, listed in the Resource Directory, or look in the government section of your white pages. You can visit, call, or write the office to request the appropriate forms and a written description of the complaint procedure. It's best, though, to visit the office to avoid slowing down your case. Be sure to ask how many days you have to file your charge.

Charges cannot be made verbally. They must be written. There is no fee for filing or for an investigation. The agency staff members are expected to be able to assist you in filing your charge. However, if the staff members are overburdened, they may have little time to explore all possibilities related to your charge. An advocacy organization can help you evaluate your case, give you information on what to include in your charge and which documents to bring, or refer you to a lawyer, if necessary. If you require an interpreter, call the EEOC office ahead of time to make arrangements.

Before the charge is drafted, a staff person will interview you in order to get as much information about the complaint as possible. Bring any documents you have that support your claim as well as the names and job titles of the people whom you are charging. The charge should include:

- your name, address, and birth date
- the name(s) and addresses of the person(s) or company you believe discriminated against you
- the reason(s) for discrimination (for example, race, color, sex, national origin, religion, disability)
- a description of the discrimination (including all incidents or types of discrimination)
- the general dates and places at which the discrimination took place

It is illegal for an employer to retaliate against an employee for filing a charge. If you have been fired, demoted or otherwise punished for filing a charge, be sure to inform the government agency as soon as possible and include it in your charge.

You must file your charge within 180 calendar days (6 months) from the discriminatory act. In states with antidiscrimination laws and authorized enforcement agencies, you have 300 days to file, but it is always best to file at the earliest possible date to keep your case timely and viable!

If you are a *federal employee,* you must speak with an EEO counselor within 45 days of the discriminatory incident or action, although there may be an extension of the time limit in certain circumstances. The procedures that you will follow to attempt to resolve the matter are different from those outlined in this section. It is imperative that you act as soon as possible. Your counselor must provide you with a written description of your rights and responsibilities.

After you file, the agency will conduct an investigation appropriate to the charge to determine whether it is likely that a violation of the law will be found. The discriminating party (called the respondent) should be notified and asked to respond. Further investigation may be done, a settlement may be attempted, if appropriate, or your charge may be dismissed. If your case proceeds, the EEOC or state/local agency must determine whether there is reasonable cause to believe that discrimination took place. If it does not find reasonable cause, it will dismiss your case. Even if the agency finds no cause, you can still sue the employer on your own.

If the agency does find cause to believe your complaint, it will try to reach an agreement between you and your employer through conciliation. If no conciliation is possible, the agency will either issue you a notification of its intent to take civil action or give you a "right-to-sue" letter, which allows you to sue in federal court. The latter is much more common. Once you receive the right-to-sue notice or notice of dismissal you have 90 days to file your lawsuit with the court.

The EEOC or state/local agency has 180 days to complete a resolution of your charge. If the agency has not completed its investigative and conciliation process within 180 days, you may request a right-to-sue letter in order to move the issue to court as swiftly as possible.

If you win in court, you may be entitled to lost wages and benefits as well as reinstatement and other types of relief. You can also get a court order, called an *injunction,* requiring your employer to do or to stop doing something. For example, an injunction might require an employer to stop using an illegal means of choosing employees or to implement an antiharassment policy.

The Civil Rights Act of 1991 amended Title VII to allow victims of intentional discrimination to sue for compensatory damages for injuries caused by the discrimination, but the amount of damages is limited by the number of employees working for your employer. In some cases, punitive damages, designed to punish an employer who acts with malice or with reckless disregard for your rights, may be available.

Filing Complaints and Charges Under the ADEA

The procedure for filing a charge under the Age Discrimination in Employment Act (ADEA) is similar to that under Title VII and the ADA. However, under the ADEA you can potentially preserve your anonymity by filing a complaint instead of a charge. But it's important to find out whether making a complaint instead of a charge will affect your ability to file a private lawsuit.

If you decide to proceed formally, you should file your charge with the EEOC within 180 days from the discriminatory act. The EEOC will attempt to conciliate the matter, just as with Title VII and ADA charges.

FILING A CHARGE WITH A STATE FAIR-EMPLOYMENT AGENCY

Filing a charge with a state fair-employment agency (where they exist) may be more advantageous than filing a federal charge because, for example, your state may have antidiscrimination laws that offer broader protection than federal law and the laws may apply to smaller companies. Contact your state or local fair-employment agency or human/civil rights commission for information on the laws in your state and the agency's procedures. The decision to file under state law, federal law, or both is one that should be made with the advice of an attorney or advocate.

OTHER TYPES OF LEGAL ACTION YOU CAN TAKE AGAINST YOUR EMPLOYER

Depending on your situation, you may be able to file a private lawsuit based on tort law. A tort occurs when an illegal wrong or injury is done to one party by another and some damage results. For example, the crimes of assault and battery are also considered to be civil wrongs. Invasion of privacy, intentional infliction of emotional distress, defamation, wrongful termination, and interference with a contract are all examples of torts. This type of lawsuit may offer higher money remedies than a suit under state or federal discrimination laws.

As mentioned previously, if you have been physically assaulted or raped at the workplace, think about calling the police and filing criminal charges. A rape crisis center or advocacy organization can help you decide what to do. See Chapter Four for more information.

TAKING LEGAL ACTION: THE PROS AND CONS

While many discrimination problems can be solved by speaking directly to the employer or person who is discriminating against or harassing you, sometimes this is not the case. Legal action may become necessary. Depending on your situation, you can file a charge with the EEOC or take other avenues. While you do not need a lawyer to file a charge with the EEOC and doing so does not create a commitment to engage in a lawsuit, independent legal action is the final step in bringing about a resolution to discrimination after all other means of problem-solving have failed.

There are many good reasons for resisting legal action. For example, you will have to see the person who discriminated against you and relive the experience during court testimony. The expenditure of time and money may be too great a price to pay to reach an uncertain conclusion. Still, a lawsuit may provide you with the only means of financial and emotional recovery.

You should neither be pressured into bringing a lawsuit nor persuaded that your single effort will have no effect. Each woman who stands up to an employer against discrimination, informally or in the courts, is making a difference for others. Employees who take action against unfair employers make working conditions better for others.

If you do decide to take legal action, there are a few important points to remember. These are not designed to dissuade you, only to give you an idea of what to expect:

- Discrimination is hard to prove, and it may be hard to find a lawyer who is willing to represent you.
- Look for an attorney specializing in *employment law* who has experience representing the *plaintiff,* not the defendant. Always look for someone who has experience handling your specific type of problem. For example, if you are the victim of sexual harassment, look for an employment lawyer with experience handling sexual harassment cases. A good lawyer can advise you on the merits of your case, help you make decisions about fil-

ing your charge, file other appropriate claims, and help you discover other means of redress.

- Talk to other people in your place of employment who you think may have experienced the same discrimination. They may be able to serve as witnesses or join you in a class action lawsuit. Your chances of success may be improved if others can show that they were subject to the same kind of treatment.

- Ask your lawyer about the possibility of mediation. A professional mediator may be able to help the parties involved settle the problem without going to court. Mediation is generally less expensive than a lawsuit and may be useful, if you are no longer working for the employer and the employer agrees to pay for the mediator.

- Employment discrimination lawsuits can take *years*. Even if your lawyer accepts your case on a contingency basis (this means you pay only if you win), you can expect to pay for depositions, filing fees, the lawyer's travel and telephone expenses, and other miscellaneous costs. These costs can add up quickly and reach an enormous sum. Some lawyers may be willing to absorb extra costs if your case is very strong or if it offers the possibility of setting legal precedent, but don't count on this.

- Be prepared for an emotionally draining experience. You will have to recount and relive the discrimination that you suffered. Discrimination suits, particularly cases of sexual harassment, can be extremely unpleasant. It may be possible for you and your attorney to settle with the defendant before the case comes to trial. But if you do go to trial, you must know that it is the job of the defendant's attorney to discredit your allegations. Victims are often made to feel as though they are to blame or as if they somehow accepted or caused the discrimination.

- If you've lost your job, get new employment as soon as you are able, even if you are seeking reinstatement. By not seeking a new job, you may weaken your case by appearing to be opportunistic or unwilling to work. As mentioned previously, you have a legal duty to "mitigate damages." Any compensation you receive may be reduced by what the court finds you could have earned had you made diligent efforts to regain employment.

- Seek emotional support. Your family and friends may be able to support you, but the difficulties of going through a long legal process can create a great deal of stress for all concerned. Women's groups, advocacy groups, your

---

DOCUMENT EVERYTHING!

The most important thing anyone anticipating a dispute with an employer can do is to document the events leading to a complaint. This is advisable for a number of reasons. Employers, especially larger companies, are usually very adept at protecting themselves from allegations by employees. Documentation produced for a human resources or personnel department is much more persuasive than an oral account of what happened. In addition, by having a written record, you can preserve crucial details of events that you may otherwise forget. An attorney will also want to see such documents to assess your case.

lawyer, and friends may be able to recommend therapists and lead you to support groups. If there are none in your community, you can form a group on your own.

- Be prepared to fight. Many employers, especially larger employers, know how to counter claims of discrimination. Stay involved with your case. Give your attorney every relevant piece of information you have, including information that might damage your claim, so that your attorney can prepare a response. An attorney cannot work in your best interest without a full understanding of your situation.

Here are some examples of the type of documents you may need, depending on your situation:

- a copy of your job application
- pay stubs or record of your wages
- a copy of your termination notice
- a copy of any written contract between you and your employer
- a copy of your personnel manual or employee handbook
- a detailed, chronological written account of what happened. Date each entry. State the time and place at which each incident occurred. Name the people involved and any witnesses. State what was said or done and what you said or did. Indicate any promises, written or spoken, made by the employer or supervisor. Record any agreements made between you and your employer.

  Keep copies of your performance evaluations. Write down any spoken words of praise for your job performance and keep copies of any written praise. In addition, document all communications with the human resources department. Do not keep this log at work. Keep it at home in a safe place.
- names, addresses, telephone numbers of any witnesses or others allegedly victimized
- a copy of your personnel file, or employment record, if possible. Although many states have laws allowing employees access to personnel files, not every state provides for this. If you can legally access and copy your file, you will have evidence of your satisfactory job performance, unless, of course, your employer has already tampered with the file
- a copy of letter(s) to the harasser, if applicable
- a copy of any material sent to you by a harasser, including messages, e-mail, cards, evidence of practical jokes, letters, and so forth

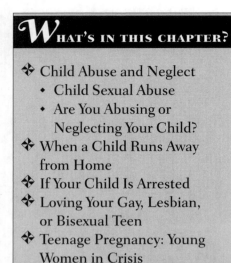

WHAT'S IN THIS CHAPTER?

❖ Child Abuse and Neglect
  • Child Sexual Abuse
  • Are You Abusing or
    Neglecting Your Child?
❖ When a Child Runs Away
  from Home
❖ If Your Child Is Arrested
❖ Loving Your Gay, Lesbian,
  or Bisexual Teen
❖ Teenage Pregnancy: Young
  Women in Crisis

❖ 2 ❖

Children in Crisis

CHILD ABUSE AND NEGLECT

CHILD SEXUAL ABUSE

Child sexual abuse is any type of sexual interaction that occurs between a child and another person through manipulation, coercion, or physical force for the gratification or profit of the offender. This includes watching a child undress for the purpose of sexual arousal, exposing oneself to a child, masturbating in front of a child, making obscene phone calls or propositions to a child, taking pornographic pictures of a child, touching, fondling, or rubbing against a child's body for sexual gratification, asking a child to touch, fondle, or rub another's body and/or his or her own body for the purpose of sexual gratification; any attempted or completed oral, vaginal, or anal intercourse, or inserting any part of an object into a child's vagina or anus for other than legitimate medical purposes.

Sexual Abuse Is a Crime

Child sexual abuse is a crime in every state. Both girls and boys are vulnerable to sexual abuse by adults and other minors. Although sexual abuse is often thought of as a crime perpetrated by strangers, most children are hurt by someone they know and often someone whom they trust — for example, a parent, grandparent, uncle, aunt, brother or sister, stepparent, or other family member not related by blood. This type of abuse, called intrafamilial sexual abuse, can

Childhelp USA:
1-800-4-A-CHILD
1-800-2-A-CHILD (TDD)
   This national hotline is available twenty-four hours a day, seven days a week, to provide crisis counseling, referrals to child abuse prevention and treatment services, emergency shelter programs, parenting education and support groups and other services to victims of child abuse, parents, and others interested in the prevention of child maltreatment. Many languages are spoken on the hotline.

Boys Town National Hotline:
1-800-448-3000
1-800-448-1833 (TDD)
   This twenty-four-hour national hotline accepts calls from children, teens, and adults about any problem, including sexual abuse, physical abuse, substance abuse, gang activity, domestic violence, running away, and parenting problems. Operators can provide counseling and referrals to helpful organizations in your area.

Parents Anonymous national office:
(909) 621-6184
   Parents Anonymous is a national self-help organization for parents who are having difficulty parenting. Groups are led by parents and facilitated by professionals in a nonjudgmental environment. Services are free. Call to find out if there is a chapter in your area. You do not have to give your name.

For more information about these and other important resources for families in crisis and for adult survivors of child abuse, refer to the Resource Directory.

occur in families of any income, racial or ethnic heritage or religious background. Children are also abused by familiar but unrelated people such as neighbors or baby-sitters. Although the majority of reported offenders in cases of child sexual abuse are male, women and girls can and do sexually abuse children. Some researchers believe that sexual abuse by female offenders is underreported.

Child Sexual Abusers Don't Necessarily Use Physical Force

Because the offender is often an adult whom the child respects and with whom the child has a close relationship, physical force is seldom needed to accomplish an abusive act. Rather, the abuser often depends on subtle forms of manipulation.

Abuse usually takes place over a long period of time and is accomplished in great secrecy with the abuser moving very gradually from less threatening, seemingly benign acts to more overt sexual behavior. In order to secure the child's cooperation, the abuser may bribe the child with gifts or special attention. Maintaining the victim's silence is crucial, and thus the abuser may threaten to kill the child, himself, or family members or the family pet if the abuse is revealed. The abuser may intimidate the child in other ways. For example, he may say, "I'll go to jail if you tell," or suggest that the family will break up or that other children will be abused if the child does not comply. The abuser may also threaten to take away a child's "special attention" or privileges if he tells.

Many children are afraid to tell because they fear they will not be believed or that they will be blamed for the abuse. In fact, abusers create an environment wherein children are made to feel completely responsible for the abuse they experience. Some children may not disclose abuse because they are too young to understand the nature of what is happening to them or because they lack the words to describe it. A child may also be confused by the perpetrator's sexual behavior and interpret being touched as an expression of affection. He or she may not want to reject the abuser for fear of losing the relationship, especially if the abuser is someone he or she loves. A child may feel ashamed or guilty. It takes a great deal of courage for a child to reveal sexual abuse.

If You Suspect That Your Child Has Been Abused

Some children disclose information about sexual abuse directly. Some may only be able to hint at the abuse or talk about it in vague terms. You may learn about the abuse from a third party, such as a teacher or relative. You may suspect that something is troubling your child but may not be able to define exactly what it is. On the other hand, you may have no indication that anything is wrong until you receive a visit from an investigator with the child protective services agency or a law enforcement officer.

Regardless of the way in which you come to know about the abuse, you will need some guidelines to help you assess what is happening. Although researchers have noted many of the effects of sexual abuse in children, child sexual abuse is not easy to detect. Children react to abuse in different ways, and it's important to remember that the behavioral indicators of sexual abuse listed below are only signs that your child may be experiencing some sort of distress and are not, by themselves, definitive markers of sexual abuse. Your child may be reacting to a divorce or separation, a family move, the death of a loved one, or another stressful event. A child who has been physically abused may also exhibit some of the same behaviors. Moreover, some sexually abused children exhibit none of these behaviors.

Behavioral Indicators of Sexual Abuse

- bed-wetting or soiling
- sleep disturbances, such as nightmares or insomnia
- excessive and/or public masturbation
- inappropriate or unusually sophisticated sexual behavior or knowledge
- sexual interaction with peers or revealing sexual organs to others
- intense, and possibly sudden, fear of certain people, for example, the abuser or someone of the abuser's gender, and certain places, such as the child's school or a relative's home
- regressive or infantile behavior
- withdrawal, sadness, or depression
- unusually aggressive or hostile behavior
- self-destructive or self-injurious behavior
- a sudden onset of school-related problems
- problems relating to peers
- extreme changes in eating habits
- psychosomatic illnesses such as headaches or stomach aches for which there are no apparent explanations
- running away
- delinquency
- suicide attempts or talk of suicide or death

Physical Indicators of Sexual Abuse

Very often, there is no physical evidence of abuse. However, if physical indicators are present, it is important to seek medical attention for your child from a physician who is experienced in the investigation of child sexual abuse. Possible physical signs of sexual abuse include:

- torn, stained, or bloody underclothing
- trouble walking or sitting
- pain, itching, swelling, or soreness in the genital area or the area around the anus
- injury to the genital or anal area

- pregnancy
- the presence of a sexually transmitted disease

What to Do If You Learn That Your Child Has Been Sexually Abused

When you first learn that your child has been abused, you may be overcome with a range of forceful emotions. You may be shocked, horrified, and enraged. You may not want to believe it. You may blame yourself because you think that you should have known about the abuse or because you recognize some of the signs in retrospect. If the abuser is someone close to you, you may feel a strong sense of betrayal, fear, grief, and confusion all at once. You may suddenly find yourself having to choose between offering support and loyalty to your child and to the person alleged to have committed the abuse.

These feelings are understandable, and it will be very important for you to express and explore them later — outside of your child's presence. It is crucial to remain calm and to focus on your child's needs first. Disclosure is the first step in your child's recovery. The way in which you react will have a significant influence on your child's ability to cope with the abuse and to heal. Your child needs to feel that you'll be there to help and that you'll be able to listen and get through this crisis together. Here are some things you can do to help your child when you first learn about the abuse:

Stay calm and be supportive. Try as hard as you can not to overreact. Your child may be very frightened and may feel ashamed, guilty, and confused. Expressions of revulsion, disbelief, anger, or blame can only increase her sense of guilt and impair the trust that you share.

Praise your child for telling you what happened. It takes courage for a child to disclose sexual abuse. If your child told someone else before coming to you, you may be feeling very hurt. Children often fear that their parents will blame them or become angry or upset if they tell. The fact that your child told someone else first does not mean that he doesn't trust you or that you are a bad parent. Let your child know that you are glad that someone was informed and that it is all right to talk to you about any uncomfortable or bad feelings at any time. Do not make statements suggestive of blame such as "Why didn't you come to me earlier?" or "Why didn't you just run away from him?"

Listen with respect and concern. Let your child explain in her own way. Be careful not to ask leading questions, such as, "Was it your uncle?" or "Did she touch your private parts?" Children may feel prompted to give adults the answer they think they want to hear. Do not interrogate your child for every detail of the abuse. Instead, let your child know of your love and concern. Tell him or her that it's all right to talk at any time. Make it clear that she can start the conversation. Otherwise, she may interpret any silence on your part as an indication not to talk about the abuse again.

Believe your child. No matter how much you wish to deny the possibility of abuse, it is vital that your child knows that you believe what he or she tells you. Although it's important to make sure that you are not misinterpreting your child's statements, it's equally important to understand that children rarely lie about being sexually abused. Often, the details of abuse given by a child indicate knowledge and experience of sexuality beyond that which is usual for the child's age and which cannot be gained solely through the media or by talking with other children. Some sexually abused children may identify the wrong person or several people as the perpetrator, because they are too scared to actually name the person who abused them. As well, some children may recant earlier statements. This may happen when a child fears retaliation by the abuser or is frightened by his or her parents' reactions.

It's crucial to proceed carefully toward an understanding of what happened. If you do not express belief in your child and allow your child to talk about his experience, you risk marring his trust in you. If your child is lying about being sexually abused, counseling may be necessary. A false allegation may be a sign of other problems in your child's life or in the family. Under no circumstances should you try to bury the matter and forget it. Child sexual abuse that remains unaddressed often results in serious problems for the child and the family.

Reassure your child that the abuse was not his or her fault and that the abuser is solely responsible for what happened. Tell her that you will always love her and that you will do your best to protect her. Many victims of child sexual abuse suffer from what is termed damaged-goods syndrome.[1] They feel as though their bodies have been permanently damaged or that they will be perceived as bad or unwanted because of the abuse. Help your child to understand that there is nothing "bad" or "wrong" about her.

Respect your child's privacy. Tell only those who need to know, such as a child protective services worker or law enforcement officer. Make sure your child understands that you will not share the information indiscriminately. Ask your child to tell you who he thinks should know.

Get Medical Attention for Your Child

Seeking emergency medical care is necessary whenever you suspect that your child has been injured and whenever there is a possibility of collecting evidence for prosecution. If the abuse was very recent (within forty-eight to seventy-two hours of the assault), especially when penetration or genital contact is suspected, your child should be taken to the emergency department of the nearest general hospital for a medical/evidentiary examination. The child protective services agency and/or the law enforcement agency will provide you with instructions, which should be followed. The purpose of the examination is to look for, document, and treat any injuries that your child may have sustained as well as to record other evidence of abuse, such as the presence of seminal material in or on your child's body. When necessary, children may also be tested for sexually transmitted diseases and/or pregnancy. The examination may be conducted with a sexual assault examination kit modified for use with children. Although it is uncommon for medical professionals to find evidence of sexual abuse, an inconclusive examination does not mean that the child was spared harm.

It may be difficult for you to define what happened to your child. That is why it is necessary to contact the child protective services (CPS) agency or law enforcement for advice on how to proceed. Do not attempt to investigate the abuse by yourself. You may destroy your child's case.

Even in nonemergency situations, a medical examination is important. Children who have been sexually abused are often concerned that they might have been injured by the abuse and thus will benefit from a professional reassurance of good health. Your caseworker or therapist can give advice on this matter.

The examination should be performed by a medical professional who has experience in child sexual abuse cases and who is sensitive to the needs of child victims. Your pediatrician may not have the necessary training to do the examination but may be able to refer you to another doctor who does. The child protective services agency can also help you find a doctor. In some communities, a multidisciplinary team of professionals work together to evaluate and address the needs of child sexual abuse victims. A team may include medical and mental health professionals, child protection advocates, police, and prosecutors.

Depending on the state in which you live and the circumstances of the abuse, reports of child sexual abuse may be made to the local child protective services agency or to the police. Law enforcement and child protective services agencies may investigate the report together.

Generally, it is advisable to call the police if the abuse was committed by a stranger or a nonfamily member such as a teacher, coach, or baby-sitter. Abuse committed by a family member and, in many states, another person in the household, such as a boyfriend or girlfriend, may be reported to the child protective agency. You can always call the police if the child protective agency is closed, for example, after normal business hours or on the weekends.

The child protective services agency is typically a division of the Department of Social (or Human) Services. (The name of the government agency may differ in your area, and the name of the child protective services agency may also differ.) Look in the front section of your telephone directory. There may be a county or statewide child abuse hotline on which to make a report. You can also call the child protective services agency directly, often through the state hotline. Check the government section of your local white pages for the telephone number. If you are having trouble locating the agency or you need help making the call, a crisis counselor with Childhelp USA may be able to help you. For the telephone number, see page 45.

If your child was abused by someone close to you or someone in your family, you may be tempted not to report the crime and to try to deal with the problem on your own. The person alleged to have committed the abuse, other family members, or friends may pressure you not to report. If the abuser is also hurting you or if you depend on the abuser for financial support, you may fear confronting the issue. However, the child's protection *must* come before all other considerations. It is likely that the person who abused your child will abuse or has abused other children. Moreover, you have a legal duty to protect your child from harm. Parents have been held liable for failure to protect their children when they chose to place other concerns above a child's safety. Placement of your child outside the home, termination of your parental rights, and criminal charges are possible results of failing to protect a child from continued harm. Confronting the abuser without doing anything more about it will not stop the abuse, and may place you and your child in greater danger. Therefore, it's in your best interests and the best interests of your child to report the abuse and to discuss the situation with a professional at the child protective services agency. Remember, abuse will not stop without intervention.

If you are also being abused, contact a women's shelter for information and support. A women's shelter or another advocacy group may be able to provide temporary refuge for you and your children, if you need it. See Chapter Four for more information.

What Will Happen When You Report Child Sexual Abuse?

Because community and agency responses to child sexual abuse differ, it is not possible to tell you precisely what will happen once a report is made. However, the following is a brief, general explanation of what to expect.

Your child may be interviewed by a law enforcement officer or a child protective services investigator or both, depending on state law and local policies as well as the nature of the abuse and the circumstances under which it occurred. A child protection team consisting of professionals from various disciplines may work together to investigate your child's case. Some communities have established *child advocacy centers* to improve coordination between agencies by providing services, including interviews, medical examinations, and counseling, in a single, child-friendly facility. Although programs differ, emphasis is on reducing the number of interviews a child must endure and decreasing the traumatic impact of the investigation.

When you first contact the child protective services or police agency, you will be asked for information about your child, your family, the abuse, and the alleged abuser. The intake worker will determine whether the incident(s) meets the legal and agency definitions of child abuse. If so, an investigation will be conducted. In most states, the investigation must take place within a certain time frame determined by state law and agency policy. If the agency feels that your child is in imminent danger, the investigation may begin immediately or within twenty-four hours.

During the initial investigation, your child may be interviewed at school or in another setting, such as an office at the child protective services agency or child advocacy center. Once your child is interviewed, you and any other children in the household may be interviewed as well, and witnesses may be sought. At some point, your child may be interviewed on videotape. A videotape can help reduce the number of times a child must recount the abuse and can help local prosecutors (often called county or district attorneys) decide whether to pursue the case. For some young children, being videotaped is a frightening experience. A child may fear disclosing the abuse or retribution from the offender or may be afraid that the information will be shown on television and will need reassurance that it will not.

It may take the agencies involved a month or more to determine whether there is enough evidence to substantiate the allegation of abuse. The case may be reviewed (or investigated) by the local prosecutor, who will decide whether it can be tried in criminal court. The decision to try the case depends on many factors, among which are the availability of evidence and a child's ability to testify.

If a decision is made to try the case, an arrest warrant will be issued for the perpetrator. If the perpetrator is arrested, you should know that he or she may have an opportunity to post bond and thus may be free until the next court appearance. Ask the local prosecutor (district or county attorney) whether special conditions, such as a criminal order of protection prohibiting the abuser from contacting you or your child, can be attached to a pretrial release. You should also be aware that the defendant may plead guilty to a lesser offense in exchange for a lighter sentence (called plea-bargaining), in which case there will not be a trial and your child will not have to testify. Otherwise, a trial date will be set.

The investigation and trial are often very long and stressful for children and families. Be sure to ask the professionals involved in your case as many questions as you have about the process and to seek outside assistance. Therapy or counseling (discussed below) can be very helpful to your child and to you.

If you are involved in another legal proceeding, such as an abuse or neglect proceeding, the judge may appoint a guardian ad litem (GAL) or court-appointed special advocate (CASA), who may be an attorney or volunteer, to represent your child's interests. (Some state laws allow for the appointment of GALs to represent children's interests during criminal proceedings.)[2] Your child may also be able to have his own attorney in a civil proceeding. For more information about the services of volunteer guardians ad litem, contact the National Court Appointed Special Advocates Association (CASA), listed in the Resource Directory.

Seeking Therapy

Early intervention with professional therapy can be very beneficial for children who have been sexually abused. Although all children do not react to sexual abuse in exactly the same way, you may have already noticed some of the behaviors indicative of abuse. Molested children often suffer from terrible guilt, anger, fear, and from feelings of low self-esteem. Depression and suicidal thoughts are not uncommon.

If unaddressed, the effects of sexual abuse can continue long into your child's adult life. Children often need help believing that the abuse was not their fault and in repairing their ability to trust. Other children in the family, who may be having a hard time dealing with events after the disclosure of abuse, and certainly siblings who have also been abused, may benefit from therapy. Professionals working with sexually abused children may recommend play therapy, individual or group therapy, or a combination of these to help a young child cope with and heal from sexual abuse.

Parents need a place to express their feelings as well. Getting support for yourself can help you to better support your child. If your husband or partner abused your child, it may be especially important for you to speak with an objective professional in order to make decisions about the future of your relationship. If you were also sexually abused as a child, your child's abuse may have revived painful memories, and you may want to explore unresolved issues related to the past.

The child protective services agency may be able to refer you to a therapist experienced in helping children who have been sexually abused and their families. A local rape crisis center may provide counseling, support groups for sexual abuse survivors, or referrals to mental health services. As well, police or medical professionals may be able to give you the names of qualified therapists. Talking to supportive family members or friends or your clergyperson can also be very helpful.

ARE YOU ABUSING OR NEGLECTING YOUR CHILD?

Even parents who love their children and want the very best for them can unintentionally harm them. All parents need help from time to time, and no parent is perfect. Recognizing a negative pattern and taking steps to address it can be the beginning of many positive changes, not only in your child's life, but in your own. Change is difficult and frightening at first. It may mean facing issues of abuse and neglect in your own childhood. Be patient with yourself. Your willingness to risk an honest appraisal of your relationship with your child(ren) is a sign of strength and an ability to grow. It takes courage, and it is challenging, but it is never too late to improve your relationship with your children and to enhance your own sense of well-being.

Are You at Risk? Questions to Ask Yourself

This section is intended to help you identify potential problems in your relationship with your child so that you can take the opportunity to improve it. Some of the questions may be hard to answer and some of the information about child abuse and neglect may be difficult to read. But, as with any other critical issue, it's important to have as much realistic information about child abuse and neglect as possible. If you recognize the need for change, be careful not to judge yourself too harshly. Rather, focus on finding a solution.

Becoming aware of a problem and addressing it doesn't mean erasing all the positive things in your life. Your strengths — your perseverance, your sense of humor, your intelligence, your ability to love — do not disappear when you accept the challenge of change. There are many avenues of support available to you, and you are not alone. Many parents have come to recognize and accept the need to look for new ways of dealing with the daily frustrations and demands of parenting, and they have improved their family lives as a result.

- Do you feel overwhelmed by parenting? Do you feel that you could use more help and support but that there is no one available to turn to?
- Are there many days when you feel depressed or anxious?
- Would you like to reduce the presence of alcohol or other drugs in your life?
- Do you sometimes feel so angry or disappointed with your child or yourself that you lash out at your child with harsh remarks such as, "You never do anything right!" or "I wish you were never born"?
- Have you ever been afraid that you might hurt your child?
- Have you ever physically hurt your child?
- Have you ever lied about how your child was injured?
- Have you ever touched your child, or any child, in a sexual manner, for example, when bathing your child? Have you fantasized about it?

The following sections will provide a general discussion of child abuse and neglect. Although forms of child maltreatment have been categorized, they often overlap. For information on what to do if you think you are maltreating your child, see the section titled Preventing or Stopping Child Abuse and Neglect on page 60.

What Is Physical Abuse?

When we think of child physical abuse, we often imagine acts of intentional cruelty committed against a child by an inhumane, unfeeling parent. While some parents may intentionally hurt their children, most physical abuse occurs when ordinary parents are trying to discipline their children. Although the legal definition of child physical abuse differs from state to state, physical abuse can generally be thought of as the infliction of any injury by other than accidental means. Pushing, hitting, shaking, spanking your child with your hand or an object, kicking, beating, pinching, pulling hair, biting, scalding, and other actions can cause injury to a child even when a parent intends only to teach the child a lesson, not to do actual harm. Parents or caregivers may repeatedly harm or threaten a child, but an injury caused in a single incident can constitute an act of child abuse. Child maltreatment, including physical abuse, is against the law. Although much of the work of child protective services agencies centers on helping families to resolve the problems that lead to abuse or neglect and on keeping families together, the legal consequences of maltreatment can be dire. For example, serious or chronic cases of maltreatment may necessitate removal of a child from the home, termination of parental rights and, depending on the circumstances, criminal charges. Women who are not directly abusing their children but who fail to intervene when another, such as a husband or partner, harms them may also face these actions. Even women who are themselves terrorized in violent and abusive relationships have been held liable for failure to protect their children. In addition, a divorced or separated parent may seek a change of custody based on child maltreatment.

If you feel that you may, or know that you have, hurt your child — or if you know that someone else is hurting your child — you must take steps to prevent or stop it. A physically abused child or adolescent suffers emotional and bodily pain. Long-term repercussions for families are often very serious. For example, children who are physically abused are at risk of becoming delinquent, running away from home, and hurting themselves with destructive behavior. Emotional support and options for learning nonviolent, effective

Shaken baby syndrome (SBS) is the term that is used to describe the damage done to a child whose head is whiplashed when shaken. Shaking, slapping, throwing or tossing a baby, even in play, can cause permanent brain damage, seizures, blindness, and death.

Very often, frustration caused by a baby's crying can lead to shaken baby syndrome. Crying is one of the first ways babies learn to communicate. Some children cry more than others and are harder to soothe. You're not a bad mother because your baby cries more than other children. Ask your pediatrician or nurse for tips on calming a crying baby and for solutions to problems with particularly fussy or colicky babies. If you are afraid of how you might react the next time your baby cries, get the help that you need to protect your child from harm. Contact a national child abuse prevention hotline (see the beginning of this chapter) or check the front pages of your local telephone directory for the number of an area- or statewide child abuse and neglect prevention hotline.

parenting skills are available to you. If you are also being hurt by a violent or abusive partner, see Chapter Four.

What is Emotional/Psychological Abuse?

Every parent has said or done things that she regrets, but emotionally abusive behavior is consistent. Emotional abuse is a habitual, often subtle, style of communication that erodes your child's sense of self-worth. Name-calling; ridiculing or belittling a child's looks, interests or hobbies, even in the spirit of fun; constantly finding reason to blame a child for things that go wrong; withholding love or affection; publicly humiliating a child; regularly threatening a child with harm or abandonment; or locking a child in a room or a closet are all forms of emotional abuse. Children who are physically or sexually abused are always emotionally abused. It's not easy to recognize this type of behavior in yourself, nor is it easy to admit that it can damage your relationship with your child. But emotional abuse is every bit as hurtful as physical abuse. Children learn about themselves through their parents' words and behavior. Listen to yourself when you speak to your child. If another adult spoke to you in the same way, how would you feel? Did someone hurt you with words when you were growing up? You do not have to hurt your child. You can change harmful patterns. There are many resources for parents who are concerned about their relationship with their children. Parents Anonymous is an excellent resource. For other ideas contact a national or local child abuse hotline.

Child Neglect

Abuse generally refers to something that a parent does, while neglect really describes something that a parent consistently fails to do. Parents have a responsibility to meet minimal standards of childcare and to provide for their children's basic needs. Although legal and community definitions of neglect are often difficult to define, the following are general descriptions of categories of neglect:

Physical neglect means failing to provide your child with safe shelter, nutrition, and clothing. Lack of adequate supervision may also be a category of neglect in many states.

Medical neglect includes delaying or failing to seek medical, dental, or psychiatric or psychological care for a child, including necessary preventative care like immunizations.

Educational neglect is the failure on the part of parents or caregivers to make sure that a child is educated. Constantly keeping a child home from school to baby-sit or work or refusing to address a child's special education needs are examples of possible educational neglect.

Emotional neglect includes the failure to love, nurture or show affection to a child, exposing a child to severe or ongoing domestic violence, allowing a child to abuse drugs or alcohol, and failing to attend to a child's need for psychological care.

How Do Abuse and Neglect Affect Children?

The effects of child maltreatment are serious. They touch children in the immediacy of their lives and often reach far into adulthood. Physical abuse can result in bruises, welts, cuts, broken bones, burns, scars, permanent disabilities, and death. Children who are left unsupervised can suffer permanent or fatal injuries that might have otherwise been avoided. A lack of medical attention can turn a relatively minor problem into a grave condition. Without a proper diet, children can develop malnutrition. In extreme cases of emotional and physical neglect, children can develop a condition called nonorganic failure to thrive (FTT), in which a child fails to gain weight and develop normally and which must usually be treated with hospitalization. Impairments in intellectual functioning can also result from abuse and neglect.

While the physical manifestations of abuse and neglect may sometimes be obvious, children who are maltreated suffer impairments that may not always be as visible. Because children are unique individuals, the ways in which they will be affected by maltreatment differ and depend on many factors. Children who are hurt, ignored, or denigrated by those who are close to them often suffer from a low sense of self-esteem and may grow up feeling unloved. Maltreated children may have problems relating to and interacting with their peers. They may seem anxious and depressed and may withdraw from social or other activities. Conversely, an abused or neglected child may be hostile and aggressive, have more academic problems than other children, and may be at greater risk for delinquency and running away. Children who are physically abused may exhibit self-destructive behaviors, such as self-mutilation and suicide attempts.

How Does Abuse and Neglect Happen?

The risk of harming your child is greatest when you are under stress. Parenting is a demanding, exhausting job. There are few parents who haven't experienced the frustration of trying to balance meeting the needs of their children with the fulfillment of other family responsibilities, the demands of work outside the home or school, and intimate relationships. During a crisis, such as divorce, or when financial problems arise, these ordinary pressures may seem unbearable.

When you're angry or tense and feel like you could hurt your child — wait. Take a deep breath. Close your eyes and count to ten. Splash cold water on your face. Sit down. If your child won't be endangered, leave the room for a moment. Play some music. Sing. Call a friend, a neighbor, or a relative to talk. Write down what you are feeling. Do whatever it takes to get through the anger and frustration. National organizations dedicated to preventing child abuse and neglect offer many free pamphlets with tips on reducing family- and work-related stress. Take time out to call for information or to speak to a counselor on a toll-free helpline about your concerns.

If you use corporal punishment, even spanking, as a parenting tool, the danger of hurting your child is always present. One of the best ways to reduce the risk of child abuse is to learn nonviolent ways of disciplining your child. Parents all over the country are taking an interest in learning new and effective parenting techniques through parent education and support groups. Parenting groups and classes offer a good way to meet other parents in your community and to gain the tools to reduce family conflict.

Unrealistic expectations of a child's behavior can create the potential for abuse. For example, many parents become frustrated when children do not toilet-train as early as they expect. Although every child is different, most children are toilet-trained between two and three and a half years of age. Prior to that time a child may not have developed the muscle control or other of the essential physical and social skills required to accomplish this complex task. Punishing or rushing a child will not produce results. Generally, children exhibit an interest in toilet training when they are ready to learn how, and they respond to praise, not to punishment. Your nurse or pediatrician can give you more practical information about child growth and development.

Alcohol and other drug abuse play a major role in child maltreatment. Loving parents can abuse or neglect their children when high or intoxicated. When under the influence of alcohol or other drugs, you are less likely to be able to reason and more likely to lose your temper and to say and do things that you wouldn't otherwise. When you're high or intoxicated you can't make sound judgments about your

If you are a new mother, you should know that it's not at all unusual to experience a range of difficult emotions after having a baby. New mothers may be exhausted, frightened about the prospect of parenting, and worried about their ability to bond with their babies. There are a lot of myths about motherhood, including the notion that a mother will instantly feel close to her baby and will "just know" how to care for her once she is born. When these expectations are not met, it's easy to feel as if something is terribly wrong. Despite the myths, all mothers need someone to assist them from time to time. Find out what support services are available to you. You may consider hiring a young person to do a few chores for you in the afternoon, or asking another trusted family member to watch your baby while you rest. The services of a professional mother's helper, although certainly more expensive, can be quite valuable. See the Resource Directory chapter Crises in Conception for information.

It's also very common for women to experience sadness, tearfulness, anxiety, irritability, anger, and mood swings after childbirth. These feelings, which usually last a short period of time, are often referred to as the baby blues. For some women, however, postpartum reactions may be prolonged or severe. Postpartum depression is a term that is used to refer to clinical depression associated with childbirth, but it is actually one in a spectrum of syndromes that may affect women after giving birth. If you feel that you can no longer care for yourself or your baby or that you may harm yourself or your baby, call your doctor or go to the emergency department of a nearby hospital *immediately*. You are in a dangerous situation. Help is available and should be sought right away. Being able to recognize and acknowledge your feelings is the first step toward getting the help that you need. There is absolutely no shame in having a postpartum disorder, and it does not mean that you are a bad mother or any less of a woman. Make sure that you get the care and attention you deserve.

child's safety. If you drink or use drugs, you probably already know these things. Nonetheless, you may find yourself underestimating the effect that drug or alcohol abuse has on your family, especially if you are still functioning at work or in other aspects of your life. But drug and alcohol abuse will eventually hurt you and your child. There is *no* shame in having a drug or alcohol problem and great benefit in seeking help. Untold numbers of people have conquered their addiction to or abuse of harmful substances, including alcohol, cocaine, heroin, amphetamines, and prescribed medicines. Chapter Seven outlines options for recovery.

Preventing or Stopping Child Abuse and Neglect

If you think that you may be in danger of abusing or neglecting your child, take advantage of the resources that are available to help you. Here are some ideas:
   Crisis hotlines. The hotlines listed at the beginning of this

chapter can provide you with immediate crisis counseling, information, and referrals to other sources of assistance in your area. Also check the front pages of your local telephone directory for the numbers of statewide or local child abuse and neglect prevention lines, if available. Some communities have also developed *parent stress- or information lines.* These services may also be listed in the front section of your local telephone directory or may be operated by a local hospital. (Call the social work department of a local hospital for information.) If available, these services can answer your questions about parenting and offer referrals to specific programs. There is no need to feel embarrassed about calling a crisis or information line. These services are developed and run by people who understand how difficult and stressful parenting can be. They are there to help.

Parents Anonymous is a national self-help organization for parents who are having difficulty parenting. Check the Resource Directory for information.

Parent education and support groups help parents learn nonviolent ways of disciplining children and provide information on a variety of parenting topics, such as childcare and development, nutrition, and budgeting. For information about parenting groups or classes or to locate a group in your area, try contacting one of the national crisis hotlines listed at the beginning of this chapter, a state/local child abuse prevention hotline, a local high school, adult school or community college, or the social work department of a hospital in your area. Also try your place of worship, an agency serving families, such as Catholic Charities or Jewish Family and Children's Services, the YWCA, the local office of the United Way, or a community mental health center. These organizations may offer parenting classes or be able to refer you to groups.

Home visiting programs. New and expectant mothers can often benefit from extra support before and after a new baby's arrival. Hospitals, clinics, social service agencies, public health departments, and high schools may provide services or referrals to in-home services for new mothers. Although many programs focus on the needs of young or first-time mothers with low incomes, voluntary programs for all families in need of assistance are becoming available. Home visitors, who may be specially trained community members or professionals, can provide you with information about prenatal care, help you to cope with the demands of new motherhood, teach or help you sharpen parenting skills, as well as help you find and use other community resources that meet your needs. Ask your health care provider, school counselor, the local government health or social services department, or the social work department of a children's hospital or general hospital to refer you to a home visitation program that suits your needs. Social service agencies, such as Catholic Charities or Jewish Family and Children's Services, may also provide referrals. Healthy Families America is a home visitation program sponsored by the National Committee to Prevent Child Abuse (NCPCA) that operates in chapters across the United States. For more information about this program or other child abuse and neglect prevention resources in your area, call 1-800-CHILDREN.

Counseling or therapy provided by a qualified professional can help you to understand and cope with troubling aspects of your life. Talking to a friend can be beneficial, but friends may not possess the objectivity and expertise necessary to help you through a life crisis or to deal with long-term issues related to past child abuse and neglect.

Help for drug and alcohol addictions. Chapter Seven offers more information about drug and alcohol abuse recovery options, including self-help groups with a spiritual or secular foundation.

Women's shelters and other advocacy programs throughout the country operate crisis lines *for women in abusive or violent relationships* and may also be able to provide a place of temporary refuge. See Chapter Four.

Respite services can provide you with temporary childcare in your home or in other settings so that you can take some time to rest or to attend to other responsibilities. Respite care can be particularly helpful when you are under stress or in a period of crisis. To find a respite care program in your area, you can contact the ARCH National Resource Center for Respite and Crisis Care Services at 1-800-7-RELIEF. The cost, quality, and duration of services vary across programs.

Other ways to find services in your community. The United Way or other community agencies may sponsor a telephone INFO-line (or I&R line) to allow community members access to information about local services. Ask a reference librarian in a public library for information or look in your local yellow pages under Social Services or Family Services for information. You can also contact the child protective services agency, which is usually located within the local Department of Social (or Human) Services. (The names of government social services departments differ from state to state.)

What you should know . . . Most of the professionals who will be able to provide you with support and assistance are mandated to report suspected cases of child abuse and/or neglect to the appropriate intervening agency.

If a Report of Child Abuse or Neglect Is Made Against You

Legislation has been enacted in every state to address the widespread problem of child abuse and neglect, and in every state certain professionals, including medical and mental health professionals, social workers, film processors, teachers, daycare providers, and police, are required by law to report suspected cases of abuse and neglect to the child protective services agency and in most states can be held criminally liable for failure to make a report. However, any person can report child abuse or neglect, and people who report suspected maltreatment are granted immunity from civil and criminal prosecution, if their reports are made in good faith. In some states there are penalties for knowingly making a false report.

The child protective services agency, often referred to as CPS (although the agency may have another name in your community) is the organization generally responsible for investigating suspected cases of child abuse and neglect and providing rehabilitative services to children and families. In some communities and in some cases, CPS and law enforcement work together.

The way in which CPS agencies will investigate and respond to reports of child maltreatment also varies widely. Therefore, it is not possible to tell you exactly what to expect if you are called upon by the agency. The following is only a general description of what might happen.

Intake workers who receive reports of maltreatment must screen out calls that do not meet legal and agency definitions of abuse or neglect and must determine whether the report warrants an investigation. Responses to reported incidents of child maltreatment are often prioritized according to the type and the severity of the alleged abuse or neglect. High priority reports often require an immediate response or a response within twenty-four hours.

Once CPS has determined that an investigation is warranted, it will become the job of the caseworker to find out if you have abused or neglected your child and to assess the risk of further harm to the child. During this process, the caseworker may interview you, any other person who is being investigated in connection with the case, and the child(ren) alleged to have been abused and/or neglected. They may also interview other members of your household, any witnesses and possibly neighbors, relatives, and teachers. The caseworker may interview your child before talking to you. For example, your child may be interviewed at school. Medical and mental health practitioners and other professionals may also be asked to examine your child or to interview you and/or your child to aid in making a determination of neglect or abuse.

Under the Adoption Assistance and Child Welfare Act of 1980, child protective services agencies must make all reasonable efforts to keep families together through the offering of supportive services before a child can be removed from the home. However, when it is felt that a child is in imminent danger, CPS and law enforcement may remove the child temporarily under protective custody and place him or her out of the home. It may be possible to place the child with a relative or trusted friend rather than in a shelter. In a number of states, CPS must have a court order before a child can be removed. However, in most states, the police may remove a child without a court order. Generally, a hearing should be held shortly after the child is removed to decide whether to continue the out of home placement until further court action is taken.

When there is evidence to substantiate a finding of abuse or neglect, CPS may offer you and your family services to help you work on the problems that led to the maltreatment. The agency will conduct a family assessment to determine why the maltreatment occurred and to develop a suitable case plan to address the identified problems. Your input in determining the services that are appropriate and necessary to help you and your family is very important. Depending on availability, services may include therapy, parent education and training, drug and alcohol abuse treatment, financial aid or counseling, respite care, and homemaker and housing assistance. Services may be available at no cost or offered on a sliding scale fee basis, in which case payment will be based on your income. Services are generally offered on a voluntary basis, but if they are refused, CPS may take court action to require you to participate or to protect your child in other ways, for example, by placing your child in foster care. In extreme cases of maltreatment or when you make no effort to remedy the problems that led to the abuse or neglect, the agency may petition the court to terminate your parental rights. Termination of parental rights usually signifies the end of the parent-child relationship and is generally done to allow a child to be adopted into another home.

If you are investigated, there are a few considerations to keep it mind:

- It is in your best interests to cooperate with the investigation, even if you think that it is unjustified or if the caseworkers and other service providers express values that are different from your own. Unique defensiveness or noncooperation may prompt the agency to take court action.
- Be honest with yourself. If there are problems in your home, take the opportunity to recognize them and to get the help that you need to work toward a solution that will benefit your child. Keep focused on your child's needs and let them dictate your course of action.
- Many CPS agencies are understaffed and overburdened, and resources may be very limited. In some areas, there may be a waiting list for services. Although it may be very difficult to access some services on your own, try to take advantage of some of the resources mentioned earlier.
- You have the right to representation by an attorney at any court proceeding concerning your child's placement outside the home. Find out whether you can have an attorney appointed to you by the court. Maintain ongoing communication with your lawyer. Learn as much as you can about your state's child abuse and neglect laws and the child protective services agency in your community. The child protective services agency should be able to furnish you with information about state laws and agency policies.
- If you feel that the investigation is being conducted in an inappropriate manner, complain to your caseworker's supervisor and/or to any higher-ranking agency official.
- If your child is removed from your home, remain in as much contact with your child as possible through visits, cards, and telephone calls, keeping your child's best interests in mind. Be sure to keep a record of all of your efforts to stay in contact with your child so that you can make it clear to caseworkers that you will not abandon your child.

WHEN A CHILD RUNS AWAY FROM HOME

This section was developed with the help of Leslie Forbes, Executive Director of Options House, a Hollywood-based shelter for runaway and homeless teens.

THE NATIONAL RUNAWAY SWITCHBOARD

1-800-621-4000

The National Runaway Switchboard is a nonprofit organization operating a nationwide telephone switchboard twenty-four hours a day, 365 days a year. Operators can provide crisis intervention, facilitate conference calls between parents and children, deliver messages from children to parents, and give referrals to other helping organizations. All calls are confidential.

Children run away from home for many reasons. You may or may not know why your child left. Possibilities will be discussed below, but it's important not to jump to conclusions. You will have time to talk with your child, to listen, and to understand later. You must remain calm and take immediate action now. Many children who run for the first time, especially younger children, stay within a relatively short distance from their homes and return within forty-eight hours. Nonetheless, a child's departure must be taken very seriously. An experienced or older child can travel far quickly.

Some parents feel relief when their children run away, especially when there has been a great deal of conflict in the family. Don't let this feeling keep you from taking steps to bring your child back home safely. The longer your child is away from home, the greater her vulnerability to exploitation and crime. It is your legal responsibility to care for your child's welfare.

A child who runs away from home may do so more than once. Acting promptly and calmly during a first episode may prevent others. Here are some things you can do:

- Take a deep breath. Don't panic. A child's departure is a frightening event, but it is not unusual. There are actions you can take and people who will help you.
- Contact family members, extended family members, your child's teachers and school administrators, her friends, employer(s), clergyperson, neighbors, or anyone who might know where your child is or may have talked to her before she left. To whom might your child have run? A favorite aunt? Your ex-husband or ex-partner? A boyfriend or girlfriend?
- Check local hospitals to find out if your child has been admitted as a patient. In life-threatening situations, hospitals will treat minors before notifying parents or guardians.
- If you have not located your child after taking the steps above, report your child as missing to the police. Give the police a *recent* photograph of your child. Remember that a child's appearance can change quickly. A child who wears heavy makeup or who cuts, spikes, or dyes his hair may look nothing like he did in his school portrait. Photographs taken from the front and side increase the possibility that someone will recognize your child if he attempts to change his looks. Supply as much descriptive information as you can, including age, height, weight, skin, hair, and eye color and any distinguishing marks or characteristics. Tell the police when your child was last seen and by whom and what he was wearing, if you know.
- If your child has a disability, needs medication, or has any special needs, let the police know! They are much more likely to investigate when a child is in unique danger.
- Under a federal law in effect in all states, the National Child Search Assistance Act of 1990, police are forbidden to impose a waiting period before taking a missing person's report for a person eighteen years or under. However, police departments, particularly urban police departments, may be overwhelmed by the sheer volume of calls they receive and may not be able to respond right away. If you feel strongly about having the police take a missing person's report and they refuse to do so,

contact your state's missing children's clearinghouse. If you live in one of the few states where there is no clearinghouse, call the state police or the National Center for Missing and Exploited Children's (NCMEC) toll-free twenty-four-hour hotline, 1-800-THE LOST. (If you use a TDD, call 1-800-826-7653.) The NCMEC or the local police can give you the number of your state's missing children's clearinghouse or the state police.

- Contact the National Runaway Switchboard and other runaway hotlines listed in the Resource Directory. Runaway hotlines are often very familiar with community resources and can offer suggestions to help you locate your child. You may want to leave a message for your child on the hotline. For example, you might want to say that you are willing to address whatever it is that caused him to run away.
- Contact your state or local missing children's or runaway hotline, if there is one. Look in the front section of your local yellow pages under Community Services or other similar headings, or dial your directory assistance or 1-800 operator.
- Start thinking about how you will respond when and if your child calls. The call will probably come when you least expect it, and being prepared can help you avoid conflict that may make matters worse. Have the number of a runaway hotline or shelter on hand. If your child does not want to come home, he or she can use these telephone numbers to find shelter and assistance.
- Make a list of the organizations and people you call. When you speak to someone over the phone, write down the date and time. Note the name, telephone number, and title of the individual to whom you're speaking and the information you are given. It's not easy to remember information when you're under stress, and you may need it to track down your child.
- If your child returns, let everyone on your list know that he or she has been found and that he is safe.

If Your Child Has Established a Pattern of Running Away

If your child has run away a number of times, take the measures as listed in the previous section and add the steps outlined below. Parents or guardians of children who have been gone for some time may also want to pursue these options:

If you have reason to believe that your child has been abducted by his or her other parent or a stranger, don't waste any time. Take the following actions. (Relevant national telephone numbers are listed in the Resource Directory.)

- Contact the police as soon as you suspect that your child is missing, or that the other parent has taken the child or will not return him from a period of visitation.
- Ask the police to take a missing person's report and enter your child's description into the FBI's National Crime Information Center (NCIC) database. In the case of parental abduction, you may need a custody order to do this, depending on where you live, but don't let this stop you from contacting the police immediately. Again, let the police know about any special medical or physical needs your child has, as they are more likely to take action.
- Next, call the National Center for Missing and Exploited Children's (NCMEC) twenty-four-hour toll-free hotline. The state's missing children's clearinghouse, the state police, and nonprofit missing children's clearinghouses that offer services at no charge can provide additional information and assistance. A few nonprofit missing children's organizations are listed in the Resource Directory. Stay away from organizations that charge a fee to help you find your child.

- Consider whether there is a pattern to your child's behavior. Why did he/she leave the last time? Is there anything that seems to trigger his/her running? A fight with his/her other parent or guardian? Skirmishes with siblings? Where did he/she go the last time? How long was he/she gone? Did he/she call? When? Thinking about what happened in the past may help you focus your search now.
- Ask the police to enter your child's description into the FBI's National Crime Information Center database. You may have to urge the police to do this. If the police will not enter your child's description into the computer, you can contact your state's missing children's clearinghouse, the state police, or the National Center for Missing and Exploited Children for assistance.
- If you think that you know where your child is, contact shelters for runaway and homeless youths in that area (or areas). Because most shelters are ethically, and often legally, bound to protect children by ensuring their confidentiality, shelter workers may not be able to tell you if they have seen your child. However, you can leave a message for him or her, asking him to call you if he visits the shelter. Shelters do not generally help parents or guardians find children, but some may be able to give you general information about the necessary steps to take to search for a child.
- Get in contact with your state missing children's clearinghouse or state police. These organizations can be valuable to parents and guardians of runaways, particularly parents of children who cross state borders, because they are generally responsible for coordinating law enforcement efforts within the state and, if need be, with other states. Your state police or clearinghouse may be able to alert police in other states of your child's possible presence there.
- Make a flyer or poster with a recent photograph of your child, his physical description, a contact number and any identifying features, including braces, eyeglasses, birthmarks, tattoos, piercings, arm or leg casts, or any other characteristics that might distinguish him from other children. If you have or are willing to buy a beeper, include that number on the flyer. Children move fast, and a caller who has spotted your child may need to reach you quickly. A flyer may be particularly useful if you think you know where your child has gone.
- Send a copy of your child's flyer with a brief cover letter

explaining your situation to law enforcement agencies and runaway shelters in the area(s) to which your child may have run. Although shelters may not have the space to post every flyer for more than a limited period of time, a flyer gives the shelter tangible information about your child. Some shelters do not post flyers because there is a risk that, if a child sees her picture as she enters the shelter, she'll walk out. Thus, some shelters keep flyers on file. State missing children's clearinghouses and nonprofit missing children's organizations can often help you create flyers and distribute them to shelters and law enforcement agencies at no cost. Again, avoid organizations that charge a fee to help you look for your child.

- Send your flyer and cover letter to other places your child might visit, such as a food kitchen or free clinic. Runaway shelters may be able to give you information about these and other relevant community agencies. You can also try contacting local offices of the United Way or local information and referral lines (see the first page of the Resource Directory) for referrals to community agencies.

If Your Child Calls

Not knowing where your child is or whether he is safe is likely to have caused you long and sleepless nights. You may be very hurt and angry at your child. These are natural feelings, but you cannot afford to express them when he calls. He may hang up, and you may lose contact.

It is not easy to contain strong emotions. Keeping a journal during your child's absence may help you to release and work through negative feelings. Try to understand that your child left home for a reason. Although you may not have caused the problem, it may still be difficult for your child to call you.

When the phone rings, your goal will be to get your child to a safe place. Accept that your child is in control of the situation. Remain calm and open. Ask your child if he or she is safe. Ask him if he wants to tell you where he is. If he doesn't want to tell you, let him know you understand. Let him know that you are prepared to work on the issues that led to his departure and that you want to listen to what he or she has to say. Then listen.

Make notes of your conversation. If your child hangs up, you may only have these notes to provide you with clues to his whereabouts. If you hear anything in the background that suggests your child's location, write it down. Do you hear traffic going by? Sounds of a familiar place, such as a train station or a local hangout? If you let them resonate, these sounds may provide you with more clues for your search.

Make it clear that your child is welcome home. If for some reason your child does not want to come home, or if there are serious problems that cannot be resolved right away, offer alternatives. Many runaway shelters offer places for young people to stay. Give your child the telephone number of a shelter or a runaway hotline. Let him know, however, that you are willing to meet at any time. Tell him that he can call you day or night. Even if your child is not ready to come home, he may agree to meet in a neutral location, such as a place of worship, the office of a runaway program, or a coffee shop. Again, resist entering into a debate or laying blame on your child or yourself. You may not like what you hear when your child calls, but your task is to focus your efforts very specifically on getting him off the streets, where he is in danger.

Why Do Children Run Away?

Many people are unable to articulate their feelings and instead express distress through action. Children are no different. Running away is usually a symptom of distress.

Sometimes a child who runs away will reveal a problem that is entirely new to a parent or guardian. On the other hand, a child's departure may be the result of problems that have been developing over time. You won't be able to define the issue that triggered this event until you talk with your child. Don't assume that you are to blame. The problem may have nothing to do with you. A child who runs away may be struggling with a personal problem that she is afraid or embarrassed to discuss. Conflicts surrounding the awareness of a pregnancy, a gay, lesbian or bisexual identity, a problem with alcohol or other drugs, with peers, or with schoolwork may prompt a young person to flee. Running away and other acting-out behaviors, such as delinquent activity, may also be symptoms of depression, a highly treatable but serious condition.

Family problems may also be at the heart of a runaway episode. Some children run to evade parental control. Discord between partners or spouses, divorce, the death of a loved one, or the introduction of a stepparent into the family may give rise to feelings so troubling that a young person may see running away as the only means of coping. Physical and sexual abuse are high on the list of reasons why teenagers leave home. A parent's or guardian's overinvolvement with alcohol or other drugs can provide another incentive to run. Even if these explanations don't seem to fit what you know about your child, it's important to realize that your child is asking for help.

When Your Child Comes Home

When your child returns, keep your calm. Let her know that you are glad to have her back. Although you may need a few days before you can sit down together, suggest a talk. When you meet, be prepared to do most of the listening. Teenagers who run away often feel misunderstood and unheard. Thus, it's important for parents or guardians to listen as their children discuss their perceptions of the problems at hand. Your child may tell you things that hurt you or make you very angry or uncomfortable. Try as hard as you can to remain in control of your emotions. Be patient with yourself as you work toward understanding.

If your child has run away for the first or second time, remember that his safe return does not put the issues that caused this crisis to rest. Children often run away again, and resolution of the problem will not occur without some effort on everyone's part.

Family counseling or therapy can offer you and your loved ones an objective look at some of the issues that may be related to the runaway event. Although many professionals prefer to have everyone in the family involved in family counseling or therapy, it's not always necessary or possible. If no one in your family is willing to go for counseling or therapy, you can go alone. A parents' support group may also be helpful.

Many shelters for runaway and homeless youths offer counseling or therapy services free of charge or on a sliding scale basis. If a shelter cannot offer you services, ask for a referral to a program in your community that will meet your needs. If your child has run away many times, you can also contact the child protective services agency, a runaway shelter, or the police to find out whether there is a program for chronic runaways in your community. Although they are not available in every community, these programs can be quite helpful where they exist. Your patience and commitment to resolving family problems will go a long way toward achieving a successful reunion and building a healthy, productive future for your child.

Juvenile justice systems vary significantly across jurisdictions and the laws affecting minors accused with delinquency are changing. This section is meant to give you an indication of what you *might* encounter when your child is taken into custody. It is not meant to describe procedures in a given jurisdiction. Likewise, the information is not meant as a substitute for legal advice. Legal advice should be sought from an attorney who is experienced with juvenile justice issues and court procedures in your area.

The arrest of a child is serious and could have long-term repercussions. Your cooperation and willingness to participate in your child's case will have a direct effect on its outcome. It is critical that you become involved at the beginning and stay involved. Ask questions. Know the names of each person dealing with your child. Be persistent in getting the facts. When you don't understand what someone is telling you, ask for a careful explanation. An interpreter may be requested, if needed.

Who Will Contact You?

Most likely, you will be contacted by a law enforcement official. A police patrol officer may bring your child home. Otherwise, you will be telephoned by a police officer at the area police department, by a juvenile detention worker, or possibly by your child.

The decision to take a minor into custody depends on many factors, including the nature and seriousness of the alleged offense. As mentioned, minors are subject to laws that apply to adults and to rules that apply only to minors. Police officers may take a minor who has committed a status offense into custody, particularly if you can't be reached or if it's after office hours.

What to Do If Your Child Is Arrested

Go immediately to the facility where your child is being held. Most often, your child will be held at a police station or juvenile detention center. Your child may also be taken to a medical facility, if it is thought that she requires immediate treatment.

Stay calm. Be prepared to cooperate and to ask questions. Your goal is to learn what caused your child to be taken into

---

DELINQUENCY AND STATUS OFFENSES

Although the definition of a delinquent act varies according to jurisdiction, most jurisdictions acknowledge two broad categories of delinquency: juvenile delinquency and status offenses.

In very general terms, a *juvenile delinquent* is a person not yet an adult who commits an act that would be criminal when committed by an adult.

A *status offender* (also called *incorrigible*) is the broad term applied to those minors who commit acts that are illegal only when done by minors. Truancy, running away, and underage drinking are examples of status offenses.

---

custody and what you can do to bring about the best outcome. Find out who is handling your child's case. Write down the name and telephone number of each person involved and the times at which he or she can be reached.

At the time of this writing, the Juvenile Justice and Delinquency Prevention Act, passed by Congress in 1974, allows minors taken into custody certain protections. For example:

- a status offender should not be held in a secure detention or secure correctional facility. A status offender should be held in a nonsecure area until transfer to another facility.[3]
- A juvenile accused with committing a delinquent offense should not be held in an adult jail. An exception may be made for juveniles against whom felony charges are filed in criminal court. In certain rural areas, a juvenile may be held in an adult jail or lockup for up to twenty-four hours (excluding weekends and holidays) in very limited and specific circumstances.

Current federal law also requires that juveniles and adults be separated by sight and sound in jail. Although most jurisdictions are making an effort to comply with this requirement, it is still possible that your child could come into contact with an adult criminal while being held in a jail. If your child may be released to you, take him or her home. Don't try to teach your child a lesson by leaving him or her in a jail or detention center. There is no guarantee of adequate supervision. He/she may be physically or sexually assaulted. Moreover, you have a legal obligation to pick up your child. If you do not pick up your child, you could be required to pay for the cost of care incurred while he/she is detained.

Do You Need an Attorney?

If your child is taken into custody and interrogated, he or she must be given *Miranda warnings*. You may be familiar with a version of the Miranda rights: "You have the right to remain silent. Anything you say can and will be used against you in a court of law. You have the right to an attorney. If you cannot afford one, one will be appointed for you." *Your child has the right to an attorney* at this point in the juvenile justice process. If your child is facing incarceration or probation, an attorney should be present during questioning.

In some counties, particularly large metropolitan areas, Miranda attorneys are available on call and can be reached without great delay. If this service is not available, your child will have to wait in detention until an attorney can be found to begin the interrogation. But if incarceration or probation is a possibility, waiting may be preferable to waiving Miranda rights without a lawyer's advice. To get an attorney, call the local bar association or public defender's office. You do not have to retain the attorney who represents your child at the Miranda hearing beyond this stage in the process. You are free to hire a different attorney to represent your child later on.

In many states, the juvenile court is beginning to function more like an adult criminal court than a civil court. However, the juvenile court is still very different from criminal court. Therefore, if you choose a private criminal defense attorney to represent your child, make very sure that the attorney is experienced in juvenile justice issues. Be aware that you will have to pay for a private attorney's services.

Your child may be entitled to representation by a public defender at no cost. However, parents may be required to make reimbursements for legal services and court costs, according to their ability to pay. If you choose a public defender, you should know that while there are excellent public defenders who are familiar with the juvenile justice system, many are overburdened by a heavy caseload. You and your child may have very little time to talk with the public defender before going to court.

Because every situation is different, no one other than a qualified professional familiar with the details of your child's case can advise you. Be certain that you have a full understanding of the issues involved before making decisions for your child.

Diversion Programs

Although there is an increasing emphasis on punishment within many juvenile courts, it is still a primary objective of the juvenile justice system to divert certain minors, usually those who are alleged to have committed less serious offenses or who are first-time offenders, away from the formal hearing process.

This effort at *diversion* takes many forms. It could mean that your child will be released with no further action or with a written warning or a reprimand. It may also mean that your child will be given a referral to a community agency that can provide services to resolve some of the problems that brought him into contact with the law. These services may include counseling, drug and alcohol rehabilitation, community service, and other services if available.

In some instances, further court action will be dependent

on your child's compliance with the conditions of diversion. In other words, if your child fails to comply, action against her will continue.

Decisions to divert depend on the nature of the offense with which the child is accused, her prior record, and the cooperation of both child and parent(s) or guardian(s). Very often, juveniles alleged to have committed more serious offenses or who are repeat offenders cannot be diverted. The use of diversion also depends on the availability of appropriate services in your area and on your ability to pay, if no public programs are available. Police patrol officers, intake and probation officers and judges all have the power to make certain decisions about diversion, although in some jurisdictions the power to make diversionary decisions rests primarily with the judge. If you are not told about the possibility of diversion, ask.

The Police Station

Once you arrive at the station, an investigating police officer should interview your child in your presence. Remember, you or your child may ask to have an attorney present before your child answers any questions. Police and juvenile justice procedures should be thoroughly explained. Your child should understand that any statements made are voluntary and may later be used against him. The purpose of the initial interview is to determine whether your child should be petitioned (charged) with an offense or if the case can be diverted. If it is felt that a petition (charges) should be filed against your child, your child's case will be referred to the next level of intake: juvenile court intake. You and your child will either go immediately to this stage in the process or you will be given an appointment to return for the intake interview.

The Juvenile Court Intake Interview

The juvenile court intake interview occurs after the police have made a decision to refer your child's case to the juvenile court. Juvenile court intake procedures vary widely across jurisdictions, but the general purpose of court intake is to determine whether your child's case will go to court and whether she should be held in detention. In most states, court intake is the responsibility of the intake or probation department but it may also be handled by the local prosecutor's (county or district attorney's) office.

First, the intake officer will determine whether your

child's referral is appropriate and review the allegations made in the police complaint for legal sufficiency. The alleged facts in the complaint must be supportable by sufficient evidence that a delinquent act was committed and that the accused juvenile did the act.[4] If it is very clear that there is no legal sufficiency to the complaint, the case should be dismissed.[5] If it is found that the allegations contained in the police complaint are legally sufficient, the next usual step for the intake officer is to decide whether to recommend a petition (charges) be filed, to dismiss your child's case, or to refer your child to an appropriate community agency for services. Resolutions, such as informal probation, can be used as a condition for suspension of court action. This involves both the supervision of your child and the offering of appropriate services to your child with your consent. Informal probation is typically reserved for youths who commit less serious offenses and who admit guilt. If your child is arrested for another offense during a period of informal probation, the original complaint will be referred to the prosecutor.

To make an intake decision, the intake officer will interview you and your child. Afterward the officer will conduct a brief investigation into your child's case, which will include a check for prior court activity and interviews with the victim, witnesses, police, school, and social service agencies. If your child is referred to court, the information in this report, often called the *social history report,* may be used to help the judge reach a decision regarding sentencing.

If a petition is filed, the intake officer must decide whether your child should be further detained or released to you with a requirement to return for a court appearance. If a decision is made to hold a juvenile in detention, a petition must be filed with the juvenile court within a period of time specified by state law.

The intake officer will then refer your child's case to the public prosecutor. The prosecutor will again review the allegations to see if there is sufficient evidence for court action. The prosecutor can close the case, seek a form of diversion for your child, send the case to juvenile court, or, in certain cases, move to have the case tried in adult criminal court.

If there is enough evidence to go to court, *you and your child have a right to be given timely notice of the charges and of the date you are to appear in court.* In most states, a summons is used to serve notice. It may be mailed or served in person. A copy of the petition should be attached to the summons.

Most often, minors are released to their parents or guardians while awaiting a hearing. But, depending on state law and local policy, your child could be detained if the nature of the alleged offense was such that it is believed that your child represents a threat to public safety, or if it appears that he will not return for a hearing. Detention is sometimes used when it is felt that harm will come to the child otherwise. Still, the decision to hold a juvenile must be supported by a reasonable belief that the minor committed the alleged offense.

Most states allow for a *detention hearing* to be held within 24 to 72 hours (depending on state law) after the juvenile's admission to a detention facility. In addition, some states allow juveniles to bail. At this point, your child's case may be dismissed, or he may be placed on conditional release while awaiting a hearing. It is also possible that your child will continue to be held at a juvenile detention center, a foster home, or a runaway shelter pending a hearing. Home detention is a possible alternative to detention in a secure or other facility.

The Juvenile Court

The juvenile (or family) court hears a variety of cases involving juveniles, including cases of delinquency. Whether your child's case will be heard in juvenile court depends largely on the nature of her offense and her age. The maximum age for delinquency differs in each state. State law also determines whether the age limits can be extended in some cases.

Some juvenile courts have established arraignment procedures. At the *arraignment,* the petition (charges) will be reviewed to see if court action is necessary. Your child should be given notice of the charges and of his rights. Your child should be asked if he requires an appointed attorney and whether he intends to admit or deny the charges. The judge may then appoint a lawyer to your child and set a date for a pretrial hearing, if necessary. A *probable cause hearing* is generally required when a minor is detained. This hearing may be combined with another hearing, such as the detention hearing. If there is not enough evidence to establish probable cause that the minor committed the alleged offense, the case may be dismissed or diverted as a result.

If your child's case is not diverted or if there is enough evidence to prosecute, an *adjudicatory hearing* will be held.

This hearing is more formal and similar to a trial in adult court, except that there are no jurors present. A minor does not have a guaranteed right to a jury trial, though in some states one may be requested.

- Juveniles accused with committing delinquent acts have a right to an attorney, the right to confront and cross-examine witnesses and to exercise the privilege against self-incrimination. As well, the court must find guilt beyond a reasonable doubt.

If the petition against your child is found to be invalid, there will be no further action. If the petition is sustained (found valid), your child will have been found delinquent and will next appear at the disposition (sentencing) hearing.

In practice, cases are often plea-bargained. When this happens, no trial is held. The young person pleads guilty to a lesser offense or to one or only some of the charges in exchange for a lighter sentence. This is an extremely serious step. A young person should understand the full implications of a decision to plea-bargain before agreeing.

Disposition (Sentencing)

If the petition against your child is upheld or if your child admits to having committed an offense, there will be a disposition (sentencing) hearing. The judge, child, parent(s) or guardian(s), attorney, and probation officer are usually in attendance. This hearing is similar to a sentencing hearing in adult court. The seriousness of the crime, your child's prior record, and the recommendations of the probation officer as well as your attitude and your child's are considered. Once a decision is reached, the court will order a specific form of disposition.

Depending on the various factors in your child's case, state law, and the community's resources, the judge may have a number of alternatives from which to choose. For example, a judge may decide to put your child on formal probation, refer your child to a community agency or treatment program, order counseling or community service, order your child to pay damages to the victim (restitution), or place your child in home detention, in foster care, in a group home, or in another type of institution or nonsecure facility. Multiple forms of disposition, such as restitution and community service, can also be used. In some states, parents can be held financially responsible for the damage caused by their child. The judge can also commit your child to a secure juvenile correctional facility. You may be able to appeal this disposition.

Formal Probation

Formal probation is the most common means of disposition. During probation, your child will remain at home while being subject to the supervision of a probation officer and to certain restrictions imposed upon his freedom. Your child should also be offered appropriate services either through an agency or through direct casework by the probation officer.

The conditions of probation vary from case to case and court to court. They may include curfew, counseling, finding a job, obeying parents, paying damages to the victim, and doing community service as well as more severe restrictions. Probation can also extend to parents or guardians. For example, you could be required to participate in family counseling.

Because probation can be revoked (both you and your child may be returned to court for a revocation hearing), you and your child should fully understand the terms of probation. Ask the probation officer to explain to you any condition that you don't understand. The length of probation will vary depending on the state in which you live and on the terms imposed by the court.

Institutions

There are primarily two types of institutions in which juveniles are held: secure and nonsecure. Secure facilities include juvenile institutions, maximum security training schools, correctional facilities, and detention centers. These are prisons. Diagnostic centers are also secure and are often used to determine the best form of disposition for adjudicated youths.

Nonsecure facilities are a less restrictive type of facility. These include farms and ranches, boot-type camps, halfway houses and shelters. These institutions may be less restrictive, but they still serve as correctional facilities.

Group homes are another type of institution. They are not run by private families, though most are community-based. Group homes typically board fewer than twelve older teenagers and are run by a paid, full-time staff. They are not all alike and many serve a specific clientele, such as pregnant teens or children with developmental disabilities. Group homes also vary in quality. Some lack funds to maintain a qualified professional staff; others provide residents with excellent services. In most states, a court order is needed to place a child in a group home.

Can Your Child Be Tried as an Adult?

Yes. Most states allow for the juvenile court to waive its jurisdiction and permit a minor to be transferred to criminal court. The age of the youth, the severity and type of offense alleged, prior offenses, and the youth's amenability to treatment are the most significant criteria for considering such a waiver. Older adolescents who commit serious crimes are typically those considered for transfer. However, restrictions on age and conduct vary from state to state. For example, some states have no restrictions on age, in other states children as young as thirteen can be tried as adults. Further, states may consider legislation to allow waiver of even younger children.

Depending on the jurisdiction, a judge or prosecutor may make the decision to try a young person as an adult. But in some areas, the decision to transfer is automatic for some offenders. Where discretion is allowed a "waiver" or "transfer" hearing must be held. (This process may also be called certification.) A juvenile has a right to attorney representation, a right to examine the records used to make the decision regarding transfer, and a right to know the reasons for transfer.

Can Parents Be Held Legally Responsible for the Actions of Their Children?

Yes. States vary on this question, but it is possible that you could be held liable for the illegal actions of your children or for damages caused by your children. A number of states and localities impose fines, restitution, or parenting classes on parents of children who commit status offenses or delinquent acts.

The California Supreme Court recently upheld California's "gang parent law." Under this law, parents may be prosecuted if their failure to reasonably supervise and control a child results in the child's delinquency.

How to Help Your Child

Every parent must judge for herself the best course of action to take with her own child, but you can have a direct effect on the outcome of your child's case. Listen objectively to what the professionals involved have to say. Decide what you believe is best for your child and then work to achieve that end. You do not have to condone or excuse your child's behavior, but you will have to work with your child and with the professionals involved to get the best results.

Don't give up. You may feel overwhelmed and extremely angry at your child. But do not abandon him. Children need to know that someone cares about what they do. Set limits on your child's behavior and enforce those limits consistently. Find out why your child is misbehaving. Your child's behavior may be an indication of deeper problems such as abuse or neglect or depression.

Preventing Juvenile Delinquency

Don't wait until your child gets into trouble to become involved in your child's life. Spend time with your child. Talk to her about her experiences. Let her know that you care about the decisions she makes. Giving more to your child may seem impossible when you are under stress or when you don't have a lot of leisure time or money, but your effort is crucial to your child's future. If you need help, a respected friend or relative may be able to assist you. You may also consider enrolling your child in a mentor program like Big Brothers/Big Sisters. Such programs have been shown to have a positive impact on children who stay involved with them.

Children of all ages need to be involved in constructive, self-esteem-building activities. Find out what your child likes to do. Get your child started in an activity that is both enjoyable and helpful in improving life skills. Take action as soon as it becomes apparent that your child is troubled. Don't ignore misbehavior or assume that it will resolve itself. It may escalate instead.

If You Feel You Cannot Control Your Child

There are options for parents with incorrigible children. Family therapy, individual therapy, and group therapy for teens are often recommended. If you are ordered to attend counseling by the court, complete the program.

Placing your child with a relative he likes and respects may be a viable possibility, provided you remain in contact with him and he is not made to feel abandoned. There is no one simple solution.

Many frustrated parents consider bringing their children under the authority of the court. Having your child declared a minor in need of supervision (MINS), or child in need of supervision (CHINS), is usually not the best option. After turning your child over to the authority of the court, you may have a very difficult time influencing any decision that the court makes about your child.

Services for Children at Risk for Delinquency

Finding services for children who are at risk for delinquency or who have been adjudged delinquent can be difficult. You are going to have to make a lot of inquiries as many valuable programs operate only at the local level. But good programs do exist, and they can be extremely beneficial. You may also want to find out about programs for yourself, such as parenting classes and parent support groups.

Start your search by asking your child's school counselor for information about local programs. Your child's probation officer may be able to help. However, probation officers often have very heavy caseloads, and those families not directly assigned to a probation officer will have difficulty getting referrals. An officer in the juvenile division of your local police department should be able to tell you about services and programs. Your area may have a Youth Service Bureau. These organizations can provide referrals to services for kids with delinquency, behavioral, and substance abuse problems. Your place of worship or the local YWCA/YMCA may be able to direct you to a good program for kids or may operate one.

LOVING YOUR GAY, LESBIAN, OR BISEXUAL TEEN

Learning About Your Child

Because adolescence is a time of biological change, sexual development, and experimentation, feelings about sexual orientation can be delicate and confusing for both parent and child.

For some children, awareness of a same-sex orientation begins early in life, while others do not realize or don't feel comfortable sharing the knowledge of this significant part of themselves until adulthood. Teens are not always certain about their sexual orientation, and for some, sexual identity varies and develops over time.

The subject of sexual orientation can come up in families in a variety of ways. Sometimes parents or guardians sense that their child is somehow "different" from others, although

---

PFLAG OFFERS
SUPPORT TO PARENTS

Parents, Families and Friends of Lesbians and Gays (PFLAG) is a national family-based organization with chapters across the U.S. and in other nations. PFLAG offers mothers, fathers, and other relatives of gay, lesbian, and bisexual people support, assistance, and educational materials. Confidential discussion groups are held on a regular basis. You can call PFLAG for information or to talk with a PFLAG parent. You can also write to another parent if it's not possible to meet with a group. For information, see the Resource Directory.

for both parent and child a true understanding of the nature of that difference may evolve gradually. Parents may be told about a child's sexual orientation by someone else, who may or may not have accurate information. Parents may also discover a child's same-sex orientation accidentally. Misconceptions about bisexual, lesbian, and gay people can lead to assumptions about a child's orientation. For instance, children who do not conform to the expectations of their gender may be regarded — rightly or wrongly — as gay or lesbian. After much introspection and doubt, some children find the courage to tell their families about themselves in a letter, a telephone call, or in conversation. Regardless of the way in which you learn about your child's sexual orientation or questions about sexual orientation, knowing how to respond can be very difficult.

Before you do anything, listen and offer your support. Let your child tell you about himself. Young people who are gay, bisexual, or lesbian or who are questioning their sexual orientation are often terrified of rejection by family and friends. Sadly, these fears are not always unfounded. You may have concerns or questions about your child's sexual orientation, but when you talk with your child, let your conversations be guided by a desire to understand.

It's very important to resist labeling your child, for example, by describing her as a lesbian or as bisexual. Labeling a child with a term that she rejects or is not ready to accept can hinder her understanding of herself and heighten the sense of isolation that she may already feel. Yet there is no reason to disbelieve a child who is very sure that he is gay or bisexual. When you tell a child that he is "just going through a phase," for example, you risk dismissing a very important aspect of his understanding of himself. As a parent, you are in a position of trust. It's important to treat the information that you receive with respect and caring.

Being able to listen to and support your child does not mean that you will understand or accept your child's sexual orientation all at once. Shock, denial, anger, guilt, fear, sadness, and depression are common responses. Parents must often mourn the loss of their child's heterosexual identity and the hopes and dreams that naturally grew from the assumption of heterosexuality. For example, many parents look forward to their child's marriage and long for grandchildren. These hopes may now seem impossible to fulfill, but many gay, lesbian, and bisexual people form lasting, loving relationships and have children. In addition to fears about relationships, many parents feel great sadness, fear, and anger when they imagine some of the difficulties their child may face. It's natural to want to do everything that you can to protect your child, and thus reflection on the hardships a gay, lesbian, or bisexual child may experience or may have already suffered is a source of profound pain to many parents.

What Is Sexual Orientation?

When you first learn about your child's sexual orientation, or about her questions, you may suddenly feel as if you don't know her. The notion of her sexual orientation may overshadow all of the other qualities that you know her to possess. You may even question your own sexual orientation. It's important to realize, however, that your child *is* the same person you've always known. Sexual orientation is only an aspect, albeit a significant aspect, of one's whole being. There is a difference between sexual behavior and sexual orientation.

Sexual orientation is not a term used to describe sexual practices. Rather, it refers to the emotional, romantic, and sexual attraction that one has for members of either gender or both. If you are heterosexual, you know that being attracted to a man often involves much more than just sexual interest and that relationships are based on mutual love, shared values, trust, respect, and admiration. Sex may be a part of heterosexual relationships, but few would assert that sex wholly defines heterosexual unions. Certainly, there are people who abstain from sex but who are nonetheless entirely heterosexual. The same is true for people with same-sex orientations, because sexual orientation describes an essential part of one's identity. It's important to remember that many teenagers who think or know that they are lesbian, bisexual, or gay may not have had any sexual experience or may have experimented with opposite sex relationships before they became aware of their same-sex orientation. This is because awareness of one's sexual orientation often occurs prior to and independent of sexual activity.

Misinformation Hurts Families

Misinformation about homosexuality and bisexuality is the source of a great deal of pain for both teenagers and parents. The notion that one may readily choose his sexual orientation and outdated theories that link a same-sex orientation to qualities in the parent-child relationship are among the most hurtful myths. Because we live in a society that is intolerant of homosexuality, it is very common for parents of gay, bisexual, and lesbian youths to feel guilty about their child's sexual orientation and to believe that it is the result of something they did. Although the "causes" of homosexuality and bisexuality are not yet known, current research suggests that sexual orientation is determined very early in life and possibly before birth. Many researchers believe that one's sexual orientation may be determined by a combination of biological factors (including genetic and hormonal factors) as well as psychological and social factors. For most, sexual orientation is not a choice.

Parents do not cause homosexuality or bisexuality in a child. Nor is one's sexual orientation the result of influence or teaching. Homosexuality and bisexuality are natural expressions of human sexual diversity. In the 1940s, noted scientist Dr. Alfred Kinsey and his associates developed the Kinsey scale which, displaying the results of their research, describes variations in human sexual behavior as existing along a continuum. These variations range from exclusive heterosexuality to exclusive homosexuality with a large portion of the survey population exhibiting varying degrees of bisexuality.[6]

Homosexuality is not an illness or disorder. In 1973, the American Psychiatric Association removed homosexuality from its handbook of psychiatric and emotional disorders. Sexual orientation cannot be altered through therapy or other means. Although some claim to be able to temporarily change behavior through therapy, the ethics of trying to change that which is essential to an individual's core identity have been seriously questioned.

Why Is It Important to Know About Your Child's Sexual Orientation?

For a teen who feels or knows that he is gay, the trials of adolescence can be exacerbated by misinformation about homosexuality and the stigma attached to a same-sex orientation. Lesbian, gay, and bisexual teens are acutely aware of the stereotypes and epithets assigned to people with a same-sex orientation and the contempt with which many view homosexuality and bisexuality. A dawning awareness of a same-sex orientation can be frightening to a young person. She may go to great lengths to deny or to conceal her sexual orientation. He may expend a tremendous amount of energy monitoring the way he behaves,[7] hoping that no one will identify him as gay or bisexual. The fear of being identified as lesbian, gay, or bisexual may cause young people to distance themselves from family members, friends, and other important people in their lives. Many young people never speak about their feelings and silently suffer the belief that there is something inherently wrong with them. Without support and guidance toward self-acceptance, some teenagers learn to hate themselves.

Most adolescents want very much to "fit in" with their peers and to be accepted. Tragically, teenagers who are perceived as having a same-sex orientation are often subjected to severe verbal and physical abuse by their peers. The sense of isolation created in the lives of many young lesbian, gay, and bisexual people and the damage to self-esteem caused by negative biases and stereotypes put bisexual, gay, and lesbian teenagers at risk for many self-destructive behaviors, such as the use of alcohol or other drugs, truancy or dropping out of school, and running away. Gay, lesbian, and bisexual youths are at very high risk for suicide.

Knowledge and acceptance of your child's sexual orientation can be life-saving. When you are able to understand and empathize with the difficulties that your child may be experiencing, you are in a better position to offer support and to help your child through a critical, sometimes painful, time in life.

Resist Drastic Action

All children need to know that they have a place within the family, that they belong. Nothing hurts a child as much as rejection, even subtle rejection, from loved ones. Some parents feel so overwhelmed by the range of powerful, visceral emotions that can accompany the discovery of a child's natural sexual orientation that they pretend it doesn't exist. Some parents respond by rejecting their children, throwing them out of the house, institutionalizing them, or physically hurting them. Regardless of the pain that you are in at present, you are strongly urged not to follow these courses of action. You must place concerns for your child's emotional well-being and physical safety ahead of all other considerations. Rejecting your child at this critical time could do irreparable harm to your relationship.

If you cannot tolerate the idea of your child's sexual orientation and feel like asking her to leave home, you should know about the danger to which you are exposing her. Children who are pushed or thrown out of their homes must often attempt to survive on the street. These children are highly vulnerable to rape, sexual exploitation, substance abuse, and HIV infection.

It is not unusual for parents to hold fast to the idea of a

"cure," at least until they come to terms with their child's sexual orientation. Some parents consider sending their children to private psychiatric hospitals advertised in the media. As previously suggested, neither the American Psychological Association nor the American Psychiatric Association view homosexuality as a disorder or illness. One must wonder then, how can an illness that doesn't exist be treated? It has been suggested that some for-profit facilities accept admissions of young people who do not have serious emotional or mental disorders.[8] Although there are times when inpatient hospitalization may be necessary, for example, when a child of any sexual orientation represents a genuine threat to himself or others, hospitalization can be very damaging to a child who is deprived of contact with family and friends, who is stigmatized by being labeled mentally ill, potentially maltreated, and told that there is something fundamentally wrong with an essential aspect of his nature.

How to Help Your Gay, Lesbian, or Bisexual Child

Young people who are lesbian, gay, or bisexual or who are questioning their sexual orientation need accurate information about homosexuality and bisexuality. They need to know that there is nothing wrong with them and that they are not "bad" or sinful. They need support. The sense of isolation and loneliness that many sexual minority children feel and the lack of opportunities for age-appropriate social and dating activities may put them at risk for involvement in sexual relationships that may not be right for them and for which they may not be ready. Young people need a place to meet other gay, lesbian, and bisexual teenagers and to explore their emerging identities in a safe, nonjudgmental, nonsexual atmosphere. They need exposure to healthy gay, lesbian, and bisexual role models. Despite all the hostility and overt discrimination that gay, lesbian, and bisexual people experience, most lead productive, ordinary lives. Lesbian, gay, and bisexual people are of all races and ethnic and religious heritages. They work in every occupation and have made significant contributions to world culture and history. As you learn more about the lesbian, gay, and bisexual community, you will come to appreciate this.

In many major cities across the country, gay and lesbian community centers provide the public with a range of services. Some offer peer support groups for gay, lesbian, bisexual, or transgender youths and teens who are questioning their sexual orientation. These organizations may sponsor youth hotlines and pen pal programs for children who have questions about their orientation and/or who can't come to the center. PFLAG also sponsors a pen pal program for teens. Young people and parents who live outside cities with gay and lesbian centers may benefit from information and support offered through other resources. University and college campuses often house gay and lesbian organizations that can be of service. You may want to find out if your local YMCA or YWCA has a support group for gay, bisexual, lesbian, and transgender teens. Some schools also offer such programs.

A young person may benefit from talking to a counselor or therapist who understands and accepts homosexuality and bisexuality. Although it can be difficult to find a professional who is skilled in addressing issues of adolescence and sexual orientation, some gay and lesbian organizations serving youths offer counseling or can make referrals. When choosing a counselor or therapist, it is critical to make certain that services will be absolutely confidential.

Many parents are concerned about the possibility of their child's exposure to HIV, and with good reason. HIV infection and other diseases transmitted through sex and needle use pose a real threat to all teenagers, who often feel invulnerable to harm. You can help your children by getting information about how HIV is transmitted and by teaching them how to protect themselves. Youth groups and school programs may offer information about HIV/AIDS, drug treatment, abstinence, and safer sex.

It bears repeating that lesbian, gay, and bisexual children need the love and nurturing of their families. You may need information and support in order to maintain the kind of relationship with your children that you value.

TEENAGE PREGNANCY: YOUNG WOMEN IN CRISIS

By the time a young woman finds the courage to tell her mother that she is pregnant, she is likely to have experienced a great deal of anxiety and fear. She may have been shocked to find out that she is pregnant and may have agonized about whether to tell you. Despite appearances, teenagers care very much about their parents' or guardians' feelings. It is difficult for a teenager to think that she has disappointed someone she loves. Facing the possibility of rejection from a parent or guardian is even harder.

You may indeed be shocked, angry, and disappointed when

you learn that your daughter is pregnant, but blaming her or yourself, calling her names, or throwing her out of the house will only worsen the situation and destroy your relationship with your child. Your daughter is facing a decision that may affect the rest of her life. In this crisis, as in others that you may have faced together, she needs your loving support and guidance.

There are many questions to be answered and plenty of information that must be gathered quickly in order to preserve as many of her options as possible. If you are having trouble accepting the news of your daughter's pregnancy or if you feel too overwhelmed to be of immediate assistance, find someone who can offer you the support that you need in order to help your daughter. Your husband or partner, a trusted relative or friend, a clergyperson, or a professional counselor or therapist may be able to talk with you objectively. If your daughter's pregnancy is the result of incest or rape, it is especially important to seek compassionate outside help.

Sometimes, the thought of being pregnant is so difficult for a young woman to accept that she reacts by denying the physical and emotional symptoms of her pregnancy in the hope that it will somehow resolve itself. Some young women may not recognize nausea, fatigue, breast tenderness, bloating, and other changes as signs of pregnancy. You may suspect that your daughter is pregnant before she is ready to face the possibility herself. Because early pregnancy detection is of paramount importance, it may be necessary to talk frankly and gently with your daughter and encourage her to find out whether she is pregnant by having a blood or urine test at a family planning clinic or through her doctor's office. Home pregnancy tests, while affording women privacy and convenience, are not always accurate.

To find a reliable family planning clinic, you can call Planned Parenthood's toll-free number listed in the Resource Directory under Crises in Conception for an automatic referral to the nearest Planned Parenthood organization. Women's or feminist health clinics, listed in the yellow pages of your local telephone directory, are another good source of assistance. School health clinics may offer pregnancy testing on campus or make testing available through a clinic that is associated with the school.

Crisis or "problem" pregnancy centers advertised in telephone directories and in newspapers often under the headings "Alternatives to Abortion" or "Crisis Pregnancy Centers" are not the best places to go for immediate medical attention and counseling. These organizations seek to attract and counsel women considering abortion but do not support a woman's right to terminate her pregnancy and may not be licensed adoption or family service agencies. While every woman's personal and spiritual beliefs about abortion must be respected, it is important that your daughter have realistic and accurate information about all of her options and professional medical care. In addition, these organizations often employ scare tactics, such as showing graphic and misleading films or videos about abortion, to try to convince women not to terminate their pregnancies. Some may harass women or tell women they are not pregnant when they are.

If your daughter's pregnancy test is positive, she should have an immediate physical examination to verify her test results and to determine the length of her pregnancy. Prenatal care should begin right away to protect her baby's health, even if termination is a possibility. Her doctor may prescribe prenatal vitamins to prevent birth defects. She must eat nutritious food, stop eating junk food, rest, and exercise sensibly. If she smokes, she must stop. She must not use drugs or alcohol, even in minimal amounts. Caffeine and artificial sweeteners must be avoided, and she must not use any medication, including aspirin, without first seeking her doctor's advice.

Your Daughter's Decision

Depending on the length of her pregnancy, your daughter may have three basic options: carrying her pregnancy to term and raising her baby; carrying her pregnancy to term and placing her baby for adoption; and terminating her pregnancy. Making a decision is never easy, and each available option presents its own challenges. Although you may have strong feelings about the course you wish your daughter to take, you must allow her to make a decision that accords with her wishes and her beliefs. There are grave consequences to forcing a decision upon your daughter. A young woman pressured to have an abortion or to place her child for adoption may get pregnant again to make up for her loss. Young women who are forced to relinquish their children for adoption without being able to arrive at this extraordinarily difficult decision themselves may have a very difficult time integrating the profound grief that is felt at the loss of a child into their lives. Some young women who are afraid to hurt or disappoint their parents by revealing an unexpected pregnancy or who are prevented from having an abortion may try to self-abort or to seek services from an unskilled, unlicensed provider. The result could be serious injury or death.

You can help your daughter reach the decision that is right for her by talking together and exploring her feelings about each of her options. Give yourself time to cool off before talking. If you are angry at each other, a constructive dialogue won't be possible. Counselors at family planning clinics, such as Planned Parenthood organizations, can provide your daughter with objective, accurate information about all of her choices and will not pressure her to choose one option over another.

Abortion and Adoption

Because every woman who is facing an unexpected pregnancy needs information about abortion and adoption, these topics are discussed in detail in Chapter Five. If a young woman has had unprotected sex within the last forty-eight to seventy-two hours, she may be an appropriate candidate for emergency contraception, which is also discussed in Chapter Five. But again, this is an extremely personal decision, and one that should never be forced. The following section will discuss considerations relevant to an option often chosen by young mothers.

Raising the Baby into Adulthood

Your daughter may be considering having and raising her baby alone or with the baby's father or her present boyfriend, if he is not the father.

You may be wondering about the possibility of marriage for your daughter and the baby's father or boyfriend. If this is an option, find out what it means to your daughter and why it is important. Will her marriage be the result of a considered decision between two people to love and support one another for a lifetime or does it feel more like "the right thing to do"? How long have your daughter and her boyfriend been thinking about marriage? Would they marry even if she were not pregnant? Who will support the child financially? What will happen if they divorce? Is your daughter prepared to raise her child alone in that event? How will she support herself? Does she really know what marriage entails? These kinds of questions should be examined honestly and carefully. Try not to use these questions to hurt your daughter or to enforce your judgment on the matter. Allow her time to assess her situation realistically. Although your daughter and her boyfriend may want to consult with you and other relatives, their clergyperson, or a marriage counselor in order to clarify their feelings about marriage, the decision should be theirs alone.

Whether or not marriage is an option, it is necessary to help your daughter understand all the challenges that she will face both as a mother and as a teenager with new, life-long responsibilities. Young people often have unrealistic expectations about motherhood and little knowledge of what it actually takes to raise a child into adulthood. Some young women may view having a baby as a means of strengthening their sense of self-worth and purpose and of fulfilling a longing for unconditional love. Where do your daughter's strengths and talents lie? What dreams does she have for the future? How will the baby fit into these plans? Does she understand that parenting is a commitment that lasts eighteen years at the very least? Does she know that it is she, rather than the infant, who must be constantly available to provide love and attention? Does she understand that she must be primarily concerned with meeting the baby's needs and that her own needs must be secondary? If her child has a disability or an illness, will she be prepared to meet his or her special needs? Who will care for the baby when she is sick?

Having a child means giving up one's own childhood. Her social life will be very restricted as most of her time will be dedicated to caring for a dependent infant. Her friends may gradually lose interest in her as she becomes less available for social events and more engaged in the tasks of mothering. On the other hand, many young women feel pressured by friends to keep and raise their babies. Your daughter may have good friends who are pregnant or raising children. How much of a role does social pressure play in shaping your daughter's desire for motherhood?

Babies are expensive. Think about who will pay for all the furniture and supplies that the baby will need, including formula, diapers, clothes, and blankets. Of course, these are only examples of a few items needed for newborns. As you know, costs related to childcare are extensive. You might talk to your daughter about some of the future childcare expenses with which she'll be confronted, such as costs related to food, housing, clothing, schooling, daycare, and medical care. If she plans to discontinue her education, she may never be able to realize the life she imagines for herself and her baby.

Give your daughter books about pregnancy, childbirth, and childcare. Encourage her to talk seriously with single mothers to learn what their experiences have been and to find out what parenting is really like. If it appears that your child is sure of her decision to raise her baby, it will be necessary to take an even closer look at some of the practical considerations that come with early parenting.

Anticipate Family Conflicts

One of the first considerations your family will have concerns living arrangements. Will your daughter live at home while raising her child or will she live with a relative? If living in a maternity home is an option, it will be important to ask many questions about the services provided, the cost of services, the requirements made of residents, the home's philosophy, and whether your daughter will be able to keep her baby when she leaves the maternity home. Some maternity homes are geared toward providing shelter and services only to women who are planning to place their children for adoption. Naturally, the decision regarding living arrangements can be made only by you and your family. The decision will depend upon the unique circumstances of your life.

You may decide that it is wise for your daughter to live at home with the baby until she finishes her education and can safely establish her independence. Because conflicts between parent/guardian or grandmother and daughter can arise even in the best of circumstances and often center on the question of who will raise the baby, this issue must be discussed before the baby is born so that everyone will have a clear understanding of the part she will play in the baby's care. For example, does your daughter expect you to be the baby's primary caretaker, or will she accept her role as the child's mother? Are you volunteering more childcare time than you really want to give? Are these services just expected of you or are they rendered as part of a flexible, mutual agreement? Is it possible to guide your daughter's early parenting education without taking over her role as mother? How will you and your daughter resolve disagreements?

Family counselors or therapists can often help mothers and daughters work through the practical and emotional issues connected to early parenting. Social service agencies meeting the needs of families and children, including family support programs and secular and religious-based family service agencies, such as Catholic Charities and Jewish Family and Children's Services, often provide counseling or case management services to families and individuals at a low cost or at no cost.

The importance of early and ongoing prenatal care cannot be overemphasized. Without adequate prenatal care, teenage mothers are more likely to have complications than other mothers and their babies are likely to suffer. For example, teenagers are at greater risk than other young mothers for a condition called pregnancy-induced hypertension, or preeclampsia (also called toxemia). If untreated, this condition can lead to eclampsia, a convulsive syndrome that can cause maternal death. Babies of mothers with pregnancy-induced hypertension (PIH) may be born prematurely or at a very low birth weight. Smaller babies are more likely to have serious medical and developmental problems and to die than other babies.

Teenagers are also extremely vulnerable to sexually transmitted diseases. If left undetected and untreated, some sexually transmitted diseases can cause severe complications for babies, including congenital defects and death. Fortunately, these and other preventable problems can be identified and successfully addressed with early, consistent prenatal care.

Planned Parenthood organizations may provide prenatal care services or referrals to prenatal care programs in your area. You can also contact general or university hospitals, women's or feminist health clinics, other community clinics, or the local department of health for information about prenatal care services. (For the telephone number of the local health department, look in the government section of your telephone directory.) If you already have a family practitioner or an obstetrician-gynecologist, she or he can either provide your daughter with prenatal care or refer your daughter to another doctor.

Encourage Your Daughter to Stay in School

Without a high school education, your daughter's ability to earn an income sufficient to support herself and her child will be extremely limited. Public assistance will not be enough. In fact, current federal law generally forbids states to provide welfare to unmarried parents under eighteen who are not in high school or its equivalent and who are not living with a relative or guardian or in an adult-supervised setting. As well, state family-based welfare programs only provide temporary assistance. (It's important that you find out exactly what requirements must be met for assistance in your state, if you are considering applying for welfare.)

Do all that you can to help your child stay in school. Your daughter has a right to her education. Among other of its provisions, Title IX of the Education Amendments of 1972, a major federal law, prohibits any school that receives federal financial assistance (for example, public schools and some private schools) from treating students differently because of their gender. Under this law, it is illegal for schools that receive any federal funding to exclude students from any program or activity because of pregnancy, false pregnancy, termination of pregnancy, or childbirth. Schools receiving federal funding cannot require a pregnant student to obtain certification from a doctor stating that she is able to continue in the regular school program unless all students who have special medical conditions are required to produce such certification. A pregnant student must be allowed to take a medical leave of absence for as long as her doctor thinks is necessary and must be reinstated to the same status as when she left, even if other students are not allowed to take a leave of absence. If home study programs are available to other students, they must also be made available to pregnant students. Although a student may volunteer to attend an alternative school or program for pregnant students, a school cannot require or pressure her to do so. For more information about Title IX, including how to file a complaint, write to the Assistant Secretary for Civil Rights, The Office for Civil Rights, 400 Maryland Avenue SW, Washington, D.C. 20202, or telephone (202) 205-5413. Complaints must be filed within 180 days of the discriminatory incident.

Alternative Schools for Pregnant Teens

In many communities, there are school programs designed to help young women complete their education and prepare to become good parents. Although they vary widely, alternative schools may offer regular classroom instruction or high school equivalency test preparation; childbirth and parenting education programs; daycare; and peer support and counseling. More extensive programs may have a health facility on-site and offer job training. Some alternative schools and other organizations have mentor programs in which a trained volunteer is matched to a pregnant teen to help her finish her education, provide her with emotional support, and help her find needed medical and social services. Alternative programs may be offered on or apart from regular high school campuses. Adult education schools may also offer alternative education programs. In some areas, pregnant students may be able to split their schedules to attend both alternative and regular classes.

To find out more about school services for pregnant or parenting teens in your area, talk to your child's school counselor, her prenatal or health care provider, and/or agencies in the community that serve pregnant and parenting teens.

Community Resources for Pregnant or Parenting Teens

Depending on where you live, there may be many programs available to help pregnant teenagers meet the emotional and practical challenges of pregnancy, childbirth, and parenting. Classes to prepare expectant mothers for childbirth may be available through local clinics or hospitals. Parenting education and support groups, which allow parents to learn basic childcare skills and to meet other parents in the community, may be offered through schools, hospitals, health clinics, religious organizations, colleges and universities or programs operated by the local Department of Social (or Human) Services. (Government social service agencies have different names in different parts of the country.) You might also try contacting the local offices of the United Way or the YWCA for a referral.

Home visitors or visiting nurse programs are among the many valuable resources that may be available to your family. Trained volunteers or professionals can provide in-home instruction on the basics of childcare and development, offer emotional support, and provide a link to other community services. To find a home visitation program that meets your needs, try calling the local Department of Health, the local Department of Social Services, prenatal care clinics or local hospitals, family support programs, and agencies that provide a range of services to children and families, such as Catholic Charities or Jewish Family and Children's Services. You may also want to inquire at your place of worship for a referral.

In some communities, there are organizations, often called family support programs, that offer a range of direct services to pregnant and parenting teenagers at a single location and/or provide assistance in locating and using other community-based and government resources. Services that may be accessible through family support programs include counseling for teens and families; parenting classes; daycare; high school or job training programs; home visiting programs; health care and family planning services; instruction in problem-solving and in other life skills; programs for young fathers; and early intervention programs to screen and address child developmental disabilities. Some family support programs and alternative schools offer support groups for grandparents as well. To locate a family support program, try asking your health care provider, a community prenatal clinic, your daughter's school counselor, the local Department of Social (or Human) Services, a family service agency, or the social work department of a local hospital.

Don't Forget the Baby's Father

Regardless of whether the baby's father and your daughter marry or continue their relationship, he can make important emotional, practical, and financial contributions to his child's life. Many young men are willing to accept parental responsibilities, if given encouragement. Some community organizations and schools offer programs designed to help young fathers become better parents.

Despite the potential benefits of the father's involvement in his child's life, there are times when the father's involvement may be inappropriate, such as when he is abusive or violent or when the pregnancy is the result of incest or rape. As with other decisions related to her pregnancy, decisions about the father's involvement should be made by your daughter, or your daughter and the child's father when appropriate.

Young unmarried mothers must also make decisions about getting legal custody of their children, establishing paternity, and seeking child support. Chapter Three provides basic information about these topics. However, only an attorney who is experienced with family law and who is familiar with your daughter's situation can offer proper legal guidance.

WHAT'S IN THIS CHAPTER?

- Annulment, Separation, and Divorce
- Finding a Lawyer
- Mediation
- Dividing Property
- Alimony (Spousal Support)
- Social Security Benefits and Welfare
- Child Custody
- Helping Your Children Cope with Divorce
- Child Support

✦ 3 ✦
Divorce

HOW MUCH DO YOU KNOW ABOUT DIVORCE?

Divorce is one of the most common and significant of life's crises. The prospect of divorce marks the beginning of what is often an intense and arduous legal process underscored by the pain of separation and loss. For many, divorce brings about unforeseen economic changes, unique parenting challenges, and a reexploration of identity and self-worth. It can also mean new opportunities for growth and positive redirection. But the issues of divorce are complex. The more you know about the divorce process, and the more equipped you are to communicate with your attorney and the other professionals who will assist you, the better able you will be to participate in a decision-making process that will affect your life for years to come. Learn and read all you can about divorce. Bookstores and libraries usually carry self-help manuals and other books on the practical aspects of divorce. When you have information, and when you are aware of your various options, you save yourself time, money, and much emotional strain.

This chapter is intended to help you communicate with your attorney and other professionals and to give you an overview of some of the issues in divorce. Nothing within it constitutes legal advice, which only your attorney can provide. For further information, please refer to the reading list at the end of this book.

If you and your husband have talked about divorce or if you are having difficulties, you may want to consider marital (or couples) therapy. Marriage and family therapists (MFTs) can help married and unmarried couples alike identify and address problems that arise within their relationships. Couples who have finalized their decision to divorce may be able to use therapy or divorce counseling as a means of arriving at a more amicable parting. Divorcing parents can be helped to refocus their attention on the needs of their children and on finding ways to parent cooperatively. However, many experts consider marital or divorce counseling to be unsafe for women in abusive or violent relationships and thus generally recommend that any contact with an abusive partner, including counseling, be avoided.

Marriage and family therapy is usually short-term and solution-focused. The emphasis is on helping couples and families learn new skills to resolve their difficulties. It is not necessary to have your husband (or partner) join you in order to visit a marriage and family therapist. You can go alone. Individual therapy can help you explore relationship issues and find new strength as you move through the divorce process. Likewise, it is usually not necessary to bring the whole family together to participate in family therapy, though some practitioners may prefer to work with the entire family.

Although therapists are not attorneys and do not give legal advice, it's important to look for a therapist who has experience working with divorcing couples and who is familiar with the divorce process and the laws governing divorce in your jurisdiction.

A friend who sought therapy in connection with divorce and who was satisfied with the outcome can be an excellent source of referral. For more information on finding and choosing a therapist or counselor, see Chapter Seven.

DIVORCE

ANNULMENT, SEPARATION, AND DIVORCE

An *annulment* nullifies the marriage contract and treats the marriage as though it never existed. Whether a marriage is void or voidable depends upon the defect that existed at the time of the marriage. Bigamy or incest may automatically void the marriage, and thus the marriage may be deemed invalid without a court determination. Grounds for an annulment determined by the court vary from state to state but usually include fraud, being underage, and duress (threats or force). Many states limit the time within which an annulment may be obtained. You can marry immediately after an annulment and in most states children born of an annulled marriage have the same rights as children born of an existing marriage. Because of the emergence of no-fault divorce laws, which make ending a marriage easier than in the past, annulments are not common.

Separation occurs when a married couple decides not to live together any longer. Although separation is often a prelude to divorce, many people do not divorce but remain separated for religious, economic, or personal reasons. Separated couples are still legally married and are therefore not free to remarry. Separation can occur by mutual consent or judicial decree. In either case, separating (and divorcing) couples often have a written separation agreement. The separation agreement is a contract between couples to live separate and apart. It usually resolves issues concerning property, child support, alimony, and child custody and visitation.

Because the laws concerning separation vary from state to state, it is wise to seek legal advice before separating and to have your attorney review your agreement. Otherwise, important rights may be lost.

Divorce (dissolution of marriage) granted under United States law legally terminates a marriage. Each state has its own statutes and caselaw (decisions made by judges) that govern the divorce process. Many states have residency requirements that must be met before a spouse can file for divorce. These requirements range from six weeks to twelve months. Common law marriages must also be dissolved by court procedure or any future marriage will be invalid.

GROUNDS FOR DIVORCE

In the past, before the advent of no-fault divorce laws, a spouse suing for divorce had to prove that the other was at fault. Today all states recognize some form of no-fault divorce based on irretrievable breakdown of the relationship, irreconcilable differences, incompatibility, or separation. In some states, divorce is granted only on a no-fault basis. In other states, no-fault grounds have been added to existing grounds, and divorce can be filed either on fault or no-fault grounds. Depending on the state, fault-based grounds for divorce can include (but are not limited to) adultery, mental or physical cruelty, desertion or abandonment, habitual drunkenness, and drug addiction. In some states, fault is considered when dividing marital property or awarding alimony (spousal support). For example, courts have denied alimony based on adultery involving heterosexual and lesbian relationships. (Also see Child Custody on page 117.)

You and your husband can lay the groundwork for your divorce yourselves. More often, couples negotiate through their separate attorneys or through a mediator. A combination of these options may be appropriate or necessary. If violence, intimidation, or lack of fair play are a part of your relationship, it may not be in your best interest to work directly with your husband either informally or with a mediator.

Issues to be resolved usually include the division of property, alimony, child custody and visitation, and child support. The written agreement that describes the arrangements to be made concerning these issues is called the separation agreement. (The terms "settlement agreement" or "property agreement" may be used, although property agreement technically refers to the settlement of property issues alone.) Your separate attorneys should always review the agreement, regardless of how it was decided. Once an agreement is reached, it will be presented to the court for judgment.

When couples agree that there should be a divorce — or when one party disagrees but doesn't plan to fight the divorce — the divorce is said to be uncontested. A divorce is also said to be uncontested when couples concur on all of the issues in their separation agreement. When couples cannot agree, the divorce is said to be contested. If the issues can't be resolved, trial may be necessary. Ordinarily this is considered the least desirable option, as it can be extremely expensive, emotionally grueling, and time-consuming. Fortunately, the vast majority of divorces do not come to trial.

FINDING A LAWYER

Do You Need an Attorney?

Although couples in short-term marriages with no children and little property may be able to proceed without an attorney, legal representation is important if you have children and property (such as income, a house, and an automobile). At the very least, you will need an attorney to advise you of your rights and to review your separation agreement. Consider that the issues at stake are those around which your economic future and well-being may turn. The more complicated your divorce or the more you stand to lose, the more important it is to shop for the attorney who can best represent you.

TEMPORARY ORDERS

If necessary, either spouse can ask the court for temporary orders (also called pendente lite or interim orders) to address the issues of temporary support, alimony, child custody and visitation, sole occupancy of the home, and other issues until final orders are made. Some orders can be granted "ex parte." This means that the order can be made without notice to the other party, although notice must be given and a hearing must be scheduled later. You may also be able to get a temporary restraining order against an abusive or violent husband. Ask your attorney for information and assistance.

Do Not Use Your Husband's Attorney

It is essential that you get independent legal counsel to negotiate or review your separation agreement. An attorney cannot fairly represent the interests of two divorcing spouses at the same time. Likewise, a lawyer who has had personal, financial, or business dealings with your husband — or with both of you — may have a conflict of interests. An attorney who represents both parties in a divorce at the same time may be acting unethically. Don't let yourself be talked into a decision that is against your best interests. Look for someone who can represent you without bias.

Look for an Experienced Attorney

As a general rule, you should look for an attorney who has experience handling the type of matter with which you are concerned. This is true of divorce cases, which can be extremely complex, covering many areas of the law. A general practitioner with experience in divorce matters may be suitable when a divorce is likely to be simple. However, it is usually advisable to seek an attorney specializing in *family law* (also called matrimonial or domestic relations law), particularly when your divorce is likely to be complex or if a business or substantial property is involved. If there are special issues connected with your divorce, such as custody issues, abuse and violence, or immigration issues, look for someone who has experience in that area as well.

In some states family lawyers may be certified, although it's not necessary to be certified in order to practice family law. Certification means that the attorney has met certain experience and examination requirements. To learn what criteria a *certified family law specialist* must meet in your state, call the Board of Legal Specialization at your state bar association. Although certification does not guarantee that an attorney is better than others, it is at least an indication that she or he has achieved a certain level of competence in family law. You should be aware, however, that certified family law specialists often only handle large marital estates.

The American Academy of Matrimonial Lawyers, a professional organization active in many states, can provide you with a list of matrimonial (family or domestic relations) attorneys in your state or area. See the Resource Directory for information.

The cost of your divorce will depend on many factors including the complexity of your case and whether it comes to trial. Factors that contribute to increased costs include contested issues, the necessity of using formal measures to obtain financial information about the other party and experts, such as appraisers, actuaries, or accountants to evaluate assets. It should be noted, however, that, depending on the issue, the services of experts or the use of discovery devices may be vital to the satisfactory resolution of your case and should not be avoided merely as a cost-saving measure; the result may be long-term financial loss.

An attorney may charge a flat fee for routine work, such as that involved in a simple uncontested divorce. However, most attorneys' services are billed at the attorney's hourly rate, which differs from place to place and is often dependent on the attorney's experience and reputation. Talk to the attorney about fees and your ability to pay at the first meeting. Insist that any agreement about fees be put in writing. Contingency fees, arrangements whereby an attorney is paid based on the percentage of the recovered award, are not usually applicable to divorce cases and may be barred in divorce cases in some states. However, attorneys may be allowed to work on a contingency fee basis when collecting past due child support or alimony.

Low-Cost Alternatives

Some legal aid organizations handle divorce cases. You must have a low income in order to qualify for legal aid. If you do not qualify for assistance, the legal aid organization may be able to refer you to an attorney who works for reasonable fees or to an attorney referral service.

Will Your Husband Pay Your Attorney's Fees?

Sometimes courts will order a woman's husband to pay her attorney's fees when she is needy and he clearly has the ability to pay. But there is no guarantee that this will happen. Thus, many attorneys will request a retainer up front and hold you responsible for paying the difference between the amount awarded by the court, if any, and the attorney's actual fees.

When you meet with your attorney, ask any and all questions that you have about your divorce. Listen carefully, take notes, and make sure that everything is explained to your satisfaction. Don't be intimidated by an attorney. Remember that you will be his or her employer.

The following are examples of basic questions that you may want to ask your attorney about your divorce, depending on your needs.

- What are grounds for divorce in my state? What is the procedure for divorce in my state?
- How is property divided in my state? What property is excluded from division?
- What is considered marital property in my state? Are private, employee, or military pensions, retirement plans, or professional degrees considered marital property? What property might I be entitled to?
- Am I entitled to alimony? What are the advantages and disadvantages of trading alimony for a larger property settlement? Are the fees that I pay you to obtain alimony tax deductible?
- What effect will a current or future romantic relationship have on my right to alimony or custody? Are there behaviors in my history that might affect custody? (Discuss the issues that concern you.)
- Are my children entitled to support? How do the guidelines for child support operate in my state? How will they affect my case?
- How can I protect myself if my husband takes more than his share of money from our joint bank account or otherwise engages in financial misconduct?
- What are the advantages and disadvantages of mediation? How do you feel about your clients working with mediators?
- Will you give me a written estimate of the time it may take to work on my divorce and the possible costs to me?
- How long do you estimate my divorce will take? Is there a waiting period after filing for divorce before a hearing/trial can take place or after which a final decree will be issued?

MEDIATION

Divorcing couples are increasingly turning to mediation to resolve their conflicts and negotiate the terms of their separation agreements. In some states mediation is mandatory when couples can't resolve certain issues, such as child custody and visitation. But mediation can also be used to tackle a range of divorce issues, including property division and alimony.

During mediation you and your partner work out the terms of your divorce with the help of a professional mediator who is trained to facilitate your negotiations. Although mediators are often psychologists, social workers, or lawyers by profession, it is important to understand that they are neutral and do not advocate on behalf of one party or the other. During mediation, an attorney mediator is not practicing law, nor is a therapist mediator doing therapy. The focus is on helping you and your husband work together toward the achievement of a mutually satisfactory settlement.

Attorneys are not usually present during the mediation sessions. However, you may seek the advice of your attorney throughout the mediation process. If you wish to do this, look for an attorney who is comfortable with mediation and a mediator who is not opposed to having clients' consult with their attorneys during mediation. Do not sign the agreement achieved in mediation, which may be the settlement agreement or a document called a memorandum of understanding, until your attorney has had a chance to review it and discuss it with you thoroughly.

How much does mediation cost?

An advantage of mediation may be that of lowering the cost of divorce. This does not mean that private mediators' fees are lower than attorneys' fees. Fees are often akin to those typically charged by members of the mediator's primary profession and will vary geographically. However, some mediators determine fees on a sliding scale basis (you pay according to your income), and fees may also be negotiable.

Naturally, the cost of mediation will be increased when you employ an attorney or other professionals in addition to a mediator in order to reach an agreement. When a couple fails to reach a satisfactory agreement in mediation and proceeds to an attorney-negotiated agreement or to court, the potential cost-saving benefits are lost.

Disadvantages of mediation

Mediation is not for everyone. When there has been a history of violence or intimidation in the relationship, mediation is not advised.

Mediation requires honesty and good faith on the part of both parties. Before negotiating property division, couples are required to fully and completely disclose all their income and assets. Mediators, unlike attorneys, do not have the power to force revelation of this information through discovery. Therefore, if you believe that your husband is hiding assets and will not be cooperative, or if your divorce involves complex economic issues, mediation may not be in your best interest.

When both partners have equal financial bargaining power, are able to assert their interests, express their concerns, and work toward a fair solution, mediation can be productive. But when one partner is intimidated by the other or has had less economic or emotional power in the marriage, mediation can be a disservice. For women who have been abused by their spouses, mediation may be ineffective and even dangerous because of the extreme imbalance of power and the possibility of coercion and increased violence. Mediation is therefore not recommended in such situations.

In some states couples may be ordered or referred to mediation to resolve certain issues of their divorce. However, there may be an exemption from mediation for victims of spousal abuse. Similarly, mediation may not be required if child abuse has occurred. Tell the mediator and your attorney about any abuse or violence that has occurred in your relationship before going ahead with mediation. Even where an exemption for victims of abuse is not provided by law, your attorney may still be able to challenge the requirement.[1] If mediation cannot be avoided, ask that measures be taken to protect your safety during the session(s). For example, request that the mediator meet with you separately. This is called private caucusing. Also, you may be able to have your attorney accompany you during mediation. Be aware, however, these measures do not guarantee your safety outside of mediation.

Because divorce or separation is an extremely dangerous time for women in abusive or violent relationships, it is important to take extra safety precautions whether you are using mediation or negotiating the terms of your divorce through your attorneys. Advocates at women's shelters can help you develop a safety plan for you and your children as well as help you find refuge if you are in danger. For more information about women's shelters, see Chapter Four.

How do you find a mediator?

Providing that mediation is a safe option, you and your husband should look for a mediator who suits you both. National organizations such as those listed in the Resource Directory may provide you with a list of mediators practicing in your state. Friends are also a good source of recommendation. If you are ordered to mediation by the court, you may be able to choose between a court mediator and a private mediator. Court mediation may not be confidential and, depending on the jurisdiction, court mediators may be able to make recommendations to the judge. Be certain to learn the conditions under which mediation will take place before working with a public mediator.

It's important to select a mediator carefully. When interviewing, find out where the mediator was trained. Is the training organization recognized by a national mediation organization? How long has the practitioner been doing mediation? How much of her or his practice is devoted to mediation? What is the hourly fee? Is a retainer or advance deposit required? Is it refundable? If you are concerned about a particular issue, such as child custody or the tax consequences of divorce, find out what expertise the mediator has, if any, in that area. Look for a mediator whom you like and trust.

DIVIDING PROPERTY

WHAT IS MARITAL PROPERTY?

Property is anything you own. It can include concrete items such as money, real estate, furniture, and jewelry, and intangible items like pensions, stocks and bonds, and government benefits.

Although each state defines marital property differently, it can generally be thought of as everything that a couple acquires during a marriage. In most states it doesn't matter whether the property is in your name or in your spouse's name. It doesn't matter who bought the property, who controls it, or if you have knowledge of its existence. If funds acquired during the marriage were used to purchase the property, it may be considered marital property. The increase in value of property bought before the marriage, such as a home, can also be considered marital property.

Depending on the state, professional licenses (for example, a license to practice medicine), businesses or professional practices, and pensions may be considered marital property. Even where licenses or degrees are not considered property, you may be entitled to reimbursement if you contributed to your husband's ability to earn a professional degree, for example, by working to put him through school. Ask your attorney to discuss any property that you may be entitled to share.

WHAT IS SEPARATE PROPERTY?

Separate property is defined differently in different states. However, as a general rule, property that is acquired before the marriage or through inheritances and gifts made solely to one partner is considered separate property. Although most states do not subject this type of property to division, some do. Once again, it is important to ask your attorney how property is distributed in your state.

If you commingle your separate property with marital assets — for example, by adding money that is considered separate property to a joint bank account or using your separate property to make a mutual purchase — it may no longer be distinguishable as yours alone and may be subject to division.

HOW IS PROPERTY DIVIDED BETWEEN SPOUSES?

In *community property* states, marital assets (earnings and property acquired during the marriage) are generally equally divided between wife and husband, although laws differ among community property states and exceptions may be made based on circumstances that might make equal division unfair. The community property states are Arizona, California, Idaho, Louisiana, Nevada, New Mexico, Texas, Washington, Wisconsin, as well as the Commonwealth of Puerto Rico.

All other states are *equitable distribution* states. In these states, distribution of property is based on what the court deems to be fair. As with other aspects of your agreement, you and your spouse may be able to decide how you want to divide your property, keeping state law in mind, or your attorneys may negotiate property distribution. If no agreement can be reached, it may have to be decided in court.

The term "equitable distribution" does not indicate that property will be divided equally by the courts. Although each state and court determines how property will be divided, factors commonly considered are the length of the marriage, the financial circumstances, the employability and earning capacity of each spouse, the age and health of each, and the financial and nonmonetary contributions that each has made to the marriage. Again, fault or misconduct can influence the division of property in some states.

While equitable distribution may seem fair on the surface, it is not always so in practice. Although equitable distribution states are increasingly adopting presumptions that property will be divided equally, courts sometimes award the spouse who has contributed the most financially, often the husband, a greater share of the property. As well, nonexistent or "rehabilitative" alimony awards made without an understanding of the problems many women face upon reentering the job market frequently leave women in strained economic circumstances.

The tax consequences of property distribution can also have a marked effect on your economic future. Consult with your attorney and an accountant to learn how taxation will affect the decisions you reach regarding property distribution.

If you expect to require assistance from government programs that base eligibility on financial need, such as Medicaid or Supplemental Security Income, ask your attorney how the property and alimony issues of your divorce will affect your ability to use these programs.

How much do you know about your family's finances?

Before property can be divided, it must be identified. In order to negotiate property division, you and your attorney must have as much information about your family's income and assets as possible. Your attorney can uncover this information without your help, but the process used to do this, called discovery, is time-consuming and very expensive. You may also have personal information relevant to your case that your lawyer would have no way of knowing without your help. Resist the temptation to let your attorney "take care" of everything. You are the one whose interests are at stake, and thus you must do everything you can to achieve the best possible outcome. You can save a lot of money, become more informed about your financial status, and improve your chances of a good result by gathering information on your own. Even if you are not contemplating divorce, it's important that you have full knowledge of and access to all financial records throughout your marriage. If you become widowed or solely responsible for handling your family's finances, you will have to be versed in these matters.

Your lawyer will tell you what information to bring to the first meeting. The following lists are intended to give you a general idea of the type of information that you may be asked to bring, depending on your financial circumstances. Gather this information as soon as possible, bringing *copies* to your attorney. Leave the originals in a secure place.

Do you have a right to part of your husband's pension?

Both civil and military pensions, as well as retirement benefits, may qualify as marital property and can be very valuable assets. For information on pensions and divorce contact:

The Women's Pension Project
Pension Rights Center
918 16th St. NW, Suite 704
Washington, D.C. 20006
(202) 296-3776.

Since 1981, the Women's Pension Project has helped individual women and groups advocate for their pension rights through educational, organizing, and legal assistance activities. The Divorce Clearinghouse offers legal assistance to divorcing women and lawyers who are having difficulty with pension issues. Literature explaining pension issues in understandable terms and legal packets for attorneys are available.

- copies of any divorce papers, if you have been served
- separation agreement, if you and your husband have written one
- marriage certificate
- record of previous marriages and divorces
- business and personal tax records dating back to a period of time specified by your lawyer, usually three to five years

Bring copies of records of separately and jointly owned property, including:

- bank account, savings, and certificate of deposit (CD) statements
- stocks and bonds
- loans receivable (money owed to you and/or your husband)
- mortgage records and deeds to all properties owned by you and/or your husband
- insurance policies
- pension and retirement plans
- titles to automobiles and other vehicles
- wills and trusts
- appraisals of jewelry, antiques, art, and other valuables
- records of furnishing, appliance, and equipment purchases
- records of the contents of your safe deposit box
- any recent loan applications (An application may reveal honest information about your husband's financial health.)

Bring copies of records of your income and your husband's, including:

- employment records
- records pertaining to your and/or your husband's business, such as tax records
- records of royalties
- records of any other income, such as government benefits and pension/retirement income

Make another list of *debts and liabilities* that you and your husband share, including:

- any mortgage or loan due
- personal notes (money that you or your husband owe)
- credit card receipts; balance on unpaid credit lines
- unpaid medical or dental bills

Some of this information may be tough to gather, particularly if your husband has kept information from you. Your attorney can tell you how to obtain copies of these documents.

CREATE A BUDGET FOR FUTURE EXPENSES

In order to get a realistic idea of what you and your children will need to live on in the future, develop an estimate of your annual expenses. To start, make a list of your past year's expenditures, if typical. Use receipts, checkbook entries, credit card billings, automatic deductions from your bank account, bank statements, and so forth. You and your attorney will use this information to negotiate property division and, possibly, alimony. Itemize the amount of each expense. Include everything that you can think of as necessary, such as rent or mortgage, real estate taxes, food, clothing, children's educational expenses, insurance, medications, medical, dental, and vision services not covered by insurance, utilities, repairs, daycare costs, your own education-related costs, work-related expenses, transportation/automobile expenses, laundry/dry cleaning expenses, pet care, children's activities and allowances, and other needs.

Will You Lose Your Health Insurance?

Provisions for medical and dental insurance are frequently a part of separation agreements. However, if you are currently covered by your husband's employee insurance policy, you should know that the Consolidated Omnibus Budget Reconciliation Act (COBRA) allows you and your children to remain covered for at least thirty-six months (three years) after a divorce or legal separation. You will be required to pay up to 102 percent of the cost of the premium, and you may convert the plan to individual coverage when the thirty-six-month period expires. COBRA only applies to businesses with twenty or more employees. If you want to exercise your rights under COBRA, notify the plan administrator of your husband's company within sixty days of the divorce. Do this in writing. Generally, the employer must notify you of your right to elect coverage within fourteen days. If you choose coverage, you must make payments within forty-five days. Another federal law, the Health Insurance Reform Act, allows employees and their dependents who were eligible for health insurance through their place of employment but

> **WARNING: DON'T SIGN ANYTHING THAT YOU DON'T UNDERSTAND**
>
> If you are in doubt about the legal effect of any document that your husband asks you to sign, do not sign it until you have received your attorney's advice. You may be signing away important rights. Never sign any form that contains blank spaces.

declined it because they were enrolled in another group plan and then lost their health insurance due to a qualifying event, such as divorce or legal separation, to enroll in their employer's plan within thirty days of the qualifying event. Be sure to discuss these and other medical and dental insurance issues with your attorney.

PROTECTING YOUR FUTURE: FINDING HIDDEN ASSETS

While divorcing partners are required to fully disclose their income and assets for the division of property, there is a possibility that one or the other spouse may not follow this directive.

Lawyers have the ability to use "discovery" in order to obtain information about income and assets. Discovery may be done informally or, when one partner is uncooperative, by using certain legal tools, including *depositions* (questions answered under oath in the presence of a court reporter); *interrogatories* (written questions answered under oath); *notice for production of documents* (such as bank statements) and *subpoenas* requiring third parties (such as banks or employers) to turn over certain documents, as well as other formal requests.

Forensic accountants can be hired to detect income and assets hidden within a business. Again, be sure to discuss your concerns with your attorney and to inquire about the services of professionals who might be able to uncover and evaluate any property that may be rightfully apportioned to you. You will generally be responsible for paying for experts' services (a considerable expense), although in some cases the court may direct your husband to defray the costs if you cannot afford them.

ALIMONY

Divorce settlements may provide for the more financially advantaged spouse to help the less advantaged partner by making payments to contribute to her or his support. This financial support is called alimony or, more often, maintenance or spousal support.

HOW IS ALIMONY DETERMINED?

Awards of alimony are guided by state law and generally based on the need of the recipient and the circumstances of the payor. Factors usually taken into account include the age and health of each spouse, the length of the marriage, the earning capacity and educational level of each spouse, the income and assets of each, the nonmonetary contributions made to the marriage by each, the couple's standard of living during the marriage, and the tax consequences of property division and alimony. In some areas, alimony is determined by formula, much as child support payments are calculated.[2]

As previously mentioned, misconduct or fault may influence the amount of alimony you will receive or whether alimony may be awarded at all. Alimony may be stipulated to be tied to the cost of living index, increases or decreases in salary, or to other conditions to which you and your husband agree.

How long will alimony continue?

In a lengthy marriage in which the wife has been a home-maker, has had little employment opportunity, or is older, alimony may be permanent or long-term. Yet, if the spouse receiving permanent alimony remarries, or the ex-spouse paying alimony dies, alimony will normally cease. In some states, courts are permitted to terminate or reduce alimony when the receiving spouse lives with another in an intimate relationship, called cohabitation. Be certain to ask your lawyer how any current or future relationships will affect your alimony.

Alimony may be awarded to a homemaker in order to help her prepare to become self-supporting. This sort of alimony, often called rehabilitative alimony, usually lasts only a few years.

Because alimony typically stops when the payor dies, it is common practice for a husband to take out an insurance policy on his life, if possible, so that in the event of his death his ex-wife's support and that of his children may continue. If you do this, it is a good idea to take responsibility for paying the premiums. Otherwise, you may lose this insurance if your husband misses his payments and lets the policy lapse.

Normally, your ex-husband cannot wipe clean his alimony debt by declaring bankruptcy; however, you should be very careful to discuss with your attorney the ramifications of taking a lump-sum payment of alimony or trading alimony for a greater share in the division of property. Payments that are not considered to be "in the nature of support" may be dischargeable through bankruptcy. Similarly, awards of attorney's fees paid to you by your husband as ordered by the court may be dischargeable if not viewed as being in the nature of support. Lastly, you will usually pay taxes on alimony but not on child support.

CAN THE AMOUNT BE CHANGED?

Many states allow an adjustment in alimony when either spouse experiences an unforseeable, significant change in circumstances. Alimony may be increased when you lose your job or reduced when you get a job. Conversely, alimony may be reduced when your ex-husband's ability to pay is reduced, or increased when his earnings rise. You and your husband can specify the terms for future alimony payments in your agreement. Be sure to ask your attorney whether the type of alimony you receive can be modified.

How Do You Collect Alimony?

Your husband can send you periodic payments directly, or he may choose to have the amount automatically deducted from his wages and deposited into your bank account. Regardless of what method you choose, make sure to keep a written record of payments. You will need this information if your ex-husband misses payments or does not send the right amount and you have to force collection.

COLLECTING ALIMONY THAT IS PAST DUE (ARREARS)

If your husband has fallen behind on his payments and will not voluntarily agree to make up the amount, you may have to ask your attorney to pursue collection. The Child Support Enforcement office may also be able to help you recover past due alimony, if the agency is collecting support for your child.

THE SOCIAL SECURITY ADMINISTRATION
1-800-772-1213 1-800-325-0778 (TTY)

SOCIAL SECURITY BENEFITS FOR DIVORCED WOMEN

If you are divorced, you may be eligible to receive benefits based on your ex-husband's work record. Providing that you are eligible, you will receive an amount equal to up to one half of your ex-husband's benefits — the same amount that you would receive as his wife. He does not necessarily have to be collecting benefits when you apply. His benefits will not be reduced, and if he remarries, his new wife's benefits will not be affected. However, if you remarry, your benefits may cease, although they can be restored if your new marriage ends.

To be eligible as a divorced spouse:

* you must be at least sixty-two
* you must have been married to your husband for at least ten years
* you must be currently unmarried
* you must not be eligible for equal or higher benefits on your own work record
* your ex-husband must be receiving disability or retirement benefits *or* he must be at least sixty-two years old and fully insured, and you must have been divorced from him for at least two years

DIVORCED WIDOW'S BENEFITS

If your ex-husband is fully insured and dies, you may be eligible to receive benefits based on his work record, if you meet the following qualifications:

* you are at least sixty years of age, or fifty to fifty-nine years old, if you are disabled
* you were married to your husband for ten years or more; or you are caring for his child who is under sixteen or disabled and eligible for Social Security benefits
* you are unmarried or did not remarry until after sixty, or fifty, if you were disabled at the time of remarriage

You cannot collect benefits based on your former spouse's work record and that of your present spouse at the same time.

As a divorced widow, you will receive an amount up to 100 percent of your ex-husband's benefits, depending on other factors that may affect your benefits.

You can apply for benefits by telephone, through the mail, or by visiting your local Social Security office. It is generally best to apply in person. When applying for benefits, bring:

* your Social Security number
* your ex-husband's Social Security number or his date of birth and parents' names
* your birth certificate
* your divorce judgment or decree

Do not wait until you have gathered all of the information above to apply. If you do not know your ex-husband's Social Security number or have lost contact with him, apply anyway. The Social Security office should be able to locate the information you need to establish your eligibility. It is important that you *apply three to six months in advance* of the birthday on which you can start collecting benefits so that you will receive them as soon as you become eligible. For more information about Social Security and benefits that may be available to you, call the number above and ask for free pamphlets about the type of benefits that interest you.

WELFARE: APPLYING FOR ASSISTANCE

There comes a time in most people's lives when asking for assistance — whether it be from a relative, a friend, or the community — is necessary in order to stay afloat financially. Many women feel hesitant about applying for public assistance. For example, you may feel that someone else needs the help more than you do or that you are demeaning yourself or your family by accepting assistance. But applying for and receiving benefits is a matter of survival. There are many reasons why women need assistance, including inadequate or nonexistent child support payments, difficulty in finding employment, and low wages. Never let anyone insult you because you are applying for or receiving assistance. Remember that you are doing what you can to help yourself and your child(ren).

At the time of this writing, the family-based welfare system formerly known as AFDC and now generally referred to as TANF (Temporary Assistance for Needy Families) is undergoing tremendous change nationwide. Family welfare programs may vary significantly from state to state, even within states, and may continue to change. It is extremely important that you find out as much as possible about the program in your state, especially the requirements that you and your family members must meet and follow in order to receive and continue receiving assistance. Also ask about applying for Medicaid (or Medi-Cal in California), the state-federal program providing medical assistance to people with low incomes. If you have lost welfare benefits because of the changes in welfare law, you can still apply for Medicaid.

At this time, local and state welfare offices administer the welfare program. The welfare office is usually a part of the Department of Social (or Human) Services, listed in the government pages of your local telephone directory. Before you go to the office to apply, find out exactly what requirements you must meet in order to receive assistance, what type of assistance is available, and what documentation you must bring with you when you go to the office. Be prepared for a long wait at the office.

CHILD CUSTODY

In a divorce or separation proceeding, either or both parents may have custody (also called access) of their children. Decisions about child custody should be made amicably by both parents whenever possible. Custody battles often end after a great amount of financial and emotional damage, and they are especially harmful to children. Mediation may help parents to make decisions in their children's best interests. In a number of states, mediation and parenting classes are mandatory for custody and visitation issues if parents might otherwise go to court.

Generally, the decisions that you and your husband reach will be written into your separation agreement. Because the agreement must be approved by the court, your negotiations should be made with a basic understanding of your state's laws concerning custody. Your attorney can provide you with information about the statutes and caselaw regarding custody in your state.

TYPES OF CUSTODY ARRANGEMENTS

There are two aspects to any child custody order: physical and legal. A parent with physical custody has responsibility for the child's daily care. The child lives with the parent who has physical custody and is subject to that parent's control. Legal custody gives a parent the right to make major decisions affecting the child's life, such as those regarding religion, school, and discipline, as well as medical decisions.

One parent may be given both rights exclusively. This is called *exclusive* or *sole custody.*

Joint custody gives each parent custody. Various joint custody arrangements are possible. For example, parents may share both legal and physical custody. Parents with joint physical custody share time with their children, though the division of time need not be equal. On the other hand, both may retain legal custody, while one parent is given sole physical custody. This is called joint legal custody. States' attitudes toward joint custody differ. In some states, there is a presumption or preference for joint custody, although most states neither favor nor disfavor the arrangement. Some states allow joint custody where both parties have agreed to it, and several require parents or the court to work out a detailed parenting plan for a joint custody agreement. In every state, the judge has the authority to approve or award joint custody.

The differing views, definitions, and criteria adopted by courts when awarding joint custody make it necessary to find out exactly what joint custody means in your state and to carefully consider the possible advantages and disadvantages.

Split custody separates siblings, with each parent having sole legal and physical custody of one child or more. This is not a typical alternative, as allowing siblings to remain together is generally felt to be in their best interests.

How are decisions about child custody made?

Parents may reach a mutual decision about child custody. If you and your husband cannot reach an agreement on your own, through mediation or your attorneys' negotiations, a judge will have to make the decision. In all states, courts make decisions about custody according to the best interests of the child. Many states have guidelines to help judges determine what is actually in a child's best interests, but judges continue to have wide discretion when making placements.

Although states use different criteria when making determinations in custody disputes, the following are examples of some of the factors that may be weighed by the court when making placements. It should be noted that these are only examples — the criteria used by your state may differ — and that no single factor is controlling. Following this list, you will find brief discussions of other potential factors.

Factors that may affect custody decisions

- the wishes of the child, considering the child's age and maturity. More weight is given to the preferences of older children. In some states, no weight is given to the preference of children under a certain age.
- the relationships between parents, child, siblings, and other significant people involved
- the child's adjustment to home, school, and community
- which parent is most likely to promote a close or continuing relationship with the child's other parent (This factor can create problems for women with abusive or violent husbands.)
- the mental and physical health of all involved. The pres-

ence of a physical disability or chronic illness should not be the basis for a denial of custody, unless it can be shown that the disability has an adverse effect on the parent's ability to raise and care for the child.

KEEP A RECORD OF ALL YOU DO FOR YOUR CHILD

Increasing importance is being placed on keeping children in the custody of the person who has contributed most to their daily care. Traditionally, women have acted as their children's primary caretaker, but as gender roles change and men begin to take on more responsibility in the home, caretaking duties may be divided. The *tender years doctrine,* a legal development of the nineteenth century that presumed it was in the best interests of young children to be placed with their mother unless she was found unfit, has been rejected in most states, and men who contest custody are often successful. Although biases in favor of women may still be influential today, you should not assume that you will be awarded custody simply because of your gender. It is therefore a good idea to document your daily activities as primary caretaker if you are seeking custody of your children. Document all that you do for your children, including preparing meals, bathing and grooming your children, buying clothes and doing laundry, helping with homework, disciplining your children, cleaning, arranging for daycare, medical care, education, transportation, and social activities, as well as any other of your responsibilities. This documentation will help your attorney argue on your behalf if it becomes necessary.

Courts often find benefit in allowing children to remain in the family home, thereby preserving the children's current relationships with friends and school. Thus, the parent with whom the child is living may have a better chance of gaining custody.

IF THERE IS ABUSE OR VIOLENCE IN YOUR RELATIONSHIP

Domestic violence is a factor in determining custody in most states. Women who have experienced violence in their relationships should consider requesting sole custody, restriction of the abusive parent's visitation rights (for example, supervised visitation), and an order of protection against the abuser. However, you and your lawyer may have to fight hard for these provisions, as judges may still have biases that affect decisions related to domestic violence, including cus-

IF YOU ARE A WOMAN WITH A DISABILITY . . .

. . . and you anticipate or are involved in a custody dispute, contact Through the Looking Glass's national clearinghouse for parents with disabilities at 1-800-644-2666 for information, attorney referrals, and consultation about parenting issues. Help is available to women with physical, psychiatric, and cognitive disabilities and their advocates. You may also find Protection and Advocacy Systems, discussed in Chapter Six, and other disability rights organizations to be useful resources.

tody decisions. It is possible for an abusive father to be granted visitation or custody. For more information about domestic violence, see Chapter Four.

Physical abuse of a child, neglect, or exposure to abuse by another are also factors to be weighed in custody determinations. When there is evidence that one parent has sexually abused the child, custody can be awarded to the other parent. However, it is extremely important to proceed carefully when alleging sexual abuse. An unproven allegation may hurt your chance of getting custody if it appears that it was made in order to deny custody to the other parent. This can happen when abuse has in fact occurred. For more information about child abuse and actions to take upon the discovery of abuse, see Chapter Two.

PROTECT YOUR CHILD FROM PARENTAL KIDNAPPING

If your spouse or partner has threatened to take your child — or if you sense that he may — take it very seriously. Contact the National Center for Missing and Exploited Children, other nonprofit national organizations for missing children (see the Resource Directory listings under Children in Crisis), your state or local police, and the local prosecutor's office (district or county attorney) to learn what measures can be taken to prevent a kidnapping and what to do in the event of an abduction. Do not delay. You must be prepared to notify police as soon as you have reason to believe that your spouse or partner has taken your child or that he is intentionally keeping your child from you.

If there is a possibility that your child may be taken outside of the United States, contact the Office of Children's Issues in the Department of State, listed in the Resource Directory under Children in Crisis. Ask for a free copy of the booklet *International Parental Child Abduction,* which describes measures that you can take to try to prevent an abduction from happening.

It is important to have a custody order (including a temporary custody order) that clarifies when each parent is to be with each child and to avoid joint custody when there is a possibility of abduction. Without a clear custody order (and a certified copy of the order that can be presented to law enforcement in the event of an abduction), each parent generally has a right of access to the child. Authorities are reluctant to get involved, unless the child is in immediate danger or at medical risk, for example, when the child needs medication that the abductor does not have.

If your husband or partner is abusive or violent and you are considering leaving with your child or going into hiding, you should be aware of some of the potential legal risks involved. (For general information, see Chapter Four.) *However, your safety and that of your children is of utmost importance and should be your primary concern.*

In order to provide information to the police in the event of a kidnapping, make sure that you have *at least* the following in a place that is safe and readily accessible to you but not accessible to your husband or partner:

- certified copies of any court order pertaining to custody and visitation
- your child's passport
- a clear, *recent* color photograph of your child, preferably one taken head-on and one in profile.
- a complete, written physical description of your child, including unusual markings and identifiers such as orthodontic braces and eyeglasses.
- a copy of your child's birth certificate
- updated copies of your child's medical and dental records and insurance cards
- a recent photograph of your husband or partner
- his full name, description, date of birth, driver's license number, vehicle description, and license plate number
- his home and work addresses and telephone numbers
- his Social Security number and your children's Social Security numbers
- his passport number

Make sure that you have the telephone numbers and addresses of your husband's or partner's family members, current and past employers, business partners, coworkers and friends.

Try to keep custody issues from becoming a source of conflict. During a divorce or separation, when tensions are high, remain alert to the possibility of an abduction. If possible, take your children to school and pick them up directly afterward. Consider where your spouse may go with your child. If you already have a protection order against your husband, make sure that everyone at your child's school, including administrators and teachers, are aware of it and will follow its guidelines. Give teachers, baby-sitters, day-care workers, or anyone else who looks after your child a copy of your custody order and make certain that they understand the custody arrangements. Thinking about some of the things that your child likes to do, places that your husband or partner wants to visit, and interests that your partner or husband maintains can provide you with clues to his whereabouts if he leaves. Teach young children their full names and their address. Instruct them how to get in touch with you at any time, including at home and at work, and how to make a long-distance collect telephone call.

WILL YOU LOSE CUSTODY IF YOU'VE HAD AN AFFAIR?

In many, but not all, states, issues of morality or marital misconduct, such as adultery, are not given weight unless it can be shown that a parent's behavior has a negative impact on the child. This does not mean that the other parent will not attempt to gain custody because of an extramarital affair or that a judge will not view an affair as harmful to your child. Your concerns should be frankly discussed with your attorney.

WILL YOUR INCOME AFFECT DECISIONS ABOUT CUSTODY?

Although the difference in income between two parents should not be the sole basis for an award or denial of custody, some states may consider a parent's financial circumstances as a factor. Unfortunately, bias against parents with lower incomes persists. Among other arguments, your attorney might assert that child support should be awarded in an amount sufficient to give the child similar advantages whether living with the higher- or lower-earning parent.

IF YOU HAVE CUSTODY, WILL YOU BE ABLE TO RELOCATE WITH YOUR CHILD?

States differ as to whether a custodial parent is free to move with the children after divorce. Some courts limit the custodial parent's ability to relocate, and some states prohibit custodial parents from moving without notice to the noncustodial parent (the parent without physical custody) or permission from the court. Ask your attorney for information about your state's laws regarding relocation and how any such restrictions will affect you.

WHEN ARE CUSTODY DECISIONS MADE? THE IMPORTANCE OF TEMPORARY CUSTODY

If you and your husband cannot agree on arrangements for the care of your children before the final custody order, a temporary custody order may be made. The temporary order will prevail until the final order is entered, or until the court changes it. As with permanent orders, the decision to order temporary custody is based on the child's best interests. It is crucial to try to obtain a temporary custody order when your spouse is violent or abusive or when there is a possibility that he will kidnap your child. As well, a parent with temporary custody may have a better chance of getting final custody, as courts generally do not like to disrupt the child's home life without good reason. If you are seeking custody, stay with your children. Do not leave them solely in the care of your husband or another. However, if you must leave without the children to escape violence, it's a good idea to talk to a lawyer about what you can do to protect your rights to custody. Some shelters and advocacy organizations offer legal counseling.

DO YOU NEED A CUSTODY ORDER IF YOU ARE UNMARRIED?

Although in some states a biological mother is considered her child's natural guardian, a court order is generally necessary to ensure the mother's sole legal custody. Once paternity is established, as is usually required before child support can be ordered, for example, both parents' rights to custody of the child may be viewed as equal. This may be suitable if both parents are involved with their child's life, but this possibility can complicate already troubled situations. If the mother does not have a custody order, the father or his family may seek to assert his legal rights as a parent and may request custody or visitation. Custody disputes between unmarried couples may then be decided by the courts in the same manner as couples who are divorcing. Very serious problems can arise for a mother who does not have legal custody if the father decides to kidnap his child. In some states, a custody order is required before the police will take a missing person's report and before criminal charges against the abductor can be filed.

A disadvantage of seeking custody, however, is that where a father may not have thought about custody previously, your action may stir his interest.[3] You will have to weigh both the advantages and disadvantages of seeking legal custody along with other important considerations, including child support issues.

Prejudicial attitudes toward lesbian mothers are changing, and many states do not view a parent's sexual orientation as a detrimental factor in making or modifying a custody order unless it can be shown that her sexual orientation has an adverse effect on her child. Nonetheless, judges have wide discretion in making custody determinations and may hold personal biases against lesbians or bisexual women that unduly influence their decisions. Attorneys representing lesbian clients in custody cases should present expert testimony that refutes assumptions and stereotypes about lesbians and bisexual women that are based on myth rather than fact. Concerns about stigma suffered by children can also be rebutted.

The same attitudes that influence custody decisions also affect decisions about visitation. Courts sometimes place restrictions on a child's visitation with a lesbian mother, such as requiring that her partner not live with her during visitation or disallowing overnight visitation when she and her partner are living together. Yet in the majority of states, harm must be shown before visitation rights can be affected.

Lesbian Moms: Where to Turn for Help with Custody Issues

As with all issues of divorce, it is best if you and your husband do everything that you can to reach an agreement without going to court.[4] But if you are fighting a custody battle, you will need the help of a knowledgeable attorney, one who is experienced in representing lesbian and gay parents in custody disputes in your state. The National Center for Lesbian Rights and CALM, listed in the Resource Directory, are good places to begin your search for information.

CAN A CHILD CUSTODY ORDER BE CHANGED?

No custody order is ever final. Custody orders can be changed in certain situations, but to modify an existing order, it is generally necessary to show that a significant change in circumstances has occurred or that the present custodial situation is harmful to the child. As well, the change must be in the child's best interests.

Physical or sexual abuse, neglect, domestic violence, or an unstable home environment are examples of situations that present harm to a child. Other changes of circumstances, such as a custodial parent's relocation or regular interference with visitation, and even an older child's preference may be sufficient to warrant a change of custody.

Some states have established time limits before which a petition to modify custody can be filed with exceptions for emergencies, such as when a child is endangered. As a practical matter, a reasonable amount of time must pass before an allegation of changed circumstances will carry any weight.

Visitation

Parents have a right to a continuing relationship with their children, one from which children typically benefit. Therefore noncustodial parents are generally entitled to reasonable visitation (also called "partial custody"), unless visitation would be contrary to the child's best interests, for example, if there is danger of harm to the child. Abuse, neglect, violence, and kidnapping threats or actual kidnapping may necessitate restrictions, such as supervised and/or specific visitation or a denial or termination of visitation.

There can be adverse consequences to restricting the father's right to visitation in the absence of a court decision. If there are strong reasons why visitation is not in your child's best interests, the best course to choose is to seek restrictions or denial of the father's right to visitation through the courts.

Custody and visitation orders should specify when the child is to be with each parent so that the likelihood of misunderstanding and conflict may be reduced. Again, it is imperative to clarify visitation rights when there is abuse or violence in your relationship or any threat that the other parent will take a child or keep a child past visitation.

HELPING YOUR CHILDREN COPE WITH DIVORCE

The painful emotions and practical concerns of divorce can often overwhelm parents, making responsible parenting difficult. But children are also profoundly affected by divorce. The way in which your children experience and cope with divorce depends a great deal on how you and your husband conduct yourselves during and after the process. Here are some general guidelines for helping your children:

- Once the decision to divorce is final, tell the children, using age-appropriate language. Be honest and direct.

Keeping information from children only causes them to become confused and worried about what is happening.

- When you tell the children about the divorce, resist any temptation to blame the other parent.
- Let your children know — and show them — that the divorce won't lessen the love you feel for them or the connection that you share.
- Be clear about any changes that may take place in your children's lives, such as those created by a move or a return to work. Children must be told in clear, simple, and reassuring terms how their daily lives will be affected. Young children need to know who will feed them, put them to bed, where they will live, and how often they will see the other parent.
- Allow your children to ask questions and express the anger or sadness that is natural when divorce occurs. Let them know that they can raise the subject of divorce with you at any time. When you don't take the time to listen or to answer your children's questions, they may not seek your help again. Instead, they may suffer silently or use negative behavior to express their feelings.
- Let your children know that they are not in any way to blame for the divorce. It's very common for young children in particular to feel that they caused the divorce by being bad.
- Because many children harbor fantasies of their parents' reunion, it is necessary to help your children understand that you and your spouse will not reunite.
- Children need a continuing relationship with both their parents and often interpret the failure of a noncustodial parent to visit as a sign of rejection or abandonment. Do all that you can to encourage a positive relationship between your children and their father. Interfering with visitation only hurts children. If there are reasons why contact with the father may not be in a child's best interest, seek the advice of your attorney. A proposed change of visitation should be handled through the legal system.
- Do not criticize the other parent in front of or around your children. Do not force your children to take sides or use your children to spy on or relay messages to their father.
- Continued hostility and bitterness between parents hurts children deeply. Although it may seem impossible, it is imperative that you and your husband strive to parent cooperatively. Marital therapy, divorce counseling, or parenting classes (sometimes available through

or mandated by the court) may help you and your spouse focus on and respond to your children's needs. However, if you are or have been abused by your husband, it is not generally advisable that you attend counseling or therapy together.

CHILD SUPPORT

WHAT IS CHILD SUPPORT?

Both parents have an obligation to support their children. When one parent has custody of a child, the noncustodial parent has an obligation to contribute to the financial support of that child, making periodic payments, usually monthly, for that purpose. A court order for child support from a divorce, separation, or establishment of paternity gives the custodial parent the right to collect child support. It is also possible to establish an order for child support if you have been deserted by your husband but not divorced.

Your attorney can help you obtain child support. If you do not have an attorney, if you are not divorcing, or if you have never been married, your local Child Support Enforcement office, often called the IV-D (4-D) agency, can also help you get and enforce an order for child support.

How Is Child Support Decided?

Federal law requires that all states and the District of Columbia, Puerto Rico, Guam, and American Samoa have guidelines for child support agreements. Although states use different guidelines to determine child support, amounts are usually based on mathematical formulas that take into consideration the needs of the child and the income and earnings of one or both parents. The ability of the noncustodial parent to pay child support is crucial. However, judges may be able to make support orders based on a parent's potential earning abilities rather than on present income.

Judges have limited discretion to lower or increase the amount of child support determined by the guidelines according to criteria within state guideline statutes or court rules. If it can be shown that application of the guidelines would be unfair or inappropriate, courts may deviate from the amount of support resulting from the guidelines, stating the reasons for deviation in writing. Here again, the criteria used for deviation differ across states. Expenses for childcare, a child's extraordinary medical or educational needs, custody and visitation arrangements, and the noncustodial parent's duty to support other dependents are common factors affecting the use of guidelines. Be sure to bring your child's daycare and special needs to the attention of your attorney or CSE caseworker. Depending on state law and your circumstances, a separation agreement may provide support for expenses that allow your children to maintain their pre-divorce lifestyle, such as costs for summer camp, private school, and college.

In a divorce, the court will review your separation agreement to determine whether it complies with the state guidelines or is otherwise acceptable. If no agreement can be reached or if your separation agreement is not approved, the decision will be made by the judge or through an administrative process. You cannot give up your child's right to financial support, for example, by trading child support for property. It's also important to note that the parent who owes child support cannot generally discharge past-due support by declaring bankruptcy.

Getting Medical Support for Your Children

No child should be without medical coverage, especially when the noncustodial parent has access to and can afford health insurance. Under the Child Support Enforcement Amendments of 1984, child support enforcement agencies are required to include health insurance in a child support order if health insurance is available to the noncustodial parent at a reasonable cost. Provisions for the medical support of your child can be included in your separation agreement or child support order.

When defining your obligations to provide for your child's medical care, your agreement or order should make clear who will pay the health insurance premiums, who will pay for expenses that are not covered by health and dental insurance and those that are covered only in part, as well as what happens when coverage is reduced or lost.

In the past, custodial parents often met with significant problems when trying to enroll a child in the noncustodial parent's employer-provided health care plan or when seeking reimbursement from the other parent for medical expenses. The Omnibus Budget Reconciliation Act of 1993 (OBRA '93) amended two major federal laws (ERISA and the Social Security Act) and created "qualified medical child support orders" (QMCSO). With a QMCSO, a custodial parent may enroll her children in the employer-provided plan and submit claims to the employer directly as well as receive reimbursement from the employer without having to rely on the noncustodial parent. Employers must make group coverage available to children of an employee who is required to carry the children on his plan and cannot deny coverage to a child because the child does not live with the noncustodial parent or because the parents weren't married. State laws provide further assistance to custodial families. For example, states are required to enact laws that, among other provisions, mandate immediate withholding of the parent's wages to pay for the insurance premiums and forbid an employer to deny coverage to a child born out of wedlock.

Among the criteria a medical support order must meet in order to be "qualified" is the requirement that it contain a reasonable description of the coverage to be provided by the plan to each child. Your attorney or CSE caseworker should be aware of QMCSOs and should obtain clear information about your husband's employer-provided health plan in order to draft the QMCSO.

How Can You Get the Best Support for Your Child?

It is important to provide your attorney or CSE caseworker with as much information as you can about your income or earning capacity and/or the other parent's current and anticipated income. If your ex-husband has quit his job or is intentionally keeping his income low in an attempt to reduce support payments, be sure to bring this to the attention of your advocate. In most states, a support order can be made on the basis of the other parent's earning capacity rather than on his actual earnings.

Much of the information that you'll bring to your lawyer initially will help your lawyer or CSE worker define your husband's income. Discovery can also be used to elicit information about your spouse's income and assets.

It's also important to develop a realistic understanding of your child's needs and to try to negotiate for everything that you think should be included in your agreement. If possible, include major future expenses, such as college tuition. Don't delay thinking about your child's future education; in many states, you will not be able to ask for support for college tuition at a later date. If you have a separation agreement, it may be possible to include provisions for the automatic adjustment of the support order to changes in the cost of living and for periodic updates of information about your ex-spouse's income.

Another important consideration for parents is the dependency tax deduction that can be taken on income tax returns. Generally, the custodial parent is given the exemption unless it is clearly negotiated and given in writing to the other parent. This is an issue that must be discussed with your attorney and accountant — one that is of unique concern to parents with joint custody.

How Long Will Child Support Last?

Child support lasts for the time specified in your child support order. Generally, support will last until the child reaches the age of majority (eighteen or twenty-one, depending on the state). Child support may also stop when a child is adopted, enters the military, gets married, or otherwise becomes emancipated, for example, by judicial determination. Some states have laws that allow for the continuation of support until a child finishes high school, or college in some cases, or for an extension beyond the statutory limits for a dependent child with a physical or mental disability. Parents must include a provision to extend child support past the age of majority in their separation agreement or child support order; these extensions are not granted automatically.

If your ex-spouse dies, child support will normally end unless the support order names your children as beneficiaries of your former husband's estate. Your ex-husband may want (or be ordered) to take out an insurance policy on his life, naming the children as beneficiaries. Consider paying the premiums yourself. If your ex-husband pays the premiums, there is a possibility that he will let the policy lapse or change beneficiaries.

How Are Child Support Payments Made?

All states now mandate immediate wage withholding unless both parents agree in writing to an alternative, such as direct payments, or if the court or administrative process allows for the use of another plan. This means that if the other parent is employed, the employer will automatically make deductions from his paycheck. When the father is self-employed or paid in cash, other methods of collection can be used.

Can the Amount of Child Support Be Changed?

Either parent may petition the court or, in many states, begin an administrative action with the CSE office, to change the amount of child support.

Generally, a significant change in circumstances for parent or child is required to modify the amount of child support. For example, if the parent who owes child support involuntarily loses a job, there may be cause for lowering support payments. However, the noncustodial parent cannot quit his job and then request a modification because of lower income. When the other parent requests modification, you must be notified and allowed to contest it.

Similarly, the other parent's substantial increase in income or a substantial increase in costs to meet your child's needs may support an increase in the amount of child support. The state child support guidelines may be used to make decisions about the need for modification and the amount of support. Under federal law, parents may request that the state review their child's support order every three years (or after a shorter period of time, depending on the state) and make changes, if appropriate. You may also be able to request a review and modification of your child's support order before such period of time, if there has been a substantial change in circumstances. You may want to seek modification if your support order was awarded before 1984 or 1988 when legislation set new guidelines for child support, particularly if health care coverage was not included in your order, or if you want to have support withheld from your husband's wages. Whether you can take these specific actions without having to show a change in circumstances depends on state law. However, it is a good idea to seek information about your state's guidelines to find out whether modification would be to your advantage before seeking a change in support. Your local CSE office can supply you with information about your state's guidelines.

Both parents may be required to update the court regarding their employment or income. If required, make sure that you do this. This may be especially important to you if your ex-husband fails to keep the court updated and you want to complain. The weight of your complaint may be lessened if you have also failed to keep your end of the bargain.

Visitation and Child Support

A child's right to support and visitation are generally viewed as independent issues, and a noncustodial parent cannot use denial of visitation as an excuse not to pay child support. If the father has fallen behind on or refuses to make child support payments, the best course is to pursue all legal avenues available to enforce compliance.

Acting on your own to deny the child's father visitation

entails some serious risks. The father can bring an action against you for interference with visitation or for contempt of court. Contempt of court proceedings can be initiated for a violation of any court order, and contempt may be punishable by fines or jail time. It's also important to remember that unless there is real justification, denying visitation hurts children. A child who is kept both from receiving child support and from contact with his or her other parent loses twice.

When problems such as abuse or neglect exist, it is advisable to seek a change of custody or visitation rather than to enforce these restrictions yourself.

Collecting Child Support: When the Father Fails to Pay

In recent years, major legislation has been passed to try to solve the serious problem of fathers' failure to pay child support. When attempting to collect past-due child support, you can return to your attorney (if you have one) or apply to the local Child Support Enforcement office. Child Support Enforcement offices have more means of collection available than private attorneys, and the services are less expensive. On the other hand, CSE agencies often have very large caseloads, the process may be slow, and you may not get the attention that you could get from a private attorney.

Depending on the situation and state, CSE agencies can use a variety of collection methods, such as immediate wage withholding from the father's paycheck, state and federal tax refund intercepts and offsets, unemployment compensation intercepts, money judgments and garnishments, seizure and sale of property, and liens. The CSE office can attempt to locate a debtor parent through the use of federal and state parent locator services. Recent welfare reform legislation requires all states to have new hire registries in place to which employers can report newly hired employees. States must also be able to withhold or restrict the use of professional, occupational, or driver's licenses and report arrearages to credit bureaus. Other provisions in the law should make child support enforcement methods more efficient, but it will take time for states to implement the law. Also, under an executive order, federal agencies can deny loans to parents who are delinquent in their child support payments. Talk to your attorney or CSE caseworker about provisions for enforcement that can be included in your separation agreement or court order.

If the other parent has the ability to pay child support but has willfully violated a support order, contempt proceedings

---

CHILD SUPPORT QUESTIONS OR PROBLEMS? ACES CAN HELP

ACES toll-free child support hotline:
1-800-537-7072

ACES, the Association for Children for Enforcement of Support, is a national nonprofit self-help advocacy organization assisting children of parents who have failed to meet their child support or visitation obligations. ACES cannot collect child support for you, but it can provide you with information to help you become the best possible advocate for your child's right to support.

can be used to coerce him to comply with the order or to punish him for noncompliance. Civil contempt must be "purgeable." In other words, the person who commits contempt of court (called the contemnor) may be given a sentence of fines or jail time and then be ordered to perform a specific, doable act, such as look for a job, within a certain period of time to exonerate himself.[5] Criminal contempt is not purgeable; it is meant to punish. In order to determine whether contempt is the best strategy to use in your case, talk to your attorney or contact ACES or other advocacy and support organizations for information.

Failure to Pay Support Is a Crime

In many states, failure to pay child support is a crime. Under the Child Support Recovery Act of 1992, it is a federal crime to willfully fail to pay past-due support for a child who lives outside the state, if the amount is over $5,000 or has been unpaid for over a year.[6] This remedy may be used against a parent who has the means to pay child support, but refuses to do so. Speak to your attorney or the U.S. attorney's office in your state about the applicability and appropriateness of state and federal criminal laws to your case. However, when you consider criminal remedies, including criminal contempt, you must weigh the value of such penalties as enforcement tools against the curtailment of the father's ability to earn while incarcerated.

The Child Support Enforcement Office

Every state has a child support enforcement program, which is usually operated through the state and local Social (or Human) Services Departments or another similar government agency. The U.S. Department of Health and Human Services' Office of Child Support Enforcement is the federal agency responsible for overseeing the regional, state, and local CSE offices.

You must apply for services through your local Child Support Enforcement (CSE) office. To locate the agency nearest you, call the nearest regional office listed in the Resource Directory or check the listings in your local white pages. ACES can also provide you with information.

Your local CSE office can help you:

- establish a court order of paternity
- locate an absent parent and access information about him and his assets and income

- obtain a court order for child support
- enforce your child support order
- obtain a court order for child medical support

Any person with a child who needs help collecting child support can apply to the program. People receiving or seeking family welfare assistance (formerly called AFDC), Medicaid, or federally assisted foster care programs may automatically receive services at no charge. Other parents or caregivers may be charged an application fee and all or part of the costs of services. Some states absorb the application fee.

Working with the CSE office is a cooperative effort. The more pertinent information that you can bring to help the CSE office locate the father and establish and enforce your child support order, the better the agency will be able to serve you. If you have any new information, be sure to keep the CSE office updated. Because of the high demand for assistance with child support many agencies are heavily backlogged, and you may need to be very insistent on individual attention to your case. The success of any collection effort depends on the father's intentions and circumstances. If he is self-employed, works for cash or commissions, is hiding assets, or has left the state, the process will be slower and much more difficult. It's important to actively pursue your case. Keep informed about its status and ask questions. Don't give up.

If He Has Moved to Another State

Your children are entitled to and can collect support even if your ex-husband has left the state, although enforcement usually takes much longer. If you have a support order, and know the name and address of your ex-husband's employer, the CSE agency or you (in some states) can use interstate wage withholding to enforce an order of support or collect back payments.

CSE caseworkers and attorneys can also use the Uniform Reciprocal Enforcement of Support Act (URESA) and the Revised Uniform Reciprocal Enforcement of Support Act (RURESA) in order to help parents establish and enforce out-of-state support orders. Each state has its own version of URESA, which allows the CSE caseworker (or other appropriate official) or private attorney to file a petition for support in the state where the other parent resides. A hearing will be held in that state. Normally there is no requirement that you be present. Enforcement under a URESA statute usually takes longer than interstate withholding.

A new law that has replaced URESA and RURESA in many states, the Uniform Interstate Family Support Act (UIFSA), contains a number of provisions intended to make interstate collection more efficient. Federal welfare reform law requires that all states adopt UIFSA by 1998.

Under UIFSA, an order for immediate wage withholding can be sent directly to the other parent's employer for enforcement or to the CSE agency in the other state. The law allows a court or administrative agency to order that any identifying information about you or your child be kept secret upon a finding that the health, safety, or liberty of either is at risk. This provision may be particularly useful when threats of parental kidnapping have been made or when the other parent is abusive or violent. As with RURESA, states adopting UIFSA may have significantly varied some of its provisions. Therefore it is important to consult with your CSE caseworker or attorney for specific information about the act.

Lastly, the Full Faith and Credit for Child Support Orders Act requires each state to enforce and not modify support orders of another state except when the original state is no longer the child's state or the residence of any contestant or when all contestants consent in writing to let the new state make a modification.

If your child's other parent is out of the country, talk to your CSE caseworker about options for enforcement.

If You Are Seeking or Receiving Welfare

Welfare programs for families are meant to meet the needs of children. However, the government will not assume the father's obligation to contribute to a child's support when he is known and can be located. In other words, welfare payments for your family comprise a debt that the father owes to the state. In order to be eligible for welfare, you may be obliged to cooperate with the CSE office to identify and locate the father unless you can show "good cause" for not cooperating. Good cause is defined by the state, but examples may include rape, incest, or instances when identifying the father is not in the children's best interests, and other possible exceptions.

If you believe you have good cause for not identifying the father, gather as much documentation as you can and get witnesses to support your claim. Seek legal assistance if necessary. However, it is vital that you not seek assistance from attorneys working with the CSE office because their interests lie with the collection of child support rather than with the protection of your right to an exemption.[7] Legal aid organizations and women's shelters (see Chapter Four) may be able to serve you in this regard.

If You Were Never Married to Your Child's Father

Before you can get an order for child support, you must legally establish that the person you claim to be your child's father is indeed the father. Paternity can be established at any time before the child's eighteenth birthday. But it is important to make a decision about establishing paternity and seeking child support as soon as possible. As time passes, you may lose contact with the father, making collection of support extremely difficult. If you decide not to pursue paternity immediately, make certain that you have your ex-partner's Social Security number and keep track of his whereabouts.

Should You Establish Paternity?

There are some significant advantages to establishing paternity. For example, the child's father will be obliged to pay child support, and your child will have inheritance rights as well as easier access to Social Security benefits on the basis of the father's work record. The father may accept a parental relationship with his child, if he has not already done so, and the child may be accepted by the father's family, if this has not already occurred. Your child will also have access to more information about his or her family and medical history.

Even if the father has no income, for example, because he is a student, unemployed, in prison, or otherwise appears not to be a source of financial support, it does not necessarily mean that there is no reason to establish paternity. The father's financial situation may change and, if paternity has been established, you could begin to collect support at any time before the child's eighteenth birthday.

What Are the Disadvantages?

There are also good arguments against establishing paternity. If the father is abusive or violent, you may fear for yourself and the child and therefore wish to avoid all contact. Once paternity is established, the father or his family may seek custody or visitation. If you are pregnant and unmarried, do not put off a decision about paternity establishment. Even if you decide not to establish paternity, it is important to consider obtaining *legal* custody of your child.

❖ 4 ❖
Violence Against Women

WHAT'S IN THIS CHAPTER?

- ◆ Rape
- ◆ Domestic Violence
- ◆ Stalking

RAPE

*W*HERE CAN YOU TURN FOR HELP? RAPE CRISIS CENTERS

Rape crisis centers across the United States offer information, assistance, and support to women who have experienced any type of sexual assault. When you call a rape crisis center, a trained volunteer or staff member, often called an advocate, will be there to listen. She can help you make decisions about seeking medical treatment and reporting the rape to the police, but she will not pressure you to make decisions. An advocate's job is to give you emotional support and information so that you can make the choices that are right for you. An advocate will believe you when you talk about the rape. She knows that rape is not your fault.

The following are free services generally available through a rape crisis center:

- ◆ Twenty-four-hour hotlines on which to speak to an advocate who can provide you with immediate crisis counseling. You do not have to give your name when you call.
- ◆ In most rape crisis centers, advocates are available twenty-four hours a day to meet you at the hospital when you seek medical assistance following a rape. They can tell you what to expect, provide you with emotional support, and protect your rights during the examination. Some rape crisis centers may be directly involved in giving the examination. If necessary, your advocate may be able to bring you a change of clothing and arrange transportation for you.
- ◆ Advocates are generally available twenty-four hours a

Depending on the type of information you need, the following organizations may be able to offer you assistance.

Women's shelters offer help for all women experiencing abuse and violence within a relationship. You'll find information about women's shelters and other resources for abused women and families in this chapter.

State coalitions against domestic violence. State coalitions provide support to shelters and work to educate state legislatures about domestic violence. Some coalitions can provide referrals to local women's shelters. The National Coalition Against Domestic Violence, listed in the Resource Directory, can refer you to local programs.

Rape crisis centers offer assistance to survivors of any type of sexual assault. Information about rape crisis centers is given in this chapter.

Local departments of aging, adult protective services, or Departments of Social Services investigate complaints of elder abuse or neglect. Many states have *elder abuse hotlines* on which to report abuse or neglect.

Victim/witness assistance programs offer assistance to crime victims and provide information about the criminal justice system. These programs are often found in the offices of your local prosecutor (district or county attorney), but are not available in all areas.

Local law enforcement agencies provide information about state and local criminal laws and police procedure for enforcing those laws.

Local prosecutor's offices provide information about state and local criminal laws, enforcement, and possible penalties for violation.

City attorney's offices provide information about state and local laws.

day to meet you at the police station, if you choose to report the rape. They can offer you information about filing a report, the investigation process, and the ways in which the criminal justice system works in your community. An advocate may be able to accompany you to court, provide transportation, help you remain informed about the progress of your case should it come to trial, and give you information about your rights as a victim. Some rape crisis centers provide attorney referrals. You do *not* need a lawyer to file a police report or to have your case heard in court, although you may have an attorney present. Also, you may need the services of an attorney if you later decide to sue the rapist or other third parties in a private civil action.

♦ Advocates can help you through the emotional crisis of rape. You may welcome talking with someone who can empathize with your feelings, who knows that you did not cause or invite the rape, and who can offer you information about your options. In addition to immediate crisis counseling over the telephone, rape crisis centers frequently offer support groups for rape survivors. Some centers offer groups for survivors of sexual abuse, significant others, and family members. Private counseling or referrals to counselors are also generally available.

♦ Rape crisis centers often work to improve rape laws and to educate the general public about rape by providing speakers and programs to schools, businesses, and other organizations. Rape crisis centers may also offer self-defense classes.[1]

How to find a rape crisis center

Rape crisis centers are also listed in your local telephone directory. Check the front section of your local yellow pages, where there may be listings of other important community services. Hospitals may also be able to call an advocate for you or to provide you with a referral. Some hospitals have advocates on call or on-site. Police are another source of referral. Your local YWCA may be able to give you the telephone number of a rape crisis center or may operate one. If you attend a college or a university, there may be a student health service or women's resource center on campus that can provide you with information about rape crisis services operating within your area or school. If there is no rape crisis center in your immediate area, call a center in another area for information and referral.

RAPE ABUSE AND INCEST NATIONAL NETWORK (RAINN)

1-800-656-HOPE

RAINN is a nonprofit organization that operates in cooperation with hundreds of rape crisis centers across the country. Your call will be automatically forwarded to the rape crisis center nearest you. All calls are toll-free and confidential.

What is rape?

Rape is a violent crime. It is an extraordinary violation of your physical, emotional, psychological, and spiritual being. It is not an expression of sexual desire. Although sexual activity is involved in rape, sex is only the weapon that the rapist uses to dominate, humiliate, and degrade the person whom he chooses to assault.

The most important thing that you have to learn about rape is that it is not your fault. The rapist is entirely responsible for committing the crime. The clothing you wear, your appearance, your behavior, your lifestyle, or the activity in which you were involved at the time of the rape did not cause it to happen. If you knew the man who raped you, consented to have sex with him in the past, or if you agreed to certain sexual acts before the rape but not to the act that constituted the rape, it is still not your fault. Rape is not sex; it's violence. No one deserves to be raped.

- Do not bathe, shower, douche, brush your teeth, comb your hair, brush off your clothing, or change your appearance in any way. If you can manage, do not use the restroom. You may have a strong — and understandable — desire to do any or all of these things, but you will destroy the physical evidence that can be used to identify and prosecute the rapist.
- Do not move or touch anything at the scene of the crime. If contacted, police may be able to collect evidence that could lead to a successful prosecution.

WHAT TO DO

Listed here are suggestions that you may choose to follow in any order that you feel is appropriate or necessary.

- Get to a safe place.
- If you are injured, call 911 or the operator for an ambulance. Police can also take you to the hospital.
- Contact someone you trust — your husband or partner, a parent, guardian or other relative, friend, and/or an advocate at a rape crisis center.
- Even if you think that you have not been badly hurt, it is still important to seek medical treatment immediately. A rape crisis center or the police can refer you to a hospital. Do not drive yourself, if at all possible. Your support person or the police can take you. A rape crisis center may also be able to arrange transportation for you. If you can, bring a change of clothing with you or have a friend, relative, or advocate bring clothing to you at the hospital. You have the right to have a friend, family member, or advocate present during your medical examination.

❖ Consider calling the police. Deciding whether to call the police is one of the most difficult decisions that you will have to make as a rape survivor. But reporting soon after the rape will increase your chance of successfully prosecuting the rapist. Reporting does not necessarily mean that you will be involved in a criminal trial. Talking with an advocate at a rape crisis center can help you to reach a decision. Remember, the choice is yours. You are in control.

You may be wondering what you did wrong, why you weren't able to avoid the rape, or whether you could have escaped somehow. You must understand that your actions do not cause or invite rape and that rape is sometimes unavoidable. Women are raped walking during the day as well as in the night; they are raped by neighbors who come to their doors as well as by strangers. You cannot tell whether someone is a rapist just by looking at or talking to him. Having a close personal relationship with someone — a husband, partner, friend, employer, coworker, parent/guardian, or other relative — does not give that person the right to rape you. Most rapes are carefully planned. The rapist may have had days, weeks, months, even years to plan how to overcome you; you may have had only seconds in which to make your decisions. You survived. The choices that you made were right.

Although men are raped, and women have raped other women and men, the vast majority of reported rapes are committed by men against women. Many women are raped by strangers, but most women are raped by someone they know, such as husbands, ex-husbands, boyfriends and ex-boyfriends, relatives, friends, or neighbors.[2] The myth that only certain "types" of women are raped serves to perpetuate another myth: that those who adjust their behavior to meet narrowly defined expectations of their gender will be spared harm. In reality, all women are vulnerable to rape. Rape happens to women of every age, race, ethnic or religious heritage, class, educational background, and profession. Women with disabilities, lesbians, and heterosexual and bisexual women are raped. Similarly, rapists are of all backgrounds and walks of life, although in statistics drawn from reported rapes, rapists are likely to be young men. Interracial rapes occur, but most rapists victimize women of their own heritage.

The legal definition of rape varies from state to state. As a result of legal reforms that began in the 1970s, many states have redefined rape as sexual assault or sexual battery and/or have included vaginal, oral, and anal contact or penetration by a person or object in legal definitions of rape. Reformed rape laws may also specify varying degrees of the crime based on factors such as penetration, injury, use of a weapon, commission of another felony in the course of the rape, and the age of the victim.

IF YOUR HUSBAND HAS FORCED YOU TO HAVE SEX

Because spousal rape often occurs within relationships where other forms of violence and abuse have taken place, it can be very hard to recognize that forced sex is, in fact, rape. Spousal rape is against the law in virtually every state. In a number of states, spousal rape is treated in the same manner as rape committed by a stranger. However, in other states, antiquated notions of women as property still survive in the way the laws are written. There may be exemptions under which a husband is immune from prosecution. Spousal rape may be afforded a lesser degree of criminality than rape committed under other circumstances, and wives may be given a very short period of time in which to report the crime. If you have been raped by your husband, you may want to contact a women's shelter as well as a rape crisis center. (Some organizations serve both rape survivors and victims of domestic violence.) You are also encouraged to seek medical examination and treatment. You have the right to decide what course of action you will take. Advocates at women's shelters and rape crisis centers can help you weigh your options and protect your safety.

It is extremely important to seek medical attention as soon as possible after the rape:

- You may have serious injuries, which, if left untreated, can worsen.
- You may have internal injuries of which you are unaware.
- You may have been exposed to sexually transmitted diseases.
- Pregnancy can result from the rape and, if you wish, emergency contraception can be provided. To be effective, this must be done as soon as possible after the rape, generally within forty-eight to seventy-two hours.
- Medical evidence taken from an examination can be used to locate, identify, and prosecute the rapist. This should also be done immediately after the rape. The more time that passes after the rape, the more likely it is that the evidence will be lost entirely.

Where Can You Get Medical Attention?

Immediate care from medical personnel at the emergency department of a local hospital is essential. Some hospitals, particularly in urban areas, have multidisciplinary teams that specialize in helping rape victims. Contact a rape crisis center or the police for a referral to a hospital with a rape trauma team, or go immediately to the nearest general hospital.

Although the importance of getting medical care as soon as possible cannot be overemphasized, you may wish to seek medical examination from a private physician, a community clinic, or women's health clinic, such as a Planned Parenthood organization. You should know, however, that private physicians and clinics may not be equipped to collect evidence of the rape for prosecution.

If You Go to the Hospital, Will You Have to Report the Rape?

Many hospitals are required to contact law enforcement agencies when victims of violent crime are treated. The fact that the police have been notified does *not* mean that you will have to talk to them when they arrive. Usually you retain the right to decide whether or not to report the crime. Advocates at local rape crisis centers can tell you what to expect when you go to the hospital and can assert your wishes during the examination. This may be necessary if hospital staff pressure you to report. Remember, you are entitled to have a friend, relative, or advocate with you during the examination.

Generally, your consent will be required before evidence taken from the medical examination can be released to the police. In some areas, evidence may be collected and held for you in case you decide to report the crime. Be sure to ask hospital staff members for information about their requirements and policies, as they differ from place to place. Also, find out whether you will be given an evidentiary examination or a regular pelvic examination if you decide not to report the crime.

According to the provisions of the Violence Against Women Act (VAWA) of 1994, women should not be charged for an evidentiary examination. However, in some areas, payment may be contingent upon reporting the crime and cooperating with the investigation.

What Will Happen at the Hospital?

When you arrive at the hospital, ask for and speak to the triage nurse (the nurse who decides in which order patients are seen) or the admitting medical attendant. You will have to state that you have been sexually assaulted so that medical personnel can give you appropriate care and treatment and, possibly, priority in the wait for services. However, there is no need to give the admitting clerk or nurse details of the assault. Most likely, you will be asked to provide information about your health insurance (if you have insurance) and to fill out an admissions form and medical history questionnaire.

Hospitals that are staffed with special rape trauma teams may have waiting rooms for survivors that are set apart from the general emergency waiting room. In other hospitals you may have to wait in the emergency room. Many hospitals have an emergency room social worker on call who can contact advocacy programs, provide you with information, and help you make decisions. It's best to ask to see the social worker, although in many emergency rooms the social worker will be summoned automatically.

The Evidentiary Examination

Medical personnel will examine, document, and treat any injuries that you have received. Depending on the extent of your injuries, X-rays may be taken. Most hospital emergency departments have sexual assault examination kits available to collect and preserve evidence so that it can be used to prosecute the rapist in court.

Although medical professionals and hospitals do not use identical protocols for examining rape victims, the following should give you a general idea of what will happen during the examination.

Before the examination begins, you should receive an explanation of the procedures and may be asked to provide your written consent. If you are not given a thorough explanation of the examination, ask for one.

You may also be asked to consent to have photographs of your injuries taken. Although you can withhold your consent, photographs may be presented in court as evidence of force used by the rapist. Because photographs must meet certain criteria in order to be admissible in court, they should be taken by someone acquainted with the requirements of courtroom photography. This can usually be done by a nurse, physician, or police officer, or in some cases, a rape crisis counselor. You may request that the photographs be taken by a woman. It may be necessary to have the police take photographs again at a later date, if you discover scratches, new bruises, or other injuries to your body. You may also want to have someone whom you trust take photographs of your injuries for your own records.

- The doctor or nurse will take a medical history from you, asking you for general information about your health. She or he may ask you for the date of your last menstrual period and of your last consensual sexual intercourse. You may be asked whether you are currently using birth control. The answers to these questions will help assess the possibility of a current pregnancy and determine whether it will be necessary to distinguish the attacker's semen, if present, from that of your consensual partner. Nonetheless, you have a right to know the reason for any question asked and should not be questioned extensively about your sexual history.
- You will be asked to describe the rape, including the time and place that it occurred and the sexual acts that took place. It may be very embarrassing and painful for you to describe the ways in which you were harmed, but it is necessary to help medical personnel look for and collect evidence of the rape, to examine and treat your injuries, and to document the assault.
- You will be asked to remove your clothing. Some or all

of the clothing that you were wearing at the time of the rape may be collected and used as evidence. You may not get this clothing back for some time.

- You may be asked to stand or sit on a sheet of paper so that any hair, dirt, leaves, grass, or other evidence from your body may be captured and collected. Your pubic and head hair may be combed for evidence of the rapist's hair, and scrapings from your fingernails may be taken for evidence of his skin or blood. These samples, if found, can be used to identify the rapist.

- Your body will be examined for external injuries. Be certain to make the doctor or nurse aware of any scratches, cuts, bruises, burns, red marks, or other injuries that you received and any areas of pain or discomfort. Any physical injuries that you received should be documented.

- Your body may be examined with an ultraviolet light, called a Wood's light, to detect sperm and acid phosphatase, an enzyme found in semen that fluoresces under the light.

- You may be given a pelvic examination and/or anal and oral examinations, if you were assaulted at these sites. The health care provider will also look for and document evidence of trauma to your genital area. Many women find pelvic examinations uncomfortable, and because you've just been raped, this examination may be very upsetting to you. Let the nurse or doctor know if you need a moment to relax. If you have not had a pelvic examination before, tell the examining professional. He or she can explain the examination to you and make you more comfortable. Specimens of seminal material on or in your body can be used to identify the attacker and to establish that intercourse took place. Evidence of the attacker's hair, clothing fibers, and other types of evidence will be sought from your body.

- Testing for sexually transmitted diseases (STDs), including gonorrhea, chlamydia, and trichomoniasis may be done. Blood samples may be drawn to test for syphilis. However, testing for sexually transmitted diseases immediately after the rape may determine only whether you had an STD before the rape occurred. Getting tested for STDs is important, but you may want to wait until the evidentiary examination is completed to have baseline testing done. You should be given information about necessary follow-up appointments for further testing and treatment. In some hospitals, you may be offered antibiotics to prevent sexually transmitted diseases. If you have a partner, it is a good idea to practice safer sex by using a latex condom and/or dental dam (latex barrier) until you know the results of your tests.

• A standard HIV antibody test offered as part of your medical examination can only confirm that you became infected with HIV prior to the rape. Therefore, you may want to wait to be tested for HIV infection at a later date. Although the risk of contracting HIV from a rape is believed to be low, testing is important. Because many hospitals cannot completely ensure that the results will be kept confidential, and because insurance companies can access medical and hospital records, it is suggested that you seek anonymous testing, if available in your state. For more information, see Chapter Eight. Your rape crisis advocate or state HIV/AIDS hotline can also give you information about testing options.

• Blood and urine samples may be taken to test for current pregnancy and to detect the presence of drugs and alcohol in your system. You may want to ask why blood and urine samples are being taken and to discuss your concerns with your advocate.

• If you are not currently pregnant and you consent, you may be offered emergency contraception. (See Chapter Five.) Make certain to ask the doctor or nurse for information about the risks, benefits, and possible success of the medication and for information about possible side effects, including nausea and vomiting. You may want to wait until you can be tested for pregnancy as a result of the rape before considering your options. If you are not offered emergency contraception and you want to receive medication, talk with hospital staff members and with a rape crisis advocate. You may have the option of going to another hospital for treatment, to a Planned Parenthood organization or a women's health clinic, or to your private physician for treatment. You may also want to contact the Emergency Contraception Hotline, listed in the Resource Directory, for the names and telephone numbers of the nearest health care providers prescribing emergency contraception. Remember that emergency contraception must generally be taken within forty-eight to seventy-two hours to be effective.

• You should be given information about the necessity of follow-up appointments for examination of your injuries and testing for sexually transmitted diseases and pregnancy. Be sure to ask where you can be tested, if you choose not to have your follow-up appointments at the hospital.

- You may be able to get a referral for counseling from a social worker or nurse in the social work department or discharge planning unit of the hospital. Rape crisis advocates can also give you information about support groups and counseling for rape survivors.

Evidence taken from your examination will be very carefully collected, stored, and labeled. It should be noted that lack of evidence of seminal material or injuries does not mean that you will not be believed or that the rapist cannot be prosecuted. In fact, according to one national study, the majority of rape survivors are not seriously physically injured.[3] If the rapist used a weapon or was very intimidating and much larger than you, you may have resisted passively in order to survive. Also, it is not uncommon for rapists to be sexually dysfunctional or not to ejaculate during a rape.

WHAT WILL YOUR VISIT TO THE HOSPITAL COST?

Under the Violence Against Women Act, costs for the evidentiary examination must be paid for by the government. However, in some states payment may be contingent upon full cooperation with the police or local prosecutor's office or may be made through the state victim compensation program, in which case reimbursement can take some time. Additionally, you may be billed for emergency room services, tests, nonevidentiary aspects of the examination, treatment, and medication.

In some cases, your insurance, including private or employee group health insurance, Medicaid (Medi-Cal) or Medicare may serve as your first source of payment, and, as mentioned, you may be eligible for reimbursement for some costs through your state victim compensation board. Depending on the state, you may be able to seek assistance with medical bills, lost wages, and payments for counseling or other expenses. A rape crisis advocate, a hospital social worker, or a victim/witness assistance advocate may be able to help you identify other sources of financial assistance.

Later, if you report the crime and the rapist is convicted, the judge may order him to compensate you for your expenses. This practice is called restitution. You may also decide to sue the rapist in a civil trial or to sue a third party, such as a hotel or landlord whose negligence and failure to protect you from foreseeable harm may have contributed to the rape.

Although there has been some improvement in laws pro-

- You have the right to refuse treatment, even if it has already begun, and to leave the hospital at any time.
- You have the right to have a friend, family member, or advocate or other support person present during the medical examination.
- You may ask that male police officers not be present during the examination. If it is necessary for a police officer to be present, you may request a female officer. You may also request that a woman physician conduct the examination. Be aware, however, that in some areas there may be no or few female police officers or physicians and that your request may be impossible to grant or may delay the examination. A nurse should always be present during the examination. You may request that the nurse be a woman.
- Except in a medical emergency or under other limited circumstances, you have the right to obtain a verbal description of the nature and purpose of any treatment that you are offered, its risks and benefits, information about treatment alternatives, any possible side effects, the probability of the treatment's success, and the likely consequence of no treatment.
- You may be asked to sign a consent form authorizing treatment. Ask the doctor any questions that you have about proposed treatments before giving your consent.

❖ If you are a minor, you may be concerned about having to get your parent/s' or guardian/s' consent before the examination can be done. You may also be wondering whether your parent(s) or guardian(s) must be notified and if the crime committed against you must be reported. The answer to these questions depends upon your age, the language of the laws in your state, and the circumstances surrounding the rape. Rape advocates can provide you with information. Remember that you do not have to give your name when you call.

viding for assistance with payment for rape examinations, the injustice of having to pay for treatment related to sexual assault clearly still persists. Anger at having to bear these costs is justifiable.

REPORTING THE RAPE TO THE POLICE

Only you can decide whether or not to report the rape to the police. Your concerns and fears about reporting should not be trivialized. You may be afraid that you won't be believed or that you will be treated with disrespect by the police. You may believe that there is nothing that the police can or will do. Or you may not want anyone to know about the rape. You may blame yourself. If the rapist is someone you know, you may be concerned about the prospect of sending him to jail or disrupting his family life. The rapist may have threatened you with retaliation. If these are your concerns, you are not alone. Many rape survivors have felt as you do. Often talking to an advocate at a rape crisis center can help you examine your concerns and assess your options. Many rape survivors do not want police involvement initially but later decide to report the crime. Remember, advocates will neither pressure you to report nor dissuade you from reporting. They will listen and let you decide.

There are good reasons to report the crime. Reporting the rape can aid you in your recovery by helping you regain a sense of control over your life and affirm that what happened to you was a violent crime. As well, the details of your report and medical examination can help the police identify and locate the assailant, if he is unknown to you. Even if he is not arrested as the result of the investigation of your rape, he may have raped or may rape other women and girls, and the information you give to police may lead to his arrest in the future. If the rapist is arrested and brought to trial, you may feel the satisfaction of knowing that you sought to protect others from harm. However, the trial process can be extremely stressful, and it is not always successful. Lastly, if you report the crime soon after it is committed, you may be eligible for victim compensation.

Reporting the crime does not mean that your case will go to trial. Criminal trials differ from civil trials in a number of ways, the chief difference being that a person found guilty in a criminal trial can be sent to jail or prison. In a civil action, individuals hire private attorneys to settle their disputes. Money damages and other kinds of relief are awarded to the successful party. Criminal cases, on the other hand, are tried on behalf of the state or "the people." That is because a crime is considered an offense against the community. At trial, you will be considered a witness for the government, rather than a victim seeking redress. Prosecutors (often called district or county attorneys) are hired by the government to prosecute the criminal. In a criminal case, the prosecutor must prove that the person alleged to have committed the crime, the defendant, is guilty beyond a reasonable doubt. This is a much higher standard of proof than in a civil trial where a "preponderance of the evidence" is needed to show that the defendant is responsible.

Both police and prosecutors have considerable discretion in considering whether to pursue a case. If the rapist is arrested, the prosecutor will determine whether to charge him (and whether to reduce the charges) and bring the case to court. Although there is a possibility that you could be called as a witness even if you decide that you don't want to press charges, in general the prosecutor is likely to be reluctant to try your case if you are the only witness and you don't want to testify. In fact, you may have to persuade the prosecutor to file charges.

If you do not want to report the crime to the police, it is possible to call a rape crisis center and make an anonymous (or third-party) report. This information can be used to establish a pattern of the rapist's activities.

When Should You Report?

Although many state laws do not require you to make a report within a given period of time (except in the case of marital rape) or allow you a certain number of years to make the report, if you choose to report the rape you should do it soon. The sooner that you report the crime, the more opportunity the police have to catch the suspect, if he is unknown to you. As the suspect moves on to other areas, it becomes increasingly difficult for police to find and arrest him. Reporting early will strengthen the possibility of police involvement and your ability to prosecute. For example, defense attorneys can introduce evidence of the time that you took to report the rape to discredit your testimony.

Whether you decide to report immediately or wait to make a decision, it's a good idea to take time to write down everything you can recall that happened before, during, and after the rape in order to prepare for your interview with the police. Documenting the rape can often help you to remember and clarify details. Having to recount the details of the rape may seem like an overwhelming task at first, but retelling the events, rather than keeping them inside, will help you release healing emotions and may help you to view the rape as a crime — a crime for which you are not to blame. Additionally, if you have not already had a medical examination, you will have to tell the attending physician or nurse what happened in order to receive proper care and treatment.

If You Decide to Report: The First Step

You may want to contact the police immediately after the rape or after you have completed your medical examination. Or, you may wish to speak with a rape crisis advocate first.

Depending on police procedure, you may be asked to give two interviews. Your first interview may be with a uniformed officer. A second, more thorough, interview may be held with a plain clothes detective who is trained in investigating sexual assault. On the other hand, you may be interviewed by a detective who will work with you throughout the investigation. If there is a second interview, it may be held soon after the rape, or you may be asked to come to the police station within the next couple of days. A rape crisis center or the police can explain the process to you and tell you what to expect. If you wish, you are entitled to have someone with you when you speak with the police. This can be a friend, a relative, a rape crisis advocate, or an attorney.

It is important that you be absolutely honest with the police and as specific about the details of the rape as you can. Any omission or untruth can greatly jeopardize your case. For example, if you were drinking or using drugs at the time of the rape, you may be afraid to admit this to the police. But again, it's important to be honest. The fact that you were drinking or using drugs does not give someone the right to rape you. You may also be worried about discussing events that occurred before the rape or about any outstanding warrants that you have. If you are an undocumented immigrant, you may fear having your immigration status revealed. You may also be very concerned about the interview if the person who raped you is your husband, partner, or a family member. These concerns are not unusual. A rape crisis advocate can discuss your fears with you and help you make a decision that is right for you.

While it is not possible to tell you precisely what you will be asked during an initial or follow-up interview, the following will give you a general sense of what to expect.

The police will ask you for your name, address, telephone number, and place of employment so that they can contact you. Your employment status should not be the subject of the inquiry. They will want to know the date, time, and location of the rape. You will be asked to give information that will help police locate and identify the suspect, such as a physical description of the rapist, a description of his vehicle, anything that he might have said to you during the attack, and whether or not he used a weapon. You will be asked to discuss what happened before, during, and after the rape. Again, offer as much detail as you can. If you are uncertain about the answer to a question, say so. If you remember finer details later, contact the police to provide them.

At some point, you will be asked to describe the specific sexual acts that took place. These questions are asked to help police identify the rapist, if he is unknown to you, and charge the crime. However, police do not have the right to ask you irrelevant and offensive questions, such as whether you enjoyed the rape. Police will also ask you about other crimes committed by the rapist, for example, if your home was burglarized or if you were kidnapped. If you do not understand the reason you are asked a certain question, you can ask the officer to explain the reason.

If you are interviewed at the scene of the crime, police may take fingerprints and photographs and look for other evidence. This is why you should not move or touch anything before they arrive. They may interview any possible witnesses.

Write down the names, badge numbers, and telephone numbers of every officer with whom you spoke. This will enable you to contact the police to find out what is happening with your case. Ask the police how to get a copy of your report so that you can review its contents.

If you have difficulty getting a police officer to take a report, speak with his or her superior.

Your Follow-up Interview

During a follow-up interview you will be asked by a detective to give a detailed account of the rape. If you do not know the suspect, you may be asked to look at mug shots or to help develop a composite portrait of the rapist. Later, if the suspect is arrested, you may be asked to identify him in a lineup. The rapist will not be able to see you.

If any new bruises have appeared on your body since your medical examination, let the detective know. Ask that new photographs be taken and marked as evidence. You may request that a female officer take the photographs. However, in some areas, this request may be impossible to grant due to a lack of female staff.

The police will present their evidence to the prosecutor's office and the prosecutor will decide whether to formally charge the assailant. It is very important to remain in contact with the police during the investigation and to make sure that they can get in touch with you. You have a right to speak with the prosecutor and to be informed regarding the progress of your case. Advocates at rape crisis centers or victim/witness assistance programs (where they exist) can help you learn more about your rights within the criminal justice system.

How does the criminal justice system work?

Knowing the procedures involved in arresting and prosecuting a rapist will help you make a decision about reporting the rape. Learning your rights and responsibilities as a victim will also help you to cope with the many surprises, delays, and possible disappointments that occur during a criminal trial.

The procedures of the criminal justice system vary from jurisdiction to jurisdiction. Therefore, it is essential to gather information from advocates and professionals working in your area. You can always telephone the police and ask for a general explanation of the ways in which rape cases are handled. The local prosecutor's office can give you information about the stages involved in the arrest of an alleged criminal and in bringing the case to trial. Of course, rape crisis centers and victim/witness assistance programs (where they exist) are excellent sources of information.

Many rape survivors are shocked and angered to learn that the assailant may be released if there is not enough evidence to justify his arrest or that the charges against him may be dismissed. He may also be given the opportunity to plea-bargain — to plead guilty to a lesser offense or to only one or some of the charges in exchange for a lighter sentence. You have the right to have your views about a possible plea-bargain heard by the prosecutor. However, the decision to accept a plea offer rests with the prosecuting attorney and, ultimately, the judge. If the case is dismissed or the defendant pleads guilty, a trial will not be held. For some rape survivors, the prosecutor's decision to plea-bargain is deeply dissatisfying; for others the decision is a relief, because the trial process is hastened and testifying is no longer necessary.

When you talk to advocates and professionals, ask about the possibility of conditioning a defendant's release upon a criminal *order of protection* or *no-contact order*, which prohibits him from contacting you. You may also want to find out whether you can deliver a *victim impact statement*, which describes the way in which the rape has affected your life and which may have an effect on sentencing, to the judge or probation officer.

Rape trials are often long and difficult to endure. For some women, a trial can be emotionally healing and for others, emotionally devastating. Despite legal reform in recent decades and the increased training of medical and legal professionals in this area, some police officers, doctors, attorneys, and judges still subscribe to old myths about rape, as may jury members. In the way of reform, the federal government and many states have enacted laws that restrict the admissibility into court of evidence regarding a rape survivor's sexual history. These are often referred to as "rape shield" laws. However, evidence may be admissible if it is deemed relevant to the defendant's trial. For example, if you had a sexual relationship with the defendant and your consent is at issue, evidence of the sexual nature of your relationship may be admissible. Information about your sexual history may also be admitted as evidence if the defendant is trying to show that he is not the source of the injuries or semen documented in your medical examination. Defendants may be required to notify the court of an intention to offer evidence of a rape victim's sexual history, and rulings on admissibility can sometimes be made in the judge's chambers.

CAN YOU SUE THE RAPIST IN COURT?

Yes. If you know the identity of your attacker, you can initiate a civil action against him for money damages. One advantage of a civil suit is that rather than the beyond-a-reasonable-doubt standard used in criminal trials, the defendant's responsibility need only be proved by a "preponderance of evidence." In other words, it must be shown that it is more probable than not that the defendant raped you. Disadvantages include having to hire a private attorney and being unable to collect money damages (or find someone to represent you) if it is discovered that the defendant has no income or assets of value. You can, however, bring a civil action against the rapist even if criminal charges have been filed. Civil rape trials are no less emotionally trying than criminal trials. It's important to discuss your fears about testifying with your advocate and attorney and to ask for truthful information about the defense attorney's likely strategies.

Some states and the Violence Against Women Act (VAWA) recognize that violence against women can be motivated by hatred or bias based on gender. The VAWA declares that "all persons within the United States shall have the right to be free from crimes motivated by gender."[4] Under the VAWA, a victim of a violent crime that would constitute a felony is allowed to sue the person who allegedly committed the crime for money damages and other relief in state or federal court. Generally, in order for a lawsuit brought under this act to succeed, it must be shown that the crime was committed because of the victim's gender. Victims of sexual assault and/or domestic violence may be in a position to utilize this act for redress.

You may also sue third parties whose negligence and failure in a duty to protect you from a foreseeable harm contributed to the rape. Depending on the circumstances, this may include a landlord or apartment manager, or other third party, such as a hotel, parking lot, bus company, school, or government. By talking with personal injury attorneys, you can determine whether you have a potentially successful case. Some rape crisis centers can make referrals to attorneys in your area.

Reactions to Rape

Each woman reacts to the trauma of rape differently and each is entitled to her own methods of coping and surviving. Nonetheless, survivors share many common responses to the experience of sexual assault. Immediately after the rape you may feel shock and disbelief. It may be hard for you to accept that you were raped. You may minimize or repress the trauma and attempt to go on with your life as though nothing happened. Fear of death and of being hurt are also natural responses to a crime during which you may have been threatened with death or injury and during which you were robbed of your sense of power and control. It's natural to feel anxious, tense, restless, confused, disoriented, angry, or depressed. You may have trouble sleeping or have nightmares or flashbacks of the rape. You may also feel a great sense of relief because you lived through it. You may be afraid that you will not be able to enjoy sex again or that being with your partner will revive painful memories of the rape. These feelings may come and go or occur all at once. Later, you may find that these feelings, which appear to have been resolved, reemerge. On the other hand, months or even years may pass before these feelings surface for the first time.

Headaches, loss of appetite, nausea, vomiting, muscle tension, and fatigue are also common responses. However, if you have any of these reactions, it's important not to ascribe them solely to emotional or psychological causes but to ask your doctor or nurse whether there may be a physical reason for your response. For example, emergency contraception may produce side effects of nausea or vomiting.

You may feel very angry about what happened to you. Anger is a difficult emotion for many women because we're often socialized to believe that it is inappropriate to express anger or rage. It may be frightening to feel so much anger at the rapist. But it is normal and appropriate, and its expression is necessary and healthy. It's also important to note that if you were treated in a less than understanding manner by medical and legal professionals, you have another reason to be angry.

Rape is both a profound personal tragedy and a social evil.

Professionals who contribute to the acceptance of rape by patronizing, disbelieving, blaming, ignoring, or verbally attacking rape survivors should be apprised of their inappropriate behavior. Of course, one of the best ways to deal with someone who mistreats you is to confront that person directly. Calmly and clearly describe the behavior to which you object and ask for an explanation. You may also want to write a letter to the professional who offended you — and, if necessary, that person's superior — asking for an apology. Another good way to channel feelings of anger is to work for continued change in the criminal justice system and in public attitudes about rape. If and when you are ready, simply talking to other people about rape is a good way to begin.

Your friends and relatives may be very supportive. On the other hand, they may react in ways that are not helpful or easy to understand. For example, if you were raped by someone you know, you may receive much less support than someone who was raped by a stranger.

Others may blame you or cause you to feel shame because they think that women secretly want to be raped or that women somehow ask to be raped by their behavior or dress. Some people subscribe to these myths about rape as a way of distancing themselves from their own vulnerability to harm. Sometimes people who love you blame you as a way of deflecting their own sense of guilt for failing to protect you, although it is not always possible to protect another from violence. If your husband, partner, or family member is having difficulty coping with the rape, you may want to suggest that that person speak to an advocate at a rape crisis center for information about any services that are available to significant others. Although family and friends may experience feelings that are similar to those of the survivor, it is not the survivor's job to help them through this crisis. You need time to fathom your own feelings. Caring for and nurturing yourself is of utmost and primary importance.

Rape is a loss similar to death. Survivors need time to mourn. Although recovery is a very individual process, you may want to utilize resources that are available to survivors. You may also want to explore private counseling or therapy. Rape crisis centers frequently offer private counseling or provide referrals. Eventually, you may want to consider becoming a volunteer at a rape crisis center. Getting involved in or creating an organization that works against rape and other forms of oppression can be very healing, empowering work.

The earlier that you seek support, the sooner you will be able to begin healing. It takes courage to acknowledge a need and to actively address it. If you do not have friends and family with whom you can talk honestly, contact a rape crisis center. Volunteers understand what you are feeling. Many

---

HELPING A RAPE SURVIVOR

- Show her that you believe her and that you care about what happened. Be available to listen.
- Reassure her that the rape was not her fault, regardless of the circumstances. Blame, criticism, and expressions of disbelief can seriously impair a survivor's ability to cope with the rape and will increase her pain and sense of isolation.
- Don't force her to talk about the rape if she doesn't want to. She may not be ready to talk about it. Let her express her feelings in her own time.
- As hard as it may be, do not take any action that might jeopardize your safety and well-being. Trying to find the rapist and hurt him will put you in danger and very possibly in jail. By doing this, you will only deepen the rape survivor's anguish and sense of responsibility.
- Encourage her to call a rape crisis center for support. In addition to emotional support, volunteers can give her information to help her make decisions about getting medical treatment and reporting the rape to the police. She will not have to give her name. Because you have also been affected by the rape, you may want to speak with a rape crisis center advocate or counselor to sort out your own feelings and to find constructive ways to help her. This is especially true if you are feeling angry at the survivor or feeling guilty. Without resolving your feelings, you may not be in the best position to help her.
- Tell the survivor how you can help her. For example, you may be able to go with her to the hospital or to the police station. You may want to invite her to stay in your home until she feels comfortable returning to her own home or offer to watch her children while she attends a support group. Be realistic about what you can do. Don't commit yourself to something that you really can't do or with which you are uncomfortable.

Try to offer her support without taking control of her life. The temptation to prescribe or limit the survivor's activities may be very great if the survivor is your daughter, and even greater if your daughter has a disability. Sometimes, attempts to exercise control over the decisions a survivor makes are really attempts to reduce feelings of guilt for not being able to protect her. But, according to a study done by the Bureau of Justice, a large percentage of rapes take place in the victim's home or in the home of a friend, relative, or neighbor.[5] Clearly, restricting your daughter's life will not protect her from rape. It's important to realize that the rape is not your fault, just as it is not the survivor's fault. One of the most devastating aspects of rape is that the victim's sense of power, autonomy, and individuality are taken from her. By depriving her of her right to make decisions for herself, according to her own schedule, you are in effect reinforcing the sense of powerlessness created by the rapist. Without trust in her ability to control her own decision-making process, emotional healing becomes more difficult. Instead of implementing your own response to her rape, support her decisions.

1-800-799-SAFE (7233)
1-800-787-3224 (TDD)

Available twenty-four hours a day
in English and Spanish. Operators
have access to translators for 139
languages.

Information, referral, and crisis intervention are available from all fifty
states, Puerto Rico, and the U.S.
Virgin Islands. Crisis intervention
services can help callers identify
problems and possible solutions, including making emergency safety
plans. The hotline provides referrals
to domestic violence and other
emergency shelters, social service
organizations, and legal services. Information about sources of assistance is also available to family
members, friends, employers, and
others who want to learn more about
domestic violence, child abuse, sexual assault, programs for batterers,
and related topics.

are rape survivors themselves. They are there twenty-four
hours a day.

DOMESTIC VIOLENCE

WHAT IS ABUSE?

Abuse describes many behaviors and takes many forms. For
example, abuse can be emotional or psychological, physical, sexual, or financial. The words "battering" and "domestic violence" are often used to refer to physical violence or
threats of violence against women by their partners, but in
reality battering and domestic violence include a range of
abusive behaviors that are used by one person to intimidate,
manipulate, control, and degrade another. Often there is a
pattern of abuse, although there may be long periods in
which the abuse seems to have lessened or disappeared. The
abusive partner may say that he or she acts out of love or may
give countless other justifications for his or her abusive behavior. But abuse is not love, and there are no acceptable
excuses for hurting another person.

Because our intimate relationships are vastly complex, it's
often very difficult to recognize the signs of abuse in our
lives. We sometimes think that abuse only happens to certain kinds of people. But women from all races, ethnic heritages, socioeconomic classes, religions, professions, and educational backgrounds experience abuse. Straight, lesbian,
and bisexual women are abused. Abused women are women
with disabilities and nondisabled women. Abuse can happen
to a woman at any age.

Abusers can be husbands and ex-husbands, boyfriends,
ex-boyfriends, women life partners, girlfriends, or ex-partners. Although this chapter focuses on intimate adult relationships, parents can abuse their children and adult children can abuse their parents. The term "partner" will be
used in this chapter to describe a member of an intimate
relationship, including a married, unmarried, or dating relationship.

Violence against women is common. Although domestic
violence is widely underreported, it is estimated that between 1.8 and 4 million women are abused each year[6] in the
United States.

There is no typical portrait of an abused woman, nor does
a woman who is being hurt by someone she loves suddenly
take on the singular identity of "battered woman." Abuse
may be a part of your life, not the whole of it. Knowing that

you are strong, capable, active, and intelligent may prevent you from considering the behavior that you find frightening, hurtful, demoralizing or just plain exhausting as abuse. Nonetheless, it is important to trust your instincts and to explore the aspects of your relationship that give you concern.

Are You Being Abused?

Does your partner:

- push, shove, slap, hit, punch, kick, choke, or burn you or hurt you in other ways?
- hurt you with weapons or objects or threaten you with weapons or objects?
- threaten to hurt you, your children, your family or pets?
- throw things at you?
- drive recklessly when you or your children are in the car?
- hold you down, lock you in a room, or intentionally lock you out of the house?
- force you to have sex?
- force you to engage in sexual acts with which you are not comfortable?
- tell you that you are dumb, ugly, lazy, worthless, or otherwise demean or hurt you with words?
- curse or yell at you?
- get very angry over little things or over nothing at all?
- constantly make fun of you or criticize you?
- make fun of things that are important to you, such as your religious or spiritual beliefs?
- insult, embarrass, or humiliate you alone or in front of others?
- accuse you of having affairs or flirting, without any justification?
- isolate you from your friends and family?
- destroy property or break things?
- control or spend your money?

Think about how you feel toward your partner.

- Are you afraid of your partner?
- Do you feel tense and anxious, wondering when he or she will explode?
- Are you hesitant to disagree with your partner or to express your feelings?
- Do you no longer make decisions on your own for fear of how your partner will react?
- Are you made to feel to blame for the abuse that you experience?

Answering and reflecting upon these questions honestly may help you to recognize abuse in your life. Usually, we know when we are being abused by someone, but in order to cope and survive, we minimize or deny the abuse. Listen to yourself. Trust yourself. If you feel as though you are being abused, you probably are.

It's Not Your Fault

The abuser may have told you that you cause the abuse. He may accuse you of provoking him. She may say that you "made" her hit you. The abuser may give various reasons for hurting you, suggesting that if you would only conform to his or her expectations, you will avoid abuse in the future. But how many times have you tried to do things differently hoping to placate your partner? Does the abuse subside? Or does it seem as if you can never please the abuser, that everything that you do is wrong? Do you sense that you can't really control the outbursts even when you know that they are coming? You cannot control abuse, because *abuse is a choice*. Your partner makes a decision to hit you or hurt you in other ways. If you have ever fought back against physical abuse, you may have a more difficult time seeing yourself as someone who is in an abusive relationship. You and other people in your life may be tempted to view the abuse in your relationship as mutual combativeness. Examine your relationship. Who is afraid of whom? Who is in control? Battering is about control. Self-defense is a means of survival. Fighting back to defend yourself does not make you an abuser.

Abusers Make Excuses for Their Behavior

Abusers do not take responsibility for their actions. They routinely place blame elsewhere. Here are a few examples of the kinds of statements abusers make to avoid responsibility:

+ You made me do it; I was provoked.
+ You're an abuser.
+ I lost my temper.
+ I lost control.
+ I was drunk (or high).
+ I was abused as a child.
+ My father beat my mother.
+ You're a bad wife (or girlfriend).
+ You're unfaithful to me.

None of these excuses justify hurting another person. For example, your partner may have experienced abuse as a child or witnessed domestic violence. While battering is in some ways learned behavior, not all people who witnessed or experienced abuse in their families grow up to be abusers. Likewise, people who have not been mistreated as children can be abusive. The person who grew up in an abusive family has no more right to hurt another person than anyone else, and while substance abuse is often associated with battering, it does not cause abuse. Many abusers hurt their partners when they are not drinking or using drugs, and many are abstinent. Getting treatment for alcohol or other drug abuse problems may not end your partner's abusive behavior.

If you or your partner has experienced racism and discrimination, you may understand the pain that he or she experiences. But does that give your partner the right to hurt you? Can the pain of racism and oppression be lessened by the hurt that you suffer?

The abuser may try to explain away the violence by blaming it on his or her past, stress, economic pressures, discrimination, substance abuse, your behavior, or anything else, but there is never any reason for one human being to hurt or degrade another.

Will Early Abuse Get Worse?

Early abuse should be taken very seriously. Verbal and emotional abuse can lead to physical abuse. Once your partner has hit you, it becomes easier for him or her to hit you again. Abuse can start at any time. Often, it begins or heightens when you move in together or marry. It may start when you become pregnant. On the other hand, abuse can erupt after many years of marriage, for example, after retirement. Once it starts, abuse usually gets worse over time, increasing in frequency and severity. If your partner has abused you in the past but the abuse has not recurred in some time, you may be tempted to view the abuse as an isolated event. However, the danger that it will happen again is always present.

Don't wait until things get worse to seek information and help. Advocates answering crisis lines at women's shelters or in other organizations can help you explore what is happening in your relationship. They will not tell you whether to leave or to stay. They understand that abuse is not your fault.

Are Your Children at Risk of Harm?

Yes. If you are being abused, there is a strong possibility that your children are being abused or will eventually be hurt. Despite myths to the contrary, people who batter women are

If you know someone who is being abused, you can help by doing the following:

- Tell her that you know what is happening.
- Believe what she tells you.
- Listen to her without judging her.
- Let her know that she isn't alone.
- Urge her to call a women's shelter or the social work department of a local hospital for information and support. Encourage her to get medical treatment for any health problems that she may have, including chronic health problems such as stomach complaints or depression.
- Discuss the ways in which you can be of help. Don't be afraid to be honest. You may have limits on what you can do. If you cannot help her directly, help her explore other avenues for information and support.
- Realize that women in abusive relationships often make several attempts to leave the relationship before ending it completely. Seeking information about abuse can help you to better understand what may be happening in your loved one's life. Contact a women's shelter to speak with an advocate.
- Allow her to make her own decisions. Give her the respect that can be conveyed by keeping communication fluid and available.

likely to abuse their children. One study found that within families with children, 70 percent of the men who abused their wives also abused their children.[7] Even when the batterer has no intention of hurting your children, they can be hurt or even killed when they attempt to come between you and your partner during a violent episode.

There is also a relationship between domestic violence and child sexual abuse. It may be extremely painful to face the possibility that your children are being sexually abused, but if you sense or know that your children are being hurt in your home, you must seek help immediately. You may feel guilty because you did not recognize it or take steps to stop it sooner. But it is not too late to get help. There are grave consequences to ignoring child abuse or hoping that it will resolve itself. Clearly, the health and well-being of your children are at risk. In addition, you may lose custody of your children, have your parental rights terminated, or be held liable for failure to protect them from abuse.

Even when children are not being directly abused, they suffer in other ways. Research suggests that children who witness abuse show symptoms similar to children who have been directly physically, sexually, or emotionally abused.[8] You should also consider that children are often aware of abuse, even when they don't see it. When children grow up in an abusive home, they learn to see violence as a way to solve problems. Children who are exposed to domestic violence are at great risk for becoming abusers or victims of abuse themselves. Children may feel guilty or blame themselves for the abuse because they can't stop it or because they believe that they caused it. It is vital that you let your children know that the abuse is not their fault. Listen to them when they express their feelings about the abuse. Trying to cover up the abuse by pretending that it doesn't happen only confuses children and tacitly reinforces the idea that abuse and violence are acceptable.[9]

VIOLENCE AGAINST WOMEN IS AGAINST THE LAW

All states and the District of Columbia have laws against domestic violence that allow for a protection order to be issued against an abuser. Assault (the attempt or threat to injure another person coupled with the ability to do so) and battery (the use of force against another) are crimes in every state, regardless of the relationship between the parties involved, but some states have laws that make domestic abuse a specific crime.

Violence Against Women Is a Hate Crime

Some states and the Violence Against Women Act of 1994 (VAWA) recognize that some acts of violence against women are hate crimes committed because of a person's gender. Victims of certain felonies, which may include domestic violence and sexual assault, may be able to sue their abusers under the VAWA for money damages in civil court.

GETTING HELP FROM THE POLICE

When Can the Police Make an Arrest?

State laws regarding domestic violence differ in many ways, including the ways in which domestic violence is defined and the circumstances under which police officers are permitted or required to make an arrest. As well, police policies regarding arrest differ from place to place.

As you read this section, remember that it is only general information about what may happen when you call the police for help. It is not meant to describe the way in which an individual officer in your community may respond to your unique situation.

Depending on state law, local policy, and the officers' own assessments, police may respond as follows to a domestic violence call. They may take your partner out of the home to calm down, attend to your injuries, take you to the hospital or to a safe place, and/or make an arrest.

- In a number of states, police officers are *mandated* to make an arrest when they have probable cause to believe that domestic violence has occurred and/or that a protection order has been violated. The way in which "probable cause" is defined also depends on state law. It may be defined as evidence of physical injury or the use of a weapon or dangerous instrument. It may also be defined as an officer's reasonable belief that there is a possibility of further abuse without intervention, that a crime has been committed, or that a protection order has been violated. (Violation of a protection order may be either a criminal or civil offense, depending on state law.)
- In most states, police are *permitted* to make an arrest if they have probable cause to believe that a crime involving domestic violence has been committed or that an order of protection has been violated.
- Police may also make an arrest if they see the abuser commit a crime.

- An arrest may be made if the police request and get a warrant, but this cannot be done immediately.

Problems with Police Intervention

Although police are being increasingly trained in the dynamics of domestic violence, it is still possible to be treated in a less than helpful manner when you call for assistance. Police may view domestic violence as a family problem in which they should not intervene. They may blame you. They may treat you with disrespect. They may not make an arrest. They may arrest both you and the abuser, particularly when they cannot determine who the primary aggressor is. Although dual arrests are discouraged under the Violence Against Women Act and some state laws, you should be aware of the possibility and find out whether it could happen to you and under what circumstances.

You have a right to be protected by the police. If they do not take the danger you are in seriously, ignore your requests for help, or refuse to take a report, get their names and badge numbers and complain to their superior. It may also be possible to press charges against the abuser, even if the police did not make an arrest.

LOCAL LAWS AND POLICIES

If it is safe — *and you are not in immediate danger* — it is a good idea to contact a women's shelter or other advocacy organization for general information about the laws in your area and your options in the event of danger. An advocate can help you develop a safety plan for you and your children.

Your local police department can also give you information about the way in which a call for assistance is likely to be handled. Your local prosecutor (district or county attorney) can tell you how the law may be enforced and the likely result of prosecution. You can find the number of the local prosecutor's office in the government section of your telephone directory. If you are an undocumented immigrant, contact a women's shelter, a legal aid organization, and immigrants' rights organizations to get as much information as possible about the ways in which police intervention may affect you. (Check the front section of your telephone directory for information.) Remember that you have a right to call the police and to be protected regardless of your immigration status.

Questions to Ask About Domestic Violence

When you call the organizations above, ask for explicit information about the laws allowing or mandating arrest in your area. By probing some of the following areas, you may be able to get a sense of what will happen if you call the police for help.

- Try to find out how long the abuser may be held, if arrested. It's possible that the abuser may be held only for a few hours or overnight.
- Find out what assistance the responding officers may be required to give you. Can they take you to the hospital or to a women's shelter or to another safe place? With what other services can they provide you? Must police officers give you information about your rights under the law?
- Are police officers required to take a report?
- Does your local police department or prosecutor's office have a special unit for handling domestic violence cases? In general, what are the attitudes of local prosecutors and judges toward domestic violence?

Most importantly, think about how the abuser might respond. Some abusers may take the involvement of police seriously, while others may increase their violence as a result. Think about how you can plan for your safety if the abuser is arrested.

Calling the Police

You have a right to call the police for help as soon as you feel at risk of harm.

- If possible, get to a safe place first.
- Dial 911. These calls are recorded and can be used as evidence of the abuse. Emergency phone systems should be equipped with TDDs for people who are deaf or who have hearing or speech impairments. Under the Americans with Disabilities Act (ADA) Title II, emergency telephone systems are required to be directly accessible to people with speech and hearing impairments through telecommunications technology. It's important, however, to make sure that your area system complies with this mandate *before* you are in danger. To do this, contact your 911 center, which is usually operated by the local police department, through the relay serv-

ice in your area. The seven-digit non-emergency number may be listed in the front section of your local telephone directory explaining 911 services. Ask whether the department has telecommunication devices for the deaf in place and whether staff are trained to answer calls directly. You can also ask to tour the center.

- If 911 is not available in your area, call the operator or dial the police directly.
- Tell the 911 operator or police dispatcher what is happening. Tell the operator if the abuser has a weapon or is drunk or high.
- State whether the abuser is violating a current protection order.
- Give your name and address or location as calmly and clearly as possible.

When the police arrive, they should take a detailed report. In some states, police are required to take a report whether or not they make an arrest. In other states, police are required to take a report when they do *not* make an arrest.[10] The information contained in the police report can be used to support an arrest or any future legal action against the abuser.

- Tell the police what happened in detail.
- Give the names of any witnesses.
- Show the police any evidence of the attack, for example, where you were hurt, the weapon or object used against you or to threaten you, and any torn or bloodied clothing or damaged property.
- Ask the police to take photographs of your injuries. You can also have your injuries photographed at a hospital.
- Write down the names of the officers, their badge numbers, and the number of the police report.
- Ask the officers how to get a copy of the police report.
- Ask the police to take you to a hospital, a safe place, or to a women's shelter, if necessary.

Seek Medical Treatment

It's extremely important that you seek medical treatment for any injuries that you received, even if you think that you were not badly hurt. Go to the emergency department of the nearest hospital immediately after an attack. The police, friends, family, or neighbors may be able to take you there. Do not wait to do this. Many injuries are not obvious. You may not be aware of broken bones, internal injuries, or other conditions caused by physical violence. For example, if internal bleeding is not recognized by physicians, you can bleed to death or get very sick and require surgery. Broken bones that are not set immediately can result in permanent deformities. Any injury that requires stitches can become infected or heal undesirably. Trauma to the head is not always immediately apparent. When you go to the hospital, ask about the signs of possible head injury so that you will know what to watch for over the next few days.

Tell the doctor how you got your injuries. The doctor may not ask you. The more information that you give the doctor about the way in which you were hurt, the better equipped she or he will be to treat you. You may fear talking honestly with the doctor, especially if the abuser accompanies you to the hospital. However, there is a chance that you will be alone with someone on staff during your visit. You can ask the staff member to ask the abuser to leave or to stay in the waiting room.

Medical professionals are becoming more aware of the needs of victims of domestic violence, but you may not be treated with the sensitivity that you deserve. One reason for this is that physicians are trained to diagnose and treat specific medical conditions and not necessarily to offer other kinds of assistance. It can be disheartening to reach out to a medical professional who does not respond as you had wished. Remember that a doctor's or nurse's limitations do not reflect upon you and that there are other sources of support.

If the treating physician or nurse is responsive, ask for information about resources that are available to you or to be referred to someone on staff who can help you, such as a social worker. The social work department of the hospital may have a good advocacy program for abused women and their families or may be able to refer you to other community programs. As you gather information, write down the names of everyone with whom you spoke.

Another reason to seek medical help is to establish a record of your injuries. If possible, have your injuries photographed or request that detailed notes documenting your injuries be taken. These records will be helpful to you if you decide to take legal action against the abuser, such as filing for a protection order, pressing criminal charges, or initiating a divorce. You can get copies of your medical records at a later date.

Although it is possible to file criminal charges even if you did not call the police at the time that the abuse took place or if the police did not make an arrest, it is best to talk with advocates at women's shelters or other advocacy programs, victim/witness assistance programs, or legal aid organizations for information and assistance before filing charges. The criminal justice system is complex and often confusing; you will need someone to guide you through the process, inform you of your rights, and help you protect your safety. Discuss your concerns about the abuser's likely response to criminal charges with an advocate. Think about whether filing charges will be effective or safe. Here again, there are a number of questions you may want to ask before filing charges:

- If arrested, will the abuser be released on bail or on personal recognizance? (A defendant released on personal recognizance makes a promise to appear in court for trial. No money need be posted.)
- What will happen if the abuser is not convicted or sentenced to pay a fine or serve probation? If a sentence of probation is given, will there be close supervision?
- Does the prosecutor's office take a strong stance against domestic violence?
- What criteria are used by the prosecutor's office to determine whether a case will be pursued?
- Is there a "no drop" policy in place that disallows you to withdraw your complaint after it has been filed? Does this apply to misdemeanor charges as well as felonies? Prosecutors are increasingly prosecuting domestic violence cases without the victim's consent or cooperation.
- Will your case be assigned to one prosecutor or will you have to repeat your story to various attorneys during its progress?
- What will happen if you fail to appear in court?

Women's shelters, victim/witness assistance programs, and police departments can tell you how to file a complaint. The following is a brief and general overview of the process:

You can file a complaint with the police or sheriff's department. The complaint will be reviewed by the local prosecutor (district or county attorney). Depending on where you live, the local prosecutor's office may be staffed with one prosecutor or numerous assistant prosecutors, often called assistant district attorneys. The prosecutor will then decide whether to authorize charges. You must realize that the prosecutor has great discretion in this area and is not compelled to take your case. If the prosecutor feels that there is enough evidence to convict, a charge will be authorized and an arrest warrant or a summons to appear in court will be issued for the abuser.

A trial is not always necessary or possible. Nor is jail time the usual result of prosecution. Depending on state law and the crime with which the abuser is charged, he or she may be sentenced to pay a fine, attend a treatment program for batterers, do public service,[11] or serve jail time or be sentenced to probation if convicted. A conviction may result in a combination of penalties. Some areas allow for diversion programs through which punishment is contingent upon completion of a certain act or acts, such as completing a treatment program. Often, abusers are given probation. If the abuser is convicted of a felony, a jail or prison sentence of more than one year is possible.

You can make a difference by staying involved in your case. Otherwise, your case may be dismissed, diverted, or plea-bargained without your knowledge, depending on what actions are permissible under state law. In a plea-bargain the defendant agrees to plead guilty to a lesser offense or to only one or some of the charges in exchange for a lighter sentence. You may also want to ask about the possibility of appearing at the bail hearing to make known the danger that the abuser poses to you. If necessary, consider asking for special conditions attached to pretrial release or to a sentence of probation, such as the issuance of a criminal protection order to prevent the abuser from contacting you. Don't hesitate to ask an advocate for help.

If your husband or partner is forcing you to have sex, you may also want to read the section on rape in this chapter. It may be almost unbearable to recall times when you were forced to have sex or touched in a manner that hurt you physically or emotionally. Telling someone may be even more difficult. Having information about rape and your legal options may help you define what is happening to you and understand available recourses.

COURT ORDERS OF PROTECTION

All states have laws that allow victims of domestic violence to obtain protection orders. A civil order of protection is a court order, usually issued by a civil court, for example, family court, that prohibits an abuser from behavior that may put you at further risk of harm. The following sections will discuss both permanent civil protection orders, which can last from a few months to a year or more depending on state law and emergency protection orders, which are issued on a temporary basis. Don't wait until an emergency arises to learn about protection orders. There is much to be considered before deciding whether a court order will serve you effectively.

Emergency Orders of Protection

Emergency orders of protection (also called temporary orders or *ex parte* orders of protection) are available to victims of domestic violence in all states. Temporary orders can be issued much faster than permanent orders of protection, sometimes within a few hours. Some courts make temporary orders available on the weekends or in the evenings. The types of behavior that can be prohibited by a temporary order of protection and the conditions that can be included in the order depend on state law. Generally, temporary orders can offer the same type of relief as permanent orders. However, in some places, relief may be limited to only the most pressing needs, such as ordering the abuser to stay away and refrain from hurting you.

You will have to file a petition for an emergency order. A hearing may be held before a judge or other appropriate court official to determine whether the order should be issued. The abuser will not be present at this hearing. However, you may have to testify about the abuse that you have experienced. Although the bases upon which an emergency order will be issued differ from state to state, it is generally necessary to show that you are in immediate danger. The length of time that the temporary order will last also depends on state law, but temporary orders are often short-term, lasting only a number of days.

Once the petition is issued, the abuser will be notified and allowed an opportunity to be heard in court. Depending on state law, the date for the full hearing, at which you and the abuser will both be present and at which the need for a permanent order of protection will be decided, will either be set by the court or must be requested by you or the abuser.[12] Notification of the abuser is called *service of process* and will usually be done by a sheriff or a police officer.

If the abuser cannot be located, it may take many weeks before service of process can be achieved.[13] You may want to take special precautions to protect yourself during this time. Find out whether the temporary order is immediately effective and whether it can be extended if the abuser cannot be located for service of process. Call the sheriff's or police department yourself to find out whether the abuser has been served. Talk to an advocate about options for protecting your safety. Keep your original, valid order and a certified copy on your person at all times. If the abuser approaches you before he or she has been served, call the police. Tell them that you have a protection order and that it is being violated. The responding officer may be able to serve the abuser with the order at that time.[14]

Permanent Orders of Protection

Permanent orders of protection, like temporary protection orders, can require the abuser to stay away from you and refrain from hurting you, as well as provide for other types of relief. This section will discuss some of the advantages that orders of protection may offer and some of the potential drawbacks.

What Types of Behavior Can a Protection Order Prohibit?

Depending on state law, protection orders can require that the abuser:

- stop abusing you
- have no contact with you. This can include staying away from your home, a relative's or another's home, your place of employment, shops and businesses, and other places that you frequent
- move out of the home
- attend a batterer's treatment program
- pay spousal and/or child support
- compensate you for lost wages, moving and medical expenses, and attorney's fees

PROTECTION ORDERS CAN GRANT YOU TEMPORARY CUSTODY OF YOUR CHILDREN

In addition, protection orders can grant you temporary custody of the children and set conditions and schedules for visitation. The possibility of a custody dispute is an unfortunate and serious reality for women who have been abused. Abusive partners or their families may wage custody battles against the victim of domestic violence. A request for spousal support (short-term alimony) or child support may incite the abuser to try to get (or change) custody. Because orders for temporary custody may affect future legal actions, for example, a divorce or permanent custody hearing, it's a good idea to seek assistance from an attorney for the full hearing, if possible. Be completely honest with your attorney about issues that may damage your ability to get temporary or permanent custody of your children so that she or he can work in your best interests. A women's shelter may be able to refer you to an attorney or to a legal aid organization for assistance.

Consider asking for supervised or restricted visitation. Under supervised visitation, the abuser may be limited to visiting the children while in the presence of a third party, such as a trusted relative, or in a public place or at a visitation center, if such a service is available in your community. It may also be possible to arrange for the children to be picked up by a third party at a designated place so that you do not have to come into contact with the abuser. Joint custody should be avoided. Although more difficult to obtain, denial of visitation may be necessary and appropriate in some cases. Visitation orders should be specific, detailing when each parent is to have access to the children and when each visitation period ends.

What Happens If the Abuser Violates the Order?

In many states, a police officer may make an arrest without a warrant if he or she has probable cause to believe that a protection order has been violated. Many states have enacted mandatory arrest laws that *require* police officers to make an arrest if there is probable cause to believe that the abuser has violated the order. It should be stated, however, that you must be willing to enforce the order. Once the order is issued, you should be sure to get a certified copy and keep it with you at all times. Call the police as soon as it appears that the abuser is going to violate it, for example, when you see the abuser nearing your home. Tell them that you have an order of protection and that it is being violated. When the police arrive, show them the order as proof that it has been issued.

Even when you are willing to enforce the order, police may be reluctant to make an arrest. This can happen even in areas where police are required to make an arrest. Ask women's shelters or advocates, the local police, and the judge who issues your order for information about the ways in which the order will be enforced, if violated.

Depending on state law, a violation of the protection order may be a misdemeanor (a crime less serious than a felony) or in criminal or civil contempt of court. In some states, a repeat violation may be a felony. Felonies are serious crimes punishable by fines and imprisonment for a year or more. The abuser can also be charged with crimes committed while violating the order, for example, breaking and entering. Penalties to be imposed depend on the nature of the violation. Generally, they can include an order to attend a batterer's treatment program, fines, jail time, probation, or a combination of sanctions. Whether the violation will be prosecuted, and the result of the prosecution, will depend a great deal on the seriousness with which the prosecutor's office and courts view domestic violence as well as upon your cooperation. Find out whether and how you can return to court to enforce the order, if the abuser violates it. If civil contempt is an available remedy in your area, you may be able to initiate contempt proceedings on your own, although this can be a trying and expensive process. It's a good idea to talk to advocates about this realm of the law and to find out how successfully it is being implemented.

Will a Court Order Protect You?

Before petitioning for an order of protection, consider the risks and benefits. The effectiveness of any court order depends on the willingness of the police and courts to enforce the order, on the abuser's likely response, and your willingness to use the courts and police if the abuser violates it. Better than anyone else, you know how the abuser is likely to react to a court order. Some persons may respect the order; others may disregard it entirely. Some abusers may intensify their violence in response. If you've had previous negative experiences with orders of protection, you may want to talk over a decision to take another type of legal action, such as filing a criminal complaint, with an advocate.

In some areas, protection orders may be issued for both victim and abuser. This practice poses significant disadvantages for women who are being abused. Most distinct is the possibility that, if the police are called regarding a violation, they may arrest both of you or do nothing at all.

Despite its potential drawbacks, an order of protection may prevent abusive behavior and make it easier for police to make an arrest. An order of protection serves as a document of the abuse and can generally be very useful to you if you decide to take other kinds of action against the abuser, such as pressing criminal charges, initiating a divorce or custody case, or applying for suspension of deportation or self-petitioning for legal residency.

Who Can Get an Order of Protection?

Protection orders are specifically intended to prevent domestic abuse and therefore only cover interpersonal relationships. The type of relationships to which protection orders extend depends on state law. In every state, wives may petition for a protection order against their husbands. Most states allow former spouses, family members, people who live with or have lived with their abuser, and people who have had a child by their abuser to obtain a court order. In many states, children can be covered in an adult's protection order. Women in relationships with women may qualify under statutes that allow people who live together or have lived together to petition or may qualify for another type of order, such as a civil harassment order. Women who have never lived with their abusers may have difficulty getting protection. However, the seriousness of violence within dating relationships is beginning to gain recognition, and some states provide protection in this area. Even if you think that you are ineligible, consider applying anyway. Courts have the power to liberally interpret the wording of the law. You may also be able to apply for a protection order under civil harassment or stalking statutes.

In addition to establishing eligibility, you will have to show the basis upon which the order should be issued. Depending on state law, protection orders may be issued based on a showing of physical or sexual abuse, threats of abuse, attempts at abuse, or on the basis of other behavior. Documentation of the abuse, including police or medical records, photographs of your injuries, statements taken from witnesses, torn clothing, weapons, or objects used as weapons may help you to obtain the order. When collecting evidence, consider whether it is safe for you or someone else to keep it until you go to court.

How to Get an Order of Protection

Advocates at battered women's shelters, as well as other victim/witness assistance programs, where they exist, can explain how and where to file a petition for an order of protection. Advocates may be able to help you fill out the forms and go with you to court. In some areas, court clerks may assist petitioners. However, clerks may unintentionally dissuade women from filing for protection orders by giving erroneous advice. If you are given information by a court clerk, remember that only the court has the authority to determine whether you should be granted an order of protection and that you have a right to file a petition.

In many states you will be able to file for a protection order without an attorney. However, there are many times when the help of a lawyer may be very valuable, for example, if the abuser is represented by counsel or if you are asking for child support, seeking temporary custody, or if there are financial issues connected to the protection order. These serious issues may be the subject of a later court date, such as a divorce, legal separation, or custody hearing. Local women's shelters may be able to refer you to an attorney who will take your case for free (pro bono) or on a sliding scale basis. In some areas, legal aid organizations offer assistance with protection orders to women of low income. There may be a waiting list, though some legal aid organizations set aside time specifically to handle protection orders. You should also be aware that your husband's income may be considered as part of your own and may thus affect your eligibility for legal aid. Talk to your advocate about any anticipated problems and make certain she understands that you do not have access to your husband's money, if that is so.

In order to receive funding under the Violence Against Women Act, a state cannot require you to pay for filing a petition for an order of protection. Although you may not be charged for filing a petition for a protection order, attempts may be made to collect from the abuser.

When filing the petition, be sure to include a description of past and recent abuse and a detailed account of what happened to you. Ask for every type of relief that you think you will need. List every place from which you want the abuser barred.

After the petition is filed, a hearing will be held at which you and the abuser will be allowed to present evidence to support or refute the necessity of an order. Your attorney, or often an advocate, can accompany you and help to arrange measures to protect your safety, either informally or with the court. You and your advocate or attorney may want to rehearse what you will say at the hearing. You should be prepared for any allegations that the abuser may make against you.

If the abuser cannot be located and served with notification of the hearing, you may want to take extra precautions to protect your safety before and at the time service of process takes place. For example, you may want to stay with a friend whom the abuser doesn't know. Also, find out whether any alternative means of notification, such as publication of notice in a newspaper, are available to you if personal service cannot be achieved.

Once the order of protection is issued, hand deliver a copy of the order to your local police department and the police department of any area in which you might come into contact with the abuser. This will help ensure a prompt response from the police if the order is violated. Also, take a copy of your protection order to your place of employment, and give copies to relatives, your child's daycare program or school, and to any other place from which the abuser is barred by the order. By doing this you will alert others that an order of protection has been issued and allow them to follow its guidelines. For example, if daycare workers or teachers or administrators at your child's school know that the abuser is prohibited from being near the children, they can call the police if he or she attempts to take your children out of school or daycare. Again, keep a copy of the order with you at all times so that you can show it to police officers in the event that you must enforce it.

OTHER LEGAL ACTIONS THAT YOU CAN TAKE AGAINST THE ABUSER

Divorce and legal separation are options for women in violent or abusive marriages. Making a formal break with the abuser can mark the beginning of renewed independence. Unfortunately, though, divorce or separation may not put an end to abuse. You should be aware that the risk of violence may be greatly increased when you decide to end your relationship. If you do not have an order of protection, consider getting a temporary restraining order when you initiate a divorce or separation action.

Chapter Three outlines basic information about divorce and separation. As you read that chapter, be aware that although it is written with awareness of some of the problems women who are abused may face upon divorce, you will need the specific advice of a family law attorney who is knowledgeable about domestic violence. You must be frank with your attorney about the abuse or violence in your relationship so that she or he can take the most appropriate, and safest, actions.

Other potential legal remedies may include suing the abuser for money damages under state domestic abuse acts (if allowed), under specific torts (an illegal wrong or injury from which damage results), or if applicable, the Violence Against Women Act. However, these options may only be realistic when the abuser has assets, such as property of any kind, or income from which to collect damages.

Deciding Whether to Leave Your Relationship

Only you can decide whether to stay or to leave your relationship. If the abuser has threatened to hurt or kill you or your family or has threatened to commit suicide, you may be afraid to leave, and with good reason. Threats should be taken literally. One of the most dangerous periods in an abused woman's life is when she leaves her partner. If you are thinking about leaving, contact advocates at women's shelters or other advocacy programs for battered women. Discuss your options and work with advocates to develop a safety plan. Trust yourself. No one knows your situation like you do. Your safety and that of your children is of primary importance.

While it is crucial to speak with advocates to explore the ways in which you can leave your relationship safely, the following are general suggestions:

- Do not tell the abuser that you are making plans to leave or where you are going.[15] Be cautious about not leaving behind clues to your whereabouts after you have gone.
- Consider where you will go. Can you go to a friend's home, a relative's? Can you go to a motel? A women's shelter? Where will you be safe? Who can help you? Is it safe for that person to help?
- Start saving as much money as you can. Put your money in a place that the abuser won't find out about. Set aside a bag of essentials for yourself and your children. Pack clothing, medication, and other important items that you will need if you have to leave quickly. Again, do *not* let the abuser know that you have made these preparations.
- Have an extra set of car and house keys made. Keep them in a safe place — one that you can get to quickly, if necessary.
- If your safety will not be jeopardized, gather as many essential documents as you can before leaving.
- Consider getting a court order of protection.
- Talk with advocates or your attorney about possible ways to keep your address secret, even if you must appear in court.

- If you are a documented or undocumented immigrant married to a U.S. citizen or lawful permanent resident (LPR) who is abusing you or your children, you and/or your children may be able to *self-petition for legal permanent residency* (a "green card") without the abuser's knowledge or consent, if you meet certain requirements. You and/or your children may also be able to apply for *cancellation of removal* (formerly called suspension of deportation) if certain requirements are met.
- If you are a conditional permanent resident, you may be able to apply for a "battered spouse waiver" so that you do not have to joint-petition to remove the conditions from your legal residency and can petition to do so on your own.

For information and help, contact a local women's shelter or your state coalition against domestic violence. The National Coalition Against Domestic Violence, listed in the Resource Directory, can refer you to your state coalition. Help may also be available from an immigration lawyer or an immigration law center, although it has been said that some immigration law groups or immigration lawyers are not current on domestic violence laws.

LEAVING WITH YOUR CHILDREN

If you have children, you probably have a number of concerns about their safety and well-being. Advocates at women's shelters can give you information about accommodations for children within the shelter and answer questions about orders for temporary custody. If the abuser is the father of your children, getting temporary custody is important, because without a custody order each parent may have equal access to the children. Getting custody can help protect your rights if the father takes or hides the children from you. However, if you leave with the children in violation of an outstanding custody order, or if the father obtains a custody order after you have gone, you may be accused with parental kidnapping or face contempt of court proceedings. In some states, there are specific requirements that women with children who are fleeing abusive relationships must meet before leaving. If there is time, *and you are not in immediate danger,* speak with advocates in women's shelters or other advocacy programs and, if possible, an attorney specializing in family law, about your options. If you cannot contact an attorney or advocate before leaving, seek legal assistance immediately after you arrive at your destination. Again, *your safety and that of your children should be placed above all other considerations.*

If You Decide to Stay

If you decide to stay, you can still take active measures to protect your safety. Keep as many options open as possible. Deciding to stay does not mean giving up your plans for the future. You still have a responsibility to care for yourself and your children. Here are some things that you can do for yourself:

- Develop several different emergency plans that you and your children can use to get out of the house quickly, if necessary. Advocates can help you create safety plans that are tailored to your individual needs.
- If you don't have a car or you don't drive, and if you don't have access to a telephone, think about how you can escape. Who can help you in an emergency? Is there a neighbor who is willing to help you, a relative, a friend? How could you signal to a neighbor for help in the event of an emergency? Will it be safe for you to tell neighbors to call the police if they hear or see you being abused?
- Keep the telephone number of the National Domestic Violence Hotline or the twenty-four-hour hotline of a local women's shelter available in a place where the abuser cannot find it — or memorize it.
- Continue seeking support from others. Even if you have been disappointed by others' lack of understanding in the past, it's important not to cut yourself off from new sources of support and information. Although some people do not understand domestic violence, there are people who *will* understand and listen to you. You can call a women's shelter or other advocacy program to talk at any time. You can attend a support group for women who are being abused without having to live at a shelter. Talk with family, friends, clergy, or counselors. People are becoming increasingly educated about the nature of domestic violence. Seek until you find someone in whom you can confide. If you give up hope, you will never find that person.
- Continue to pursue your personal goals. You may be able to further your education or to begin or advance in a job or career. By doing this, you can renew your sense of emotional or financial independence. Cultivate your interests, hobbies, and pleasures — the gifts that make you unique, that satisfy and challenge you. Your partner may try to undermine your confidence in your abilities in order to control you. By privately maintaining your

sense of individuality through the use of your talents, you will be able to see evidence of your own importance and worth, even if the abuser demeans you.

WHERE CAN YOU GO WHEN YOU ARE IN DANGER? WOMEN'S SHELTERS AND OTHER HELPING ORGANIZATIONS

There are shelters for abused and battered women in many communities throughout the country. Women's shelters can offer you refuge from violence and time to think about your options. As well, women's shelters offer a range of services that can help you to reestablish your independence. Shelters are intended as temporary residences. Most allow women to stay from about one week to thirty days. Some services are available to abused women outside the shelter.

Although women's shelters differ from one another in size, staffing, atmosphere, house rules, and in many other ways, many shelters can provide you with:

- someone to talk to on a crisis line that operates twenty-four hours a day. Staff members answering crisis lines can offer you support, information, and referrals
- help in devising a plan to protect your safety and your children's safety
- temporary shelter and help finding transitional housing
- information and assistance needed to apply for welfare, food stamps, and other social service programs
- support groups for women in abusive relationships
- individual counseling or referrals to counselors for yourself and/or your children
- help in learning nonviolent parenting skills
- help in learning money management and job-seeking skills
- legal and medical advocacy. For example, an advocate may be able to help you get an order of protection, accompany you to court, or go with you to the hospital. Referrals to legal aid organizations or to private attorneys may also be provided

Not everyone will be immediately comfortable in a shelter. Most shelters are communal living spaces. Generally, women of different classes, races, ethnic backgrounds, religions, and cultures live together. Residents are usually expected to help with cooking and cleaning and other tasks that are necessary to keep the shelter running. In order to protect the safety of all residents, most shelters have very strict rules about confidentiality and will not allow you to tell anyone about the shelter's location. Many have curfews that must be followed as well. Usually, you will not be allowed to use alcohol or nonprescription drugs. You may not be allowed to spank your children at a shelter.

In some areas, particularly urban areas, shelters are often full to capacity. It may be difficult to find space in a shelter. If you live in a rural area, the shelter may be far away. Do not give up. Staff members at women's shelters are usually very familiar with other shelters and resources in your area and will do their best to find you a safe place to stay.

In addition or as a possible alternative to shelter programs, you may find excellent assistance in advocacy programs based in medical centers or local hospitals and in local social service agencies serving families and children, such as Jewish Family and Children's Services, Catholic Charities, or other religious-based or secular agencies. Contact the social work department of your local hospital(s) to find out what services may be available to you. A local office of the United Way or Family Service America (see the Resource Directory for the national number) may be able to give you a referral to a family service agency with a domestic violence program in your area. You can also check the front section of your local telephone directory or the yellow pages listings under Social Service Organizations, Family Services, or other similar headings. Look for organizations serving women or families.

Safe living spaces should be available to any woman who is being abused. It should not matter whether you are being abused by a husband, boyfriend, woman life partner, girlfriend, or an adult child or caregiver. However, women with disabilities, older women, and women in relationships with women face special concerns.

It is extraordinarily difficult for an older woman to leave her home of many years, particularly when she is in delicate health or has a disability that the shelter cannot accommodate. Older women and women of all ages with disabilities may face unique access, transportation, and economic barriers to leaving an abusive relationship and finding refuge. Some women's shelters are not equipped to serve women who are in ill health or who employ a daily personal attendant or home health aide. There may also be an overlap between domestic violence laws and laws meant to protect against elder abuse by caregivers and the abuse of adults who are deemed to be vulnerable because of a physical or mental impairment. Depending on state law and an individual's circumstances, an older woman or a woman with a disability may be referred to adult protective services (APS) for help, particularly if she is being abused by an adult child or if her abuser also serves as her caregiver. Adult protective services personnel may or may not be trained to recognize and address domestic violence. However, depending on the resources available, APS caseworkers may be able to find temporary refuge for a woman who needs some help with activities of daily living in an assisted living facility, board and care home, nursing home, or other place where appropriate care can be delivered.

Although some women's shelters are limited in their ability to serve older women and women with disabilities, there are a few shelters that are specifically designed to meet the needs of both disabled and older women. Again, family service agencies and hospitals may have established domestic violence and/or elder abuse programs, and some women may be more comfortable in these programs. If you are a woman with a disability or an older woman, it may be more difficult to find help, but there are many people who care about what happens to you. Domestic violence advocates, advocates for older women, advocates for women with disabilities, and advocates in adult protective services systems are working very hard to improve services, and although change is slow, progress is being made. Keep looking for help. If you have a disability, let the shelter know about your needs. If the shelter can't find a way to meet your needs, ask for a referral to a shelter that can.

If you are not in immediate danger, and you are in an abusive relationship with a woman, you may want to frankly discuss with advocates any fears that you have about staying in a shelter. If you identify yourself as lesbian or bisexual, you may be worried about coming out in the shelter. Although many shelters are sensitive to the concerns of women in relationships with women, it is possible that you'll encounter negative attitudes among the women within the shelter or from the staff. The decision to come out is yours, and you are entitled to your privacy. Still, you may want to ask how participants in support groups for abused women are screened and to find out what measures will be taken to keep a woman abuser from trying to participate in a support group.

How to Find a Shelter

There are many ways to find a women's shelter. You can call the *National Domestic Violence Hotline* (1-800-799-SAFE) for the telephone number of a shelter nearest you, or you can look in the front pages of your local telephone directory. (These pages often have blue edges.) There you may find a section titled Emergency Numbers or Community Services. Look for the telephone numbers of domestic/family violence hotlines or shelters. Rape crisis hotlines, YWCAs, and police departments may also be able to give you referrals. Again, social services organizations and hospitals may run advocacy programs or provide you with a referral. Some communities have information and referral (I&R) lines that may be able to supply you with the telephone numbers of local shelters and other support services. Look in the yellow pages under Social Services Organizations or similar headings or call your local directory assistance operator.

What to Bring with You to the Shelter

If there is time, and it will not compromise your safety by raising the abuser's suspicions, take any important documents that you can, including:

- your identification, for example, driver's license, passport, or immigration papers
- Social Security cards (yours and your children's)
- your children's birth certificates
- copies of any existing custody order for each child
- marriage certificates or divorce papers
- bankbook and credit cards
- your children's school and immunization records (you'll need these to enroll your children in a new school district)
- any prescription medication that you or your children need
- a small bag of clothes for you and your children
- each child's favorite toy, stuffed animal, book, or game

If there is no time to gather these items before you leave, don't worry. Your safety is more important than anything else! If you are in danger, leave.

Shelters often provide meals for residents, sometimes until food stamps can be obtained. Likewise, if you have no time to pack clothing, many shelters can provide you with clothing. If you cannot come to the shelter on your own or with the help of police, staff members can often arrange transportation for you.

Will It Be Safe?

One of the chief goals of women's shelters is to provide a safe place for you and your children. Therefore, shelters usually keep the location of their residence confidential and take security precautions, which may include security gates, bars on windows, and surveillance cameras.

STALKING

Although stalking first gained national attention through highly publicized accounts of celebrities stalked by obsessed "fans," most victims of stalking are pursued by someone they know, such as ex-partners or ex-spouses, coworkers, ex-employees, rejected dates, casual acquaintances, and others. Stalking is often a continuation of domestic violence. Abusers may stalk their partners after an attempt is made to leave the relationship. Nonetheless, stalkers can also be complete strangers. Regardless of who is stalking you, it is important to understand that you did not cause or provoke the stalking and that it is not your fault. Stalking can happen to anyone.

WHAT IS STALKING?

Most states have passed antistalking legislation, and all states have some type of legislation that can be used to try to combat stalking. Although the definition of stalking differs from state to state, many states outlaw willful, malicious, and repeated following or harassing of another person. Usually, the behavior must be such that it would cause a reasonable person to suffer substantial emotional distress or a reasonable fear for one's safety. Some states require that the stalker make an overt threat before he or she can be charged with stalking, although some states recognize that threats can be implied by action.

A stalking offense may be a misdemeanor (a crime less serious than a felony, punishable by fines and/or up to a year in jail) or a felony. A felony is punishable by a year or more in jail or prison. In many states, a first-time offense may be classified as a misdemeanor with a subsequent violation punishable as a felony, although in a few states a first stalking offense may be a felony. It is a federal crime to cross state lines with the intent to injure or harass another person and to place that person or that person's family members in fear of death or serious bodily injury. Because the laws concerning stalking differ, it is important to get information about the explicit provisions of the stalking law in your state and to find out how it is enforced. Your local prosecutor's office, police department, women's shelter, or victim/witness assistance program (where available) may be able to provide you with this information. If you want to read the law, ask where it can be found among your state's statutes or, if possible, for a copy of the law. County and university law libraries and many public libraries contain volumes of your state statutes. You can also ask the reference librarian to help you find the law.

What to Do If You're Being Stalked

The following are some very general suggestions that may help you cope with a stalker. It's best to discuss your options with an advocate or attorney.

- Report stalking, and each incident of stalking, including threats, to the police. If you have any trouble getting a police officer to respond to your concerns, don't hesitate to speak to his or her superior.
- Document all incidents of stalking. This will help to prosecute the stalker. Keep a journal in which to record exactly what happens during each incident with the stalker. Write down the time and date. Take photographs of any property that is damaged by the stalker.[16] Find witnesses to the stalking. Keep and date any letters or notes from the stalker and any answering machine cassettes on which the stalker has left messages. Remember, however, that your words and behavior will be recorded on audio or videotape, which may be admissible in court.
- Do not communicate with the stalker. Direct confrontation with the stalker may result in increased stalking activity.
- Contact a women's shelter for help in developing a safety plan that you and your children can use in the event of an emergency.
- Take extra security precautions. If you can, install an alarm system in your home. You may also want to consider getting a cellular phone so that you can call for emergency assistance away from home. If possible, vary your daily routine and your route to work in order to make it more difficult for the stalker to predict where you will be and when. If you are being followed in your car, do not drive home. Drive to the nearest police or fire station.
- If you live in an apartment building, give a picture or description of the stalker to whoever may be responsible for letting people into the building, such as a security guard, doorman, or apartment manager. Tell family members, neighbors, coworkers, and friends not to give

out any information about you to the stalker or to any other person. As a general rule, don't give out personal information about yourself to strangers.

- Consider changing your telephone number and keeping it unlisted. Contact your local telephone company and police department for information about tracing and tapping phone calls.

- Have your mail sent to a post office box rented from a private company. A private company may be preferable to the U.S. Postal Service, because the stalker may be able to locate your box at the post office and wait for you there when you come to collect your mail. If you do rent a box with the U.S. Postal Service, do not list as a business, because business addresses are not confidential. According to the Violence Against Women Act, you may keep your address confidential by showing a valid outstanding protection order to an appropriate U.S. postal official.

- Consider getting a restraining order or protection order against the stalker. The advantage of such an order is that a violation of it may provide for harsher penalties, depending on the state. However, there are disadvantages, including the possibility of heightened stalking activity in response. If you have a protection or restraining order, deliver a copy to the police station and keep a copy on your person at all times, so that you can show it to the police in case of a violation.

WHAT'S IN THIS CHAPTER?

- ✦ Emergency Contraception
- ✦ Facing an Unexpected Pregnancy
- ✦ Where to Turn for Information
- ✦ Abortion
- ✦ Placing Your Child for Adoption
- ✦ Pregnancy and Infant Loss
- ✦ Postpartum Depression
- ✦ Sexually Transmitted Diseases

✤ 5 ✤

Crises in Conception and Sexuality

EMERGENCY CONTRACEPTION

This section is meant to offer information to women who are facing an unexpected pregnancy and who are wondering about their options. In addition to the choices discussed below, there is another possible alternative for women who have recently had unprotected sex and do not want to be pregnant: emergency contraception. If you are already pregnant, emergency contraception will not work for you.

The contraceptive methods discussed here should be used only in an emergency and only with a prescription written by a licensed health care provider. If you already have a health care provider, it's best to contact him or her and ask about emergency contraception before using the Hotline. If you do not have a steady provider or you do not wish to confer with your regular clinician, you can contact the Emergency Contraception Hotline (1-800-584-9911) for information about the providers nearest you who can prescribe emergency contraception.

Even when couples use birth control methods consistently and correctly, contraception can fail. For example, condoms can break or slip off, or a diaphragm or cervical cap can be dislodged. It is also not uncommon for women to forget to use contraception, to make a mistake with their regular method, or to lack access to birth control. If you have had such a contraceptive emergency, or if you have been raped, you may want to consider emergency contraception. Although emergency contraceptive pills are commonly referred to as the "morning after pill," women do not have to wait until the morning after to use the method. The window of opportunity to use emergency contraceptive pills ranges from immediately after unprotected sex to up to seventy-two hours after unprotected sex. The IUD can be used up to seven days after unprotected sex has occurred.

At the time of this writing, there were three emergency contraceptive methods that could be prescribed by a licensed health care provider: an estrogen-progestin combination pill (regular birth control pills), progestin-only birth control pills, often referred to as "minipills," and copper-T IUD insertion. Other, potentially improved methods may be on the horizon.

Some, but not all, combined estrogen-progestin pills that are already on the market as routine oral contraceptives can be used as emergency contraceptives. A certain prescribed dosage must be taken within seventy-two hours of unprotected sex, with a second dosage taken twelve hours later.

For women who cannot take estrogen, progestin-only minipills may be preferable to the regimen above. This method must be used within forty-eight hours of unprotected sex. A second dose is taken twelve hours later.

Emergency contraception works by affecting ovulation, fertilization, or implantation. Emergency contraceptive pills prevent pregnancy primarily by making the uterine lining temporarily inhospitable to implantation. They may also prevent fertilization by impairing the sperm's ability to move through the fallopian tube and, depending on where you are in your cycle, by inhibiting ovulation. Because emergency contraceptives may act to prevent the development of pregnancy after fertilization has occurred, some women may have religious, spiritual, moral, or other objections to these methods.

Both combination birth control pills and minipills reduce the chance of pregnancy by around 75 percent. (However, you should be aware that if an ectopic pregnancy has already occurred, emergency contraceptive pills will not interrupt it. An ectopic pregnancy is a dangerous condition in which a pregnancy develops outside the uterus.) Although safe for most women to take, emergency oral contraceptives have a few possible contraindications. Therefore, it's important to talk to your health care provider before using birth control pills as an emergency measure.

No long-term consequences or serious side effects of emergency contraceptives have been reported. Temporary side effects include nausea, vomiting, breast tenderness, dizziness, and headache. Be sure to ask your health care pro-

---

EMERGENCY CONTRACEPTION HOTLINE

1-800-584-9911

This is a national toll-free automated hotline run by the Reproductive Health Technologies Project, a nonprofit organization whose mission is to advance the right of every woman to achieve full reproductive freedom through increased information and access to a wide range of safe and effective means for controlling fertility and protecting her health; and Bridging the Gap Communications, a publishing and distribution company that specializes in family planning, women's health, and sex education.

Accessible from any telephone, the Hotline provides callers with prerecorded information about emergency contraception in English and Spanish and the names and telephone numbers of the three nearest providers prescribing emergency contraception. Be advised, however, that in some areas, especially in rural areas, providers may be several hours away.

The Hotline is completely confidential. Its purpose is to provide you with information, not to identify you.

If you would like more information about emergency and ongoing methods of contraception, you can also order a book on these topics through the Emergency Contraception Hotline.

vider for information about side effects and what you can do to alleviate them.

As mentioned, pregnancy prevention cannot be completely guaranteed with emergency contraceptives. There are no known risks to the developing fetus caused by emergency or continued oral contraceptive use, but because the risks are uncertain, you may want to talk to your health care provider and to further consider your options should emergency contraceptive pills fail.

COPPER-T IUD INSERTION

Another method of emergency pregnancy prevention is copper-T IUD insertion. Copper-T IUD insertion can be done up to seven days after unprotected sex and works primarily by disrupting egg implantation. The chance of averting pregnancy is far greater with emergency IUD insertion than with combination pills or minipills, but not every woman is a candidate for copper-T IUD use.

IUD use has been associated with an increased risk for pelvic inflammatory disease (PID). If untreated, PID can lead to infertility, ectopic pregnancy, and chronic pain. The risk of PID associated with IUD use is slight for women who are not at risk for sexually transmitted diseases, but it is much greater in women who are at risk for STDs, such as chlamydia and gonorrhea, which can cause PID. For this reason IUD use should usually be avoided by women at risk for sexually transmitted diseases, including rape victims. Likewise, only a health professional trained in IUD insertion should perform the procedure, as there is a rare risk of perforating the uterus during insertion. These risks and other potential drawbacks to IUD use should be carefully discussed with your health care provider.

As with emergency contraceptive pills, emergency IUD insertion will not interrupt an ectopic pregnancy that has already occurred. Emergency IUD insertion is also the most expensive emergency contraceptive method. However, a copper-T IUD can remain in place for up to ten years after insertion, providing very effective contraception and thus making it an economical alternative in the long run.

If you have had unprotected sex and feel that emergency contraception would be right for you, contact your health care provider or another licensed clinician as soon as possible. If you are not already using birth control and STD prevention techniques, or if you are not happy with your current methods, this may also be a good time to talk to your provider about birth control options most suited to your needs. If you do not have a normal menstrual period in the three weeks following use of emergency contraception, see your health care provider immediately.

FACING AN UNEXPECTED PREGNANCY

An unexpected pregnancy can precipitate a crisis. If you think that you may be pregnant, it is important to find out right away in order to preserve as many of your options as possible and to seek prenatal care immediately, if you are considering carrying to term.

Home pregnancy kits, available in local pharmacies or supermarkets, are one way to detect pregnancy. However, since home tests are not always accurate, it is wise to have a blood or urine test and physical examination done at a family planning clinic or through your doctor's office to confirm the pregnancy. *Some of the signs of early pregnancy* include missing a period or having a very light period, breast tenderness, fatigue, nausea, and bloating.

Every woman has the right to determine her own response to an unanticipated pregnancy. You may decide to parent your child, to have an abortion, to place your child for adoption, or to arrange for temporary care of your child with a relative or foster parents until you are able to resume your role as mother. This is a decision that only you, or you and the significant others in your life, can make.

There is often a great deal to be gained by speaking with a professional who is knowledgeable about available resources and who can help you to examine each one of your options in depth. This service is often referred to as "options counseling" or "pregnancy counseling." A family planning clinic, such as a Planned Parenthood organization, a family service agency providing a range of services to families and children, or a mental health center in your community are good resources for initial assistance. The national referral number for Planned Parenthood organizations is listed in the Resource Directory. Your local office of the United Way or the national office of Family Service America, also listed in the Resource Directory, can refer you to organizations providing counseling and other services to women and families.

Crisis pregnancy centers also seek to help women facing unplanned pregnancies. You should know that crisis pregnancy centers, often listed in local telephone directories under Abortion Alternatives or Health Care Services may be operated by groups that are opposed to abortion. Although every woman's spiritual and personal beliefs concerning

THE STAGES OF PREGNANCY

Conception typically occurs about fourteen days after the first day of a woman's last menstrual period. However, women's cycles differ and it is generally not possible to estimate precisely when conception occurs. Therefore, pregnancy is usually dated starting from the first day of your last menstrual period. So, for example, when you are said to be four weeks pregnant, the embryo is actually about two weeks old. Likewise, if you are twelve weeks pregnant, the fetus is ten weeks old.

Pregnancy is described as taking place over three trimesters. For example: the first trimester is 1 to 12 weeks; the second trimester is 13 to 24 weeks; the third trimester is 25 weeks to delivery.

abortion must be respected, there are several reasons why crisis pregnancy centers are not suggested as sources for pregnancy counseling. These agencies often employ scare tactics such as the display of graphic and inaccurate videos or films or other forms of harassment to dissuade women from having abortions. They may pressure women to place their children for adoption or may not provide unbiased, accurate, or complete information about all of the possible resolutions to an unexpected pregnancy.

This section focuses on two possible resolutions to an unexpected pregnancy: abortion and adoption. Many women want to parent their children but lack the financial security to feel confident about the future. If this is true for you, a pregnancy options counselor may be able to help you identify sources of support that you haven't considered and tell you about any community and government resources for which you may be eligible.

ABORTION

WHAT IS ABORTION?

Abortion is a process whereby a developing embryo or fetus is expelled or removed from a woman's uterus.

A legal abortion is a very safe procedure. In fact, a legal abortion done in the first trimester of pregnancy is one of the safest of all medical procedures. Complications associated with first-trimester abortions occur less than 1 percent of the time with an experienced provider[1] although the risk of complications increases when abortions are done during later stages of pregnancy.

Most clinics will not perform a standard suction abortion until at least seven to eight weeks from your last menstrual period. (See the sections on nonsurgical methods of abortion for information about options prior to seven to eight weeks.) It is important to try to schedule your abortion as soon as you have made your decision, because abortions done in the first twelve weeks are safer, more available, and less expensive than abortions performed in the second trimester. If you put off your decision for too long, you may run into unexpected delays. For example, clinics are often overburdened. Even if there is a clinic in your area, you may not be able to schedule an appointment right away. Likewise, a few states have laws requiring women to wait for a period of time after an initial visit to a clinic before returning to the clinic for the abortion procedure. If you are a young person, the law in your state may require you to notify your parent(s) or to obtain their consent before having an abortion, or you may have to get permission from a judge.

Will Abortion Affect Your Ability to Bear Children in the Future?

Although having one or two abortions will not affect your chances of having a healthy baby in the future, there is some evidence that repeated abortions may increase the rate of miscarriage or preterm birth in later pregnancies.

Unsafe Methods of Abortion

Prior to the Supreme Court's 1973 decision in *Roe* v. *Wade* that struck down abortion bans in the United States, women often resorted to dangerous methods to attempt to end their pregnancies. Many sought abortions illegally from unskilled providers; others attempted to induce abortion themselves. These attempts at abortion ranged from using coat hangers or knitting needles to introducing toxic agents into the cervix or vagina. Infection, perforation of the uterus, sterility, and death were not uncommon results of these unsafe methods. Some women took varieties of herbs that were usually ineffective in ending pregnancy but which caused sickness and death in many cases. Others threw themselves down stairs or deliberately injured themselves in other ways in an attempt to cause a miscarriage.

Despite the legalization of abortion, many women still face obstacles to a safe, legal abortion. Regardless of the situation you are in and the desperation that you feel, you are urged *not* to try any of the unsafe methods listed above, or to do anything to risk your life or health. There are people who can help you. The National Abortion Federation, Planned Parenthood clinics, and other clinics performing abortions or giving abortion referrals are good sources of help and information.

How to Find an Abortion Provider

Most abortions are done in the first trimester in clinics that specialize in abortions. However, abortions may also be done in doctors' offices, outpatient facilities, and, less frequently, in hospitals. In most states, only a licensed doctor can perform an abortion. You may have to travel outside your area to obtain services, as most U.S. counties have no abortion provider. Abortion clinics are more likely to be found in or near cities and towns. Although complications resulting from an abortion are unusual, it's important to make certain that the provider you choose is located near a hospital into which you could be admitted in case of an emergency.

If you are in your second trimester, it will be more difficult to find a provider, especially after sixteen to twenty weeks. Even clinics that regularly perform abortions may not do abortions past twelve to sixteen weeks. For more information about the availability of second-trimester abortions in your area, contact the National Abortion Federation or local clinics or doctors providing abortion services.

To find a clinic or doctor in your area, contact the National Abortion Federation. Planned Parenthood organizations, operating in most states, may provide abortions or may give you a referral to a provider. To get an automatic referral to a Planned Parenthood organization near you (if there is one), call 1-800-230-PLAN. You can also look in the yellow pages of your local telephone directory under Abortion Services. As previously mentioned, it's important to beware of agencies that falsely advertise themselves as abortion clinics or family planning clinics. One of the best ways to determine whether an agency is really an abortion provider is to ask whether they perform abortions or give referrals to abortion providers. If they do not or if they give a vague or indirect answer, look elsewhere. If you are not certain of the services offered by a clinic that you plan to visit, take a friend with you so that it will be easier to leave, if necessary.

You may also be concerned about the presence of anti-abortion protesters. Although many clinics are able to conduct their businesses without harassment, some clinics are regularly targeted by protesters. Call the clinic where you plan to have your abortion to find out whether protesters are expected and how patients' arrivals are handled. Many clinics who have been plagued by antichoice harassment provide volunteer escorts to shield patients coming for services. Confrontation by protesters can be a frightening, humiliating, often infuriating experience. Remember that only you have the right to decide whether or not you will bear a child. No one else can or should have the right to look into the circumstances of your life and decide your destiny. Although protesters may want you to feel guilty or ashamed about exercising your right to reproductive freedom, there are countless women and men across the country who defend your right to make this extraordinarily personal decision.

The following sections will discuss surgical abortion procedures during the first and second trimester of pregnancy. This is only intended as general information. Be certain to get a thorough explanation of the procedure from your provider and to ask any and all questions that you have about the procedure, costs, and availability of counseling services.

*T*HE FIRST-TRIMESTER ABORTION PROCEDURE

Before your first-trimester abortion, you should receive information about the abortion procedure, either privately or with a group of women who are also waiting for abortion services. The counselor should tell you what to expect during and after the abortion and answer any questions that you have. If you wish, you may speak to a counselor privately. Your counselor can help you to explore your feelings about having an abortion so that you can make certain that it is the right decision for you. Don't hesitate to be honest about your concerns. Clinic counselors are dedicated to helping women explore *all their options* when faced with an unexpected pregnancy. They should not pressure you or try to persuade you to have an abortion. They are there to help you do what you believe is best. Sometimes, women feel pressured to have an abortion by parents or significant others. It's important to note that you can ask to speak to your counselor alone, even if you are a minor.

State law and medical ethics require that a patient be informed of the risks and benefits of any medical procedure before giving her consent. Once the risks and benefits of the abortion procedure have been explained to you, you will be asked to sign a consent form. In some states, providers are required by law to furnish information that is intended to dissuade women from having an abortion. Because the information required to be given is standardized and not tailored to an individual patient's needs, some of the contents of a state-mandated lecture may seem inappropriate or insensitive. For example, a woman who has been raped may be told that the father is liable for child support, or a woman who must terminate her pregnancy for genetic or medical reasons may be informed of the probable gestational age of the fetus and given a list of state agencies that can help her carry the child to term. Providers who are required to give this information may be just as concerned about its relevance as you are. Be sure to let your counselor know what you are feeling and to ask as many questions as you have about the information with which you are presented. If you would like more information about abortion, you can contact NAF or the Center for Reproductive Law and Policy, listed in the Resource Directory.

The Abortion Procedure

Most first-trimester abortions are done using a method called vacuum aspiration (also known as suction curettage or suction abortion). You will be asked to lie down on an examining table with your feet raised in stirrups. Before beginning the procedure, the doctor should do a pelvic examination to confirm the length of your pregnancy. Let the doctor know if you have not had a pelvic examination before. She or he can explain the procedure and help you feel more comfortable.

Next, the doctor will place a speculum into your vagina and clean your cervix with an antiseptic solution. Then, a long clamplike instrument called a tenaculum will be used to hold your cervix in place while the doctor injects a local anesthetic. At this point, you may feel pressure or a pinching sensation.

After the anesthetic takes effect, the doctor may use dilators to widen your cervix so that the instrument used to perform the abortion, the cannula, can be introduced. As the cervix dilates you will most likely feel menstrual-like cramping.

The cannula is a small flexible tube attached to a machine called an aspirator. The aspirator creates the vacuum used to produce suction in the cannula. The abortion is actually done when the doctor places the cannula into your cervix, turns on the aspirator, and moves the cannula around the inside of the uterus to remove its contents. During this time you will probably feel strong cramping. Sometimes, doctors will use a curette, a small, sharp-edged, spoonlike instrument, to gently remove any remaining tissue from the uterine walls. The actual abortion procedure takes about ten to fifteen minutes.

Most first-trimester abortions are performed using a local anesthetic, which involves injecting a numbing medication into the cervix to reduce the discomfort of dilation. General anesthesia, which renders you unconscious, is usually reserved for late-second-trimester abortions, although it will occasionally be offered for a first-trimester abortion. The use of general anesthesia increases the risk of complications and the length of time it takes to recover from the procedure. Thus, it is generally not recommended for abortions done within the first trimester.

After your abortion, you should be taken to a recovery room to rest for a brief period of time. A nurse will check your blood pressure and other vital signs, give you instructions for care after the abortion, and make sure that your cramping is lessened and that you are not experiencing too much bleeding.

THE SECOND-TRIMESTER ABORTION

An abortion in the second trimester of pregnancy (between thirteen and twenty-four weeks) is more costly than a first-trimester abortion and the risks and complications are greater. A second-trimester abortion can also be much more difficult emotionally. Only about 10 percent of abortions in the United States are done during the second trimester.

Most second-trimester abortions are done using a procedure called *dilatation and evacuation (D&E)*. The procedure is very similar to a first-trimester abortion, with a few exceptions. Before the procedure — usually a day before — small sticks of laminaria (dry, sterile seaweed) are inserted into the cervical canal to begin the process of dilation. The seaweed absorbs moisture and expands, causing the cervix to slowly dilate. The process may cause menstrual-like cramping. Ask your provider whether the placement of the laminaria will affect your daily activities.

During the D&E procedure, the doctor uses forceps to remove fetal parts in addition to a curette to scrape the uterine walls. Suction is used to remove blood and the remaining contents from the uterus. Recovery after a second-trimester abortion generally takes about one to two hours, depending on the type of anesthetic used.

Another method used in second-trimester abortions, usually in late-second-trimester abortions, is called *induction abortion* (or instillation or labor-inducing abortion). This type of abortion can be physically and emotionally painful for a woman to endure. But women undergoing interruptions because of a fetal or genetic abnormality may have strong personal reasons for choosing either method. In an induction abortion, the doctor instills a drug or solution that causes abortion either by way of a vaginal suppository, IV medication, or injection into the uterus through the abdomen. Prostaglandin, which causes the uterus to contract, is the most commonly used agent, but others, such as saline, urea, or oxytocin may be used. Prostaglandin should not be used by women with certain contraindications, such as asthma or seizures (epilepsy), in their medical history. These considerations should be fully discussed with your doctor. Induction is generally done in a hospital. During an induction abortion, a woman goes through a process very similar to labor, in which the fetus and placenta are expelled. Delivery may occur hours after the induction begins, usually within twelve to twenty-four hours.

Hysterotomy (not to be confused with hysterectomy) is a technique used when no other method can be used. The procedure is similar to a cesarean section (C-section) and is done during the second trimester.

You may have cramping for a few hours or up to a few days after your abortion. Most women have some bleeding afterward, which may range from spotting to bleeding that is similar to a menstrual period. It may last for up to two to three weeks and may stop and start or be continuous.

Your clinic or doctor should give you a written list of dos and don'ts after your abortion. It is very important not to put anything into your vagina for at least two to three weeks in order to prevent infection. This means no tampons, no douching, and no sexual intercourse. Many also advise against taking tub baths for at least a week or while you are still bleeding. You can become pregnant right away after having an abortion, so it's important to immediately resume or begin using a suitable method of birth control if you are sexually active. Your provider should be able to talk to you about your options.

A follow-up appointment should be scheduled about two weeks after your abortion. A follow-up is necessary to make sure that your uterus has returned to its normal size, that the cervix is closed, and that you do not have any uterine tenderness or other signs that a problem may be developing.

COMPLICATIONS OF AN ABORTION

Before you leave, you should be given a number to call over the next twenty-four hours in case a complication develops after your abortion. Although uncommon, possible complications of an abortion include uterine perforation, hemorrhage, incomplete abortion, and infection. If you experience any of the following symptoms, call your clinic or doctor or go to the nearest hospital emergency department:

- signs of pregnancy, such as nausea and fatigue, that last more than a week

- fever of more than 100.4 degrees Fahrenheit
- very heavy bleeding or bleeding such that you must use more than one menstrual pad per hour
- severe abdominal pain
- vaginal discharge with a strong, unpleasant odor

YOUR EMOTIONS AFTER AN ABORTION

The decision to have an abortion is clearly a very personal one, which most women make only after a considerable amount of thought. Because the decision is so personal and so unique to the circumstances of each woman's life, it's not possible to tell you exactly how you will feel before or after your abortion. Most women feel a sense of relief after an abortion. But you may also feel a sense of loss and sadness. You may feel guilt and anger, even though you may feel that you made the best decision in your circumstances. The social criticism and ostracism that many women face because of a decision to end a pregnancy can be a further source of emotional pain. But there is only one person who can understand the complexities of your life and the intricacies of your decision to end your pregnancy — and that is you.

Although serious emotional difficulties after an abortion are uncommon, each woman's experience is very different. If you are contemplating abortion, it's important to fully examine your feelings and the possible long-term impact of your decision before having the procedure done, particularly if you feel you are being forced to have an abortion by someone close to you or if you are opposed to abortion. Talking to a counselor at the clinic where you plan to have the procedure done, your husband or partner, or a family member or friend can also help you to look more closely at your decision. Talking to a counselor or therapist can be helpful after your abortion, especially if you experience continued difficult feelings.

If you have interrupted your pregnancy for medical or genetic reasons, or if you feel that you made the wrong decision, your feelings may be quite different from those described thus far. You may be feeling intense grief over the loss of your child. The section Pregnancy and Infant Loss, in this chapter, may be helpful to you.

PAYING FOR YOUR ABORTION

In 1996, the average cost of a first-trimester abortion performed in a clinic ranged from about $200 to $450. A dilatation and evacuation abortion done in a clinic ranged from about $600 to $2,000 or more. The cost increases considerably when services are performed in a hospital. Some insurance policies cover abortion. Look closely at your policy to see whether abortion is covered. In a number of states, Medicaid (or Medi-Cal in California) covers abortions in all or most circumstances. But in most states, Medicaid only covers abortion services in cases of rape, incest, or when a woman's life is endangered. To find out whether Medicaid funding is available to you in your state and under what circumstances, contact the National Abortion Federation. If Medicaid does cover needed services in your state, NAF may be able to give you information about clinics that accept Medicaid. Because cost is a barrier to reproductive freedom for so many women, a number of organizations are working to ensure that all women have access to abortion services in ways that include providing small grants or loans to women who cannot afford an abortion. To find out what assistance may be available to you, contact the National Network of Abortion Funds, listed in the Resource Directory, or the National Abortion Federation.

When inquiring about abortion services, always ask for an explanation of all the charges that you will be required to pay for, including additional tests or other treatments that may be necessary and follow-up visits.

OBSTACLES TO A SAFE AND LEGAL ABORTION

Reproductive freedom for women living in the United States continues to be precarious. The scant number of providers and the limited availability of services under Medicaid may render an individual woman's right to choose whether or not she will bear a child nearly meaningless. But other obstacles can make an abortion difficult to obtain or delay timely services. In some states, laws requiring a woman to endure a waiting period after an initial visit are being enforced. If you must travel outside your area for services, this could mean additional time away from home and further expenses. Depending on how long you have been pregnant, this could also mean having to find a provider to perform a second-trimester abortion.

FOR YOUNG WOMEN CONSIDERING ABORTION

In most states, young women under eighteen (or seventeen, depending on state law) are required to notify one or both

---

QUESTIONS TO ASK ABOUT THE ABORTION PROCEDURE AND THE CLINIC

- Approximately how much time will I spend at the clinic?
- What type of procedure will be done?
- What sort of anesthesia is available?
- How are emergencies handled? What will happen if I experience a complication?
- What is the cost of the abortion? What additional charges will I incur?
- What types of insurance do you accept?
- Do you require full payment up front?
- Will I be able to have a counselor or a friend with me during the abortion?

Don't hesitate to ask any question that you have about the procedure or the facility at any time.

parents or to obtain the consent of one or both parents (or other relatives in some states, for example, a grandparent, aunt, uncle, or adult sibling) before having an abortion. In some states, however, parental notification/consent laws are not generally enforced.

You can find out whether your state has a parental consent or notification law by calling the National Abortion Federation or by speaking to a counselor at a clinic that provides abortion services in your state.

If you have a good relationship with your parent(s), you probably know that despite possible displays of anger or disappointment, they will help you. Telling your parent(s) can be hard, but chances are they care about you and want to be there for you. If you choose to have an abortion, you may be able to meet a parental notification or consent requirement without much difficulty. For some young women, however, meeting these requirements may be very difficult, if not impossible. For example, a young woman who is a victim of incest or who fears physical abuse from family members may have understandable fears about notifying her parent(s) or getting consent to have an abortion. If this is true for you, or if there are other reasons why parental notification or consent may be impractical or impossible, there are some alternatives. States with a parental consent or notification law must allow young women to bypass consent or notification requirements. This usually means that a young woman must go to court in order to get permission from a judge to have an abortion without her parents' involvement. Generally, a judge must determine that a young person is mature enough to make the decision by herself or that parental involvement would not be in her best interests. In a few states, a physician can waive notice requirements,[2] but this is not common.

The prospect of going to court to talk to a judge about a matter as intensely personal and private as the decision to terminate your pregnancy may be unthinkable. But there are people concerned about the lives of young women and who are willing to help. If you feel that you cannot discuss your options with your parent(s) safely, you can call the National Abortion Federation for more information and go to a clinic and ask for help. The procedure for bypass should be swift and confidential. As mentioned above, unsafe and illegal methods of terminating a pregnancy can cause serious harm to your health — even death. Before you take any risks with your life, seek assistance. It may be difficult to get through this time, but it is not impossible.

Mifepristone is a drug that works by blocking the action of progesterone, one of the female hormones that plays an important role in establishing and maintaining pregnancy. When the uterine lining is deprived of progesterone, the placenta, which supports the fertilized egg, is disrupted and termination of the pregnancy results. Mifepristone is used in conjunction with another hormone, prostaglandin (in this case misoprostol), which causes the uterus to contract and helps to expel its contents. When used together, these hormones are about 95 to 96 percent effective in ending pregnancy.

This method of abortion, which may soon be available in the United States, is effective when used up until forty-nine days from your last menstrual period. To use mifepristone, you must make at least three visits to your doctor or clinic. Mifepristone and prostaglandin can cause fetal deformities, if the abortion is not complete. Therefore, a vacuum aspiration abortion is usually recommended when this method of termination fails.

Advantages of Mifepristone

A major benefit of mifepristone is that it allows women to terminate their pregnancies earlier than is possible with a surgical vacuum aspiration abortion. It can be used soon after pregnancy is determined. There is no risk of perforation of the uterus by medical instruments and the risk of infection is lower.[3] In addition, once mifepristone is widely available, your regular doctor will be able to prescribe it for you, making a trip to a clinic unnecessary. However, doctors prescribing mifepristone should be specifically trained in its use, and you must be sure to ask your doctor for explicit information about the procedure before using it.

Disadvantages

There are possible side effects to mifepristone and to prostaglandin. These include cramping and prolonged bleeding. Approximately one in one thousand women will require a transfusion due to blood loss. Other possible side effects include nausea, vomiting, and diarrhea. Another disadvantage is that more visits to the clinic or doctor are required than with a vacuum aspiration abortion.

A NEW OPTION FOR WOMEN: COMBINED METHOTREXATE AND MISOPROSTOL

Two drugs that have been on the market for years — methotrexate, used to treat ectopic pregnancies, certain autoimmune diseases and cancer, in higher doses, and misoprostol, an ulcer drug and the same prostaglandin used with mifepristone — may soon be widely available in combination to allow women safe, effective, early abortions without having to travel to an abortion clinic. As with mifepristone (RU-486) and misoprostol, at least three visits to your health care provider are needed for the procedure, and doctors who offer this procedure should be specifically trained in its use.

Methotrexate, given intramuscularly in clinical studies, works by inhibiting the division of fetal cells and possibly by interfering with the attachment of the embryo to the uterine wall. Misoprostol, given intravaginally, is a prostaglandin that causes uterine contractions, which expel the embryo. The combination has been shown to be safe and effective in women seeking terminations up to seven to nine weeks of pregnancy. Because of the possibility of failure and of excessive bleeding, access to surgical abortion services is still necessary for women seeking medical abortions. Women undergoing this procedure should also receive counseling in order to learn what to expect before giving their informed consent.

PLACING YOUR INFANT FOR ADOPTION

This section concerns the voluntary placement of an infant for adoption and does not address other adoptions, such as those involving older children.

THINKING ABOUT PLACING YOUR CHILD FOR ADOPTION

The decision to place a child for adoption is perhaps the most difficult decision a woman can make during her lifetime. The consequences of a decision to place a child for adoption are serious and long-term. Once an adoption is final, it is permanent. Generally, a mother of a child who has been adopted by someone else has no legal right to see her child again or to know of her child's whereabouts, although in some adoptions there is a possibility of voluntary contact between birth families and adoptive families. Because of the

---

> **WHERE TO GET INFORMATION ABOUT ADOPTION**
>
> The National Adoption Information Clearinghouse
> (703) 352-3488 or toll-free 1-888-251-0075
>
> The National Adoption Information Clearinghouse provides a number of free services to people interested in adoption. In addition to offering information on a range of topics of interest to birth parents and adoptive parents, the NAIC can give inquirers information about birth parent/adult adoptee search and support groups, counselors who work with birth parents, as well as books, magazines, and on-line services for birth parents. For the address and more information about the NAIC, see the Resource Directory.

---

permanent nature of adoption, all alternatives to adoption should be considered in addition to adoption. It's important to remember that you have many choices and time to explore them. Birth mothers (mothers who have placed their children for adoption) and advocates for birth mothers emphasize the importance of waiting until after your baby is born to make a decision about adoption.

Even when adoption is the best choice for you, your partner, and your child, it can be an extraordinarily painful life experience. Before choosing adoption, you must be as prepared as possible for the grief that accompanies the loss of a child. A good way to become acquainted with the adoption experience is to talk with women who have placed a child for adoption. The Resource Directory contains listings of national support organizations for birth parents, adoptive parents, and adoptees. Some groups may be able to refer you to a birth mother who can talk with you over the telephone. The National Adoption Information Clearinghouse and some state adoption specialists can also refer you to birth mother support groups.

Because private adoption agencies and attorneys are in the business of facilitating adoptions, it's wise not to talk to an adoption agency or attorney while you are deciding what to do. Instead, talk with someone who can be unbiased and who will help you examine *all of your options,* including parenting your child, identifying a family member who can care for your child temporarily, placing your child in temporary foster care, placing your child for adoption, or having an abortion. For example, if you want to raise your baby but are uncertain of how you will be able to support your family, a counselor should be able to tell you about any financial or other assistance available to you. Your financial situation may be quite different in the future and the resources that you and your counselor identify may serve as a bridge to better times. A counselor should also be able to tell you about foster care and legal mechanisms that will enable a trusted relative to assume responsibility for your child without completely terminating your parental rights.

Social service agencies that provide a range of services to families and children, often referred to as "multiservice family agencies," are perhaps the best places to go for pregnancy counseling and/or adoption services, because they do not rely solely on adoptions as a source of income. Wherever you seek services, you should be treated with respect and be given plenty of support and information. A pregnancy counselor should not make you feel guilty, shame you, condescend to you, or suggest that you are unfit to parent in order to persuade you to place your child for adoption. If you feel uncomfortable with the direction of any counseling that you receive, leave. Always remember that you have a right to make a decision without pressure from anyone, including your partner, family members, counselors, advocates, attorneys, agency staff members, or prospective adoptive parents.

Inquiring about adoption or seeking information about the services of an agency or attorney does not commit you to placing your child for adoption. In fact, until you sign a legal document consenting to adoption or relinquishing your child for purposes of adoption to an agency, you remain your child's legal parent. Ask as many questions as you have and make sure that you are satisfied with the answers that you receive. Be certain to get information in writing about the services offered to you and your rights as a birth mother. Do not sign any document without being absolutely sure that you understand its meaning and that you are completely confident of your decision.

Read as much as you can about adoption from the perspective of birth parents, adoptees (adopted children), and adoptive parents in order to get a realistic understanding of adoption as experienced by all of the people involved. The reading resource list at the end of this book offers some suggestions.

WHAT IS ADOPTION?

Adoption is the legal process by which biological parents' rights and responsibilities to care for a child are permanently given to another person or couple. Adoption laws vary considerably from state to state and are currently changing. For information about the laws governing adoption in your state, contact the National Adoption Information Clearinghouse or your state adoption specialist.

Until fairly recently, all adoptions were carried out confidentially. An adoption agency, attorney, or doctor chose the adoptive parents for a woman's child and she received very little information, if any, about them. If a mother had any contact with her child after birth, it ended once the baby was placed with the adoptive family. Today, a birth mother can often choose the type of adoption plan that she wants to make for her child. In addition to a traditional or confidential adoption, you can choose from various open adoption plans, which will be discussed below. Depending on state law, you may be able to choose between working with an adoption agency or an adoption attorney. These possibilities will also be discussed in the following sections.

TYPES OF ADOPTION

There are basically three different types of adoption. You have a right to choose the type of plan that you feel will best meet your child's needs and your own.

Traditional (also called closed or confidential) adoption. In this type of adoption, the agency chooses the adoptive parents for a child. The birth parents and adoptive parents do not meet, but they may receive nonidentifying information about each other, such as social and medical histories. While this type of adoption is still widely available, it has been affected by the movement toward greater openness in adoption. For example, a few states now allow adoptees who have attained a certain age to see their original birth certificates upon request.

In an *open adoption*, there is communication or contact between birth parent(s) and adoptive parent(s). The meaning of the term "open adoption" and the degrees of openness that are available to birth parents and adoptive families can vary, often depending on an agency's policies or an attorney's attitude toward open adoption and the desires of birth parents and adoptive parents. Levels of openness can range from a face-to-face meeting where only first names are given to the periodic exchange of letters and pictures to ongoing visits with the adoptive family. Many birth parents and advocates for birth parents and adoptees favor open adoptions where identifying information, such as names, addresses, and Social Security numbers, are exchanged. This is because, providing that everyone adheres to the agreement regarding openness, a birth mother will have access to information about her child's whereabouts and well-being, the adoptee will have knowledge of his or her birth parent(s), and the family can have ready access to important information, such as medical information, that must be updated as it evolves.

Because some agencies do not facilitate open adoptions and because the term "open adoption" may be defined differently by agencies and attorneys, it's very important to ask whether open adoption is available and to learn exactly how open adoption is defined when contacting people or agencies for information. Some agencies offering open adoptions work with a definition that is similar to traditional adoption. Always ask whether there will be any restrictions on contact outside the limitations that you and the adoptive parent(s) impose. Ask how information will be conveyed between birth parents and adoptive parents. For example, if you wish to send letters to the adoptive parents, will you be able to send them directly to the parents if they agree, or will the agency or attorney act as a go-between? As with traditional adoptions, open adoptions may be affected by changing laws.

Two of the most important elements of a successful open adoption are the match between birth parents' and adoptive parents' expectations of future contact and the commitment that each has to keeping a mutually defined agree-

---

THE IMPORTANCE OF COUNSELING AND SUPPORT

For most, the separation of mother and child is an intensely painful event. The grief experienced when a child is lost through an open or closed adoption is much like that felt at a child's death. Yet, because a child who is adopted into another family is not dead and because there is little societal acknowledgment of the grief birth mothers feel, it can be very difficult for women who have placed their children for adoption to find a sense of closure and to receive the loving support they need to mourn. If you have ever grieved for someone you have loved and lost, you know that the pain does not ever completely resolve and that many years can pass before you are able to fully accept the loss. It is common for grief over the loss of a child to resurface in the future, for example, on the anniversary of the child's birth or at major milestones, such as the birth of another child. Some birth mothers have said that the grief never ends.

Even though it's painful, it's important to seek support from counselors and others who are knowledgeable about grief and adoption. Unresolved grief can create serious problems in other areas of your life, particularly in relationships. A family service agency or community mental health center may be able to provide initial counseling services. Adoption and multiservice family agencies offer counseling and support groups for birth mothers who are seriously contemplating placing a child for adoption.

Ideally, agencies should make certain that women are not pressured, however subtly, into making a decision to place their children for adoption. Although many adoption counselors are knowledgeable about the emotional complexities of adoption, it is still possible to encounter a counselor who is more concerned with facilitating an adoption than with helping you to reach a decision that you can accept. If your counselor does not provide you with information about adoption, abortion, and any assistance that might be available to allow you to raise your child, or if you feel that you are being pressured or guided toward a decision that the counselor thinks is best, talk with someone else.

You do not have to work with a counselor at an agency or with the counselor recommended by your attorney. In addition to the low-cost options mentioned above, there is also the possibility of working with a private counselor. The American Adoption Congress, listed in the Resource Directory, and the National Adoption Information Clearinghouse can provide you with a list of counselors or therapists who specialize in working with birth parents. If no counselor is listed in your area, try calling birth mother support groups for referrals.

---

ment. Many disappointments are the result of unclear and differing ideas about the level and frequency of contact or changes in heart after an agreement is made. In most states, agreements regarding contact between birth parents and adoptive parents are *not* enforceable. Thus, birth mothers and adoptive parents must generally rely on each other's promises to keep the commitment that they have made to one another. Each parent must be very honest about her or his reasons for choosing open adoption.

If you are interested in making an open adoption plan, ask to interview prospective adoptive parents personally. If possible, your child's father may also want to be involved in choosing the adoptive family. When you speak to prospective adoptive parents, find out why they are interested in open adoption. This may begin a dialogue that can help you assess an adoptive family's commitment to open adoption and help you to examine your own feelings about open adoption. If, upon greater introspection, you find that you are more comfortable with limited contact, you may want to maintain your relationship with your child simply by sending an annual birthday or holiday card.[4] This simple form of contact can mean a lot to a child when it is consistent. It's also important that each party in an open adoption respect the boundaries of the open adoption agreement. For example, you must understand that, even in an open adoption, you will generally not be able to have a say in the way your child is raised.

RELATIVE ADOPTION

People who are related by blood or marriage, for example, grandparents, aunts, and uncles, may adopt a birth mother's child. Attorneys or legal aid organizations are often used to facilitate this type of adoption. Even when a trusted relative is planning to adopt your child, it is wise for both parties to have independent legal counsel, if possible. As with other methods of adoption, relatives may be subject to a home study by a social worker or other professional.

The prospect of adoption by a relative gives rise to special concerns. For example, you will have no more right to make decisions about your child's upbringing in a relative adoption than you would if your child were adopted by a stranger. If the fact of the adoption is kept secret, difficulties can be created for all concerned, including the adoptee. It may be hard to hear your child call your relative "mother," if this is how your child will refer to your relative. It may not be easy to think about how you will feel in the future, but it is necessary to discuss these issues thoroughly with a counselor to make sure relative adoption is the choice for you. Legal aid organizations or attorneys may not offer you counseling, but you can seek objective counseling on your own.

HOW ARE ADOPTIONS ARRANGED? AGENCY AND INDEPENDENT ADOPTIONS

As you begin to examine the possibility of a traditional, relative, or open adoption, you will also want to consider whether to work with a multiservice family agency, an adoption agency, or an adoption attorney (independent adoption — see page 212). The following is a very basic overview of these three distinct alternatives.

Many women considering adoption assume that they have very little control over the process. But in fact birth mothers have the right to as much involvement in the adoption process as they wish, although some agencies and attorneys encourage more involvement than others. You can choose to work with an agency or attorney who will respect your needs. Talk to as many agencies or attorneys as necessary. An agency or attorney should not charge you for inquiring. But of course, it's always wise to make sure before setting an appointment.

Licensed Multiservice Family Agencies

In all states, agencies may facilitate adoptions. Some agencies provide adoption and foster care services only and some agencies, called multiservice family agencies, provide a wide range of services to the public, including programs for mothers who place their children for adoption and those who do not.

As mentioned earlier, licensed multiservice family agencies are often the best sources for adoption counseling and services. Many, but not all, private adoption agencies rely heavily on fees from adoption transactions for income. Thus, there may be a greater risk of being pressured or feeling obligated to place your child for adoption when you work with a private adoption agency. If you are considering working with a licensed multiservice family agency, look for an agency that is a member in good standing with the Child Welfare League of America.

Adoption Agencies

There are two types of adoption agencies: private agencies and public agencies. Public agencies, which are run by the government, generally assist children who have been abused, abandoned, or neglected. Private agencies may be for-profit or nonprofit and may or may not be associated with a religious organization. Some advocates suggest that nonprofit private agencies may be more reputable than for-profit organizations. A private adoption agency should be state-licensed.

What Services Do Licensed Multiservice Family Agencies and Licensed Adoption Agencies Offer?

Licensed multiservice family agencies and licensed adoption agencies provide a range of services to birth parents and to prospective adoptive parents. These services encompass most aspects of the adoption process and usually involve:

- providing information about adoption
- locating and screening adoptive parents
- offering counseling and support groups for birth parents before and after adoption
- offering parenting classes for mothers who decide against adoption (This service is more typical of licensed multiservice family agencies.)
- giving referrals to or making arrangements for legal services and medical care. An agency may help you apply for Medicaid (or Medi-Cal in California), if you are eligible. Your insurance or your parent's insurance may cover the cost of your care. Some agencies may be able to help with other expenses, such as housing or clothing expenses.

A relatively new form of agency adoption, called *identified adoption* allows birth parents and adoptive parents who find one another without agency assistance to use an agency's services to arrange the adoption. This form of adoption is not available through all agencies, nor is it legal in all states.

The Agency Adoption Process

Once you have settled on an agency, you and your adoption counselor will begin to formulate an *adoption plan* for your child. A social worker at the agency will ask you for information about your medical and psychological history, prenatal care, and your use of alcohol or other drugs. Adoptive parents will need as much accurate medical information as possible in order to provide the best care for your child.

In any agency adoption, people who want to become adoptive parents are required to submit to a *home study* by which the agency evaluates their readiness to parent and the environment into which a child will be placed. In some states, couples or individuals are required to be certified or licensed by the court before they can be approved as potential adoptive parents. Information gathered about prospective adoptive parents varies, but may include facts about their educational and social background; financial status; their marital status and previous marriages, if any; the neighborhood and home in which they live; their religious affiliations; the reasons why they want to adopt a child; as well as information about their health status, references, a criminal background check, and any complaints of child abuse or neglect made to government child protective services agencies. The components of a home study cannot be taken for granted. It's a good idea to find out exactly how the agency evaluates applicants' suitability for parenthood and, further, how the agency will determine a couple's or individual's fitness to parent your particular child.

You may want to ask about the type of people an agency serves. Some agencies serve a specific clientele, such as people of a particular faith. (Agencies do not usually ask that birth mothers be of a specific religious heritage.) Some agencies include a range of prospective parents in their client base, including married and single people and gay and lesbian people. Some agencies may require couples to be married for a certain length of time or set age limits over which applicants may be ineligible.

Depending on the agency's policies and your wishes, you may be able to choose the adoptive parent(s) for your child, selecting from profiles of adoptive parents who have already completed a home study and been approved by the agency. This is one of the advantages of working with an agency. However, you do not have to be involved in the selection process if you don't want to be. It's important that you do what you think is best.

If you have preferences about the type of parents you wish for your child, ask the agency whether you will be able to choose adoptive parents with characteristics that you think are important. In many instances, you may be able to be fairly specific about the qualities you would like to see in your child's adoptive family. For example, you may prefer that your child's adoptive parents be a couple or live in a city or rural area. You should be aware, however, that although you may be able to choose the adoptive parents for your child, in most agency adoptions there is no absolute guarantee that the agency will place your child with the parents you select. For example, the adoptive parents may not go through with the adoption and your child may have to be returned to the agency. Moreover, there is no guarantee that adoptive parents will be able to raise your child as well as you might wish. The agency adoption process is quite rigorous, however, and those who endure it want a child very much.

If you are interested in choosing the adoptive parent(s) for your child, you may be concerned about how much control you will have over the selection process. If it's important to you, ask an agency whether you can look at the entire client base and read the home studies of the parents who interest you. If you want to meet with prospective adoptive parents, you may want to know how many times you can meet and whether any restrictions will be placed upon your meetings.

There are special considerations to bear in mind if your child is of color. The Multiethnic Placement Act (MEPA) of 1994, which applies to agencies that receive federal financial assistance, including some private (nongovernment) agencies,[5] prohibits agencies from creating policies that have the effect of delaying or denying a child placement in a qualified home, including policies that establish time periods during which an agency will only search for adoptive parents who match a child racially or ethnically.[6] At the same time, the law requires agencies to make diligent efforts to recruit potential adoptive and foster parents who reflect the ethnic and racial diversity of children who need adoptive homes.[7] One of the goals of the act is to reduce the time that children, particularly children of color, spend in foster care while waiting for adoption.[8] You may have concerns about the necessity of foster care and the racial, ethnic, or cultural background of prospective adoptive parents, which you should discuss with agencies. If it is important to you that your child be placed with adoptive parents of the same racial or ethnic background, you may want to work with agencies that specialize in placing children of color, if available in your area. These agencies may be able to place your child with a couple or individual of the same heritage more readily than agencies that are not specialized. The National Adoption Information Clearinghouse can give you information about agencies that focus on the needs of children of color.

The Indian Child Welfare Act is a federal law that applies to Native American children. It requires that preference for adoptive parents be given to members of a child's extended family, other members of the child's tribe, or other Native American families. The tribe must receive notice of the adoption and may intervene. Under this law, a consent to adoption taken before birth or within ten days of birth will not be valid.[9] If a Native American birth parent or custodian cannot afford a lawyer to represent her in a placement proceeding, she may have an attorney appointed to her by the court.[10] If you are Native American or of Native American descent, be sure to ask the agency or attorney with whom you are working about the applicability of this law to your child's adoption. The Multiethnic Placement Act does not apply to Native American children.

Agency Adoptions: After Your Baby Is Born

The most important aspect of the adoption process is the consent to adoption or relinquishment of a child for adoption to an agency after birth. Because of its importance, it is discussed in a separate section below. Following that section are other important topics that you should know about regardless of whether you are thinking of working with an agency or attorney.

Although many agencies allow for the direct placement of a child with adoptive parents, you may be asked to place your child in foster care before the placement is made. Be sure to ask about agencies' policies regarding foster care before you proceed. Some agencies have set policies about foster care and some will consider your wishes. If you need more time to think about your decision once your baby is born, you may want to voluntarily place your child in foster care or you may want to take your child home with you, as is your legal right. If you decide to place your child in temporary foster care, ask to know what rights you have to remove your child from foster care.

After your child is placed with the adoptive family and before the adoption is finalized, the agency will continue to monitor the family for a certain period of time, usually at least six months. The adoptive parents will petition the court for adoption. A hearing will be held, and if the prospective adoptive parents are approved as parents, the adoption will be finalized. A new birth certificate will be issued with the name that the adoptive parents have chosen for your child, and the baby's original birth certificate will be sealed. Be aware, however, that laws regarding adoption procedures and the time frames in which adoptions are finalized vary greatly from state to state. The above outline is only an example. Make certain that you have an explicit understanding of the agency adoption process in your state before you agree to make an adoption plan.

Looking for an Adoption Agency

To find a licensed multiservice family agency or adoption agency in your area, contact the Child Welfare League of America or Family Service America, listed in the Resource Directory. A counselor at a family planning clinic, such as a Planned Parenthood organization, or the local office of the United Way may also be able to give you various referrals, but you may not be able to tell whether these referrals are multiservice family agencies, for-profit, or nonprofit adoption agencies. It's a good idea to try to get in touch with other birth mothers in your area, if you can, for additional recommendations.

It's important to find out whether any agency is licensed and whether any complaints have been made against it. To do this, you can call your *state adoption specialist* and ask for the name of the organization that licenses agencies providing adoption services. The state adoption specialist or unit is usually located in the state Department of Social Services. (The name of this agency differs from state to state. For example, it may be called the Department of Children and Family Services or the Department of Health and Welfare.) Look in the government section of your local white pages under State Government Offices. Find out when the adoption agency was last reviewed by the licensing agency. You may have to visit the licensing office in your area to review the agency's records. Another possible way to find out if any complaints have been registered against an agency is to call the Better Business Bureau. Licensing, however, is only an indication that the agency is in compliance with state licensing laws and is not in itself a guarantee of quality. The adoption specialist in your state may be able to give you a general sense of an agency's reputation. Again, another possible way to test for quality is to find out whether the agency is a member in good standing with a major child welfare organization, such as the Child Welfare League of America.

Independent Adoption

Independent adoption (or attorney-facilitated adoption) is a method of adoption that is frequently chosen by birth mothers and adoptive parents. It is legal in most, but not every, state. In an independent (private) adoption, birth parents and adoptive parents find each other, often through an intermediary, such as a lawyer, doctor, or clergyperson, and work with their separate attorneys to arrange the adoption.

Before considering this alternative, it is imperative that you find out whether it is legal in your state. Your state adoption specialist or a licensed multiservice family agency or adoption agency can give you this information. The state adoption specialist may also be able to give you a copy of your state's adoption law. If you are planning an adoption with a couple who live out of state, you should know that the adoption laws for both states may have to be met. For more information about interstate adoption, consult with your attorney. Also, ask the state adoption specialist for the location and telephone number of the Interstate Compact specialist in your region. This is the professional who coordinates the Interstate Compact on the Placement of Children, with which adoptive and birth parents must generally comply.

If you choose independent adoption, you are strongly urged to have your own lawyer and not to rely on the lawyer hired by the adoptive parents, whose interests are separate from yours. In some states, birth parents are required by law to have separate counsel.

Depending on the state, a licensed social worker or psychologist may be required to do a home study of the prospective adoptive family in an independent adoption. Some states may not require that the home study be conducted until after a child is placed with adoptive parents. Home studies for independent adoptions may not be as thorough as the studies done for adoption agencies. Therefore, you may not have access to the same kind of information about prospective adoptive parents in an independent adoption as you would in an agency adoption. However, if you choose an open adoption plan in which you meet the potential adoptive parents, you can ask them questions directly to get a sense of their suitability.

Another difficulty associated with independent adoptions concerns the expenses that can legally be paid to you by adoptive parents. Taking money in exchange for a child is illegal in all states. However, state laws differ widely regarding the type of financial assistance that may be legally given to the birth mother by the adoptive parents. Depending on the state, these may include legal, medical, counseling, and living expenses and reasonable attorney fees. Generally, these costs must be court-approved. Be aware that accepting financial assistance from prospective adoptive parents may have the effect of making you feel obligated to place your child for adoption and may complicate your decision-making process, even when adoptive parents have no desire to pressure you.

Some attorneys may not refer you to counseling before and after your child is placed for adoption, but experienced adoption attorneys often realize the far-reaching consequences of adoption and will recommend that clients receive counseling. Nonetheless, it is a good idea to seek the services of someone who can be neutral. A counselor or therapist recommended by an attorney or paid for by adoptive parents may not be able to be unbiased. It's to the benefit of everyone involved that you receive the kind of assistance needed to make an honest, considered decision, even if it means deciding against adoption.

Looking for an Adoption Attorney

If you wish to arrange an independent adoption and it is legal in your state, you will need to locate an attorney and adoptive parents. Adoptive parents may be permitted to pay for the services rendered by an attorney who is hired to represent you. It is best to choose an attorney yourself, not to have the attorney of the adoptive parent(s) refer you to one. If you have a low income you may be able to find an attorney who will assist you for free or for a reasonable cost by contacting a legal aid organization or law school clinic in your area. Private attorneys are much more expensive than those associated with legal aid organizations. A support group for birth mothers may also be a source of private attorney referrals. If possible, look for an attorney whose practice focuses on adoptions and who has long experience in the field. Adoption laws are complex and constantly changing. When you find an attorney with whom you are comfortable, contact the state bar association, which may be listed under State Government Offices in your local white pages, to make certain that the attorney is licensed.

Independent Adoptions: Finding Adoptive Parents

There are a number of ways to find prospective adoptive parents. One of the best ways to find prospective adoptive families is to ask relatives, friends, and others whom you trust whether they know of anyone who is trying to adopt a child. You might also try asking your doctor or clergyperson if she or he knows of any couples or singles with qualifications that you consider important. Contacting adoptive parent support groups in your area is another way to locate prospective parents with whom you feel a connection. The state adoption specialist or other adoption organizations may be able to give you information about local support groups for adoptive families. It's a good idea to meet with all the prospective adoptive parents you are considering a few times before deciding to pursue an adoption together. As soon as you have decided upon the adoptive parent(s) for your child, let the other prospective parents know so as not to unfairly delay their search for a child.

Independent Adoptions: After Your Baby Is Born

Independent adoptions often allow for the direct placement of a child into the adoptive home. You may be asked to sign a form to give the adoptive parents temporary custody of your baby before you sign the form consenting to adoption, which may be executed several weeks or months later. These forms are easily confused. Be certain that you understand the nature of any form you are asked to sign and to have your attorney review it.

The Consent or Relinquishment Form

Before any voluntary adoption plan can proceed, either in an agency adoption or an attorney adoption, a birth mother (and birth father, see the following section) must consent to the adoption or formally give her child to an agency for placement. Your formal consent or relinquishment does not end the adoption process, but it is a crucial step in the direction of its completion. Once you have consented to adoption or relinquished your child to the agency, it can be very difficult, if not impossible, to change your mind and get your baby back.

Laws concerning consents and relinquishments vary dramatically from state to state. The name of the form that birth mothers are asked to sign also differs. It may be called a consent to adoption, a relinquishment or surrender of parental rights or may be given another name, depending on the area and whether the adoption is being arranged by an agency or attorney. Before signing adoption papers, consider the following facts.

- Most states require that the consent or relinquishment be signed only *after* the birth of the baby. Advocates often recommend that you do not sign or consider signing a consent or relinquishment form (or even think about planning an adoption) until after your child is born and certainly not until you have recovered from the physical trauma of delivery. Once your baby is born, you may want to reconsider your decision. If you do not want to sign adoption papers or select an adoptive family for your child until after your child is born, make this clear to the agency or attorney. In many states, your consent or relinquishment may be obtained only after a specific period of time has elapsed from birth. The length of these *waiting periods* varies greatly across states with such laws. Always find out how much time you will have before a social worker or attorney will ask you to sign adoption papers.

- If you are a minor (under eighteen or twenty-one, depending on state law), you may be required to obtain your parent/s' consent before agreeing to place your child for adoption.

- Generally, once the consent or relinquishment form is signed, your parental rights will be terminated. Depending on state law, you may not be able to alter the decision to place your child for adoption after this point. In some states, you may be able to change your mind during a limited period of time after you sign adoption papers, but in others, there are no such provisions in the law. It is very important to find out what revocation period, if any, exists in your state. Likewise, the laws regarding reasons for revocation of consent or appeal vary. For example, depending on the state and circumstances, you may have to prove that the consent or relinquishment was obtained by fraud or under duress, or that it is not in the child's best interests, among other permissible reasons. However, waging a legal battle to get your baby back can be extremely difficult. Be certain that adoption is the *only* choice for you and your child when you sign.

- Adoptive parents are also entitled to change their minds about adoption. Make sure that you discuss this possibility with your agency or attorney.

State laws regarding the way in which the consent or relinquishment must be taken also differ. Your state may require that the consent form be signed in front of a judge, a witness such as a licensed social worker, or a notary public.

Before signing a consent or relinquishment form, *you must be absolutely sure of your decision.* Make certain that you have read the form carefully, that you understand its provisions and have had all of your questions answered to your satisfaction. It is best to have your own attorney review any legal document that you are asked to sign.

Safeguarding your adoption plan: the father's rights

Generally, before a child can be adopted, the parental rights of both birth parents must be terminated. Therefore, state law may require notification of the father (or any possible father) so that he can either consent to the adoption, if he doesn't want custody of his child, or formally deny paternity, if he doesn't think that he is the father. The father may have a right to argue for custody of his child. If measures aren't taken to secure his consent or denial of paternity before the adoption proceeds, there is a possibility that he could establish his paternity, object to the adoption and ask the court to allow him to raise his child. If you are married, your husband must consent to the adoption, even if he is not the child's biological father.

There are various ways to make sure obligations concerning the father's rights are met and to protect the adoption, even if you do not know the father's identity or where he is living. Fathers' rights concerning adoption vary significantly from state to state. Your adoption agency or attorney must take the proper measures to comply with the law. Again, this is very important. If this matter is not handled properly, the secure placement of your child in his or her new home may be jeopardized.

Your time with your baby

You have the right to see and spend time with your baby in the hospital once you give birth. You have the right to hold and feed your baby and to take pictures of your child. Seeing and holding your child can help you through the grieving process. You also have the right to decide who you want to be with you during delivery. These issues should be discussed with your adoption counselor and/or your child's prospective adoptive parents, but the decision is yours. You can also name your child on the original birth certificate, although the adoptive parents may change the name.

Will you be able to see your child again after adoption?

If you choose an open adoption plan for your child, you may be able to send letters and pictures to your child, visit your child periodically or maintain contact in other ways. If you do not choose open adoption or if you lose contact with the adoptive family, there are a few things that you can do to promote the possibility of future contact.

A few states allow adoptees who have reached a certain age to have access to their original birth certificates upon request. In most states, however, adoption records are permanently sealed and an adult adoptee may have to go to court in order to try to show that there is "good cause," usually an urgent medical need, to open identifying records. Alternatively, a growing number of states allow adoptees over a certain age and birth parents to receive identifying information about each other through mutual consent, often through mutual consent registries. In order for these registries to work, both parties must consent to disclose information to each other. When there is a "match," information can be released. Some states allow intermediaries to help older adoptees search for their birth parents. In these states, a birth mother may file a waiver of confidentiality with an adoption agency or court. If no waiver is on file, a birth mother may be contacted by an agency or intermediary and asked whether she wants to release her name or other identifying information to the adult adoptee.

Some private organizations concerned with adoption maintain reunion registries through which birth parents and adoptees can notify each other of their desire to be contacted. The International Soundex Reunion Registry, which is free, the Concerned United Birthparents Registry, and the registry maintained by the Adoptees' Liberty Movement Association are some examples. See the Resource Directory for addresses and telephone numbers. If the adult adoptee does not have enough correct information about you, or if your address and telephone number are not kept current, she or he may not be able to locate you through a registry.

Most people have a strong, inherent need for connections to their family, their community, and their past. Adoptees are no different. Unfortunately, for many adult adoptees the kind of information that might give them a greater sense of identity and belonging is unavailable. Although people differ, it can be devastating for a child not to know anything about his or her birth parents or the truth about why he or she was placed for adoption. Today, many birth parents provide this information by writing a letter to place in their child's adoption file. By writing such a letter and working with an agency or attorney who will place it in your child's file for your child to read at a later date, you can express your love for your child and honestly explain the reasons why you chose adoption. Although a letter written to your child is an extremely personal document, and you alone must decide upon its contents, you may want to include plenty of information about yourself and the birth father, if possible, as well as your thoughts about your child and the memories that you have of your time together. Your child may yearn to see a picture of you and of the birth father, if possible. You may also want to include facts about your family history, such as where your family members were born and where they lived. Information about your religious or spiritual beliefs and those of your family can also help an adoptee develop a fuller sense of his background. In your letter, you can state whether you would like future contact and give your name and address. Although most states gather vital nonidentifying information, such as medical histories, from birth parents, gaining access to current medical information is a serious problem faced by many adoptees. Because the knowledge you have about your health status changes over time, it's necessary to update information about your medical history. If you develop a medical condition that may be hereditary, your child should know about it. Ask the agency or attorney you plan to work with how you will be able to update this information.

Agencies may have restrictions on what information can be placed in your file and what can be conveyed to the adoptive parents, so be sure to ask about this before you agree to work with a particular agency. There are also some realistic risks in giving a letter to an agency or attorney. The agency or attorney may not be in business when your child is old enough to have access to the records, the records may be lost, or the agency may not have the funds to search for them. Therefore, depending on the type of adoption arrangement you have, you may want to think about handing the information to the adoptive parents directly so that they can pass it on to the adoptee. There is always the possibility, however, that the adoptive parents may choose not to share this information with your child. Birth parent support and self-help groups across the country can provide you with information about these and other important adoption issues.

QUESTIONS TO ASK AGENCIES OR ATTORNEYS

Questions to Ask an Adoption Agency

Because agencies differ, it's a good idea to learn as much as you can about the agencies with which you are thinking of working and to ask as many questions about the agencies as you have. Here are some suggestions in addition to those offered in the sections above:

- What is your philosophy and mission?
- What are my legal rights and obligations as a birth mother? Whose rights does the agency represent, my rights or those of the adoptive parent(s)? May I have legal counseling from an attorney who does not represent the agency's interests? How can such counseling be arranged?
- What services do you offer in addition to adoption services? (Multiservice family agencies offer a broad range of services.)
- Will I be able to choose my child's adoptive parents? May I make an open adoption plan? How does this agency define the term "open adoption"? What levels of openness are available? How long has your agency been involved in doing open adoptions? Are there any restrictions on contact between birth parents and adoptive parents? How will communications between birth parents and adoptive parents be conveyed?
- May I make a traditional (confidential) adoption plan for my child? Can you explain confidential adoption to me? What are the advantages and disadvantages?
- Generally, what services will be offered to me before I have my child and after my child is placed with the adoptive parents? May I have a written statement concerning the services offered? Who pays for services provided by the agency? What will happen if I change my mind and decide against placing my child for adoption? Will I be responsible for paying for these services?
- Will counseling be available to me during my pregnancy and after my child is adopted? Who will provide counseling services? May I bring someone close to me, such as my husband or partner or my parent(s) or other close relatives to counseling? Are there costs for counseling services? Are support groups for birth mothers available?
- Of the women seeking counseling services, how many have actually placed their children for adoption?[11] (A high percentage may indicate a risk of pressure.)
- Are adoptive parents charged a fee for the adoption? What is the amount?
- How are prospective adoptive parents selected? What initial requirements are made of applicants? What does the home study require of parents? Can you give me written information about the way adoptive parents are chosen and are qualified?
- What rights does the father of my child have to consent to or challenge the adoption?

- What will happen if the adoptive parents decide against adopting my baby? What will happen if my baby needs expensive medical care immediately after birth? Will I be responsible for these expenses?
- At what point after my child's birth will I be asked to sign a relinquishment or surrender form? Will you allow me to take as much time as I need to make my decision? Is there a period after I sign during which I may change my mind? Are there any restrictions on this right?
- Will my baby be placed in foster care before she or he goes home with the adoptive parent(s)? If I need more time to consider my decision after I have my baby, will I be able to take my baby home with me? Will foster care services be available to me? Will I have to pay for foster care, and if so, what will the cost be to me?
- Are adoption records open in my state? What is the agency's policy about searches for an adoptee or a birth parent? Will the agency assist in searches?

Questions to Ask an Attorney

You may want to ask an attorney many of the same questions that you will ask an agency. Here are some additional suggestions:

- Whose interests are you obligated to represent, mine or those of the adoptive parent(s)? What are my legal rights and obligations? Can you explain the adoption law in this state to me? (Also ask about the laws in the other state, if you are planning an interstate adoption.) Do any federal laws regarding adoption apply to my adoption plan?
- How many adoptions have you helped arrange in the past? How many did you arrange last year? Will you facilitate an open or traditional (confidential) adoption? What are your feelings about open adoption? How many open adoptions have you arranged?
- Will a home study of the prospective adoptive parents be conducted? Who will do the study? What does it involve? Will it be done after or before my child is placed with the adoptive family? Who pays for it? What will happen if the prospective adoptive parents' home study is not approved?
- What type of financial assistance may I legally receive in connection with my adoption plan? Will I be responsible for any of these expenses if I change my mind and

decide not to proceed with the adoption? Will you collect fees from me if I decide against adoption?

- Do you consider counseling for birth parents to be important? Why or why not? May I work with a counselor of my own choosing?
- When will I be asked to give my formal consent to adoption? Is there a period after formally consenting to the adoption when I have the legal right to change my mind? Are there limitations on this right? What is the name of the form that I will be asked to sign? What other forms might I be asked to sign? How long will I have to reexamine my decision before I give my consent?
- Will my child be released directly to the adoptive parent(s) or is there a period of time during which my child will stay in foster care?
- What rights does the father of my child have to consent to or challenge the adoption?
- What will happen to my child if the adoptive parent(s) change their minds about the adoption?

When interviewing attorneys, look for someone who has a clear concern for you and for your child's future. If an attorney speaks to you in a condescending manner, brushes aside your concerns, directs you toward an adoption plan with which you disagree, consistently uses terms that you don't understand, fails to answer your questions satisfactorily, or seems undesirable for other reasons, look for another attorney.

PREGNANCY AND INFANT LOSS

This section is meant for anyone who has lost a child during pregnancy, at birth, or shortly after. Information about the loss of a young child is presented here because of its close relationship with other crises in pregnancy and early motherhood, not because it is any less tragic or profound than the loss of someone who lived longer.

Because this section is meant to provide general information, bereaved parents, their relatives, and close friends may benefit from continued reading on the crisis of pregnancy and infant loss. Recommendations for further reading are given at the end of the book. There also are many national organizations that specialize in helping bereaved parents, many of which are listed in the Resource Directory. Many of the services that these organizations offer will be discussed in this section. Chapter Ten contains additional information for people who are mourning the loss of someone they love and describes some of the common feelings associated with grief.

GRIEVING THE LOSS OF YOUR CHILD

The first parts of this section are meant for all women who have suffered a miscarriage or the loss of an infant. Following are discussions specific to certain types of loss. You are encouraged to read any section that seems helpful to you. The term "partner" will be used in this chapter to describe a member of an intimate relationship, including a married or unmarried relationship, and is meant to be inclusive of relationships between a woman and a man and between two women.

There is perhaps nothing in life as painful and as difficult to accept as the loss of a child. When a child dies at any stage of life parents must not only mourn the loss of their special, irreplaceable child but also all the hopes and dreams that they had for their baby and for their future as a family.

When you first learn of your child's death, you may feel shock or numbness. You may not be able to absorb the full reality of your loss and may feel as though you are moving through life on "automatic pilot." Later, you may feel tremendous anger and guilt. These are very natural feelings. It's natural to want to blame yourself or others for what has happened, to feel deep sorrow, depression, fear, loneliness, confusion, and emptiness. The loss of a child can strike at the core of your feelings about yourself as a mother and as a woman. If you have had a previous loss, or if you have lost a twin or children in a multiple birth, and/or struggled with infertility, your feelings of grief may be intensified.

In addition to severe emotional pain, you may also experience physical manifestations of grief. Grieving parents sometimes feel pressure or tightness in the chest. Many parents feel a literal aching in their arms to hold their child and imagine that they hear their baby's cry. If you were lactating at the time of your baby's death, your breasts may be engorged with milk. Having your breasts full when there is no baby to nourish may deepen your anguish. It may be helpful to wear a binding bra and to avoid touching or stimulating your breasts until your milk production stops.

Although the loss of a child is inexpressibly painful, allowing yourself to grieve will help you to begin to accept what has happened and to heal. Healing does not mean forgetting. It simply means that you will be able to live, learning how to cope with your loss and with the pain. Each person's grieving process is different. There is no correct or "appropriate" way to grieve. Normal grief reactions include a wide range of feelings and behavior. It's all right to trust your feelings and do what feels natural to you. Take as much time as you need, and don't hesitate to ask for support from others.

The experience of grief is a long and difficult one — much longer than most parents expect — and the process is not necessarily orderly. You may feel different emotions at different times. They may overlap and pour into one another. Although the intensity of your pain will lessen over time, it is normal for feelings of grief to resurface, even many years later. For example, it is common to grieve at the anniversaries of your baby's birth and death or at the time that your baby should have been born.

Hospitals are becoming increasingly aware of the needs of bereaved families and many have health care professionals on staff specially trained to help people who have suffered a miscarriage or infant loss. If you are in the hospital as a patient, a perinatal bereavement team may be available to you. The team may include a nurse, a physician or midwife, a social worker, and a pastoral counselor or chaplain. These same professionals may be able to help you even if they are not formal members of a bereavement team. A perinatal bereavement counselor or other support person may visit you in your room. However, in some hospitals, you may have to ask for someone to visit you. If your hospital does not provide this service, ask your nurse or a hospital social worker to put you in touch with a local organization for bereaved parents or with one of the national support organizations for bereaved parents listed in the Resource Directory.

When a baby dies at home or in a daycare center, you may visit the hospital only briefly or not at all. Even in these circumstances, you can ask the hospital social worker, nurse, or a funeral director for a referral to a program designed to help families immediately after the death of a child, if there is one in your area. Even if you don't use this information right away, it may help to know that there are people to talk to.

Making Decisions

One of the hardest things about the loss of a very young child is that you will be asked to make many difficult decisions while you are still numb and in shock. Some of the decisions that you will be asked to make involve individual choices that may help you to accept the death of your baby and begin to grieve. Some decisions may have to be made soon, but others can be put off for a while. You do have choices. Don't hesitate to ask for the time that you need to make them.

If your baby died in the hospital, someone from the hospital should ask if you would like to see and hold your baby and if you would like to bathe, dress, and photograph your child. This may be a nurse, a social worker, a clergyperson, or a doctor. If the hospital does not ask you if you would like to do this, you may have to ask. It can be very beneficial for parents to see and hold their child. Parents who are not offered this option may wonder what their baby looked like and/or regret that they did not have the chance to say good-bye. However, the decision is yours. You shouldn't be forced to do something that isn't right for you. You should not be rushed. If you are not up to seeing your baby right away, ask your health care provider if you can wait and if your baby can be made available to you later when you are ready.

You may have concerns about how your baby will look. You can ask the staff person helping you to prepare you ahead of time. Many people who assist bereaved parents say that parents are often surprised at how easily they are able to overlook any physical defects the baby might possess and how readily they see the beautiful aspects of their child. When you see your baby, ask not to be hurried. Spend as much time as you need. If you wish, you can ask to see your child again later.

Although it may initially seem inappropriate or odd to have photographs taken of your child, you may later wish that you had a picture of your baby to help preserve your memories. If you were not offered a photograph in the hospital, it's possible that the hospital took a photograph of the baby as a matter of course. You may want to contact the hospital to find out whether this is so, and if the photograph can be made available to you. Naming your baby (if you have not done so already) is another way to honor your child and endow him or her with a special place in your family. Naming your child can make your loss more concrete and help you to grieve. You may also want to ask for mementos of your baby's life, such as your child's blanket, crib card, hospital records, handprints, a footprint, or a lock of hair. Depending on your child's age, a birth certificate and death certificate may have been completed. If available, you may want to request a copy of these documents.

If your child was taken to the emergency room from home or elsewhere, you may also have to make a request to see and hold your baby and to say good-bye. Hospitals are becoming increasingly aware and understanding of the strong need parents have to be with their child, but not all parents' experiences with hospitals are good.

If you have had a very early loss, the above suggestions may not be possible or may seem inappropriate to you. Likewise, parents who have made the decision to interrupt their pregnancy for medical or genetic reasons by dilatation and evacuation may not have the opportunity to see their child. It's important, however, to recognize your needs. Many parents find that making a memorial to their child is very helpful to their emotional recovery. You can honor your child's life by planting a tree, engraving or setting a stone in a charm, making a donation in your baby's name, or in other ways.

When a baby dies, some hospitals will automatically move the mother off the maternity floor; others will ask if she would like to be moved. Hearing other babies cry can be very painful, but you may have many good reasons for wanting to remain on the maternity floor. For example, staff members on the floor may know you and be attentive to your emotional and physical needs, the visiting hours may be better, or you may feel that being on the maternity floor rather than in another area of the hospital validates your motherhood and provides you with some comfort as you grieve. You should be able to request the location you desire. Because you may need your partner, parent(s), guardian(s), or other supportive person after normal visiting hours, you may want to find out if the hospital staff can stretch some of the visiting rules. However, you should be aware that it will not always be possible for the hospital to do this.

You may be asked to make a decision about autopsy. If no one can tell you why your baby died, an autopsy may provide a reason. However, this may not always be the case, and parents may have personal reasons for declining autopsy. You may also want to consider organ donation, if appropriate and meaningful to you.

Making Funeral Arrangements

Depending on your wishes and/or the traditions of your faith, you may want to have a funeral or memorial service for your child. A service can be a part of your healing process. It helps to acknowledge your child's death and to share your sorrow with family and friends. The funeral does not have to be held right away. If you are in the hospital as a patient, it may be possible to delay the service until you're feeling well enough to attend. Talk with your doctor about your physical condition.

Deciding upon funeral or memorial arrangements can be extremely painful. You may need time to think about how you want to care for your child's body. Keeping the hospital staff informed is very important. Tell them (or ask your support person to tell them) that you are deciding whether to have services for your baby. This way the hospital will know not to act without your consent and you can learn about your options for saying good-bye.

If you are a concerned friend or relative, now is an excellent time to step in and help by making the necessary contacts and telephone calls. Hospital perinatal bereavement counselors, social workers, or a funeral home director can be contacted for information about local requirements concerning burial or cremation. A representative from a bereaved parents' support organization may be able to give you general information about your options. If the parents wish to follow the guidance of their faith, their clergyperson or the hospital chaplain should be consulted for help in making funeral arrangements.

Funeral directors often provide services at a minimal cost to families who have lost a very young child. Your hospital social worker or bereavement counselor should know about available sources of financial assistance. The hospital may offer burial or cremation services. However, it's wise to ask exactly what the hospital's policy is so that you can be certain your baby's body will be cared for in a way that is acceptable to you.

Support for Parents Who Have Lost a Child

Many parents who have lost a child feel very alone and isolated, especially after family and friends have paid their condolences and have begun to go on with their lives. The deep, unique grief felt at the loss of a child cannot be compared to any other type of grief, and your loss of your child cannot be compared to any other parent's loss. However, many parents find it helpful to speak with others who have had a similar experience. Those who have also lost a baby are perhaps the only people who can truly empathize with what you are feeling. Bereaved parents' organizations can refer you to a support group where you can express your grief without fear of judgment. Of course, support groups are not for everyone, and not all support groups will meet everyone's immediate needs. If you are interested in attending a support group, you may want to first talk to the group leader. Ask whether the group is facilitated by a professional, what her or his credentials are, and what types of loss group members have experienced. You may want to attend once or twice to get a sense of whether the group will be helpful to you.

There are times when the extra support of a counselor or therapist experienced in issues of perinatal loss or bereavement can be helpful. Your health care provider or hospital bereavement counselor can give you the name of a therapist, or you can gather referrals to experienced therapists by attending a bereaved parents' group.

You and Your Partner

If you are part of a couple, you may be aware of the challenges to a relationship that the loss of a child can create. Although many couples become closer as a result of their experience, grief and loss can also strain a relationship. You may find yourself confronted with expectations from your partner about the way you should grieve or find that you have expectations about your partner's response. It's important to remember that individuals can grieve the same loss differently. When these differences are not understood and respected, relationships can suffer. Sometimes people who respond to loss by crying openly and talking about their emotions feel that this is the only way in which grief is expressed. But grief does not always display itself as expected. You or your partner may not be comfortable talking about painful feelings. Men are especially subject to cultural pressures not to convey emotion and to appear strong and impassive. A man may respond to loss by trying to put the experience quickly behind him and may worry about his partner and the intensity of her grief. Because your partner hasn't experienced the same physical attachment to your baby as you did during your pregnancy, he or she may also have a less tangible relationship with your child. If you had a complicated pregnancy experience, your partner's grief over the loss of your child may be mixed with relief and gratitude that your life was spared.

If your partner's response is different from yours, it may make you feel as though he or she doesn't care or isn't grieving for your child. It's important not to make these assumptions. To prevent misunderstandings, talk honestly with your partner. Describe your feelings. Respect your partner's style of grieving. If it's possible, put aside a little time each day to be together to share your feelings or to be close without words. If your partner cannot be with you or support you right now, reach out to other listening, caring people.

Talking to Your Other Children

Children also grieve. They often understand and feel more than they are able to express. If you have other children, it's important to help them by honestly explaining what happened in words they can understand and by answering their questions. Let them know that you love them and that you will be available to them. If you are feeling overwhelmed by grief and would like help attending to the needs of your other children, ask a close friend or relative to step in and look after them for part of the day. Because it's very common for young children to believe that their negative thoughts or feelings can cause bad things to happen, they must be reassured that nothing they said, did, or felt caused the baby to die. Children may find death frightening and confusing. Your love can help them through this very difficult time, and their love can help you.

There are books that can help children understand this loss in age-appropriate terms. You, your partner, or a close friend or relative may find reading with your child to be a helpful way of sharing feelings. Some suggestions are given at the end of the book. The loss of a child can create feelings of extreme vulnerability. It's not unusual for parents who have lost a child to be very fearful for the safety of their surviving children and the other people they love. Likewise, it's natural to feel angry or irritated with those close to you, including your surviving children. Recognizing these feelings as a natural part of grief may help you to cope with them.

Your Family and Friends

Many people feel uncomfortable talking about the death of a child. It's hard to know what to do or say. Although family members and close friends may be grieving themselves, they may unintentionally say things that don't help you very much, such as, "You can always have another baby" or "It's probably for the best." In these instances, it's very likely that others are looking for a way to ease your pain and don't mean to trivialize your loss. But it's all right to tell others what you need, how they can help you, and what is unhelpful. If your hospital or other helping agency provides follow-up telephone or home visits with a staff person, you may want to ask the caregiver to talk to you and to your family members about ways to get through this crisis together.

The death of a child has a different meaning for each family member, because each had a different relationship to the child. Friends and family members may not have had the same feelings about your pregnancy or may not have known your child in the same way that you did. If you were at the beginning of your pregnancy when you lost your child, some people may not have been aware that you were pregnant. Because their attachment to your child is different from yours, those you love may be able to move on from the loss sooner than you can. This doesn't mean that they didn't care about your baby; it just means that their experience was different.

Someone You Care About Lost a Child

The loss of a child affects everyone close to the child and to the parents. Grandparents often suffer a double burden, grieving the loss of their grandchild and suffering as their

---

HOW TO HELP SOMEONE WHO HAS LOST A CHILD

Here are a few simple things you can do to help someone who is grieving the loss of a child. For additional information on ways friends and family members can be of help following a death, please see Chapter Ten.

- Listen. Parents may need to talk about their loss many times. Take your cues from your friend or relative. If she or he doesn't want to talk, don't force conversation. Let your loved one know that you will continue to be available to listen.
- Remember that you cannot take away someone else's pain, nor should you try. Rather than philosophy, parents may appreciate a heartfelt "I'm sorry."
- Avoid statements like, "You can always have another baby," or "Just be glad the child wasn't older when you would have been more attached." Many people feel awkward and unsure of how to respond when someone suffers a loss, but these statements, though well meaning, can be very hurtful. Remember that children cannot be "replaced," that every child is special, that some couples may not want to or be able to have other children, and that no phrase, however well crafted, can ease the pain of loss.
- As time passes, don't be afraid to speak about your loved one's child, to refer to him or her by name, and to acknowledge the anniversary of his or her birth and death. Understandably, you may not want to upset your friend or relative by bringing up the child, but she or he may already be sad and distraught. When others are afraid to acknowledge a child's life, it may seem to the parent as though they are denying the child's existence. Parents may cherish the opportunity to talk about the fond and painful memories they have.
- Allow your friend or relative time to grieve. Many grief experts say that it is normal for parents to need one to three years, or more time, to begin to recover from the loss of a child.

Try not to measure the depth of your loved one's grief by the age of the child who died. The meaning of loss is different for each person. At the same time, it's important not to judge a person's style of grieving. Everyone grieves in her own way and in her own time.

---

own children mourn. When a baby dies at a daycare center or in the hospital, caregivers are also profoundly affected and may feel tremendous guilt and grief. If you are a grandparent, other relative, friend, or caregiver, you may find it helpful to talk to others about your loss and the emotions you're experiencing. In some areas, support groups are available for grandparents or caregivers. In some cases, significant others affected by the death of a child may participate in support groups for parents. A national or local support organization, hospital social worker, or counselor may be able to refer you to a group in your area.

SPECIAL SITUATIONS

STILLBIRTH AND THE DEATH OF A NEWBORN

Stillbirth is defined as the loss of an infant during pregnancy any time after twenty weeks' gestation. Although it is not uncommon for a woman who is grieving to wonder whether she did anything to cause her baby's death, it is very unlikely that the stillbirth could have been prevented. In more than half of all stillbirths, no explanation for the baby's death can be offered.[12] When a cause can be determined, there are a number of possibilities, for example, stillbirth can result from a congenital defect or chromosomal abnormality, or a knot or other problem with the umbilical cord, maternal hypertension (preeclampsia), or separation of the placenta from the uterus and subsequent hemorrhage.

When a newborn dies just after birth or some time after, there may also be definable causes. Premature delivery, chromosomal defects, and infectious illness are some of the causes of neonatal death. Even when causes can be defined, as with stillbirth, they are often completely outside a mother's or father's control. It can be very difficult to accept the lack of control that we have over life and death, especially when the loss of a much loved, much wanted child causes so much pain. Although you may know that you are not to blame, it can be very difficult to accept this emotionally. It's natural to want to find a reason for your baby's death, even if only by blaming yourself. Talking with your doctor, asking as many questions as you have, spending time with supportive listeners and writing in a journal are good ways to help release the feelings of guilt that are a natural part of the grieving process. Even if you think that there is something you could have done differently, try not to be hard on yourself. No one ever deserves to lose a child.

Sudden Infant Death Syndrome (SIDS)

Sudden infant death syndrome (SIDS) is "the sudden death of an infant under one year of age which remains unexplained after a thorough postmortem case investigation, including performance of a complete autopsy, examination of the death scene, and review of the clinical history."[13] Sometimes called "crib death," SIDS is estimated to take the lives of about 3,500 to 5,000 infants each year. It is the leading cause of death among babies between one month and one year of age and occurs most commonly between the ages of two and four months.

The loss of an infant to SIDS is sudden and inexplicable. One moment an apparently healthy baby is put down to sleep and minutes or hours later he or she is found dead. There are no signs of suffering, no cries, no warnings. Without any apparent reason, a child is taken and a family is altered forever.

Not knowing why your baby died, not having a clear answer, may be agonizing. SIDS is often referred to as a diagnosis of exclusion. In other words, examiners must rule out other causes of death before a SIDS diagnosis can be made. Although researchers aren't sure what causes SIDS, it is very clear from thirty years of ongoing research that SIDS is not contagious, it is not hereditary, and it is not caused by vomiting or choking, minor illnesses such as colds, or from vaccines or child abuse.[14] At present, SIDS is not predictable or preventable. Parents do not cause SIDS. You are not at fault. You are not to blame. You did not cause your baby's death.

Even when you know that you are not to blame, the diagnosis of SIDS is difficult to accept. In the absence of a clearly defined cause of death, it is natural to blame yourself, your doctor, your partner, or others. Many parents of children who die of SIDS feel an abiding sense of guilt. You may replay the moment in which your infant died or was found dead over and again in your mind and be plagued by a constant sense that had you done something differently — not gone back to work, not taken your child to daycare, or checked your child once more in the middle of the night — she or he might have lived. We know that SIDS is not caused by anything parents or caregivers do or do not do. While the feeling of guilt is a natural part of grief, it is very important to talk many times with supportive family members, clergy, friends, nurses, bereavement counselors, and/or other parents who have lost a child to SIDS before you can begin to acknowledge that you are not to blame and that you did not fail your child.

Although the exact cause(s) of SIDS have eluded scientists for years, most believe that it is likely SIDS has more than one cause and that there are different conditions that make infants more vulnerable. Medical research is currently focused on cardiac causes, respiratory causes, and other physiologic or metabolic crises. Yet the medical model of research hasn't succeeded in finding the cause(s) of SIDS. Newer theories suggest that SIDS is an interaction of developmental, physiologic, and environmental factors.[15]

Autopsy plays a vital role in establishing a SIDS diagnosis and in aiding SIDS research. An autopsy can be used to rule out other possible causes of death, such as major infection or a congenital disorder, and can provide assurance that any cause of death determination is accurate. It can also help parents better understand a SIDS diagnosis and may relieve parents of the feeling that they caused or contributed to their child's death. However, some parents are disturbed by the prospect of autopsy, especially when a child has endured prolonged medical procedures.

In many areas, an autopsy is required whenever anyone, including a child, dies suddenly or unexpectedly. In some areas an autopsy is required before a SIDS diagnosis can be entered on the death certificate. However, in a few places an autopsy may not be done unless parents request it. You may have to ask for the autopsy results, but in most cases you should be told the results as soon as possible.

Some parents don't want to see the autopsy report; others have a strong desire for this information. Because grief is unpredictable, and you may not know how you'll feel when the autopsy report is completed, ask your doctor how you will receive the report. You may want to find out whether the report will be or can be sent to your health care provider rather than to your home. If you have a good relationship with your provider and feel comfortable discussing important issues with him or her, you can make an appointment to meet and discuss the results. This way you can better control when and how you hear the information. The coroner/medical examiner or the public health nurse may also be able to meet with you and explain the results.

In many jurisdictions, death scene investigations are done by the police or investigators as a routine response to any sudden or unexpected death. The death scene investigation can, along with autopsy, help the coroner or medical examiner make a proper diagnosis. Some officials may refer to the death scene investigation as a crime scene investigation, although usually it is not the latter. Professionals can help by being sensitive to the shock and grief felt by parents by treating the baby with respect and care, and by explaining what they are doing and why.

Although it can be extremely upsetting, a death scene investigation and history taken from family members and others may help you in the long run by allowing you the opportunity to give as much information as you have to investigators and possibly by providing you with the knowledge that the utmost was done to determine the cause of your baby's death. It's important to get as much information as you can about the investigation and to ask as many questions as you want to. If there are problems with the investigation, you may want to contact the state SIDS program or another support organization for guidance.

When a child dies of SIDS, parents may have limited or no contact with a hospital and thus may be unable to avail themselves of bereavement programs established for hospital patients and their families. Although many families receive strong and loving support from relatives and friends and from their places of worship, there are additional sources of help. In many states, SIDS programs are available to help parents in crisis and to educate the public about SIDS. Often available through the state and local health departments or independent, professional programs, SIDS programs may provide parents and others with crisis intervention, counseling, education about SIDS, and support groups or referrals to support groups and peer contacts. Depending on where you live and the program, a nurse or social worker may visit you in your home, if you wish. You may also be able to speak with another parent who has lost an infant to SIDS. Talking with others who've had a similar experience can be extremely helpful.

Sometimes, doctors or members of the emergency room staff will contact a SIDS program on the family's behalf. The coroner or medical examiner may also notify the state SIDS program of your loss or refer you to the program. The program may then contact you by letter or by telephone to let you know how they can help. You or a trusted relative or friend may want to contact such programs personally.

SIDS is a medical event that is seldom discussed, and misinformation and myths about SIDS are still prevalent. Thus, you and your loved ones may want to have additional, accurate information about sudden infant death syndrome. The National Sudden Infant Death Syndrome Resource Center, the Sudden Infant Death Syndrome Alliance, and other organizations listed in the Resource Directory may prove a useful source of information about SIDS, its possible causes, state SIDS programs, and issues of concern to grieving parents. Support groups can also provide written information about SIDS and the ways in which the death of a child can affect each member of the family.

For Parents Facing a Prenatal Diagnosis

The intensity of the grief felt by parents facing a prenatal diagnosis of a genetic or fetal abnormality is as profound as the grief felt by other bereaved parents. Yet there are issues that may be of particular importance to parents who are given the additional responsibility of choosing to continue or interrupt their pregnancy.

Choosing to continue or interrupt a much wanted pregnancy may have been one of the most difficult decisions of your life. You may have begun to grieve as soon as you received your child's diagnosis and may have mourned or may be mourning all the dreams and plans that you had for your child and for your family. Although feelings of responsibility, guilt, and self-blame are a natural part of the grieving process, these feelings may be greatly magnified for a woman or couple who are faced with a decision to continue or interrupt their pregnancy.

You may have had very little time to think about your options. Both decisions — to continue your pregnancy or to interrupt your pregnancy — may have given rise to intensely painful experiences. If you chose to interrupt your pregnancy, you may have had to endure procedures for second-trimester pregnancy interruption, which can be both physically and emotionally traumatic. Although procedures done earlier in pregnancy may be less physically painful, they are no less emotionally wrenching. If you chose to continue your pregnancy, you may have had scant information about how to manage day to day and little support to help you prepare for your child's birth.

Parents may receive a tremendous amount of love and support from family, friends, and their clergypeople. But this is not always so. Those who would ordinarily be a part of your support system may have a hard time helping you either because they are unaware of the traumatic nature of your experience or because they may have negative feelings about pregnancy interruption or your decision to continue your pregnancy. Your own religious, spiritual, or personal beliefs may have made your decision particularly complex.

If you have been through this experience, you may appreciate the information and support available from organizations for bereaved parents. *A Heartbreaking Choice* is a newsletter for parents who have interrupted a pregnancy because of a prenatal diagnosis. Abiding Hearts provides support for parents who have chosen to continue a pregnancy. Pen Parents, also listed in the directory, can provide you with information about these services.

If you are facing a decision related to prenatal diagnosis now, it's important to talk with your doctor, a geneticist, and a genetic counselor for as much information as possible. Generally, your obstetrician will be able to make a referral to a local genetics center. Otherwise, you may want to contact the National Society of Genetic Counselors, listed in the Resource Directory, or a university human genetics department for possible referrals. The additional opinions of a perinatologist (a doctor who specializes in the care of mother and child, especially during high-risk pregnancies) and a neonatologist may also further your decision-making process. It's important to discuss the meaning of the diagnosis for you (and your partner), your child, and your family, as well as the medical, social, financial, emotional, spiritual, and religious considerations affecting your decision and the parenting issues that may be involved. Each element of your decision has far-reaching consequences. You should not be pressured into a decision that only you (and your partner) can make. You may also want to discuss the meaning of this diagnosis for future pregnancies.

In addition to a second medical opinion, you may find the support and guidance needed to make this most difficult decision by talking with trusted friends and relatives, your clergyperson, and/or others who have been placed in a similar position. Your doctor or genetic counselor may be able to arrange a meeting or conversation with other parents who are willing to share their experiences.

If your child has been diagnosed with a specific disorder, you may want to contact support and advocacy groups dedicated to serving the needs of people with similar disabilities or conditions. The March of Dimes and other organizations providing information about birth defects are also good resources to help enhance your understanding of your child's condition and its challenges. (See the Resource Directory listings under Disabilities.)

Although not necessarily a less emotionally painful alternative, adoption may be an option for some parents. Some parents who are considering carrying their child to term may want to know what their child will look like and how they can best prepare to welcome their child into their family and to say good-bye. Once again, medical professionals and Abiding Hearts can be helpful resources.

Finally, you may also want to consult the reading resource list at the end of this book for titles that explore in greater depth the decision-making process related to prenatal diagnosis.

Multifetal Pregnancy Reduction (Selective Reduction)

With the advent and increased use of reproductive technology, women who have endured the considerable stress related to infertility and the struggle to conceive are being faced with a new and painful dilemma. Whether facilitated by reproductive technology or not, women who are pregnant with multiple children may be presented with a choice between continuing a multiple pregnancy and risking extreme prematurity, with its possible consequences of newborn death or illness, or terminating some fetuses in order to try to protect the health and lives of as many of the others as possible. Very real economic and parenting issues may also be part of a decision to undergo selective reduction.

For many parents, the decision is an agonizing one. You may have spent months, even years, enduring the emotionally and physically trying process of infertility treatment. You may have expected or may not have been told about the risk of conceiving multiple children, or you may have already been through a selective reduction and fear going through it again. If you are facing this decision now, ask for as much time as possible to consider it. Only you (and your partner) can make this choice. You should not be pressured. Because the decision is one that may stay with you for many years, it's likely that you will want as much information about the medical and emotional risks of the procedure suggested to you.

You may be anxious about pain during the procedure and extremely concerned about the risks of losing all of the children you're carrying. It's important to learn as much as you can about the risks of delivering prematurely and of miscarriage with or without the procedure. Ask for information about the health risks for children who are born prematurely and about the signs of premature labor. Equally necessary are conversations about your religious or spiritual beliefs regarding pregnancy termination.

Parents are often referred by their physicians to genetic counselors, who can aid in their decision-making processes. If you are not referred, you may want to try to locate a genetic counselor on your own. Look for a genetic counselor experienced in working with parents with higher multiple births and, if possible, someone who has personal experience with multifetal pregnancy reduction. The National Society of Genetic Counselors, listed in the Resource Directory, may be able to provide referrals for you to investigate, or you may be able to get a referral from a genetic counselor in your community. You can also contact university medical centers with human genetics departments for referrals.

If feasible, it's a good idea to seek a second opinion. Thus, in addition to talking to a geneticist and genetic counselor, you may want to speak with a neonatal doctor and a perinatologist for further opinions on prognosis. You may also want to ask your doctor or genetic counselor about the possibility of arranging a conversation with a woman or couple of similar background who went through the procedure you are contemplating.

If you have had a multifetal reduction, you may feel or may have felt acute grief. Even if you know that you made the best decision that you could and with the best interests of your children in mind, you may still feel sadness and guilt. You may think about your lost children often, wondering about them and longing for them. It may be difficult to hear glowing media reports of multiple births or to see others' twins, triplets, or higher multiples. Feelings of grief may be mixed with happiness at the birth of your surviving child(ren). But if you later lost one, more, or all of your children, your grief may be intense and abiding. If you endured infertility treatments or had a difficult pregnancy, you may feel anger not only at the injustice of your loss but at the seemingly vain investment of emotion, pain, time, income, and effort made in order to become a mother. Your religious or spiritual beliefs may have made your decision all the more difficult. This may be especially true if others who are close to you could not support or discuss your decision because of their beliefs.

Remember that each individual's experience is completely different and that there is no right or wrong way to feel. You may have some or none of these feelings. It may help to talk with your partner, trusted family members, friends, or others whom you believe to be supportive and caring. For very personal reasons, some women and couples choose never to discuss their decision to undergo selective reduction. Yet more and more women are writing about their experiences. The Center for Loss in Multiple Birth (CLIMB) and Pen Parents, listed in the Resource Directory, offer a forum for parents who have experienced loss. You may want to connect with these or other organizations or to look at some of the literature in the Recommended Reading list on pages 620 to 622. Books that discuss selective reduction often contain writings by women who have been through the experience. Reading their stories and knowing that you are not alone may bring you some comfort.

Miscarriage

A miscarriage is the spontaneous loss of a pregnancy before twenty weeks' gestation. Statistics suggest that about one in every five or six confirmed pregnancies will end in miscarriage, although the overall rate of miscarriage may be even higher.[16] Certainly, statistics mean little when you have lost your child, but they are presented here to let you know that you are not alone.

Doctors commonly refer to miscarriages as "spontaneous abortions" and categorize them according to type. The word "abortion" may trigger a strong emotional response, but in this instance, it is not meant to refer to the controversial procedure. Although medical terminology is used here to help you better understand miscarriage and request information from your doctor, the language can sometimes be hurtful and can contribute to a sense of loss and failure. Remember that medical terms are just words and do not reflect on your worth as a woman.

A *threatened miscarriage* describes a situation in which a woman experiences symptoms of miscarriage but her cervix remains closed. When miscarriage is threatened, a woman has about a 50 percent chance of completing a healthy pregnancy. An *inevitable miscarriage* has occurred once the cervix has already begun to dilate. Upon examination, a doctor will be able to tell you if this is happening. When a miscarriage is inevitable, a considerable amount of bleeding and cramping may have already taken place, and you may have already passed tissue. A *blighted ovum* is the term used when a woman miscarries a pregnancy in which only the placenta, but no fetus, has formed in her uterus. This condition is just as traumatic for a woman as any other type of pregnancy loss. An *incomplete miscarriage* occurs when some of the fetal tissue and/or blood clots are not completely expelled and remain in the uterus after a miscarriage. In this case, a woman usually experiences prolonged bleeding and cramping and will require a D&C (dilatation and curettage) to remove the remaining products of conception. A *missed miscarriage* results when the fetus dies in the womb but is not expelled. There are often no symptoms. But the signs of pregnancy diminish with time. In this case, a D&C or induction of labor may be suggested depending on the length of your pregnancy.

What Causes a Miscarriage?

Although the causes of miscarriage are largely unknown, some possible causes are understood. For example, miscarriage can be caused by chromosomal abnormalities or by an infection. Both of these possibilities can usually be determined by testing tissue recovered from the miscarriage. Fetal genetic abnormalities are the most common causes of miscarriage early in pregnancy, and although they are less likely to be causes as pregnancy progresses, they can still cause a loss as late as the third trimester.

Some other possible causes of miscarriage include a hormonal imbalance, a uterine abnormality, problems with your cervix, certain immunologic factors, and exposure to environmental toxins. Remember, however, that in most cases, your doctor may not be able to give you a reason why your baby died.

Generally, women who have had one miscarriage have about the same chance of having a healthy pregnancy and baby as women who have never had a miscarriage. After two or more miscarriages, the chances of a subsequent miscarriage slowly begin to increase. However, even after two miscarriages, there is still a very good chance that the next pregnancy will be successful. Although some doctors advocate tests after two miscarriages, most will begin doing some work-up to help determine the cause after three miscarriages.

Your Feelings After Miscarriage

The depth of a woman's grief is not determined by the length or circumstances of her pregnancy. You may have begun to envision and build upon your life with your child when your happiness was devastated. You may feel betrayed by your body and very wounded in your sense of yourself as a woman and as a mother. Family and friends may not realize what your pregnancy meant to you and may not be fully able to understand and empathize with your grief.

You have a right to cry and to mourn. On the other hand, you may not feel grief, or you may feel some, but not all, of the feelings associated with loss. There is no right or wrong way to react to the experience of miscarriage.

Many women feel a sense of guilt after a miscarriage and

search for ways in which they might have contributed to their loss. It's not uncommon to wonder whether having sexual intercourse, engaging in too much activity, having had a drink or two during your pregnancy or before you knew you were pregnant, or being under a great deal of stress might have caused your miscarriage. Generally, it's very unlikely these activities will be defined as the source of your loss. Yet, it's important to talk to your doctor about any activities that you feel may have contributed to your miscarriage, for example, regular alcohol or other drug use or episodes of illness. She or he can help you understand whether these factors are potentially significant and discuss their relevance to any plans that you have for future pregnancies. Although you may know that you shouldn't blame yourself, you may need time to talk to supportive people and to express these normal feelings in order to work through them. Writing about your feelings in a journal, meeting with other women who have lost children through miscarriage, and reading about miscarriage can also help you to heal emotionally.

ECTOPIC PREGNANCY

Ectopic pregnancy is any pregnancy that develops outside of the uterus. It is a very dangerous condition that causes the loss of a fetus and puts a woman at risk of life-threatening hemorrhage. Undetected ectopic pregnancy is one of the leading causes of death in pregnant women.

Ectopic pregnancies will rarely develop in the abdomen, ovary, or cervix; most often ectopics occur within the fallopian tube. This is sometimes called tubal pregnancy. Ectopic pregnancies are more likely to occur in a tube in which there is some abnormality. Women who have had pelvic inflammatory disease (PID), tubal surgery, or a previous ectopic pregnancy; women whose mothers took DES (diethylstilbestrol) while they were pregnant or who were born with an abnormality of the fallopian tube; women with endometriosis; and women using an IUD are at greater risk. If you have pelvic pain and irregular bleeding — especially if you've missed your last period or if you have any risk factors for ectopic pregnancy — contact your doctor or go to the nearest hospital emergency room immediately. Some women with ectopics may feel extremely nauseous, vomit, develop a fever, feel very weak or faint, or pass out. Occasionally, women feel pain in the shoulder as well. When you get to the emergency room, make sure that the staff members are aware of the severity of your symptoms. Do not allow them to let you wait. Ectopic pregnancy is a medical emergency.

If it was necessary to remove one of your fallopian tubes because of an ectopic pregnancy, you won't be able to get pregnant when an egg is released from the ovary on the same side where the tube was removed. However, it is still usually possible to get pregnant when the egg is released on the other side. Overall, women who have had an ectopic pregnancy have about a 30 to 40 percent chance of having a future successful pregnancy.[17] If, on the other hand, an ectopic is found early and the fallopian tube is saved, the likelihood of having a subsequent intrauterine pregnancy is higher.[18] There is also about a 10 to 20 percent chance of having another ectopic pregnancy.[19]

If you have had recurrent ectopic pregnancies and/or you have lost both fallopian tubes, you may want to consider other options for motherhood. Facing the possibility of infertility is extraordinarily painful for many women and couples, but there are possibilities. You may want to start a search by contacting the organization RESOLVE, the largest nationwide support group for people facing an infertility crisis, at (617) 623-0744. Adoption is also an option to consider.

Your Feelings After an Ectopic Pregnancy

It's natural to grieve the loss of a child because of an ectopic pregnancy. Because you may have also been through a medical crisis, your concerns may first center on the near loss of your life, the experience of surgery and hospitalization, and worries about your reproductive health. You may mourn the loss of your fertility. Feelings of grief may emerge months later, especially around the time when your baby would have been born, or you may not have an emotional response. If you had surgery, you may grieve the loss of part of your body and, if you have any scarring, changes in your physical appearance. Everyone responds to an ectopic pregnancy in her own way. There is no "right" way to feel.

Discussing your feelings with others who care about you, involving yourself in a support group for people who have had a pregnancy or infant loss, and reading about ectopic pregnancy are good ways to begin to heal from your experience. Having information about the way in which an ectopic pregnancy will affect your future reproductive capacity is necessary in order to discuss and weigh your options thoroughly with your doctor.

EMOTIONS AFTER THE ARRIVAL OF A NEW CHILD

The arrival of a new child by birth, adoption, or other means is a major life event, one that is usually followed by a significant period of adjustment. For some women, the transition into motherhood is relatively uneventful; for others it can be extremely challenging.

The joys and rewards of early motherhood are easily extolled, but the struggles remain largely undiscussed. There are many myths about motherhood which, if left unaddressed, can impair a mother's sense of confidence and create serious disappointments. For instance, many women are told that the early days of mothering are always smooth and blissful, that mothers instantly bond with their children and will "just know" how to care for them from the start of their long relationship. In reality, mothering is a stressful job, and mothering skills must be learned. There is no such thing as a perfect parent — all parents make mistakes. Bonding does not always happen right away; it can take a little time to develop.

All mothers need support. If you are planning a pregnancy, are pregnant or have a new baby, think about who can help you during the first few months after your baby is born. For example, is there someone in your family, your husband/partner, mother, grandmother, sister, aunt — or in your community — a trusted friend, neighbor, or other mother — who can stay with you during the day, do a chore or two, watch the baby while you nap, look after your other young children, or fix a meal for you? Do you have older children who can be enlisted to help around the house or run an errand? Can you hire a young person to go to the market for you or do some cleaning after school? If you are enrolled in childbirth classes, ask other women what they're going to do to make the postpartum period easier. Childbirth education programs may also offer formal support groups for new mothers. In some communities, home visitation programs are available for new or young families. A home visitor, who may be a trained volunteer or professional, can offer you emotional support and information about parenting and childcare techniques and help you find community resources that might be valuable to you. Although home visitation programs generally focus on the needs of families with low incomes, they are becoming increasingly available to all families. To find out if there is a home visitation program in your area, contact the social work department of a local children's hospital, a well-baby or family clinic, or a social service agency serving families.

Although more costly, a Visiting Nurse Association (usually listed in the yellow pages of your telephone directory) can provide daily homemaker services to new mothers. Another very valuable resource for the new mother is the doula. Doulas are professional nonmedical caregivers who can provide new mothers with a wide variety of services, including meal preparation, light housekeeping, breast-feeding consultation, and ideas and information about baby care. For more information about doulas you can call the National Association of Postpartum Care Services, listed in the Resource Directory.

Asking for support does *not* mean that you are an inadequate mother. This important point cannot be overemphasized. You may have to consciously work at allowing yourself to ask for what you need without feeling guilty or like a failure. When family members or friends offer to help, tell them exactly what you would like them to do. Try not to feel as though you must entertain those who come to help you. If possible, try not to rely on relatives or friends who will be a greater source of stress than assistance. If you can't avoid this, be clear about what will be helpful to you and what will be hurtful. Have this discussion before the baby arrives. You may want to ask for the support of an objective but close friend who can advocate for your wishes without causing more friction in the family.

Becoming knowledgeable about emotional changes after birth is another necessary part of every woman's postpartum planning. The following section will discuss some common feelings after childbirth, including the "baby blues" and postpartum disorders.

Postpartum disorders

Emotional upheaval after the birth of a baby is very common and usually occurs quite unexpectedly. Signs of depression, anxiety, or in very rare cases, psychosis may surface even after a positive and much anticipated birth. Women are rarely warned about these conditions either by family members, friends, or medical professionals, yet when they occur, they can be devastating. Postpartum reactions can affect women of every age, social and economic class, and cultural background. Single women and married women are equally vulnerable. Postpartum disorders can strike new mothers and veteran moms alike.

Although this section focuses on the self-resolving "baby blues," on postpartum depression and postpartum psychosis, postpartum disorders actually occur along a continuum and include postpartum panic disorder, postpartum obsessive-compulsive disorder, and postpartum fatigue.

Symptoms of a postpartum disorder may not always be consistent; they may ebb and flow from day to day and may range from mild to severe. One type of postpartum reaction may overlap with or be followed by another.

Having a postpartum disorder does not mean that you are a bad mother or that you cannot parent. It does not mean that you are weak, incompetent, or that you are any less of a woman. Postpartum disorders are real, treatable illnesses.

The "Baby Blues"

Postpartum blues, often referred to as the "baby blues" are extremely common, affecting up to about 50 to 80 percent of new mothers. Signs and symptoms include sadness, crying, anxiety, irritability, anger, and mood swings. Onset usually occurs around the second or third day after delivery. The baby blues require no specific treatment and usually resolve with support, love, rest, and by finding a little time for yourself. However, symptoms that do not resolve after a week or two may be a sign of postpartum depression.

Postpartum Depression

Postpartum depression may begin soon after birth or up to six months to a year later. About 10 to over 20 percent of new mothers will experience postpartum depression. Possible symptoms of a postpartum disorder include:

- nervousness, worry, anxiety, panic attacks
- crying, sadness, a sense of hopelessness
- irritability
- extreme fatigue
- marked changes in sleeping and eating habits
- lack of concentration, confusion
- pronounced anxiety about the baby's well-being
- anger at or absence of feeling for the baby
- mood swings
- fear of hurting yourself or the baby

Postpartum Psychosis

Postpartum psychosis is a much rarer disorder, affecting about one to two new mothers in every thousand, usually within the first two to three weeks after delivery. Symptoms of postpartum psychosis may include hearing sounds or voices that are not there (hallucinations), extreme confusion, clearly irrational beliefs (delusions), obtrusive thoughts, insomnia, refusal to eat, excessive energy, loss of memory, and fear of harming yourself or the baby. *Postpartum psychosis is a medical emergency.* If you are having any of these symptoms, you must seek help immediately. Call your doctor or have someone take you to the emergency department of the nearest hospital right away. Postpartum psychosis requires immediate medical attention and hospitalization until you can care for yourself and your baby again.

What Causes a Postpartum Disorder?

The causes of postpartum disorders are not known, but it is widely believed that the enormous hormonal changes that occur after childbirth are a significant contributing factor. As well, stress and the emotional, psychological, sociological, and environmental factors associated with or triggered by the arrival of a new child may contribute to or cause a postpartum disorder. For some women postpartum reactions may be due entirely to biological causes. It's also important to note that some purely physical conditions, for example, a thyroid disorder, can mimic postpartum depression. Psychosocial and biological factors may work together to create postpartum distress. As well, the causes may have no biologic aspect. Adoptive mothers, for example, are just as vulnerable to the stress and complications of being a new parent as mothers who have given birth.

Although there are known risk factors for postpartum disorders, most women have no comparable experience in their histories and do not anticipate having a postpartum reaction. Having a risk factor in your life does not mean that you will have a postpartum reaction, only that you may be more vulnerable.

Possible risk factors for postpartum disorders include:

* history of postpartum depression, or history in a blood relative, such as a mother or sister
* history of depression, manic-depressive illness (bipolar disorder), or other mental illness
* a difficult or unexpected childbirth experience, for ex-

ample, having a cesarean section, having a premature delivery, a child with a disability, or twins
- grief over the loss of a child
- other crises, such as a new move or the loss of a family member around the time of the child's arrival
- sleep deprivation
- unrealistic expectations of motherhood
- an unsupportive or abusive partner
- problems in your relationship or marriage
- unresolved past issues, including difficulties in your relationships with your parents or child abuse and/or neglect

TREATMENT OF POSTPARTUM DISORDERS

When unrecognized and untreated, postpartum disorders can worsen and cause considerable suffering. One of the barriers to recognizing a postpartum reaction is the difficulty in diagnosis. Therefore, it's best to work with a professional who is knowledgeable about postpartum disorders. Assessment and treatment should be individualized and based on the type and severity of symptoms. Depending on the diagnosis and the individual, treatment may consist of education about postpartum disorders, participation in a support group, bolstering the support and nurturing that you are able to receive at home, psychotherapy, and medication. For more information about postpartum depression and medication, talk to your doctor. You may also want to contact Depression After Delivery, listed below, or look at the reading list.

If you think that you may be experiencing a postpartum reaction, contact your family practitioner, obstetrician, or nurse midwife. Your doctor or nurse may refer you to another professional, such as a psychiatrist, psychologist, or social worker. National support organizations can also provide you with referrals to knowledgeable professionals. When interviewing professionals you might ask how frequently they see women with postpartum disorders in their practice and whether they are familiar with the various treatment possibilities. Seek someone who makes you feel comfortable and with whom you can speak freely.

Unfortunately, there is still a stigma attached to the notion of working with a mental health professional. Family and friends may urge you to just "snap out of it" or "pull yourself together" and may belittle your attempts to find the appropriate, sensitive care that you need. It's critical to take care of yourself during this time. Fearing that others will disapprove of your desire for professional assistance is no reason

---

HELP FOR WOMEN EXPERIENCING POSTPARTUM REACTIONS

Depression After Delivery: 1-800-944-4PPD (4773)

Postpartum Support, International: (805) 967-7636

These national support organizations offer educational packets, referrals to medical and mental health professionals, and connections with other women who have had a similar postpartum experience.

to continue suffering. Happiness is one of the best gifts that a woman can give herself, her child, and her family.

SEXUALLY TRANSMITTED DISEASES

Also see the section on HIV Infection and AIDS in Chapter Eight.

WHERE TO GET INFORMATION ABOUT STDs

The American Social Health Association (ASHA), a non-profit organization dedicated to the prevention and control of sexually transmitted diseases, provides the public with information about sexually transmitted diseases through its publications and programs. In addition to the following hot-line services, ASHA operates the HPV (human papilloma-virus) Support Program and the Women's Health Program.

The CDC National AIDS Hotline
1-800-342-AIDS (2437); 1-800-243-7889 (TTY);
1-800-344-7432 (Spanish)

Health communication specialists can answer basic questions about HIV/AIDS, HIV antibody testing, and AIDS service organizations. Services are available on the main number twenty-four hours a day, 365 days a year.

The National STD Hotline
1-800-227-8922

This national toll-free hotline offers basic information about STDs, free written information, and national referrals to clinics for testing and treatment from 8 A.M. to 11 P.M. EST Monday through Friday. All services are confidential. You will not be asked to give your name.

The National Herpes Hotline
(919) 361-8488

The Herpes Resource Center provides a range of services to the public including the National Herpes Hotline. The hotline operates Monday through Friday 9 A.M. to 7 P.M. EST. Trained health educators can provide basic and sensitive information about herpes prevention, transmission, treatment, and research as well as emotional issues related to herpes. Support groups, called HELP groups, are located in most metropolitan areas of the United States and Canada and in Australia. You can ask to have free information about herpes mailed to you in an unmarked envelope. All services are confidential. A quarterly journal, brochures, videos, and audiocassettes about herpes are also available.

ARE YOU AT RISK FOR STDS?

Many people are aware of the risks and gravity of human immunodeficiency virus (HIV) infection, but we often forget about the prevalence and seriousness of other diseases that can be transmitted sexually and/or through sharing needles. According to the American Social Health Association, about one in four adults in the United States has a sexually transmitted disease.[20] Anyone who has sex can contract an STD. This includes people of all ages, races, ethnic and religious backgrounds, incomes, and occupations. Women who have sex with men and women who have sex with women are at risk. Young adults and teenagers are at especially high risk for STDs. Women are more vulnerable to STDs than men. For example, women are ten to twenty times more likely to contract HIV from unprotected heterosexual sex than are men and twice as likely to contract gonorrhea and chlamydia.[21]

WHAT ARE THE SYMPTOMS OF STDS?

One of the most important facts to know about STDs is that, with many, there are often *no symptoms* in women or men. In fact, many women have no symptoms until they have severe disease. If symptoms do occur, they can appear immediately after the initial infection or weeks, months, or years later. Sometimes, symptoms come and go, but even if the symptoms do resolve, when no treatment is given, the disease may still be present. Keep in mind that when your partner has symptoms and you do not (or vice versa), you may both actually be infected and should both be seen by a health care provider as soon as possible.

Here is a list of symptoms of common STDs, reprinted with permission from the brochure *For Teens,* published by the American Social Health Association, a nonprofit organization dedicated to stopping STDs and their harmful consequences.

Symptoms of STDs in both men and women:

- sores, bumps, or blisters near your genitals or mouth
- burning and pain when you urinate

- swelling in the area around your sexual organs
- rectal itching, pain, or discharge
- a swelling or redness in your throat
- fever, chills, and aches

Symptoms of STDs in women:

- unusual discharge or smell from your vagina
- pain in your pelvic area (the area between your belly button and sex organs)
- burning or itching around your vagina
- bleeding from your vagina that is not your regular period
- pain deep inside your vagina when you have sex

Symptoms of STDs in men only:

- a drip or discharge from the penis

WHAT TO DO IF YOU THINK YOU HAVE AN STD

If you think that you have an STD or have been exposed to an STD, visit your doctor, clinic, or local health department right away. You may understandably be frightened, embarrassed, or angry, but these are not reasons to avoid protecting your health and the health of others. The consequences of an untreated sexually transmitted disease can be very serious. For example, if allowed to go untreated, STDs like gonorrhea, chlamydia, and syphilis can lead to infertility, chronic pain, ectopic pregnancy (a dangerous condition in which a fertilized egg implants outside the uterus), and in the case of syphilis, heart disease and blindness. Yet these same STDs are completely curable if treated early. (For information about specific STDs, see the section Common Sexually Transmitted Diseases.)

Many local health departments offer free or low-cost confidential testing. An advantage of going to a public health department clinic for testing and treatment may be that of not having to use your insurance. However, it's best to find out what the clinic's payment policies are ahead of time, especially if you are a member of a managed care plan. For the location of the public health department nearest you, call the National STD Hotline.

In most states, minors (persons under eighteen or twenty-one, depending on state law) do not need their parent/s' or guardian/s' consent to be tested and treated. However, state laws differ regarding physicians' ability to notify parents or guardians without a minor's consent after treatment.

If you are a young person, it's always best to talk to your health care provider about the need to notify your parent(s) or guardian(s).

IF YOU ARE PREGNANT . . .
CAN AN STD AFFECT YOUR BABY?

Infants can be infected with STDs if their mothers are infected and can suffer serious conditions, such as congenital defects, eye problems and blindness, and even death. Getting tested for sexually transmitted diseases like syphilis, hepatitis B, gonorrhea, and chlamydia is especially important if you are pregnant because the serious problems STDs can cause in infants can often be prevented or treated easily. Enrolling in early and ongoing prenatal care is very important. You should be tested for most common STDs in the course of your prenatal care, but be certain to discuss STD screening and testing for HIV infection with your health care provider. Do not assume that your doctor has tested you. This is especially true regarding testing for HIV infection. Often, you will need to sign a separate informed consent form to test for HIV. If you are pregnant and HIV-positive, important decisions must be made about treatment. For more information, see the section HIV Infection and AIDS in Chapter Eight. Also see the sections Common Sexually Transmitted Diseases and Take an Active Role in STD Prevention in this chapter.

YOUR EMOTIONS AND STDS

If you think you have an STD or you have been diagnosed with an STD, you may be shocked, ashamed, saddened, angry at yourself or at the person you believe transmitted the disease to you. Although an STD diagnosis may give rise to other issues in your relationship, it's important to stay calm and to deal with the health issue first. Remember, many people do not know that they have a sexually transmitted disease, even when they have given it to another. An STD can lie dormant for months or years without being detected. It's also possible for both partners to have an STD even when only one member of the couple has symptoms.

It's also important to remember that a sexually transmitted disease is just that — a disease — not a reflection of your moral character. Don't let a disease harm your sense of self-worth and sexuality. Millions of people have contracted STDs and have learned to cope with both the physical and emotional effects. They are ordinary people who came into contact with an STD.

Taking care of yourself includes attending to your emotional needs as well as your physical health. Be good to yourself during this time. Reach out to someone who can be a supportive listener and who will treat the information that you divulge with sensitivity, respect, and confidentiality. If you are feeling upset, anxious, or sad about having an STD, it can really help to talk to someone. If you don't feel comfortable talking to friends, family members, or others, call the National STD Hotline, listed at the beginning of this section. An operator can give you the number of a local crisis intervention hotline. If you have been diagnosed with herpes, contact the Herpes Resource Center to talk with a counselor.

You can also look in the front pages of your local telephone directory or call your operator for the telephone number of a crisis intervention line, if there is one in your area. There is no need to feel ashamed or embarrassed about calling. Volunteers on crisis lines are there to talk about almost any subject that concerns you.

You may also want to talk to a counselor or therapist. Chapter Seven, "Crises in Mental Health," offers information about finding and choosing mental health services, including services available at a low cost.

TELLING YOUR PARTNER

It's important to tell your partner(s) that you have a sexually transmitted disease and to name the disease. Without treatment your partner may suffer the devastating consequences of some STDs, such as infertility, and possibly infect others or continue to infect you. Lawsuits and even criminal charges have been filed against people who have lied about having an STD and who have knowingly infected their partners.

You may be apprehensive about your partner's reaction or you may be angry. Again, it's important to stay calm and to emphasize your concern for your partner's health and the necessity of diagnosis and treatment. If you are afraid that your partner may become violent or abusive when you disclose the information, contact a women's shelter or other women's advocacy program first to talk to an advocate. Women's shelters and advocacy programs will not ask you to come to a shelter. Advocates can, however, help you think about your options. For more information about shelters and advocacy programs for women, please see Chapter Four.

Although it will generally be your responsibility to tell your sexual or needle-sharing partner(s) that you have an STD so that your partner(s) can receive appropriate testing, counseling, and treatment, your local or state health department may be able to help you notify your partner anonymously, if you wish. You may give your health care provider the names of those to be notified so that she or he can supply them to the health department. Or, you may be interviewed by a professional from the health department, who will ask you for the names of those to be contacted. Partner notification may not be possible with every STD, but most states have partner notification programs for people with HIV infection, syphilis, gonorrhea, and chlamydia. Partner notification is completely confidential. Your identity will not be disclosed. (Also see the section HIV Infection and AIDS in Chapter Eight for information about partner notification and HIV/AIDS.)

All states require that cases of syphilis, gonorrhea, and AIDS be reported to the local or state health department. Requirements for other STDs vary from state to state. For example, HIV infection is reportable in some states. Reporting is done to assess the prevalence of sexually transmitted diseases as well as to try to ensure that exposed partners are treated. Reports are strictly confidential and may be done by your doctor or clinic or directly by the laboratory that processed your STD test. Your local health department should be able to tell you what sexually transmitted diseases must be reported in your state and what efforts are taken to try to contact partners.

PROTECTING YOURSELF FROM SEXUALLY TRANSMITTED DISEASES

You can contract a sexually transmitted disease from having vaginal, anal, or oral sex. The infectious organisms that cause many STDs are passed from one person to the other through bodily fluids, such as semen, vaginal secretions, and blood. However, some STDs, such as herpes and human papillomavirus, which causes genital warts, can be transmitted by simple skin-to-skin contact. Your chances of contracting an STD increase with the number of sexual partners you have and the number of times you have sex without using latex condoms or barriers.

The best way to protect yourself from STDs is, of course, by not having sex or by having sex with only one person who does not have an STD and who has sex only with you. Otherwise, the best way to protect yourself is by having your male partner(s) use latex condoms and other barrier protection methods, such as the female condom or dental dam, every time you have vaginal, anal, or oral sex. Barrier protection, such as dental dams, should be used by female partners. However, condoms and other latex barrier methods don't provide complete protection against herpes and genital warts (HPV), as these materials don't cover the entire genital area. This certainly doesn't mean that you should forgo condom use. Rather, you must take additional precautions if you or your partner have herpes or genital warts. (See the following sections pertaining to these conditions.) If you use a nonbarrier method of birth control, such as oral contraceptives, Norplant, Depo-Provera, or an IUD, it's important to remember that these methods provide protection against pregnancy, but little or no protection against STDs. Adding a barrier method, such as the male or female condom, to your usual nonbarrier method of birth control is necessary to help prevent STDs.

Spermicides, which can help prevent pregnancy, can kill some infectious agents, but not all. They should be used with condoms, not in place of condoms. Nonoxynol-9, an ingredient found in some spermicides, may provide some protection against infections for some women but may cause vaginal irritation. Talk to your doctor about whether Nonoxynol-9 is right for you.

Many women believe that douching will help prevent STDs, but the opposite may be true. It is thought that douching may push infectious organisms higher up in the reproductive tract, predisposing a woman to pelvic inflammatory disease, a serious complication of sexually transmitted infections.

You cannot always tell whether your partner has an STD by examining him or her. But it's always a good idea to look closely at your partner's genitals and surrounding areas for any open sores, rashes, bumps, discharge, redness, swelling in the groin, or anything else unusual. If you see anything unusual, don't have sex. If your partner does have signs or symptoms of an STD, he or she should be examined by a doctor and treated, if necessary.

The best type of condom to use is a male latex condom. The next best is the female condom, which is made of polyurethane. Contact your local pharmacy to learn whether female condoms are available for sale. An unlubricated male latex condom cut into a square or a latex barrier, which can be bought at an adult erotica shop or medical supply store, can be used for male-to-female or female-to-female oral sex. Sex toys should be kept clean, covered by condoms, and not shared. Both condoms and latex barriers, if used correctly, can help prevent transmission of HIV and many other sexually transmitted diseases.

When shopping for male condoms, do not buy natural membrane or lambskin condoms for STD prevention. These condoms have large pores through which STD infectious organisms can pass. Do not use oil-based lubricants, such as Vaseline, hand lotion, or mineral oil. These lubricants can damage a latex condom and cause it to break more easily. Use only water-based lubricants, such as K-Y Jelly (which can be purchased in many pharmacies), Wet, Astroglide, or other brands.

Many HIV/AIDS hotlines and educational organizations make free information about condom and barrier use available to the public. Call your state or local HIV/AIDS hotline or the CDC National AIDS Hotline for information. Some hotline services make it their policy to send out written materials to callers in a discreet manner, but it's best to request this, if it concerns you. For more information about HIV/AIDS hotlines and other organizations offering safer sex education information, see the HIV/AIDS section in Chapter Eight and in the corresponding Resource Directory chapter.

Remember that some STDs, such as HIV and hepatitis B, can also be transmitted by sharing needles for intravenous (IV) drug use or other purposes. Therefore, if you use drugs intravenously, don't share needles. If you are sexually active with a partner who uses IV drugs, be sure to use condoms every time you have sex. The section HIV Infection and AIDS in Chapter Eight describes safer needle use practices. If you are thinking about getting a tattoo or a piercing (including ear piercing), always ask how customers are protected from contracting hepatitis B and HIV infection. Do not undertake piercing or tattooing on your own and *never* share needles.

DISCUSSING SAFER SEX WITH YOUR PARTNER

It may be overstating the obvious to say that many good, intelligent, and responsible people have or have had sexually transmitted diseases. Although some people may lie about their sexual histories or about whether they have an STD, others may just not know that they are infected, especially when symptoms are very mild or when there are no symptoms.

It's always necessary to talk openly about sexually transmitted diseases *before* becoming intimate. Plan a time when you and your partner can talk privately and honestly together about safer sex. Most people are concerned about sexually transmitted diseases, even if they find it hard to talk about them. Your partner may be relieved that you took the initiative to broach the subject. Talking about safer sex before you become intimate can give you time to get to know your partner better, and to make sure that you want to have sex with him or her and that you will have condoms or latex barriers available when you need them.

Many women feel awkward or afraid to bring up the topic of safer sex with their partners. Many women feel embarrassed about buying and carrying condoms or latex barriers, and many have not used a condom or latex barrier before. If you are hesitant about introducing condoms or barriers into your sex life, you're not alone. If you have a close friend or relative who is comfortable talking about sex and who uses condoms and/or barriers, you may want to ask her how she introduced barriers and/or condoms into her relationship.

Practice talking about safer sex by writing down some of the things you'd like to say to your partner and your partner's likely responses. Some people who don't want to use condoms or barriers offer a variety of excuses or comments meant to discourage responsible sex, such as "It doesn't feel the same," "It cuts off my circulation," "I get an allergic reaction," "Heterosexuals really aren't at risk for most STDs," "Lesbians really aren't at risk for most STDs," "I don't have an STD," "Don't you trust me?" "Does this mean that you're seeing someone else?" It's natural to want to please your partner and to be frightened of rejection. But you must put your life, health, and fertility first. Discussions about safer sex with your partner can center on options and goals. For instance, you can try different condoms and different spermicides to see which brands are suitable for the both of you. Experiment with different lubricants. Talk about who will be responsible for buying condoms or barriers and where you will keep them. Make this something that you do together, as a couple.

If your partner refuses to wear condoms or use latex barriers or makes you feel bad or inadequate because of your desire for safer sex, it may be worth your while to think about the value of a relationship in which your health and well-being aren't priorities. There are times when protecting your health means more than mutual conversation about safer sex practices. If there is violence or abuse in your relationship, you may want to talk to a women's shelter or other advocacy organization in order to clarify your options. Again, advocates will not tell you to leave your relationship, nor will they ask you to go to a shelter. They are there to discuss your concerns and help you explore your options. See Chapter Four for more information.

TAKE AN ACTIVE ROLE IN STD PREVENTION: GET CHECKED FOR STDS

If you have been with a new sexual partner, if you or your partner have sex with more than one person, or if you think that your partner has had sex with someone other than you, see your health care provider soon and get checked for STDs every six months. Do not assume that you have been tested for STDs because you have had a recent physical exam, pelvic exam, or Pap smear. Doctors do not routinely test for STDs. Generally, you must ask to be tested. You also have the option of testing at a public health clinic.

Before starting a new relationship, think about visiting an STD clinic with your partner for testing. By doing this, each will have truthful information about the other's health status. You may also want to visit an anonymous HIV testing site, if available in your state. For more information about HIV antibody testing and making a decision about getting tested, see the HIV/AIDS section in Chapter Eight.

COMMON SEXUALLY TRANSMITTED DISEASES

This section will provide you with basic information about common sexually transmitted diseases. It is not a substitute for medical advice, which only your health care provider can give you. Following, and in specific sections, you will find general information about treatment.

Chlamydia

Chlamydia is currently one of the most common sexually transmitted diseases in the United States, with about 4 million new cases diagnosed each year. Unfortunately, most women have no symptoms until chlamydia causes significant damage, including pelvic inflammatory disease, which can lead to infertility, chronic pain, ectopic pregnancy (see the section Pregnancy and Infant Loss) and infection to newborns causing conjunctivitis, an infection of the eye, or pneumonia. In men, it can cause infection in the testicles (epididymitis), which can lead to infertility.

Gonorrhea

Gonorrhea currently affects more than 1 million people each year. Like chlamydia, it can cause pelvic inflammatory disease. Other long-term consequences of gonorrhea that can occur in both men and women include arthritis, skin eruptions, and in rare instances, heart disease (endocarditis) and infection of the outer surface of the brain (meningitis). Gonorrhea can also cause infection in men's testicles, which can lead to sterility. It can affect the throat in both men and women, causing pharyngitis, an infection of the throat.

In the past, gonorrhea caused blindness in many newborns. Today, antibiotic drops are usually put into the eyes of all newborns at the time of delivery to prevent gonorrheal infection at birth.

Pelvic Inflammatory Disease (PID)

Pelvic inflammatory disease is an infection that affects women's reproductive organs, specifically the upper genital tract, which includes the uterus, the fallopian tubes, and the ovaries. PID can be caused by a variety of organisms, but most often it results from an infection caused by an STD, usually untreated gonorrhea or chlamydia. PID can develop in a short time or months after the original infection. An intrauterine device (IUD) can predispose a woman to PID, but the increased risk is highest during the first four months after its placement.

The long-term effects of PID can be very serious and include infertility, ectopic pregnancy, chronic pain, and recurrent infection. The symptoms of PID include:

- tenderness in the lower abdominal or pelvic area
- fever, chills, nausea, vomiting
- increased vaginal discharge
- bleeding between periods
- pain during sex

Sometimes only very mild symptoms occur, or there are no symptoms. But even in this case, serious damage to the reproductive system can result.

Early diagnosis of PID is crucial. If you have any symptoms of PID or are at risk for STDs, see your doctor *as soon as possible*. The sooner PID is diagnosed and treated, the less chance there is of permanent damage to your reproductive health.

Depending on the severity of the disease and on other circumstances, hospitalization may be required. In other cases, women can be treated on an outpatient basis. As with other reproductive tract infections, sex should be avoided until treatment is completed, and your partner should be encouraged to seek STD testing and treatment, if infected. Otherwise, you can be reinfected with an STD, acquire another case of PID, and risk further harm to your reproductive health.

HPV and Genital Warts

The rate of genital warts is increasing rapidly in the United States. The human papillomavirus (HPV) is the virus that causes genital warts. There are currently more than seventy identified subtypes of HPV. Some subtypes of HPV cause warts on the hands or feet, which are not thought to be transmittable to the genital area. Other types cause warts in the genital area through sexual contact. Skin-to-skin genital contact with an infected partner is all that is needed to spread HPV. Because areas that are infected and shedding the virus cannot always be covered by condoms or barriers, these methods are not completely effective in preventing the transmission of HPV. It's important to note that genital warts may be present on the cervix where they cannot be seen by the naked eye. Genital warts along the vaginal walls may also go undetected, or be too small to see. When an HPV infection shows no outward signs or symptoms, this is called subclinical infection. Thus, even if you use condoms every time you have sex and see no visible warts, there is still a chance that you can become infected with HPV.

Genital warts may appear weeks or months after exposure to HPV, or they may never appear. When genital warts are visible, they appear as bumps or growths in and around the sexual organs, including the vulva, vagina, cervix, and anus and in men on the penis, scrotum, and anus. You may see one wart or many. They may be flat or raised and clustered together forming cauliflower-like structures. Generally, they're painless and skin-colored, although they can occasionally cause symptoms, such as itching, burning, and bleeding. Unfortunately, HPV can't be cured. This is because the virus can be present in skin cells even after warts have been removed. The goal of treatment is to remove visible warts and to relieve any symptoms.[22] There are many possible treatments for genital warts, including cryotherapy (freezing with liquid nitrogen), use of chemical compounds which can be applied topically, usually by your health care provider (although most topical agents are not recommended during pregnancy), use of an electric current to remove warts, and laser therapy. Whatever treatment you and your doctor decide upon, be sure to have your doctor carefully explain what it involves and what side effects are possible. Make sure that you understand any instructions for follow-up care and what to do if you experience side effects.

Genital Warts and Pregnancy

Pregnancy often causes genital warts to grow and sometimes to bleed. Warts do not generally interfere with pregnancy and delivery unless they are blocking the birth canal or cause a significant amount of bleeding. In rare instances, babies are infected with HPV. Cesarean section does not appear to prevent transmission to newborns. However, this is a subject that must be discussed with your doctor.

HPV and Cervical Cancer

If you have genital warts, you may be concerned about the possibility of cervical cancer. However, only the subtypes of HPV that infect the cervix (subclinical infection) have been linked to cervical cancer. There is a relatively low association between cervical cancer and the type of HPV that causes visible genital warts, although there are exceptions.

Many women died of cervical cancer before the advent of the Pap smear,[23] which is used to detect precancerous conditions and early signs of abnormal cervical cell development. Today, fewer women die of cervical cancer because it is preventable as a result of early detection methods. Doctors can treat early cell changes (dysplasia) and in most cases prevent cancer from developing. This is why having a regular Pap smear is so important, especially to women who have had or have an STD.

Hepatitis B

Hepatitis B is a sexually transmitted disease, which, like HIV (the virus that causes AIDS), can also be transmitted through exposure to contaminated blood. However, hepatitis B is much more infectious than HIV and can be passed from one person to another by sharing personal items on which infected blood may be present, such as razors or toothbrushes.

A person with hepatitis B may have no symptoms at all or may become very ill with symptoms similar to those of a stomach virus. One may also develop jaundice (yellowing of the eyes and skin) and abdominal pain and tenderness around the area of the liver (upper right side of your body below your breasts). In some cases, the disease resolves completely even without treatment, but a certain percentage of people with hepatitis B will go on to have chronic liver infection. Many people who have chronic hepatitis are not aware that they have the disease.[24] They can infect others throughout their lives and are at risk for developing cirrhosis of the liver, liver failure, and/or liver cancer.

You can protect yourself against hepatitis B by practicing

safer sex and by not sharing needles for drug use or for other purposes including acupuncture, tattooing, or piercing.

Fortunately, there is a vaccine against hepatitis B. It is given as a series of three shots, all three of which must be completed. If you use IV drugs and share needles, have more than one sexual partner, are a health care worker, and/or live in or travel frequently to areas where the disease is prevalent, such as Alaska, the Pacific Islands, Africa, Asia, or the Amazon region of South America, you may want to talk to your health care provider about getting the vaccine. The CDC and public health officials recommend the vaccine for all infants.[25] Vaccination is also recommended for young adolescents who have not had the hepatitis B vaccine.[26] If you are interested in getting the vaccine, talk to your doctor or contact your local health department for information. If your sexual partner or someone in your home gets hepatitis, a shot can be given to help prevent transmission. This shot should be followed by the vaccination series.

Hepatitis B can be transmitted from a pregnant mother to her developing infant. Talk to your doctor about screening for hepatitis B if you are pregnant.

Herpes

Herpes is caused by the herpes simplex virus, of which there are two possible types. One primarily affects the area on or around the mouth, causing cold sores (also called fever blisters). This is called herpes simplex virus type I (HSV-I). The other primarily affects the genital area and is called herpes simplex virus type II. But HSV-I can be transmitted to the genital area and HSV-II can be transmitted to the oral area through oral sex.

It's important to remember that both kinds of herpes can be transmitted by simple skin-to-skin contact. For example, HSV-I is often transmitted by kissing and HSV-II is generally transmitted during sexual intercourse.

If you contract herpes, you may not experience any symptoms. But if there are symptoms, a first episode may include a painful tingling, itching, or burning sensation at the infected area. This is called the prodromal period of the disease. Your skin may then become red and inflamed. Soon after, little blisters may appear which eventually open, crust over, and heal. It's not uncommon to develop flu-like symptoms during a first outbreak. Sometimes herpes causes a vaginal discharge and may affect the urethra causing pain, burning, or difficulty with urination. Initial symptoms may occur anytime from a day to a month or even longer after initial infection, and may last as long as one to three weeks.

Herpes is most likely to be transmitted during an outbreak. It is also true that many people acquire herpes from people who have no signs or symptoms and, in fact, are not even aware that they have herpes. When the virus is present on the skin but causes no symptoms, it is called asymptomatic shedding.

The frequency of recurrence is quite variable. Some people have no further outbreaks; some have occasional recurrences; and some have many. Those who do not have initial symptoms may still develop symptoms later. The frequency of recurrence tends to diminish with time.

If you think you have herpes, try to go to your doctor while your sores are still present. If you do this, it will be easier for your doctor to test you for herpes.

Although there is no cure for herpes, there are many ways it can be controlled. Your doctor may prescribe a drug (acyclovir), which, if taken early, may shorten the course of an initial outbreak. If you know that you have or your partner has herpes, it is a good idea to use condoms every time you have sex and to abstain from sex from the time the infected partner experiences prodromal symptoms to the time that the lesions are completely healed.

Never touch an open herpes sore. You can transmit the infection to other parts of your body, including your eyes. If you do touch an open sore, wash your hands with soap and water.

Herpes and Pregnancy

Herpes can be transmitted to infants during delivery and can cause serious disease to newborns. Though herpes simplex virus in newborns is rare, it is more likely to occur if a woman contracts her first case of herpes during pregnancy. Complications can sometimes be avoided if the baby is delivered by cesarean section. Therefore, if you or your partner have herpes and you get pregnant or begin planning a pregnancy, it's important to let your doctor know so that you and your health care provider can follow specific guidelines during pregnancy and at the time of delivery. Inform your doctor as soon as possible if you experience an outbreak, especially a first outbreak. Your doctor will examine you carefully and take the necessary precautions.

Because the risk of transmitting the virus to your baby is greatest during a first episode of infection, you must vigilantly protect your reproductive health during your pregnancy, especially during the third trimester. Do not have sex with anyone who has herpes or could have herpes.

Syphilis can be an extremely serious disease if not detected early, and unfortunately, the signs and symptoms of syphilis are not easy to recognize. Anyone who has syphilis or thinks she may have been exposed to a person with syphilis at any stage of the disease should be seen by a doctor for testing and follow-up treatment, if infected. Syphilis can be acquired by sexual contact, but it can also be contracted by kissing someone who has a syphilitic sore (chancre, pronounced "shanker") on or around his or her mouth[27] or by contact with infectious skin lesions in the second stage. (See below.)

There are three stages of syphilis, although not every person who has syphilis will pass through each stage. The first stage occurs about one to twelve weeks after exposure to an infected person. In this stage, a painless ulcer, called a chancre, appears at the site of the initial infection, usually on the genitals. But the chancre can also appear on the mouth, or in areas where it may go unnoticed, such as the anal area, inside the vagina, or on the cervix. Although the chancre disappears in about one to six weeks, if untreated, a person with syphilis remains infected and can infect others.

The brain can be affected at any stage of syphilis. Neurosyphilis can result in brain damage and blindness. In addition, syphilis can cause a variety of congenital defects in infants born to mothers who are infected.

In the second stage — about six weeks to six months after the chancre appears — a rash appears along with flu-like symptoms. The rash may occur on the trunk, arms and legs, face, the palms, the soles of the feet, or on the entire body. Swollen lymph glands are common, and patchy bald spots may occur on the scalp. Raised areas (warts) may appear on the genitals. These warts are very infectious. White patches in the mouth and mucous membranes of the genitals may be noticeable and are also very contagious. Eventually these symptoms disappear as well, although this may take weeks or months. These same symptoms may appear and resolve again. However, the disappearance of symptoms doesn't mean the disease is gone: if untreated, the disease remains.

Between the second and third stage, there may be a long period in which no symptoms are evident. This period, called the latent period, may last five to ten years or longer. During this period, the organism that causes syphilis continues to multiply until the damage becomes clear in the third and final stage of syphilis.[28] In this third (tertiary) stage, heart disease and changes in bones become apparent. The progression of syphilis to its advanced stages can be prevented with early treatment of the infection.

HOW ARE STDs DIAGNOSED AND TREATED?

Many STDs are diagnosed and treated in similar ways. For example, chlamydia and gonorrhea are generally diagnosed by taking a small sample from the infected area, which is usually the cervix or vagina, with a cotton swab and sending it to a laboratory for analysis. However, a urine test for chlamydia has recently come into use[29] and may become widely available.

Other STDs are diagnosed in different ways. For example, if you have a sore, such as a chancre or herpes sore, your doctor will probably take a small sample from the sore and have it evaluated. Syphilis can be diagnosed by a blood test, although a blood test may not become positive for up to three months after initial infection. HIV infection is usually diagnosed by a blood test, although new and simpler diagnostic techniques are currently being researched. (See the HIV/AIDS section in Chapter Eight.) Genital warts are often diagnosed by examination of the lesions alone, or HPV may be discovered on a routine Pap smear. PID and hepatitis are diagnosed by the presence of certain symptoms and by blood tests. (See the sections on these diseases on pages 258 and 260.)

Many STDs are treated with antibiotics specific for the type of infection. Antibiotic shots or pills may be given for chlamydia, gonorrhea, syphilis, and trichomoniasis. Herpes, human papillomavirus (genital warts), HIV, and hepatitis are viruses and cannot be treated with antibiotics. (See the section HIV Infection and AIDS in Chapter Eight.) If you are pregnant or think that you may be, let your doctor know. Just as with any medication, certain antibiotics are not safe to take during pregnancy and, often, alternative medications can be prescribed.

It is extremely important to take all of the medication prescribed by your doctor, even if your symptoms subside. If you do not, the infection may not be completely treated and you could suffer the long-term effects of the STD. You should be very sure to return to all of the follow-up visits advised by your doctor. Your partner must also be treated for his or her own health and to prevent your reinfection. Do not have sex until you (and your partner) have finished all of the medication prescribed by your doctor.

If you have any questions or ongoing concerns about STDs, telephone counseling, support groups, and written information are available to you by calling the hotline numbers at the beginning of this section.

❖ 6 ❖

Resources for Adults and Children with Disabilities

PART ONE: RESOURCES FOR ADULTS
WITH DISABILITIES

Finding information and assistance

This chapter is intended to present an overview of resources that may be of interest to women with disabilities or chronic illnesses, or spouses, partners, friends, and family members of people with disabilities. It's not always easy to find the help or the information that you want. Health care and other service systems are often fragmented and poorly coordinated. As well, financial and budget constraints may limit available resources, and not every service will meet your needs or be delivered in a manner that is acceptable to you. Although it may take some time — and considerable use of your consumer skills and creativity — to find desired and appropriate resources, the results of your research can be rewarding. Be persistent, and keep in mind that you are the best judge of the value of the resources you discover.

Be prepared to ask many questions of service providers. Speak with the person responsible for making decisions. Don't be shy about going to the head of the department or organization. These professionals are in the business of providing services to the public and should be available and accountable to consumers. You are entitled to responsible and thoughtful answers to your questions. If you are told no, ask why not. Examine all your alternatives and trust your

Wʜᴀᴛ's ɪɴ ᴛʜɪs ᴄʜᴀᴘᴛᴇʀ?

❖ PART ONE:
Resources for Adults with Disabilities
 • Finding Information and Assistance
 • Medical Rehabilitation
 • Centers for Independent Living
 • Going Back to Work: Vocational Rehabilitation
 • Discrimination and Legal Assistance
 • Social Security Benefits
 • Workers' Compensation

❖ PART TWO:
Resources for Children with Disabilities
Part Two of this chapter is devoted exclusively to information regarding children. However, this section also contains information that can be valuable to parents of children with disabilities, particularly parents of young adults.
 • Who Can Help You Get the Services Your Child Needs?
 • Services for Newborns and Toddlers: Early Intervention
 • Special Education
 • Head Start
 • EPSDT: Health Services for Children
 • Respite Care: Time Off for Caregivers

instincts. You, after all, have final authority over your own body and destiny.

Starting your Search for Information

Before you begin your search, it's a good idea to buy a notebook in which to record the names of the people you contact, the date of your conversations, and the information that you receive, as well as necessary follow-up calls. This way, you'll be better equipped to track down and use the services available to you.

Support and Advocacy Groups

There are literally hundreds of organizations serving the needs of people with disabilities. In fact, there are so many potentially helpful organizations that it's often hard to know where to begin a search for resources. One of the best places to start is with a support and advocacy group. Support and advocacy groups are dedicated to the concerns of people with a particular disability, illness, or condition and usually offer a number of services to the public. While the range and availability of services varies widely among organizations, many offer information and referral services, emotional support groups, and publications. Many support and advocacy groups, such as the American Amputee Foundation, the American Heart Association, and the National Brain Injury Association, offer referrals to local rehabilitation facilities. Some organizations offer employment-related services, networks of parents of children with disabilities, or other forms of assistance relevant to the needs of those served. As with any type of organization, each support and advocacy group has its own philosophy and particular set of concerns. It's important to look for an organization whose views and objectives are compatible with your own.

How can you find a support and advocacy group? The Resource Directory lists major disability-specific organizations. In addition, local offices of the United Way, Area Agencies on Aging (see Chapter Nine), senior centers, medical social workers, nurses, and hospital discharge planners may be able to help you find a group that fits your needs.

Key National Organizations

Depending on your concerns, you may find the information you need quickly and at no charge by contacting one of the following organizations. Addresses and telephone numbers are listed in the Resource Directory, among other potentially helpful listings.

The National Council on Independent Living (NCIL) can refer you to the nearest independent living center.

The National Clearinghouse on Women and Girls with Disabilities offers information about services available to women and girls with disabilities across the country, including women's groups, grassroots support and advocacy groups, Planned Parenthood programs, and university and college offices for students with disabilities.

Among its other activities, the *Office of Special Education and Rehabilitation Services (OSERS)* in the U.S. Department of Education offers the free *Pocket Guide to Federal Help for Individuals with Disabilities.*

The National Rehabilitation Information Center (NARIC). Information specialists can answer basic questions about disability and perform low-cost document searches in various areas of disability and rehabilitation research. A list of state agencies on disability is available at no charge. NARIC can provide callers with information regarding rehabilitation facilities and independent living centers, but does not make recommendations.

ABLEDATA is a national database of information on assistive technology. (Assistive devices can help you perform everyday tasks in order to live more independently. They range from the very simple, for example, a zipper pull, to the relatively complex, such as a power wheelchair or voice-activated computer.)

Don't Forget Your Local Telephone Directory!

Your local telephone directory contains the addresses and telephone numbers of local and state agencies that may be of assistance, including departments of aging, health, mental health, and developmental disabilities, Governor's Committees on Employment of People with Disabilities, and local commissions on disabilities, which can provide you with information about resources in your area.

MEDICAL REHABILITATION

What Is Medical Rehabilitation?

Medical rehabilitation is a process involving certain exercises and treatments that are performed by, or under the direction of, medical professionals. Rehabilitation may also involve the provision of other services and goods designed to reduce limitations caused by an impairment.

The goal of medical rehabilitation is to help people with disabilities live as independently as possible. Among the various gains to be made through rehabilitation are improvements in the ability to perform activities of daily living (ADL), such as walking, eating, dressing, and bathing; help in the management of problems related to bowel and bladder function; instruction in the use of prostheses (artificial substitutes for body parts, such as limbs or arms); help learning wheelchair skills (including the skills necessary for transfer from wheelchair to bed or car or elsewhere); or the mastery of other mobility aids.

People who are disabled as a result of stroke, head injury, cancer, amputation, hip fractures and replacements, burns, arthritis, Parkinson's disease, birth defects and inherited conditions, as well as many other conditions, may benefit from rehabilitation.

When Should Rehabilitation Begin?

There is wide support for the belief that medical rehabilitation should be part of a continuum of care beginning with early intervention soon after an injury, episode of illness, or the identification of a medical condition. Still, many people with long-term disabilities may also benefit from rehabilitation.

Is Rehabilitation Appropriate for You?

Your doctor is the first person to whom you should speak about the possibility of rehabilitation. If you believe that you (or a family member) could benefit from rehabilitation, ask for an evaluation. Not all doctors are aware of the various options for rehabilitation, nor are all doctors knowledgeable about rehabilitation. If you cannot get an evaluation from your doctor or through your hospital as an inpatient, seek an evaluation from a local physiatrist (a doctor who specializes in physical medicine and rehabilitation, also called PM&R) or from an outpatient rehabilitation facility. The American Academy of Physical Medicine and Rehabilitation, listed in the Resource Directory, can provide referrals to member physiatrists in your area.

Your need for rehabilitation, the intensity and types of services prescribed, and the goals you set for rehabilitation will depend on your individual circumstances and will change over time. It's hard to predict the outcome of rehabilitation.

Its appropriateness and effectiveness may be influenced by a number of factors, including the nature of the injury or illness that caused your disability, your health, the potential that exists for improvement in function, the quality and co-ordination of the services you receive, and support from family and friends during the rehabilitation process.

Your motivation and desire for rehabilitation is very important. As the consumer of rehabilitation services, you should be able to determine what goals are appropriate for you and to participate fully in all treatment decisions.

MEDICAL REHABILITATION PROFESSIONALS AND THE SERVICES THEY PROVIDE

To get a better understanding of the rehabilitation process and how it may benefit you, it will be helpful to know what kind of therapies and services are performed during rehabilitation and something about the professionals who provide them.

Rehabilitation professionals work in diverse settings. For example, some work alone in private practice, while others act as members of interdisciplinary teams at comprehensive rehabilitation hospitals. Some professionals specialize in a particular area of rehabilitation, such as the treatment of people with spinal cord injuries.

Physical therapists evaluate, teach, and treat people with disabilities in order to restore and maintain physical function, prevent further disability, regain strength and mobility, and alleviate pain, among other goals. The techniques that physical therapists employ include the therapeutic uses of exercise, heat, cold, water, electricity, and massage. Physical therapists should have graduate degrees in physical therapy from a school accredited by the American Physical Therapy Association and should be state-licensed.

Occupational therapists provide treatment to people with physical as well as psychosocial needs. They instruct and assist people in the performance of activities of daily living (ADL), such as personal care, feeding, dressing, and home-making tasks. In addition, occupational therapists address swallowing problems, suggest and order adaptive devices that help make doing everyday tasks easier, and often prepare people for reentry into the workforce. Evaluation of your functional limitation is necessary before beginning any instruction or treatment. Occupational therapists hold bachelor's or master's degrees in occupational therapy and must pass a national examination. Certified occupational therapy assistants (COTAs) have associate degrees in occupational therapy and must also pass a national certification examination. All occupational therapy academic programs must be accredited by the Accreditation Council for Occupational Therapy Education. State licensing requirements vary.

Speech and hearing therapists evaluate and treat problems related to communication. Some professionals treat both speech and hearing impairments; however, many work only in one area, either as audiologists or speech-language pathologists. A therapist may work in conjunction with other rehabilitation professionals to help people achieve a variety of goals. For example, a speech therapist may work with an occupational therapist to help people who have difficulty swallowing. The American Speech-Language-Hearing Association (ASHA) offers certification programs for individual members. Successful candidates receive a Certificate of Clinical Competence (CCC). Licensing is required in some states.

Respiratory therapists diagnose, treat, and help prevent respiratory problems. Respiratory therapists are either Certified Respiratory Therapy Technicians (CRTT) or Registered Respiratory Therapists (RRT). Many states require respiratory therapists to be licensed.

Rehabilitation nurses supervise the course of a rehabilitation program and help patients and families integrate the variety of skills learned through other therapies by teaching and reinforcing rehabilitation techniques. Rehabilitation nurses are registered nurses who have passed the Association of Rehabilitation Nurses' certification examination to become Certified Rehabilitation Registered Nurses (CRRN). Nurses must be licensed.

Medical social workers help patients and families cope with the emotional and practical aspects of hospitalization and rehabilitation. Social workers often provide crisis intervention, financial and insurance counseling, and help coordinate community services needed after hospital discharge. Medical social workers hold graduate or, in some cases, doctorate degrees in social work. Licensing requirements vary from state to state.

Rehabilitation psychologists. The diagnosis of a serious illness or the experience of traumatic injury is an extraordinarily stressful life event that can give rise to substantial physical, emotional, psychological, and spiritual challenges. A disability can affect your sense of identity, self-worth, and self-confidence. You may find yourself grappling once again or for the first time with narrowly defined or stereotypical ideals of feminine beauty and worth. There may be challenges to your relationships, for example, with your husband, partner, family members and/or friends. You may be confronted with prejudices about people with disabilities — even your own biases — and may have fears about the way others will view you and interact with you. These are normal reactions. Likewise, shock, denial, anger, frustration, depression, sadness, anxiety, and the mourning of functional losses are normal responses to illness or impairment. Adaptation to a disability is a process that differs for each person. Rehabilitation psychologists, working either as part of an interdisciplinary rehabilitation team or in private practice, can help you and the important people in your life address issues that arise during the course of rehabilitation and beyond. Acting as consultants to other members of the rehabilitation team, rehabilitation psychologists can also help you work with medical professionals to develop a course of care most suited to your needs.

Rehabilitation psychologists have varied backgrounds. Some train specifically in rehabilitation psychology, while many come from backgrounds in clinical, counseling, or social psychology or other fields and have taken courses in rehabilitation psychology or gained experience on the job. When choosing or working with a rehabilitation psychologist, it's important to look for someone with whom you are comfortable and with whom you feel a connection. Find out how much experience the psychologist has working with people with physical disabilities. As with every aspect of rehabilitation, it's necessary to trust your instincts about what works for you and what doesn't. You may need a few sessions together with the psychologist to get a feel for whether you will be able to work well together. If you are looking for a rehabilitation psychologist in private practice, you might try contacting local rehabilitation centers, if possible, or a physiatrist, and asking for the names of a few rehabilitation psychologists to interview.

Orientation and mobility (O&M) instructors teach people who are blind, or who have low vision, safe travel techniques, including instruction in cane use. *Rehabilitation teachers* (also called independent living specialists), who assist people with disabilities to reach independent living goals, may work with O&M instructors and can provide information on adaptations that can be made in the home to improve safety and convenience, teach adaptive skills, and provide referrals to community support services. Although O&M instructors and rehabilitation teachers often work in rehabilitation facilities, they may also be found in state vocational rehabilitation agencies, schools for the blind, low-vision clinics associated with ophthalmologists' offices, and in private practice. Rehabilitation teachers should have a bachelor's or master's degree in rehabilitation teaching or in a related field. At minimum, orientation and mobility instructors should have a bachelor's degree with an emphasis on O&M.[1]

Physiatrists (or PM&Rs) are board-certified physicians specializing in physical medicine and rehabilitation (PM&R). In hospitals where professional rehabilitation teams work together to address patients' complex needs, the physiatrist typically oversees the work of the entire team. Some physiatrists are in private practice. The American Academy of Physical and Medical Rehabilitation, a professional organization listed in the Resource Directory, can furnish you with more information about physiatry.

In addition to the above functions, rehabilitation services may include the design and fitting of prostheses (artificial substitutes for body parts) and orthotics (devices that aid mobility, such as braces or wheelchairs), neuropsychological testing, sexuality counseling, pastoral counseling, vocational rehabilitation, nutrition counseling, and recreational therapy.

Where Are Rehabilitation Services Delivered?

Medical rehabilitation services are delivered in a range of settings, including general hospitals, inpatient or outpatient rehabilitation units within or connected with general hospitals, comprehensive outpatient rehabilitation facilities (CORFs), medical rehabilitation hospitals, outpatient departments of rehabilitation hospitals, and VA hospitals, as well as through home health agencies and the private practices of rehabilitation professionals. Skilled nursing facilities (nursing homes) also offer rehabilitation services.

The range of settings and the various types and styles of services provided within each setting can make choosing the right facility extremely difficult. The following brief discussion of various facilities offering rehabilitation services may help you select a provider and negotiate a course of treatment. Keep in mind that some providers, such as acute-care general hospitals, may offer services in one or more of these settings and that insurance may limit your choices.

When deciding on a course of care, remember that it is possible, and often necessary, to blend your treatment options. For example, treatment in an acute-care hospital may be followed with a referral to an inpatient rehabilitation facility and then continued with outpatient or home health services.

Acute-care settings. Rehabilitation that takes place in the hospital following an acute episode of illness or injury is intended to prevent or limit a disability and to develop a plan for continuing care. Individual physical therapy, occupational therapy, respiratory therapy, or speech-language therapy services may be provided. Because the length of patients' stays in hospitals is much shorter today than in the past (often due to payment systems that provide hospitals with incentives for earlier discharge), rehabilitation in the acute-care setting may also be short. The focus is on teaching you and your family appropriate exercises and self-care techniques. Rehabilitation in acute-care settings, although vital, may not be sufficient by itself.

Inpatient rehabilitation programs are offered through rehabilitation hospitals, which may be independent, contained within larger hospital complexes, or offered through rehabilitation departments in general hospitals. Sometimes inpatient programs specialize in providing care for people with common needs, for example, heart patients or people with traumatic brain injuries. Generally, rehabilitation facilities accept and treat people who are medically stable and likely to benefit from rehabilitation. Some facilities offer both inpatient and outpatient services. As well, some facilities offer housing for families of people with disabilities who are receiving treatment. Costs for hospital inpatient services are likely to be high.

Inpatient rehabilitation programs in which an interdisciplinary team of rehabilitation professionals work together under the direction of a physician to address a range of client needs — including physical, psychological, and social needs — are called *comprehensive rehabilitation facilities.* Comprehensive inpatient rehabilitation facilities that are accredited by the Commission on Accreditation of Rehabilitation Facilities (CARF) and/or the Joint Commission on Accreditation of Healthcare Organizations are considered to have met at least the minimum standards of a high-quality facility.[2]

Outpatient services may be available through outpatient departments of general hospitals and rehabilitation hospitals, as well as independent outpatient rehabilitation facilities. Outpatient programs offer a source of rehabilitation for people who do not require inpatient services or who are seeking continued care after leaving an inpatient program. Outpatient services may also provide an alternative for people who don't have enough insurance coverage for inpatient services.[3] Outpatient programs that provide comprehensive care are called *comprehensive outpatient rehabilitation facilities (CORFs)*. Medicare-certified CORFs are required to meet certain standards for participation, including the requirement that people accepted into the facility be referred by a physician. If you are seeking outpatient care, make certain to get a prescription for rehabilitation from your doctor.

Skilled nursing facilities provide skilled nursing care or rehabilitation services. A patient may be referred to a skilled nursing facility (a nursing home) when she is medically unstable or unable to receive care at home. Medicare requires a physician referral to skilled nursing facilities.

Home health care. Individual rehabilitation services delivered at home can be an important source of continuing rehabilitation for people who have been discharged from a hospital or inpatient rehabilitation facility, or who are unable to travel to outpatient services. For more information about home care, see Chapter Nine.

How to Find Medical Rehabilitation Services

While you are in the hospital, you or a family member should discuss your need for rehabilitation with the specialist or attending physician, the nurse, discharge planner, social worker, and/or case manager. Taking an active role in your plans for aftercare is important. Don't assume that rehabilitation plans will be made without your having to ask, and sometimes push, for them. If you do not advocate for yourself, you may find yourself discharged with little or no plan for continued care.

The physician's role in planning for aftercare services is a vital one since your doctor must make an assessment of your needs and refer you to an appropriate source of rehabilitation. Doctors can help you secure reimbursement from your insurer by certifying that a referral to a rehabilitation facility or home health care agency is medically necessary. It's best to initiate a conversation about rehabilitation as early as possible.

Most hospitals have *discharge planning units* or social work departments that, in addition to other tasks, develop and coordinate realistic plans for aftercare. According to federal law,[4] hospitals that participate in the Medicare program (most hospitals) are required to provide discharge planning evaluation for all patients who are likely to suffer adverse health consequences without such services and to those who request it.

How Can the Medical Social Worker Help You?

Many people think that social workers only help patients through emotional or psychological difficulties. In fact, medical social workers often serve as primary resources for financial and insurance information and can help patients connect to community resources like home care and Meals on Wheels. The medical social worker, who may function as a discharge planner, should be able to tell you about available options for rehabilitation.

The Case Manager: Meeting Complex Needs

Medical case management is one method hospitals use to contain costs. Patients with complex and expensive needs may be referred to a case manager, whose job it is to keep costs for aftercare down without risking quality. Sometimes hospital case managers or discharge planners perform this function. However, case managers may also be associated with insurance companies and HMOs, Medicaid programs (Medi-Cal in California), or large employers. Sometimes conflicts about the desirability and appropriateness of services develop when communication problems exist between the patient and family members, the hospital discharge planner, and an outside case manager.[5]

Your Attorney Can Help You Find Services

If you have a workers' compensation claim or are involved in a lawsuit related to your disability, your attorney should be able to help you locate medical or vocational rehabilitation services. Attorneys specializing in elder law may also be able to provide information and referrals.

You Are Your Best Resource

You, a family member, or trusted friend can investigate possibilities for rehabilitation, although your insurance plan may limit your choices. In addition to contacting support and advocacy groups and other organizations listed at the beginning of this chapter, you can also check the main branch of your local public library. Ask the reference librarian for information about books listing rehabilitation and health care facilities. Also, many libraries maintain current files of community resources, and you may be able to access information about local rehabilitation and home health care services by telephone, in person, or through computer bulletin boards.

PAYING FOR REHABILITATION

Private Insurance and HMOs

Paying for medical rehabilitative services can be difficult, especially without insurance. Private and group health insurance plans often cover inpatient and outpatient services. Be sure to read your policy carefully. Check for any restrictions on the use of the plan, and get any assurances about covered services in writing. HMOs may only offer limited rehabilitation benefits. However, insurers may sometimes pay for services, such as home care and rehabilitative services, if it will mean saving on expensive inpatient care. If you're seeking care that isn't covered by your insurer, try presenting this idea to your social worker, case manager, and/or insurer.

It is important to note that most health or medical insurance coverage contains a provision that allows the insurer to seek repayment of health benefits paid to you or to your account from a third wrongdoing party or its insurer. For example, if you were injured in an automobile accident and received health care benefits from your vehicle insurance carrier, then later sued the wrongdoing party and received a settlement, the vehicle insurance carrier is entitled to a reimbursement of the amount initially paid out to you or your account.

Medicare

Medicare helps pay for certain inpatient and outpatient rehabilitation services, certain services delivered in a comprehensive outpatient rehabilitation facility (CORF), and part-time or intermittent home health services for people who are homebound. If you use an assistive device (for example, a walker or wheelchair) or the help of another person to leave your home and leave only infrequently for medical appointments, you may be considered homebound.[6]

Medicare will only pay for services that are determined to be medically necessary. This is why it is important to have your doctor write the prescription for services. If you have a Medicare handbook, read it carefully. You can order a free current edition of the Medicare handbook by calling the Medicare hotline at 1-800-638-6833 or 1-800-820-1202 (TTY) or the Social Security Administration's toll-free number

1-800-772-1213 or 1-800-325-0778 (TTY). The Medicare hotline offers Medicare information on cassette as well.

In order for Medicare to reimburse a stay at a *skilled nursing facility*, you must require daily skilled nursing or rehabilitative services that, as a practical matter, can only be provided in a skilled nursing facility. (See Chapter Nine or check your Medicare handbook for information about the criteria that must be met for coverage.) If you believe skilled nursing or rehabilitative care is necessary, consult with your doctor about the possibility of a referral. In addition to rehabilitative services likely to bring about some improvement in your condition, examples of skilled nursing care that might be necessary include treatment for pressure sores, catheter insertion, and injections.

Remember that in certain situations, Medicare may be your *secondary* insurer, for example, if you have received or expect to receive payments from workers' compensation, no-fault, or liability insurance. This may also be true for certain beneficiaries who are covered by insurance through employment. Medicare payments are also affected by veterans' benefits.

You have a right to appeal official determinations by Medicare regarding coverage for treatment. To get an official determination on Part A (hospital) services (for example, skilled nursing or home health care), your provider must submit a claim to Medicare. You may have to insist on this. But it is your legal right to have the claim submitted. Without an initial determination, an appeal is not possible.[7]

Medicaid

Medicaid (or Medi-Cal in California) is the state-federal program intended to provide medical assistance to eligible people with low incomes and few assets, and in many states, people with limited resources whose medical bills exceed their incomes. At the time of this writing, Medicaid covers a broad range of services that may include physical therapy, occupational therapy and speech, hearing or language therapy, private duty nursing services, nursing home and home health care, medical equipment and supplies, and prosthetic devices among other medically necessary services. Many states have been granted *home and community-based (HCB) waivers* to furnish services to people who without such services would require institutional care. Services that *may* be available in your state include habilitation, case management, homemaker/home health aide services, personal care services, adult daycare, and respite care, among other services. At the time of this writing, advocates are urging that Medicaid guarantee the availability of home-based services. For information about Medicaid and what services may be available to you, contact your local Medicaid or welfare office or speak to your medical social worker or discharge planner.

States must allow applicants who have been denied Medicaid claims a fair hearing before the state Medicaid agency. Decisions may be appealed in court.[8] If your claim has been denied, contact a local legal aid organization, which may be able to assist you.

Other Payment Sources

Workers' compensation and no-fault auto insurance may also serve as payment sources for rehabilitation. State vocational rehabilitation agencies may help pay for rehabilitation services for clients with low incomes in some circumstances. If you have been the victim of a violent crime, including domestic violence, you may be eligible for your state victim-compensation program, which may help with some of your medical bills. However, victim-compensation funds will not cover expenses paid for by a third-party insurer. In some states, financial need must be shown in order for victims to receive assistance. Generally, you must report the crime soon after it occurs, usually within twenty-four to forty-eight hours, to be eligible for compensation. For more information, talk to your local prosecutor (district or county attorney) or ask for a referral to a victim/witness assistance program.

PREPARING FOR YOUR RETURN HOME: DO YOU HAVE THE ASSISTANCE YOU NEED?

Many important gains made during rehabilitation may be lost with a return to an environment that poses barriers. This may mean going home without the support of the home health care or personal assistant services necessary to help you with everyday activities and prevent potential medical problems.[9] It may mean facing architectural and other barriers at home, in the community, and on the job. Discrimination is an unfortunate reality for people with disabilities. As you make plans for your return home from the hospital or rehabilitation facility, you may want to speak with members of the rehabilitation staff, your nurse, discharge planner, or social worker about any home modifications, assistive devices, personal assistance or home health care services or other services that you need. If you need an assistive device (for example, a wheelchair), remember that you do not necessarily have to purchase the device from your hospital or rehabilitation facility. Other sources may offer devices at a lower cost. If you can, shop around for products that suit your needs. Independent living centers and support and advocacy groups are good sources of additional information about assistive devices. Networking with people with similar disabilities is, of course, one of the best ways to get information about affordable, reliable services and products and to share experiences.

CENTERS FOR INDEPENDENT LIVING

Centers for independent living are nonprofit, nonresidential community-based organizations that provide an array of services to people with disabilities. A product of the disability civil rights movement of the late 1960s and '70s, independent living centers were founded on the philosophy of self-help and self-determination and fostered by peer support and advocacy for the removal of architectural, communication, attitudinal, economic, and other barriers that prevent people with disabilities from full participation in community life.

What sets independent living centers apart from traditional services is the requirement that agencies meet certain standards to ensure that the services are consumer-controlled. Independent living centers are governed by the Rehabilitation Act of 1973, as amended, and by federal regulations, which are used to implement the law. According to federal law, more than half of an independent living center's staff positions must be filled by people with disabilities. As well, a majority of those serving on the center's board of directors must be people with disabilities. Independent living centers must serve people with all different types of significant disabilities.[10]

In contrast to some traditional service models, which may place a person with a disability in the passive role of "patient" or "client," independent living centers regard the people they serve as consumers. Staff members are directed to assist you to continue or to begin living independently by helping you reach your identified goals. You should remain in control of the decision-making process and the manner in which services are delivered. Further, you should be able to define independent living in your own way.

As with any type of organization, quality among indepen-

dent living centers may differ. You may want to think of independent living centers as one resource among many and, if
possible, shop for a center that meets your needs, using the
center in conjunction with other services.

What Services Are Offered by Independent Living Centers?

Independent living centers are not identical. They differ in
size, the variety and type of services offered, and the manner
in which services are delivered. However, each must offer
the following core services:

Information and referral. An independent living center can
tell you about the services it offers and help you locate other
potentially useful community resources. Some independent
living centers may also offer information on disability-sensi-
tive gynecological services.

Peer support. Talking with other people with disabilities,
forming a support base, and sharing information can be part
of the process of adapting to and accepting a disability, as
well as a means of reaching into the community and finding
new friends. Independent living centers offer you this opportunity either through group discussions or by introducing
you to another person with a disability who, acting as mentor
or adviser, can help you to develop or clarify your independent living goals. These meetings are not intended as
professional therapy or counseling; rather they are meant
toprovide the kind of assistance that can only come from
someone who knows from experience what it means to have
a disability.

Independent living skills. Your ability to live independently
may be enhanced by learning or refining independent living
skills. These skills include financial management, personal
care, daily living skills, cooking, job readiness, or any other
activity in which you have an interest. Although instruction
may be offered in a group setting, it is very often done on an
individual basis to meet your specific needs.

Advocacy. Centers for independent living promote self-advocacy among consumers and work to bring about wider
opportunities for people with disabilities and equal access to
all aspects of community life. As part of their advocacy services, many independent living centers offer benefits and entitlements advisement. If you need information or assistance
applying for Social Security disability benefits, Supplemental Security Income, Medicare or Medicaid, your local independent living center may be able to assist you. Likewise, if
you are initially denied benefits, you may want to confer with

an independent living center for advice or assistance appealing the decision. If the center cannot help you directly, ask for a referral to another appropriate organization.

Many independent living centers offer additional services or special programs, including, but not limited to:

Housing information. Independent living centers often provide information on modifying homes or apartments for greater accessibility. Some centers may be able to help you find housing, although in many areas, housing shortages and discrimination limit consumers' choices. Also, if you (or someone you care about) is a veteran with a service-connected disability, you may be eligible for a grant for home adaptation. For more information, contact the regional VA office or the Superintendent of Documents, P.O. Box 371954, Pittsburgh, PA 15250-7954; (202) 512-1800, for a current edition of *Federal Benefits for Veterans and Dependents.* Look in your telephone directory under United States Government Offices for the telephone number of the regional VA office.

Personal care attendant information and registry. For some people with disabilities, having a personal assistant to help with activities of daily living is a key to independent living. Independent living centers can often provide information on finding and hiring a personal care assistant and becoming an effective employer. Some centers have personal assistant registries.

Transportation. Some independent living centers offer direct transportation services; others may be able to answer questions about local, accessible transportation resources.

Other services. Counseling services, rehabilitation technology, mobility training, interpreter and reader services (or referrals), supported living, physical therapy, the provision of prostheses and other devices, and social and recreational services may also be offered.

How to Find an Independent Living Center

Every state has at least one independent living center, and some states, like California, have many. Centers for independent living often network with other agencies within the state. Although there are acknowledged barriers to independent living in rural areas, independent living centers continue to work with communities to overcome difficulties in serving rural populations.

You can get a referral to a local independent living center by contacting the National Council on Independent Living

(NCIL) or NARIC. (See the beginning of this chapter.) State vocational rehabilitation departments, which can refer you to community-based independent living centers, may offer certain independent living services, including visual screening, peer counseling, guide and reader services, and mobility training to people who are blind and fifty-five years of age or older. In a few states, vocational rehabilitation (VR) departments offer independent living to people with significant disabilities.

The Rehabilitation Act of 1973 provides for the creation of Statewide Independent Living Councils (SILCs) to monitor, review, and evaluate the state plan for independent living centers and the relationship between independent living centers, vocational rehabilitation programs, and other organizations providing services to people with disabilities. If there are specific needs that are not being met in your area, you can make them known by communicating with the SILC or attending public meetings held by the SILC.

Who May Use an Independent Living Center?

Independent living centers must serve people of diverse disabilities. Spouses, partners, family members, and friends of people with disabilities may also be eligible for services. Each center determines its own eligibility criteria, but eligibility must not be based on a specific type of disability.[11] Generally, there is no financial test for eligibility. However, centers may restrict some services, such as financial help with home modification (if available), to people with low incomes.

How Much Do Services Cost?

Generally, independent living centers charge no fee for core services. Fees may be set for some services, such as interpreter services, when provided. When there is an initial charge for basic services, it is usually nominal, and many independent living centers allow for a waiver of fees or set them according to a sliding scale, if appropriate.

AIDS Service Organizations

Women with HIV infection or AIDS may also find community AIDS service organizations to be useful sources of information and assistance. While AIDS service organizations (ASOs) are not independent living centers, many offer comparable services. For more information, see Chapter Eight.

Vocational rehabilitation agencies offer various resources for people with disabilities who want to return to work, retrain for a new type of employment, enter the workforce for the first time, or live more independently within the community. Employment can mean full- or part-time employment, the practice of a profession, homemaking, self-employment, farm or family work, home-based employment, sheltered or supported employment, and other kinds of work.

While vocational rehabilitation may be offered through private or nonprofit agencies, or as part of a medical rehabilitation program, this section focuses on the services offered by state-federal vocational rehabilitation agencies, which are structured to assist people with significant disabilities in reaching employment and independent living goals.

As you read this section, you must consider that state vocational rehabilitation agencies have in the past been both lauded as a source of education, training, services, and equipment to which many people with disabilities might not ordinarily have access and severely criticized for having too few resources to serve the many who apply, as well as eligibility requirements that unfairly exclude many potentially successful candidates. Nonetheless, state vocational rehabilitation agencies can provide access to valuable resources, such as personal assistance services to help you do your job, or the identification of other comparable services and benefits.

Always remember that you have the right to appeal any unfavorable decision. Do not hesitate to exercise that right. Also, keep in mind that this section concerns federal (national) laws and regulations. A state may impose its own requirements on the operation of vocational rehabilitation programs.

Where to Find Vocational Rehabilitation Agencies

State vocational rehabilitation programs can generally be found on the state, regional, and local level. Some vocational programs are part of a larger agency such as the state Department of Social (or Human) Services, the Department of Education, or the Department of Labor. In other states, vocational rehabilitation agencies function as independent departments.

To locate the address and telephone number of your state vocational rehabilitation office, check the state government listings of your local telephone directory. The Client Assistance Program (CAP) can provide you with information and answer questions about the vocational rehabilitation program. Although CAPs are usually operated through agencies that are separate from vocational rehabilitation offices, the telephone number may be listed among the telephone number(s) for the state rehabilitation office.

Independent living centers, Protection and Advocacy organizations (which sometimes run CAPs), social workers, medical rehabilitation professionals, educational institutions, and local mental health departments can also give you the number of the vocational rehabilitation office or refer you. However, you do not need a referral to apply. Any person with a disability may apply directly.

In about half the states, services are provided to people who are blind through a separate department. Some states mandate that a person be legally blind in order to be eligible for these services. However, many vocational rehabilitation agencies serve people who are not blind but who have visual impairments.

What Services Do Vocational Rehabilitation Agencies Offer?

The following is a list of many of the individualized services provided by state vocational rehabilitation agencies.

- evaluation of your vocational rehabilitation potential
- counseling and guidance, including personal adjustment counseling
- job training and other training services
- books and tools and other training materials
- aid in paying for basic living expenses necessary to allow you to benefit from vocational rehabilitation (called maintenance)
- transportation related to VR services
- services to your family, if necessary for your vocational rehabilitation
- interpreter services for deaf people and tactile interpreter services for persons who are deaf-blind
- reader services, rehabilitation teaching services, note-taking services, and orientation and mobility services for people who are blind
- telecommunication, sensory, and other technical aids
- recruitment and training services to provide new job opportunities in the field of rehabilitation and other public service employment
- placement in suitable employment

- postemployment services, if necessary to maintain employment or find other suitable work
- occupational licenses and permits
- rehabilitation technology services and devices (including equipment needed by an employee to perform her job or to make her home more accessible)
- personal assistance services.[12] A personal assistant helps you with everyday activities, such as bathing, grooming, and eating.
- supported employment services (ongoing support for workers with significant disabilities or chronic mental illness.[13] For example, you may have a job coach who teaches you how to perform the tasks of your job and who will help you get the services you need to continue in your job.)
- Restorative services are also available. These services are considered when it is necessary to correct or modify a mental or physical condition that is stable or slowly progressive so that a consumer may further her rehabilitation goals. These services include medical rehabilitation, prostheses and orthotics, eyeglasses, hearing aids, necessary hospitalization in connection with surgery or treatment, and clinic services; however, they are usually provided on a short-term basis. The vocational rehabilitation agency must identify other potential sources of payment before funding restorative services.
- Other goods and services that may help you become employed may also be available.[14]

Who is Eligible for Vocational Rehabilitation?

In order to become eligible for vocational rehabilitation under federal law, you must have a mental or physical disability which, for you, constitutes a substantial impediment to employment, and there must be a reasonable expectation that you will be able to benefit from vocational rehabilitation services in terms of employment. However, the vocational rehabilitation agency should assume that you can benefit from the services unless it can, by clear and convincing evidence, demonstrate otherwise.[15]

SSI recipients under the age of sixty-five who are referred to state vocational rehabilitation agencies may lose their benefits or be denied benefits, if they refuse to participate in the program without good cause. In certain situations, SSDI/SSI beneficiaries who recover from blindness or disability while participating in vocational rehabilitation may continue to receive benefits until the program's completion. Contact the Social Security Administration for information.

Although *every person with a disability has a right to apply for vocational rehabilitation services* and eligibility determinations are made on an individual basis, states that cannot immediately serve all eligible applicants must give priority to people with the most severe disabilities. Other eligible people will be placed on a waiting list. States may not, however, base an order of selection on type of disability, race, gender, color, creed, national origin, source of referral, expected employment outcome, the need for a specific service or the anticipated cost of services, or personal income.[16]

Federal law also requires that services be provided without discrimination on the basis of sex, race, creed, color, national origin, or age. There is no legal age limit for eligibility, but because of the emphasis given to employment and the availability of more appropriate services for children, vocational rehabilitation agencies do not generally serve young children directly. Vocational rehabilitation agencies do serve youth moving from special education into employment.

How Are Eligibility Decisions Made?

Preliminary evaluations are given to determine your eligibility and to assess your vocational needs. Your rehabilitation counselor will collect information to make the decision, including information about your disability, your work history, education, interests, and abilities. This information may be gathered from various sources including you, your employer, school, the Social Security Administration, or the hospital that treated you. Depending on your disability, you may also be asked to take a medical, psychological, vision, hearing, or other type of examination. These diagnostic evaluations are made without cost to you.

The evaluation period usually lasts no longer than sixty days. However, states may extend the evaluation period in some situations, during which time services will be provided until a final determination of your eligibility is made. The extended evaluation period may last no longer than eighteen months. You must be notified in writing of a determination of ineligibility, given the reasons for the decision, and informed of your rights to have the decision reviewed.

The Individualized Written Rehabilitation Program

Once you have been determined eligible for vocational rehabilitation services, you will be given a thorough evaluation to determine the nature and scope of the services needed in order to reach your goals. Then you (or if appropriate, a parent, family member, guardian, advocate, or other representative) and your rehabilitation counselor will jointly decide upon a suitable rehabilitation plan. This plan is called the individualized written rehabilitation program (IWRP) and should be designed to meet your employment objectives and reflect your unique strengths, resources, priorities, concerns, and capabilities. The IWRP must contain a statement from you (or your representative) describing how you were informed of and involved in developing the plan, information regarding your rights, a description of the Client Assistance Program, and other related services and benefits provided through a federal, state, or local program that will enhance your ability to achieve your vocational goals. You should receive a copy of the plan and any updates.

How Much Does Vocational Rehabilitation Cost?

In some states, a financial means test may be applied to certain services. In other words, if you are able, you may be asked to participate in payment for these services. However, evaluation of your rehabilitation potential, counseling, guidance and referral services, and job placement services must be available without charge regardless of your income.[17]

There may be a charge for some services. If you cannot afford to pay for services, the vocational rehabilitation agency may provide them at no cost. However, the agency must make efforts to find comparable services and benefits, such as private insurance, Medicaid (Medi-Cal in California), or Pell grants, before paying for certain services, unless locating other payment sources would delay services to a person at extreme medical risk.

How Long Will Vocational Rehabilitation Take?

Since rehabilitation efforts should be tailored to meet your unique needs, there is no real way to estimate the length of time it will take for you to complete the program. For example, you may undergo an extended evaluation period, require restorative services, or need extensive training or further education to achieve your objectives.

Generally, once you have maintained suitable employment for at least sixty days, your case will be closed, unless you and your counselor have agreed upon a plan for extended or postemployment services.

Many community colleges and universities have offices on campus that are organized to serve enrolled students with disabilities, often called Disabled Student Services (DSS). If you are interested in returning to college to retrain for a new career, these offices may offer an alternative or an additional route to information and assistance.

DSS offices provide many services to students, but many do not have a specific program. Rather, staff members work in various ways to help students meet their educational goals. For example, students with learning disabilities may consult with the DSS office to arrive at solutions to problems related to test-taking or to get information regarding diagnosis. DSS offices often provide information regarding transportation, housing, program modification, and discrimination. Some DSS offices provide nonstudents with referrals to information sources within the community.

Handling VR Denials and Complaints

Vocational rehabilitation agencies exist to serve you. You have a right to apply for services and to request a timely review of any determination made by the rehabilitation counselor regarding services or a denial of services. At minimum, formal review procedures must include a hearing before an impartial hearing officer within forty-five days of a request.[18] If you have a problem regarding vocational rehabilitation, or if you are denied services, it's best to talk it over with your rehabilitation counselor first. If this proves unsatisfactory, speak to the counselor's supervisor. If no resolution can be achieved, contact the Client Assistance Program for advice and help.

The Rehabilitation Act requires states to establish Client Assistance Programs (CAPs) to assist vocational rehabilitation consumers. A CAP must provide you with information about vocational rehabilitation services, inform you of your rights and responsibilities within the program, and help you resolve any problems you might have during rehabilitation, including conflicts that arise in your relationship with the program or staff members. CAPs can also help you if you decide to pursue a complaint against the vocational rehabilitation agency through administrative or legal processes. There is no charge for services.

DISCRIMINATION AND LEGAL ASSISTANCE

Unfortunately, discrimination is still one of the greatest barriers to employment, education, and full participation in community life for people with disabilities. Discrimination due to a disability is often compounded by discrimination based on gender, race, ethnicity, religion, and/or sexual orientation. Becoming familiar with your rights under federal, state, and local antidiscrimination laws and from advocacy organizations providing information or legal assistance to people with disabilities is the best way to prepare yourself to deal with discrimination should it occur.

The following are brief descriptions of major federal laws forbidding discrimination against people with disabilities:

The Rehabilitation Act of 1973

The Rehabilitation Act of 1973, as amended, prohibits discrimination against people with disabilities by the federal government, organizations receiving federal funds, and federal contractors. The law protects any person who has a physical or mental impairment that substantially limits one or more major life activities; has a record of such an impairment; or is regarded as having such an impairment.[19] In order to be protected by the law, you must be "qualified" either as a job applicant, employee, student or prospective student, or as a person eligible for other covered services.

Section 504 of the Rehabilitation Act provides that "no otherwise qualified individual with a disability in the United States . . . shall solely by reason of her or his disability, be excluded from participation in, or denied the benefits of, or be subjected to discrimination under any program or activity receiving Federal financial assistance or under any program or activity conducted by any Executive agency or by the United States Postal Service."[20]

Section 504 prohibits discrimination against people with disabilities in numerous institutions receiving federal assistance, including (but not limited to) elementary and secondary schools, colleges and universities, vocational rehabilitation agencies, vocational schools, libraries, police and fire departments, hospitals and other health, welfare, and social services.

Section 501 of the Rehabilitation Act prohibits employment discrimination by the federal government against people with disabilities. *Section 503* forbids federal contractors and subcontractors to discriminate. Both sections of the law require employers to take affirmative action to recruit, hire, train, and advance people with disabilities.

The Americans with Disabilities Act of 1990

The Americans with Disabilities Act (ADA) is a landmark piece of legislation intended to allow the millions of Americans with disabilities greater access to employment, public services, and transportation.

Title I of the ADA addresses employment discrimination in the private sector. For more information, see Chapter One.

Title II prohibits discrimination by public entities, including state and local governments. The provision covers all services, programs, and activities of public entities, such as police and fire departments, regardless of the size of the entity and whether it receives federal funds. Title II also contains provisions for making public transportation services accessible to people with disabilities.

Title III forbids discrimination in public accommodations, such as restaurants, hotels, private schools, lawyers' and doctors' offices, hospitals, pharmacies, retail stores, daycare

---

EMPLOYMENT RESOURCES

The following organizations provide employment-related resources and information. Addresses and telephone numbers are listed in the Resource Directory on page 523.

Job Accommodation Network (JAN) is a service of the President's Committee on the Employment of People with Disabilities, providing employers and people with disabilities toll-free information on job-site accommodations, hiring, retraining, and promotion of people with disabilities, and the employment provisions of the Americans with Disabilities Act.

Job Opportunities for the Blind (JOB), a project of the National Federation of the Blind and the Department of Labor, provides job seekers with a national reference and job referral service, a recorded job magazine, and recorded literature on job information and career-planning seminars, among other services. JOB also offers introductions to blind peers working in fields which are of interest to job seekers. Services are free.

Mainstream, Inc. assists employers in developing job opportunities for people with disabilities and operates a job placement service in Dallas, Texas, and Washington, D.C.

centers, homeless shelters, libraries, theaters, museums and many other places, except private clubs and religious organizations.

Although it's important to seek professional assistance soon after a discriminatory incident to examine all of your options for redress, complaints regarding a violation of Title II and III of the ADA can be sent to the U.S. Department of Justice, Civil Rights Division, Disability Rights Section, P.O. Box 66738, Washington, D.C. 20035-6738.

Title IV requires that telephone companies provide telephone relay services for people who use telecommunication devices for the deaf (TDD) or other nonvoice terminal devices.

A final miscellaneous title makes it illegal to coerce, intimidate, threaten, or interfere with a person with a disability who exercises a right under the ADA and waives state government immunity for violations of the act, among other provisions.

The Congressional Accountability Act provides for the application of the ADA and the Rehabilitation Act, as well as other civil rights and workplace laws, to the federal government and amends the ADA to prohibit disability discrimination in congressional public services and accommodations.

Airline services are covered by the *Air Carriers Access Act.* For general information about this law, you can contact the Office of the Secretary, U.S. Department of Transportation, listed in the box.

Disability laws are complex and the procedures for seeking redress varied. If you feel that you have been discriminated against because of your disability, consider contacting the local civil/human rights commission, listed in the government section of your telephone directory, or your state's Protection and Advocacy organization (see page 293) for more information. It is best to act as soon as possible, because there are limits on the time during which legal action may be taken.

Housing Discrimination

Under the federal Fair Housing Act of 1968, as amended, people with disabilities (as defined in the Rehabilitation Act) are entitled to protection against discrimination when renting or buying residential housing. The act, which is very broad and cannot be discussed in detail here, forbids discrimination based on race, skin color, religion, national origin, sex, family status (people with children under nineteen and pregnant women), and mental or physical disability.

FOR FREE INFORMATION ABOUT THE ADA AND OTHER DISABILITY LAWS

- ADA information line: U.S. Department of Justice at 1-800-514-0301 (voice) or 1-800-514-0383 (TDD)
- NARIC: 1-800-346-2742 or (301) 495-5626 (TTY)
- Job Accommodation Network: 1-800-526-7234 (voice/TDD)
- Federal Communications Commission (Title IV of the ADA) (202) 418-0190 (voice); (202) 418-2555 (TDD)
- Architectural and Transportation Barriers Compliance Board: 1-800-USA-ABLE (voice/TDD). Provides information about building accessibility and transportation.
- U.S. Department of Transportation: (202) 366-4000 (voice). Disability-related information: (202) 366-9306 or (202) 755-7687 (TDD).

The law covers almost all types of private residential housing, including mobile home parks and federally assisted housing. Some states have fair housing laws that are comparable, and some go beyond the federal law by forbidding discrimination on marital status, sexual orientation, or source of income among other possibilities.

A biased landlord may find many excuses not to rent to a person with a disability. She may say that the apartment is too small for you or that you must have a full-time personal attendant to take care of you. But landlords may not make presumptions about you or your needs, treat you differently than other prospective tenants, or use information about your disability to discriminate against you.

A landlord may ask you questions related to your qualifications as a prospective tenant, provided they are asked of *all* prospective tenants. These may include questions about your past tenancies, requests for references or for financial information, or whether you are currently using drugs.

Federal regulations prohibit a landlord from asking questions to determine if you have a disability or to determine the nature or severity of your disability.[21] A private landlord or public housing provider may not ask whether you can live independently in order to evaluate your eligibility for a tenancy,[22] unless you are applying for housing specifically designed for people with disabilities. In this case, a housing provider may ask questions to determine your eligibility, but the questions should not exceed their purpose.

It is possible for a landlord to reject your application based on *objective* evidence that your tenancy would directly threaten the health or safety of others, although this determination cannot be based on presumptions or fears about your disability but must be based on evidence from prior behavior. Further, the landlord must consider whether the direct threat can be eliminated through reasonable accommodation.[23]

If you need to make modifications to your home, or if changes in the rules, policies, practices, or services of the premises are necessary to allow you an equal opportunity to use and enjoy your home, you should know that under the Fair Housing Act a landlord must allow you reasonable accommodations, if they do not cause the landlord undue hardship.

For example, a landlord cannot refuse to allow you to install grab bars in the bathroom or ramp the steps leading to your apartment if you pay for the improvements. The landlord can require that you restore the premises to their original condition when you leave (normal wear and tear excepted), if the request is reasonable. Granting permission to widen a door in order to accommodate a wheelchair on the condition that it be narrowed when you leave is generally considered unreasonable.[24]

If you wish to make reasonable accommodations, you must inform the landlord of your needs. When extensive changes are proposed, your landlord may negotiate an agreement to set aside a reasonable amount of money, not to exceed the cost of restoration, in an interest-bearing escrow account in order to make sure that funds will be available to restore the unit.

Changes in rules, policies, practices, or services can often be made very simply. For example:

- a no-pets policy must exempt guide dogs or other "service" animals; likewise,
- a companion or "service" animal that is necessary to your well-being may be exempt from a no-pets policy. A note from a doctor, rehabilitation counselor, therapist, or other appropriate professional, or registration can verify the need.
- A person with a mobility impairment may be given a parking space near her apartment, if she desires and needs the accommodation.
- A deaf person may request that visual smoke alarms be installed in her apartment and in the common areas of the building.
- A person receiving retirement income or government assistance may be able to make arrangements with her landlord to pay rent on the date the check is actually received, rather than on the first of the month in order to avoid late fees or possible eviction for repeated late payments. Remember, it's always best to get any promises in writing.

The possibilities for these kinds of accommodation will depend on your needs. You and your landlord will have to work together to arrive at creative solutions to specific problems. For more information about housing discrimination laws, including accessibility requirements for new buildings, you can contact the federal Department of Housing and Urban Development (HUD), a legal aid organization, a protection and advocacy organization, or a local fair housing organization, if there is one in your area. The National Fair Housing Alliance, listed in the Resource Directory, can give you a referral to any available local fair housing center, or you can contact city hall or a legal aid organization.

For more information about federal housing discrimination law, you can call or write the Office of Fair Housing and Equal Opportunity, Room 5116, Department of Housing and Urban Development (HUD), 451 Seventh Street SW, Washington, D.C. 20410-2000; 1-800-669-9777 or 1-800-927-9275 (TDD).

If you suspect discrimination, be sure to document all that happened, including the date, place, and time at which the alleged discrimination took place, the address of the property, what was said and done by each party, and the names of any witnesses. Keep copies of all relevant papers, including advertisements, applications, your lease or rental agreement, bills and receipts, and any correspondence. *Retaliation for filing a complaint with HUD is illegal.* If your landlord gives you an eviction notice or raises your rent, or threatens to, because you filed a complaint, contact HUD or the agency investigating your complaint immediately.

PROTECTION AND ADVOCACY SYSTEMS

In every state, there is a protection and advocacy organization (P&A) that is mandated by law to investigate, negotiate, and mediate problems expressed by eligible clients who have developmental disabilities and people with significant mental or emotional disabilities who are currently residing in twenty-four-hour care and treatment facilities or have been discharged from a facility in the past ninety days.

Many protection and advocacy organizations operate state Client Assistance Programs (CAPs). In addition, some P&As have programs called Protection and Advocacy for Individual Rights (PAIR). These programs offer services to people with disabilities who do not necessarily fit into other eligibility categories.

Common areas of focus by P&As include:

+ Abuse and neglect in residential facilities
+ Discrimination
+ Habilitation and rehabilitation
+ Information and referral
+ Social Security benefits advocacy
+ Special education
+ Changing practices or policies that interfere with consumers' ability to access assistive technology devices or services

Protection and advocacy organizations may offer additional services in the areas of homelessness, landlord and tenant problems, and criminal justice. Priority must be given to those with the greatest need for services or to eligible people previously unserved or underserved.[25]

To locate a P&A organization in your area, contact the National Association of Protection & Advocacy Systems, Inc. (NAPAS), listed in the Resource Directory.

Income for People with Disabilities: Social Security Benefits

If you have a disability or chronic illness, you may be eligible for either Social Security disability insurance (SSDI) or for supplemental security income (SSI). The following are very brief explanations of these programs.

Social Security Disability Insurance

Social Security disability insurance (SSDI) is a federal disability insurance program. Workers contribute to the Social Security trust fund through payroll taxes. Benefits are meant to provide you and your family with income when you are no longer able to work because of a disability.

Who may be eligible? In order to be eligible for SSDI on your own work record, you must:

- have become disabled before the age of sixty-five
- have worked long enough to become "insured"
- have a medically determinable mental or physical impairment that is expected to last at least twelve months *or* to result in death
- be unable to do any kind of substantial work because of your disability. This is referred to as substantial gainful activity (SGA).

It is important to note that under the Social Security Administration's definition of disability, you must not only be considered unable to perform your previous work but *any* other kind of work that exists in the national economy, considering your age, education, and past work experience. Generally, earnings of over $500 a month are considered substantial for people with disabilities and over $960 for people who are blind (1996).[26] The Social Security Administration does offer work incentives to allow you to earn income without losing your benefits.

Special rule for people who are blind and at least fifty-five: If you are legally blind and cannot engage in work that requires the skills or abilities comparable to those used in your previous employment, you may also be eligible for benefits. These criteria are different from those mentioned above. Your eye doctor (ophthalmologist) can tell you if you are legally blind. Sometimes a person who is not legally blind, but whose condition prevents her from working can qualify for Social Security benefits as a person with a disability.

Benefits for family members. You may also be eligible for benefits if you are a disabled widow aged fifty to fifty-nine or a surviving divorced spouse aged fifty to fifty-nine with a disability. In addition, children and adult daughters and sons with disabilities may be entitled to SSDI benefits. Benefits may be subject to a family maximum amount.

How long will you wait for benefits? Your disability benefits will not begin *until the sixth full calendar month of disability.* The wait may be longer if you are denied benefits and have to appeal. Social Security disability benefits are retroactive for up to twelve months (excluding the waiting period). Spousal disability benefits are retroactive for six months.

How does SSDI affect other benefits? You and your family's disability benefits combined with other benefits that you receive, including workers' compensation, cannot be greater than 80 percent of your highest average monthly earnings shortly before you became disabled. SSDI recipients with low incomes may be eligible for SSI to supplement their benefits.

When you have been eligible for SSDI for twenty-four months, you can begin Medicare coverage. Medicare beneficiaries with low incomes and limited resources may be eligible for the Qualified Medicare Beneficiaries (QMB) or the Specified Low-Income Medicare Beneficiaries (SLMB) programs through which the state Medicaid agency pays Medicare out-of-pocket costs.

Supplemental Security Income

Supplemental security income (SSI) is a federal cash assistance program intended to provide a minimum level of income to people sixty-five years of age or older and to people of *any age,* including children, who are blind or disabled. In order to be eligible, you must have a low income and limited resources. Many people qualify for both Social Security and SSI benefits.

In the past, a child under age eighteen was considered to be disabled when a mental or physical impairment limited the child's ability to function like other children of the same age to such an extent that the impairment was of comparable severity to that which would disable an adult. In 1996 this provision was repealed, and the definition of disability for children was changed. While there is a different standard for determining eligibility for children, the program is still avail-

Adults and children who are applicants for SSI may be considered *presumptively disabled* and qualify for payments for up to six months before an eligibility decision is made. Conditions considered to automatically qualify a person as disabled include:

- AIDS or HIV infection, if severity criteria are met[28]
- amputation of two limbs
- amputation of a leg at the hip
- total blindness or deafness
- bed confinement or immobility without the use of a wheelchair, walker, or crutches because of a long-standing condition
- stroke more than three months in the past with continued or marked difficulty in walking or using an arm or hand
- cerebral palsy, muscular dystrophy, or muscular atrophy and marked difficulty in walking (for example, you use braces), speaking, or coordination of the hands or arms
- diabetes with amputation of one foot
- Down syndrome
- significant mental deficiency (for a person at least age seven)[29]

First-time SSI applicants who need assistance before the time their first check arrives may qualify for *emergency advance payments* when there is a strong likelihood of meeting the qualifications for eligibility. *Immediate payments* may also be available to certain SSI applicants or recipients who have established their eligibility and who are facing a financial emergency causing a lack of food or shelter or danger to health or safety.

able and parents of children with significant disabilities are still eligible to apply.

Benefit amounts vary depending on the state in which you live. Most states supplement SSI benefits. In some states, you must make a separate application for supplementary payments.

The amount of your benefits may also be affected by your marital status and living arrangements. For example, married couples who are living together are paid at the rate for couples; married couples who separated are paid at the individual rate after the first month of separation.[27] Likewise, children's benefits will be affected when living with a parent whose income and resources are deemed to be available to the child.

Generally, if you are considered eligible for SSI, you will also be eligible for Medicaid (also called Medi-Cal or Medical Assistance). In some states your eligibility is automatic; in others, you must make a separate application for Medicaid. In all states (except California, which includes extra

Resources for Adults and Children with Disabilities

cash payments in SSI checks), you will also be eligible for food stamps.

SSI recipients may want to learn about the PASS (Plan for Achieving Self-Support) program. Under the PASS program, you may set aside income and resources to pursue a business, job training or educational goals without jeopardizing benefits. Centers for independent living can often assist consumers with PASS applications.

Tips on applying for benefits

- Do not wait to apply for benefits. Because of the delay caused by the waiting period and any further delays due to an initial denial, it is important to apply *as soon as possible*. You will need to gather many documents to verify your disability. It's best to be as prepared as possible, but don't let the time involved in preparing your documentation delay your application unnecessarily. Talk to an advocacy organization or the Social Security Administration as soon as you can.
- If possible, seek the advice of an advocate or advocacy organization before applying. Also ask whether your state has its own disability insurance programs for workers.
- It is generally best to file in person. In order to avoid a long wait, call to find out whether you can make an appointment. If you are too sick to visit the Social Security office, the office may send a representative to help you fill out the forms, if necessary.
- It is not uncommon to be turned down for benefits the first time you apply. If you are denied SSI or SSDI benefits, you have the right to file a written request for a reconsideration within sixty days. If you are denied a reconsideration, you can then make a written request for a hearing before an administrative law judge within sixty days from the date you receive the notice of the reconsideration determination. You may submit new evidence to support your claim and may be represented by an attorney or advocate. If you are still dissatisfied with the decision, you can request a review by the appeals council. You can request a review in federal court within sixty days after an unfavorable appeals council decision or a denial of review.

Here are a few organizations that may be able to help you prepare your application for government benefits and assist you when problems arise.

Benefits and entitlements: who can help?

Applying for government benefits and entitlements can be a frustrating experience. But you have the right to apply and to appeal a denial. You should never be made to feel as though it is wrong to assert these rights. Everyone has a need for assistance at some time in life. Access to financial or medical assistance is often a matter of survival. Although you may feel that you are "taking" something from your community, you may also want to consider the many ways in which you can, and do, give to your community and to those you love every day.

- *Independent living centers* can often provide assistance or refer people to other helpful organizations.
- *Area Agencies on Aging (AAA)* can direct you to any available free or low cost insurance counseling programs serving older people who have questions about Medicare, Medigap, and long-term-care insurance. The AAA may also tell you about any free *legal services* programs in your area available to older people. See Chapter Nine for more information.
- *Legal aid organizations* may be able to assist you, but funding restrictions may limit legal services availability.
- *AIDS service organizations* often provide benefits advisement or referrals to legal aid organizations dedicated to serving people with HIV infection or AIDS. (See Chapter Eight.)
- *Protection and advocacy systems* may be able to assist eligible clients.
- *Disabled American Veterans (DAV),* a nonprofit organization, provides advisement and advocacy for veteran's benefits free of charge to veterans and their families. It is not necessary to be a member to utilize DAV's benefits services. For more information about DAV, refer to the Resource Directory.
- If you are a patient in a hospital, ask to speak with a medical social worker for assistance.

WORKERS' COMPENSATION

All states have workers' compensation laws that require employers to assume the cost of accidental work-related injuries and diseases. In general, disability and death benefits are paid regardless of who is at fault. In return for no-fault coverage, benefits are limited and employees cannot usually sue their employers for damages, though in some states there are exceptions to this rule. In most states employees can sue their employers for intentional injuries.

Workers' compensation laws differ from state to state, and not every type of employment is covered. For example, state law often allows employers to exclude farm workers and domestic workers from the system. In many states, employers of any number of employees must insure their workers; but in some states, only employers of a certain number (typically three to five) are covered by the law. Civilian employees of the federal government are covered by the Federal Employees' Compensation Act (FECA).

Although many employers purchase workers' compensation from state insurance funds or private insurers, most states allow employers to self-insure. Self-insurance is not really insurance. Rather, employers are allowed to set up a fund to pay workers' compensation benefits.

Generally, workers' compensation benefits are only payable for injuries or diseases, including mental or physical injuries "arising out of and in the course of employment." The cause of illness or injury must be linked to employment and, typically, must have occurred while you were doing your job.

Depending on the extent of the injury, an injured worker may be entitled to medical benefits or cash impairment or disability benefits. Medical rehabilitation is available to workers who sustain severe disabilities; and many states allow for vocational rehabilitation when necessary. In some states, and under the Federal Employees' Compensation Act, participation in rehabilitation is compulsory.

The type and duration of benefits you receive will depend on state law and the extent of your injury or illness. Cash benefits, paid in weekly installments, are limited to a percentage (typically, about two-thirds) of your average weekly wage. Where there has been a loss of an organ, limb, or other body part, "scheduled" or "fixed" benefits are awarded at an amount set by the state.

In many states, payments for "permanent total" disabilities last through the remainder of the insured worker's life. Death benefits are usually paid to the widow (or widower) of an insured worker until she (or he) remarries and to children until they reach a certain age. In recent years, some courts have awarded benefits to unmarried partners.

As mentioned above, workers' compensation benefits combined with Social Security disability insurance payments cannot exceed 80 percent of your average weekly wage prior to your becoming disabled.

What to Do If You Have Been Injured at Work

You should notify your employer, get treatment for your injury, and file a claim with the state agency that administers workers' compensation as soon as possible. In most states, workers' compensation laws are administered by a board or commission typically called the Workers' Compensation Commission or Department of Industrial Relations (or Accidents). In a few states, laws are administered by the workers' compensation court.

Each state sets a different time limit in which employees must notify their employers, but limits are usually very short.

Most states allow longer periods for reporting work-related diseases.

If your claim is contested, it is advisable to seek the services of a workers' compensation attorney. You and your employer or the insurer have an opportunity for a hearing. If the hearing is unsatisfactory, either side can ask for an administrative review and, in most states, appeal in court. As with similar legal disputes, workers' compensation cases can be lengthy and emotionally painful. You will have to balance the compensation you stand to gain against other potential losses.

PART TWO: RESOURCES FOR CHILDREN WITH DISABILITIES

You may not view your child as having a disability, but the term "disability" is very broad, encompassing such diverse conditions as cerebral palsy, hearing impairments, autism, emotional disorders, and learning disabilities, among many others. If your child has special needs, you may want to know about a major educational law, called the Individuals with Disabilities Education Act (IDEA), which is designed to protect children with disabilities. Through the IDEA, your child may have access to early intervention and education programs, which can enhance his or her developmental and educational growth. These programs will be discussed in this section. Be advised that, at the time of this writing, the IDEA was undergoing reauthorization and that some of its provisions may have been changed.

The first step on the path toward getting treatment and services for your child is to consult with your child's pediatrician. Your health care professional can help you understand your child's condition and provide you with resources for continued information and support. Having information will not only help you to resolve any fears that you have about your child's disability, it will help you advocate for your child and make necessary decisions regarding services that are available under the IDEA and other programs.

Support and advocacy groups, many of which are listed in the Resource Directory, and the organizations discussed below can provide you with additional information about your child's condition and the IDEA. Don't forget local public libraries and bookstores. There is a variety of good books written for parents of children with disabilities. The reading list at the end of this book offers some general suggestions.

The task of finding services, treatment, and financial assistance to meet your child's needs is often a daunting one. However, there are a number of organizations that can help along the way. Relevant telephone numbers and addresses of the following are listed in the Resource Directory.

National Information Center for Children and Youth with Disabilities (NICHCY) is an information clearinghouse providing free information on disabilities and disability-related issues. NICHCY can send you a state resource sheet, which lists government and private organizations offering support and advocacy services. Publications that cover the IDEA, respite care, assistive devices, sibling issues, medical bills, and many other topics are available. Information specialists can answer questions about the IDEA and other legal matters.

Parent Training and Information Centers (PTI) are federally funded organizations that teach parents of children with disabilities how to become active participants in their children's education and development. They offer workshops, information and advice over the telephone, and literature to help parents secure the school services to which their children are entitled. NICHCY's state resource sheets include information about Parent Training and Information Centers. (Also see Federation for Children with Special Needs in the Resource Directory.)

Protection and Advocacy Systems may be able to assist you and your child with legal matters involving special education and discrimination. (See Part One of this chapter.)

Are there additional services in your state? In addition to learning about federal programs for children with disabilities, contact your state's educational, health, and social service agencies to find out whether there are state programs that might benefit your child.

Services for newborns and toddlers: early intervention

If your child is between birth and three years of age and has recently been diagnosed with a disability, or if you suspect that your child has a disability, you should know about early intervention. Early intervention is a federal-state program that was created under Part H of the IDEA. It is designed to identify and treat problems in child development as early as possible and allows access to a range of services that can enhance your child's growth and decrease the possibility of a developmental delay. The kinds of services that are right for your child and the frequency with which they will be delivered depend on the nature of his or her needs, the family's needs, your schedule, and other factors.

Each state is allowed to develop its own early intervention program. To get your child started, contact your state's lead agency for early intervention. This is usually the state department of education or health, which oversees and coordinates the early intervention program and can refer you to the appropriate initial contact. The *National Information Center*

Evaluation refers to the procedures used to determine a child's eligibility for early intervention, including a determination of your child's developmental status.

Assessment means the ongoing process used to identify your child's unique needs, your family's strengths and needs related to your child's development, and the nature and extent of the services necessary to meet those needs.

IFSP, the Individualized Family Service Plan, is a written plan for early intervention services. It is based on the evaluation and assessment and is developed by you and the professionals involved in providing early intervention services.

for *Children and Youth with Disabilities* (NICHCY) can help you locate your state's lead agency. Call and request a copy of a resource sheet for your state.

If your baby is still in the hospital, ask the discharge planner or medical social worker for a referral to your state's early intervention program.

How to Get Early Intervention: Assessment and Evaluation

When you contact the lead agency, you'll be given an appointment for an evaluation and assessment. A multidisciplinary team of professionals, usually comprised of a psychologist, an early interventionist, and an occupational or physical therapist, will test all areas of your child's development to determine whether she or he qualifies for early intervention.

It's possible that the assessment, evaluation, and IFSP development will take place all in one day. Therefore you should be prepared for that day with enough information about early intervention and your child's needs to make decisions regarding the service plan. Parent training information centers and support and advocacy groups can help you better understand the nature of your child's disability and the needs she or he may have.

Under current law, the evaluation and assessment, and the first IFSP meeting, must take place within forty-five days of the initial referral to the lead agency, unless exceptional circumstances, such as your child's illness, make it impossible.

Both the evaluation and the assessment must be given in your family's native language or mode of communication, including sign language. This can be accomplished through the use of an interpreter. The assessment must not be racially or culturally discriminatory and cannot be given without your written consent.

Evaluation and assessment are done without charge and, in most cases, the services your child needs will be provided at no cost. Because states develop different policies, it is possible that you will be asked to pay for some services on a sliding scale basis. However, you must not be denied services simply because you cannot afford to pay.

How Is Eligibility Determined?

There are three ways in which children are determined to be eligible for services. Children who are considered to have developmental delays are generally eligible. These include delays in cognitive development — cognition refers to the act or process of knowing or perceiving — physical development (including vision and hearing), language and speech development, emotional or social development, and self-help skills.

A child may also be determined eligible for early intervention services if he or she is diagnosed with a physical or mental condition that has a high probability of resulting in a developmental delay. Down syndrome and chromosomal abnormalities, vision and hearing impairments, fetal alcohol syndrome, and seizure disorders are examples of conditions that are known to have developmental consequences.

Infants who are at risk of having developmental delays if early intervention services are not provided to them may also be eligible. At-risk conditions include low birth weight, respiratory distress experienced at birth, lack of oxygen, brain hemorrhage, nutritional deprivation, infection, and a history of abuse or neglect.[30] Contact the lead agency to find out whether your state's program is available to at-risk infants.

Securing Early Intervention: The IFSP

If your child is found eligible for early intervention services, you and the evaluation team will develop an *Individualized Family Service Plan (IFSP)*. Based on your child's evaluation and assessment, the IFSP identifies the early intervention services that will benefit your child's development and commits the state to provide them. The completed IFSP must include information about your child's present developmental status; a specific description of the early intervention services to be provided; when, where, how often and by what method they will be provided, and how long they will last; and a statement of the major outcomes expected to be achieved for the child and family. (Outcomes of early intervention services cannot be guaranteed. The IFSP merely requires the state to provide them.) Further, the IFSP should include medical and other services that your child needs but which are not required to be provided by law and a plan for transition into preschool services.[31]

Your family will be assigned a service coordinator, who will ensure that the goals of the IFSP are being carried out and help you coordinate community services for your child. The name of the service coordinator should be written into the IFSP.

With your consent, the IFSP will include information about your family's resources, priorities, and concerns related to the enhancement of your child's development. Although you do not have to supply the evaluation team with information about your family, it's a good idea to discuss any problems you might have in carrying out the plan, such as language barriers, transportation problems, or even personal issues, so that assistance can be arranged.

It is possible to receive services before an IFSP has been developed. To do this, you must give your consent to develop an interim IFSP with the service coordinator.

Early Intervention Services

The following are examples of services that can be provided to your child through the early intervention program, if appropriate. Remember that services that are appropriate for your child must be written into the IFSP. Like all laws, the IDEA is subject to change. Contact NICHCY and other relevant groups for any new information.

- audiology (identification of hearing loss and services to help prevent or adapt to hearing loss)
- coordination of the services provided
- family training and counseling and home visits
- medical services delivered by a physician, generally for diagnosis and evaluation purposes
- nursing services
- nutrition services
- occupational therapy
- physical therapy
- psychological services
- social work services
- special instruction
- speech-language therapy
- transportation costs necessary to enable your child and family to receive services
- vision services
- assistive technology devices (such as speech synthesizers and computer-type enlargers)
- health services necessary for your child to benefit from early intervention, except services that are purely medical in nature, surgical services, devices necessary to treat or control a condition, and well-baby care. Examples of services that can be included are intermittent clean catheterization, tube feeding, and changing of dressings or colostomy collection bags.[32]

You do not have to accept a service that you believe is inappropriate for your child. Be certain to talk over your concerns with the professionals involved and to discuss any problems that you foresee in carrying out the plan at the meeting. Don't sign the IFSP until you understand and approve of its contents. The IFSP must be reviewed periodically and evaluated annually.

Where Will Your Child Receive Services?

Services can be given at home, in early intervention centers, hospitals, clinics, or in a combination of settings. To the maximum extent appropriate, efforts must be made to deliver services in settings in which nondisabled children participate.[33]

Therapists may work individually with your child or they may instruct you or a teacher in ways to aid in your child's development.

Families' and Children's Rights

The law provides for many procedural safeguards to ensure your rights and those of your child. The lead agency is responsible for establishing and implementing these safeguards. For example:

- You must be given the opportunity to inspect and review records relating to the evaluation and assessment, eligibility determination, implementation of the IFSP, any individual complaints dealing with your child, and other pertinent records.
- You must be given written notice before an agency or service provider proposes, or refuses, to begin or change the identification, evaluation, or placement of your child, or to provide early intervention services.[34]
- You have a right to confidentiality of any information that may identify your child and a right to written notice of and consent to any exchange of information among agencies.[35]

Dispute Resolutions: Problems with the IFSP

If you and the agency disagree about services to be included in the IFSP, it is best to try to resolve the issue at the IFSP meeting. Resolving conflicts through administrative procedures can be difficult and time-consuming. However, regulations governing the IDEA require states to have procedures in place in order to bring about a timely resolution of parents' complaints, either through the method used to resolve complaints regarding special education (described below),

Throughout the country, there are public residential schools for blind and visually impaired students and for deaf and hearing-impaired students. Serving children in grades kindergarten through twelve, public residential schools for blind children offer instruction in mobility training, Braille, and skills for independent living in addition to regular coursework. Schools for children who are deaf or hearing impaired begin enrollment from infancy and continue through the twelfth grade. Students receive instruction in sign language and lip-reading as well as in traditional subject matter. To learn more about special needs schools, contact your local school district.

or by developing another method that meets similar standards. Contact your lead agency to find out what process your state uses and how to file a complaint.

From the time of filing and throughout the hearing process, your child is entitled to continue receiving services, unless you and the lead agency agree to discontinue services.

If you are dissatisfied with the result of the administrative hearing, you have the right to bring a civil action in state or federal court.

CHILDREN AGED THREE TO TWENTY-ONE: SPECIAL EDUCATION

The Individuals with Disabilities Education Act requires that school districts provide a free, appropriate public education, including necessary related services, for children and youth with disabilities, beginning at age three, in the least restrictive environment. If for some reason your child cannot be assured of a free, appropriate education in a public school, your child may be entitled to placement (with your consent) in a private school or facility at no cost to you. Note, however, that a free, appropriate education is usually interpreted by the school district to mean adequate and not necessarily the best.

Getting an Evaluation for Special Education

If you think that special education may be appropriate for your child, contact the principal of your child's school and ask how to request an evaluation. Make sure to put your request for an evaluation in writing. Parent training and information centers (PTI) can give you information on getting an evaluation for your child. Your child's school, teacher, or doctor may also refer your child for an evaluation, but this cannot happen without your written consent.

How Is Eligibility Determined?

Before your child can be placed in a special education program, an evaluation must be done to determine his or her educational needs. An evaluation consists of a series of tests in all areas of development, including, if appropriate, health, vision, hearing, social and emotional status, general intelligence, academic performance, communicative ability, and motor skills.[36] Conclusions drawn from the evaluation may not be based on the results of one test alone.

The evaluation may only be conducted with your consent and must be given without charge. Tests must be administered by a multidisciplinary team of professionals and should not discriminate against your child. For example, tests should not be given in a manner that is racially or culturally discriminatory and must be administered in the language or mode of communication with which your child is most familiar, including sign language and Braille. In addition, any personally identifiable information regarding your child must be kept confidential. As a parent, you have a right to inspect and review any educational records relating to your child.[37]

Children who are eligible for special education are those who, through the evaluation process, are determined to need special education and related services (i.e., have to have a qualifying disability and be determined to need special education because of that disability) and to have one or more of the following: mental retardation; hearing impairments, including deafness; speech or language impairments; visual impairments, including blindness; serious emotional disturbance; orthopedic impairments; autism; traumatic brain injury; other health impairments, such as epilepsy, hemophilia, or diabetes; specific learning disabilities; or deaf-blindness.[38]

The evaluation process will result in the formation of an *Individualized Education Program (IEP)*. The IEP represents a commitment by the education agency to provide a learning program designed especially for your child, including related services. However, the IEP does not guarantee specific results, only that the services identified in the document will be delivered.

If you disagree with the results of the evaluation, you are entitled to an *independent educational evaluation (IEE)*. You may want to consider getting an IEE if you believe that the evaluations were administered incorrectly or conducted in a discriminatory manner. This second evaluation must be considered when your child's IEP is made. You can request that the school give you a copy of all evaluations and records concerning your child.

The Individualized Education Program

When your child is found eligible for special education, a meeting will be held to identify your child's educational goals and the services needed in order to reach them. At the meeting you, your child's teacher(s), a representative from the school district, and a member of the evaluation team (if your child is being evaluated for the first time) will develop the individualized education program (IEP).

You have the right to attend the IEP meeting and to be accompanied by your husband or partner, an advocate who is familiar with the IDEA, or anyone you wish. In fact, it is vital that you attend this meeting. Many parents are tempted to let the experts take over in the development of the IEP. But your involvement is crucial and can make a difference in the nature of your child's education. You will be asked to share your knowledge of your child and your beliefs regarding his or her education. Your child may also attend the IEP meeting, if you feel it would be appropriate and beneficial.

The IEP should be tailored to meet your child's needs. It should not be based on what services the school district has available. It should contain a statement of:

- your child's present levels of educational performance
- short-term and annual instructional objectives
- specific special education and related services to be provided
- when and for how long services will be delivered
- appropriate objective criteria and procedures to determine whether short-term instructional goals are being met; and
- a transition plan after graduation into postschool activities.[39]

Preparing for the IEP Meeting

It is best to prepare for the IEP meeting as much as possible. Become familiar with your state's policies and the mandates of the IDEA. Review any and all of your child's developmental evaluations. Think about which programs and services will best meet your child's needs. NICHCY can provide you with information on the IDEA. Advocacy organizations can give you information about the needs of children with similar disabilities. Parent Training and Information Centers can offer advice and guidance.

The process of creating an IEP should be a cooperative one, with parents and school personnel working together. Ask any questions that you have regarding the IEP at the meeting. If you disagree with something that is suggested, say as much, and ask for clarification. Although it is important to respect the knowledge and special training of professionals in the education field, you have a unique understanding and knowledge of your child. Your input is equally valid and important.

It is essential that you approach the meeting from an open, rather than an adversarial perspective even if you have had negative experiences with schools in the past. The possibility of a dispute is minimized when each party listens objectively and respectfully to the other. Try to resolve any differences of opinion at the meeting. You can call another IEP meeting if the established plan is not satisfactory, and if disputes arise, you have the right to a due process hearing.

What Services Will Your Child Need in Order to Benefit from Special Education?

As mentioned, the IDEA mandates school districts to provide a free, appropriate public education, including necessary related services, to children with disabilities. The following is a list of services the school district must offer your child, if needed. Again, it's important to remember that laws change and to contact NICHCY and other organizations for ongoing information.

School districts have the option of offering other developmental, corrective, and supportive services, such as art, music, and dance therapy. You and those in attendance at the IEP meeting will determine what services the school will offer your child.

- early identification and assessment
- transportation
- speech therapy
- audiology (identification and help to prevent and adapt to hearing loss)
- psychological services
- recreation and recreation therapy
- rehabilitation counseling
- physical therapy
- occupational therapy
- counseling services
- medical services (for diagnosis or evaluation)
- parent counseling and training
- school health services
- social work services in school
- transitional services[40]

Where Will Your Child Receive Special Education Services?

Special education services can be delivered in a variety of ways, but because the law states that children must be placed in the least restrictive environment, schools attempt to place children with disabilities in as regular a classroom setting as possible. For example, your child may attend regular classes for most of the day and then go to a resource room within the school where specialized attention or therapy is given. If the school lacks resources to serve your child on the grounds, arrangements may be made for specialized instruction to be given at another facility.

Resolving Disagreements: Due Process

It is best to try to resolve disagreements about your child's evaluation, IEP, or suggested related services at the initial IEP meeting. Although parents and the school district have the right to a hearing before an informed and impartial hearing examiner, this formal exercise of due process can be a long and difficult one. However, states are required to establish procedures for due process, which may begin either with a hearing before the public agency directly responsible for the education of your child or the state education agency. To find out which method your state uses and how to begin due process, contact the school district's office of special education or the school superintendent. NICHCY and support and advocacy groups can also give you information about due process.

Another Way to Get the Services Your Child Needs:
Section 504

There is a possibility that your child's disability will not qualify him or her for special education or related services under the IDEA, as has happened in the past with students who have Attention Deficit Disorder. Section 504 of the Rehabilitation Act presents a possible means of obtaining related services for your child.

Section 504 forbids discrimination against people with disabilities in federally funded programs. The regulations governing educational programs are very similar to the IDEA and require public schools to provide a free, appropriate education to each qualified person with a disability regardless of the nature or severity of the disability.

Two aspects of Section 504 are useful to parents attempting to secure related services for their child. Unlike the IDEA, Section 504 does not require that students be enrolled in special education to receive related services. As well, Section 504 defines disability more broadly than the IDEA. Section 504 protects people who have a physical or mental impairment that substantially limits one or more major life activities and people with a record of such an impairment or who are regarded as having such an impairment.

In order to be protected by the act, people with disabilities must be qualified to participate in the program or activity. With respect to public education, a qualified person with a disability (as defined above) is:

- of an age during which nondisabled students are provided such services;
- of any age during which it is mandatory under state law to provide such services for people with disabilities; or
- a person for whom the state is required to provide a free, appropriate education under Section 612 of the Education of the Handicapped Act (currently known as the IDEA)[41]

Parents who believe that their child is not receiving a free, appropriate education can contact the special education director from the school district that the child attends and request a Section 504 review. The resource sheet for your state offered by NICHCY lists the name of your special education director. If the school's 504 review is unsatisfactory, you may also file a complaint with the office of civil rights in the Department of Education. You also have the right to bring a civil action in state or federal court.

HEAD START

Head Start is a federally assisted child development program for low-income children of three to five years of age. It operates in nonprofit organizations and school systems throughout the country. Head Start programs work in the areas of education, health, parent involvement, and social services to address a child's total developmental needs.

Head Start programs must reserve 10 percent of their enrollment for children with disabilities. Generally, local schools work with Head Start programs to create an IEP and share resources to deliver related services. For example, a child may receive instruction both at the regular school and the Head Start school. In most Head Start schools, a special services coordinator arranges the community services that children need.

Although many children are referred to Head Start programs by another agency, such as the local Department of Social Services or their school, you can go directly to the Head Start school and apply. However, the program may have a waiting list, prioritized according to need.

EPSDT: GETTING HEALTH SERVICES FOR YOUR CHILDREN

If your children are eligible for Medicaid (or Medi-Cal, in California), you should know about the EPSDT program. EPSDT stands for Early and Periodic Screening, Diagnosis, and Treatment. Although not widely advertised, it is a good way to get the health care your child needs. It's part of the Medicaid program and is designed to serve children ages birth through eighteen or twenty-one, depending on the state. Under the program, states are required to provide eligible children with routine screenings for physical and mental health problems, including developmental delays. At minimum, these screenings should include a comprehensive physical examination and history, and vision, hearing, and dental testing. If through the EPSDT screenings a physical or mental health problem is discovered, the state must provide necessary medical services to your child, which can include almost any service funded by Medicaid, even if these services are not offered to other Medicaid recipients or are provided only in a limited amount or duration. For example, a child may be able to receive cleft palate surgery or rehabilitative services, if medically necessary. Necessary scheduling and transportation assistance must also be provided. Children who are found to have disabling conditions can be referred to the state's early intervention program for a full developmental assessment.

If you have applied for Medicaid (or Medi-Cal), ask your intake worker or caseworker about getting an EPSDT screening for your child. (If you have a low income, you may be eligible for Medicaid and not know it. For more information, contact your state or local Medicaid office. Check the state or local government sections of your telephone directory. The names of the agencies under which the office may be located differ from state to state. In general, look for social services, health, or public welfare departments.) Although the name of the EPSDT program varies from state to state, your worker should know what EPSDT is. Do not wait for your worker to give you this information — ask! You are entitled to a complete description of the program and the services that may be available to your child.

RESPITE CARE: TIME OFF FOR CAREGIVERS

Respite care is a service that provides temporary care to children with disabilities so that parents and caregivers can relax, rest, or tend to other family concerns. It is easy to become overwhelmed by the financial and time demands caring for a child with a disability may present, and although you may be reluctant to use a respite service, the benefits of having time to rest and rejuvenate cannot be overestimated. With time off from caregiving, you may find it easier to handle the everyday pressures of parenting or to give extra time to your nondisabled children.

Respite care can be arranged to last from several hours to several weeks. Services can be provided in your home as well as in family daycare settings, group homes, hospital-based programs, and parent cooperatives.

Respite care services may be provided by your local department of social services or department of education, public and private respite care agencies, and support and advocacy groups. Most respite services are offered on a sliding scale basis, although there are exceptions. Licensing requirements for organizations providing respite care differ from state to state and depend on the nature of the organization offering care.

Most likely, you will have to do some searching for a center that meets your needs and approval. You can call the ARCH National Resource Center for Respite and Crisis Care Services at 1-800-7-RELIEF for the names of respite care centers in your area, although the National Resource Center does not make recommendations. Also, contact parent support groups, Parent Training and Information Centers, your child's social worker, or your child's special education or IFSP service coordinator.

Foster parents must contact the foster care licensing authority in their area, since children in foster care may only receive respite care from programs licensed by the foster care licensing authority.

For more information about choosing a respite center or home respite providers, contact Access to Care and Help (ARCH) at ARCH National Resource Center Coordinating Office, Chapel Hill Training-Outreach Project, 800 Eastowne Drive, Suite 105, Chapel Hill, NC 27514. Telephone: 1-800-473-1727 or 1-800-7-RELIEF. Single copies of fact sheets are free.

WHAT'S IN THIS CHAPTER?

❖ Suicide Prevention
❖ Crisis Intervention: Sources of Help
❖ Seeking Mental Health Care
  ◆ Finding Your Way Through the Mental Health System
  ◆ Psychotherapy
  ◆ Medication
❖ Hospitalization
❖ Paying for Mental Health Care
❖ Women and Alcohol and Other Drugs

❖ 7 ❖

Crises in Mental Health

SUICIDE PREVENTION

People of all ages, races, ethnic heritages, professional backgrounds, and socioeconomic classes die by suicide. Adults over sixty-five have the highest suicide rate in the United States. Suicide is also the third leading cause of death in young people between the ages of fourteen and twenty-four, and the sixth leading cause of death in children ages five to fourteen.

Someone to whom death seems the only answer may be suffering a penetrating sense of hopelessness, for which relief may be unimaginable. She may have experienced a series of overwhelming problems or stressful life events and/or may be suffering from depression, a highly treatable but serious condition. A child or teenager experiencing a painful life event may not have a concrete sense of death's finality and may in some degree view death as a temporary respite from pain or anguish.

All talk of suicide, gestures, and attempts at suicide must be taken very seriously. The notion that most people who talk about suicide don't kill themselves is a myth. Suicide threats, whether overt or veiled, are significant among warning signs for suicide. A suicide attempt is a genuine cry for help, not merely an attention-seeking device. Attempts may result in permanent impairments and, eventually, in completed suicide.

POSSIBLE RISK FACTORS FOR SUICIDE

It is not always possible to identify someone at risk for suicide, nor is it always possible to stop someone from suicide.

Although the act of suicide is highly complex and individual, there are risk factors and warnings signs, which this section will discuss.

Bear in mind that no single risk factor is predictive of suicide. A number of risk factors and warning signs, however, can be significant.

People at particular risk are those with:

- a prior suicide attempt
- a family history of depression or suicide
- experience of a series of stressful life events such as: the death of a loved one; loss of employment, income, status, or independence; or a new move. For teenagers, humiliating or painful experiences, such as the breakup of a relationship or an academic failure, may precipitate a suicidal crisis.
- a psychiatric diagnosis such as schizophrenia in addition to depression
- an alcohol and/or other drug abuse problem
- a diagnosis of a serious medical illness, especially if coupled with depression or persistent pain
- the experience of being isolated or feeling alone
- depression. Signs of depression include:

  > persistent depressed mood (feeling sad or empty or being tearful)
  > loss of interest or pleasure in activities
  > weight gain or significant weight loss without dieting
  > decrease or increase in appetite
  > trouble sleeping (including early morning waking) or sleeping too much
  > apparent restlessness or slowness

- fatigue or loss of energy
- feelings of worthlessness or excessive or inappropriate guilt
- difficulty concentrating or indecisiveness
- recurrent thoughts of suicide or death or a suicide attempt[1]

Depression does not always present itself in a straightforward manner. For example, a young person who is depressed may exhibit the symptoms above, but sudden changes in attitude and behavior, such as withdrawing from others, becoming very anxious, irritable or disruptive, may also indicate depression. Symptoms of depression experienced by older people are similar to symptoms at any stage of life, but may be marked by irritability, loss of appetite, physical complaints, memory problems, and confusion. Because it is difficult to diagnose, depression in an elderly person may be mistaken for dementia. Sometimes depression is disregarded since it is perceived as a natural part of the aging process or of illness, which it is not.

Some Warning Signs of Suicide

As with risk factors, no single warning sign, *with the exception of talk or threats of suicide,* is an indication of suicide risk. Again, a cluster of clues should be taken very seriously:

- talk of suicide or death or preoccupation with death or violent themes
- significant or sudden changes in personality or behavior
- depression and feelings of hopelessness
- sudden lift out of a depression. The risk of suicide is greater when someone who has previously suffered from debilitating depression seems suddenly to have recovered energy. A firm decision to commit suicide or the dissipation of the immobilizing aspects of depression may give someone with depression enough energy to undertake self-destruction.
- "putting one's affairs in order" — mending a friendship, taking a sudden or urgent interest in writing or changing a will without any particular reason, taking out an insurance plan suddenly, or giving away valued possessions
- acquiring the means to commit suicide, for example, buying a gun or amassing prescription medications. Failing to take needed medications can also be a sign of an intent to end one's life.[2]

What to Do If You Think Someone You Know Is at Risk for Suicide

If you think someone you know may be depressed or suicidal, don't avoid the subject. Talk to your friend or relative. Tell her that you care and want to know what is troubling her. Let your concern and empathy show. If your relative or friend suggests suicide as a possibility, resist the temptation to argue or offer platitudes such as, "You have everything to live for." Stock encouragements or criticisms may not be meaningful to someone who is suffering from depression and may only aggravate feelings of guilt or alienation. Instead, try to listen without judgment. Understand that people experience and perceive life problems and crises dif-

---

In addition to other risk factors for suicide, the following are especially relevant to young people:
- physical or sexual abuse
- family conflict or disruption
- being lesbian, gay, or bisexual in the absence of familial or other support
- school problems or undue pressure to succeed
- perfectionism
- alcohol and/or other drug abuse
- troublesome behavior, for example, getting into fights, committing crimes or running away
- cluster suicides. The suicide of another teenager or the suicide of a celebrity may increase the risk of suicide for vulnerable teens.

---

ferently. For example, adults who have lived through many different experiences often forget how deeply a young person can be affected by the breakup of a romantic relationship or by academic defeats or other losses. Help your loved one look for other solutions to the problems with which he is struggling. As you talk together, remind him that even the most difficult of situations can change and that the success rate for treatment of problems like depression is high.

Don't be afraid to ask directly, "Are you thinking about killing yourself?" Talking about suicide will not induce someone to take his or her own life. Rather, your relative or friend may be relieved to know that it is safe to discuss the subject with you. Calmly and gently ask how long your loved one has been feeling depressed or upset and whether he has made any plans or taken steps to end his life. The risk for suicide is highest when someone has a clear, defined plan. Let your friend or relative know how much you care and how much you would hurt if he or she were gone. Remove any means of suicide, such as a gun, drugs, and cutting instruments. If you think that your relative or friend is in danger of self-harm, seek professional help immediately. Unless you are in danger, don't leave your relative or friend alone until help is obtained. Here are some possible options:

- In a medical emergency or when violence is imminent, dial 911 or your local emergency telephone service for an ambulance or the police.
- Contact your friend or relative's doctor or therapist.
- Contact a suicide prevention or crisis intervention hotline. Dial 411 or 0 for the telephone number or look in the front section of your yellow pages under Community Services or another, similar heading.
- In some areas, psychiatric crisis services are able to help people without hospitalization, although it is not always possible to avoid being hospitalized. A crisis or suicide hotline may be connected to or aware of these services. You may also be able to locate psychiatric crisis intervention services by calling a community mental health center or local mental health association. Also, check your yellow pages for listings.
- Take your friend or relative to the emergency department of the nearest hospital.

Once help is found, it's important to start thinking about aftercare. Problems that lead to suicide attempts don't resolve easily and the risk of suicide does not necessarily decrease once the initial crisis has passed. Individual, group, or family therapy may be recommended.

There are events in women's lives that can create an overwhelming sense of despair, hopelessness, and isolation. For example, sexual or physical abuse; sexual assault; abandonment; domestic violence; the loss of a loved one, including the loss of an infant or a pregnancy; the breakup of a family, marriage, or an important relationship; physical pain; and fears about one's health or future are sources of anguish for many women. But these are only examples. What you are feeling may be different.

Some people in severe emotional pain are suffering from depression. This is a serious condition that can cause suicidal thoughts and lead to suicide attempts if left untreated. It's important to understand that depression is not the result of weakness or an inability to "pull yourself together." Depression can be biological in nature or have a biological aspect and can be a reaction to crises such as those mentioned above, or other stressful life events and problems. Women who are raising children alone and struggling to make ends meet are at high risk for depression. Depression can occur along with physical illnesses like cancer, HIV infection/AIDS, heart disease or stroke, as well as with other psychiatric conditions. One of the worst things about depression is that it can make you feel hopeless and worthless. It can make you feel as though you don't deserve help and that seeking therapy or counseling is useless. But the majority of people who seek treatment for depression can be helped — and that means you can be helped. Finding a good therapist, learning about depression and, if necessary, finding the right medication can make a tremendous difference in the way that you feel.

If you are thinking about killing yourself, don't be ashamed or embarrassed by your feelings. Suicidal thoughts are not unusual. Talk to someone you trust. Give that someone a chance to help you. Contact a relative, a friend, your clergyperson, or your therapist, if you have one — anyone with whom you feel comfortable. You can also contact a suicide prevention or crisis intervention hotline. If there is such a service in your area, the telephone number can be found by dialing 411 or 0 or looking in the front section of your local yellow pages. You can also contact an agency that offers psychiatric crisis intervention services, if available (see below), or go to the emergency department of the nearest hospital for help. Do not stay by yourself. Try to remember that there are solutions, even modest solutions, to the most difficult problems — and as long as you are living you can find them. You do not have to end your life to stop the pain.

CRISIS INTERVENTION: SOURCES OF HELP

Situational Crises

When painful or stressful life events occur — even positive events, such as the birth of a child — it's natural to feel anxiety, fear, and a sense of helplessness for a while. It's not unusual for one stressful event to lead to another, overwhelming your usual coping skills and creating a crisis. In such situations, you may be able to benefit from crisis intervention services offering short-term emotional support and help in problem-solving to reestablish your equilibrium.

The following are various organizations that provide services to people in crisis. These services range from face-to-face crisis counseling to telephone crisis counseling and referral.

Remember that you will find practical suggestions for coping with specific life crises throughout this book and that various helping organizations relevant to the given topics are mentioned in each chapter and in the Resource Directory.

Some family service agencies, other community counseling agencies, and community mental health centers provide face-to-face crisis counseling. See this chapter.

Advocates at rape crisis centers offer crisis counseling for victims of sexual assault through twenty-four-hour telephone hotlines. Support groups, individual counseling, or referrals to counselors and therapists may also be provided. See Chapter Four.

Women's shelters and advocacy programs frequently operate twenty-four-hour hotlines for women experiencing abuse or violence or who have questions about the possibility of abuse or violence in their relationships. Support groups and counseling, or referrals, may be available for women and children. See Chapter Four.

National or local child abuse hotlines can often provide you with immediate counseling over the telephone and referrals to programs or practitioners helping children, adults, and families who have been affected by child abuse and neglect or other problems. See Chapter Two or the Resource Directory chapter for more information.

National organizations serving people experiencing particular crises, for example, a diagnosis of a life-threatening illness or the loss of an infant or pregnancy, may offer telephone counseling with a volunteer or staff member and referrals to counselors and therapists.

Hospital social work departments can often provide services and referrals to community services available to meet patients' needs.

Psychiatric Crisis Intervention

During periods of intense emotional turmoil, such as an episode of severe depression, suicidal feelings, or during crises related to other psychiatric conditions, such as schizophrenia or bipolar disorder (manic-depressive illness), intervention may be necessary. Although hospitalization is warranted when someone represents a clear danger to herself or others or has a critical medical problem, it may not be the only alternative. Depending on where you live, services may be available to assess crisis situations, help you stabilize and resolve problems that may have contributed to the crisis without hospitalization, if possible, and connect you to other community services for further assistance.[3]

Psychiatric crisis services may be offered through community mental health centers, a separate crisis intervention agency, some psychosocial rehabilitation programs, and hospitals. Depending on the agency, services may include mobile outreach (a crisis team will come to your home or other settings, if necessary), telephone and walk-in crisis services, and residential (live-in) programs. However, residential programs are much less frequently available than other crisis services.

Despite common goals, psychiatric crisis intervention services are unique. The type of services offered, the length of time that can be spent with an individual during a given crisis period, and approaches to intervention vary widely across agencies. Many psychiatric crisis intervention centers will become involved in involuntary hospitalizations, if necessary. However, in a few areas of the country, people who have experience with the mental health system as ex-patients are developing or participating in the creation of alternatives to traditional crisis intervention in order to give people more choices for healing.

Residential (live-in) crisis programs, where they exist, can be a viable option for people who need more time and assistance than other intervention programs are able to provide. Programs may offer individual, group, and family therapy, psychosocial rehabilitation, medication, case management, education groups, and recreational activities, among other services.[4] Some residential programs are less structured and medically oriented than others. For example, a few residential crisis programs serve small groups of people in homelike environments, rely less on medication than other models of intervention, and provide services without the use of restraints or seclusion. These programs may be called crisis hostels or houses. (They are sometimes confused with group homes, which they are not.) Lastly, some residential programs offer help in crisis apartments or rooms for which staff are on call.

Although psychiatric crisis services can be very important resources, consumers of mental health services and their families have noted problems with their use. A serious problem associated with the mental health system in general is the scarcity of services, especially where residential alternatives to hospitalization are concerned. People with a dual diagnosis (for example, a substance abuse problem and another psychiatric diagnosis) may have an especially hard time finding help. Some programs may not operate twenty-four hours a day. In some situations, staff answering the telephone after hours may not have training to assess crisis situations and may only be able to take a message.

If you feel that you may need crisis intervention services in the future, it's best to become familiar with the types of services available in your area, if there are any, before a crisis occurs. Find out how they are delivered, by whom and what the costs will be, if any, as well as what the admission or eligibility criteria are. Visit residential programs to find out what services are offered and to decide whether the atmosphere seems healing and helpful to you.

To find a crisis intervention center, you can contact a community mental health center, your therapist or doctor, case manager, police, local hospitals, women's shelters, homeless shelters, or your local mental health association, if there is one in your area. Also, contact the Department of Mental Health (or similar state/local agency) to find out whether you can get a list of residential crisis services in your area, if there are any, or suggestions for finding residential services. A national consumer/survivor organization (see below) may be able to give you information about alternative crisis services in development.

GETTING MENTAL HEALTH CARE

The National Mental Health Services Knowledge Exchange Network at 1-800-789-2647 or (301) 443-9006 (TTY). The Substance Abuse and Mental Health Services Administration sponsors this referral system offering information about federal, state, and local mental health agencies, other national clearinghouses, mental health associations, professional organizations, and consumer and family advocacy organizations, among others.

The Mental Health Information Center at 1-800-969-NMHA (6642), sponsored by the National Mental Health Association, offers referrals to local mental health associations, federal and state agencies on mental health, national support groups, Protection and Advocacy Systems, and other agencies, and offers many free publications.

FINDING YOUR WAY THROUGH THE MENTAL HEALTH SYSTEM

The mental health system is very fragmented and extremely difficult for anyone who needs more than just one type of service to negotiate. If you are interested in finding a therapist in private practice, you might want to skip ahead to the section titled Psychotherapy. If you are looking for referrals to community mental health centers, low-cost non-profit counseling clinics, support groups, or if your needs are multi-faceted, the following resources may be especially helpful. There should be no charge to you for referrals or for basic information. Remember that organizations providing referrals do not make recommendations and that you will have to personally determine whether an individual practitioner, service, or support group is right for you.

Local mental health associations, established in many states, are very diverse organizations. Each mental health association has a different focus, but most include mental health referrals to support groups as well as local and low-cost outpatient clinics. Some mental health associations provide referrals to psychiatrists and psychologists, and some do not. Likewise, some can make referrals for children, and others are limited in this area. A mental health association may also offer general information about topics in mental health/mental illness; conduct educational programs or workshops in schools or for the public; advocate for change within the mental health system; and in some cases, provide psychosocial rehabilitation services. When you call a mental health association for a referral, be prepared to provide a brief description of your problem and to give your general location. You may also be asked whether you have insurance so that the person assisting you can get a sense of your options when researching services that fit your needs.

The National Alliance for the Mentally Ill (NAMI) Helpline at 1-800-950-NAMI. NAMI provides a wide array of support and educational services for people and families of people with severe mental illnesses, such as schizophrenia, major depression, and bipolar disorder, and is a leading advocate for improved mental health services. The consumers and family members answering NAMI's Helpline can provide you with information about local self-help groups and mental health resources in your area as well as send you free brochures about severe mental illness and related issues. You may also be interested in learning about the special interest networks NAMI coordinates. These include a sibling network, multicultural and religious networks, and children's issues networks.

Local Alliances for the Mentally Ill (AMI) groups are comprised of families and people with severe mental illnesses who know from experience how difficult a psychiatric diagnosis can be. They are very familiar with local services and can serve as an invaluable resource for anyone with multiple needs. Some local groups publish resource guides for families and consumers that cover a range of important topics, such as education about mental illness, the impact of mental illness on the family, medication, hospitals, community services, jail diversion, and SSDI/SSI and other financial considerations. Many AMI groups offer a twelve-session family education and support program taught by other families trained to give the course. *Journey of Hope* enables families to learn more about mental illness and medication, to work on problem-solving and communication skills, empathy, and self-care. For more information about NAMI and local AMI groups, call the number above or see the Resource Directory.

There is a burgeoning movement of mental health consumers and survivors of maltreatment within the mental health care system of which anyone contemplating use of mental health services should be aware. While the philosophies of consumers/survivors differ, the guiding principles of the consumer/survivor movement are those of self-determination, empowerment, and egalitarianism, the expansion of civil rights for people who use mental health systems, and participation in decision-making processes that affect people with psychiatric disabilities. Two significant agencies serving the consumer/survivor movement are:

- *The National Mental Health Consumers' Self-Help Clearinghouse* at 1-800-553-4KEY is a consumer-run organization that can provide you with information about the consumer/survivor movement and articles/literature on an array of topics in mental health/mental illness. The clearinghouse can also help you find self-help groups.
- *The National Empowerment Center* (NEC) at 1-800-769-3728 (voice/TDD) is an organization that offers consumers/survivors an avenue for networking and coalition-building. In addition to its other activities, NEC can offer information on topics of potential interest to consumers/survivors and give referrals to mutual support groups, drop-in centers, and statewide consumer organizations.

Statewide consumer organizations are independent organizations that embrace the principles of the consumer/survivor movement. Although organizations differ, many feature advocacy and promote self-help and educational activities. Referrals to local drop-in centers, self-help groups, and other consumer activities may be available through statewide consumer organizations.

Other national support and advocacy groups can provide you with resources, and are often very current on research being done in their area of concern. The Resource Directory contains listings of many support and advocacy groups. (NAMI and Depression After Delivery are examples.) If you don't find a support and advocacy group that meets your needs in the Resource Directory, the referral services above may be able to assist you.

When should you seek mental health care?

Sometimes life presents challenges that can be difficult to overcome without objective, empathic support and help in problem-solving. In times of crisis, family, friends, and clergy can serve as a tremendous source of assistance, and additional help may not be desired or needed. As well, many personal dilemmas can be resolved through the use of supports that are not traditionally associated with professional mental health care. For example, a woman who loses her job and is having trouble finding another one may be helped more by a career counselor than a psychotherapist.

Situational crisis intervention services can be of great help when you are faced with an immediate, overwhelming problem and you don't know what to do. Counseling services, often available through family service and other community organizations, as well as from medical center social work departments, can differ from psychotherapy services. For example, counseling services often focus on providing information, enhancing coping skills, and problem-solving, and therefore may be more useful than psychotherapy for those who need immediate guidance in approaching a current life problem. Support groups are also excellent sources of information, practical assistance, and emotional comfort.

Psychotherapy can be beneficial when you haven't been able to resolve problems that interfere with the quality of your life either by talking to friends and family or through the use of other informal supports. Therapy may be useful in conjunction with support groups and as follow-up to crisis intervention services, and certainly in addition to the emotional warmth that others can offer.

Sometimes people who would easily see reason in asking for solutions to physical pain or help with practical problems like job loss or financial trouble dismiss emotional or mental pain as the result of personal weakness or a lack of initiative. Psychological or emotional problems do not arise from weakness or laziness. Real life problems have a genuine effect on our emotional health. Emotional or psychological problems may also have a biological basis that cannot be overcome by "trying harder" or "snapping out of it." Ignoring mental health problems can be dangerous, especially when one considers that problems often worsen and become critical when unaddressed. Asking for help is not a sign of inadequacy; rather it is an indication of resourcefulness, openness, and strength.

Deeper beneath the reluctance to seek professional mental health care is the pervasive and historical misunderstanding we have about mental health and mental illness. Images of people with mental illness as violent, uncontrollable, unintelligent, and unproductive abound in our culture. In reality, millions of people with mental illness (or who have recovered from a mental illness) live ordinary, productive lives, contributing to their families and to their communities. If you or someone you know has been given a psychiatric diagnosis, try to remember that a label can never define the complexity of any individual's experience and that you are not alone.

Psychotherapy

Psychotherapy can help you to reduce emotional distress, to discover new coping skills, and to grow as an individual. There are literally hundreds of types of psychotherapy. Some therapies are designed to address acute, temporary problems, while others can help you to understand and address long-standing issues. Some therapeutic goals can be accomplished in a relatively short period of time, while others take longer to realize. Therapy may be talk-oriented or may include an action-oriented approach to problem-solving.

Therapists often use a variety of techniques when addressing an individual's needs, and many believe that varied and flexible approaches to therapy yield the best results for most clients. Following are some commonly practiced forms of therapy. Many therapies, including the following, can be used in individual, family, couples, or group settings.

Supportive psychotherapy is provided to relieve distress and to offer emotional support and practical help with everyday problem-solving. This type of therapy can be useful to people in situational crises and people with long-term mental illnesses.

Psychodynamic psychotherapy explores past experiences and conflicts within the unconscious mind in order to resolve current difficulties. Although derived from the principles of psychoanalysis, a prolonged, intensive type of therapy, the goals of psychodynamic psychotherapy are more limited and the process is much less time-consuming.

Rather than delving into the underlying causes of current problems, *behavior therapy* (also called *behavior modification*) attempts to change behavior. Its practice centers on the theory that troubling behavior is the result of learned, maladaptive responses and can be changed through the use of specific techniques. Behavior therapy can be combined with other therapies and can be used to treat a range of disorders, including phobias. Methods include systematic desensitization (incremental exposure to feared situations), operant conditioning (positive reinforcement for desired behaviors) and relaxation techniques, among others.

Cognitive therapy (often combined with behavior therapy and called cognitive-behavioral therapy) addresses the link between the way we think and the way we feel and behave. For example, negative and distorted thinking can lead to negative feelings and self-defeating behaviors. The goal of cognitive (or cognitive-behavioral) therapy is to identify and change negative thought patterns and replace them with more realistic thoughts and beliefs, thereby affecting behavior. This type of therapy is usually short-term and is thought to be particularly useful in treating depression and some anxiety disorders.

Interpersonal therapy focuses on the present and addresses interactions with other people, such as a husband or partner or coworkers, as the source of emotional pain. Short-term interpersonal therapy has been found to be particularly useful in treating depression.

Therapy is widely offered on an *individual* basis. Here, the therapist and client work face to face to address issues of specific concern to the client.

Group therapy is conducted with a small group of people, often with similar concerns. This type of therapy offers the possibility of emotional support and improved interactions with others. It's usually cheaper than individual therapy, although both forms of therapy can be combined. Before considering group therapy, meet with the therapist leading the group to find out more about the therapist, what type of therapy is used, what to expect from the group, and whether you would be a good candidate.

Family and couples (or *marital*) *therapy* helps families (including extended family members and important others) and married or unmarried couples to solve problems and improve their interactions. It may not be necessary to have the whole family enter therapy together, although some therapists prefer to work with the entire family.

Young children often feel more than they are able to express. As its name implies, *play therapy* allows a young child to communicate feelings through the use of toys. Depending on a young person's needs, art therapy or dance and movement therapy may also be suggested. Many believe that children's needs are best served when the entire family is involved in treatment.

Your choice of practitioner may be determined by the nature of your concerns, costs, the restrictions of your insurance (if you have insurance), the availability of professionals in your area, and personal preference. Telephone numbers and addresses of many of the following mental health practitioners' professional organizations are listed in the Resource Directory.

Psychiatrists are medical doctors who treat emotional and mental disorders. Some psychiatrists may specialize in child psychiatry or geriatric psychiatry. Only psychiatrists and other medical doctors may prescribe medication. Psychiatrists have completed medical school, a year-long internship, and a psychiatric residency program of three to four years or more. They must be licensed to practice by the state medical board. In order to become board-certified, a psychiatrist must have been in practice for at least two years and have passed the American Board of Psychiatry and Neurology examinations. There are special requirements for certification in child psychiatry. However, board certification is not required to practice psychiatry. Although some psychiatrists practice therapy, they often work with other mental health professionals who provide therapy, such as social workers and psychologists. *Professional organizations*: American Psychiatric Association. See also the American Medical Association, Black Psychiatrists of America.

Clinical psychologists are trained to practice psychotherapy. In most states, clinical psychologists must have a doctoral degree, for example, a Ph.D. (Doctor of Philosophy) or a Psy.D. (Doctor of Psychology), and at least two years of supervised experience in order to practice independently. Psychologists must be licensed or certified in every state and the District of Columbia. *Professional organizations*: American Psychological Association, the Association of Black Psychologists.

Clinical social workers also practice psychotherapy. Because social workers' services are often more available and generally of lesser cost than psychologists' services, they have a wide appeal. Clinical social workers must have a master's degree and training practicing therapy under supervision (called field placement). (Ph.D.s are offered in this field, but training may be directed toward attaining academic or administrative positions.) Most states require clinical social workers to be licensed, certified, or registered. *Professional organizations:* National Association of Social Workers, the Association of Black Social Workers.

Pastoral counselors. Clergy have long attended to the needs of their congregations with or without formal training in counseling or psychotherapy. However, in addition to qualifications required to serve their congregations, some clergy may be licensed psychologists or social workers or members of other mental health care professions. Pastoral counselors who meet certain requirements may be certified by the American Association of Pastoral Counselors. *Professional association:* American Association of Pastoral Counselors.

Marriage and family therapists or counselors may be of various professional backgrounds. For example, they may be psychiatrists, psychologists, or social workers. The standard-setting organization in the field, the American Association for Marriage and Family Therapy (AAMFT), requires that Clinical Members have a minimum master's degree in marriage and family therapy and at least two years of supervised clinical practice in marriage and family therapy. *Professional association:* American Association for Marriage and Family Therapy.

Clinical mental health counselors must have a master's degree in counseling, have practiced under clinical supervision and passed an examination for certification by the National Academy of Certified Clinical Mental Health Counselors. In most states, counselors must be licensed to practice. *Professional association:* American Mental Health Counselors' Association.

Psychiatric nurses are registered nurses who specialize in mental health care. Psychiatric nurses have nursing degrees at the master's level or above and may be involved in prescribing and giving medications or in education or administration. In some states, psychiatric nurses are licensed to practice psychotherapy independently. Those who meet certain qualifications can be certified by the American Nurses' Association. *Professional organizations:* American Nurses' Association, American Psychiatric Nurses' Association.

Finding and Choosing a Therapist

Looking for a good mental health care practitioner can be difficult, especially during periods of emotional distress when your inclination may be to settle on the first available therapist. It's important, however, to shop around, if you are able. There are many competent, caring professionals practicing psychotherapy, but as in any field, there are those who are not as capable as others or who may simply be unable to meet your unique needs. The following sections will give you an overview of various options for psychotherapy.

FINDING MENTAL HEALTH CARE: OUTPATIENT SETTINGS

Mental health care professionals work in a range of settings, including hospitals, hospices, residential programs, community clinics, and private offices. For many people, outpatient services provided by professionals in private practice or in community settings offer the most appropriate form of assistance. The following are examples of outpatient settings:

- private offices
- community mental health centers (see below).
- family service agencies (see below) and other nonprofit community counseling agencies
- clinics associated with a private psychotherapy or psychoanalytic training institute. Therapists in these clinics may specialize in a particular type of therapy, for example, psychoanalysis or behavior therapy.
- clinics associated with universities, colleges, or academic medical centers. University and college clinics may offer low-cost counseling services to students and nonstudents.
- Private clinics affiliated with a university, although not necessarily low cost, may be good sources of specialized care for particular disorders.
- clinics associated with the psychiatric or social work department of a local general or psychiatric hospital
- social service organizations such as the following:

    AIDS service organizations
    gay and lesbian centers
    programs for homeless and runaway youth
    rape crisis centers
    shelters for victims of domestic violence

- Area Agencies on Aging can refer callers to hospitals or clinics providing geriatric assessment services to evaluate the needs of older people who are in fragile health or who are experiencing memory or behavioral problems. (See Chapter Nine.)
- Hospital and hospice social workers or psychologists may offer counseling or referrals to patients and their families. For example, they may offer counseling or facilitate support groups for patients with chronic or ter-

minal illness and their families or provide referrals. Bereavement programs are often available through hospitals and hospices. (See Chapter Ten.)

Getting Help from a Clinic

Although clinics or community-based counseling organizations can generally be thought of as sources of affordable mental health care, costs in a clinic can range from almost nothing to nearly the same price as you would pay with a private practitioner, depending on the type of clinic you choose and your income. Always ask for an estimate of the costs before scheduling an appointment.

As mentioned in the section earlier, local mental health associations and family or consumer groups can be good sources of referrals to community clinics. Because a single source of referral may not be entirely comprehensive, you

---

FOCUS ON COMMUNITY TREATMENT:
FAMILY SERVICE AGENCIES AND COMMUNITY MENTAL HEALTH CENTERS (CMHC)

Family service agencies are nonprofit social service agencies. Although services vary depending on the agency, many offer crisis counseling and services that address issues particular to family life, such as marital counseling, help with parenting difficulties, pregnancy counseling, adoption and foster care services, and elder care. Services are usually short-term, and fees are typically determined on a sliding scale according to clients' incomes. To find a family service agency, start by contacting the local office of the United Way, your local Catholic Charities organization, Jewish Family and Children's Services, or other similar religious-based or secular organizations. Also see Family Service America, listed in the Resource Directory.

Community mental health centers (CMHCs) are usually private nonprofit or public agencies that receive funding from state and local governments and other sources. CMHCs may provide a single service or a range of mental health services to the public. Services may include individual and group therapy, case management, partial hospitalization/day treatment, medication management, and psychosocial rehabilitation or vocational rehabilitation programs. Residential, inpatient, and substance abuse services and services for people with mental retardation may be offered by some centers. CMHCs may be independent clinics or part of a psychiatric or general hospital. Some services may be covered by Medicaid (Medi-Cal in California) or Medicare, although this may depend on where services are delivered and on other factors. Services may also be free or available for a fee that is based on your ability to pay. As funding becomes more restricted, however, CMHCs may only be able to serve those covered by insurance or people with severe psychiatric disabilities. For referrals to a local CMHC, you can contact your local mental health association, AMI group, or your state or local department of mental health. (See the government pages of your local telephone directory.) If you are a member of a managed care/Medicaid program, you may be referred to a CMHC by your primary care doctor or another mental health agency.

---

may want to use many sources. For example, you may want to call a local mental health association, a university or college, if you live nearby, and ask friends and family for recommendations. If your needs concern sexual assault or domestic abuse, contact a rape crisis center or a women's shelter. (See Chapter Four.)

Mental health clinics staff practitioners of varying professional backgrounds and often serve as training environments for student therapists, who should be closely supervised. Working with a student therapist does not necessarily put you at a disadvantage. Training and experience are important, but a talented student who is being properly supervised can still be very helpful. A true disadvantage of working with clinics (and some managed care plans) is that although you can and should specify your preferences regarding a practitioner, you may not have the opportunity to choose your therapist personally. In some training clinics, such as university or college clinics, sessions may be videotaped or audiotaped for educational purposes. You may want to inquire about the way in which your sessions will be supervised and make another choice if you are not comfortable with the clinic's procedures.

Some clinics specialize in particular type(s) of therapy, such as cognitive-behavioral therapy. As well, some clinics may offer short-term services only, and the number of visits that you can schedule may depend on restrictions imposed by your insurance plan. Lastly, agencies providing mental health care should be state-licensed, usually by the Department of Mental Health or the Department of Health.[5]

When you call for an appointment with a clinic, give the staff a general sense of your problem. Find out what type of services are provided and by whom. Ask how closely your therapist will be supervised and by whom and how long the wait for services will be. Ask any questions that you have about cost and insurance. Although an assessment can sometimes be done over the telephone, you may be given a date to meet for an intake appointment. The intake interview will help the staff determine if you can be treated at the clinic or whether you should be given a referral to a more appropriate provider. After your intake appointment, clinic staff may then discuss the issue with which you are concerned at a meeting and assign you to the most appropriate or most available therapist.

Despite some limitations on choice, clinic clients should not resign themselves to therapy that does not feel helpful and should be able to change therapists, if the need arises, although in some clinics this may be problematic.

Self-help/mutual support groups are some of the most available and accessible sources of ongoing emotional and practical assistance. There are hundreds of self-help groups throughout the United States, varying in size, structure, and philosophy, and covering a wide range of concerns. Most support groups were originated by ordinary people who came together to help one another with shared problems and are entirely peer-led, although some involve or are facilitated by professionals.

Self-help groups offer more than just a place to receive and give emotional support. They are among the best sources of information for tackling practical problems related to the group's area of concern. For example, members of local support groups often have personal experience negotiating mental health, health care, and/or social service systems.

For some people, support groups can be a primary source of assistance. For others, support groups are best used as adjuncts to professional services. Members or groups may offer referrals to therapists or counselors. As well, support and advocacy organizations addressing specific life crises, such as life-threatening illness, pregnancy and infant loss, and bereavement, may have mental health programs or offer referrals to clinicians who are particularly knowledgeable and sensitive to such issues. Even when a support group does not meet your treatment needs directly, it can help you to cope with everyday stress and offer a means of connecting with others who share similar life experiences.

Before taking part in a group, talk to the facilitator. Ask about her or his experience in the group's area of concern. Find out what the group's function is, when it meets, and who participates. You may want to attend once or twice before deciding if the group is right for you.

❖ There are many ways to find a support group of interest to you. Many national groups are listed in various chapters of the Resource Directory. You can also find support groups by calling your local mental health association, if there is one in your area, or the National Mental Health Consumers' Self-Help Clearinghouse. The American Self-Help Clearinghouse and the National Self-Help Clearinghouse, which can also provide referrals, are listed on the first page of the Resource Directory. Lastly, your state may have a self-help clearinghouse. Check the front section of your yellow pages under Community Services or a similar heading.

Some local support groups are housed within nonprofit social service organizations and are difficult to find through clearinghouses, national support and advocacy groups, or other referral sources. If you're interested in finding a local support group for victims of sexual assault, sexual abuse, or domestic violence, a rape crisis center or women's shelter may be the best place to start your search (see Chapter Four). Centers for independent living offer peer-support groups for all people with disabilities (see Chapter Six). Drop-in centers offer support and peer counseling for people with mental illness. As well, AIDS service organizations (ASOs) offer support and counseling to people with HIV infection and AIDS (see Chapter Eight). Some gay and lesbian centers, often available in metropolitan areas, offer support groups and counseling to lesbian, bisexual, gay, and transgender youth and may offer counseling, therapy, and informal drop-in or rap sessions for adults. Hospitals may offer informal support groups for medical patients and their families or may make referrals to groups outside the hospital. Your place of worship or local community college may also offer support groups of interest to you.

Choosing a Therapist Who's Right for You

Because much of therapy involves talking to another person, albeit a trained professional, we often think of therapy as a rather benign process and may believe that one therapist is probably just as good as another. Therapy can be an enriching, illuminating, if not laborious, process, but along with the benefits, there are risks, as there are with any type of treatment. Therapy can be unhelpful, even harmful, when practiced by someone who is not competent to treat your problem or who behaves abusively or irresponsibly.

The qualifications mental health professionals must meet in order to practice are but minimal criteria for selecting a therapist. Aside from experience, other criteria are more subjective. This section offers general guidelines to use when choosing a therapist, but your instincts will serve you well when you are looking for someone to help you. The therapist-client relationship is one of mutual trust and responsibility, and thus a good personality match between client and therapist is essential. When you talk to therapists over the phone, trust your gut feelings about your potential compatibility.

Start your search for a therapist by gathering referrals from sources that you deem trustworthy and appropriate. (See below for ideas.) Once you have some good suggestions, you can begin your initial investigation. Interview as many candidates as you can briefly over the telephone. When you have your candidates narrowed, arrange to meet two or three in person, if at all possible. Once you find a therapist in whom you have some confidence, you may have to spend a number of sessions with him or her to determine if you will be productive together.

Here are some additional suggestions:

- Look for someone who has recent and frequent experience working with people whose concerns are similar to yours. Talking with a friend, advocate, or clergyperson may help you to identify the matter troubling you. If you're looking for a therapist for a child, consider only those whose training and experience qualify them to work with children or adolescents and with the problem your child is experiencing.

- Let therapist candidates know about your problem as you view it and your life circumstances. For example, it may be very difficult to tell a therapist that you are being hurt by someone you love, but if you don't let therapists know about the source of your pain, it will be harder to find someone who can help you. You may also want to question the therapist regarding her or his views on the issue of concern to you. For example, some therapists may have beliefs about sexual abuse, sexual assault, sexual harassment, or domestic violence that minimize the impact of violence and abuse or emphasize the victim's responsibility.

- The gender, age, race, ethnic, religious, and cultural background, sexual orientation and/or socioeconomic class of your therapist may be important to you. Mental health professionals are as much a part of society as anyone else, and encountering prejudice, antipathy toward or ignorance of your cultural values and/or the experiences that may have shaped your life is as much of a reality in therapy as it is elsewhere. Nonetheless, it's not always possible to find a therapist who shares characteristics identical to your own, and similarities in background do not necessarily guarantee mutual understanding. If you can't find someone with a similar background, it may be necessary to question therapists about their beliefs and experiences, to be alert to bias, trust your instincts, and move on when you encounter prejudice or sense an inability to understand your concerns.

- Look for someone whom you like and trust and with whom you can work as a partner. (If you're looking for a therapist for a child, choose someone whom your child likes and trusts.) A therapist should be open and sincere. He or she should be someone with whom you feel comfortable enough to express yourself honestly, who conveys respect for you, and makes you feel understood.

- Avoid a therapist who is rigid, dictatorial, patronizing, defensive, evasive (especially about her or his education and training), or guarantees success in treatment.

- Many people prefer a therapist who offers feedback and

some advice. If you want feedback, ask the therapist whether this is part of her or his style.

- Look for a therapist who has had therapy.

Questions to Ask a Therapist

Some therapists may prefer that the following questions be asked during your first face-to-face interview. However, it may not be economically feasible to wait until you actually visit the therapist to make at least a preliminary judgment about whether he or she is right for you. You should be able to get basic information about the service the therapist has to offer over the telephone. Briefly explain your problem and ask:

- Can you tell me something about your education and training? What degrees and licenses or certifications do you hold? How many years have you been in practice? Are you a member of any professional organizations? Most therapists will not object to these questions.
- How much experience do you have helping people with problems similar to mine? Do you specialize in this area?
- Can you tell me something about your theoretical orientation(s) and approach to therapy?
- What are your hourly fees? Do you accept payment on a sliding scale basis? What is your policy about billing insurance companies?
- Do you have time to see me? What hours do you have available?
- How long are sessions and how often are they held? If you need more than the time typically allotted (usually fifty minutes) or more sessions than normally scheduled per week (typically one), ask about this possibility.
- At your first visit, be sure to ask for clarification about billing procedures, policies regarding and charges for cancellations and telephone consultations, and the therapist's availability for emergencies.

Things to keep in mind when considering therapy:

- You may want to get a medical evaluation before seeking therapy, advising your doctor of the symptoms you're experiencing. Some medical conditions as well as prescription and street drugs can produce troubling psychological symptoms.
- Therapy is a commodity. You are a consumer of a service and as such you have the right and responsibility to

determine whether a particular therapist is helping you and to make active decisions about your treatment.

- Costs can often be negotiated. Higher fees are not necessarily an indication of better quality.

- You have a right to know the therapist's diagnosis of your problem and to know who has access to any records pertaining to your treatment. A number of states allow clients to see their medical and mental health records, although there may be limitations on this right.

- You are entitled to express your doubts and dissatisfactions about therapy and to have your concerns addressed seriously.

- Growth and independence are the goals of therapy. A therapist who promotes dependence on his or her services may do more harm than good. You have the right to leave therapy at any time.

- You have a right not to be touched in any manner that makes you uncomfortable. Sexual contact between a therapist and a client is always considered unethical. In some states, it is a crime for a therapist to have sex with a client, and sexual misconduct may be the basis for a lawsuit. If a therapist makes or suggests sexual contact with you, leave. Tell someone — a friend or relative — what happened. Don't keep it to yourself. Complain to the therapist's professional organization and state licensing agency or to the therapist's supervisor. You can call the state/local Department of Mental Health (or similar agency) or a local mental health association to get the name of the agency responsible for licensing. If you have been sexually assaulted in any way, consider calling the police. A rape crisis center can give you a sense of your options and provide you with various types of assistance, even if you are not sure whether what happened to you was illegal or inappropriate. (See Chapter Four.)

- Generally, conversations between a therapist and client must be kept strictly confidential. Although federal and state laws and professional codes regarding confidentiality differ and are very complex, there are a few common exceptions to the confidentiality usually recognized as part of the therapist-client relationship. For example, the therapist-patient privilege, which protects a client from disclosure of information in court, may be implicitly waived when a client raises the issue of her mental health in a court proceeding or is ordered by a court to undergo a psychiatric examination. Other common exceptions to the confidentiality necessary to the therapeutic process include the requirement that therapists report suspected instances of child abuse and neglect, the need to take appropriate action when a client presents a danger to herself or others, and the potential duty to warn someone against whom threats of harm are made. In order to establish coverage, an insurance company may also have access to information about your diagnosis with your informed consent. (Please note that access to information about a loved one's treatment is a complex issue, one that is beyond the scope of this discussion. Support and advocacy groups for families, such as the National Alliance for the Mentally Ill, may be able to offer you information on this topic.)

MEDICATION

Medication can be used to reduce or relieve symptoms of psychiatric disorders such as depression and bipolar disorder (manic-depressive illness), anxiety disorders, and schizophrenia, but it cannot cure mental disorders. Medication is thought by many to be most effective in combination with appropriate psychotherapy.

Although psychotropic medications have been widely accepted as effective means of treating psychiatric disorders, debate about the role drugs play in mental health care continues. Discussions about the use of psychotropic medication are especially important to women since, in the United States, prescriptions for psychotropic drugs are more likely to be written for women than for men. Ironically, most research into the effects of psychotropic drugs has been done with men and younger adults.

Still, broad generalizations about the use of medication cannot be made. Psychotropic drugs can be life-saving for some, unhelpful to others, and can be harmful when prescribed negligently. Not everyone needs medication. Psychotherapy or other forms of treatment and support may be just as effective as medication for some. For others, psychiatric medications play a significant role in long-term treatment.

If medication is suggested to you, educate yourself about the diagnosis that you have been given and the drug prescribed. All medications have potential benefits and risks. Become familiar with them. Know what to expect when you use the drug, and report any side effects to your doctor. Do not discontinue your medication without your doctor's advice, because sudden withdrawal from some drugs can produce adverse reactions.

SEEKING THE NAMES OF THERAPISTS

When looking for a therapist, gather names from a variety of sources. Here are some suggestions:
- Family members and friends who have had therapy
- Clergy, advocates, and other therapists
- Support and advocacy groups
- A medical center's department of social work
- A rape crisis center or women's shelter can often recommend therapists or counselors to people who have been the victims of sexual abuse, sexual assault, or domestic violence.
- Local child protective services agencies and child abuse and neglect hotlines may be able to offer the names of therapists who specialize in helping children who have been abused or neglected.
- Your child's school counselor, pediatrician, or primary care doctor may be able to make appropriate referrals for your son or daughter.

❖ Your physician may recommend a therapist, but a medical doctor is more likely to recommend a psychiatrist than other referral sources. If you are a member of an HMO and you wish to pay for services with your insurance, you may have to rely on your primary care physician for a recommendation.

When considering the need for medication, it's important not to disregard the impact that life circumstances have on your mental health. For example, physical, sexual, and emotional abuse, violence, stress, discrimination, and other external factors can cause great unhappiness. You may be able to address these concerns directly through therapy and/or with the practical help available from support groups, women's shelters, rape crisis centers, and legal assistance organizations.

Not everyone responds to the same medication in the same way. It may take some time before you and your doctor are able to find the right dosage. Emerging evidence suggests that there may be differences in the way psychotropic drugs affect men and women[6] as well as people of different racial and ethnic heritages.[7] Your age (or a child's age), your health status, and other factors can also affect your response to medication. Thus it's a good idea to look for a doctor who has experience treating the disorder with which you have been diagnosed as well as experience treating women, people of your age group (or your child's age group), and people of your racial and ethnic heritage, if at all possible. Women who are pregnant or planning a pregnancy should inform their doctors immediately. Expectant women considering psychotropic drugs should carefully discuss the risk of birth defects with their doctors. If you are nursing, you and your doctor will have to weigh the advantages and disadvantages of weaning or stopping medication.

If you are having trouble finding the right drug treatment, you may want to consider consulting with a psychiatrist trained in psychopharmacology (the uses and actions of psychotropic drugs). An academic medical center or other teaching hospital may have such a professional on staff.

You are strongly urged not to stop at this book for guidelines to making decisions about medication. Consultations with your doctor and other mental health professionals and continued reading can provide you with various perspectives about treatment. *The Physician's Desk Reference,* available in most libraries, contains explicit information about prescription drugs. A layperson's version, *The PDR Family Guide to Prescription Drugs,* or other guides to prescription drugs may also be available in bookstores and libraries.

If medication is recommended to you, you can do the following:

♦ Get a medical evaluation. You may have a medical condition that precludes or affects the use of a certain drug. Moreover, some medical conditions can mimic psychiatric disorders. For example, a thyroid disorder can produce symptoms similar to those of depression. Some over-the-counter medications and prescription drugs, including birth control pills, can also produce depressive symptoms.

* Get a second opinion.
* Tell your physician if you are pregnant, nursing, or planning a pregnancy.
* Give your doctor as much information about your medical history as possible, including complete information about all other drugs you are taking. List birth control pills and other prescription drugs, over-the-counter medications, home remedies, alcohol and street drugs. (The combination of some psychotropic drugs and other drugs can produce negative, and in some cases, life-threatening effects.) If you occasionally borrow prescription drugs from someone else, don't leave them off your list. Incidentally, borrowing drugs from others is dangerous because doctors prescribe medication based on an individual's unique medical history. Medication that may have beneficial effects in one person can create adverse reactions in another.
* Ask questions about the drug. Bring a pad of paper and a pen with you to the doctor's office, or ask a friend or relative to come with you to listen or take notes. Here are some suggested questions:

> What is the name of the drug and what is its purpose?
> What are the risks and benefits of this drug? How will it affect me physically and emotionally?
> Do I have any medical conditions that might make taking this drug unsafe?
> What are the short-term side effects of this medication?
> What is known about the long-term effects of this drug?
> What should I do if I experience side effects?
> What alternatives are there to this treatment, including nonmedical alternatives?
> What is the likely result if I decide against treatment?
> What dosage are you prescribing for me and why?
> How and when should I take this medication?
> When should I expect to feel some of the benefits of this drug? Will some of my symptoms be reduced or alleviated before others?

Should I be monitored while on this medication?

Are there any foods, beverages, or other medicines/drugs that I should avoid while taking this medication?

Is this medication addictive? (Certain antianxiety medications, such as Xanax and Valium, can be addictive.)

When should I expect to stop taking this medication?

How will use of this drug affect my daily activities? Will I be able to drive? How will my sexual functioning be affected?

- Before you leave, ask for written information about the medication(s) you are given.
- When filling your prescription, talk to your pharmacist about the medication. Ask about the purpose of the drug, how it may interact with other medications you are taking, and what the possible side effects are, even if you have already spoken to your doctor. Make sure the pharmacist has filled the prescription correctly by comparing the label on the medication to your doctor's prescription. Ask your pharmacist to keep a computer or written profile of the drugs you are taking so that potentially hazardous drug interactions can be detected before a prescription is filled.
- Report experiences of positive and negative effects of the drug to your doctor.

Older Women and Medications

The physical changes that take place as we age make us more susceptible to the side effects of medication, and because the incidence of disease increases as we grow older, we are more likely to be taking multiple medications. Combinations of drugs, including over-the-counter drugs, can interact and may increase the levels in the blood of some medications, raising the risk of side effects or negative reactions. Skipping medications and doubling doses accidentally can also cause trouble. Sometimes the side effects of medication are confused with symptoms of dementia or depression or are wrongly shrugged off as the natural effects of aging. If you are an older woman, it's critical that you and your doctor follow your medications closely. In order to help your doctor evaluate the drugs you're taking, you can implement what is commonly referred to as the "brown bag test." Periodically put all your medications, including over-the-counter medications like aspirin and decongestants, and any home remedies you use, into a brown bag and take them to your doctor for review. You'll want to know whether they are appropriate for you and whether they interact poorly. If possible, discuss the ways in which you can safely reduce the number of medications you are taking.

If you or a loved one are experiencing symptoms such as memory loss, confusion, or behavioral changes, you might consider having a complete geriatric assessment (see Chapter Nine) to learn the root of the problem. Sometimes such symptoms are caused by overmedication and other problems that are temporary or can be easily remedied.

IF YOU HAVE MORE EXTENSIVE NEEDS

If your needs extend beyond psychotherapy and/or medication, you may be interested in some of the services described in this section. Costs of services mentioned here vary widely. For example, drop-in centers, where they exist, may charge no fees or only minimal dues for membership. Inpatient psychiatric hospital services, of course, can be extremely expensive, and your insurance will most likely dictate your choices. Some communities lack the resources to provide a range of services to people in need, while others are able to do more.

A hospital social worker, case manager, or your therapist may be able to connect you with available services in your area. Consumer organizations and self-help groups are excellent sources of information and support.

Case management services range from connecting consumers to other agencies within the mental health system to working directly with consumers to accomplish rehabilitation goals. In some areas, the availability of case management services may be very limited, and case managers may be overburdened with high caseloads.

Psychosocial rehabilitation describes various services aimed at helping people to live as independently as desired within the community. Although there are various philosophies and approaches to rehabilitation, programs generally focus on providing practical support (for example, help getting food, clothing, housing, benefits, and health care), goal-oriented recreational activities, vocational and social skills training, and case management. Sometimes these programs help people meet their educational goals. You may find psychosocial rehabilitation services in comprehensive mental health care programs, such as hospitals, community psychosocial rehabilitation centers, community mental health centers, clubhouses, or through other organizations. Clubhouses and Fairweather Lodges are examples of psychosocial rehabilitation concepts.

Clubhouses are a type of psychosocial rehabilitation service. Clubhouses typically provide consumers, who are called members, with housing options, social services, and educational and employment opportunities. Many clubhouses are based on the Fountain House model established in 1948 in New York, which was developed using the concept of transitional employment. In a transitional employment program, members work in the clubhouse on a voluntary basis to gain or relearn skills and bolster confidence. Voluntary work is often done in preparation for a part-time supported position in the competitive workforce. Members may then go on to work independently with varying levels of support when needed. Some clubhouses offer support groups and other services. The activities and philosophy of a particular clubhouse may depend on the needs identified within the community.

Fairweather Lodges are groups of ex-patients who work and live together.

Vocational rehabilitation programs offer various employment development opportunities, including sheltered employment (people with disabilities work together in a supportive environment) and other models of vocational rehabilitation that allow for varying levels of participation in the competitive workforce with support as needed. As mentioned, vocational rehabilitation services may be part of various types of programs offering psychosocial rehabilitation services. State/federal vocational rehabilitation programs are also available to people with psychiatric disabilities.

Drop-in centers are places where you can go to socialize, attend mutual support groups and peer counseling sessions, and participate in recreational and advocacy activities. Drop-in centers are often described as places where consumers are not treated as patients but as equals among equals. Participation is wholly voluntary. Information about other community services, food, clothing, and help with Social Security benefits may also be available. Centers are often open on the weekends or evenings when traditional services are usually closed. Many are run by the persons who use the center's services. They may be found in nontraditional spaces, such as churches and store-front settings, or may be set in community mental health centers or other agencies. To find a drop-in center, contact your local community mental health center or your consumer statewide advocacy organizations. (See the section titled Getting Mental Health Care on page 321.)

Housing options are in short supply for many mental health consumers, who face extraordinary discrimination and who may have specific needs. If you need some support to live independently, there are possibilities for assistance, although options vary greatly from place to place. A psychosocial rehabilitation program may provide or arrange for support. If you have a low income, government subsidy programs may be available, but the wait for housing is often very long and in some areas no new applications are being accepted. Other options include group homes with staff on-site, apartments owned or leased by psychosocial rehabilitation and other agencies, and transitional housing programs that help residents hone skills for independent living.

In some areas programs are filled to capacity, and the quality of housing can vary dramatically. It's extremely important to visit the site yourself or to have a family member or friend visit to inspect the quality of the premises and interview staff members. Likewise, residential programs may not be structured for families, so it will be necessary to find out what the policies are, if you have children. For information about the availability of housing opportunities in your area and possible financial assistance, contact a community mental health center, your case manager or social worker, the social work department of a general or psychiatric hospital, or a consumer/survivor or family organization. Being aware of antidiscrimination laws and options for assistance will help if you have trouble finding desired housing.

Discrimination laws. Discrimination against people with psychiatric disabilities is pervasive. The Rehabilitation Act of 1973, the Americans with Disabilities Act, and the Fair Housing Act are examples of federal laws specifically designed to protect people with disabilities. For more information about these laws, see Chapters One and Six.

Supplemental security income (SSI) and Social Security disability insurance (SSDI) are vital sources of income for many consumers/survivors. A hospital social worker, case manager, drop-in center, or legal aid organization may be able to help you apply for benefits. Centers for independent living are another possible source of assistance. See Chapter Six.

Legal assistance. Information and legal assistance may be provided to eligible individuals through a Protection and Advocacy organization, legal aid organizations, or a fair housing organization, if there is one in your area.

Partial hospitalization (day treatment) allows a person who needs more care than is offered through an outpatient program and less than is provided within a hospital to receive intensive services during the day, evening, night or on weekends while remaining in the community. Partial hospitalization services may provide an alternative to hospitalization in a period of crisis or serve as a source of extended counseling and rehabilitation services. Community mental health centers and general or psychiatric hospitals may offer these services.

Hospitals. In periods of crisis, hospitalization may be necessary. But hospitalization stays are generally brief and discharge planning begins almost immediately upon admission. If there is a possibility that you will use a hospital, it's best to become familiar with available hospitals before a crisis occurs. Although your choice may be limited to those hospitals covered by your insurance plan and with which your doctor is affiliated, the state or local Department of Mental Health (or similar agency) may be able to give you a list of facilities providing inpatient psychiatric care. Likewise, a psychiatric social worker or support and advocacy group such as a local AMI group or consumer organization may be able to advise you about facilities.

Accreditation by the Joint Commission on Accreditation of Healthcare Organizations suggests that the hospital has met at least *minimal* standards of care. Ask about the facility's services and specializations, approaches to treatment, specific costs for all services rendered as well as any possible extra charges, and the extent to which your insurance plan will cover your stay. You will probably want to know the facility's philosophy regarding medication, restraints, and seclusion. In 1996, the Joint Commission issued new standards that call for organizations to limit the use of restraints and seclusion to situations with adequate, appropriate clinical justification.[8] For a copy of the standards, contact the Joint Commission at the customer service number in the Resource Directory.

Ask others in your community, such as your therapist, case manager, or clergyperson about the hospital's reputation. Whenever you go into a hospital to stay overnight, either for medical or psychiatric care, it's a good idea to take an advocate, family member, or friend with you when you are admitted and to make sure that the person will look out for your best interests during your stay. Try to choose someone who is assertive and unafraid to speak on your behalf, if need be. If residential (live-in) crisis or partial hospitalization services are available to you, you may want to consider investigating these options, asking the same types of questions.

Many women who are entering the hospital worry about losing custody of their children. If possible, try to make arrangements for your child(ren) to stay with a trusted relative or friend. For more information and to ask questions about custody issues as they affect women with psychiatric disabilities, contact Through the Looking Glass's toll-free hotline, listed in the Resource Directory. Protection and Advocacy organizations are another possible source of information and assistance.

General hospitals with psychiatric units or beds may provide care on an emergency or short-term basis and may accept only voluntary patients who meet certain admissions requirements. Because general hospitals vary in their ability to help people with psychiatric emergencies, it's a good idea to contact general hospital(s) in your area in advance to find out what level and types of psychiatric services they offer.

Hospitals that are associated with medical schools are often referred to as *teaching hospitals*. These may be community or university hospitals and are often known for attracting high-quality staff. If you are looking for a specialist in eating disorders, schizophrenia, or depression, for example, university-based hospitals or academic medical centers may be a useful resource. Support and advocacy groups can often provide information about university hospitals conducting research in their areas of interest.

Private psychiatric hospitals are often for-profit institutions. Most private hospitals offer only short-term care and may focus on treating a specific type of problem, for example, substance abuse problems or eating disorders. There is a great deal of variation in quality among private hospitals. While private hospitals can provide high-quality care, there have been charges that some private hospitals attempt to keep and treat patients up until the day their insurance coverage runs out.[9] *Public hospitals* may be the only resources available to people without insurance or with low incomes and to those whose resources have been exhausted by the high cost of mental health care. Intensive short-term as well as long-term care may be available. *Veterans Administration (VA) hospitals* are government-funded hospitals that offer medical and psychiatric care to veterans. Services provided are similar to those available through other hospitals and are free to veterans. With both VA and state/county hospitals, quality varies widely.

A *medical advance directive* is a document that allows

you to give instructions regarding your treatment and/or appoint someone to make treatment decisions for you in the event that you become incapacitated. All states recognize some form of advance directive for health care, and a few states provide specifically for advance directives for mental health care. In an advance directive, you may be able to state what treatment you want or do not want, or that you want no treatment. You may be very specific about the scope of authority given to the person appointed to represent your interests. State law may limit your proxy's authority as well. Because advance directives for mental health care are very new, there is little caselaw (decisions made by judges) by which to interpret their effectiveness, and there appear to be definite and varied limitations to their use. Nonetheless, there are many benefits to having a document over which you can dialogue with the person designated as your agent (assuming that he or she is willing and able to act in that capacity) and your mental health care provider(s). Even if you don't create an advance directive, it's important to discuss your feelings regarding treatment and the reasons for your choices with those who may be involved in your care.

In a few states, Protection and Advocacy organizations may be able to give you more information about advance directives or help you create one. A mental health lawyer should also be able to inform you about advance directives. Of course, you will have to pay for a lawyer's services. If you do execute an advance directive, you must make others aware that you have one. You may want to fill out or create a notification card to carry in your purse or wallet. Give a copy of your advance directive to your appointed agent and any alternate agents as well as to your health care provider(s) and any hospital where you are likely to be treated. A copy should be kept with your medical records. Keep your original in a safe, accessible place.

Hospitalization

In an emergency situation, such as when a person represents a clear danger to herself or others, it is possible to be hospitalized involuntarily for a period of examination. The time allowed for an emergency commitment period varies, but it is usually short (seventy-two hours, for example, not including weekends or holidays). Once the emergency evaluation period ends, you must either be discharged, must accept commitment voluntarily, or a petition must be filed in court to extend the commitment period. To extend the commitment period, a hearing must be held at which you are entitled to attorney representation. Laws, procedures, grounds, and standards of proof regarding involuntary commitment differ from state to state.

Generally, the time periods for extensions of an involuntary commitment are time-limited, and a periodic review must be conducted to ensure that individuals are not being hospitalized unnecessarily. If recommitment is undertaken, procedures are usually quite similar to those of the initial commitment. Even in the case of an involuntary commitment, you or your family members may be held liable for the cost of hospital care.[10]

Many people seek hospitalization voluntarily. This alternative can be preferable to involuntary commitment. Generally, there are two types of voluntary commitment. In an "informal" voluntary commitment, an individual may leave the facility at virtually any time. A conditional or "traditional" voluntary commitment may require that you give notice of an intention to leave the hospital. However, a hospital may start procedures to prevent you from leaving if there are grounds, for example, that you represent a clear danger to yourself or others.

Except in emergency situations or when judged incompetent, you generally have the right to refuse treatment. Once an emergency has passed, your informed consent should be obtained, unless you have been found to lack capacity.[11] Depending on the state, a substitute decisionmaker may be appointed to make treatment decisions for someone who has been declared legally incompetent. This may be a family member, appointed guardian, or judge, depending on the circumstances and state law. When faced with decisions about treatment, some courts rely on the "substituted judgment standard" (or a combination of this and a standard that attempts to clarify what is in the individual's best interests). Using the substituted judgment standard, the court must try to ascertain what the consumer would want if she did not lack capacity to decide. It has been suggested that an advance directive providing instruction might be very useful under these circumstances.[12]

PAYING FOR MENTAL HEALTH CARE

What you will pay for mental health care — and whether you will be able to afford services — is largely determined by the type and length of the care you need, the range of services available in your community, and your insurance coverage, if any.

Generally, psychiatrists' fees are the highest of all mental

FOR INFORMATION ABOUT YOUR RIGHTS AND LEGAL ADVOCACY

Every state has a Protection and Advocacy (P&A) System designated to protect the rights of people with disabilities. Protection and Advocacy for Individuals with Mental Illness (PAIMI), a P&A Systems program, is designed to serve people with significant mental illness or emotional impairment who are residing in, or are being admitted to, a mental health facility providing care and treatment or who experience a problem within ninety days of discharge from a facility. Mental health facilities may include psychiatric facilities, nursing homes, supervised group living arrangements, juvenile detention facilities, jails, and prisons. The Protection and Advocacy for Individual Rights (PAIR) program serves people with disabilities who are not eligible for other P&A programs, including PAIMI. Your local legal aid organization may also be of help or may refer you to other organizations that represent the interests of people with disabilities.

health professionals; psychologists' fees are less expensive; and social workers' and psychiatric nurses' fees are the least costly. However, fees are often negotiable. It's perfectly acceptable to ask a private practitioner about the possibility of a fee reduction, about the availability of sliding scale fees or whether he or she will provide services on assignment from Medicare. Services offered through publicly funded or non-profit clinics, such as a community mental health center, may be low-cost or determined on a sliding scale based on your income. However, it's always necessary to get an estimate of what the costs will be for each session before you consider working with a particular clinic.

You may or may not want to use your insurance to pay for part of the cost of mental health services. Although insurance can help cover the costs of mental health care, it is necessary for a client to be assigned a psychiatric diagnosis before a claim can be submitted. Thus, people who prefer not to be given a specific diagnosis may want to consider paying for mental health services out-of-pocket when possible, for example, when seeking elective outpatient services.

If you plan to use your private insurance, be sure to check your policy before starting or planning for mental health care. Coverage for mental health services is, at present, treated very differently from coverage for physical health care, and benefits are usually limited. However, a federal law that takes effect in January 1998 prohibits insurers covering employers of fifty-one or more employees from placing lifetime or annual limits on benefits for mental health services that are different from those placed on medical services unless premiums rise 1 percent or more. Find out whether your plan covers mental health services at all (some plans do not) and under what circumstances. As you review your plan, you may want to ask the following questions:

- Must you be referred to treatment by your physician?
- Does the plan limit your choice of providers? For example, does it cover only the services of certain professionals, such as psychiatrists or psychologists, or those with certain levels of training or licensing?
- How far does your coverage extend? Are there limits on visits to therapists and/or limits on hospitalization? (There usually are.) Is a co-payment required? How much is it? Does your insurance cover the cost of prescription drugs? Are there limitations on coverage for preexisting conditions?
- If you are a member of an HMO or other managed care plan will you have access to professionals who special-

ize in treating your type of problem? Will you be able to choose the specialist you want? If you find a specialist who is qualified to treat you outside of the plan, can that provider be added to the plan's provider network? Will you have to pay more in that event? If you encounter problems as an HMO member, complain to your primary care doctor or to the appropriate authority immediately. You may have to be very vocal and insistent about getting the care that you need and deserve.

If you are covered by Medicare, be sure to check a current Medicare handbook for specific information about your coverage before researching treatment options. If you do not have a current Medicare handbook, you can get a free copy by calling 1-800-638-6833 (8 A.M. to 8 P.M. EST Monday through Friday) or 1-800-820-1202 (TDD).

The range of services covered by Medicaid (Medi-Cal or similar state programs) varies from state to state. There may be restrictions on the use of services and limits on the number of visits that you can have with a provider. Again, you may have to get a referral through your primary care physician if you are in a managed care/Medicaid program. Contact your local Medicaid or welfare office to find out what services are covered.

The Health Care Financing Administration is the federal agency charged with overseeing Medicare and the federal portion of Medicaid programs. The agency's regional offices should be able to give you information on all services for which beneficiaries qualify and provide information about making complaints regarding the quality of services. For a referral to your regional office, contact the federal office listed in the Resource Directory.

WOMEN AND ALCOHOL AND OTHER DRUGS

Women of all ages, socioeconomic classes, cultural, racial, ethnic, and religious heritages, and educational backgrounds can become overinvolved with alcohol and/or other drugs. We may drink or use other drugs to relax, to be sociable and to feel less unsure of ourselves and, certainly, because it's pleasurable.

Many of us grew up in families where alcohol and other drug use was common. Drinking and/or other drug use may be a part of our current relationships with family members, husbands or partners, and friends. We may use alcohol or other drugs to escape the daily stress of caregiving, work in unsatisfying or demanding jobs, financial worries, discrimination, or to try to dull the pain caused by the loss of a loved one through death, divorce, or separation. When we are ill, lonely, or isolated from other people, we may turn to alcohol or other drugs for comfort. Many women who use alcohol or other substances are or were physically, sexually, or emotionally abused or sexually assaulted. Here again, alcohol or other drug use may be an attempt to numb the pain and anger caused by these violations. Some women use mind-altering substances to avoid coming to terms with a lesbian or bisexual identity or to avoid dealing with societal or internalized homophobia.

Depression and anxiety often underlie substance abuse. Ironically, we may drink or use other drugs to try to relieve symptoms of anxiety and depression; mind-altering substances can actually cause these conditions. Tranquilizers or sedatives prescribed by some doctors to relieve symptoms can create a dangerous cross-addiction in women who are using alcohol and/or other drugs.

Whenever you use alcohol or other drugs, there is a possibility of becoming physically and psychologically dependent. Withdrawal symptoms may surface when you stop drinking or using. A great deal of your time may be spent thinking about, getting and using a substance, then hiding your use. Sometimes it's hard to see the damaging effects of substance abuse. In fact, denial is one of the strongest features of abuse and addiction. When you are using or drinking, negative life events — the loss of a job, difficulties in school, accidents, problems with children — may seem unrelated, but may have a common root in substance abuse.

Why is it so hard for us to recognize a problem with alcohol or other drugs? Certainly, each woman's relationship to alcohol or other drugs is different and each has her own reasons for drinking or using. Yet there is a stigma attached to substance abuse by women that can create a great deal of shame and embarrassment and keep many women from coming to terms with a substance abuse problem and seeking treatment. While the underlying issues connected to women's abuse of alcohol or other drugs — violence, discrimination, and depression, for example — are frequently disregarded, women who drink or use other drugs are often characterized by a failure to meet the expectations of their gender. A "good" or "strong" woman is expected to be abstemious and available to attend to others' needs, not impaired by alcohol or other drugs, and certainly not involved in nursing her own pain. A woman who uses alcohol or other drugs is made to feel selfish, weak, sloppy, and indulgent. The myth that associates alcohol or other drug use by women with sexual promiscuity or aggressiveness is perhaps the most damaging; yet it has little basis in reality. Women are far more likely to be sexually or physically assaulted when drinking or using other drugs than to be forceful themselves. When we accept degrading myths as truths, we lose the opportunity for change. Certainly, it's hard to feel good about yourself when alcohol and/or other drugs are controlling your life. You may not even feel that you deserve to live differently. But you do. Having a substance abuse problem does not make you a bad or weak person. Relapsing does not make you a failure. A substance abuse problem is a health problem that can be treated.

Treatment works. Recovery isn't easy, it's a life-long process, but it can happen. Even if you have tried to quit many times before, there is always another chance. You may have to be persistent and determined to find a treatment program that's right for you, but it can be done. Moreover, twelve-step programs such as Alcoholics Anonymous and Cocaine Anonymous and secular programs are widely available and free.

Quitting alcohol or other drugs is something that you do for yourself. Others in your life may try to keep you from living differently or criticize you without offering any support, but in the end, it's your health and your future that you must think about. If you think that you would like to stop drinking or using other drugs, this chapter will give you resources for assistance. Living without alcohol or other drugs is a big change, and change can be frightening. Being sober won't solve all your problems, and the tangible rewards of sobriety don't come all in one day, but living without the problems caused by substance abuse can give you a new sense of freedom and can open up possibilities in your life that might otherwise have gone unexplored.

HEALTH FACTS ABOUT ALCOHOL AND OTHER DRUGS

The health risks associated with alcohol and other drugs are serious for everyone, but particularly for women, who develop alcohol-related health problems after drinking lower levels of alcohol than men for shorter periods of time. If you drink or use other drugs, you are entitled to know some of the health problems that substance abuse can create. For example, in addition to the possibility of death and severe injury from traffic accidents, violence, and suicide, alcohol

---

DO YOU HAVE A PROBLEM WITH ALCOHOL OR OTHER DRUGS?

According to the Center for Substance Abuse Prevention, you may have a problem if . . .

- No matter how many promises you make to yourself about cutting down, you frequently wind up under the influence of alcohol or other drugs.
- You're uncomfortable when alcohol or other drugs are not available. You have a few extra drinks before the evening begins that others don't know about.
- You regret things that you've said or done under the influence.
- You handle all social celebrations with alcohol or other drugs. You drink alcohol or use other drugs heavily after a confrontation or argument. When faced with a problem, your immediate reaction is to drink or use other drugs.
- It takes more alcohol or other drugs than it used to to get the same effect.
- You've missed work or school because of your substance-abusing behavior or you've been arrested for driving under the influence.
- You're angry or alarmed when others mention your substance-abusing behavior.[13]

use can damage your heart and liver, cause pancreatitis, worsen high blood pressure, and cause menstrual irregularity and possible problems getting pregnant. Studies have also linked alcohol consumption to increased risk for breast cancer. Cocaine can cause sudden death at any time from stroke or heart attack or other causes. Smoking cocaine can cause permanent lung damage. Heroin and other injectable drug use can cause bacterial endocarditis, an infection of the lining of your heart, lung damage, brain abscess, liver and kidney disease, and other problems, including HIV infection from sharing needles and works. Amphetamines can cause stroke and convulsions. Some sedative-hypnotics can be addictive and deadly in combination with alcohol. Inhalants like "poppers" and household products like glue and spray cans can cause heart, lung, liver, kidney, and brain damage.

If You Are Pregnant

Drinking beer, wine, liqueurs, mixed drinks, or other alcoholic beverages and using other drugs of any kind, including cigarettes and marijuana, can be extremely harmful to a developing fetus. Being pregnant and having a substance abuse problem can be frightening. You may worry about the effect alcohol or other drugs will have on your baby. You may know that using alcohol or other drugs can harm your child but may wonder if you can live without them. You may be afraid of how others will react when you tell them that you think you have a substance abuse problem. Even confiding in a friend can be difficult because of the stigma attached to drinking or other drug use by a pregnant woman. You may fear that others will see you as a bad person or someone who doesn't care about her child(ren). But if you are reading this section, you are probably quite concerned about the health of your child and your own health. That is the first and most important step in seeking the compassionate care that you deserve.

The effects of alcohol or other drug use during pregnancy are varied and often severe:

- Babies exposed to drugs while in the womb can be born physically dependent and may go through a painful withdrawal period that is difficult for even the most experienced caregiver to handle. For example, a baby going through narcotic withdrawal may be irritable, may constantly scream and cry, may be unable to sleep, and may vomit, have diarrhea, breathing problems, fever, tremors, seizures, and difficulty feeding, among other problems.

- Babies exposed to alcohol and other drugs, including cigarette smoke, may be born prematurely or at a low birth weight. Smaller babies are more vulnerable to disease and death than other babies.

- One of the most widely known consequences of alcohol use during pregnancy is fetal alcohol syndrome (FAS). FAS refers to a collection of medical problems, including mental retardation, congenital defects of the face and eyes, developmental delay, and growth retardation. Fetal alcohol effects (FAE) is the term used to describe less severe effects of alcohol exposure in children. Children with FAS and FAE can have organ defects, learning disabilities, and serious behavioral problems, as well as visual, hearing, and speech problems. These effects continue into adulthood and are not reversible. Since alcohol affects each woman and developing fetus differently, and even minimal amounts can be dangerous, it is best to talk to your obstetrician about the safety of alcohol use during pregnancy.

- Regular drinking and the use of other drugs during pregnancy are associated with an increased risk of miscarriage and stillbirth. Drugs like heroin, cocaine, and cigarettes are linked with a higher than average rate of sudden infant death syndrome (SIDS), although there are other possible risk factors for SIDS, and the cause(s) of SIDS are at present unknown.

- Alcohol and drug use can affect your ability to parent. When you are intoxicated or high, you may say and do things that you wouldn't otherwise. You may lose your patience easily or forget to do important things for your baby. Life can be unpredictable when you are drinking or using other drugs. You may find yourself spending less time with your child(ren) than you would if you didn't have to invest so much energy in drinking or getting and using other substances. Mothers who love their children very much can become abusive and/or neglectful when they are gripped by alcohol or other drugs.

Reading about some of the possible effects of alcohol or other drug use on your baby isn't easy. It's painful to imagine that your child might suffer from some of these problems. Sometimes when thoughts are too painful to handle, we try to push them away. You may be tempted to ignore some of the risks of smoking, drinking, or using other drugs. You may have smoked cigarettes and used alcohol or other drugs during another pregnancy and had a healthy baby — or you may know someone who had a similar experience. Of course, some children escape the harmful effects of alcohol or other drug use, but some do not. In fact, medical researchers have only just begun to understand and identify the effects of alcohol or other drugs in children. It is not possible to predict whether your child will be born with or develop problems as the result of alcohol or other drug use. It *is* possible to avoid the risk. You do not have to take chances with your baby's life. There are options. The good news is that treatment is becoming more available for pregnant women and that it works. You can improve your chances of having a healthy baby *whenever* you decide to stop using alcohol or other drugs during pregnancy, even in your third trimester. It's never too late to stop. Even if you've sought treatment in the past and found yourself unable to quit, you can still succeed this time. Each day that you stay in treatment without using alcohol or other drugs, you give yourself — and your baby — new hope. There is no reason to wait until a problem with alcohol or other drugs gets worse to seek treatment. By seeking treatment and prenatal care, you can protect your baby's health and your own.

WHERE CAN YOU GO WHEN YOU NEED HELP?

Not everyone who uses alcohol or other drugs will need to participate in a formal treatment program. In fact, a great many people get the help that they need through a twelve-step recovery program. However, for some people professional assistance is necessary. Unsupervised withdrawal from some drugs, for example, heavy alcohol use or a class of drugs called benzodiazepines — for example, Valium or Xanax — can be very dangerous. Medical problems can also complicate withdrawal and recovery. Pregnant women may need a formal treatment program because sudden withdrawal during pregnancy from some substances, like heroin, can be harmful and even fatal to a fetus.

Because you may not be able to predict your needs yourself, it may be necessary to seek a professional assessment of the extent of the problem and an appropriate recommendation for treatment before beginning your recovery. You can do this by:

- contacting your state or local alcohol and drug abuse agency for information about getting a free or sliding scale assessment and/or referrals to treatment programs. You can get an automatic referral to your state's alcohol and drug abuse agency by calling the National Drug Information and Treatment Hotline at 1-800-662-HELP or by looking in the government pages of your local telephone directory. The agency may be listed independently or under the Department of Health or Mental Health. Also check the front pages of your telephone directory for listings of community services.

- You can also call treatment programs directly. You can find out about treatment programs that meet your needs by calling one of the national hotlines listed on page 361.
- Many large companies maintain Employee Assistance Programs that can help you find substance abuse treatment. Contact the personnel or human resources department within your company to find out if such a service is available.
- If you have a social worker or case manager, she or he may be able to give you a referral or give you more information about programs that meet your needs.
- If you are concerned about a young person, it's important to get an evaluation from someone who is knowledgeable about child and adolescent substance abuse. Your child's school psychologist, counselor, or pediatrician may be a good source of assistance.

AN OVERVIEW OF SUBSTANCE ABUSE TREATMENT OPTIONS

Treatment for serious substance abuse problems can include various phases. For example, an inpatient program may be followed by aftercare in an outpatient program and twelve-step meetings. Likewise, continued individual and/or group therapy can be very valuable in helping you uncover and work on some of the issues at the heart of your involvement with alcohol and other drugs. A good treatment program should help you transition to the next level of care and not merely offer you a telephone referral to another facility.

The following are brief descriptions of various aspects of care for alcohol and other drug addictions. Again, a professional assessment may be necessary to determine the course of care most appropriate for you.

Detoxification. Detoxification is the process through which a person who is physically dependent on a substance is helped to withdraw under supervision. Detoxification can be accomplished on an outpatient basis or within a residential or inpatient treatment program. Detoxification alone is not considered adequate treatment for alcohol or other drug addiction problems, but rather the first step toward treatment for those who need it.

Drug-free outpatient programs. Outpatient programs, frequently offered through hospitals and independent drug treatment programs and in some community mental health centers, allow clients to receive treatment while living at home. The intensity and variety of outpatient programs vary widely. Programs may require participation in support groups as well as individual, group, and family counseling or therapy and twelve-step meetings. Visits may be required once or twice a week or every day, depending on the program, and sessions can be quite lengthy. Depending on their length and intensity, outpatient services may be a reasonable alternative for women with children or women who cannot afford to be away from their jobs for any length of time.

Methadone programs. Methadone is a synthetic opiate (or, narcotic) that is used to treat addiction to heroin and other opiates by suppressing withdrawal symptoms and reducing drug cravings. Methadone maintenance programs, which provide eligible clients with regular doses of methadone, are usually offered through special clinics and are considered to be a last resort for people who have been unable to live without opiates. Methadone maintenance, together with prenatal care, is often recommended for pregnant women because withdrawal from opiates, such as heroin, can be harmful, even fatal, to a developing baby.

Inpatient programs are structured twenty-four-hour programs, usually offered in specialized inpatient treatment facilities or in general hospitals. Typically lasting anywhere from two to six weeks, these programs may offer detoxification (see above), medical care, twelve-step meetings, individual, group, and family counseling/therapy as well as other therapies specifically designed to address substance-abuse-related issues and behavior. Aftercare is an essential part of any inpatient program and may involve outpatient treatment, continued group counseling or therapy, and/or participation in twelve-step programs.

Residential therapeutic communities (TCs) are highly structured programs in which people combating substance abuse problems live together for a long period of time — anywhere from six months to two years. Although program philosophies differ, they generally serve those with the most severe substance abuse problems and strive to change behavior that may have contributed to or resulted from chronic substance abuse. Residents are given gradually increasing levels of responsibility within the therapeutic community and are slowly prepared for a return to life outside. Group discussions and individual and group therapy sessions are part of therapeutic community programs, in which recovering substance abusers may serve as counselors or role models. Some TCs use confrontational tactics with residents that are thought by some to be counterproductive for women, who may respond better to a more supportive approach. Because it may be difficult to find a TC that incorporates services especially for women and one that allows children to live on the premises, some women may not be able to benefit. However, there are a few TCs designed especially for women, and it may be worth your while to seek information about them.

Twelve-Step Programs

If you want to stop using alcohol or other drugs, there is one source of assistance that may be available to you regardless of your income or where you live. Twelve-step programs based on the Alcoholics Anonymous model are free, generally anonymous, and located in communities throughout the United States. They include the following groups:

• Alcoholics Anonymous
• Cocaine Anonymous
• Narcotics Anonymous
• Marijuana Anonymous
• Nicotine Anonymous

These are among the best known of the self-help groups, which usually stress total abstinence from alcohol or other drugs through fellowship with others in recovery. Meetings are usually led by peers rather than by professionals. Although twelve-step programs have a strong spiritual base, they do not represent the beliefs of any one religious organization.

One of the best things about attending a self-help/mutual support group is the opportunity you have to develop new, positive relationships and to meet others who have "been there" and who can share similar experiences. Knowing that you are not alone can mean a lot as you begin your recovery process. Depending on the area in which you live, there may be specialized AA groups for women only, lesbians and bisexual women, people of specific cultural heritages, and young people. A local twelve-step program should be able to tell you which special-interest meetings are available in your area. Check the Resource Directory for more information.

Not everyone is comfortable with the idea of a spiritually based twelve-step program, and some women may be more at home in a program with a feminist/woman-centered or secular foundation. Other groups also listed in the Resource Directory have been formed to address these needs:

- Women for Sobriety (WFS)
- Secular Organizations for Sobriety/Save our Selves (SOS)

Alcohol and Other Drug Abuse Is a Family Problem

Because family members and significant others are adversely affected by a loved one's drinking and/or other drug use, twelve-step programs have been established to help children, partners, spouses, parents, and friends of substance abusers deal with the pain and problems associated with a loved one's addiction:

- Al-Anon/Alateen
- Families Anonymous
- Adult Children of Alcoholics

There are also groups designed for people of various cultural, religious, and professional backgrounds. Look in the business section of your local white pages or contact national organizations for more information.

FINDING TREATMENT MAY NOT BE EASY, BUT IT'S POSSIBLE

You may have to be very persistent to find a formal treatment program, but it can be done. Your age, the area in which you live, the substance that you are using, the severity of your substance abuse problem, and the extent of your insurance coverage, if any, may all influence the type of program you will need and the difficulty you'll have in finding services. You may have to wait for an assessment and for treatment in publicly funded programs.

If you are a single woman with children, you may have a very difficult time finding inpatient or residential programs that allow your children to stay with you while you are in treatment. Likewise, outpatient programs intensive enough to make childcare arrangements necessary may not provide these services themselves. It may be possible, however, to have a trusted relative or friend look after your children during the time that you are in treatment.

At present, some states allow pregnant women top priority

in waiting lists for public services. In some areas there are programs specifically designed for pregnant women; in other areas, pregnant women may have fewer options. If you're pregnant, let the referral sources you contact know, because they may be able to get you into treatment sooner.

Women with disabilities should know that substance abuse treatment programs, whether public or private, are subject to the Americans with Disabilities Act (ADA), a federal antidiscrimination law. To be considered a person with a disability under the ADA, you must have a physical or mental impairment that substantially limits one or more major life activities, a record of such impairment, or be perceived as having such an impairment. (See pages 32 to 35 for a slightly broader discussion of disability in this context.) In addition to prohibiting other types of discrimination, the ADA requires that programs remove physical and communicative barriers to participation, if this can be done without an undue burden to the facility (usually a financial burden) or provide an alternate method of serving you, if possible. If you encounter discrimination in a substance abuse treatment program, the first step is usually to try to reach a solution within the program. Government-sponsored programs with more than fifty employees are required to have an ADA coordinator (or disability coordinator) available to resolve grievances. Smaller programs may have someone designated to perform this task, but it is not required. The ADA coordinator should be able to tell you what additional steps to take if the matter cannot be easily resolved. You can also contact the Department of Justice's general ADA information line at 1-800-514-0301 (voice) or 1-800-514-0383 (TDD) for information about filing a complaint.

It may be difficult to find a program that specifically fits your needs. Although it's important not to disqualify an available program because it lacks some services, there are a few features you may want to look for when evaluating a treatment program. Of course, childcare and services for children are a top priority for many women with children. As well, many advocates feel that in order for a treatment program to serve women adequately, it must either be designed for women, offer women-only group meetings where issues like incest, sexual abuse, sexual assault, domestic violence, and relationships can be openly discussed, or offer access to a staff member who is knowledgeable about women's issues. It's also important to look for a facility that offers programming that is sensitive to your cultural values and the issues that inform your daily experience. This may mean looking for a program designed especially for women of your cultural, racial, ethnic, religious heritage and/or sexual orientation or one that will actively strive to address the concerns of all its clientele. For example, you may want to ask about bilingual services, the composition of the staff and/or the ways in which the program will work to ensure that services are provided with knowledge, sensitivity, and respect for your community's history and values. You may also want to probe for knowledge and sensitivity regarding issues affecting lesbian or bisexual women and programs that reflect your religious values and/or incorporate spiritually based or secular programs. If you have a disability, check for accessibility problems and patronizing or brazenly discriminatory attitudes toward people with disabilities.

Beyond substance abuse treatment and the relevance of services to your life experience, writers and professionals in the field have also cited the following as being of particular value in a program for women: a range of treatment options; individual, group, and family counseling; support groups and twelve-step programs; health care services, including prenatal care (ideally with obstetricians with whom you are comfortable and who are familiar with substance abuse issues); parenting education and support; job counseling and training; help in sharpening assertiveness and stress management skills; transportation options; and a solid case management program to help you connect with the next level of treatment and to get other social services like housing, food, and further therapy or counseling.

Paying for substance abuse treatment

Cost is a major barrier to treatment for many women, but there are options if you have a low income or no insurance coverage. Government-run programs often provide services for low fees or allow you to pay according to your income and may accept Medicaid (also called Medical Assistance, or Medi-Cal in California). Some services are available at no cost. Your insurance may dictate the type of program that you will be able to use and the length of your treatment. Before beginning an investigation of your options, be sure to find out what type of treatment your insurance covers, if any, and how much coverage you have.

Be cautious about assessments and recommendations made by insurance-based programs. Substance abuse treatment programs can be extremely expensive, and your insurance benefits may provide some programs with an incentive to find you in need of formalized treatment or, more precisely, the treatment plan offered by the program. Moreover,

The following are hotlines that you can use to start looking for treatment programs in your area. To widen your options, it's best to call all available and relevant hotlines. Also, look in the front section of your local yellow pages under Community Services or a similar heading for the telephone numbers of any local drug and alcohol hotlines.

When you contact a referral line or treatment program, be sure to clarify your needs. For example, the operator will probably need to know how old you are, what substances you are using, how long you have been using, if you are pregnant, whether you have private insurance, Medicaid, or no insurance and need a low-cost program. You may also want to ask about programs specifically for women and programs that allow children to live with their mothers during treatment, and to make any other requests related to your needs. You do not have to give your name when you call.

Before you dial, it's a good idea to get out a notepad and pen to write down the information you are given so that you can compare and follow up on available programs.

The National Drug Information and Treatment Referral Hotline at 1-800-662-HELP will automatically connect callers with a touchtone phone to their state drug and alcohol resource center, which can then provide information about local programs. Printed material is also available.

1-800-COCAINE. The Phoenix House operates this twenty-four-hour helpline, which offers referrals to treatment programs. You do not need to have a cocaine addiction to use this hotline.

American Council on Alcoholism at 1-800-527-5344 provides counseling, referrals, and consultation.

The National Council on Alcoholism and Drug Dependence offers an information and referral service at 1-800-NCA-CALL. Callers with touchtone phones will automatically be referred to the NCADD affiliate in their area or the state drug and alcohol abuse agency. Printed information is available.

❖ *The Cancer Information Service* (CIS) at 1-800-4-CANCER (9 A.M. to 7 P.M. Monday through Friday) sponsored by the National Cancer Institute can provide information about smoking cessation programs, among its many other activities.

some programs make exorbitant claims about their success rate that cannot be substantiated. When you request an assessment from a treatment program, make sure to ask for referrals to other programs so that you will have options from which to choose, and remember that the cost of a program is not indicative of its quality. Be wary of any program in which staff members attempt to pressure you or guide you into their services.

Life-Threatening Illness

This chapter offers an overview of three major life-threatening illnesses and provides information about resources for people with cancer. It does not offer medical advice, which only your doctor can give you. When you speak with your doctor, you may want to take notes or have a family member or friend take notes for you so that you can remember the information you're given. If asked before the visit, some doctors will allow you to tape-record your conversation. It's natural to feel nervous in a doctor's office or to forget what your doctor tells you, especially when you are facing a medical crisis. Ask as many questions as you need to and don't be embarrassed to ask your doctor to repeat information. After all, your health and well-being are most important.

The following topics are covered in this chapter:

- ✦ Stroke
- ✦ Women and Heart Disease
- ✦ Hormone Replacement Therapy
- ✦ Resources for Cancer Information
- ✦ HIV Infection and AIDS
- ✦ Assistance in Buying Medication

STROKE

W HAT TO DO IF YOU THINK YOU OR SOMEONE ELSE MAY BE HAVING A STROKE

A stroke is a medical emergency. If you or someone you know is exhibiting any of the symptoms listed on page 363, go immediately to the nearest hospital emergency department. Call for an ambulance or have someone drive you to the hospital. Do not drive yourself.

Until very recently, doctors could do little to limit or stop the progress of damage done by stroke. Today, there may be a chance at intervention for some stroke victims who reach medical help in time. A new class of drugs known as thrombolytics may be available to your doctor. Commonly referred to as "clotbusters," these drugs, which have been used for years to treat heart attacks, are now being used to try to break up blood clots that are the cause of some strokes. But in order to be effective, they must be given within three hours of stroke onset. The potential availability of these and other medications make it more important than ever to get to the hospital as soon as possible in the event of a stroke.

In the Emergency Room

When you arrive at the emergency room, locate the triage nurse. This is the nurse who decides in what order patients will be seen. State your name or the name of your friend or family member. Tell the nurse that you (or your friend or relative) are having a stroke. If you are a relative or friend, make note of the nurse's name so that you can locate the nurse for new information about the patient's progress.

Wʜᴀᴛ ɪs ᴀ sᴛʀᴏᴋᴇ?

A stroke occurs when the blood supply to the brain is disrupted. The brain, which controls every function of the body, needs constant replenishment of oxygen and nutrients from blood. When blood flow to an area of the brain is compromised, that area may die or become damaged due to lack of oxygen, and since every area of the brain controls a specific function of the body, the result may be the loss of a corresponding function. Death can also occur as the result of a stroke.

Hᴏᴡ ᴅᴏᴇs ᴀ sᴛʀᴏᴋᴇ ʜᴀᴘᴘᴇɴ?

There are two principle ways in which blood flow to the brain can be jeopardized: the blood vessels that carry blood to the brain, the arteries, can become clogged; or these blood vessels can rupture.

A stroke that is caused by a blocked artery is called an *ischemic stroke* or a *cerebral infarction*. The process of atherosclerosis (also known as hardening of the arteries) is often a key factor in the development of this type of stroke. Atherosclerosis is caused by damage to the blood vessel lining. The damage can occur from a number of different causes, such as smoking, high blood pressure, or high cholesterol. Over time, fatty deposits, calcium (plaque), and blood clots (thrombi) can build up on the vessel walls. The blood vessels may become increasingly narrow until there is little room for blood to flow. If a complete blockage occurs, a type of ischemic stroke called a *thrombotic stroke* results. When a small blood clot formed in another part of the body, often the heart, travels to the brain and gets caught in a narrowed artery, the resultant ischemic stroke is called an *embolic stroke*.

A *hemorrhagic stroke* occurs when an artery bursts inside or on the surface of the brain. When this type of stroke occurs, there is bleeding into the brain, which can put pressure on the brain and destroy tissue. As with an ischemic stroke, hemorrhagic stroke can also result in decreased blood flow to certain parts of the brain.

If a hemorrhagic stroke occurs, the rupture may be the result of degenerative changes within the blood vessel caused by atherosclerosis and/or chronic hypertension. It may also

---

Eᴀʀʟʏ ᴡᴀʀɴɪɴɢ sɪɢɴs ᴏf sᴛʀᴏᴋᴇ

- Sudden weakness, numbness, or lack of control of the face, arm, or leg on one side of the body
- Sudden dimness, blurriness, double vision, or loss of vision, especially in one eye
- Slurred speech, inability to speak or understand speech
- Sudden severe headache
- Loss of coordination, unsteadiness, dizziness or sudden falls, especially when combined with other warning signs

---

Transient ischemic attacks (TIAs) occur when the blood flow to the brain is temporarily disrupted. The symptoms of a TIA are the same as those of a stroke, but last only briefly and leave no residual effect. These ministrokes are an important warning sign that you may be at risk for stroke, and should never, under any circumstances, be ignored. A person who has had a TIA may have ten times the risk of stroke as someone who has not had a TIA. TIAs are believed to be caused by emboli. An embolus is a clot that has broken off from the inner lining of a blood vessel and traveled upstream to lodge in another, smaller vessel.

TIAs typically come on rapidly and last for a short period of time, usually one to fifteen minutes, though they can last up to twenty-four hours. If you think that you have had a TIA, have someone take you to the nearest hospital emergency department or call 911 or your local emergency response number. You should be evaluated by a physician immediately.

be due to the bursting of an aneurysm, which is more likely to occur in a person who has a congenital weak spot in an artery in the brain, or to a condition called arteriovenous malformation (AVM). An AVM is a tangle of abnormal blood vessels that can occur in the brain and is also congenital. Other causes of hemorrhagic stroke include the use of drugs like cocaine and amphetamines, trauma to the head, a brain tumor, and complications from anticoagulant therapy, such as heparin or Coumadin.

WHAT TESTS WILL YOU BE GIVEN IN THE HOSPITAL?

In the emergency room, a doctor should examine you and ask you (or your friend or relative) specific questions about aspects of your medical history and risk factors for stroke. Vital signs will be checked and routine laboratory testing will be done. Depending on the suspected cause of the stroke, routine lab testing may include blood work, urinalysis, an EKG (or an ECG — an electrocardiogram), and/or a chest X-ray. A CT scan, also called CAT scan (computerized axial tomography), may be done. Although very different from a standard X-ray, a CT scan uses X-rays to produce a highly detailed image of the brain. CT scans are most useful for ruling out hemorrhagic stroke.

Immediate treatment for stroke usually involves close monitoring to prevent the stroke from progressing, if possible. Initial management may involve treating swelling of the brain (brain edema), which can occur after a stroke and can cause further damage. Other procedures may include:

- *MRI (magnetic resonance imaging)* uses radio waves to build a three-dimensional computer-generated image of the brain. Evidence of ischemic stroke (a stroke caused by a blockage in a blood vessel) will generally show up sooner on an MRI than on a CT scan. Some areas and structures in the brain are also better visualized with an MRI than with a CT scan.
- A variety of *ultrasound techniques* may also be done to image the arteries in the neck and at the base of the skull.
- An *echocardiogram* is an ultrasound picture of the heart that may be used to determine if a clot has formed in the heart or if there are any heart abnormalities that might allow a clot to form.
- *Arteriography* involves injecting a special dye into a catheter that has been inserted into the arteries under

investigation and then taking X-rays to image the cerebrovascular system. This is done to try to identify the cause of the stroke and look for trouble spots in the arteries. It may be done in conjunction with the administration of "clotbusters." It is also done when a type of surgery called *carotid endarterectomy* is being considered or if malformations of the blood vessels, AVMs or aneurysms are suspected but not seen on other tests. Complications are rare, but arteriography is an invasive procedure that carries with it more risks than the noninvasive procedures previously described. Possible complications include tearing of the artery by the catheter and the possibility of causing another stroke if a small piece of plaque is dislodged from the artery when the catheter is placed. A technique called magnetic resonance angiography (MRA), which is done with an MRI scanner, has recently been developed. MRA allows the cerebral and neck blood vessels to be imaged without an invasive procedure. This technique may someday replace angiography.

OTHER TREATMENTS FOR STROKE

Medications. In some cases, a heart problem is discovered as the cause of a stroke or TIA. Treatment may require tak-

---

"CLOTBUSTERS": NEW DRUGS FOR EMERGENCY TREATMENT OF STROKE

As mentioned earlier, certain patients with ischemic strokes may be candidates for thrombolytic drugs. If administered in time, these drugs, the most current of which is t-PA (short for tissue plasminogen activator), may limit or stop the damage caused by a stroke. Despite the improvement in stroke treatment that these drugs represent, there are serious drawbacks to their use, and they should only be given after a full explanation of the short- and long-term risks and benefits. Only physicians experienced in their use in hospitals equipped to respond to complications should administer them.[1] Clotbusters can cause bleeding in the brain, which can be fatal or can worsen the outcome of any stroke. Thrombolytics should never be given to patients with hemorrhagic strokes, and therefore, doctors must rule out hemorrhagic stroke before using them. As with all medications, thrombolytic drugs do not always work.

In addition to the medical complications of thrombolytics, there are practical complications as well. These drugs are new, and due to the changing nature of stroke treatment, many members of the public and some emergency service health care workers are not fully aware of the use of clotbusters and the emergent nature of stroke. If you know that you're at risk for stroke, talk to your doctor about the use of clotbusters, their pros and cons, and their local availability. Many new drugs are being tested for stroke treatment, and it's hoped that in the future, they'll widen options for doctors and patients.

---

ing medication, often an anticoagulant (blood thinner) like Coumadin (also known as warfarin). Be aware, however, that there are significant risks to taking anticoagulants (blood thinners), the most dangerous of which is cerebral hemorrhage.

One of the most common treatments for the prevention of blood clots are blood platelet antiaggregants, such as aspirin and Ticlid. Aspirin and ticlopidine (Ticlid) both work to keep clots from forming by preventing the blood platelets from sticking together. There is much evidence to suggest that aspirin is beneficial for people who have had a stroke or TIA, but thus far there is no evidence that aspirin is beneficial for women who have not had a stroke, TIA, heart attack, or heart disease. There are risks associated with aspirin including allergy, stomach upset, ulcers, and bleeding problems in some people. In women, Ticlid may be more effective than aspirin in preventing a first or recurrent stroke. However, it's much more expensive than aspirin and some of its side effects are very serious. If you are taking Ticlid, your doctor will probably ask that you be closely followed with blood tests, particularly in the initial stages of treatment. Always ask your doctor to explain the nature and purpose of any medication prescribed to you, it side effects, what to do if you experience side effects, the alternatives that exist, and whether other drugs and over-the-counter medications you are taking will interfere with the prescribed medication.

Surgery. The carotid arteries are the two main arteries that travel along the front of the neck. These arteries and the basilar artery, which runs along the back of the neck, carry blood to the brain. Atherosclerotic plaque can easily build up in the carotid arteries, leaving one at risk for stroke. *Carotid endarterectomy* is a surgical procedure that involves removing atherosclerotic plaque from a carotid artery. It is done as an attempt to prevent an ischemic stroke. The risks of this type of surgery may, however, be quite high. They include the possibility of stroke and heart attack, or death. Therefore, it's important to choose a physician and hospital with significant experience in this procedure. Surgery may also be indicated if an aneurysm or AVM is found, because once a leak from a site has occurred it's very likely that it will leak or rupture again.

HOW DOES A STROKE AFFECT THE SURVIVOR?

When the blood supply to an area is disrupted, the brain tissue that was fed by the artery doesn't always die. Sometimes, nearby arteries are able to take over and supply the area with blood. When this happens, the area may recover, though this is less likely to happen with large strokes.

The effects of stroke, though very individualized, generally depend on the location and severity of the stroke. For some survivors stroke can result in paralysis of one side of the body, such as the side of the face, an arm, and/or a leg, or the whole side of the body. For others, slurred speech, inability to speak, dizziness, loss of vision, personality and behavior changes, or a combination of these effects may result.

The largest part of the brain, the cerebrum, is divided into two hemispheres. Generally, the left hemisphere and the right hemisphere each control the opposite side of the body. In general, when the right hemisphere is affected, the result may be left-sided paralysis, memory deficits, impulsive behavior, and/or spatial or perceptual defects. When the left side is affected, the result may be right-sided paralysis, cautious behavior, and/or speech, language, or memory deficits. Still, it should be remembered that no two stroke survivors are alike and no two will experience the effects of stroke in the same way.

For some survivors, stroke results in behavioral changes that can confuse and worry the survivor, family members, and friends. For example, a survivor may be able to understand language but not be able to speak or write. This is a form of aphasia, a speech and language disorder. Of course, this is just one example. There are many degrees and types of aphasia. As well, other types of deficits may occur. Some have both a physical and psychological basis and can pose significant challenges to stroke survivors and their families. If you are a family member who has noticed behavior changes in a survivor, you'll need information about the way in which the stroke may have affected the survivor. It's important not to make assumptions about the causes of behavior that you observe. Talk to your doctor or rehabilitation professionals about the behavior that concerns you. Your local chapter of the American Heart Association may be able to provide you with free, general information about the ways in which stroke affects behavior. For the national address and telephone number, refer to the Resource Directory.

Many survivors experience depression after a stroke. Depression and grieving for the losses that accompany stroke are understandable. But depression can also have medical causes. Sometimes the specific injury to the brain can cause an effect that is mistaken for depression. For example, the injury can produce uncontrolled crying spells that can begin for no apparent reason and are, in fact, not the result of depression.

Although diagnosis of depression may be difficult in stroke survivors because of the functional deficits caused by stroke, potential signs may include thoughts of suicide, a change in personality, a sense of guilt or worthlessness, loss of interest in life, irritability, sleeplessness, or loss of appetite. Again, sadness after a stroke is normal, but if any of these symptoms are very pronounced or prolonged, it is a good idea to seek your doctor's advice. It's important for your doctor, who may be a primary care physician or a neurologist, to try to determine whether there are medical causes for the behavior experienced before referring you or your family member for further treatment.

For some stroke survivors experiencing depression, short-term individual therapy may be helpful as may participation in a stroke support group. In many areas of the country, stroke support groups and clubs are available to put survivors and their family members or caregivers in touch with others who have also survived a stroke. There, survivors and loved ones can share experiences and learn more about adapting to the limitations that can be imposed by a stroke.

Short-term antidepressant medication may also help to lift a stroke survivor's depression so that she or he can begin the rehabilitation process. Beginning rehabilitation as soon as possible is paramount. Time must not be unnecessarily lost due to depression that goes unrecognized and untreated.

COMPLICATIONS THAT CAN OCCUR AFTER A STROKE

Survivors and family members should be aware of some of the health problems that may occur after a stroke so that care can be taken to avoid them and they can be addressed if and when they present themselves. Be sure to speak to your doctor or rehabilitation professionals about these or any other complications.

- *Blood vessel* problems. Blood clots may form in legs that are inactive due to weakness or paralysis. Blood clots in the legs can be particularly dangerous because they can sometimes travel to the lungs, causing pain, shortness of breath and even death. Talk to your doctor about any measures that you can take to prevent clotting. Doctors often prescribe special leg stockings and encourage physical therapy as soon as possible to prevent immobility. Sometimes, doctors may prescribe anticoagulant medication, if the risk of clotting is thought to be particularly serious.

- *Bedsores* (also called pressure sores or decubitus ulcers) can occur if a person is left lying or sitting in one position for too long. Means of preventing them include keeping the skin clean and dry and maintaining a nutritious diet. Also, a person lying in bed must be turned frequently. If the survivor uses a wheelchair, emphasis should be placed on shifting frequently, and, if possible, getting out of the wheelchair occasionally. Sterile dressings should be applied to bedsores that have already developed.
- *Limb contractures,* or freezing or stiffening of the joints, may occur when a survivor is paralyzed and range-of-motion exercises are not undertaken.
- Some survivors may experience *seizures,* usually soon after the stroke. Seizures generally respond well to conventional anticonvulsant medication. People with seizures may experience an "aura" before the seizure, which they come to recognize as a warning sign. Ask your doctor or nurse for information about what to do in the event of a seizure so that you can reduce the chances of injury.

REHABILITATION FOR STROKE SURVIVORS

Although almost every stroke survivor experiences some permanent loss of functional ability, rehabilitation can help survivors learn how to compensate for their losses by using different parts of the brain or by finding new ways of doing old tasks. Rehabilitation is not easy. The battle for progress is hard and generally very slow. However, progress can often be made even if the survivor's deficits initially appear to be significant. In the past, it was generally felt that survivors wouldn't make real gains after the first six months following a stroke. However, it is becoming increasingly recognized that stroke survivors can continue to make progress well after that six-month period.

Rehabilitation should start as soon as you are medically stable and, if possible, while you are still in the hospital. However, if you are not referred to a medical rehabilitation facility or given information about available options for rehabilitation, you may want to contact a nearby rehabilitation program (if there is one in your area) or get an evaluation from a local physiatrist (also called a PM&R specialist). These are doctors who specialize in physical medicine and rehabilitation. (See Chapter Six.)

During rehabilitation, you may need the support of many professionals, including your doctor, a physical therapist, speech therapist, an occupational therapist, nutritionist, and/or a social worker. But you, the survivor, and your family play the most important role in recovery. Survivors need encouragement, care, and understanding during the long and frustrating path toward rehabilitation. Families also need support and information about stroke, rehabilitation, and the ways in which stroke is likely to affect the survivor's life. Here again, stroke support groups and clubs can be very beneficial.

ARE THERE RISK FACTORS FOR STROKE?

There are important risk factors for stroke, some of which can be changed and some that cannot. It is important to remember that if you have more than one risk factor, your risk for stroke increases several times.

Although stroke can happen at any age, three quarters of all strokes occur in people sixty-five years of age or older. Men are more likely to have a stroke than women, but stroke is the third leading cause of death for women in the United States. African-American women are much more likely to have a stroke and to die of a stroke than white women. This may be due to the increased incidence of high blood pressure among African Americans and possibly to inadequate access to health care services.

People with diabetes are at increased risk of stroke, heart disease, or other blood vessel disorders. It's a good idea to have your doctor check you for diabetes, if you have a family history of diabetes, if you are overweight, or if you are pregnant or have high blood pressure, especially if you are Latina, Native American, or African American, since people of these heritages have a high incidence of diabetes. People with sickle cell anemia, even children, are at a greatly increased risk of stroke. As well, persons with certain types of heart conditions and those who have had a ministroke or a previous stroke are at increased risk. There is also evidence of an association between stroke and recent infection, particularly bacterial infection. Speak to your health care professional about steps you can take to reduce your risk for stroke.

The following are risk factors that can be changed. High blood pressure is the most important risk factor for stroke. High cholesterol, smoking, being overweight, and the consumption of more than one or two alcoholic beverages a day are also associated with an increased risk of atherosclerosis and thus stroke. Recreational drug use, especially the use of stimulants like cocaine and amphetamines, increases the risk of stroke in people of any age.

Studies on the effect of birth control pills on high blood pressure, heart disease, and stroke were done with higher dose estrogen pills that are not in general use today. More studies must be done with today's low-dose estrogen pills to determine if a significant risk for high blood pressure, stroke, and heart disease exists. However, it has been determined that smokers who use birth control pills are at increased risk for stroke.

There is disagreement about the effect of hormone replacement therapy on stroke. However, new studies indicate a risk for blood clots in the legs associated with even low doses of hormone replacements. If you know that you are at risk for stroke, carefully discuss the advantages and disadvantages of hormone therapy with your doctor or doctors before deciding to use it.

WOMEN AND HEART DISEASE

If you have had angina, you can distinguish a heart attack from angina by the pain, which may be much more severe and which does not generally stop or decrease with rest and/or by taking a nitroglycerin tablet or spray.

Heart attacks can also occur without pain. These are called silent heart attacks. Older people and people with diabetes may have blunted sensitivity to pain and therefore may be more likely to have silent heart attacks. Silent heart attacks are every bit as serious as heart attacks that can be felt.

If you have any of these symptoms at rest *for more than two minutes* or the symptoms do not respond to nitroglycerin tablets or spray taken as prescribed by your doctor, immediately call 911 for an ambulance, or call the emergency telephone number in your area. If it would be quicker, have a friend or relative drive you directly to a hospital emergency room. Do not drive yourself. There is a possibility that you could pass out in the car and further endanger yourself and the lives of others.

Do not minimize the seriousness of your symptoms. Women are less likely than men to have classic heart attack symptoms. Rather, when having a heart attack, we may have nausea and nonspecific symptoms, such as indigestion-like symptoms, weakness or lethargy, or shortness of breath. Do not worry about being perceived as a hypochondriac or as

SIGNS OF A HEART ATTACK

You may be having a heart attack if you have any of the following symptoms:

- pain near the center of your chest which lasts longer than two to three minutes and is not relieved by rest or changing positions
- pain that ranges from mild to severe and feels like tightness, heaviness, a squeezing sensation, intense pressure, or crushing pain
- pain that radiates into your jaw, shoulders, back or neck, or down your arms (usually, but not always, the left arm)
- nausea, shortness of breath, fatigue, feeling faint or light-headed, sweating, or a sense of impending doom
- severe indigestion that does not subside by using antacids or burping

someone who is overreacting in the emergency room. If the blood supply to the heart is compromised for more than thirty minutes, irreversible injury can occur. Thus, any delay in treatment could lead to loss of heart muscle, which can cause increased disability or even death. The risk of potential embarrassment is far outweighed by the possibility of saving your life. Many people have died because they did not get medical help in time.

If you know that you are at risk for heart disease, talk to your doctor about what to do in the event of an emergency. Ask for information about the hospitals in your area best equipped to respond to and care for heart patients.

IN THE EMERGENCY ROOM

As soon as you arrive, you or the person who has brought you to the emergency room should locate the triage nurse (the nurse who decides in what order patients will be seen) or the charge nurse and tell him or her that you are having a heart attack. Do not downplay the potential seriousness of your condition and do not let the staff make you wait for medical attention.

It may take physicians a few hours to establish the diagnosis of a heart attack. This is done primarily by taking a history of your symptoms, observing changes on your electrocardiogram (EKG, or ECG), and studying the results of a special blood test called a cardiac enzyme panel. The cardiac enzyme panel measures an enzyme called creatine kinase, which is released from dying or injured heart muscle cells and which, at certain critical levels, can indicate a heart attack.

Initial treatment of a heart attack may include the use of a number of different medications. If you get to the hospital early enough, a new type of medication popularly referred to as "clotbusters" (also called thrombolytics) may be given. A drug called t-PA (or tissue plasminogen activator) is among the most common of these drugs in use today. A blockage in a coronary artery, often caused by a blood clot, can cause a heart attack. Clotbusters can help to dissolve a clot in a coronary artery, but only if administered soon enough. Optimally, thrombolytics should be given within the first one to two hours after symptoms appear.

In addition to the procedures above, emergency angioplasty or bypass surgery may be done in some cases.

If there is any question that you are having a heart attack, you will be transferred to the coronary care unit (CCU) or the intensive care unit (ICU) for continuous monitoring. It

---

CPR — CARDIOPULMONARY RESUSCITATION

When someone who is having a heart attack is not breathing, has no pulse, or is passed out and unresponsive, CPR should be started by a person who is trained in its use. Ideally, everyone should be trained in CPR, but if you live with someone who has heart disease, it is especially important to learn this life-saving technique. Your local branch of the American Red Cross, American Heart Association, or your local fire department may offer classes for a low cost.

is likely that you will stay in the hospital from twenty-four to thirty-six hours or more, depending on whether or not you've had a heart attack. This is because serious complications can develop as the result of a heart attack. An arrhythmia, which is an irregularity of the heart's rhythm, is a common and feared complication that can cause sudden death. In an emergency situation, such as in the case of a life-threatening arrhythmia, medical professionals may use a defibrillator to send an electric shock to the heart to help it return to its normal rhythm. Alternatively, intravenous medication may be used to help restore a normal rhythm. If complications do arise from your heart attack, your hospital stay may be extended over a period of weeks.

Congestive heart failure is another problem associated with heart attack, although it can result from other causes. Very generally, congestive heart failure occurs when the heart is unable to pump efficiently and as a result blood (fluid) backs up behind the heart. This may cause fluid to build up in the lungs, causing shortness of breath or swelling in the feet, depending on which part of the heart is affected. Doctors may give diuretics to remove excess fluid from the body or administer other medications to help the heart pump more efficiently.

WHAT IS CORONARY ARTERY DISEASE?

This section focuses on coronary artery disease (also called coronary heart disease), which is the most common form of heart disease. However, there are other forms of heart disease about which women should be educated. To that end, suggestions for further reading are given at the end of this book.

To understand coronary artery disease (CAD), you must first have a basic understanding of the anatomy of the heart. The heart, like other organs of the body, requires nutrients and oxygen in order to function. These essentials are brought to the heart through blood supplied by its own specialized system of arteries. These are called the coronary arteries. When the blood supply through these arteries is insufficient, the result is chest pain (angina) or a heart attack. A heart attack will occur if an artery is completely blocked and a portion of the heart muscle is deprived of oxygen delivered by the blood for more than thirty minutes. Atherosclerosis (hardening of the arteries) is the most common cause of narrowing of the arteries which predisposes one to heart attack.

Atherosclerosis is thought to be caused by damage to the

WHAT IS ANGINA?

Angina pectoris is the name for classic cardiac pain that, like a heart attack, is caused by an inadequate blood supply to the heart. Although angina is usually caused by a narrowing of the arteries rather than a complete blockage, it is an important indicator of increased risk for a heart attack. Angina often occurs with physical exertion, especially in cold weather or after a meal, or from stress that causes the heart to beat faster. Generally, angina will subside quickly with rest or when a nitroglycerin tablet is taken according to your doctor's instructions. The pain of angina is similar to that of a heart attack. But it can sometimes be felt in atypical, subtle ways, such as an aching or sharp chest pain or as pain that occurs only in the arm or shoulder. If you experience symptoms suggestive of angina, you must seek medical evaluation as soon as possible. These symptoms could be a signal that you have coronary artery disease and may mean that a potentially preventable heart attack is around the corner.

Unstable angina describes chest pain that is new, occurs at rest, or that lasts longer, occurs more frequently, or develops with increasingly less activity than chest pain you have felt in the past. If you think that you are experiencing unstable angina, notify your doctor immediately. Unstable angina can progress rapidly to a heart attack and often requires hospitalization.

inner lining of the arteries. In response to the damage, fatty deposits (or plaques) build up in the arteries over time. This buildup slowly causes the arteries to narrow. Eventually, the arteries may become so narrow that the blood supply that nourishes the heart can barely pass through them, or a small blood clot may develop and block the artery completely. Certain risk factors are associated with atherosclerosis and may speed its development. Some risk factors are modifiable. For example, you may be able to reduce your risk for atherosclerosis by no longer smoking if you do smoke, avoiding foods that are high in fat and cholesterol, exercising, and if you are overweight, losing weight.

A DANGEROUS MYTH: WOMEN DON'T GET HEART DISEASE

Many people, including some doctors, minimize the risk of coronary heart disease in women. However, heart disease is the number one killer of American women. Each year approximately 240,000 women die of heart disease. Heart disease kills more women than all types of cancer combined.

How did this dangerous myth come into being? Perhaps it did because many women appear to be protected from heart disease by the female sex hormone estrogen until menopause. At menopause women gradually begin to lose this advantage, and by the age of sixty or sixty-five, women are at an almost equal risk for heart disease as men.

Not only are we at great risk for heart disease, when we get sick, the outcome is usually worse than it is for men. A woman's chance of dying of a first heart attack is greater than a man's, as is her chance of having a second heart attack. Reasons for this may include the possibility of subtler symptoms in women, the tendency some doctors have not to treat women's heart symptoms as seriously or aggressively as men's complaints, and the tendency some women have to deny or minimize their symptoms. Treatment may be delayed until women are both more advanced in age and in extent of heart disease, at which time the likelihood of complications is greater.

The most important thing an individual woman can do to reduce her risk of heart disease and its dangers is to become aware of the risk factors and the warning signs of heart attack, to take those warnings seriously, and to insist that her doctor or medical team do the same. If your doctor won't take your concerns seriously, do find another doctor, if possible.

The treatment options for heart disease depend on many factors. The severity of disease, the existence of associated problems, and complications that occur after a heart attack all influence the type of treatment your doctor will advise.

Decisions about treatment are complex and individual. The more you know about your condition and its treatment, the better informed you will be to take part in the decision-making process and take charge of your health care. Arm yourself with plenty of information. There are many books on the market that provide an overview of treatment options and enable readers to evaluate the advantages and disadvantages of available treatments in conjunction with their doctors' advice. Take a look at the reading resource list at the end of this book for ideas, and check your local bookstores and libraries. Remember that no treatment eradicates heart disease. Once again, what is needed to help improve the outcome of any treatment is commitment to changing those factors that affect your risk of disease — diet, smoking, alcohol or drug use, stress levels, and exercise.

Your doctor may prescribe *medication* after your heart attack, especially if you have angina, hypertension, congestive heart failure, or certain arrhythmias. Aspirin therapy may also be suggested. Studies have found that even in small doses aspirin can reduce the risk of death and nonfatal heart attack in people who have had a previous heart attack, coronary artery bypass graft (CABG), stroke, or a transient ischemic attack (TIA). However, there is as yet no conclusive evidence that aspirin therapy is beneficial to women who have not been diagnosed with some type of coronary artery disease or cerebral artery disease, although studies examining the potential benefits are under way.

Aspirin is sometimes mistakenly considered a benign drug, and you may be tempted to start an aspirin regimen on your own to prevent a heart attack. But aspirin can cause complications, such as stomach upset, ulcers, and higher risk of bleeding problems, including hemorrhagic stroke. No aspirin therapy should be undertaken without first consulting your doctor.

Angioplasty. Before discussing this procedure, it's important to have an understanding of a diagnostic procedure called *cardiac catheterization* (also known as coronary angiography), which will be done before angioplasty. Cardiac catheterization is an invasive procedure (the skin is penetrated) used to look directly at the arteries to determine if

WHAT CAUSES A HEART ATTACK?

Risk factors for a heart attack include age (your risk increases as you get older), family history (heart attack in a parent, grandparent, brother or sister under the age of fifty-five, or sixty-five for a female), smoking, heavy alcohol consumption, and recreational drug use, especially cocaine. Risk factors also include being overweight, a lack of adequate exercise, an abnormal cholesterol profile, hypertension, and diabetes. While some studies have shown a link between coronary artery disease and aggressive type A behavior in men, further studies are being done to try to determine whether there really is a connection. As yet no evidence has shown this connection in women. Some studies suggest that holding anger inside may increase heart disease risk in women. It is recognized that stress can lead to unhealthy behaviors such as smoking, drinking, and overeating, which certainly can affect your risk of heart attack.

It's important to note that if you have more than one risk factor, your risk for heart attack can be several times greater than if you had a single risk factor.

and by how much they are narrowed. During the test, you will be awake, although possibly sedated. A fine tubing called a catheter will be inserted into an artery in the groin (or, more rarely, in the arm) and advanced until it sits in the heart. To help visualize the blockage, a small amount of dye will be injected into the heart through the catheter while the heart is being filmed. A 35mm motion picture of your heart displaying all the coronary arteries will be produced. Most people report that this procedure is uncomfortable but not painful. There are a few but significant risks associated with cardiac catheterization, including the risk of infection, heart attack, or stroke. The risk is greater for people who are elderly, frail, or have severe heart disease.

Angioplasty (also called percutaneous transluminal coronary angioplasty, PTCA) may be done after a cardiac catheterization to try to open a blocked artery. A special catheter with a tiny balloon on the tip is introduced through an artery in the groin and again advanced until it reaches the heart. When it reaches the point of blockage, it is inflated and held in position for a few seconds or minutes. Complications include possibly injury or puncture of an artery, requiring emergency coronary artery bypass graft surgery; clot formation at the site of angioplasty, which could lead to a heart attack; and death. While these risks are small, it is still critical to schedule the angioplasty (or cardiac catheterization) at a hospital where a significant number of PTCAs are performed, one with an experienced surgical team that includes a cardiovascular surgeon who is available to perform coronary artery bypass surgery, if necessary. The American College of Cardiology and the American Heart Association recommend that physicians performing adult cardiac catheterizations have a caseload of at least 150 cases a year and at least 50 PTCAs a year in order to maintain proficiency.[2]

A significant, common problem associated with angioplasty is the possibility that the opened artery may become blocked again or "re-stenosed." If this happens, angioplasty must usually be repeated.

In the early years of angioplasty, the procedure was considered riskier and less successful for women. Women, who are usually smaller than men, tend to have smaller arteries, and the problems in performing angioplasty were generally felt to be due to the size of the balloon used in the procedure. When a smaller balloon is used, the death and complication rate is much less but still slightly higher for women. Ask your doctor to discuss the risks and benefits of angioplasty versus medical management or CABG in your situation. Keep in mind that only certain types of blockages can be treated with angioplasty. The location and length of the blockage, as well as its hardness from calcium deposits, are factors that influence whether angioplasty can be used.

Another alternative to surgery may include atherectomy. *Atherectomy* is similar to angioplasty, but instead of a balloon, the catheter is tipped with a special instrument equipped with rotating blades or a small drill tip that is used to remove plaque buildup from the arteries. *Coronary artery stents* are tiny, mesh, stainless steel scaffoldings that can be put in place during angioplasty to keep an artery open. Ask your doctors about the advantages and disadvantages of stents for women and, in particular, for you.

At the time of this writing, *laser angioplasty,* which is used on blockages in leg arteries, is being used on a limited basis in the treatment of coronary artery disease.

Coronary artery bypass graft (CABG). Like PTCA, the goal of bypass surgery is to restore blood flow to the heart. CABG is major surgery during which a vein or artery is taken from another part of the body, usually a leg vein or mammary artery, and grafted on to the vessels of the heart so that blockage can be effectively bypassed and the blood can flow freely to the heart. CABG has been shown to relieve severe angina that won't subside with medication alone and to prolong life in certain people with heart disease.

Complications of Bypass Surgery

Coronary artery bypass surgery may be riskier for women than for men. There may be several reasons for this. Women with heart disease tend to be older than male heart patients and therefore may be more likely to require emergency surgery. We also tend to have smaller, more delicate arteries than men, which makes surgery more difficult. If you are in doubt about your need for surgery, seek a second and even a third opinion, if necessary, from a cardiovascular surgeon or another cardiologist.

Choosing Your Surgeon

Your cardiologist will usually recommend a cardiac surgeon. Depending on your insurance coverage, you can also look for a surgeon yourself. In either case, get two or three names. When you choose a surgeon, you are effectively choosing the hospital where you will be treated, since most surgeons generally operate only in one or two hospitals. The more CABGs a hospital does each year, the better the outcome of the operation is likely to be. University-affiliated hospitals, medical centers, and large community hospitals tend to be the biggest hospitals and thus tend to have the highest volume. Ask your surgeon and/or call the hospital and ask about the numbers of CABGs done annually. In general, it is suggested that the hospital do a minimum of two hundred to three hundred CABGs a year. Also, ask your surgeon for his mortality rate (the number of people who have died as a result of the operation) and for his complication rate.

Cardiac Rehabilitation

Cardiac rehabilitation should begin in the hospital as soon as you are medically stable. Initially, emphasis will be placed on preventing loss of mobility and muscle tone and on steadily increasing your activity. Once you are discharged from the hospital, your exercise program will be slowly increased under the supervision of your doctor, who will also order periodic testing. Cardiac rehabilitation can help you learn more about your heart condition, make important lifestyle changes, understand what to expect during your recovery, and help you to adjust physically and emotionally. Don't wait for your doctor to tell you about rehabilitation, ask. Your local chapter of the American Heart Association can also refer you to a rehabilitation program, if there is one in your area.

Depression and sadness are common responses to heart attack. They tend to lessen as time goes on and as you return to your usual activities. But if feelings of sadness or depression continue, consider talking to your doctor and rehabilitation staff members. You may also wish to seek a therapist or support group to discuss feelings related to heart disease. Your mental health is just as important as your physical health and should never be neglected. Note that some cardiovascular medications can cause depression, so be sure to discuss your symptoms with your doctor.

HORMONE REPLACEMENT THERAPY

If you are a woman going through or approaching menopause, you are likely to be facing the difficult question of whether or not to take hormone replacement therapy (HRT). The decision-making process is indeed a challenging one as each woman's medical history and feelings about hormone therapy make her situation unique. There really are no simple answers. After you've learned as much information about HRT and its alternatives as possible, evaluated your personal risk factors, and consulted with your doctor, you must make the decision that best suits you. You are strongly urged to continue your investigation into the pros and cons of HRT beyond this section. Books and articles on the subject abound and will most likely continue to be printed as new research becomes available.

Initially, hormone replacements were taken by women to relieve problems associated with menopause such as hot flashes, night sweats, vaginal dryness, and decreased sexual desire. Today, however, many doctors advocate HRT for the prevention of osteoporosis (the loss of bone density that causes weakening of the bones and can lead to fractures) and to reduce the risk of coronary artery disease in women. But recent evidence suggests that HRT may increase the risk of breast cancer. Thus, the discussion of whether or not women should use HRT after menopause remains a controversial one.

Possible benefits of HRT

Studies have shown that hormone therapy may reduce the risk of coronary artery disease in women by as much as 50 percent. Because heart disease is the most common cause of death in women in the United States, more common than breast cancer, the possible benefits can be quite significant. Nonetheless, there is still some disagreement among authorities about HRT's cardioprotective benefits.

Although the use of HRT to prevent osteoporosis is well known, most studies show that the benefits are not significant until a woman has been using HRT for at least seven years. In addition to hormone therapy, you may want to ask your doctor about the pros and cons of some nonhormonal osteoporosis treatments if you have or think you are at risk for osteoporosis. As a further benefit, recent studies have also suggested that HRT may reduce the risk of colon cancer.

Possible risks of HRT

Breast, uterine, and the rare but often fatal ovarian cancer have all been implicated as possible risks associated with HRT. A study published in 1995 involving more than 120,000 women found that the risk of breast cancer increased about 46 percent in women who used HRT for more than five years as compared to women who had never taken hormone replacements. The risk increased to about 70 percent in women between the ages of sixty-five to sixty-nine.[3] At the same time, this study found no increased risk to women under fifty. To add to the confusion, a smaller, subsequent study contradicted the findings of this larger study. As with HRT's cardiovascular benefits, the relationship between breast cancer and long-term HRT is still being studied and debated.

It's long been known that women who have not had hysterectomies using estrogen alone are at increased risk of uterine cancer. Today, however, estrogen is generally prescribed with progestin (a synthetic version of the natural female hormone progesterone) to women who have not had a hysterectomy, and the risk of uterine cancer has been reduced. But, predictably, there may be a downside to the addition of progestin to estrogen therapy. There is still some question about whether its addition reduces the positive cardiovascular benefits of hormone therapy.

HRT is generally not recommended for women who have liver disease, and women with breast cancer or a history of breast cancer. It may be inadvisable for women who have migraine headaches, gallbladder disease, blood clots in the legs or lungs (pulmonary embolism), or a history of uterine cancer. Unfortunately, there is also disagreement about the benefits of HRT for women with high blood pressure and for women who already have heart disease or who have had a stroke. Thus, if you have or have had one of these conditions, you will want to look closely at the risks and benefits and discuss the issue thoroughly with your doctor. You may also consider looking into natural food alternatives to hormone therapy, although their benefits have not been studied.

If you are on hormone replacement therapy, watch for possible symptoms of uterine or breast cancer and blood clots in the legs or lungs. These symptoms include abnormal vaginal bleeding, breast lumps, pain in the calves or chest, and shortness of breath. Contact your doctor immediately if you have any of these symptoms.

CANCER AND RESOURCES FOR INFORMATION

Cancer occurs when normal cells undergo uncontrolled division, usually resulting in a lump of tissue called a tumor, although not all cancers create tumors. Generally, if you have a tumor, you will not be able to feel or see it in the early stages of cancer.

Tumors can either be benign or malignant. If a tumor is benign, it is not cancer. While many cancers are contained in the original area, some can invade other parts of the body, usually by traveling through the bloodstream or lymph system. This is called *metastasis*. Types of cancer are often categorized by the name of the organ in which they originate. For example, cancer that originates in the breast is called breast cancer.

Cancer symptoms vary and depend on where the cancer originates. According to the American Cancer Society, the warning signs of cancer include a sore that doesn't get better, a nagging cough or unusually hoarse voice, indigestion (a very bad upset stomach more than once in a while) or problems with swallowing, changes in a wart or mole, unusual bleeding or discharge, a thick spot or lump in a breast or anywhere else, and a change in bowel or bladder habits.[4] Most certainly, a person can have such symptoms and not have cancer. However, if you have any of these symptoms, report them to your doctor.

IF YOU HAVE BEEN DIAGNOSED WITH CANCER

Finding out that you have cancer is frightening. But it's important to understand that cancer is most often not a death sentence. There are 8.5 million cancer survivors in the United States today, and this number is growing.

If you have received a cancer diagnosis, you may want more information about the type of cancer you have and about your treatment options. Taking an active role in your recovery can be beneficial. For example, having information can help you gain a better understanding of your treatment options, get a second or third opinion about your diagnosis, find sources of financial assistance, and address problems that arise with your insurance provider or at the workplace. Information can also help you seek sources of emotional support, if desired.

The following sections will help you find low-cost sources of information about cancer and cancer care. In the Resource Directory, you'll find information about organizations that provide support and information to people with cancer. The reading resource list at the end of the book provides information about books on cancer and treatment.

The following are national organizations that offer the public information about cancer and cancer-related issues. For more information about these organizations, refer to the Resource Directory.

The Cancer Information Service
1-800-4-CANCER (1-800-422-6237); 1-800-332-8615 (TTY)

This toll-free, nationwide telephone information and education network is sponsored by the National Cancer Institute (NCI), one of the National Institutes of Health. When you call the toll-free number, your call will be automatically routed to one of NCI's regional Cancer Information Service (CIS) offices, which operate from 9 A.M. to 4:30 P.M., Monday through Friday. Information specialists can answer questions and send you written information on cancer topics, although they cannot diagnose cancer or offer recommendations for treatment. All calls are kept confidential. CIS offices can also provide referrals to FDA-certified mammography facilities.

Each CIS office has access to NCI's PDQ database. The *Physician Data Query (PDQ)* database was developed by the National Cancer Institute to give health professionals and patients accurate, up-to-date information about cancer and cancer treatment. The PDQ provides information about types of cancer, cancer care, available clinical trials, and the names of physicians and hospitals involved in the care of cancer patients. You may want to ask about referrals to NCI-supported programs and cancer centers to help you get a second opinion about your diagnosis. Your CIS office can also do a PDQ clinical trials search for you.

You and your physician can access the PDQ database with a computer modem, communications software, and a PDQ access code or through a medical library with on-line searching capability. PDQ access may also be obtained by facsimile through CANCERFAX, by e-mail, and via the Internet.

In addition to other services, the National Cancer Institute's CIS offices offer many booklets on cancer topics. At the time of this printing, some of the booklets offered include *Chemotherapy and You: A Guide to Self-Help During Treatment, Radiation Therapy and You, When Cancer Recurs: Meeting the Challenge Again, What You Need to Know About Breast Cancer,* and *Taking Time: Support for People with Cancer and the People Who Care About Them.*

SEEKING INFORMATION AT THE LIBRARY

In addition to newsletters and other publications offered by support and advocacy organizations, you may want to explore additional sources of information. Public libraries often carry a variety of books, magazines, and journals that contain information about cancer treatment. In addition, many public libraries provide access to databases that make searching for information and printing out articles fairly simple. Ask your reference librarian how to find the information you're seeking. For more in-depth searches, you may

The American Cancer Society
1-800-ACS-2345

The American Cancer Society offers the public information about cancer and its treatment and, depending on the state, a range of other services for people with cancer and their families. Other services may include peer support and visitor programs, transportation for people who cannot otherwise get to facilities for medical treatments, information and advocacy for people who experience problems in the workplace, summer camps for children, and overnight housing near major treatment centers for eligible persons. Call the toll-free number for more information about services in your community.

The National Coalition for Cancer Survivorship
(301) 650-8868; (301) 565-9670 (fax)

The NCCS is a coalition of individuals, cancer support organizations, and treatment centers that advocates on behalf of the cancer survivorship community. It serves as a clearinghouse for a wide range of issues of concern to people with cancer and specifically addresses employment discrimination and insurance problems. Low-cost publications include *You Have the Right to Be Hopeful, Teamwork: The Cancer Patient's Guide to Talking with Your Doctor, Working It Out: Your Employment Rights as a Cancer Survivor,* and *What Cancer Survivors Need to Know About Health Insurance.*

Other advocacy and support organizations meeting the needs of people with cancer and their families offer resources ranging from free or low-cost reading material to peer counseling, free lectures on treatment issues, and various referrals.

want to visit the biomedical library of a university or college, if there is one in your area. Call to find out if the library has access to the National Library of Medicine's computerized MEDLARS program, which offers access to a database called CANCERLIT, as well as PDQ, and a larger database called MEDLINE, from which CANCERLIT is drawn. CANCERLIT contains over a million citations and abstracts of articles on cancer published since 1963. For information about accessing the database with your home computer, write or call MEDLARS Management Section, National Library of Medicine, 8600 Rockville Pike, Bethesda, MD 20894; (301) 402-1076. If you subscribe to an on-line service or have access to the Internet you may also be able to access some of the National Library of Medicine's databases and other sources of information, such as user forums where laypeople and professionals share information on-line.

In recent years, the public and some medical professionals have taken an increased interest in complementary (also called alternative) medicine and the connection between the mind and physical well-being. You may not think of prayer, meditation, and stress reduction and visualization techniques as alternative therapies, but these practices have helped many to summon the inner strength to cope with cancer and possibly to enhance their bodies' ability to fight disease.

Generally, it's best not to ignore traditional medicine in favor of an alternative practice. This is because little research has been done on complementary therapies and because many types of cancer are treatable, especially in the early stages. Complementary practices are best thought of as additions to traditional therapies.

If you are considering a complementary therapy, seek information about the proposed treatment before accepting its use. Ask your doctor whether the therapy you are considering could affect your medical treatment. Ask specific questions about the complementary treatment. For example, what is the treatment's purpose? What are the possible results of the treatment? What are its proven benefits? What side effects may result? What is the cost? Ask for copies of published research on the treatment. If you are researching a clinic, find out how long it has been in business. If you are working with an individual practitioner, find out how long she or he has been in business and ask for information about the practitioner's background and training. Ask to speak to others who've undergone the treatment. If you are offered a treatment that is purported to cure cancer, you should be extremely skeptical. There are no known alternative remedies for curing cancer.

A good place to begin a search for information about complementary therapies is the National Institutes of Health's Office of Alternative Medicine. It was established in 1992 to evaluate alternative therapies.[5] The office does not make referrals, but it can provide you with a copy of the *Directory of Alternative Healthcare Associations* and fact sheets on various topics. The American Cancer Society also publishes the booklet *Questionable Methods of Cancer Treatment* to help consumers make informed decisions about their health care. Call the main office number of the American Cancer Society, listed in the Resource Directory under Life-Threatening Illness, for more information.

HIV INFECTION AND AIDS

WHAT IS HIV?

HIV stands for human immunodeficiency virus, the virus that causes AIDS. When the virus enters the bloodstream, it gradually disrupts and weakens the body's immune system. As HIV infection progresses, the immune system can become increasingly deficient. Opportunistic infections, such as pneumocystis carinii pneumonia (PCP), a type of pneumonia, may appear. These infections are called opportunistic because they are caused by organisms that take the op-

The CDC National AIDS Hotline
1-800-342-AIDS (2437); 1-800-243-7889 (TTY); 1-800-344-7432 (Spanish)

Health communications specialists can answer basic questions about HIV/AIDS, HIV antibody testing, and AIDS service organizations. Services are available on the main number twenty-four hours a day, 365 days a year.

National AIDS Clearinghouse
1-800-458-5231; 1-800-243-7012 (TDD)

This clearinghouse offers information and publications on HIV/AIDS.

The National Pediatric and Family HIV Resource Center
1-800-362-0071 or (201) 268-8251

NPHRC is primarily a resource for health care providers, but also offers educational materials and guidelines for the care of children, youth, and families with HIV infection and AIDS.

Your state or local AIDS/HIV hotline

These telephone hotlines can answer basic questions about HIV infection and AIDS and help you find information about resources in your area. Check your local telephone directory or call the National CDC AIDS hotline for the telephone number.

Aids service organizations (ASOs)

AIDS service organizations are multifaceted organizations offering a range of services to people with AIDS and HIV infection.

---

portunity to invade and replicate in the body while the immune system is compromised.

AIDS, which stands for Acquired Immunodeficiency Syndrome, is the late stage of HIV disease. When a person with HIV infection develops one or more of the illnesses that are defined by the Centers for Disease Control as being AIDS-related or has a CD4 cell count of less than 200 per cubic millimeter (mm^3), she will be diagnosed with AIDS. (The Centers for Disease Control (CDC) is the federal agency mandated to control infectious diseases.) It is vitally important to understand that not everyone's immune system reacts to HIV in the same way and that there are many documented cases of people who have continued to remain healthy despite HIV infection.

The decision to take the HIV antibody test is not one that is easily made. Testing for HIV can be frightening, especially if you have reason to believe that you've been exposed to the virus. However, it is extremely important to know your immune status. Negative results — results that indicate you are not HIV-positive — are often a reminder of the need to take care of yourself and to practice safer sex and/or safer needle use.

If you are HIV-positive and you know your immune status, you can take control of your health and health care. There are many ways that people with HIV infection and AIDS can enhance their health and prolong their lives. There are decisions to be made about medication, nutrition, and, possibly, lifestyle changes to strengthen your immune system. New medication regimens that appear to be more effective than older therapies in suppressing HIV replication are becoming available, and the decision about whether to introduce medication into your course of care is perhaps one of the first and most crucial decisions you and your doctor will make during treatment.

Knowing your HIV status can also allow you to protect the health of others. If you are HIV-positive you can pass the virus to your husband or partner and to your child before birth, during delivery, or after birth through breast-feeding. You can also transmit HIV to others by sharing needles or by donating blood (or semen, for men).

Should You Really Be Tested? Assessing the Risks

While anyone who is concerned about HIV infection should be tested, there are some explicit indications for testing. If you have any of the following risk factors or are not sure whether you do, you may want to think seriously about testing:

* you have had unprotected sex with someone who is HIV-positive or whose status is unknown
* you use injectable drugs
* you have had sex with someone who uses injectable drugs
* you have sex or have had sex with a gay or bisexual man

- you have or have had sex with more than one partner
- your partner has more than one partner
- you are pregnant or planning a pregnancy
- you have or have had a sexually transmitted disease or you have severe gynecological problems, such as recurrent yeast infections
- you received blood products between the years 1978 and 1985 or you have had sex with someone who received blood products between those years

THE HIV ANTIBODY TEST

There are differing types of HIV tests that can be used in various circumstances, and new diagnostic techniques are being developed. But this section will discuss the tests in most frequent use. The standard HIV antibody test is actually comprised of two tests: ELISA (enzyme-linked immunosorbent assay), which is a screening test, and a confirmatory test called the Western blot. When you are tested, your blood will be drawn, labeled, and sent to a laboratory for analysis. Generally, if the first ELISA is positive, the laboratory will run a second ELISA on the same sample. Then the Western blot will be run to confirm the ELISA result. A second confirmatory test may also be run. There is no risk of contracting HIV through the HIV antibody test. At all testing sites, blood will be drawn with a new, sterile needle, used once per patient, and then thrown away. If you test at a clinic or doctor's office, you will most likely take the test on one day and return for your results on another. It is very important that you do come back for your results; otherwise, you will not know your health status.

The HIV antibody test is not a test for AIDS. It cannot be used to determine how long you've been infected with HIV or whether you will develop AIDS. The ELISA and Western blot are used to detect the presence of antibodies to the human immunodeficiency virus (HIV) in the bloodstream. Antibodies are proteins developed by the immune system in response to the presence of a foreign (nonself) substance within the body, such as HIV.

Where Should You Be Tested: Anonymous Versus Confidential Testing Sites

Depending on where you live, testing may be available through public health departments, AIDS service organizations, community health and STD clinics, family planning clinics, hospitals, or doctors' offices. Home testing kits, which will be discussed shortly, are also available. You can get referrals to local testing agencies by calling the CDC National AIDS hotline, AIDS service organizations, or a state or local AIDS/HIV hotline.

Before considering where to test, it's important to know the difference between anonymous and confidential testing services. Some testings sites offer both options. Anonymous testing is the best way to ensure your privacy. When you are tested anonymously, your name is never used. Instead, you are given a number and/or a combination of letters as identification. The results are known only to you. Nothing will be written in your medical record.

Maintaining confidentiality through anonymous testing is extremely important since insurers may be able to access medical and hospital records. If you test HIV-positive before securing health insurance, you may have a very difficult time getting coverage. Also, insurers may exclude coverage for preexisting conditions, such as HIV infection, for a certain period of time. Under federal law, this exclusionary period can last no longer than twelve months for employees of large companies with employer-provided health benefits. State law may further limit waiting periods.

State law may allow insurers to require that you test for HIV infection as part of your application for an individual insurance policy. Look over your policy before testing or consider what recourse you have to coverage for medical care, if you don't have insurance. You may want to talk to an AIDS service organization for more information about testing for HIV infection and potential insurance-related problems. See the section Where to Find Information, Services, and Support: AIDS Service Organizations for information about ASOs.

Anonymous testing is offered through public health departments and AIDS service organizations across the country, but it is not available in every state. To find out whether anonymous testing is available where you live, call your local AIDS/HIV hotline, an AIDS service organization, or the state or local health department. A disadvantage of going to an anonymous testing site is that you may have to wait to make an appointment and/or to get your test results.

Confidential testing is another option. Depending on the test site, you may be able to choose between using your name or a false name when you test confidentially. If you give your name, the results can be written in your medical record, and therefore may be accessible to insurance companies and to others. Medical ethics and many state laws require doctors to keep HIV-related medical records confidential, although there are exceptions to this principle, and abuses are possible.

If you choose or must accept confidential testing, ask how the facility ensures confidentiality. Some employees or volunteers booking appointments may not be able to answer all your questions. Ask to speak to someone at the site who can. Ask if you will be required to give your name at any point during the testing process. If you are required to give your name or any type of identification, the test will not be performed anonymously. Always ask whether the results will be written in your medical record, who will have access to the results (including insurance companies), and how the medical records are stored. Don't assume that testing services offered through community clinics are anonymous; they may not be.

The risk of having your test results entered into your medical record is greatest when you test with your doctor or at a hospital. However, it's likely that you'll get the results sooner if you test through a private physician's office. It is often said that private physicians are ill-equipped to offer full or even adequate pre- and posttest counseling. This may be changing due to physicians' growing awareness of the increasing risk of HIV infection among women, but it is something you may want to think about. Of course, if you have a good relationship with your provider and he or she is sensitive to the issues that affect people with HIV infection and AIDS, the benefits of receiving testing and counseling with your health care provider may outweigh the advantages of anonymity. The choice is yours.

In a few places where testing is offered, the results from the ELISA and then, if necessary, the Western blot, may not be given at the same time. When considering where to test, you might ask whether you will receive the results of both tests at your return appointment. Otherwise, you may have to wait for the results of the Western blot, a potentially agonizing experience.

The Importance of Counseling Before and After the Test

Taking the HIV antibody test can be extremely stressful. Even if you don't think you are at risk, it's natural to be frightened and anxious while waiting for the test results. If possible, tell someone you trust that you are being tested so that you will have someone to talk to during the waiting period. Your husband or partner, a trusted relative or friend, or your clergyperson or a counselor can help you through the difficult moments. If you can, ask your support person to come with you to hear the results. If you are very anxious and upset, a crisis intervention or suicide prevention hotline can be of help too. (Check the front pages of your local telephone directory for listings of community services.)

Before you take an HIV antibody test, ask whether face-to-face pre- and posttest counseling is available on-site. It's inadvisable to take the test without counseling. At your pretest appointment you should be told about the nature of HIV infection and how the virus is transmitted. You and your counselor should discuss your risks for infection. Your counselor can then help you further consider whether you should be tested. Your counselor should give you information about the nature of the test, the possibility of a false positive or false negative, and the level of confidentiality provided by the testing site. It's also very important to discuss what you might do if your results are positive. Don't hesitate to bring up any concerns or questions you have with your counselor.

When you return for your second appointment, you should be told your results. If the results are negative, you should be given information about follow-up testing and on the ways you can protect yourself and others from the virus.

If the test shows that you are HIV-positive, you and your counselor should talk about the meaning of the results. Depending on the site and state, a social worker and a representative from the health department may also be available to you. You should be linked to services for continuing medical and psychological care and be given information on ways to reduce the spread of the virus. Thus, before you test, ask to know what services are available on-site or by referral and how you will be connected to these services. It's preferable to test at a facility that offers comprehensive medical and psychological services on-site, if possible.

Home testing kits are now available nationwide. These tests have been subject to criticism because of doubts about the adequacy of telephone counseling that should accompany positive or inconclusive test results and the potential for abuse by parents, employers, and others. On the other hand, proponents of home testing argue that home kits make testing more available to people who do not want or cannot take advantage of testing offered through public or community agencies. If you decide to use home testing, take the same measures as you would before deciding to test at a clinic. Finding someone to act as your support person to be with you when you hear the results is important no matter where you receive them.

When Should You Be Tested?

It takes time for the body to develop an immune reaction to the presence of HIV, usually about forty-five days to three months after infection. But it can take six months or longer, depending on the individual. If you are tested too soon after infection, antibodies may not be detectable by the standard HIV antibody test. Therefore, it is suggested that you wait six months after your first HIV test to be retested. In order to ensure the most accurate results, you should not engage in any high risk behavior, such as unprotected sex or unsafe needle use, during this time.

What Do the Results Mean?

A person in whom antibodies are detected is said to be HIV-positive (HIV1). She may assume that she is infected with HIV. If no antibodies are detected, the person undergoing the test will be considered HIV-negative (HIV-). A person who is HIV-negative may usually assume that she is not infected, although retesting is suggested to be certain. A negative result doesn't mean that you won't contract the virus. If you continue high risk behaviors such as unprotected sex or unsafe needle use, your risk of HIV infection remains.

Sometimes a person will receive an indeterminate result. This may be an indication of early infection or factors such as human error made in the laboratory or other medical conditions. It is often recommended that people who receive indeterminate test results retest in the near future.

How Accurate Are the Test Results?

The combination of ELISA and Western blot is extremely accurate, but there is a slight possibility of receiving a false positive or false negative result. A false positive result is one that tells you that you are HIV-positive when you are not. A false positive may be an indication of other medical conditions. If you are in doubt about an HIV-positive test result, you may want to retest to verify it. Consult your health care provider or HIV posttest counselor about this possibility.

It is also possible for a person to receive a false negative result, that is, a result that tells a person who has contracted

HIV that she is negative. As mentioned, this may be due to testing too soon after exposure to the virus.

What Will the Test Cost?

The cost for HIV antibody testing varies depending on where you test. Alternative testing sites and clinics may offer testing free of charge, for a small donation, or for a fee. If you order testing through a doctor's office, you could pay much more than at a clinic or health department. Before making an appointment for testing, ask what the charges will be. If you do not want your insurer to know that you were tested for HIV infection, do not pay for the test with your insurance.

Mandatory HIV Testing

There are some situations in which HIV antibody testing is mandatory, for example, upon entrance into the military, foreign service, or Peace Corps. Immigrants applying for permanent residency and federal prisoners must also be tested.

In many states, insurance companies may require HIV testing to determine your eligibility for an individual health, disability, or life insurance policy. You have the right to refuse the test and look for another insurer. Because laws regarding testing for insurance vary from state to state, you may want to contact the state HIV/AIDS hotline or AIDS service organization nearest you to find out what tests insurers may legally require you to take when applying for an insurance policy.

It is also possible that you could be asked to take an HIV test after you have received a job offer, but only if the requirement extends to all employees in the same job category and the test is both job-related and a business necessity. State law may also restrict HIV testing by employers. An AIDS service organization or legal group serving people with HIV/AIDS or an employment lawyer should be able to provide you with information about relevant laws.

Anonymous testing of blood samples taken for purposes other than HIV testing may also take place in hospitals to determine the rate of HIV infection in the area. Any personal identification on samples is removed.

Many states have allowed the routine anonymous testing of newborns in order to track the spread of HIV infection. In New York State, a woman may learn the results of her newborn's anonymous test, and thus her own health status, by signing a consent form. At the time of this printing, New York was also the first state to mandate HIV counseling for pregnant women seeking prenatal care services, with the exception of women seeking services from a private provider working outside a health maintenance organization. For more information about mandatory testing or counseling, you can call the CDC National AIDS Hotline or your state or local HIV/AIDS hotline.

LIVING WITH HIV INFECTION

When you first learn that you are HIV-positive, you may be shocked. You may feel panicked, frightened, depressed, and angry. It may seem as though you have been cheated of everything you've worked for, all your dreams and ambitions. You may feel alone and afraid that other people will reject you if they know that you are HIV-positive. If you have a child who is HIV-positive, your fear, anger, and grief may seem unbearable. You may blame yourself for contracting HIV or for giving the virus to your child. But you must realize that HIV infection is a disease to which everyone is vulnerable, and it is not your fault that you or your child contracted the virus. There are many challenges ahead and carrying the extra burden of guilt or self-blame won't be helpful to you or to your family. In fact, feelings of guilt or denial about HIV infection can sometimes lead to missed medical appointments, which can do real harm to you or other HIV-positive family members. Getting good, early medical care is critical for HIV-positive women and children.

You may be feeling very isolated, but you are not alone. There are many women learning to live with HIV infection and AIDS. Talking with other HIV-positive women in support groups or with a private counselor at an AIDS service organization can be the first step toward coping with HIV infection and the many conflicting and difficult feelings a life-threatening diagnosis can bring. Eventually, those close to you may find support groups helpful as well. Many AIDS service organizations can also match you to a "buddy," a volunteer who can provide you with emotional support and practical assistance when you need it. You may not be interested in or ready to accept outside help right now, but in the long run, you may welcome it.

- Think about how you can build a strong support system for yourself. There will be times when you'll need someone to listen. There may be other times when you'll need someone to do simple, everyday things, such as run an errand for you, take care of your children for an afternoon, or help you when you are feeling tired or ill. Stress has a profoundly negative effect on your immune system. Recognizing that you will need support and thinking carefully about the people you want to invite into your life to help you can reduce some of the stress you may already be feeling. Support groups are another way of finding the understanding and empathy so necessary to your spiritual and emotional well-being, and they can be particularly helpful if you are not yet ready to talk to friends and family about your diagnosis. Support groups can also help you anticipate and solve some of the problems associated with HIV/AIDS and learn more about treatment options and resources in your community.

    It is not uncommon for people who are facing the diagnosis of a life-threatening illness to experience clinical depression. You may want to take a look at the signs of depression listed in the section on suicide in Chapter Seven. If you recognize signs of depression in yourself, consider seeking professional assistance. Depression is a serious condition, but it can be treated. Chapter Seven offers information about mental health services and suggestions for finding affordable care. A case manager at an AIDS service organization should also be able to help you find the help that you need. Remember that taking care of your mental health is an integral part of your overall health care and that you deserve sensitive, competent attention.

- Contact an AIDS service organization, if there is one in your community. A case manager at an AIDS service organization or comprehensive care program can help you find and coordinate available community services.

- If you don't have insurance, start looking for health coverage right away. Talking to a case manager at an AIDS service organization can help you to assess your options.

- Seek medical care from an HIV-knowledgeable medical team or doctor experienced in treating people with HIV and AIDS.

- Strengthen your immune system by eating well, exercising, resting when you can, reducing the amount of stress in your life and, if necessary, getting into a program to help you stop smoking, drinking, or using other drugs. Alcohol or other drug use can further compromise your immune system. If you use intravenous (IV) drugs, you are at risk for additional health problems like bacterial endocarditis, an infection of the lining of the heart, and hepatitis. If possible, look for a comprehensive treatment program, one that focuses on the needs of people with HIV and AIDS. Your state/local HIV/AIDS hotline, AIDS service organization, or HIV antibody testing counselor are good sources of information about available programs.

- Learn all you can about HIV and AIDS. Treatment journals and newsletters are excellent sources of information. See the reading list at the end of this book for ideas.

AIDS service organizations (ASOs) exist in many major cities and in other areas of the United States. Although the styles and resources of ASOs differ, many, especially major organizations offer a broad array of services. A case manager at an ASO (or in another setting, such as a hospital comprehensive care program) is the person who can help you find services that meet your needs. Although finding some types of assistance can be difficult, such as housing assistance and chemical dependency programs that address the needs of HIV-positive women, your case manager can assist you and keep you informed as services become available. It's a good idea to seek case management services right away so that you'll be better equipped to deal with any problems you experience when they arise.

Here are some of the services your local ASO may offer:

- buddy programs (volunteers who offer practical help and emotional support)
- case management
- counseling
- emergency financial assistance
- emotional support groups for HIV-positive women, significant others, children, and other family members
- food services
- HIV testing and counseling
- home health care
- hospice and housing referral
- legal services or referral
- public benefits and entitlements counseling
- medical evaluation and physician/clinic referral
- referral to alcohol and other drug abuse treatment programs
- information on HIV/AIDS research and treatment
- transportation services

Some ASOs and health care organizations offer services designed especially to meet the needs of women who are HIV-positive or who have AIDS. In addition to other activities, these organizations may offer childcare assistance, gynecological evaluation and treatment, and family planning services. Information about your health status is kept confidential, and services are usually free or low-cost.

You can find an ASO by calling the CDC National AIDS Hotline or your state or local HIV/AIDS hotline. You can also use your state or local hotline to find out about other services available for people with AIDS and HIV infection. Check the front pages of your local telephone directory under Community Services or other, similar headings or dial your directory assistance operator for the number. If you live outside a city, it may be more difficult to find the services you need. But it's still a good idea to contact the ASO nearest you for assistance. The CDC National AIDS Hotline can provide you with telephone numbers and addresses. Major ASOs are generally very familiar with the kinds of services that are available to people with AIDS and HIV infection and can help you explore possibilities.

Getting Good Medical Care

As women, we often focus our attentions on others' needs and may sometimes dismiss or minimize our own concerns. Taking care of children, other loved ones, working, and simply meeting the demands of everyday living take a lot of time and energy. But getting good medical care soon after learning that you are HIV-positive is vital, even if you have no symptoms and you're feeling healthy. As your immune system becomes compromised, potentially fatal opportunistic infections can develop. But with close monitoring by your doctor, some life-threatening infections like pneumocystis carinii pneumonia (PCP) and tuberculosis can be delayed or prevented, and many other opportunistic infections can be treated when they occur. You and your doctor may want to begin medication that may slow the progression of HIV infection. Monitoring your CD_4 count and viral load will help you and your physician determine when and if to begin medication.

There are a number of approaches you might take to finding medical care, depending on your insurance coverage and the community in which you live. A case manager at an AIDS service organization can tell you about your options.

Ideally, health care should be sought from a doctor or team of doctors experienced in treating people with HIV or AIDS. Knowledge about HIV infection and AIDS changes very rapidly, and a physician with less experience with HIV/AIDS may not be aware of current developments. The difference in knowledge could make a real difference in the quality of health care you receive. You may also want to find out about clinical trials by contacting the AIDS Clinical Trial Information Service, listed in the Resource Directory.

When looking for a physician, bear in mind that there are many different types of doctors with special knowledge in HIV/AIDS care. In the early stages of infection, many people with HIV choose to work with their primary care physician, who may be an internist or a family practitioner. Your primary care doctor will maintain an ongoing relationship with you but will refer you to specialists for specific treatment, if necessary. As HIV disease becomes more advanced, it may be necessary to see a specialist on a more regular basis. Infectious disease specialists have the requisite training and experience to care for most of the problems people with HIV infection and AIDS encounter. There are also physicians from many other specialities, such as family practice, internal medicine, oncology, dermatology, and pulmonology who may have developed a special interest in HIV/AIDS, who see many HIV-positive patients in their practice, and who may be just as valuable to your care, if not more so in some cases, than an infectious disease specialist.

AIDS service organizations or HIV/AIDS hotlines are good places to begin your search for an HIV-knowledgeable doctor. If you are in a support group for women with AIDS and HIV infection, ask others for recommendations. You can also call an HIV/AIDS hotline in your area for referrals.

If you are covered by Medicaid (or Medi-Cal), your best resource is a comprehensive care program designed especially for HIV-positive people, or better yet, one that is specifically focused on the needs of HIV-positive women and children. HIV/AIDS comprehensive care programs are usually affiliated with teaching hospitals, for example, university hospitals. Care is delivered by physicians and nurses who are knowledgeable and up-to-date about the treatment of HIV infection and AIDS. Other services, such as nutrition counseling, emotional support, chemical dependency counseling, or referrals to drug and alcohol treatment programs are typically provided. You may be referred to a comprehensive care program when you test positive for HIV.

If you are already seeing a private doctor who has experience treating people with HIV infection, find out whether you can continue to do so under Medicaid or through your Medicaid/managed care organization. Other resources for Medicaid recipients include women's health clinics that provide care for women with HIV infection and AIDS and local health departments. A Planned Parenthood organization may be able to provide you with some services.

Before you meet or during your first appointment, ask

your doctor how much experience she or he has treating people with HIV or AIDS, especially women. Ask whether fees are calculated on a sliding scale based on your income. Find out with which hospital(s) the doctor is affiliated and whether these hospital(s) have experience treating HIV and AIDS patients. Make sure that your insurance will be accepted there. If you're in or thinking about joining an HMO, find out whether the specialists and medications you need will be accessible.

LEARNING ABOUT HIV: TAKING CHARGE

Researchers are constantly learning about the course and treatment of HIV infection. Thus, there are many treatment options to explore with your doctor. For example, a new group of drugs known as protease inhibitors, used in combination with other antiviral medications, appear to be extremely effective in suppressing HIV replication in some people, although not enough is known about these drugs at present and many studies have not included women. Nonetheless, when you are educated about HIV and AIDS, you can become your own best advocate and take an equal role with your doctor in directing your course of care.

Because there is much debate and change in the field of HIV research, you'll need information from many sources. Information derived from a single source may give you only a narrow view of current thinking about a particular issue. To start your search for information, contact an AIDS service organization or HIV/AIDS hotline to find out whether newsletters, booklets, or pamphlets are available for free or at a low cost. The reading list at the end of this book contains information about selected treatment journals and newsletters. Call local libraries to find out whether they subscribe to these or other journals, or become a subscriber yourself.

To begin a deeper search for information, you may want to call or write the CDC National AIDS Information Clearinghouse for a copy of the publication *A Guide to Locating Information about HIV/AIDS.* (See the reading list at the end of this book.) Public libraries and bookstores often carry books on HIV/AIDS treatment and related issues. University or medical libraries may have access to the National Library of Medicine's information databases, including AIDSLINE. If you have a computer and modem, you can get on-line access to information about HIV and AIDS at home. Ask your nearest ASO for information about on-line services. Talking with other HIV-positive people in support groups is, again,

---

LEARN MORE ABOUT TREATMENT OPTIONS BY TELEPHONE

AIDS Treatment Information Service (ATIS)
1-800-458-5231
1-800-243-7012 (TDD/TTY)

As part of the CDC National AIDS Clearinghouse, this telephone service provides information about treatment options and other HIV/AIDS resources Monday through Friday 9 A.M. to 7 P.M. EST.

Project Inform HIV/AIDS Treatment Hotline
National: 1-800-822-7422
California callers: 1-800-334-7422

Project Inform offers callers across the United States information about HIV testing, HIV/AIDS treatment options, and support Monday through Friday 9 A.M. to 5 P.M. PST and Saturdays 10 A.M. to 5 P.M. PST.

Check the reading resource list at the end of this book for other informational resources. Your state or local HIV/AIDS hotline or local ASO may also be able to refer you to other sources of information about treatment and other resources in your area.

another excellent way of getting and sharing information about HIV/AIDS treatment and related issues.

Starting Your Doctor-Patient Relationship

Once you find a doctor with whom you feel comfortable, you'll probably want to use your initial visits to get a general idea of your health status and current treatment options. Make a list of questions that you want to ask and bring your list with you on your visit.

Here are some questions that you might ask during your early visits:

- What is the overall status of my health?
- Do you recommend any treatment? If so, why?
- What is known about the short- and long-term effects of the treatments that you recommend?
- Are there symptoms that I should be watching out for? What symptoms should I report to you and when?
- How often should I see you? How often should my CD4 cell count and viral load be tested? Can you explain the purposes of and procedures for these tests to me?
- When is the best time to call you, and how can I get in touch with you in an emergency?
- Are there others working with you who may be of serv-

ALTERNATIVE THERAPIES FOR PEOPLE WITH HIV/AIDS

Some people with HIV or AIDS use alternative therapies as a complement to medically prescribed treatments. These therapies may include acupuncture, herbal or holistic therapies, meditation, visualization, and stress reduction techniques. While some therapies like meditation are clearly not dangerous and may prove significantly beneficial, it's always important to be well informed about any actual treatment, including an alternative treatment, before embarking on it. Ask the same questions about an alternative product or practice as you would about a traditional therapy. For example, ask for a discussion of the possible long-term and short-term side effects of the therapy. Confer with your doctor to make certain that the treatment will not interfere with other conventional and alternative treatments that you are taking. Ask if there is any published research on the treatment. Find out how much it will cost and whether your health insurance policy covers experimental therapies — many do not — and ask whether services are available for sliding scale fees.

There are several organizations and journals that provide people with information about alternative therapies. The reading resource list at the end of this book offers a few ideas. You can also contact an ASO for suggestions. If you choose to implement alternative practices, look for a physician who is not opposed to their use. Always inform your doctor before starting an alternative treatment. Your health should be monitored and any problems that develop should be addressed immediately.

ice to me? For example, is there a nurse or social worker available? What are their hours?

Monitoring Your Health: Tests That You May Need and Why

On your first visit with your doctor, you will be asked to supply information about your medical history. Bring your prior medical records, including any records related to recent hospitalizations, to your visit or have them sent to your doctor's office.

You will be given a physical examination, and your blood may be drawn for a battery of blood tests, which may include some or all of those discussed below. These tests will help you and your doctor evaluate the extent to which your immune system is being compromised and will help tailor your treatment plan. It's a good idea to start keeping track of the results of your lab tests right away and to learn how to interpret them so that you can compare the results with future tests.

The following tests may be done on your first appointment with your doctor. Ask your doctor and your AIDS service organization for information about other tests that may help you take greater control of your health. You may also want to do further reading in journals, books, and newsletters to address your ongoing concerns.

CD4 cell count. CD4 cells (also known as T4 cells) are white blood cells. They are a part of the immune system and play an important role in fighting certain infections. The CD4 test is the test most commonly used to evaluate the progression of HIV infection. It's also used to decide when to begin certain preventive, or "prophylactic," treatments and/or when to start medication. Because CD4 counts can vary widely from day to day and laboratory to laboratory, it's important to pay attention to the general trend of your CD4 counts rather than to a single number.

Viral load. These tests provide a means of measuring the amount of HIV in your blood and can give clinicians information about disease progression. It is also thought that these tests may be useful in making treatment decisions. Your physician may suggest a baseline test and monitoring.

A test for syphilis may be done after your diagnosis and then annually. Many HIV-positive people are also at risk for syphilis, which can be more severe when the immune system is compromised. You may also want to be tested for other STDs.

People with HIV infection are very vulnerable to tuberculosis. Thus, it's usually suggested that HIV-positive people have a *tuberculosis skin test* at least annually. An *anergy panel* should be included with the TB skin test. The anergy panel is made of additional skin tests and is used with the TB skin test to determine the status of your immune response. If your TB skin test is negative, the anergy panel will verify that the negative result is due to a lack of TB infection rather than to an immune system that is too weak to register a skin response. If either test is abnormal, your health care provider may recommend a chest X-ray and further evaluation for TB.

Pap smear. A Pap smear is a screen for cervical cancer. It can also sometimes detect human papillomavirus (HPV). HPV is a sexually transmitted virus that increases the risk for cervical cancer. HIV-positive women are at higher risk for HPV and cervical cancer than HIV-negative women. Thus, your doctor may suggest that you have a Pap smear that screens for both conditions as well as a routine gynecological exam soon after your HIV diagnosis. Talk to your doctor about how often you should have a Pap smear and whether you should have colposcopy with your Pap. A colposcope is a device that allows a doctor to see a magnification of your cervix and is sometimes done with a biopsy in which a small piece of tissue is taken. Some feel that colposcopy is a more reliable test for cervical cancer in HIV-positive women and recommend that all HIV-positive women receive colposcopy with their Pap. All women should receive colposcopy whenever a Pap smear is abnormal, regardless of their immune status.

A test for hepatitis B. Hepatitis B is transmitted through needle use, sexual activity, and possibly through blood products — just as HIV is transmitted. Your doctor may recommend a test for hepatitis B. If the test is negative, she or he may suggest a vaccine against hepatitis B. If the test is positive, it means that you have had the disease or the vaccination in the past and cannot be infected or reinfected. Your doctor may do some blood tests to help determine whether your liver has been affected as a result of previous hepatitis B infection.

Toxoplasmosis is an opportunistic infection that can affect the brain of people with suppressed immune systems. You may have a *baseline test for toxoplasmosis.*

Cytomegalovirus (CMV) is a virus that very often affects people with HIV. It can attack many different organs in the body and can result in eye problems as well as problems with the digestive system and the lungs. Everyone who is HIV-positive should have *regular eye examinations* by an eye doctor (ophthalmologist) to check for the presence of CMV.

Many of the medical problems associated with HIV and AIDS can be treated if recognized early. Ask your doctor for a list of symptoms to watch out for. Here are some symptoms that may require immediate medical attention:

- unusually severe headache or severe headache combined with fever, nausea, vomiting, memory loss, or confusion
- abdominal pain and fever
- shortness of breath, especially on exertion
- persistent cough, especially a dry cough
- drenching night-sweats
- confusion or memory loss
- problems with your vision — for example, blurred vision or visual defects
- persistent liquid bowel movements or diarrhea
- temperature above 100 degrees Fahrenheit for two days or more
- sudden swollen lymph nodes
- pain when swallowing
- unusual and persistent fatigue
- unexplained loss of more than 10 percent of your body weight
- vaginal bleeding at times other than during your regular menstrual period
- persistent vaginal itching or discharge
- skin rash
- white patches or sores in your mouth

This is done so that, if necessary, treatment can be initiated as early as possible.

A baseline *dental exam* and teeth cleaning should be done and repeated regularly. People with HIV infection tend to have more dental problems than HIV-negative people and the problems tend to be more severe. Ask your doctor or an AIDS service organization for a referral to a dentist who is HIV-knowledgeable and sensitive to the concerns of HIV-positive people.

Telling Others

After learning of your immune status, you may want to keep the information to yourself until you can come to terms with it. Deciding whom to tell and when requires very careful thought. Talking openly with the important people in your life can very often bring you closer together. But unfortunately, not everyone understands HIV infection, and many people still carry unfounded prejudices against people with HIV infection and AIDS. Facing negative reactions (or seeing those you love face ostracism and prejudice) at a time when you most need love and support can be devastating. Talking with HIV-positive women in a support group, a therapist or counselor at an AIDS service organization, or a trusted friend can help you make decisions about revealing your status to others.

Telling your family, including your husband or partner, is perhaps one of the most difficult of considerations. An HIV diagnosis may mean having to come to terms with high-risk behaviors — even those of the distant past — for the first time. It may mean finding out about your partner's past or present high-risk behaviors. You may be afraid that your partner will leave you if he or she learns that you are HIV-positive. Many women with HIV and AIDS share your concerns. Conversation in support groups or with private counselors can help you prepare to tell your partner or husband. However, if you are in a relationship where there is violence or abuse, it is wise to contact a women's shelter or domestic violence advocacy program. Advocates at women's shelters and advocacy programs are available to help you twenty-four hours a day. They will not tell you to leave your relationship, nor will they ask you to come to a shelter, but they can help you explore your options. For more information about sources of help for women in abusive relationships, refer to Chapter Four.

Although you may want to take some time to prepare yourself before telling your partner, it is vitally important to do so. You must begin or continue to practice safer sex and urge your husband or partner to get HIV testing and counseling. Your children should also be tested. It's important to tell anyone with whom you've had sex (including oral, anal, or vaginal sex) and anyone with whom you've shared needles that they may have been exposed to HIV. If telling your partner or others with whom you have had sex or shared needles is too difficult, you can ask your health care provider for assistance. Many state or local health departments can help you notify sexual or needle-sharing partners. You or your health care provider may give a representative of the health department the names of those to be notified. In some states where confidential testing is done and positive results are reported to the health department, the health department may contact you either at the time you test or later to talk about partner notification and to ask you to provide the names of those affected so that they can be notified. Neither your name nor any personal identification will be used when notifying others who may have been exposed. You have the right to tell the health department that you wish to inform your partner(s) personally.

All states and Washington, D.C., require the reporting of AIDS cases to the Centers for Disease Control and to the state health department. Some states require the reporting of positive HIV test results. Reporting may be done by name, if available, or by demographic characteristics only. Some states have no HIV reporting requirements. Your ASO, state or local HIV/AIDS hotline, or state health department should be able to tell you what information must be reported. Information collected in the reporting of test results must be kept highly confidential.

Many women struggle with the questions of whether and how to tell their children about their diagnoses and/or about a family member's diagnosis. The decision-making process can be difficult and may give rise to many deep and complicated feelings. Parents may fear that their children will suffer from the stigma sometimes associated with HIV/AIDS as well as isolation from their community should the diagnosis become known. Fears of rejection from those close to you and uncertainty about the prospect of discussing painful issues such as illness and death may also pose barriers to disclosure. Among the most difficult emotions are feelings of guilt and shame about being ill and perhaps about the way in which the virus was transmitted. Cultural beliefs about illness and death may also prevent you from talking openly with family and close friends. Yet there are benefits to telling your children and to beginning an ongoing discussion with them when you are ready. For example, you may be relieved of the stress of keeping your diagnosis a secret; your children may have an opportunity to discuss their feelings with you and to feel included in all the events that affect your family; and you may be better able to approach and include your children in the process of planning for their future by choosing a trusted person to care for them should you die. These are extremely painful issues, and it's not always easy to think about them. Your feelings may be different from those discussed here, but it's important to examine and understand them. Talking with others whom you trust, a professional, such as a social worker or psychologist, or participating in a support group with other parents affected by HIV/AIDS may help.

Physicians have an ethical, and often legal, duty to respect patient confidentiality. However, a doctor may also have a duty to warn the sexual or needle-sharing partners of an HIV-positive patient who refuses to tell others about possible exposure to the virus. If you are HIV-positive and want to notify anyone who might have been exposed, tell your doctor that you will do this personally. If you refuse, there is a possibility that your physician will notify your partner or the health department without your consent.

Because there is no risk of HIV transmission through casual contact, you don't have to tell your landlord, coworkers, or employer about your health status. If any information becomes available to your employer, for example, because of HIV-related insurance claims, it should be kept strictly confidential. Negative actions taken against you because of your diagnosis may be a violation of federal, state, or local discrimination laws.

Unfortunately, discrimination against people with HIV infection and AIDS is not uncommon. One of the best ways to avoid discrimination and to respond when it occurs is to get information about your legal rights. There are laws prohibiting discrimination against people with HIV infection and other people with disabilities in the workplace, in housing, in public places such as doctors' offices and daycare centers, and in federal programs and activities. (See Chapter Six.) AIDS service organizations can often help you with discrimination issues or refer you to legal organizations helping people with AIDS and HIV infection. Legal and other advocacy groups may also offer literature about legal issues.

It's necessary to tell the doctor or dentist who is treating you about your HIV status so that you can receive appropriate care. AIDS service organizations can often provide the names of doctors and dentists with experience and sensitivity in treating people with HIV infection and AIDS. Refusal to treat a person because she has AIDS or is HIV-positive is a violation of federal law and possibly state or local laws. If you are denied treatment because of your health status, contact an AIDS service organization and/or an HIV/AIDS legal service group to discuss what happened.

PRACTICING SAFER SEX

Decisions about your sexual life are clearly very personal. But if you are HIV-positive, there is still a need to continue or to begin practicing safer sex, even if your partner is also HIV-positive. It is thought that there are aggressive and passive forms of the virus as well as drug-resistant strains. When you have unsafe sex, you risk increasing the number of virus particles (viral load) in your bloodstream. You could also acquire another sexually transmitted disease, such as herpes or syphilis, both of which may worsen the course of HIV infection. Contact the nearest AIDS service organization or comprehensive care program or your state/local HIV/AIDS hotline and ask to be sent confidential information about safer sex techniques and safer needle use.

HIV INFECTION AND PREGNANCY

The decision to have a child is a profound and personal one. If you are pregnant or are planning a pregnancy, it will be important to talk to your doctor about the effect that pregnancy may have on your health and on your baby's health. There is a risk of transmitting HIV to your child. It is currently estimated that 15 to 30 percent of babies born to HIV-positive mothers will also be infected with HIV. In a clinical trial, AZT (an antiretroviral medication) was found to reduce the risk of transmission from HIV-positive mothers to their infants by about two-thirds. Therefore, it is now thought to be in the best interest of every pregnant woman to receive counseling and to take a voluntary HIV antibody test. When your immune status is known, you and your doctor can discuss the risks and benefits of taking medication.

Because there is also risk of transmitting HIV through breast milk, breast-feeding is not generally recommended for HIV-positive women in the United States.

For some pregnant women with life-threatening illnesses, such as HIV infection, there are painful choices to make. In addition to raising your child, you may be contemplating placing your child for adoption, kinship, or foster care, or ending your pregnancy. You have a right to accurate information about the effect of your pregnancy on your health and your baby's health and to make your family planning decisions without pressure from others.

If you are thinking about the possibility of pregnancy interruption, it's best to talk with a physician and an advocate at an AIDS service organization or comprehensive care program before the third month of your pregnancy, when the risks of complications are fewer. Choosing to end a much-wanted pregnancy is an extremely complex and painful decision. In addition to medical and practical support, you may appreciate help from others who have either had personal experience with pregnancy loss or who assist bereaved parents professionally. The section Pregnancy and Infant Loss in Chapter Five offers information about sources of emotional support.

Because Medicaid coverage for abortion services is restricted in many states, finding and paying for services can be extremely difficult, if you have a low income. However, your advocate can help you weigh your options and perhaps help you find services that you can afford, if you choose to end your pregnancy. Your advocate can also help you find resources for your child's medical care and for other types of assistance that your family may need, if you choose not to end your pregnancy.

CHILDREN WITH HIV INFECTION

All babies born to HIV-positive women will test positive on an HIV antibody test for about fifteen to eighteen months after delivery. This is because infants initially acquire their mothers' immune system, which remains active until sometime around that age. In other words, the mother's antibodies to HIV will remain in her child's blood until the child's immune system takes over and begins producing its own antibodies in response to HIV. Because standard HIV antibody tests cannot define whether your child is truly HIV-positive, other tests designed specifically for infants should be done as soon as possible to begin to determine your baby's HIV status. Because of the complexity of HIV diagnosis in children, an HIV pediatric specialist should be involved in your child's care whenever possible.

Some children with HIV infection will begin to have symptoms within the first year and may get very sick, while others may not have symptoms for years. But children with HIV tend to develop problems sooner than adults and are more vulnerable to certain opportunistic infections. Children's CD4 cell counts are often higher than adults, even when their immune systems are significantly impaired. Thus, children may be sicker at higher CD4 cell counts. Many children with HIV have neurological problems, such as delays in development. If you have other, HIV-negative children, you may notice that your HIV-positive child is talking or sitting up later than his or her siblings. This may be a sign of a developmental delay. If you suspect that your child is experiencing a developmental delay, learn about your state's early intervention program for children with disabilities. (See Chapter Six.) Some hospital comprehensive care programs offer early intervention services on-site.

Like all children, children with HIV can develop typical childhood illnesses such as colds and flus, ear infections, and fevers. However, these infections may be more severe in HIV-positive children, and it is often hard to tell the difference between a common childhood illness and a more serious medical problem. Because your child may catch infectious diseases more easily than other children, it's necessary to take some simple measures to try to protect your child from these and other illnesses. Ask your health care provider for infection control guidelines. Learning about the ways in which HIV affects children can help you give your child the very best care. Ask your clinic, doctor, and AIDS service organization for information. You can also call the National Pediatric and Family HIV Resource Center, which makes free or low-cost information available to professionals and families affected by HIV/AIDS. See the box at the beginning of this section for information.

Taking care of yourself is also a crucial part of your child's care. Like many mothers, you may feel the need to pour all your energies into helping your child. But caring for your health by resting and attending to your own medical needs will serve you and your family best.

Finding Health Care for Your Child

AIDS service organizations can help you find resources for your child's care. The National Pediatric and Family HIV Resource Center and city or state health departments can also tell you if there is a program offering comprehensive care to children and families in your area. (Check the government listings of your local white pages.) A local children's hospital may be another good source of information.

A pediatrician who is aware of and knowledgeable about the effects of HIV in children should follow your child's growth and development closely and consider whether preventive treatment regimens are needed. You may also want to talk to your provider about the availability of clinical trials for children.

Remember that you have a right to complete and sensitive health care. You have a right to ask questions about your child's health care plan and your own. If someone cannot answer your questions, ask for the name of someone who can. You may want to buy a notebook in which to record the information that you receive about your child's medical care and other services. Note the names of the people to whom you speak, the dates and times of your conversations, and what was said. By keeping a notebook, you will be better able to track your child's care, and you'll get a better sense of what services are available to you and how you can follow up on them.

Benefits for You and Your Children

You and/or your children may be eligible for benefits and services, such as Medicaid (Medi-Cal); EPSDT, a health service for children covered by Medicaid; and early intervention programs for children with disabilities (see Chapter Six). You may also qualify for Social Security disability insurance or SSI, welfare, and/or the WIC program, which provides supplemental foods such as infant cereals and juice, nutrition education, and referrals to health care programs to qualified women who are pregnant, postpartum, or who have a child under the age of five.

Visiting nurses may be able to provide health care services for you or your child at home. Respite care services can provide you with temporary childcare in your home or in other settings, giving you time to rest or to take care of other responsibilities. Most hospital social work departments and AIDS service organizations can advise you about benefits and services for which you and your child may be eligible.

ASSISTANCE IN BUYING PRESCRIPTION DRUGS

The high cost of prescription drugs is a source of great financial strain and worry for many people with life-threatening illnesses. If you are having difficulty paying for prescription drugs, you may be eligible to receive medications free of charge or to buy medication at a reduced cost. Member companies of the Pharmaceutical Research and Manufacturers of America (PhRMA) that provide medications to qualified patients are listed in the PhRMA Directory of Patient Drug Assistance Programs. Eligibility criteria vary depending on the manufacturer. Your doctor can get information about the directory and how to apply for assistance by calling 1-800-PMA-INFO or writing the Pharmaceutical Research and Manufacturers Association of America, P.O. Box 29075, Phoenix, AZ 85038-8663.

Mail-order prescription or buyers' clubs are another source of reduced-cost prescriptions. The American Association for Retired Persons (AARP) at 601 E St. NW, Washington, D.C. 20049 or national disability- or illness-specific organizations may be able to provide information about discounts. (See the Resource Directory.)

If you are HIV-positive, the nearest ASO should be able to tell you about programs available to help people pay for the cost of medication. In addition, you can contact the National AIDS Clearinghouse at 1-800-458-5231 to order a free copy of the current *AIDS/HIV Treatment Directory,* which describes patient assistance/reimbursement programs in addition to treatment options for HIV infection and opportunistic infections and clinical trials. Mail delivery for the directory may take two to three weeks, so you may want to order it soon.

WHAT'S IN THIS CHAPTER?

- Your Keys to Information: The Eldercare Locator and Area Agencies on Aging
- Maintaining Your Independence at Home
- When You Need Help at Home: Home Care
- Caregivers
- Nursing Homes and Alternative Housing Options
- Elder Abuse and Neglect

✦ 9 ✦

Crises in Aging

BEFORE A CRISIS OCCURS: BE PREPARED

The rewards of growing older are many: a sense of confidence and self-worth that comes with experience and, for many, freedom from child-rearing responsibilities and opportunities to explore new career, educational, or avocational interests. But older women may also experience increased health problems, economic limitations, further caregiving responsibilities, and the loss of partners, family members, and friends. This chapter focuses on some of the difficulties of aging, and most particularly on resources for long-term care.

Long-term care refers to a combination of medical and personal care services that can be delivered at home, in alternative housing arrangements, or in institutional settings. While there were once few options for women experiencing limitations due to changing health, today there are varied possibilities. Many services that were performed only in hospitals can now be delivered safely at home. Community and government programs form a patchwork of programs to help older people remain in their own homes longer, and alternative housing arrangements offer people who need some assistance, but not enough to warrant nursing home care, more independence than in institutional settings. In order to find these services and use them effectively, you must be an informed and critical consumer. Whether you are looking for resources for yourself or caring for someone else, planning is essential. Crises can occur without warning. A stroke, for example, can change your life in an instant. Thus, it's ideal for families to discuss the possibility of a need for care before it arises, and certainly as soon as it appears to be a dawning reality.

Be aware that laws change and many of the programs and

services discussed in this chapter are dependent on government funding. Therefore, it is extremely important to seek current information about the availability of these programs. This chapter will point out key sources of information and assistance.

If you don't like the idea of asking for help, you're not alone. Most people prize their independence and to some, asking for help seems like an admission of decline and the beginning of a loss of autonomy. In fact, many forms of assistance can actually increase your independence by allowing you to continue to do the things that are important to you. Many people also have concerns about privacy and wonder whether those called upon for help will respect their individuality and dignity. These are very valid concerns, which underscore the necessity of a thorough, organized search for assistance and of trusting your instincts about those who come into your life.

YOUR KEYS TO INFORMATION:
THE ELDERCARE LOCATOR AND
AREA AGENCIES ON AGING

The Eldercare Locator
1-800-677-1116
9 A.M. to 11 P.M. Monday to Friday (EST)

More often than not, getting help in times of crisis requires perseverance, patience, and a lot of telephone calls, especially if you are a caregiver who lives at a distance from the one you love. The Eldercare Locator, funded by the federal Older Americans Act, can connect you with state and local information and referral sources across the country, and put you in touch with your Area Agency on Aging (AAA). Through the AAA and other referral sources, you can get answers to questions about:

- home-delivered meals
- legal assistance
- housing options
- adult daycare
- senior center programs
- home health services
- health insurance counseling
- nursing home ombudsman programs
- elder abuse prevention
- transportation services and more

When you call, you will be asked to give your ZIP code and/or the ZIP code of the person for whom you are calling and a brief description of your problem. Remember that the Eldercare Locator can provide you with telephone numbers, but its staff members do not make recommendations.

Area Agencies on Aging

Across the country, there are at present about 670 Area Agencies on Aging (AAA), which may also be called Offices on Aging. You can contact the AAA with almost any question you have about resources for older people, although the capabilities and resources of each office and the type of services developed in various communities differ. For example, more services may be available in urban areas than in rural communities. Many offices offer brochures or booklets describing services available locally and throughout the state. Depending on the area, you may find information about housing, heating and weatherization programs, home health aide/homemaker services, respite and adult daycare, transportation, medical care and mental health care options, services for people with disabilities, nutrition, educational programs, senior centers, advocacy groups, discounts, volunteer opportunities, and more. Some AAAs provide direct services or contract with other providers to offer services in addition to information and referral. If the AAA can't help you find the services you need, ask for the number of an organization or person who can. For the telephone number of the AAA nearest you, you can contact the Eldercare Locator (above), or look in the government section of your local telephone directory. Some states also sponsor statewide senior information and referral lines, which may automatically route your call to the local AAA. Check the front pages of your local telephone directory or ask your directory assistance operator or reference librarian for the telephone number.

OTHER SOURCES OF INFORMATION

Area Agencies on Aging are excellent conduits to information and assistance, but they may not be the only sources of help. Many cities and counties have information and referral systems that provide callers with information about community services. (Look in the front pages of your local telephone directory or ask a reference librarian at a public library for information.) Hospitals, the geriatrics or gerontology departments of universities, and local offices of the

In addition to the telephone numbers for the Eldercare Locator, Area Agencies on Aging, and senior centers, you may also want to note the following:

The *Family Service America* Helpline, 1-800-221-2681 (CST), can refer you to local member organizations providing services to families, including eldercare services. Family service agencies such as Jewish Family and Children's Services, Catholic Charities, Lutheran Social Services, or other religious-based or secular agencies may provide services for older people and families. Services may be available for a low cost or for a fee based on your income. For further information, look in the front section of your local telephone directory or contact the local United Way office or a reference librarian at a public library.

The United Way local offices may be able to provide you with a list or brochure of community services. Look in the business section of your telephone directory for the telephone number.

Hospitals and universities may have a geriatrician or geriatric center that serves as a resource for help with medical and community services. If you have a primary care physician, be sure to tell him or her about your changing needs and about any services you are receiving or contemplating. You will give your doctor a better picture of your overall health status and allow him or her to help you access needed forms of assistance.

Local places of worship are also good sources of information about resources for older people and may provide direct services to the community as well. Friendly Visitors programs, congregate meals, volunteer home repair programs, and other services may be available to those who need them.

Support and advocacy groups. Disability-specific or caregiver organizations such as the Alzheimer's Association or Children of Aging Parents, listed in the Resource Directory, are often able to help callers find appropriate services in their communities. (See the Disabilities and Crises in Aging sections.) Local branches of some organizations may sponsor support groups where people can meet to share practical suggestions for coping with everyday problems, exchange tips on using health care and social services systems, and express feelings in the company of others who can empathize. Some support groups are facilitated by professionals; others are run by participants. A few support and advocacy groups provide limited financial assistance to qualified applicants for specific types of services. For information about disability-specific organizations, refer to the Resource Directory.

The Better Business Bureau offers information about complaints made against local businesses. Check with this agency before using any business providing services for older people. Look in the business section of your local telephone directory for the number.

The state Office of Consumer Affairs (also called the Consumer Protection Agency) provides information and referrals to agencies involved in regulating consumer services and accepts complaints regarding certain services. Check the state government listing of your local telephone directory.

The state/local long-term-care ombudsman. Under the Older Americans Act, each state must have a full-time ombudsman to investigate and resolve complaints in nursing homes. The ombudsman program may also help residents of alternative housing, such as assisted living facilities, and in some states, recipients of home health care. Many localities also have long-term-care ombudsman programs.

Centers for independent living (CIL). In many areas of the country, you will find centers for independent living serving the needs and interests of people with disabilities. This chapter will discuss some of the ways in which CILs can be of help. Refer to the chapter Resources for Adults and Children with Disabilities for a broader discussion of these centers.

United Way may also offer information and referral services, as may the local senior center.

Senior centers are often very knowledgeable about community resources. Depending on the size of your community, people at the senior center may be able to give you a sense of the reputation of local service providers and make recommendations. If you live in an urban area, you may find a number of senior centers serving diverse communities. Contact your AAA or consult your local telephone directory for the name and telephone number of a senior center near you.

Your *state unit on aging,* which may be called the Commission on Aging, the Department of Elder Affairs or Aging Services, among other titles, is mandated to provide the public with information about services for older people. If you need more information than can be offered through the Area Agency on Aging (or if there is no AAA in your community), contact your state unit for help. The Eldercare Locator can give you the telephone number, or you can look in the state government section of your telephone book for information. Also, many cities and counties have departments of aging that provide services and referrals.

ORGANIZE A NOTEBOOK

If you're looking for more than one service or arranging care for someone else, it's a good idea to keep a notebook in which to record your calls as you make them, including the date and time of your call, the name and title of the person to whom you spoke, his or her telephone number, and the substance of your conversation. By doing this, you can document the information you were given, keep track of the services you've uncovered, and note any pertinent information for later use. Don't hesitate to contact government or nonprofit agencies. The people working with these agencies are there to serve you, and most are genuinely concerned about the lives of older people. Remember, though, that some people will be better equipped to answer your questions than others. If you aren't satisfied with the information you receive from one person, ask to speak to someone else.

MAINTAINING YOUR INDEPENDENCE AT HOME

Most people would prefer to stay at home rather than move to a new environment should the need arise for assistance with the tasks of daily living. There are many community and government services that may help you to maintain your independence at home. Home health and personal care services, adult day programs, home repair, and home modification services are examples of services that can be used to assist older people and families. This section and the following sections present an overview of these options.

Friendly Visitors. If you are homebound, isolated, or just need some company, you may want to inquire about Friendly Visitors programs. These are usually volunteer programs organized by senior centers, places of worship, family service agencies, or other community groups. Program volunteers will come to your residence to socialize, check up on you, or to help you write letters or do other small tasks. Friendly Visitors can also help caregivers by providing a little time off to rest or take care of other responsibilities. Additionally, Friendly Visitors offer the reassurance that someone will be in contact with you or with your loved one on a regular basis. Some home health care or personal care agencies provide paid companions who perform similar services.

Telephone reassurance and personal emergency response systems (PERS). If you live alone, you may be interested in telephone reassurance programs through which you and a volunteer make daily telephone contact at a set time to make sure that everything is all right. If you don't answer at the designated time, a friend or neighbor will be notified or an emergency response will be generated. The Area Agency on Aging, your place of worship, a family service agency, or a senior center can usually provide you with more information about these services.

Another option that allows for more flexible scheduling is a personal emergency response system (PERS). When a problem occurs, you can contact a local response center by pushing a call button that you wear around your neck. The central agency will contact you, and depending on the situation, a neighbor, relative, or anyone whom you designate will be summoned, or a call for emergency help will be made. Private businesses, family service and other social service agencies, and some home health care agencies offer this service. The AARP offers an excellent publication on the subject; it is listed in the reading resource list at the end of this book.

Meals on Wheels or other in-home meal delivery services offer older adults who cannot do their own cooking a way to receive at least one regular meal a day. Hot meals are usually delivered once a day five days a week. Depending on the community, no-salt, diabetic, kosher, and ethnic meals may be available, and meals may be available on weekends and evenings. It may be difficult to get home meal delivery in some rural areas, although programs often look for innovative ways to help older people in remote settings, for example, by delivering frozen meals on a weekly basis. There are also waiting lists in many areas. Planning ahead can help you make the best use of these services. For example, if you are scheduled to have major surgery and know that you won't be able to cook for yourself, you might want to find out how long the waiting list is, if there is one in your area, and whether you can sign up for the program in advance. If you can afford to pay privately, you might also ask about any private businesses supplying home-delivered meals.

Nutrition programs, where meals are taken together with others, may be available at senior centers or places of worship. Programs are usually free or available for an optional donation.

For information about meal programs, contact your Area Agency on Aging, state unit on aging, senior center, or family service agency.

Transportation. Transportation and escort services are available in many communities to help older people reach shopping areas and get to medical appointments. Reduced bus fares for older people and paratransit services for people who use wheelchairs may also be available. If you live in an urban area and have a disability, you might contact the local Department of Transportation to find out if cab vouchers are available to help people with disabilities pay for the cost of taxi services. In addition, Medicaid may pay for transportation to medical appointments by way of cab vouchers or coaches. If you are planning a visit to a social service agency, ask whether there are any transportation services available to pick up clients. Also, senior centers may provide van transportation services to shopping areas, doctors' appointments, and special events. Contact your AAA, senior centers, centers for independent living, local branches of disability-specific support and advocacy groups, or your place of worship for information about transportation services, schedules, and fees. Check the front section of your telephone directory under the heading Community Services or another similar heading for information about paratransit services. Transportation services may be more widely available in urban areas than in rural or suburban communities.

Legal assistance. In many states, certain legal counseling services are available for free or on a sliding scale basis to all people over sixty, regardless of income. In many communities you'll also find legal aid organizations that assist low-income clientele with basic legal problems for free or for a low fee. However, funding constraints have limited organizations' ability to provide services, and there may be a waiting list. Area Agencies on Aging may be able to link older clients to attorneys who will take select cases for no fee (called pro bono services). Contact your local AAA or state unit on aging for more information. There are also private attorneys who specialize in elder law, a field that covers many of the issues discussed in this chapter.

Insurance counseling. Many states provide insurance counseling programs in which trained volunteers assist older people with questions about Medicare, Medicare supplemental insurance (Medigap), Medicaid, and long-term-care insurance. The AAA or state unit on aging can help you find this service, which may be provided by the Department of Insurance or another government agency.

Counseling and other community services. The Area Agency on Aging or local mental health association (if there is one in your area) can usually refer you to community mental health centers (CMHCs). These centers provide a range of services to the public, which may include mental and physical health assessments. (See the box on page 445.) Family service agencies and other nonprofit community counseling agencies offer a range of counseling and support services aimed at addressing issues affecting family life. Although agencies differ, you may find help with problems related to stress, grief and loss, and conflicts between family members' caring for a loved one, among other issues. Geriatric care managers (see the box on page 436) may also be able to help families resolve problems that arise in the course of caring for a loved one. For information about community mental health centers, mental health associations, resources for counseling and therapy, and paying for mental health services, see Chapter Seven. You can also contact your AAA or senior center for more information. As mentioned earlier, support groups for caregivers or groups sponsored by disability- or disease-specific organizations are excellent sources of practical and emotional assistance.

Find out how *local businesses* can help. Sometimes, individual businesses offer special services or discounts to older people. For example, your local supermarket or pharmacy may offer free or low-cost home delivery to senior citizens.

Respite care. Time off for caregivers is essential. Without time to rest, caregivers risk illness, injury, and emotional burnout. Respite care is a way of giving caregivers a break and, depending on the source of care, respite may be available for a few hours, a few weeks, or overnight. Volunteers may provide relief to caregivers at home or through the services of an adult daycare center. Some nursing homes, assisted living facilities, and group homes with vacancies will care for residents on a temporary basis, and home health care agencies may be utilized for this purpose as well. If you are a caregiver and you work for a large company, you might also consult with your Employee Assistance Program or human resources or personnel department to find out if there are any respite or adult daycare benefits for employees. For more information about respite care, call your AAA, senior centers, local places of worship, disability-specific or caregiver groups, the local offices of the United Way, family service agencies, and/or community mental health centers. This is one service for which advanced emotional and practical planning is critical. Do not wait until you are completely exhausted to start investigating your options.

What Will These Services Cost?

Costs for in-home and community services vary. Some services are funded by the Older Americans Act, Social Service Block Grants, Medicaid, and other state and local sources or through donations. Depending on the way in which the services are funded, they may be available for free, for a low fee or co-payment, or for a fee that is based on your income. Of course, unless they are providing a special free service to older people, private businesses charge for their services. Your insurance may or may not cover the costs. The way in which the service is funded will also determine whether you are eligible to participate. But don't be put off by the seeming complexity of arrangements for these services. Just call the AAA and other appropriate resources to find out what's available in your area. There may be waiting lists for some services, so the sooner you call the better.

Making Your Home Safer and More Accessible

As your needs and abilities change, your own home can become a barrier to independent living. If you are thinking about moving, you may want to first consider whether making some basic changes in your home will allow you to stay. Some accommodations necessitate major changes and require professional help. For example, if you use a wheelchair, you may have to widen doorways, modify sinks, or lower kitchen cabinets. But other modifications, such as installing grab bars on the sides of the tub and in the shower and replacing doorknobs or other handles with lever or loop handles, can be done fairly easily. You can make some changes

Adult daycare provides a range of services and activities in a group setting for older people with functional impairments who are in need of some supervision and assistance. Usually open one to five days during the work week, adult daycare centers provide older adults with opportunities for socialization and stimulating recreational and educational activities and give caregivers time to work or rest during the day. In addition to recreational and educational activities, services may include meals, exercise, health monitoring, counseling, nursing, personal care, and information and referral to other services. Medically oriented adult day health programs also provide rehabilitative services, such as physical, speech, occupational, and other therapies. Depending on the program, transportation may be available to and from the center.

Some programs specialize in caring for people with Alzheimer's disease and other dementias, and a few programs provide care for young adults with mental illness. Unless preference dictates otherwise, it is not usually necessary to segregate people with Alzheimer's disease or other dementias from those without such conditions if the needs of all people in the program can be met with appropriate activities and social opportunities. If your loved one has special needs, inquire about any functional eligibility criteria the center maintains. Families with loved ones in fragile health should be careful to look for a center staffed by certified nurse's aides and supervised by a registered nurse.

Most adult daycare programs are nonprofit or public organizations,[1] although some are proprietary. Adult daycare centers may be run by local governments, hospitals, private agencies, nursing homes, and community social service or religious organizations. Out-of-pocket costs for adult daycare vary widely and can run from a small donation to between $40 and $100 a day, depending on where you live. The availability of low-cost and publicly funded programs can vary dramatically from state to state and area to area. Quality also differs, and there may be waiting lists. When considering costs, you may have to weigh the expense of, say, five days of adult daycare to other options, such as a home health aide, and even to the cost of alternative or institutional living arrangements.

Adult daycare centers are licensed or certified in most states. At present, the only national standards for adult daycare are those developed by the National Institute on Adult Daycare (NIAD), which may be voluntarily met.[2] Thus, when choice is a possibility, ask whether centers you're considering follow the standards and guidelines established by NIAD or any state-developed guidelines.

To find an adult daycare center in your area, contact your AAA, senior center, or state unit on aging. If you or your loved one has a specific disability or condition, check with organizations representing the concerns of people with that disability or illness for advice on choosing a center best suited to your needs. (See the Resource Directory listings for the chapters Disabilities, Life-Threatening Illness, and Crises in Mental Health.)

yourself or with the help of community groups, civic or religious organizations, or family members.

Again, it's a good idea to talk to your primary care physician first. By informing your doctor of your changing needs, you will allow her or him to better address your health concerns. You will also enable your physician to order home health care for you, if necessary. Consultation with an occupational therapist, who may be part of a home health care agency team, can help you make adjustments — even minor adjustments such as grab bars and bath benches — that are most suitable to your individual needs. Check your Medicare handbook for information about coverage for home health care. Among other criteria, a doctor must prescribe home health care in order for Medicare to cover the cost.

For information about other simple things that you can do to prevent accidents in the home, you can order a free copy of *Safety for Older Consumers: Home Safety Checklist* by writing the U.S. Consumer Product Safety Commission, Office of Information and Public Affairs, Washington, D.C., 20207. If you use a wheelchair or walker and want information about making more extensive changes, you might be interested in obtaining a copy of *A Consumer's Guide to Home Adaptation*, listed in the reading resource list. *The 36-Hour Day*, also cited in the reading resource list, offers plenty of ideas for making everyday life safer for someone with Alzheimer's disease.

Assistive Devices for Everyday Living

Assistive devices are products that make everyday tasks simpler to do. They can be as high-tech as a voice-activated computer or as simple as a zipper pull or reaching device. Walkers, talking clocks, thick-handled spoons, devices that aid people with communication difficulties, reading machines, seat-lift chairs, and voice-activated telephones are all examples of assistive devices. There are virtually endless varieties that can be tailored to an individual's distinct needs. You can buy, rent, or even make some assistive devices, and you may be able to borrow them. If you are interested in learning more about high-tech and "low-tech" solutions to everyday problems, contact your AAA for information about any programs designed to make technology and assistive devices available to people with disabilities in your area. Another route to information is the state vocational rehabilitation agency. (See Chapter Six.) You can also call the *National Rehabilitation Information Center*, listed in the Resource Directory under Disabilities for general information about accessible housing, bath lifts, stair lifts, wheelchairs, assistive devices for people with arthritis, and other aids. NARIC can also give you the telephone number of a local center for independent living, if there is one in your area. Centers for independent living, which serve people with disabilities in various ways, can often provide information about assistive devices, home modification, and community services. You might also call disability-specific organizations for resource suggestions. Some organizations may run assistive device loan programs or make financial assistance available to eligible people. A church or civic group may also be of help.

If you or a family member have a visual impairment or are blind, contact your Area Agency on Aging for information about organizations helping people to adjust to loss of vision. You might also ask your ophthalmologist to refer you to a low-vision clinic. In low-vision clinics, special teachers, called orientation and mobility instructors, teach people with visual disabilities safe-travel techniques and suggest simple home improvements to make everyday life easier. If you are poor, over sixty-five, and need an eye doctor, you may be able to get a list of ophthalmologists who can help you by contacting the National Eye Care Project, listed in the Resource Directory under Disabilities. Services may also be available to you through your state vocational rehabilitation program.

The American Speech-Language-Hearing Association at 1-800-638-8255 or (301) 897-5700 (voice/TDD) can send you free pamphlets on assistive listening devices, such as hearing aid-compatible telephones or telecommunication devices for the deaf (TDD). A TDD is a typewriter-like instrument that allows people with speech or hearing impairments to utilize the telephone. Your AAA may be able to refer you to local services for people who are deaf or hard of hearing or who have speech impairments. Also check the Resource Directory for other listings of national organizations serving people with hearing- or speech-related disabilities. Many of these organizations can answer questions about hearing disabilities and help you find resources to meet your needs.

Before You Buy Medical Equipment

If you're thinking of buying or renting medical equipment, such as a hospital bed, you may want to ask your hospital discharge planner, doctor, and/or an occupational therapist to assess your needs first. Occupational therapists can help you learn new ways of doing everyday tasks and can order assistive devices for you. These services are often available through home health agencies. Check your Medicare handbook and your insurance policy, or contact your insurance agent to find out whether occupational therapists' services and major medical equipment and supply purchases are covered.

WHEN YOU NEED HELP AT HOME: HOME HEALTH CARE

Home health care and personal care are terms that describe a vast and growing field of services for people who need continuing care after an illness or injury or assistance with everyday activities in order to live independently at home. Because patients are discharged from hospitals much more quickly today than in the past, home health care is often needed to assist in recovery from a hospital stay and, depending on an individual's circumstances, may be an alternative to temporary nursing home care. Home health care services can be delivered in your own home as well as in a supportive housing environment such as a board and care home or assisted-living facility.

Although many older people benefit from in-home services, children, new mothers, women with difficult pregnancies, and women and men with disabilities may all use a form of home care at one time or another. Hospice care, a specialized form of home health care delivered to people who are dying and their families, is discussed in Chapter Ten. Before you consider whether home health care or personal care will meet your needs, it's important to understand the distinctions between these two types of care, which can be provided simultaneously.

Home *health* care refers to a range of medically oriented services usually provided on a limited basis by professionals and aides. Basic services often include:

- skilled nursing care, such as the administration of medications, wound care, and injections
- rehabilitative services, such as physical therapy, speech therapy, occupational therapy, and respiratory therapy, among other types of therapy
- medical social work services
- dietitian services, and
- medical supplies and equipment

Some home health care agencies provide specialized care such as dialysis, intravenous therapy, and oxygen therapy, or focus on serving a particular patient group such as children or people with heart conditions.

Personal care (also called custodial care) is another extremely important aspect of home care. Personal care describes help with activities of daily living such as grooming, dressing, bathing, toileting, walking, and eating. These services are provided by *home health aides* or personal assistants. *Housekeeping and chore services* may also be part of personal care services.

Other community services such as Meals on Wheels, companion services, Friendly Visitors, transportation, and home repair and modification may be added to an agency's or individual's services to complete a home health care plan.

When Might You Need Home Health Care or Personal Care?

Skilled nursing and rehabilitative services are usually ordered by a doctor to help a patient recover from an acute episode of illness or an injury after hospitalization. If you think that you could benefit from home health care, be certain to speak to your doctor or discharge planner about your needs. Services may not be ordered without your suggestion.

There are many people who do not need medically oriented care but who nonetheless require help with everyday activities in order to remain safely at home. Having someone come to your home to do light housekeeping or to help you bathe, for example, can be key to your independence, especially when you combine these services with other supportive services, such as home-delivered meals. To a caregiver, even a few hours of relief provided by a home health aide or other caregiver can mean a period of much-needed rest or time to attend to various responsibilities.

Where Can You Find Home Health Care or Personal Care Services?

There are a number of providers of home health care and personal care services on the market, so many in fact that finding services to fit your needs can be confusing. Where you will find care depends on the services you need, what you can pay, and what your insurance will cover. But before you can choose a provider, you must have an overview of your options.

HOME HEALTH CARE AGENCIES

Home health care agencies are organizations that provide both medical and personal care services to the public. They may be independent nonprofit agencies (including Visiting Nurse Associations, also called Visiting Nurse Services)

A *physician* (usually your doctor) writes the order for skilled nursing and rehabilitative services, which a home health care agency implements. A doctor or registered nurse should supervise home health care services.

A *registered nurse* evaluates patients' needs and, in conjunction with a doctor, develops a plan of care. A registered nurse can administer intravenous or injectable medications, draw blood, provide wound care, change catheters, supervise your care plan, and teach you and your family about various aspects of your care, including problem prevention. She or he can monitor your health, and tell when you may be in need of further medical attention.

Licensed practical nurses (LPNs), sometimes called Licensed Vocational Nurses, are trained medical assistants who can handle routine medical tasks, such as monitoring your blood pressure and pulse and administering oxygen and some prescribed medications under the supervision of a registered nurse.

The *home health aide* is the person who has the most intimate and frequent contact with the person receiving care. Nurse practice laws dictate the type of medical duties that a home health aide can perform, but an aide can generally provide help with grooming, dressing, walking, eating, toileting, and other services permitted by law, such as simple range-of-motion exercises and assistance with self-administered medications under a nurse's supervision. Home health aides working with Medicare-certified agencies must have successfully completed a competency evaluation, consisting of a skills test and a written test. In some states, at least seventy-five hours of training is also required.

If you are in doubt about what an aide can do in your home, call your home health agency, the agency that licenses nurses in your state (check the government pages of your local telephone directory), or a local nurses' association. Some home health aides help with light housekeeping and simple meal preparation. However, these chores are generally limited, especially when actual hands-on-care requirements are heavy. *Homemakers,* on the other hand, do concentrate on housework, shopping, laundry, and errands and may provide transportation to doctor's appointments as well.

Medical social workers with appropriate qualifications can provide care-related therapy or counseling. For example, a social worker may help family members cope with personal problems that impede their ability to care for a loved one at home. They can also provide information about community resources and assist with financial and insurance issues.

Rehabilitation professionals. Professional physical therapy, occupational therapy, and speech therapy can be provided through home health care agencies. A certified rehabilitation nurse may oversee rehabilitation professionals' services. For a description of rehabilitation therapists' jobs, refer to Chapter Six.

Dietitians plan special diets for people with medical conditions.

or public (government) or for-profit agencies. They may be community-based, hospital-based, or connected to social service agencies. Some agencies even contract with other agencies to provide the services of aides or professionals. Some providers accept Medicare only; some serve both Medicare beneficiaries and Medicaid recipients, and some, but not all, accept private pay.

Levels of care offered differ from agency to agency, but generally include the services of registered nurses (RNs), licensed practical nurses (LPNs), rehabilitation therapists, medical social workers, as well as homemakers and home health aides. Home health care agencies providing skilled nursing and rehabilitative services are usually certified to participate in the Medicare and Medicaid programs, an important indicator of quality. Medicaid and Medicare will only pay for care from certified providers.

The costs of skilled nursing and rehabilitative services vary from agency to agency, and shopping for price and quality is important. Some nonprofit home health agencies will assist a limited number of patients without any means to pay, although the demand for financial assistance appears to have outstripped agencies' abilities to respond to public need.

Personal Care Agencies

Some agencies offer personal care (also called custodial care) only. These agencies can be very valuable to those who do not need and are unlikely to need skilled nursing and rehabilitative services, because the cost of personal care is usually lower than that provided by home health care agencies. Nonetheless, there may be a serious drawback to working with these agencies. They are not certified and, depending on state law, may not be licensed. You must be very careful when working with an agency that is unlicensed, uncertified, or unaccredited, because there are no standards or requirements which the agency must meet to do business and no government oversight. If something goes wrong, you will have little recourse, other than perhaps to file a complaint with the Better Business Bureau. When you work with an unregulated agency, it's vital to question the agency's policies and capabilities thoroughly.

The Area Agency on Aging and Home Care

Going to a private agency for care is not the only way to get in-home services. The Older Americans Act funds a variety of services for persons aged sixty and older, including some homemaker and chore services. Although there are no limitations on who can receive help through the OAA, financially needy people are given priority in most states. Social Service Block Grants may also help states fund limited homemaker services or home health care services. Depending on the program, services may be available at no charge or on a sliding scale basis with fees set according to clients' incomes.

Another avenue toward home health care is through the Medicaid *home and community-based waiver program,* currently used in most states. Unfortunately, many of these programs are filled to capacity and often there are waiting lists. This does not mean that you should ignore this avenue. Some people start out by using agency help and then, when insurance will no longer cover the services they need, move on to community-based and government services. Thus, if there is a waiting list, it may help to get on it.

Family Service Agencies and Other Social Service Organizations

Family service agencies such as Jewish Family and Children's Services, Catholic Charities, Lutheran Social Services, or other religious-based and secular agencies may also offer a variety of services to older people, including personal care and homemaker/chore services and some home health care. They may do this by contracting with Medicare-certified agencies or other home care agencies. Services may be available for a fee based on your income. One advantage of working with a family service agency is that you may have easier access to other important resources, such as care management, counseling, and support groups for caregivers and for people with serious or chronic illnesses. The number of services offered by a family service agency depends on its size. Some are multifaceted organizations; others are very small.

AIDS service organizations and comprehensive care programs, discussed in Chapter Eight, offer another potential avenue toward limited, low-cost home health care for people with HIV infection or AIDS. Eligibility for services may depend on the way in which the program is funded.

Combining Options to Tailor Your Plan of Care

Agency or attendant help may not be enough to meet all your needs now or in the future. As you think about who can provide assistance to you, remember that you can combine

For the most part, care that is available through private or public agencies is of limited duration. Long-term or round-the-clock care can be tough to find. Although the need for twenty-four-hour supervision and skilled nursing care may be an indication that nursing home care is warranted, there are other options.

Nurse registries, where they exist, may be a good resource for patients and families who need extensive skilled care and are willing and able to act as employers. Yet nurse registries are not usually licensed. If the agency is unlicensed, you may encounter the same problems as you would working with an unlicensed personal care agency — there may be no supervision and quality of care may be unpredictable.

If you need extensive assistance with activities of daily living, but not skilled care, hiring an *independent home health aide* or personal care assistant may suit your needs well. People with disabilities of all ages have successfully employed personal care assistants for decades, and many older people are beginning to realize the benefit of hiring and coordinating their own personal care services. The advantage of acting as employer is that you have more control over the selection of your personal attendant, the cost can be lower and, providing you are able to pay for it, you can hire someone to provide care for as long as you like. The disadvantage is, of course, that you will be in charge of hiring, training, scheduling, and, if need be, firing, your attendant. You must also pay employment taxes and workers' compensation (depending on state law) and look at the cost of theft and liability insurance to protect yourself in the event that something is stolen or that your caregiver has an accident in your home. You will also be responsible for finding a substitute when your attendant cannot work as well as for days off, weekends, and holidays. Home health agency services may be useful in these situations.

Another problem with hiring your own personal attendant or aide concerns quality of care. Wages for private, nonmedical aides are not high, the benefits are few, there is little room for advancement, and, in most states, there are no necessary qualifications to do the job. Although many people, especially women, who seek this type of work do so because they have experience as caregivers in their own families and genuinely want to help people, the possibility of receiving negligent or abusive care is very real. Even when you trust your caregiver implicitly, a lack of training or skill in transferring someone from wheelchair to bed, for example, can lead to injury to you or your caregiver.

❖ If you decide to hire an independent provider, make sure that you interview prospective employees personally. Ask for and carefully check personal and employer references. Give your aide/homemaker specific, *written* instructions about the care you wish her to provide. Put your agreement about your caregiver's fees and explicit responsibilities in writing for you both to sign. Do not isolate yourself. Your risk of abuse and neglect rises when you have infrequent contact with others. If you are homebound, ask trustworthy friends, family members, neighbors, or Friendly Visitors to check in on you frequently.

options. For example, many people coordinate help from relatives, friends, neighbors, and members of their place of worship with services available through public and private agencies and community services, such as adult daycare and home-delivered meals, to develop a plan of care that works for them.

Reputable home health agencies are often knowledgeable about local in-home services, including those that are available to people with low incomes through government and community-based programs and should at least refer you to appropriate services if they can't meet your needs. If you are being served by an agency as a Medicare beneficiary and your coverage runs out, the agency should arrange to have your care needs met by other appropriate sources, such as services accessible through the Area Agency on Aging or the Department of Social Services.

If you are feeling overwhelmed by the idea of arranging for care and you can afford to pay for assistance, you might consider hiring a geriatric care manager to help you through the maze of options. (See the box titled Geriatric Care Managers on page 436.)

Weighing Your Alternatives

For the many people whose care needs are extensive, it is often necessary to think realistically about choosing an alternative housing facility or nursing home. Although these may be alternatives of last resort, it's wise to do some research into the quality of facilities in your area. Even if you never intend to move from your home, if a crisis occurs, you will be in a far better position to find quality care if you have a sense of what's available to you.

Paying for Agency Home and Personal Care

Payment for agency home health and personal care may come from a variety of sources including Medicare, Medicaid, the Veterans Administration, CHAMPUS, other state and federal government sources, private insurance, HMOs, and your own pocketbook.

What Does Medicare Cover?

Medicare covers only part-time or intermittent skilled nursing care and rehabilitative care such as speech therapy and physical therapy, and, *in conjunction* with these services, occupational therapy, medical social worker services, and some home health aide/homemaker services. Homemaker/home health aides may only be covered for those with no family support at home. With few exceptions, Medicare pays for acute rather than long-term care. Medicare will *not* pay for personal care services alone, nor will it pay for twenty-four-hour nursing care at home. In some cases, someone who needs a skilled nursing service over a certain period of time — for example, a weekly injection — may be able to access other services, such as home health aide visits for the same duration. When it is determined that you no longer need skilled nursing or rehabilitative care or when you are no longer homebound, Medicare reimbursements will end.

In order to qualify for Medicare reimbursement:

- You must be homebound. This generally can be construed to mean that you are unable to leave the home without the help of assistive devices, such as a walker or wheelchair, or another person, and that you leave only infrequently for medical appointments.
- You must need intermittent skilled nursing care, physical therapy, or speech therapy.
- You must be under the care of a doctor who orders home health care, sets up a plan of services for you, and periodically reviews your need for services.
- The services you choose must be provided through a Medicare-certified agency. If not, Medicare won't pay.

For more information about Medicare coverage, order a copy of the current Medicare handbook by calling the Medicare Hotline at 1-800-638-6833 or TTY 1-800-820-1202 (8 A.M. to 8 P.M. EST Monday through Friday).

Denials of coverage are not infrequent. If you apply for coverage under Medicare and are denied, appeal the decision as soon as possible, as detailed in the Medicare handbook.

What Does Medicaid Cover?

Medicaid is a state-federal program providing medical assistance to eligible people with low incomes and few assets and, in many states, to people with limited assets and medical expenses that exceed their incomes. Eligibility requirements vary from state to state, but if you think you might qualify, contact your AAA, state or local Department of Health or Social Services, or local welfare agency to learn about the eligibility requirements and services available.

Medicaid pays for limited home health services furnished by a Medicaid-certified provider, including intermittent skilled nursing care and medical supplies and equipment and, in some states, extended-duty nursing services. Personal care, which includes help with activities of daily living and housekeeping, is available in a number of states and may be provided by an agency or individual.[3] Most, but not all, states have been granted "home- and community-based" waivers to offer case management, homemaker services, respite care and personal care, and other services to Medicaid recipients. Waiver programs are usually targeted to needy people who would otherwise need placement in a nursing home. There may also be limits on the duration of services and, often, waiting lists. In some states, a co-payment for services may be required.

The cost of home care paid for out-of-pocket adds up quickly. As an alternative to nursing home care, some people consider spending their assets in order to qualify for home care programs covered by Medicaid. There are significant risks involved in doing this. It's prudent to find out exactly what services are covered by Medicaid in your state and what services are likely to remain covered in these changing times before taking any action. Medicaid laws are extremely complex, and lack of knowledge about the laws and rules governing the program could imperil your eligibility. Thus, it is crucial to speak to an attorney specializing in Medicaid law and estate planning, or a Medicaid-knowledgeable attorney specializing in elder law before taking action. The Area Agency on Aging, legal aid organizations, or the state or local long-term-care ombudsman may be able to help you find legal services that suit your needs.

Private Insurance and HMOs

Private insurance may cover the cost of home health care only in part and/or with certain restrictions attached. Check your policy or call your insurance agent to find out what type of coverage you have and what restrictions and limitations may be placed on your coverage. Health maintenance organizations may cover services if authorized by your doctor and provided through an agency contracting with the HMO. In some cases, HMOs and private insurance providers will pay for home health care if it will be less expensive than necessary care provided in an inpatient setting.

Private long-term-care insurance policies have been criticized for not providing sufficient coverage for home care.

Veterans' Benefits

Certain veterans or spouses of veterans may be eligible for VA home care. For information, contact the regional or local Department of Veterans Affairs. (Look in your telephone directory under the United States Government listings.)

Other Means of Payment

Government programs accessible through the Area Agency on Aging may be free or available for a sliding scale fee or co-payment. Some nonprofit organizations, such as family service agencies, may also provide services on a sliding scale based on your income. In some cases, funding may be available through the United Way. If you have been injured at work, workers' compensation may cover the costs of home health care.

Starting Your Search for Home Care

If you are interested in home care and want to learn more, start by collecting names of recommended agencies:

- Your doctor may be familiar with home health care agencies, although this is not always the case. You may have to introduce your doctor to the idea of home health care and tell her or him what you need. The agency you ultimately select can also talk to your doctor about your need to secure and develop a plan of care.
- If you are in the hospital, ask to speak to someone from the discharge planning or social work department and for a *list* of home health care agencies. Although hospitals sometimes attempt to steer patients toward their own home health care agencies, you have a right to choose from other providers.
- Word of mouth is one of the best sources of referrals. If possible, ask relatives, friends, and neighbors who have used home health agencies to provide you with recommendations.
- Contact the Area Agency on Aging. The Eldercare Locator can help you find your AAA.
- Senior centers, your place of worship or other religious groups, and civic organizations such as the Lions Club or Rotary Club, family service agencies, or the United Way may sponsor or refer to chore, homemaker, or home health services.

- If you or your loved one has a particular disability or illness, you may want to consider contacting or joining a disability-specific support and advocacy group, such as the Alzheimer's Association.
- Centers for independent living often maintain registries of nonmedical personal care attendants and provide education on hiring and training attendants. These resources, where available, are valuable to people of all ages who are willing and able to direct the care they receive. (See Chapter Six.)
- The state or area Department of Health or Social Services may also be able to give you a list of Medicare- and Medicaid-certified agencies or other licensed agencies and information about other programs available to the public.
- In some states, long-term-care ombudsmen can give consumers information about choosing home health care agencies and may be able to provide you with some factual information about a particular agency. However, the ombudsman program will not make specific recommendations.

Once you have a few recommendations, it's time to do some preliminary research. You will have to put some serious questions to each agency, compare services and prices, and trust your instincts when choosing a provider. Remember that professionals and aides working with the agency will be coming into your home and doing a job that requires skill, dedication, and genuine concern for others. Quality care can save your life, but poor or negligent care can be disastrous.

There are as yet no universally recognized standards of care in the home health care field and state government regulation varies. Some states license home health care agencies and personal care providers, and some do not. If licensing or certification is done by your state, it is the first criterion about which you should inquire.

Home health agencies that wish to participate in the Medicare and Medicaid programs must be inspected and certified. Although no single criterion defines quality, Medicare certification is thought to be a good initial indicator of this complex commodity because such programs must comply with stringent federal regulations. For example, when you receive care from a Medicare-certified agency, your doctor will order home care. A registered nurse or therapist will further develop an assessment of your needs, and, with your input, devise an individualized, written plan of care. The plan should cover all pertinent diagnoses, your level of functioning, prognosis, your potential for rehabilitation, frequency of in-home visits, medications and treatment, and safety measures to protect you against injury. Medicare regulations require that a registered nurse (or rehabilitation therapist) make a home visit no less frequently than every two weeks if you are receiving skilled nursing care.

Accreditation from the Joint Commission on Accreditation of Healthcare Organizations, the Community Health Accreditation Program/National League for Nursing, and/or the Foundation for Hospice and Homecare are additional marks of quality care, although accreditation is voluntary and absence of accreditation does not mean that an agency provides inferior care. In states with no licensing requirement, accreditation may be the best preliminary measure of quality. In each and every case — regardless of your source of recommendation or the agency's licensing, certification, or accreditation — you must be cautious when considering home health care services and ask a broad range of investigative questions to try to gauge the provider's reliability.

Questions to Ask When Choosing a Home Care Provider

- Is the agency Medicare-certified? Medicaid-certified? Remember that agencies must be certified to participate in Medicare or Medicaid in order for these government programs to pay.
- Is it licensed or certified by the state? What standards must be met by the agency to be state-certified or licensed?
- Is the agency accredited? By what accrediting body? When was the agency last inspected?
- Is the agency bonded? (Bonding refers to an insurance policy the individual/provider carries to cover claims against the agency or individual, such as incidents of theft.) Could I be held responsible if a caregiver hurts herself in my home? Does the agency provide malpractice insurance to its professional caregivers?
- How long has the agency been in business in this community?
- What levels of care are available? (Levels of care include RNs, LPNs or LVNs, rehabilitative services, and homemaker/home health aides.)
- Are flexible schedules available? Are services available in the evening or on weekends? Can you arrange to have the same caregiver come to my home each day? It takes

time to develop trust in a professional or aide, particularly when care that requires respect for privacy and dignity is being performed. Yet continuity of care is very difficult to find.

- Will the agency guarantee a replacement, if I don't like the caregiver assigned to me or if he or she fails to show up for work?
- Is there a nurse who can be reached twenty-four hours a day in case of an emergency?
- What are the hourly or per visit fees? What forms of payment are accepted? What will my insurance cover? Will the agency help me find reimbursement for services? When my insurance runs out, will you help me find care in the community? Will you give me a telephone number or actually help me connect with another program?
- Is private payment accepted?
- Is there a minimum number of hours for which caregivers must be hired?
- How will my care plan be devised and supervised? Will a face-to-face initial assessment be conducted by a nurse or social worker? Will a nurse or therapist visit regularly to monitor the care plan? What level of education and experience must agency nurses, therapists, and their assistants have? What training do aides receive before they are hired and thereafter? Are professionals currently licensed or certified? You may want to ask agencies to provide you with written information about caregivers' backgrounds and training.
- May I see the references supplied by agency caregivers?
- Are workers hired by this agency or another? Who takes responsibility for the quality of care provided by workers who come through another agency?
- Are criminal background checks done on caregivers? Are these checks done before the caregiver is hired and sent to work? Does the state have an elder abuse or nurse's aide registry, and if so, is it checked before employees are hired? State law and/or agency policy may dictate whether criminal background checks are done, when they are done, and the type of employee subject to them. Do not assume that statewide criminal background checks are done routinely or are even required by state law. Not all states have the capability to do this, although legislation regarding this issue has increased.
- How are complaints handled?
- Can you give me the name of previous clients who might serve as references?

- Will you provide me with written information about the fees and services provided?
- May I have a copy of the *Patient's Bill of Rights*? Medicare requires that participating agencies give you notice of your rights before delivering care or during the initial assessment before treatment begins.

If the agencies to which you speak are unable or hesitant to answer your questions, consider looking elsewhere. One of the most predictable signs of quality is an agency's openness and its willingness to understand and respond to your concerns. If the agency pressures you, is defensive, or dismisses your concerns as unimportant, you can expect similar treatment once you become a client.

When you have narrowed your selection, ask friends, clergy, doctors, senior centers, local support and advocacy groups, nurses, and discharge planners for their impression of the reputation of the agencies you're considering. Contact the Better Business Bureau for information about any complaints against the agency. Every state has a home health hotline, the number of which can be obtained by calling a home health agency or the state or local department of health. Under Medicare regulations, home health agencies must give you this number if you request it. Callers to the hotline are supposed to be able to learn whether any complaints have been made against a particular agency or whether the agency has failed to meet certain essential requirements for participation in Medicare, but real problems with the hotlines have been reported. Some hotlines simply will not give out this information.

You may also want to read the agency's recent Medicare survey, which may tell you whether the agency is meeting the requirements of participation. However, you may need assistance from a health care professional and/or long-term-care ombudsman to interpret it.

Caregivers

According to the Older Women's League, 72 percent of caregivers to the elderly are women.[4] Many women who provide care for a husband, partner, or parent must also work full-time outside the home and care for children. The result is often mental and physical depletion, loss of income, and emotional pain, mixed as it may be with the knowledge that all that can be done for a loved one is being done.

If you are suddenly faced with caregiving duties, here are

Finding reliable services and putting together a plan of care for yourself or a loved one can be time-consuming, stressful, and nearly impossible for caregivers who live far away from family members who need assistance. It may be difficult to assess how much care you actually need now and to anticipate the ways in which your needs will change over time. Thus, long-distance caregivers and people with complex and changing needs may find the services of a geriatric care manager particularly useful.

Geriatric care managers are professionals who work with older people and their families to evaluate the need for assistance and to identify, plan, locate, coordinate, and monitor an individually tailored plan of care. Care managers should have at least a bachelor's degree in social work, nursing, psychology or counseling, or gerontology and two years of work experience. They do not act as substitutes for family members providing care, but rather enhance the family's ability to help. Among the types of services geriatric care managers can arrange and oversee are home health care services, alternative housing options, and institutional care.

Geriatric care managers work in a variety of settings, including government and family service agencies and other social service agencies. In these settings, care managers provide various levels of assistance for costs that range from nothing to fees calculated based on the client's income. To locate organizations offering geriatric care managers' services, try calling the Area Agency on Aging (use the Eldercare Locator to reach the AAA nearest a loved one's home), family service agencies, such as Jewish Family Services or Catholic Charities, senior centers, the county Department of Social Services (or a similar government agency), and/or a hospital social worker or discharge planner.

Those who can afford to pay more may want to hire a private geriatric care manager. These professionals provide services similar to those described above and may specialize in certain areas, such as crisis intervention, guardianship and conservatorship, or nursing home placement.

Private care management is expensive. An initial evaluation can cost between $200 and $400, and hourly rates thereafter, if needed, can be in the area of $30 to $150. Some private care managers charge flat monthly or annual fees for ongoing services. Insurers do not usually reimburse care managers' services, but what you will pay depends very much on your needs and the service(s) the care manager will perform. Moreover, if you are a long-distance caregiver, the services of a good care manager may compare favorably to traveling costs and time taken off work to assist your loved one.

Because there are as yet no universally accepted standards for care managers and no regulation of the field, you must be very careful when choosing a geriatric care manager. If you choose a care management agency, ask your doctor, clergyperson, senior center, and Better Business Bureau about its reputation. Ask for client references and check the caregiver's credentials with the licensing, accreditation, or certification program of her or his background profession. A care manager with suitable credentials and experience should not hesitate to give you this type of information. Find out what the care manager's current caseload is and whether he or she will be able to give you sufficient attention. Look for someone who will be available in emergencies, on evenings, and weekends. Ask how and how often your care manager will confer with you. Always get fee agreements in an itemized written statement. If you are a caregiver, monitor the care manager's activities and be sure to ask your loved one whether she or he is satisfied with the services.

You may also want to look for a provider who is a member of a professional organization, such as the National Association of Professional Geriatric Care Managers, which has adopted a set of standards for its members. For a copy of these standards and a list of member providers in your area, you can call or write the National Association of Professional Geriatric Care Managers, listed in the Resource Directory.

some things that you can do to prevent problems and give yourself a greater sense of control:

- Try to get as much information about your loved one's condition and prognosis as possible. Go with him or her to doctors' appointments and talk to the professionals providing care and treatment. If your loved one is in the hospital, ask to speak to the hospital social worker or discharge planner as soon as possible to begin coordinating a plan of care. Many people facing the prospect of caring for another greatly underestimate the amount of work involved as well as the length of the time commitment. It's important that you have an explicit understanding of the nature of your friend or relative's condition and any changes that are likely to develop over time before you attempt to provide care on an ongoing basis. If you have a sense of what the future is likely to hold, you'll be in a better position to realistically assess your loved one's needs and your ability to meet them.

- If relevant, ask your doctor, social worker, or reference librarian for reading suggestions to help you learn more about the condition of the person for whom you're caring.

- Make sure that your loved one wants your help. Sometimes people have little choice about receiving or giving care, but it's important not to make assumptions. Involve the ill person in planning and decision-making processes as much as possible. Declining health brings with it many losses — the loss of independence, security, privacy, and the sense of identity formerly maintained through social and professional roles, and a caregiver may unintentionally reinforce a sense of loss of control and helplessness.

- Be honest with yourself. There is often a difference between what we would like to do, or what we believe is right, and what we are actually capable of doing. Examine your situation. Do you know what the job demands? Are you up to it physically? Do you have an illness or disability that might prevent you from giving responsible care? For example, if your loved one is bedfast, can you turn her or him safely? Are your other family responsibilities already too great? How will you balance work and caregiving? What will the long-term economic consequences of caregiving be? Is there enough space in your home to ensure sufficient privacy for everyone? Can you find support among family, friends, neighbors, and community agencies? Is there a difficult history between you and the ill person that could complicate your ability to provide consistent, loving care? Don't defer thinking seriously about these issues. Unrealistic expectations often lead to unintended results, such as poor care and neglect.[5]

* Confer with other family members. Wives, partners, and daughters are often expected to provide care without any assistance and with ample criticism from other family members and friends. Try to hold a family meeting to discuss what each person can do to help, and keep them informed of all that you are doing for your family member. Qualified care managers and family service agencies may provide counseling to help facilitate family discussions.

Caregiving can be deeply rewarding, but it can also be lonely and frustrating. Family members and friends may not offer help and may indeed retreat when asked. If family members won't provide hands-on assistance, think about other ways in which they can help. For example, can someone look into the availability of community services, research information about your relative's condition, or provide financial assistance? Don't be afraid to delegate small tasks to anyone who asks, "Is there something I can do?" For example, ask willing friends and neighbors to pick up items for you when they go to the market or pharmacy.

* Talk to your employer about resources that might be available to you. If your company has an Employee Assistance Program (EAP), find out whether counseling, support groups, respite care, adult daycare, flex time, or other benefits are available. Also remember that the Family and Medical Leave Act provides limited unpaid leave for certain employees of large companies. (See Chapter One for general information.)
* Consider taking a course on caregiving so that you will know how to prevent and handle problems. Hospitals, community colleges, the Red Cross, local chapters of the Alzheimer's Association, and other community agencies may offer programs to teach basic caregiving skills. Home health agency nurses or therapists can also teach families how to care for their loved ones safely. Contact your Area Agency on Aging, hospital social worker or discharge planner, Visiting Nurse Association, or the Red Cross to find out what help may be available in your community.
* Contact a support group for caregivers. Support groups can be:

a vital link to information about community and general resources;

a source of practical suggestions for coping with everyday problems;

a way of getting the external validation for your efforts so necessary to your spiritual and emotional well-being;

a means of relief from isolation; and

a place where difficult feelings can be vented and friendships can be formed.

See the Resource Directory for listings of national caregiver groups. National support organizations, hospital discharge planners, social workers, or the Area Agency on Aging may be able to tell you about other local support groups. You can also look in the front pages of your local telephone directory under Community Services or Human Services or other similar headings for information. Before choosing a support group, speak to the facilitator and ask about the group's composition, how it functions, when it meets, the facilitator's experience, and whether the group will be right for you.

- Read some books on caregiving. There are several good manuals and "how-to" guides on the market that provide emotional support and practical information to those caring for sick or dying people at home. Some suggestions are given in the reading resource list at the end of this book and in Chapter Ten. If you can't get to a bookstore or library, you can order books directly from a bookstore or publisher over the telephone.

- Organize all important documents (see Chapter Ten). Someone who is ill or elderly can become incapacitated without warning. A will, a durable power of attorney, living will and/or health care proxy will be enormously helpful in such an event.

Most importantly:

- Prepare to accept help. *No one* can provide care to another person alone. Explore resources for home health care, personal care, respite and adult daycare and other community-based and volunteer support options early on. Don't delay until you are exhausted and can't continue providing care. It is extremely difficult to find assistance in a crisis and the availability of services can vary dramatically from community to community. Even if you don't think you'll need help for a while, you'll be very glad you know where to find it when you do.

- Take care of yourself. If you do not, expect to become ill or to injure yourself. Many caregivers feel guilty asking for help or letting someone else provide care. The ill person may even tenaciously resist the idea. But when a caregiver also becomes ill, no one wins. Someone who is morally, emotionally, and physically depleted cannot provide help at home safely and may even become abusive or neglectful.

Depression and/or anger may be signs that you are exhausted and under too much stress and need rest. Support groups and books for caregivers often provide suggestions on getting sleep, relaxing, and coping with stress and guilt. Be aware that there may come a time when your loved one's needs will surpass your abilities to provide care. The decision to opt for more formalized care is an excruciating one for all involved, but when the demands of caregiving become overwhelming, a nursing home or alternative housing option can be the safest, most responsible choice.

ALTERNATIVE HOUSING: WHEN YOU NEED MORE HELP THAN YOU CAN GET AT HOME

If you need more help at home and are considering moving, you may have a range of possible options. This section will discuss informal and more formal sources of assistance and care.

Moving in with your children. If you can no longer live in your own home, this option may be suitable providing both you and your children agree to it. But misunderstandings can develop very quickly when open and frank discussions involving all family members do not take place. Sometimes adult children assume that their parents would prefer to live with them. Some parents are loath to give up their independence and privacy, but are afraid to offend their children by rejecting an offer to live together. On the other hand, children may be uncomfortable voicing mixed feelings about living with their parents. Space, economic considerations, differences in values and lifestyles, and a host of other factors may color a decision that should be mutual. If this option presents itself, be very careful to explore it thoroughly with your children. Otherwise, your relationship may suffer.

ECHO Housing. ECHO stands for Elder Cottage Housing Opportunity. ECHO housing units are self-contained, often prefabricated units that are designed to meet the needs of older people and that can be placed near existing housing. Because the unit has a separate entrance, you can live inde-

The National Shared Housing Resource Center
(410) 235-4454

Shared housing or "match-up" programs are designed to match prospective tenants to compatible apartment dwellers or homeowners to share or rent space. They often connect people who have a particular need, such as a need for help with household chores, to tenants who will fulfill that need in exchange for reduced rent. However, this type of arrangement is not mandatory. The prospective tenant can pay full rent and forgo the exchange of services. Shared housing programs have long been beneficial to older women and are increasingly finding placements for younger people and, often, single-parent families.

The National Shared Housing Resource Center maintains a directory of shared housing services across the country. For information, send a self-addressed stamped envelope to the center at 321 East 25th St., Baltimore, MD 21218. Your local AAA or senior center may also be able to tell you about any community match-up services. Services are often free of charge. If there is a fee, it's usually minimal.

The time it will take to find arrangements depends on the availability of housing, your needs, and the needs of your prospective roommate. In addition, the sort of background check run by the service will affect the wait for a match. Some programs run criminal background checks on applicants. Generally, you will be required to provide references and interview with the service so that your needs may be evaluated.

Not everyone is comfortable sharing housing. The best arrangements are made between people who can easily communicate their desires and expectations. For example, sharing a home with someone does not mean that you will have to give up your independence or take on caregiving duties. Many shared housing services have staff members who can assist in creating an agreement between roommates and mediate any problems that arise.

❖ If you are considering sharing housing with two or more people of your acquaintance, it is a good idea to check the local zoning board to find out whether zoning laws permit a number of unrelated people to live together and to find out what effect your living arrangement will have on the receipt of any government assistance you receive, such as Supplemental Security Income. As well, your rights and legal responsibilities as co-tenants under a rental agreement or as landlord and tenant should be clearly defined and understood.

pendently of your children or other relatives but still maintain closeness. Before planning to purchase ECHO housing, however, contact the local zoning board for information about any restrictions due to zoning laws.

Another alternative is to construct a self-contained unit in your home. These units, called accessory apartments, can be very expensive to build and necessitate the work of a contractor. Here again, zoning laws must be consulted. You may also want to find out how sharing a home will affect your taxes and any government benefits you receive, such as Supplemental Security Income. For more information on these housing options, contact your Area Agency on Aging. Contact the state Office of Consumer Affairs or the local agency that licenses contractors (check the state and local listings in your telephone directory) to find out whether the agency can send you free booklets or brochures about hiring and using a contractor.

NURSING HOMES AND ALTERNATIVE HOUSING OPTIONS

This section discusses nursing homes and alternatives to nursing homes. Because the decision to move to an alternative environment or nursing home is a significant one, one that is best made with as much information as possible, plenty of information is provided. However, being confronted with a lot of information can be overwhelming, especially in a crisis. Although it's best to read the entire section and to turn to other sources of information as well, it may help to read the sections that meet your immediate needs first and other sections later.

Be advised that federal laws regarding nursing homes and their residents' rights have been targeted for change in recent years. It will be important to talk to your long-term-care ombudsman and/or nursing home citizen advocacy group, services that will be discussed shortly, for current information about laws affecting nursing home care.

WHO CAN HELP? RESOURCES FOR YOU AND YOUR FAMILY

The National Citizens' Coalition for Nursing Home Reform (NCCNHR) is a consumer organization with membership that includes several hundred grassroots nursing home advocacy groups, ombudsman programs, and individual advocates across the United States. In addition to working for legal protections for nursing home residents and monitoring enforcement of these laws, NCCNHR can refer you to a local advocacy organization or ombudsman program that offers advice and answers questions about nursing home care, if there is one in your area. In addition, NCCNHR offers a number of publications to nursing home staff members and the public. For information, call (202) 332-2275.

In many, but not all, states across the U.S., there are nursing home citizen advocacy groups working for the improvement of nursing home residents' lives and helping families to get the information they need to find good care for their family member. These groups are varied; they range from sophisticated advocacy organizations to smaller, more grassroots groups. Many produce free or low-cost booklets and newsletters providing consumers with information on choosing a nursing home.

Because each organization is distinct, each approaches its task in a different way. Some organizations are able to provide detailed information indicating the quality of care in specific homes and are very direct in discussing their experiences with particular facilities. Others are not able to expand on the merits or problems of certain homes, but if you listen closely, you can draw enough from the organization's response about a given home to learn whether it provides quality care. Be aware, however, that a nursing home advocacy group may not have information on every home in their area or state and that there is no substitute for personal observation of the homes you're considering.

The Long-Term-Care Ombudsman

Under the federal Older Americans Act, every state is required to have a Long-Term-Care Ombudsman Program to receive, investigate, and resolve complaints about nursing homes and board-and-care facilities. Some states have an extensive network of regional ombudsman programs, including trained citizen volunteers. In addition to working to resolve problems of individual residents, ombudsman programs identify and work with others to address systemic problems like inadequate staffing and Medicaid discrimination.

Ombudsmen can inform you of residents' rights under state and federal law and answer a myriad of questions about nursing home care. The ombudsman does not have powers of enforcement, however. That is usually the province of the licensing and certification agency, and states' willingness to enforce laws written to protect nursing home residents varies.

Because they have the most contact with individual homes, local ombudsmen are often the best sources of information about the facilities from which you'll be choosing. Many state and local ombudsman programs provide booklets and pamphlets about selecting nursing homes or licensed alternative housing facilities, and in some states, home health care agencies.

Long-term-care ombudsmen do not generally rate facilities or give recommendations. However, many will be able to give you a general sense of a nursing home's care and assist you in being an informed consumer. They can help you think of questions to ask or provide you with a list of questions, and tell you what to look for when you visit facilities. They can also tell you where to find and how to interpret the annual nursing home surveys.

As with most resources, ombudsman programs are very different from one another. This is true when it comes to handling residents' complaints and problems. Some may limit their intervention to advising residents and families how to proceed when a problem with a nursing home arises. Others are able to visit facilities and advocate as necessary on residents' behalf. One of the most significant problems faced by many ombudsman programs is a lack of funding. Ombudsmen must often stretch their efforts across a broad range of concerns and in some areas must prioritize calls. In some cases, political constraints limit what ombudsmen are able to do to solve problems. It's important to remember that ombudsmen represent the interests of nursing home residents and do not solve family problems. However, for those families who are acting upon the wishes of their loved ones, a good ombudsman can be a tremendous ally. To get a referral to your local and/or state ombudsman program, call the NCCNHR, the Eldercare Locator, the Area Agency on Aging, or the state unit on aging. (See the beginning of this chapter for information.)

Support and Advocacy Groups

If you have special concerns, support and advocacy groups representing the interests of people with your particular illness, disability, or condition may also be able to provide advice on choosing a nursing home or alternative facility suited to your needs. Contact the national office or local branches of organizations relevant to your concerns, for example, the Alzheimer's Association, to find out what information is available. For information about various illness- or disability-specific national organizations, see the Resource Directory.

If You Are in the Hospital

If you are referred to a facility directly by the hospital social work or discharge planning department or are given the

You and your family members may have a number of concerns about your health, which should be addressed before making a major move. Health, memory, behavioral, and personality changes may be signs of a need for increased care. The causes may be easily remedied. For example, adverse reactions to medication can produce symptoms similar to depression or dementia. In any case, health and memory changes should never be dismissed as the inevitable effects of "old age." Your doctor should be able to give you a good picture of your current health condition and the likely outlook for the future. If practicable and necessary, she or he may also refer you to a geriatric specialist or geriatric assessment program, usually located in hospitals or major medical centers. A geriatric assessment team, which may include a doctor, nurse, social worker, or psychologist and rehabilitation professionals, can provide a complete medical, neurological, and psychological examination in order to evaluate your needs and suggest the type of assistance most appropriate for you.

If you are seeking home health care, remember that your doctor must authorize your need for care if insurance is to pay. Home health agencies will provide this type of needs evaluation, if you are likely to become a client. The Area Agency on Aging, private nonprofit social service agencies, or private geriatric care managers may also provide basic assessments either separately or as part of the services that you receive. If you are receiving services under the Medicaid "home- and community-based waiver," assessment and care management are usually part of the program.

names of nursing homes, it is still very important to visit and investigate the hospital's referrals, if feasible. Discharge planners may be under great pressure to move patients out of the hospital and into a nursing home as soon as possible and may not know everything about the homes they recommend, particularly in larger communities.

A Care Manager's Help

Depending on your resources, a geriatric care manager whom you trust may be able to help you do some of the necessary investigation and paperwork involved in choosing a home or alternative housing option.

Alternative housing options

In the past nursing homes were the only option for people who could not stay in their own homes because of a need for assistance. Today, there is a growing alternative housing industry to which older adults can look for a range of supportive housing options.

There are both significant advantages and disadvantages

to alternative housing options. An alternative housing facility can provide more independence than a nursing home, but the costs can be very high, and residents generally pay out of pocket. One must be cautious when choosing a facility because at present alternative housing options are less regulated than nursing homes. The lack of consistent oversight and the presence of homes operating illegally in some areas make alternative housing facilities potential sites of abuse and neglect. Likewise, someone who really needs nursing care, or who is likely to need such assistance in the near future, may be unsafe in an environment where no medical personnel are on staff.

This section briefly outlines two options for alternative housing and provides a list of questions to use when considering your choices. The types of housing arrangements available in each community and the names by which they are identified differ widely from place to place. In order to find out what alternatives exist in your community, what services are offered, and how they are regulated, start by contacting your state long-term-care ombudsman or nursing home advocacy organization.

Assisted-Living Facilities

Assisted living is a form of congregate housing typically provided for ambulatory people who are in need of some assistance with activities of daily living but not enough to warrant nursing home care. These residences may be called board-and-care homes, personal care homes, homes for the aged, rest homes, residential care facilities, or domiciliary care homes, among other names. Depending on the facility, the number of occupants can range from a handful to hundreds.

Services usually provided in exchange for monthly fees include meals, help with dressing, feeding, eating, toileting, grooming, assistance managing medications, laundry, social and recreational activities, and transportation. Quality of care varies dramatically as do costs and the availability of state or local subsidies for older people with low incomes. Medicaid and Medicare do not generally pay for assisted-living care, but in some areas alternative living facilities accept Social Security checks, including SSI, as payment. For the most part, however, residents pay privately, and costs can be exorbitant.

Most assisted-living facilities are licensed, but some are not. Information can usually be obtained through the licensing agency, which may be housed in the state Department of Social Services or state Department of Health. However, licensing requirements, particularly when unenforced, may afford residents little or no protection. Thus, it is important to visit the facility, or have a trusted friend or relative visit if you cannot, and ask as many questions as you can, getting as much information as possible in writing.

Assisted-living facilities should not be confused with Life Care Communities or Continuing Care Retirement Communities, which are communities of apartments or houses offering graduated levels of supportive housing including nursing home care from a facility on-site or nearby. In exchange for a hefty lump-sum entrance fee and monthly payments, these facilities contract to care for residents for as long as they remain in the community. Because of the enormous investment and possible risks involved, the state long-term-care ombudsman, a financial adviser, and/or an attorney — preferably an elder law attorney or other lawyer who has experience with Life Care Communities — should be consulted for planning.

Congregate Housing

Congregate housing arrangements are usually residential apartments or large, modified homes equipped to meet the needs of older people. Residents pay for a package that typically includes a private bedroom with or without a kitchen and services such as group dining, laundry, housekeeping, transportation and, sometimes, medical services. Congregate housing can be expensive, particularly when owned and operated by private companies. But if you are of low to moderate income, you can contact your Area Agency on Aging and ask to be directed to housing facilities run by public and nonprofit organizations.

Always visit the facility, speak with staff members and other service providers on-site, and before moving in, talk to residents about their experiences in the facility. The next section will offer some general questions to ask when considering any facility.

QUESTIONS TO ASK ABOUT AN ALTERNATIVE HOUSING FACILITY

Here are some basic questions to ask about an alternative housing facility. Your local or state ombudsman can provide you with additional information.

- Ask your doctor, clergyperson, senior center, and local long-term-care ombudsman about the facility's reputation. In some areas, local ombudsmen or nursing home advocacy groups can supply concerned callers with factual information reflecting the quality of care provided in a given facility.

- Ask the administrator or other appropriate staff person the following questions and note the answers and your observations:
  - Is the facility licensed?
  - Is there twenty-four-hour assistance for help with activities of daily living, including eating, toileting, bathing, dressing, mobility, and other services? Is there a twenty-four-hour emergency response system available from each unit? Are additional services such as physical therapy available, or can such services be purchased from an outside agency and delivered in the facility?
  - Ask whether an assessment will be done to determine your eligibility for the facility. What are the criteria for eligibility? How will the assessment be done? Who will conduct it? Will a written plan of care be developed for each resident?
  - What is the attitude and philosophy of the staff? What qualifications do staff members need to perform their duties? Is there a licensed registered nurse on staff or on call? If assistance with medication is needed, who provides this service? How is this person supervised?
  - What steps are followed in the event of a personal medical emergency? Does the facility have arrangements with a nearby hospital?
  - If you must leave the facility for a period of time, for example, if you become ill and must stay in the hospital or in a skilled nursing care facility, will you be able to maintain your unit? Will you continue to pay for rent and other services during this time?
  - What steps are taken to get people out of the building in an emergency? Does the building meet state and local safety codes? Does it have a sprinkler system in case of a fire?
  - How will your privacy, security, and personal property be protected?
  - What will the costs be, including additional charges for services not included in your rent? Is assistance available to help people with low incomes defray costs?
  - Under what circumstances can you be discharged

from the facility? For example, can you be asked to leave if your health declines?

- How are complaints handled?
- Be certain that any agreement you make with the facility is in writing, including the reasons and procedures for termination of the living arrangement and the facility's refund policy.

For more information on finding and choosing assisted-living facilities and congregate housing in your community, contact the Area Agency on Aging, state unit on aging, state long-term-care ombudsman, or the Assisted Living Facilities Association, listed in the Resource Directory.

NURSING HOME CARE

PART ONE: PLANNING AHEAD

Nursing home placements usually occur when rehabilitative or medical services are needed on a short-term basis after a serious illness or injury (although home health care may be a viable alternative), when you need twenty-four-hour skilled nursing care or help with the activities of daily living, and/or when your loved ones can no longer provide care at home safely.

Very often, the transition to a nursing home is made in a crisis — for example, after a stroke or accident — when there isn't much time to investigate options. Even when there is time, the decision to move to a nursing home is often an agonizing one for both the prospective resident and his or her family. Sometimes it's the only realistic choice. There *are* good nursing homes, but information, as much advance planning as possible, and on-site inspections are the keys to finding them. If you have any sense that you may need nursing home care soon or in the near future, or if you have been diagnosed with a progressive disease, such as Alzheimer's disease or Parkinson's disease, now is the time to begin your research. You may never actually need a nursing home, but by being prepared, you'll be in a much better position to find a good one if you do. Depending on your circumstances, you may want to put your name on the waiting lists of desirable homes.

Whether you have one day to prepare for the transition to a nursing home or more time to think about other options, this section will help you by providing a basic overview of the process of seeking and choosing a home. However, it is not possible to cover all the details that are so vital to this most difficult task. You are urged to gather information from various sources (see the reading resource list), to visit the nursing homes you're thinking of entering, and, above all, to trust your instincts about the quality of care that you believe a particular institution will be able to provide.

PAYING FOR NURSING HOME CARE

By all standards, nursing home care is an extraordinary expense, one that can easily wipe out a lifetime of savings. The average yearly cost of nursing home care is about $37,000 and, contrary to popular belief, Medicare does not pay for a significant portion of nursing home costs. Medicare and Medigap will only pay for a limited amount of skilled care under very specific circumstances.

Many nursing home residents ultimately exhaust their resources and come to rely on Medicaid (also called Medical Assistance, or Medi-Cal in California), the state-federal program of medical assistance to the poor, to help them pay for the cost of care. This is one reason why it is advisable to limit your selection to nursing homes that are certified for participation in both the Medicaid and Medicare programs. A home that is not Medicaid-certified can ask you to leave once you can no longer afford to pay privately and can in fact exclude Medicaid residents entirely. Moreover, nursing homes certified to participate in the Medicaid and Medicare programs must observe federal laws and regulations protecting nursing home residents' rights.

Despite the fact that many people must rely on Medicaid to defray costs, many nursing homes openly prefer those who can pay out of their own pockets, or who are covered by Medicare, because the daily rates for private pay and Medicare are often much higher than the Medicaid reimbursement rate. State laws may affect the prioritizing of private pay residents, nonetheless. To learn about your rights under state law, contact your state and local long-term-care ombudsmen.

Will Medicare Pay for Nursing Home Care?

Medicare does not pay for custodial care, that is, help with activities of daily living such as eating, walking, grooming, and toileting, when that is the only type of care you need.[6]

Medicare will only pay for nursing home care under the following conditions:

- You must have a condition that requires daily skilled nursing or skilled rehabilitation that can only be provided in a skilled nursing facility (or skilled nursing area of a nursing home). Examples of skilled nursing care include tube feeding, injections, and catheter insertion. Physical therapy, occupational therapy, and speech therapy are examples of rehabilitative care. These services must be performed by or under the supervision of licensed professionals.
- The skilled nursing facility or area must be participating in the Medicare program.
- You must have been in a hospital at least 3 days in a row (not counting the day of discharge) before you are admitted to a skilled nursing facility.
- You must be admitted to the facility within a short time (generally 30 days) after you leave the hospital.
- Your care in the facility must be for a condition that was treated in the hospital.
- A doctor must certify that you need skilled nursing or rehabilitation services on a daily basis.

As long as you meet all the criteria above and continue to need daily skilled nursing or rehabilitative care and to show improvement, Medicare will help pay for a maximum of 100 days of skilled nursing care per benefit period.

Medicare will pay in full for all covered services during the first 20 days of care per benefit period. Thereafter, Medicare will only pay for part of the cost, which a Medigap policy may help cover. Many families do not receive assistance with or do not need 100 days of care. The average length of Medicare coverage is about 25 to 30 days.

You are entitled to notification by the nursing home of a determination that you are not eligible or no longer eligible for skilled nursing care and to appeal that denial. Immediately contact your ombudsman, state insurance counseling program for seniors (see page 417), or consult your Medicare handbook for information on how to appeal.

Medicaid and Nursing Homes

As mentioned, Medicaid (Medi-Cal or Medical Assistance) is currently the major source of assistance for people receiving nursing home care. If you meet your state's eligibility criteria for Medicaid, *need nursing home care as a matter of*

If you think that you or someone you love may need nursing home care, it's vital that you firmly establish your medical eligibility and make sure that nursing home care is really your best option. Neither Medicare nor Medicaid will pay for care that is not medically necessary, and Medicaid's medical eligibility requirements are becoming increasingly stringent in some states. If you enter a nursing home without a genuine need for nursing home care and later apply for Medicaid, your application may be denied. You may then find yourself with no financial assistance and, if you have exhausted your resources, no place else to go.

Your private physician may assess your need for care, although not all doctors are familiar with the level of care required for nursing home eligibility. In some instances, a physician subspecializing in geriatric medicine may be best suited to provide an evaluation. Some states require that people already covered by Medicaid receive a government assessment, although people who plan to pay privately may be able to use the state's assessment program. Some states require prospective residents to undergo a government assessment regardless of income. A call to your local or state ombudsman's office may help you clarify the requirements you must meet and point you in the direction of the best source for a thorough assessment.

medical necessity, and receive care in a Medicaid-certified facility, Medicaid will cover skilled nursing care as well as health-related care and services above the level of room and board.

States have different criteria for determining Medicaid eligibility. While the program is designed to help poor people, in most states people with limited assets and with incomes that are lower than their medical bills ("medically needy" people) can also become eligible for Medicaid by spending their incomes on allowable expenses until they reach the eligibility income limit.

Medicaid coverage of nursing home care is not free of charge. A nursing home resident will use most or all of her monthly income, including pension and Social Security benefits, less a small personal allowance and other state allowances, to pay for nursing home care. (This is called the share of cost.) Medicaid will then make up the difference between what the resident is able to pay and the Medicaid per diem rate. At present, special rules apply to married couples when one member is in a nursing home and the other isn't so that the non-institutionalized spouse (called the community spouse) can retain a certain amount of assets and income.

Veterans' Benefits

Nursing care in a VA or private nursing facility may be provided to veterans with service-connected disabilities, certain other veterans, and veterans who meet income eligibility guidelines. For more information, contact your regional Department of Veterans Affairs or the Superintendent of Documents, P.O. Box 371954, Pittsburgh, PA 15250-7954; (202) 512-1800 for a current copy of the booklet *Federal Benefits for Veterans and Dependents.* (Look in the United States government section of your telephone book for the telephone number.)

Will You Have a Choice of Nursing Homes?
Will You Be Able to Stay Once You're Accepted?

Depending on where you live, you may have a difficult time getting into a nursing home if you are a Medicaid recipient or become a Medicaid recipient before moving to a nursing home. For example, you may be told that there is a long waiting list, or you may find no acceptance at all. Nursing homes can and do discriminate against Medicaid recipients, although the legality of this kind of discrimination, the protections offered by state law, and the state's willingness to enforce them differ. Federal law also offers some protection for nursing home residents who receive Medicaid, but these protections are subject to change. Thus, it's important to contact your state/local ombudsman for ongoing information.

Don't make the mistake of thinking that the problems associated with Medicaid discrimination only apply to people with low incomes. It is not uncommon for people with substantial incomes to go to great lengths planning for Medicaid eligibility, only to find that no nursing home will accept them once they qualify. Likewise, it may be necessary for some people to accept placement in a less desirable nursing home while awaiting an opening in a preferred home. Yet transferring from one home to another as a Medicaid recipient can present identical problems with discrimination.

Once admitted to a home, residents covered by Medicaid may experience subtler forms of discrimination. For example, they may be moved to a less desirable area of the home. If this happens to you, contact your ombudsman immediately. Also, talk to your state and local ombudsman to get a sense of the potential for discrimination in your area.

You may encounter problems based on the amount of care you need, especially if you are a Medicaid recipient or you are nearing Medicaid eligibility. Depending on the state in which you live and the way in which reimbursements are structured, you may find nursing homes hesitant to accept people who require a great deal of care or who have complex medical needs. In areas where nursing homes receive greater reimbursements for people with heavy care needs, people who don't require as much care may also find themselves looking longer for a nursing home that will accept them. If you suspect this kind of discrimination, discuss the matter with your ombudsman and, if possible, a nursing home advocacy group to get a sense of your options.

Once you are accepted into a home that accepts Medicaid or Medicare, federal law offers you a little more protection against discrimination. At present, it is illegal for nursing homes to:

* request people who are eligible for Medicaid to make a donation, gift, or other consideration for admission
* require you to waive Medicaid or Medicare benefits or promise that you won't apply for them for a certain period of time. In fact, nursing homes are required by federal law to provide you with information on how to apply for Medicaid or Medicare.

- require a guarantee of payment from a third party, such as a family member, as a condition of admission. If you are asked to sign as a "responsible party," consult your ombudsman, lawyer, or legal aid organization about the lawfulness of this request.
- discriminate in the provision of services on the basis of the source of payment or deliver different or inferior services to Medicaid recipients
- A deposit cannot be required as a condition of admission for a resident who is covered by Medicaid or Medicare, unless for desired items that are not covered. A deposit may be required by facilities accepting only private pay residents. It is illegal for a nursing home to require that you deposit your personal funds with the establishment. If you choose to have the nursing home hold money for you, it must deposit any amount of your personal funds that exceed $100 in a separate interest-bearing account.[7]

These minimal protections have been under attack in recent years. It's a good idea to keep abreast of current law by consulting your state or local ombudsman, an advocacy group, or an attorney familiar with nursing home law.

Protect Yourself: Get Legal Advice

Medicaid law is extremely complex and always changing. Many people have misconceptions about Medicaid and how they can qualify for assistance with nursing home care. It is a good idea to consult with your state or local ombudsman, Area Agency on Aging, and/or a lawyer familiar with Medicaid, as well as to gather more information about the program in your state at the earliest possible date and certainly before you transfer any assets.

You do not need a lawyer to apply for Medicaid, but an attorney can help you understand eligibility requirements, guide your financial planning, and help you prepare for the future. For example, a state may recover payments made by Medicaid on behalf of nursing home residents. Some states may attach liens to residents' assets, such as their homes, if the nursing home resident, spouse, and certain relatives are no longer living there, and may seek recovery from a property's sale or after the death of the nursing home resident and spouse in some circumstances. States may also elect to seek recovery of other, nonprobatable assets in which the Medicaid recipient had interest or title at the time of death, such as a living trust.

Advance planning for nursing home care must be done with extreme caution. It is absolutely vital that you thoroughly understand your rights and the rules that govern the Medicaid program, especially before taking any action that might be construed as a violation of the rules. For example, you may meet with a significant period of ineligibility, if you transfer assets within a certain time frame (at present thirty-six months prior to applying for Medicaid, and sixty months for transfers from trusts). If you transfer assets improperly, you may have to pay for care out of pocket during the waiting period, thus effectively undoing months of planning.

If you own your home, have substantial assets or income, and/or plan to transfer significant assets to another person, it's wise to seek advice from an attorney specializing in elder law, a field of law that addresses many of the issues discussed in this chapter, or in Medicaid law *and* estate planning as soon as possible. If you have a low income, you may find the help that you need through a legal aid program serving older people. Your local or state ombudsman or Area Agency on Aging can refer you to free or low-cost services, and in some cases may be able to help you find an attorney who will offer her or his services pro bono. An attorney who is not familiar with the complexities of Medicaid law and the potential discrimination Medicaid recipients face is probably not in the best position to advise you. (Look under the National Academy of Elder Law Attorneys in the Resource Directory.)

It's also wise to speak to the appropriate staff member at your managed care organization, such as a health maintenance organization or Medicaid/managed care organization for information about available benefits for skilled nursing care, coordination of care, and/or for nursing home referrals.

PART TWO: STARTING YOUR SEARCH FOR A NURSING HOME

Taking Steps to Find a Good Nursing Home

Once you have determined that nursing home care is appropriate for you or your family member, you must

- get information about nursing home care, payment options, and your rights as a resident as soon as possible. Contact the long-term-care ombudsman and/or nursing home advocacy group in your area and ask to be sent any booklets or pamphlets on nursing home care and a list of questions to ask when choosing a facility.

LONG-TERM INSURANCE

If you have significant assets to protect, you may want to investigate options for long-term insurance. Long-term insurance policies may offer consumers a means of paying for nursing home care or an assisted-living facility without decimating their savings. However, buyers must choose very carefully and educate themselves about the limitations and risks involved. There are a number of sources of information about long-term-care insurance. Your state or local ombudsman, nursing home advocacy or other senior advocacy group, or your state's insurance counseling program for seniors are good places to start your search. To find these organizations, contact your Area Agency on Aging or the Eldercare Locator. Premiums for "tax-qualified" long-term-care policies are treated as tax-deductible medical expenses. Qualified long-term-care services are also deductible. Thus, if you do buy long-term-care insurance, ask your tax adviser and state insurance counseling program for additional information before choosing a policy.

- gather references to nursing homes
- narrow your selection
- visit and personally observe select nursing homes

If you are planning care for someone else, remember that the decision to move should be mutual and that your loved one should be involved in the decision-making process to the maximum extent possible. Think how you would feel if someone moved you out of your home to another location without your consent or involvement.

Collect Names and Information

Good sources for the names of nursing homes in your area include ombudsmen, nursing home advocacy organizations, local branches of support and advocacy groups, clergy, hospital discharge planners, social workers, senior citizens' centers, and geriatric care managers.

Narrow Your Selection: Questions to Ask Over the Telephone

Once you have the names of nursing homes recommended by more than one person, telephone each and ask some questions to eliminate them as candidates or qualify them further. For example, contact the nursing home administrator or person in charge of admissions and ask:

- Is there a waiting list? How long is the wait? Can I apply to the home or put my name on the waiting list? The wait may be shorter if you can pay privately. But remember that it is illegal for a nursing home certified for participation in Medicare or Medicaid to request or to require that you pay privately for a period of time before applying for benefits.
- Is the nursing home certified for participation in Medicare and Medicaid?
- Does the nursing home offer the level of care that you need? For example, if you need skilled nursing care or rehabilitative care initially and personal care (assistance with the tasks of daily living) later, does the home focus on both types of services or does it specialize in rehabilitation services alone? Some nursing homes offer wonderful care in one area and lack quality in another.
- If you or your loved one has an illness or condition that requires special care, find out whether the nursing home will be able to provide that care. Be especially cautious when assessing the services of facilities

or units that advertise care for people with Alzheimer's disease. What credentials or training do staff members have that uniquely qualify them to work with this group of patients? How will services and activities meet your loved one's particular needs? How will the staff meet patients' changing needs? Is there a safe place for residents with Alzheimer's disease to walk? What are the various ways staff members respond to residents who wander? Is there a wanderer alert system in place?

- What are the admission requirements?
- Where is the facility located? Because visits from family and friends are so important to residents' health and well-being, it is often best to choose a home that is close to relatives and important others. Regular visits from concerned family members and friends may help to ensure better care from the staff. However, proximity may be less important than quality of care. If you cannot find a quality nursing home in your area, you may wish to consider the advantage of using a better home that is farther away.

Tour the Facilities on Your List

The best way to gauge the quality of care and the environment in a nursing home is to tour it yourself, asking questions of all key staff members — the administrator or assistant administrator, the director of nursing, the food service manager and/or dietitian, the social worker, activity director, nurses, and nurse's assistants. Your local ombudsman or nursing home advocacy organization can usually give you a list of questions to ask while touring the facility or tell you what to look for. When you visit, bring your checklist and a notepad to record responses to your questions. Keen observation, interviews with residents, and a review of the facility's inspection report(s) (also called surveys) are key to understanding what life in a particular nursing home might be like.

Never be intimidated by staff members. Nursing homes are businesses, dependent on your money and/or insurance, whether public or private, to stay afloat. Staff members may tell you what you want to hear, but it is your job to look beyond pat responses to your questions. Stay away from nursing homes where staff members appear hesitant or actually resistant to your requests for information.

If you're looking for care for someone else, ask yourself, "Is this where I would like to live? Would I be happy here?" Try to empathize with your loved one as he or she is about to make the transition and keep your loved one's likes, dislikes, and specific medical needs at the fore of your thinking.

If you cannot visit yourself, ask a trusted relative or friend to visit for you. You can either schedule an appointment to tour the facility — in which case you may be shown only those features of the home that the administrator wants you to see — or arrive unannounced. Regardless of the way in which you first see the facility, you should visit any nursing home that you are considering at least twice. Choose different times of the day, such as mid-morning and evening. Visit during the work week and on weekends, when fewer staff members are likely to be on duty.

A Wealth of Information: The Inspection Report

Under current federal law, nursing homes are required to make available to the public a copy of their most recent standard survey (also called inspection report). Standard surveys must be conducted at least every twelve to fifteen months by a multidisciplinary team, including a registered nurse, from the state licensing certification agency. If you have any time at all, read the survey. You may need an ombudsman's help to interpret some of the findings, but they can tell you a lot about the quality of care provided by the home. Because it's unlikely that you will find a nursing home without any deficiencies, look at both the number and seriousness of the home's problems, paying attention to problems that affect residents' well-being, such as incidents involving nursing and personal care. The quality of care in a nursing home can change quickly. Thus, it's a good idea to review past surveys. Although a facility's unwillingness to make the recent survey available to you is probably a sign that it isn't very proud of its record, if the survey isn't posted and the administrator will not share the information with you, contact the state or local ombudsman or state licensing and certification agency. Ask the ombudsman for the telephone number of the licensing and certification agency or contact the state Department of Health for information. In some places, the survey is available in public libraries.

Chemical and Physical Restraints

Under federal law, nursing home residents have a right to be free from physical restraints or chemical restraints (drugs) that are used for the convenience of the staff or to discipline or punish a resident and not for the purpose of treating medical conditions. Restraints may only be used upon a

One of the most important questions to ask a facility concerns the length of time that your bed will be held if you must leave the home for medical reasons or if you simply want to visit family and friends. If you are paying privately, you should be able to keep your room as long as you continue paying. State regulations determine how long Medicaid recipients can expect to have their beds held. When a resident's leave exceeds the bed-hold time, the nursing home may fill her bed, but Medicaid recipients are entitled to a semiprivate room as soon as one becomes available.

At present, there are also protections against involuntary discharge. If you have any questions or receive a notice of involuntary discharge, contact your local or state ombudsman. Under federal law, nursing homes that are certified for participation in Medicare or Medicaid may not evict or transfer you unless

- it is necessary for your welfare and your welfare cannot be met in the nursing home
- your health has improved sufficiently so that you no longer need the services provided in the nursing home
- the health or safety of others in the nursing home would otherwise be endangered
- you have failed to pay (or have benefits paid) for nursing home care after reasonable and appropriate notice
- the nursing home closes

You must be given advance notice of the proposed transfer or discharge and the notice must include instructions on how to appeal. An appeal should be undertaken immediately.

You have a right under federal law to refuse transfer from a part of the nursing home that is a skilled nursing facility to another part of the home that isn't a skilled nursing area.

doctor's written orders and a resident's (or a resident's representative's) informed consent or in order to protect the safety of the resident or other residents. You have a right to know the benefits and risks of restraint use, and the alternatives to restraints. When you know the potential consequences of restraints, you will be in a better position to make an informed decision about their use.

There are very few instances when physical or chemical restraints are warranted. Good nursing homes find various ways to address residents' needs without restraints. Certified homes must explore alternative ways of meeting residents' needs before resorting to the use of drugs or physical restraints. Even when restraints are used, facilities must continually look for ways to remove them or decrease their use.

Psychotropic drugs (drugs used to treat symptoms of mental or emotional disorders) may only be given upon a doctor's orders, according to a care plan, and only if an independent consultant reviews the appropriateness of their use at least once a year. Unless clinically contraindicated, the dosage of psychotropic drugs must be gradually reduced or behavior interventions must be employed in their place.

All residents have the right not be subjected to sexual, verbal or mental abuse, involuntary seclusion or corporal punishment.

Advance Directives and Durable Powers of Attorney

Many people fear the loss of control over health care decisions at the end of life and would feel secure knowing that if they cannot voice their wishes, someone they trust will have the right to advocate on their behalf. Using an advance directive, you can make your wishes known to those you trust and provide instructions regarding end-of-life decisions should you become incapacitated. Advocates strongly urge people entering nursing homes to consider medical advance directives because, in truth, the older we get, the more realistic it is that we will face severe medical crises or death. Without an advance directive, the decisions about care at the end of your life may have to be made by family members, doctors, administrators, or even by judges. The person given authority to make health care decisions for you in an advanced directive will also be in a better position to access your medical records and to monitor your care in the nursing home. If you do execute an advance directive, make sure that the nursing home you choose will honor it and all staff members know that it exists.

Durable powers of attorney allow you to designate someone you trust to manage your financial affairs if you can no longer do so. This is also an important document for prospective nursing home residents to consider. Without completion of such a document, conservatorship or guardianship may be the only means to help someone who is no longer competent to handle her own affairs. For more information about advanced directives and durable powers of attorney, see Chapter Ten.

Financial Issues and Services

Once the home is familiar with your needs, ask for a written statement of charges for basic services and for a list of items and services not covered by your payment source. This information should be given to you at admission. If you are a Medicaid recipient, you should not be charged for services already covered by Medicaid. Ask the nursing home administrator and your state or local long-term-care ombudsman for a list of basic services that are covered by Medicare or Medicaid and those that are not.

- Ask for a copy of the contract, the nursing home's refund policy, and any other pertinent documents to study at home.
- The contract should contain a statement of your rights and responsibilities, information about prices for items and services, the nursing home's bed-hold policy, and a statement of whether the facility is Medicare- and Medicaid-certified.
- The contract is legally binding. Before you sign, it is best to have a lawyer review it and/or to ask ombudsmen any questions you have about the contract.
- Be absolutely certain that you understand the contract before you sign. Do not sign any contract that contains blank spaces.

PARTICIPATING IN YOUR CARE PLAN

Under the Nursing Home Reform Act (also called Omnibus Budget Reconciliation Act [OBRA] of 1987), nursing homes receiving Medicaid or Medicare payments must provide services that allow each resident "to attain or maintain the highest practicable physical, mental and psychological well-being." Promptly on admission, but no later than fourteen days afterward, a registered nurse (with appropriate participation of other health professionals) must conduct or coordinate an assessment of your ability to perform activities of daily living, such as walking, speaking, bathing, dressing, and your medical needs. An individualized plan of care describing your medical, nursing, psychological, and social needs must be developed by a team that includes a doctor and registered nurse. The plan should describe your needs and preferences and how the staff will meet them. You, your family, a legal representative, an advocate, or anyone you want can — and should — participate in developing this plan, which should be reviewed every three months and when your physical or mental condition changes significantly. Although the assessment is conducted annually, every three months the resident's progress should be reevaluated and, if necessary, changes can be made to the plan. A physician and members from each department of the nursing home should participate in developing the plan with you.

Be sure to go to the care-planning conference. This is your opportunity to bring up your concerns and questions. For example, you may want to discuss your preferences for certain foods, bathing times, and sleep schedules, and review the plan for any treatments and/or medications that you are receiving. Whatever your concerns are, speak up. If no one knows what your needs are, they cannot possibly be met. Let the staff members know where your strengths are, what you like and don't like, and where you need help. Ask questions if you don't understand the terms used by staff. If you disagree with a recommendation or if you want to discuss alternatives, don't hesitate to say so.

Sometimes the prospect of going to a care-planning meeting can be intimidating. It might help to speak to staff members and others about your concerns prior to the meeting or to ask someone to speak on your behalf, for example, a family member, ombudsman, or other advocate. You should never have to suffer unmet needs in silence.

RESOLVING PROBLEMS IN NURSING HOMES

Your quality of life in a nursing home is dependent on the amount of individualized attention, care, and respect that you receive from staff members. When problems arise, you and your family have a right to expect that your concerns will be addressed appropriately.

Many people fear retaliation if they complain about a problem. Retaliation, while illegal, does happen, especially subtler forms of retaliation. You can't be certain that you won't experience repercussions if you complain, but you can be sure that a problem will continue and even worsen if you don't.

One of the difficulties of living in a nursing home is that you are among many others with varying and often serious needs. Staff members may come and go and may appear quite rushed at times. Thus, approaching a problem requires both tact and firmness.

It is generally best to approach a problem by acting quickly and going through the nursing home's "chain of command" in ascending order. However, when a problem that threatens your health or well-being (or that of your loved one) develops, such as an injury or suspected abuse or neglect, don't waste time. Go to the director of nursing, the administrator, ombudsman program, the licensing agency, and/or in certain life-threatening situations such as abuse, the police. Otherwise,

- Speak to the person involved. This is usually the nurse's aide. You might say something like, "I realize how busy

you are, but when you have a moment, would you mind
_____."

- If you get no results, speak to the charge nurse. This is the person in charge of the nurses on your floor. Or speak to the person in charge of relevant services, for example, the dietitian or activities director.
- If you are unsatisfied, ask to speak to the director of nursing. This is the person who supervises all nurses in the nursing home. Next, go to the assistant administrator or administrator.
- The local long-term-care ombudsman can also help you determine what action to take and can investigate and mediate problems. Nursing homes are required to post the ombudsman's telephone number, but if you can't get it from the home, call the Area Agency on Aging. If there is a nursing home advocacy organization in your state, they may also provide advice.
- The agency that licenses and certifies nursing homes, usually the state Department of Health, should be contacted when other channels fail or when the problem is immediate and serious. You may want to contact your doctor as well.
- As a resident, you can contact the resident's council. Depending on how active the council is in addressing complaints, you may find a solution there. Family members should contact the family council. If there isn't one, form one. Other families may have similar complaints. There is strength in numbers. You and others may want to put your mutual grievances to the administrator, ombudsmen, or licensing agency or take other action.
- If nothing else works or if the problem is severe, you may want to consider contacting a private or legal aid attorney. Whether legal action is warranted and possible will depend on the facts and circumstances surrounding your case, the availability of experienced attorneys willing to take on nursing homes in your area, and your resources.

Nursing home placement is never easy. There are many considerations to resolve before choosing — a task that is difficult to do when a crisis arises. You may wonder if you have done the right thing by moving or facilitating a move to a nursing home. Sometimes there are no clear answers. There are good homes, bad homes, and some that lie in between. You may not know which you have chosen until you

If you have reason to believe that a loved one in a nursing home is being abused, neglected, or otherwise maltreated:

- Take immediate action. In addition to the actions described, you can do the following:
- Document everything. Take photographs. Keep a log of all that is said to you and all that you say to others. Maintain records of all written and telephone correspondence between you and the staff members, administrators, and owners.
- Contact the police and local prosecutor (district or county attorney). Be aware, however, that law enforcement's response to and effectiveness in dealing with elder abuse differs across communities.
- In some states, adult protective services will investigate reports of abuse and neglect in various care facilities. In other states, the licensing and certification agency will investigate. You can call the Area Agency on Aging or the Eldercare Locator or consult the government pages of your local telephone directory for the number. (See the beginning of this chapter for information.)
- You may want to contact Protection and Advocacy Systems for assistance (see Chapter Six) if your loved one has a developmental or mental disability.
- Move your loved one from the home, if possible. Nursing home residents are always free to leave.

(or your loved one) become a resident. Nonetheless, nursing home experiences can be positive. The keys are knowing your rights, speaking up when you have problems, and, for family members, visiting frequently and staying involved by reviewing medical records, talking to staff members, and being unafraid to take action when it's needed.

ELDER ABUSE AND NEGLECT

Elder abuse and neglect can happen anywhere — within hospitals, nursing homes, supportive housing environments, and at home. Institutional staff members, other residents and visitors, hired aides and companions, friends, and even family members can be perpetrators of maltreatment. Abuse and neglect can happen to anyone regardless of gender, ethnicity, race, religious background, educational level, or socioeconomic status.

Some forms of maltreatment can be intentional, while others may be less the result of malice than of other factors such as poor caregiver skills. Although the legal and research definitions of abuse and neglect vary, one may generally think of neglect and abuse in the following ways:

Neglect describes a caregiver's failure to adequately meet the needs of the person receiving care. Examples are failure to feed and provide water to someone, failing to turn someone who is bedfast to prevent pressure sores, not cleaning clothes or bedding, or neglecting to provide a hearing aid, dentures, or eyeglasses to someone who needs them. Many older people suffer from *self-neglect,* an inability or refusal to care for themselves. Self-neglect is a serious and widespread problem.

Psychological or emotional abuse describes the infliction of mental anguish, for example, by yelling or cursing at, ignoring, threatening, isolating, insulting, or verbally humiliating an older person or treating an adult like a child.

Financial abuse involves the misuse of an older person's income, resources, and property, such as stealing Social Security checks or forcing someone to alter a will, a durable power of attorney, or other financial instrument.

Physical abuse is any nonaccidental use of physical force that results in bodily injury, pain, or impairment.[8] Pinching, hitting, cutting, burning, kicking, striking with objects, overmedicating, force-feeding, and physically restraining someone inappropriately are all acts of physical abuse. Sexual abuse is any form of nonconsensual sexual conduct.

It is often very difficult to detect abuse and/or neglect, especially if an older person is unable to communicate his or her distress. Yet there are signs that may indicate abuse or neglect or the existence of other problems warranting further investigation. The following section lists possible physical and behavioral indicators of abuse or neglect.

Indicators of physical abuse

- bruises, especially a combination of old and new bruises
- burns
- other injuries; and
- explanations given for injuries that don't make sense

Physical indicators of neglect

- malnourishment and/or dehydration
- injuries that haven't been addressed
- bedsores
- signs that a person hasn't been bathed or groomed, such as odor or matted hair
- dirty clothing and soiled bedding
- lost or missing medications, eyeglasses, and/or dentures

Physical indicators of sexual abuse

- recurring vaginal or urinary tract infections
- vaginal or rectal bleeding

Physical indicators of financial abuse

- sudden poverty or inability to pay for basic necessities
- missing valuables
- lack of knowledge or confusion about finances

Behavioral indicators of abuse and neglect include:

- depression
- anxiety
- withdrawal
- sluggishness
- unresponsiveness
- confusion
- hostility or agitation
- fearfulness
- isolation

Again, not every sign or condition described above is an unequivocal indicator of abuse or neglect, but if you recognize these indicators in someone you care about, it's important to try to discover the cause with appropriate professional assistance. The following sections will provide you with more information.

Caregivers Can Become Abusive or Neglectful

Caring for an older person with multiple or serious needs is one of the most difficult, demanding jobs that anyone can do. The relentless work, stress, frustration, and isolation ripen the potential for abuse and neglect even when a caregiver has the very best of intentions. For example, a caregiver can become so tired or overwhelmed that she puts off bathing her loved one or changing her loved one's clothes, or stops performing these tasks altogether. A caregiver may begin to use physical force against someone who wanders or who becomes unruly or abusive. Lack of proper training or skills in caregiving can lead to situations that are dangerous for both the caregiver and the person receiving care. Some caregivers are so ill or fragile themselves that completing everyday tasks becomes an agonizing impossibility.

This chapter discusses a variety of ways in which caregivers who are under stress can find some relief. Adult daycare, respite care, Friendly Visitors, homemakers, companions and home health aides, support groups, family, friends, and neighbors can all provide different types of help. If you are a caregiver, you *must* seek out this assistance. No one can care for another person alone. All people need rest, time for relaxation, and interaction with others. Sadly, many caregivers, who sacrifice a good part of their lives to help others, feel guilty about asking for help themselves. Asking for outside assistance is not an admission of failure. It is a sign that a caregiver is informed and conscientious. No caregiver whose heart is in the right place ever fails, *except* perhaps when she ignores the risks for abuse and neglect. Trying to do it all can put everybody in jeopardy. You may have to persist to find it, but help is available. Make certain that family, friends, relatives, neighbors, members of your place of worship, and others know that you need assistance.

If You Are Being Abused or Neglected
by Someone Close to You

If you are being abused, neglected, or exploited by someone you know, you must believe that it is not your fault and that you do not deserve to be maltreated. No one should have to tolerate behavior that demeans or imperils one's life and dignity. Shame and embarrassment prevent many people who suffer abuse, neglect, or exploitation from reporting it. This is especially true when the person responsible is the victim's own child and when the child has serious life problems, such as alcohol or other drug abuse problems. Many people live in constant fear or in unbearable conditions because they are uncertain of how intervention will affect them or their family members. These are real concerns, and there are no easy answers. But one thing is certain: abuse or neglect that is left unchecked will continue and worsen. The result could be fatal. The following sections will discuss the types of assistance available and help you decide what to do if you are being maltreated.

Older Women and Domestic Violence

If you are being abused by your husband or partner, a women's shelter or other domestic violence advocacy organization can help. Chapter Four offers a full discussion of domestic violence and resources for assistance. As mentioned in that chapter, older women and women with disabilities of all ages who are being abused face more difficulty in getting help than other women. One of the most frustrating problems concerns the overlap and gaps in the laws against elder and adult abuse and the laws against domestic violence. Depending on state law and other factors, an older woman or a woman with a disability who is being abused by a partner or husband may be referred to adult protective services (APS). This may be especially true if her partner or husband is caring for her. Thus, you may benefit by reading the section on adult protective services below as well as the section titled Domestic Violence in Chapter Four. Although there is room for improvement in the coordination of agency efforts, women's shelters, adult protective services, and family service agencies such as Jewish Family and Children's Services or Catholic Charities or other religious-based and secular agencies may all be able to help you or refer you to an agency that can. Do not give up hope. Keep looking for help. If you persist, you will find someone who can assist you. There is no excuse for domestic violence. You do not deserve to be hurt.

ADULT PROTECTIVE SERVICES

Adult protective services agencies were established to respond to the needs of adults who are being abused and/or neglected (or self-neglected) in their homes, and in some states, in institutions.

The scope and language of the laws protecting older people from abuse and neglect differ greatly from area to area. Therefore, it is difficult to generalize about who can be helped by the APS system and under what circumstances. In most states, adult protective services workers act on behalf of vulnerable older people and other adults who are dependent on another person or who may be vulnerable to abuse and neglect due to a physical or mental disability. Depending on state law, people over eighteen, sixty, or sixty-five may be served by the agency. Most, but not all, states require that certain people, usually health care workers, social workers, and law enforcement personnel, report suspected cases of elder abuse and neglect.

Depending on state law, the nature of the abuse and/or neglect, where it took place, and who allegedly committed it, the local or state APS and/or law enforcement agency will investigate once a report is made. There may be a different protocol for investigating complaints in nursing homes or other care facilities.

Once a report is made, most state laws require the APS agency to respond immediately or within a specified number of hours or days, depending on the nature and severity of the alleged maltreatment. If you are calling APS to make a report, it's important to know that the agency may visit the alleged victim of maltreatment with or without contacting her first. Although client safety is a priority for APS workers, state laws differ and, as with other incidents of family violence, the possibility of retaliation exists for someone who is being intentionally hurt by another. The way in which each agency goes about investigating a case of suspected abuse and/or neglect differs, but typically agencies will interview the alleged victim and perpetrator and talk to any witnesses. If abuse or neglect is substantiated, which can take some time, the agency can offer either the victim or caregiver a variety of health, social, and legal services, either directly or through other community agencies. Depending on the situation and resources available, the agency may be able to provide emergency food and water, mental and physical health assessments, home health aide/housekeeping services, counseling, adult daycare, transportation, emergency shelter, help with financial management, and legal assistance. APS may take action to remove an abusive person from the home if she or he is not the owner. APS can also help victims obtain emergency orders of protection.

Unfortunately, because of a lack of funding, some in-home resources are difficult to gain access to in some areas. There may be waiting lists, just as there are for services requested directly from the Area Agency on Aging. (See the beginning of this chapter.) Understaffing and high caseloads also arise from lack of funding. APS caseworkers must often extend their efforts over scores of cases.

Many people hesitate to call APS because of fears that they will be taken to a nursing home. Although nursing care, when properly delivered, can certainly be superior to a future of abuse and neglect, most state laws require that the agency seek the least restrictive remedies available, and competent adults have the right to refuse services. However, many states have procedures that allow for intervention without an individual's consent when it is felt that an emergency exists and/or when a court has deemed someone incapable of decision-making. APS may petition the court for guardianship or conservatorship, and in some cases, a person who is declared incapacitated by a court of law may be placed in a nursing home, an alternative living facility, or group living situation, but these actions are usually taken only as a last resort and in very dire circumstances.

WHAT TO DO IF YOU ARE BEING HURT OR SUSPECT THAT AN OLDER PERSON IS BEING ABUSED OR NEGLECTED

If you are being hurt or you suspect that an older person is being abused or neglected, call the police or the adult protective services agency, which may be housed in the Department of Social or Human Services, a law enforcement agency, the state unit on aging, the Area Agency on Aging, or other government offices. The best place to start is with your Area Agency on Aging. The agency will either refer you to APS or take your report, if it is designated to do so. Many states have twenty-four-hour toll-free elder abuse and neglect hotlines on which confidential reports can be made. You can call your directory assistance operator or look in the front section of your local telephone directory under Community Services, Human Services, or another similar heading for information.

Abuse and Neglect Flourish in Isolation

To avoid undetected abuse or neglect, try to maintain as much contact with other people as you can. Intentional abuse or neglect is a choice. Abusers count on an older person's isolation and sometimes loneliness in order to exploit and control. Keep in contact with relatives, friends, neighbors, your clergyperson, members of your place of worship, or others. If you are being abused or neglected, don't keep it to yourself. Tell someone what is happening to you. If you're feeling isolated or if you live at a distance from family and friends, try to get involved with a program like Meals on Wheels or Friendly Visitors so that someone will make regular contact with you and can report abuse if they know about it or suspect it. If you are a family member, keep in touch with your loved one by visiting or calling as often as possible. Relatives who live far away might arrange for a trusted neighbor or geriatric care manager (see the box titled Geriatric Care Managers on page 436) to keep an eye on a loved one who has few social contacts.

✤ 10 ✤

Death and Dying

WHAT'S IN THIS CHAPTER?

Nothing can ever prepare one for death. No amount of information can assuage what is for each individual an intensely personal, deeply painful experience. However, this chapter may serve to answer a few questions you have about practical matters and point you in the direction of individuals and organizations that may be of assistance to you and your family.

- Support for People Who Are Terminally Ill and Their Families
- Putting Paperwork in Order
- Wills and Property
- A Letter of Instruction
- Durable Power of Attorney
- Planning for Your Children's Future: Guardianships and Adoption
- Advance Directives
- Pain Control
- Hospices
- After the Death of a Loved One
- Making Funeral Arrangements
- After the Funeral: Important Things to Do
- Grief and Mourning

SUPPORT FOR PEOPLE WHO ARE TERMINALLY ILL AND THEIR FAMILIES

Every person, every family, is unique. Your response to a life-threatening or terminal diagnosis and your needs will be different from those of any other. But you and your family need not be isolated from sources of assistance. In the coming days, you may want to explore resources to help you or your family members cope with some of the emotional challenges and practical problems a diagnosis of a very serious illness can present. Here are some ideas:

Support groups. There are support groups throughout the country for individuals and families coping with terminal illness. Intense, overwhelming feelings of fear, anger, sorrow and depression, frustration, guilt, and other natural but difficult reactions can be discussed with others with similar experiences in a nonjudgmental environment. Talking to others can be a way out of isolation and of enhancing your ability to cope with problems and conflicts that sometimes arise between family members during stressful times. Group members often exchange referrals to home health care, hospice, and other services, and discuss issues related to medical care, insurance, finances, and resources for assistance. Virtually every concern regarding serious illness can be discussed in a support group.

Many people hesitate to join a support group. You may wonder what a group can really offer you. Before going to a group, talk to the facilitator to get a sense of how the group works, if it is right for you, and whether you are a good candidate for it. You may want to attend once or twice before making a decision about continuing. Many groups are informal and don't require that you make a commitment to participate. Talking is not always easy. You may just want to listen at first. If you are not comfortable in a group setting or need more time and attention than a group affords, you may want to consider other ways of getting the support you need, such as counseling or therapy.

The Candlelighters Childhood Cancer Foundation and the Leukemia Society of America are examples of national organizations serving individuals and families through local support groups. Groups for caregivers may also be beneficial. You'll find the addresses and telephone numbers of these and other national groups in relevant chapters of the Resource Directory. If there you don't find an organization that meets your needs, contact the self-help clearinghouses listed at the front of the Resource Directory. Hospital social workers and discharge planners and your doctor may also be able to direct you to a support group that meets in or outside the hospital. AIDS service organizations, discussed in Chapter Eight, frequently offer groups for individuals, spouses, and partners and other family members or provide referrals to peer support groups.

Counseling or therapy. Often, the most meaningful support can come from someone who is willing to listen or just be with you. Friends and family often provide this close connection and empathic listening. But those who care the most may also be struggling with their response to terminal illness and may not be able to help. A therapist or counselor trained and experienced in assisting people with terminal or life-threatening illnesses and their families can offer a listening ear and address specific issues and feelings including fear, anxiety, shame, anger, guilt, and depression, concerns about body image, sexuality, role changes in the family, family conflict, and the need many people have to review life events and to resolve past regrets. Not every therapist, counselor, or clergyperson is equipped to help people in this way. That's why it's important to look for someone with appropriate training and experience. Your hospital social worker, discharge planner, or doctor may be able to refer you to a professional who works inside or outside of the hospital. Hospices may also offer professional services or contract with other organizations to provide counseling or therapy. You may find services available to families, couples, groups, or individuals. With any counseling or therapy referral — whether from family, friends, social workers, or a helping organization — you must assess the value of the services provided by your therapist or counselor.

Practical matters. You may have questions about insurance

and legal assistance. Insurance counseling programs that provide information about Medicare, Medicaid, Medicare supplemental insurance (Medigap), and long-term-care insurance policies are available free of charge to older people in many states. Area Agencies on Aging can direct you to these and other services for seniors. (See Chapter Nine.) Local organizations, such as AIDS service organizations, support groups, legal aid organizations, and places of worship will help you locate resources for practical assistance. The National Coalition for Cancer Survivorship, the Candlelighters Childhood Cancer Foundation Ombudsman Program, and the American Cancer Society can provide cancer patients and their families with information about insurance.

Financial help. Astronomical medical bills and the reduced ability to work leave many people with serious or terminal illnesses in dire financial circumstances. Accelerated life insurance benefit payments and viatical settlements are two options that may be available to help people who are terminally ill gain access to greater resources. Accelerated benefits offered by a number of insurance companies allow people with life insurance policies and limited life expectancies (usually six months to a year) to immediately receive a certain percentage of their benefits. With viatical settlements, an individual sells her life insurance policy at a discount to a viatical settlement company. The latter option has raised serious questions about the potential for abuse in an industry that is still largely unregulated. Some viatical settlement companies have gone bankrupt. Both options have disadvantages, including the possibility of leaving fewer resources for your beneficiaries. It is wise to do as much research as possible on all available options and to call your state department of insurance for more information. Check the government listings of your local telephone directory.

Limited financial assistance may also be available for eligible people through local support and advocacy organizations, such as the Alzheimer's Association or the American Cancer Society, as well as through AIDS service organizations. Sometimes professional societies make emergency grants or loans available to members who are ill or in crisis. Charitable foundations may offer small grants for the same purpose. Hospital and other social workers may be able to help you find sources of financial help. If one person or agency can't help you, ask for a referral to someone else who can.

Searching for resources can be a time-consuming, frustrating job. If you are feeling overwhelmed, ask assertive friends or relatives to help you research answers to your practical questions. Remember that friends and relatives can be good sources of direct assistance themselves and may be able to provide loans or gifts as well as recommend professionals who can assist you.

Reading resources. A number of authors have described their own emotional, psychological, physical, and spiritual challenges and articulated their thoughts on coping with some of the practical realities of terminal illness. The reading resource list at the end of the book offers some suggestions. Friends, support group members, therapists, and others may have good suggestions as well.

PUTTING PAPERWORK IN ORDER

There is no easy way to talk about practical matters concerning death. To some people with a life-threatening or terminal condition, discussion of such matters may seem an indication of lost hope and submission. But taking care of practical matters, like writing a will or an advance directive, does not mean giving up. In truth, every adult should have these documents prepared, most particularly people with children and those who want to leave property to an unmarried partner or friend. Putting paperwork in order can help alleviate worries about your family's future or your medical care. It's important to do this work as soon as possible, because some illnesses may lead to a period of incompetency when you (or your relative or friend) will no longer be able to participate in vital decision-making processes. The following can be done by you, your husband or partner, a close friend or relative, or another person whom you trust.

Create a File for Important Documents

Before you get started, it will be helpful to take an inventory of all that you own (your assets) and owe (your liabilities), and gather vital documents. A file for assets and liabilities can include: information about and documentation of real estate (such as a copy of the deed to your home), bank accounts, retirement accounts, insurance policies, stocks, bonds, pensions, motor vehicles, furniture, valuables, and debts such as mortgages. Vital personal documents to collect may include your marriage certificate, divorce papers, family birth certificates, including children's birth certificates, military discharge papers, citizen certification, recent tax returns, and any advance directive that you have completed. Once you have completed this task:

- It will be easier to think concretely about how you want your property to be distributed and what devices you may need to simplify the process.
- You will be in a better position to do some realistic budgeting and planning.
- Your executor and survivors will be spared the emotionally taxing, stressful job of trying to locate documents needed to probate your will and/or conduct other transactions after death.

If you don't have an original copy of your marriage, birth, or divorce papers, you can write the U.S. Government Printing Office, Superintendent of Documents, Mail Stop, SSOP, Washington, D.C. 20402-9328 for a copy of *Where to Write for Vital Records,* which lists the addresses of government offices where you can obtain these documents. One can usually locate them at the state Department of Vital Records or Vital Statistics.

Make sure that you keep originals or copies of these documents in a safe place, such as a fireproof box. In some states, safe-deposit boxes are sealed at death until the contents can be examined by a tax official. Thus, access to important documents may be delayed. Before storing important papers in your safe-deposit box, ask the bank manager about the necessary procedure to open a safe-deposit box after death. Let at least one person know where you have placed your collection of documents.

WILLS AND PROPERTY

There are two major reasons why people create a will: to appoint a guardian for their children and to distribute their property. If you should die intestate (without a will), your estate (all that you are entitled to transfer to others, including your home, bank accounts, and personal belongings) will be distributed among your heirs according to state law. The result may conflict with your wishes. For example, if you are in an unmarried relationship and have no children, your property will be given to relatives, such as parents and siblings, unless you have made a will or taken other measures to ensure that your property will go to your partner. Even if you are married, it's likely that you'll want more control over the distribution of your property than state law allows. If you have no relatives, or none that can be found, your property will go to the state if you die without a will.

You may have written a will some time ago, in which case it would be wise to review and update it, if necessary. Your life and family composition may have changed significantly over the years.

What You Will Need to Write Your Will

Depending on how you plan to distribute your property, you (or a family member or friend) may want to inventory all that you own, if you have not done so already. You will also need:

- the full names, addresses, and telephone numbers of the people you want to name as beneficiaries (those who will inherit through your will) and the person you've nominated as personal guardian for your children
- the full name, address, and telephone number of the person you choose to be your *executor* or *executrix* (also called personal representative in some states). This is the person who will manage your estate from the time of your death until all the assets have been distributed and debts and taxes have been paid. If you die without a will, an administrator will be appointed by the probate court to perform the same duties.

You may appoint almost any adult you wish to act as your executor, including a beneficiary. It's not necessary that your executor have legal expertise — she or he can hire an attorney to oversee the settling of your estate — but it's essential to choose someone who is organized, intelligent about financial matters, and completely trustworthy. You can also appoint two people to serve as coexecutors. A trust department of a bank or other financial institution may be elected, but institutions are not as likely to be as concerned about fairness to your beneficiaries as someone who knows your family. Financial institutions also charge fees for their services. (An executor may be given a fee as well, though he normally waives this privilege. His expenses, such as for attorney's fees, are normally paid by the estate.) Of course, it's crucial that you ask the person whom you wish to appoint whether he or she is willing and able to do the job. You must also name a successor in case your first choice becomes unavailable. It's best to choose someone who lives in the same state as you do, because it will be easier for him to perform his duties and, in some states, out-of-state executors are required to post a bond.

Your Will Must Be Typed, Signed, and Witnessed

Generally only a will that is typed, signed, and witnessed will be recognized as valid. Handwritten wills (called holographic wills) are not valid in many states and are not recommended because probate courts are disinclined to view them as legitimate. Most state laws require at least two competent adults to witness a will, and some require three. Beneficiaries should not be asked to sign as witnesses, and generally you and the witnesses must sign and date the will in each other's presence. Witnesses should be easy to locate in case they are needed to appear in probate court, although many states provide procedures for "self-proving" wills, which makes court appearances unnecessary.

Do You Need an Attorney to Make a Will?

It is possible to write a valid will without the help of an attorney. However, a professionally drafted will is most likely to produce the results that you really want. Working with an attorney to plan your estate is critical when you want to create a trust, when you have a child with a disability who will need assistance through adulthood, when you want to try to protect your assets from being depleted by expensive medical bills, and in many other instances. A private attorney or a legal aid organization can provide the services you need. There are also many books and software programs on the market to help consumers prepare their wills. Reading such books, allowing that they are current editions, can help you understand the various issues connected to estate planning and help you get the most out of your lawyer's services.

Where to Put Your Will

The original will must be kept in a safe place. If it is lost or destroyed, the court may presume that the destruction was intentional and that the copies are invalid. Be careful about keeping your will in a safe-deposit box. In some states, safe-deposit boxes, even when held in joint tenancy, may be sealed after death, thus delaying access to the important documents inside. Ask your bank manager for information about laws and procedures in your state. As a matter of practice, many attorneys who draft wills keep the originals in their offices hoping to probate the estate. A lawyer's office can be a secure place, but an awkward situation can arise if your executor does not intend to hire the attorney who drafted your will to probate the estate, which he is under no obligation to do. The will may be retrieved from the lawyer and another attorney may be sought, if desired. Another possibility is to keep the will at home in a fireproof safe or box. Wherever you decide to keep your will — in a safe place at your home or office or your lawyer's office — make sure that your executor knows where it is and how to get it. Your executor (and beneficiaries, if you like) should have an unsigned copy of the will — one that is clearly stamped "copy."

Changing Your Will

It's recommended that you review and revise your will when life circumstances change. Marriage, divorce, the birth or death of a beneficiary, major financial changes, and a move out of state are examples of changes that necessitate a will review. You can change your will by adding a codicil (an amendment) or by writing a new will with your attorney. Never type over or write in changes on your current will. A codicil must be typewritten, signed, dated, and witnessed just like the original. If you have many changes to make, it may be easier to write a new will. Be sure that the new will states that you revoke all past wills. Destroy the old will, including any copies, and ask anyone to whom you have given a copy to destroy their old copy.

What Is Probate?

Probate is the name of the legal process through which a will is proven to be valid, the estate is inventoried, debts and taxes are paid, and property is distributed to beneficiaries. Most states have created simplified procedures for handling small estates. To find out what conditions may qualify your estate for simplified procedures, contact your county probate (or surrogate's) court. For estates too large to qualify, the probate process can take many months or even years if there are complications. Information about what you own and to whom it is bequeathed becomes a matter of public record and beneficiaries' access to their inheritances can be significantly delayed.

Most people have more property than they realize, especially if they own a home and a life insurance policy. That's why it's a good idea to take a look at your assets and liabilities and to think about whether or not probate avoidance techniques will serve your needs. There are a few instances, however, in which probate is advantageous, for example, when there are many creditors with claims against the estate. However, a decision to utilize or avoid probate should only be made between you and your professional adviser. For example, you must carefully compare the cost of preparing, funding, and managing a trust to the cost of probate before making any decisions. Generally speaking, probate avoidance techniques such as the following do not do away with the need for a will, which disposes of assets not covered by these methods and of property acquired after death.

If you die without a will, the probate court must still oversee the distribution of your property according to the intestacy laws of your state. This process can be more time-consuming and costly to your beneficiaries than if you had written a will.

AVOIDING PROBATE: OTHER WAYS TO GIVE PROPERTY TO YOUR LOVED ONES

To avoid probate and to give your beneficiaries faster access to money that may be needed to live on and pay funeral expenses, you may want to consider some probate avoidance techniques. These techniques may also be useful if you think someone might contest your will, as may happen when you want to leave property to a nonrelative, such as a life partner or friend. Examples of probate avoidance techniques include a *revocable living trust* (also called an inter vivos trust), pay-on-death bank accounts, and property held in joint tenancy with right of survivorship. Life insurance policies and retirement and other benefits with named beneficiaries are also payable on death and not subject to probate.

Currently, you are allowed to give away as much as $10,000 to any individual or organization annually without incurring a federal gift tax. Couples can give as much as $20,000 per person or institution each year. But, as a precaution, find out whether your state levies a gift tax. Consult your financial adviser or attorney for information on other tax-exempt forms of gift-giving. When considering making major gifts, especially those of appreciated property such as a home or stocks, or giving a gift over the annual tax exempt limit, it's important to discuss all the tax consequences with your accountant or attorney before taking action. Likewise, discuss the consequences of making major gifts if you should later apply for Medicaid. The gift may violate laws concerning the Medicaid program and also make you ineligible for Medicaid for a period of time.

Revocable living trusts and other probate avoidance techniques can reduce the size of your probate estate, but will not save income or estate taxes. Also, keep in mind that techniques like living trusts are not for everyone. For example, if you have very few assets, you probably have little need for an instrument that involves some cost and time to create. Again, it's important to find out how a living trust will affect your eligibility for Medicaid, if you apply, and whether your state will place a lien on your trust after you die to recover expenses paid by Medicaid.

Leaving Money to Children

Many people leave property to their spouses with the expectation that their minor children (children under eighteen or twenty-one, depending on state law) will be provided for and that the estate will pass to their children when their spouse dies. However, you can also leave money outright to a child, appointing a guardian to manage the inheritance for a minor child, establish a trust for your children, or use the Uniform Transfer to Minors Act (if available in your state) to appoint a custodian who will usually be permitted to act without court supervision.[1] Leaving property to minors can be complicated and involve various tax considerations. Careful planning with the help of a lawyer is advised when substantial property is involved.

If you have a child with a disability who will need government assistance throughout his or her childhood and into adulthood, expert advice is imperative. Receipt of an inheritance can disqualify a child for certain government benefits, such as Supplementary Security Income and Medicaid or other government programs and services. A special needs trust is one possible solution to this problem. This trust, which cannot be established in the name of the child with a disability but only in another's name, allows for payment of necessities to supplement those provided by government benefits. If after examining your options, you decide to establish a special needs trust, you will need the services of a lawyer who specializes in this field. You may also want to contact the National Information Center for Children and Youth with Disabilities or other groups serving parents of children with disabilities, listed in the Resource Directory under Disabilities, for more information about estate planning options.

A Letter of Instruction

A letter of instruction, which can be done in your handwriting, summarizes all the information your executor and survivors will need to have in the event of your death. The necessity of such a letter, which saves survivors many hours of searching for vital information, cannot be overemphasized. If you have already gathered such information, this letter should be fairly easy to create. A close friend or relative can also help you write this letter. It should include:

- complete personal data including your full legal name, address, Social Security number, date and place of birth, your father's name and mother's maiden name, their birthplaces, your occupation and place of employment, veteran status, marital status, and educational degrees. Indicate the location of documents that can be used to verify this information.
- all your assets and liabilities. List the names, addresses, and telephone numbers of the institutions/individuals holding your assets. You may have personal belongings not mentioned in your will that you wish to pass along to certain people in your family and circle of friends. Putting this information in a letter of instruction can reduce the possibility of arguments, which can occur between grieving relatives when you least expect it. It's important, however, to make sure that these designations do not conflict with any designations made in your will.
- debts owed and debts to be paid. List the names, addresses, and telephone numbers of those who owe you money or those to whom you are indebted.
- location of your original will
- the names, addresses, and telephone numbers of your lawyer and other professionals, such as your tax attorney or accountant, life insurance agent, and clergyperson
- the location of other important papers
- the location of your safe-deposit box and keys
- the names of people to be notified immediately after your death
- description of any funeral plans that you have made and instructions for carrying them out. Include the name of anyone given authority to make your funeral arrangements, especially if not your next of kin. This designation must be in writing — if not, your next of kin will have authority to make the arrangements.

Your letter of instruction should be dated and copies should be made and distributed to those who will need them, such as your executor and beneficiaries. Updates can be made as needed. Your personal copy of this letter should be kept in a safe, accessible place.

Many people provide instructions for their funeral and/or memorial service in a letter of instruction. Planning ahead can be a loving service to grieving family members who, in their pain, are seldom in the frame of mind to make considered decisions. For example, a family member who doesn't know that you prefer a simple burial and committal service with a few close friends in attendance may be pressured to prepare an elaborate and expensive funeral by relatives or by a funeral director. On the other hand, you and your family may want to celebrate your life with a traditional funeral in the company of many mourners. These choices are clearly personal. There is no right or wrong decision. But bitter conflict can arise between family members when no instructions are left. Preplanning does not necessarily entail prepayment, which can be risky and is generally discouraged by consumer advocates. If you want to leave money for your funeral (and/or memorial) service, you can do this by setting up a special bank account or trust specifically for this purpose.

You may not want to be detailed about your funeral plans, or you may want to choose music, a poem or passage to be read, or design other features of a celebration that will serve as a true reflection of your life and values. You may also want to ask a particular clergyperson or speaker to preside over your services. The section titled Making Funeral Arrangements on page 497 gives an idea of some of the practical considerations involved. You or a family member may even want to compare prices for funeral items now so that your family will not be vulnerable to consumer abuses later. Even if you do not want to think about the way in which you would like to be put to rest, you may feel very strongly about what you don't want. Your family will be grateful to know this much.

DURABLE POWER OF ATTORNEY

A durable power of attorney is a document that allows you to appoint someone to manage your affairs if you should become incapable of doing so because of illness or incapacitation. The person you appoint, referred to as your "attorney in fact" or "agent," can be given very narrow authority over your financial or legal affairs, for example, the authority to utilize a certain bank account or to collect your Social Security check. She can also be given authority in wide scope. Normally, a durable power of attorney becomes effective on signing and will continue in force after you become incapacitated. (Thus the term "durable.") However, many states allow for "springing" or "standby" durable powers of attorney that become effective only upon your incapacity.

You can appoint more than one person to act as your agent. You may designate your agents to act independently or to act together, in which case they must agree on how to handle your affairs. More important, you should name one person to act as attorney in fact and another to serve if the first person becomes unavailable. People often appoint the successor to a trust that they have set up to act as their attorney in fact. This allows their agent to handle income outside the trust in addition to property within. You can revoke the durable power of attorney as long as you are competent by destroying it and providing written notification to your agent(s) and any institutions using it. The durable power of attorney terminates at death.

For someone who is still competent, a durable power of attorney is preferable to a conservatorship or guardianship, because these appointments must be made through a court process that is often expensive and time-consuming and, depending on the type of guardianship chosen, can result in a significant loss of autonomy. In any event, you must be very certain that the person you appoint as your attorney in fact or agent is someone whom you trust absolutely and who is capable of making prudent decisions in the areas that you have specified. Although you don't necessarily need a lawyer to create a durable power of attorney, consulting an attorney is wise, particularly when you plan to give your agent broad powers. A lawyer can explain your various options and can draft the document using language required by state law.

Planning for your children's future: guardianship and adoption

Normally, your child's father will have sole custody of your child should you die. But many women must look to other options to ensure their children's future security. Some options may be useful to you and your children when you are sick or in the hospital for a long period of time; others will help you plan for the future. It may be deeply painful to think about asking someone else to care for your children. Yet knowing that your children will be cared for by someone you trust may bring you a sense of relief. Hospice social workers, AIDS service organizations, legal aid organizations, adoption agencies, and private attorneys may help you to determine what types of arrangements will be best suited to your needs now and in the future, and can help you make plans. Here are some possible options:

Kinship foster care. This arrangement allows a relative to act as foster caregiver and receive payments to help care for your children. Relatives selected as foster caregivers must be approved by the appropriate government agency.

Guardianship. You can petition the court (usually family, probate, or surrogate's court) to appoint a guardian for your child while you are living. A guardian has the legal right and responsibility to care for your children until adulthood. Although the guardian you select will have the right to make important decisions for your child, for example, decisions regarding medical treatment, you and the person you've chosen can agree that you will continue living with your children and acting as parent in other ways. If you want to name someone other than your child's natural father as guardian, be sure to get professional advice, because the father may have a right to object and request custody. Of course, you must also make certain that the person you propose as guardian is willing to act in that capacity and is able to care for your children. Listed here are some alternatives.

- *Propose a personal guardian* for your children in your will. However, a judge must approve the person you've nominated, taking your children's best interests into consideration, guardianship may not take effect until letters of guardianship have been issued. Unless the person selected is obviously unfit, a judge will usually approve your choice of guardian. Again, professional advice is needed if you plan to name someone other than a relative or the children's father. All parents, whether divorced or separated, regardless of their life circumstances, should take the time to propose a guardian in whom they both trust to look after their children in the event of their simultaneous deaths.
- *Standby guardianships.* A few states allow parents to appoint guardians for their children to act as soon as they become incapacitated or die but not before.
- *Adoption* is a way to give your child a permanent placement with caregivers. Adoption is a very serious and difficult step, as both parents' rights to care for their children must be terminated or relinquished so that they can be given to the adoptive parents. Adoptive parents may be relatives or strangers, but the adoption must always be court-approved.

- *Voluntary foster care placement.* Sometimes parents have no choice but to place their children in foster care for a limited time. This alternative has some distinct disadvantages, however. When children are placed in foster care they become wards of the state, and parents have little control over their care. There is a risk of losing custody if, for example, you cannot maintain contact with your child or if the child protective services agency believes that your child will be harmed upon a return home and petitions the court to keep your child in foster care. It is wise to consult with a lawyer before using this option or the other above options.

MAKING MEDICAL CARE DECISIONS: ADVANCE DIRECTIVES

Many people fear having their lives prolonged by technology and wish to be allowed to die naturally when the time comes. Doctors are trained to prolong life at all costs and, unless presented with clear and convincing evidence of a patient's wishes to the contrary, may initiate measures to sustain a dying person's life. If you do not want doctors to take measures to prolong your life when death is imminent, you must provide evidence of your wishes by specifying instructions for your medical care and/or appointing an agent to act on your behalf should you lose the ability to express your wishes. You can do this by using simple documents generically referred to as "advance directives." Living wills and durable powers of attorney for health care (also called health care proxies) are the most common advance directives. Every state has passed legislation authorizing the use of advance directives, and in many states livings wills and health care proxies are combined in a single document. A few states recognize only the health care proxy or the living will. Despite any limitations imposed by state statutes, everyone has a common-law and constitutional right to refuse unwanted medical treatment.

Refusal of measures to prolong your life (if that is your desire) does not mean giving up other kinds of care. For example, you may decide that you do not want your life prolonged by technology but want measures taken to make you as free of pain and as comfortable as possible. You can specify the type of care you want and do not want in your advance directive.

Advance directives can benefit everyone — patients and families alike. But if you are in an unmarried relationship and want to make certain that your partner will be able to

---

CHOICE IN DYING

1-800-989-WILL
(212) 366-5540

Choice in Dying (formerly Concern for Dying/Society for the Right to Die) is a national not-for-profit organization dedicated to serving the dying and their families. Among other activities and services, the organization advocates for the rights of people to make their own medical decisions at the end of life, answers questions about end-of-life issues, helps health facilities comply with patient wishes and with state and federal laws, offers reasonably priced educational materials to the public, and will send you a copy of your state's advance directive for a small charge. Choice in Dying also offers the pamphlet *Talking About Your Choices,* which can help you and your loved ones talk about advance directives, understand commonly used life-support measures, and learn more about pain management.

(202) 434-2120

The Legal Counsel for the Elderly, sponsored by the American Association of Retired Persons, also offers low-cost self-help planning guides with state-specific advance directive forms. Call the Legal Counsel for the Elderly for an order form or write to the organization at P.O. Box 96474, Washington, D.C., 20090-6474.

visit you in the hospital and make decisions on your behalf, advance directives are crucial. Otherwise, your partner may be excluded from any decision-making process regarding your care, and, depending on the hospital's policies, may not be able to visit you.

A Living Will

A living will is an advance directive that provides instructions to your doctor if you are unable to communicate your wishes, for example, if you are unconscious. In such situations, you may wish to withhold, withdraw, or consent to life-sustaining treatment. Because most states limit the applicability of living wills to certain conditions, such as a terminal condition, permanent unconsciousness, and/or a persistent vegetative state, living wills may not reach conditions such as Alzheimer's disease and stroke, among others. Therefore, you may want to consider completing a durable power of attorney for health care in addition to a living will for the most protection, unless you live in a state where they are already combined. The health care proxy is a more flexible document, allowing for decision-making in any medical situation.

As you contemplate making a living will, it is important to talk to your doctor about the procedures most likely to be used in your situation, what they involve, and what the likely result will be if they are given, withheld, or withdrawn. For introductory information about these issues, contact Choice in Dying or the Legal Counsel for the Elderly, mentioned earlier. You may also want to discuss the religious perspective on the withholding or withdrawing of life-sustaining measures with your clergyperson.

A Durable Power of Attorney for Health Care

Using this document, which is also called a health care proxy, you can appoint someone to make health care decisions for you in the event that you are unable to do so. You should appoint one agent (or proxy) and an alternate to act in case the principal agent cannot serve. Your agent or proxy has no authority to make decisions on your behalf until you become incapacitated. But once the health care proxy is in effect, depending on the state in which you live, you can give your agent wide latitude in making health care decisions for you. However, you can also limit his authority. Many states restrict who you can choose as your proxy. For example, you cannot usually name your doctor or other health care provider as your agent. Choose someone you trust completely to carry out your wishes.

Because a durable power of attorney can be used in a wide range of situations and can be highly personalized, it is usually considered to be more helpful than a living will. But if there is no one whom you trust to speak for you, a living will may be preferable.

Preparing an Advance Directive

State laws regarding advance directives and the guidelines for preparing them differ greatly. Most states have forms that can be used to create an advance directive. You can get a form for your state by writing or calling Choice in Dying or the Legal Counsel for the Elderly. It's usually not necessary to have a lawyer's advice to complete an advance directive, but you may want to have legal advice in some situations, for example, if you think that family members will object to your decisions.

Many states require that advance directives be witnessed by two adults and notarized. State law may restrict your choice of witnesses. For example, you may be precluded from asking someone who stands to inherit from you, such as a child, to act as witness. You can personalize the advance directive by adding information about your specific instructions for and general philosophy regarding treatment. This may help family members and health care professionals to better apply your wishes to a range of circumstances. In many states, you can authorize organ donations in your advance directive as well.

Your agent and alternates should have a copy of your advance directive(s), and the original(s) should be kept in a safe, accessible place. Give your doctor and other health care providers a copy of your advance directive(s) to be kept with your records. Take a copy with you when you go to the hospital, again making sure that it is attached to your medical records. You can revoke or revise your advance directive, but when you do, make certain that your agent and anyone else who has a copy destroys the old document.

The Patient Self-Determination Act, a federal law, requires hospitals, nursing homes, or other medical facilities receiving Medicaid or Medicare payments to inform you on admission of your right to complete an advance directive and of their policies regarding advance directives. However, an institution may not compel you to make out an advance directive. You should understand the policies of any facility that you expect to enter so you'll know whether the institution will be able to honor your wishes.

It is important that you discuss your preferences with your doctor so that you understand the issues ahead and are sure that your doctor will be able to carry them out. If your doctor cannot honor your advance directive, you may want to consider switching doctors, if possible. State laws often require that you be transferred to another facility or health care provider if a disagreement of this nature arises. Above all, be sure to discuss your feelings with your family. Talking honestly with the important people in your life can help them to help you in your most critical period of need and reduce the possibility of conflict between family members in a time of extreme stress and emotional turmoil.

Do-Not-Resuscitate (DNR) Orders

Do-not-resuscitate orders are orders from a doctor to hospital staff members not to attempt resuscitative measures in the event a patient's heart stops beating or she stops breathing. These instructions, also called no-code orders, are attached to one's medical chart. To ensure that you understand measures included in the cardiopulmonary resuscitation process and the possible outcomes in your situation, ask your doctor to discuss this issue with you in detail. Your doctor may not initiate this conversation. It's also important to know your hospital's policy regarding DNR orders. Talking with your doctor does not commit you to a decision about requesting a DNR order, but can promote continued discussion. Those who may have to make a decision for you in the event that you cannot express your wishes should also know your feelings about this critical issue.

PAIN CONTROL

The fear of progressively worsening pain or of a painful death is common to people with life-threatening or terminal illnesses. Although not everyone who has a terminal illness or who dies experiences pain, for most, pain can be effectively managed with appropriate therapy. Yet pain in terminal illness is still undertreated. For this reason, it's important to initiate a discussion about pain control with your doctor. Part of your doctor's role in treating you should be to help you minimize any discomfort you feel and give you as much control over your pain as possible. If you feel that your doc-

---

IF YOU MUST MAKE LIFE-SUPPORT DECISIONS FOR A LOVED ONE WHO HAS LEFT NO ADVANCE DIRECTIVE

Many states allow next of kin to make decisions about life support for loved ones who are unable to communicate their wishes and who have made no statements, written or otherwise, about their desires. Generally, surrogate decisionmakers must substitute their judgment for that of the patient's, attempting to define what the patient would have wanted if she were able to decide.

If you must make a decision immediately, you may find your loved one's physician and nurses helpful, but you may want additional perspectives. Talk with a social worker or patient representative or ask for a meeting with the hospital ethics committee or ethicist. This is helpful particularly when conflicts arise. You can also contact Choice in Dying for more information. As noted above, transportation to another facility is an option when serious disagreements exist between families and care facilities.

tor is not doing all that she or he can to treat your pain, consider asking for a referral to a pain specialist or pain control team, or switching doctors, if necessary.

Most doctors take a step-wise approach to pain control management. That is, they begin with medication that has the fewest side effects and the least toxicity, such as non-prescription medications like aspirin and nonsteroidal anti-inflammatory drugs (for example, ibuprofen and naproxen), and move toward stronger medication with more potential side effects for moderate to severe pain.

When you discuss medication with your doctor, ask for a complete explanation of the benefits of medications as well as a written list of possible physical and mental side effects so that you will know what to expect and can discuss methods of alleviating some of the negative effects. If your pain disappears or can be controlled by other means than medication, it is usually possible to be taken off the medication by tapering doses.

Pain medication can be given in a variety of ways. Depending on the medication, it may be given orally, rectally, transdermally (across the skin by means of a patch), by injection into the skin or muscle, or intravenously. Oral medication is usually preferred since it can give you the most control over your pain management and is most cost-effective. For severe pain, patient-controlled analgesia may provide the best benefits. Medication can usually be dispensed intravenously and in set doses through an infusion pump.

Most pain experts strongly advise that medication be given in doses scheduled for certain times during the day and not on an "as-needed" basis. When pain medication is given on a schedule, pain can be prevented from starting and increasing. Moreover, it is usually possible to use lower doses of medication and patients are spared having to make repeated requests for a drug. In order to gauge appropriate doses, your doctor should assess your pain at regular intervals. Once a scheduled dose regimen is established, he or she may prescribe a short-acting narcotic to be available on an as-needed basis in the event of "breakthrough" pain.

Many people are reluctant to ask for pain medication because of the fear of addiction to narcotics that may be used to treat moderate to severe pain. Most experts agree, however, that the dependency people in pain have on medication is quite different from that developed in people who use drugs for their euphoric effects. Evidence suggests that people using narcotics for pain control are very unlikely to develop an emotional and psychological dependence on the drug manifested, for example, by cravings and compulsive use. On the other hand, there is some evidence that inadequate pain control may foster addiction, as a person in pain may be perpetually focused on getting the next dosage for relief.

Your mood can influence your perception of pain. Depression and/or anxiety, for example, may intensify pain, and treatment of these conditions, if experienced, can sometimes contribute to better pain control. Psychotherapy and antidepressants (for depression) and sedatives (for anxiety) may be helpful. Antidepressants may also be useful for people who are not depressed, because they have independent pain-relieving properties. Family and friends can help by paying loving attention to the person in pain, listening, talking, or simply sitting quietly together.

There are nonmedical therapies to relieve pain as well, such as the application of heat and cold, massage, pressure and vibration, exercise, transcutaneous electrical nerve stimulation (a device that stimulates nerves beneath the skin to block pain), acupuncture, various relaxation techniques, biofeedback, hypnosis, and meeting with support groups. Radiation therapy, nerve blocks (local injection or infusions), or certain surgical or neurosurgical procedures are useful for pain unresponsive to other treatment methods.

Many sophisticated pain control techniques can be implemented in the hospital or home. You may want to explore the possibility of home health care or hospice, a philosophy of care that emphasizes pain control.

Remember that you are the only authority on the pain you're experiencing. Let your caregivers know about any pain you're feeling so that it can be properly addressed. You need not minimize the level of discomfort you are experiencing or feel embarrassed or weak if you ask for pain control. You deserve to be as comfortable as possible. For more information about pain control or help in locating a pain specialist or program, talk to your doctor. You can also call the American Cancer Society and the Cancer Information Service, listed in the Resource Directory under Life-Threatening Illness.

ALTERNATIVES TO DYING IN THE HOSPITAL

Many people would prefer to die at home near family and friends and in familiar surroundings. The decision to remain at home rather than in a hospital is a very personal one, and may depend on preference, resources, space, and the willingness or ability of family and friends to help, in addition to other considerations. If you are a family member or friend who is thinking about caring for a loved one at home, or, if you are a person desirous of home health care, hospice programs and home health agencies can help.

This section will discuss hospice programs. These are unique organizations focused on providing care for dying people and their caregivers. Home health care, discussed in Chapter Nine, may also be an option for people who do not want or are not ready for hospice care. You may want to compare the services of both hospice and home health care programs, considering your personal needs and desires as well as the extent of your insurance coverage and other sources of financial assistance available for either type of care.

HOSPICE

Hospice describes a philosophy of care embodied in a flexible set of services offered to dying people and their caregivers. The hospice team, which generally includes physicians (usually the patient's doctor and the hospice medical director), a nurse, social worker, home health aide, chaplain, trained volunteers, and sometimes other professionals, strives to meet the patient's and family's physical, spiritual, emotional, social, and psychological needs. The goal of hospice care is to encourage a person who is in the terminal stage of an illness to remain as alert and as comfortable as possible so that her final days may be of quality, lived in dignity. Depending on the hospice program, services may be available to adults and/or children.

Although most people think of hospice as a place rather than a philosophy, most hospice agencies help families care for their loved ones at home. Families are often frightened by the prospect of taking care of someone who is dying and doubt their capabilities. The hospice team can help by providing ongoing education and practical support. Families and significant others learn to perform many of the routine tasks of caregiving, including administering medication, moving the patient, and attending to her personal care needs. Hospice staff members make coordinated visits to the home, and nurses are on call twenty-four hours a day seven days a week to counsel and help in emergencies.

Because hospice programs are dedicated to serving the dying person and her family as a unit, bereavement counseling services are available for up to a year after a loved one has died. Some hospice programs will assist in making funeral arrangements as well.

Although the majority of people enrolled in hospice programs are people with cancer, hospice care is not limited by diagnosis. However, most hospice programs require that clients be terminally ill and have a limited prognosis. Medicare and some insurers require a prognosis of less than six months to live. Patients' doctors must also agree that hospice is appropriate and consent to hospice care. Some hospices recognize that the requirement regarding prognosis can be an obstacle to care and thus will vary or extend the period on an individual basis.

Hospice care is focused on comfort rather than cure. Some treatments ordinarily considered aggressive, such as radiation therapy or AZT, may be used to control symptoms or reduce pain. Admission policies are determined by individual hospices on a case-by-case basis. If after being admitted to hospice you decide to leave the program and return to curative forms of treatment, that is possible. The important thing to remember about hospice care is that it should be flexible, and that services should be tailored to your needs insofar as possible. Hospice programs should not impose a rigid set of services upon individuals or families. You and your loved ones should be the ones in control of the tone and direction of the services you receive.

Some hospices delivering care at home require that the patient have a primary caregiver — one person who will be responsible for and oversee the care on a daily basis. The barrier that this requirement presents to the many who would otherwise be candidates for hospice services is being increasingly addressed by hospices that look for creative ways to serve people without a principal support person. For instance, a hospice may help to organize and coordinate assistance by friends, neighbors, volunteers, and church and community groups. If you feel that you would like hospice care but are discouraged by the primary caregiver requirement, it's still worthwhile to contact various hospice organizations to see what's available to you.

In some places, residential hospices serve people who do not have a primary caregiver or whose caregivers are no longer able to provide support at home. Inpatient care is sometimes used when home care is not an option, although it is normally provided on a temporary basis to manage symptoms. Respite care may also be available to give caregivers a period of rest. This type of hospice care may be provided in a separate wing or area within a hospital or nursing home or in a free-standing hospice. In order to create a homelike environment, inpatient hospices will extend visiting hours and allow children, and even pets, to visit.

Payment for hospice services is covered by Medicare and Medicaid and, usually, in part or in full by private insurance. In order to qualify for Medicare reimbursement, the hospice you choose must be Medicare-certified. Health maintenance organizations may contract for hospice services or operate their own hospice programs for members. A social worker or other hospice staff member can help you explore various options for payment. Some hospices offer services on a sliding scale basis, and most will not refuse someone access to care based on inability to pay.

If you or your loved one has been diagnosed with a terminal illness, it is best to look into your options for hospice as early as possible so that you can develop a sense of trust and confidence in a particular agency should you desire its services later on. Hospice care is provided by hospice programs connected to hospitals and home health agencies, as well as independent community hospice programs and nursing homes. Your physician, hospital discharge planner or social worker, clergyperson, or county health department may be able to refer you to Medicare-certified and other hospices. Many hospice organizations, such as some of those listed in the Resource Directory, have help lines that consumers can use to call for information and referral to hospices. Also see the entry on the Cancer Information Service.

Choosing a Hospice

When inquiring about a hospice's services, you may want to ask some or all of the following questions to determine whether the program meets with your initial approval:

- Is the program licensed by the state? Is it Medicare-certified? In order for Medicare to pay for hospice care, the hospice program must be certified for participation in Medicare. Is the program accredited? By whom?
- How long has the hospice been in operation?
- Exactly what services does the hospice provide?
- What professionals comprise the hospice team? Who will be involved in my care?
- Is there a staff nurse available twenty-four hours a day in case of an emergency? Who will answer the telephone when I call? How are messages relayed to the nursing staff?
- How often do staff members visit? If a staff member is late or can't come, will there always be another staff member available to fill in?
- How many nurses are on the hospice staff? How many

patients does each nurse see on average? What training do the nurses have in pain management and in working with dying patients? Are any of the nurses certified hospice nurses?

- How many volunteers are in the program? How are they trained?
- Are patients required to have a primary caregiver? Are services available to people without a primary caregiver? How are they arranged?
- Are inpatient services provided, if needed? Where and how are they provided? Are residential (live-in) services available? What type of services are offered to residents? How much does the inpatient program cost? How much will I pay for room and board? Are clients in the residence female or of both genders? Is privacy an issue? If so, how is it handled?
- Will a written plan of care be tailored to my specific needs? Will my doctor continue to take part in my care and in developing my plan of care? Can the plan be changed if there are problems or new needs arise?
- How are complaints resolved? With whom do I speak if I have a problem? Is this person located in this office or in another office?
- How soon can services be provided? Is there a waiting list?
- What kind of bereavement services are offered? Is individual, family, or group counseling available? What other help is offered to survivors? How long does the bereavement program last?
- Will the hospice honor my advance directive?
- How much will hospice services cost? What services are covered by my insurance? What services are not covered? Are sliding scale fees available? Is care available to people with limited or no ability to pay?
- Try to get a sense of how staff members feel about their jobs. Why did they choose to serve hospice patients? Do they seem genuine, compassionate, and caring?
- Ask for written information about the hospice's policies and services.

If you would like more information about hospice programs, see the reading resource list at the end of the book and refer to the Resource Directory.

For general information about hospice and Medicare, refer to your Medicare handbook. If you do not have a current edition, you can get one by calling the Medicare hotline at

1-800-638-6833 or 1-800-820-1202 (TTY) or the Social Security Administration's toll-free number: 1-800-772-1213 or 1-800-325-0778 (TTY).

AFTER THE DEATH OF A LOVED ONE

Because the period following the death of someone you love is one of great shock and severe emotional distress, it may help you to have a list of important things to do. If you are a friend or relative of the person who is grieving, you can provide a tremendous amount of support by helping your friend or relative to make the following arrangements. Here are some suggestions:

Contact Your Clergyperson or Spiritual Adviser

If death is anticipated, you may want to contact your clergyperson or spiritual adviser for emotional support and/or to perform any religious rituals related to preparation for death, for example, the Last Rites. If you are planning to have your clergyperson officiate at funeral or memorial services, he or she will need time to prepare.

Did Your Loved One Leave Written Instructions or a Will?

If your loved one left a letter describing funeral or other arrangements to be made after death (see the section A Letter of Instruction earlier in this chapter) or a will that contains such instructions, look to that document for help. If your loved one was a member of a memorial or funeral society, he or she may have carried a card with the name of the society and instructions.[2]

Contact Funeral Homes or Memorial Societies

If pre-arrangements have been made, contact the funeral home or memorial society selected by your loved one. Likewise, if a medical school has been chosen for donation, contact the school.

When no arrangements have been made, survivors will have to make arrangements rather quickly. It's a good idea to work closely with your clergyperson if you wish to observe the traditions of your faith. Unless you are certain that you want to work with a particular mortuary, contact (or ask a friend or relative to contact) several funeral homes and cemeteries to compare prices before choosing one. Prices can vary widely from one establishment to the next. Under the Federal Trade Commission's Funeral Rule, funeral directors are required to give accurate price information over the telephone when asked.[3] Look for a funeral home where staff members treat you with respect and caring and where you will not be rushed or pressured into decisions.

Transportation of the Body to the Funeral Home

Once you have selected a funeral home, the funeral director will be able to transport the body from the place of death to the mortuary at any time of day or night. Sometimes, death occurs away from home and families want the body returned for burial. In such cases, it will probably be necessary to work with two funeral directors. A funeral director in your area should be able to coordinate the deceased's return with a funeral director in the area where death occurred. It's a good idea to compare prices for air and ground transportation and to pay close attention to the charges both funeral directors make for services. The cost of transportation and the services of two funeral directors can be quite expensive, particularly when services and charges are duplicated. If death occurs outside the United States, contact the American embassy or consulate for help.

If your loved one died in a hospital or nursing facility, you may be able to defer decision-making for a few hours. Ask the staff for the extra time that you need. Another possibility is to request that a funeral home hold the body in refrigeration for a short period of time, although you may be charged a fee for this service, especially if you go to another funeral home for services.

Contact Close Relatives and Friends

While it's important to contact those who are very close to your loved one as soon as possible, even if the hour is late, you can wait to contact others and delegate this task to someone in your family or to another supportive person. If the deceased left a letter of instruction, it may contain a list of people to be contacted immediately.

Relatives' Transportation

Airfares are often available at discount prices to immediate family members attending funeral services. The name and telephone number of the mortuary and name of the deceased are required to confirm legitimate use of the fare. However, other discounts, such as companion fares, may be just as reasonable or of lower cost than bereavement fares.

The Death Certificate

If an anticipated death occurs at home, contact your attending physician. A physician will also sign the death certificate if the death occurred in a hospital or nursing home. The county coroner or medical examiner must usually be notified when death occurs unexpectedly; when someone who has not been under a doctor's care dies; or when death is the result of an accident, a suicide, or a homicide. If you have any doubts, the coroner's/medical examiner's office, police, or a doctor should be able to answer your questions.

You will need several certified copies of the death certificate in order to conduct necessary financial business later. For a fee, a funeral director will complete and file the death certificate and will help you obtain official copies. You can also contact the appropriate government agency, usually the state or county health department, to find out how to obtain copies on your own.

Autopsy

An autopsy is performed to find out why a person died and in some cases to advance medical knowledge. Unless legally required, as in cases of suspected homicide, suicide, sudden or unattended deaths, a family may decline autopsy. If there is no objection, an autopsy may be helpful when uncertainty surrounds the cause of death or when the family has questions about hereditary disease. Autopsy may also play an important role in any anticipated legal proceeding. However, autopsy may interfere with plans for body donation and in some cases alter funeral plans or raise the price of embalming.

MAKING FUNERAL ARRANGEMENTS

This section is designed to help readers in crisis, but everyone can benefit from planning and arranging for funeral or memorial services in advance. Making funeral arrangements for your loved one may be one of the hardest things that you will ever have to do. If your loved one left no instructions, you may find yourself faced with an array of confusing options at a time when you are least able to protect yourself as a consumer. If you have a support person, such as a close friend or relative, ask her or him to go with you to the funeral home to help make the arrangements. Your support person will be better able to ask consumer-oriented questions and make judgments about purchases.

Funerals and memorial services help survivors to accept the reality of death, to grieve openly, and to receive emotional support from family and friends. Communities reaffirm their ties and their commitment to their beliefs through the funeral ritual. When survivors begin to accept that the death has actually taken place, it becomes easier to mourn. Yet funerals can also be an extraordinary expense. Traditional funerals coordinated by commercial funeral homes may run into thousands of dollars. For some families, expense is less important than the cathartic beauty of a traditional or lavish funeral; other families prefer a simple, economical disposition and services that focus less on ceremony than on the life of the deceased. These choices are personal and depend on the deceased's wishes as well as the family's emotional and spiritual needs and economic limitations.

What Choices Must Be Made?

Initially, you will have two different types of decisions to make. You must decide what you would like to do with your loved one's body (called disposition) and what ceremonies, if any, will accompany disposition.

Here is an overview of *disposition options:*

- burial in the ground (interment)
- cremation
- entombment
- donation to a medical school
- organ donation followed by burial or cremation

Common ceremonies include:

- a funeral (a service with the body present)
- a memorial service (a service without the body present commemorating the deceased's life). This service can take place days after the death or much later. It can replace or follow a funeral.
- visitation (also called a wake or calling hours), a period in which the deceased is placed in a casket for viewing by those who come to pay their last respects. Some religious funeral traditions do not allow visitation or open caskets.
- a committal service, a brief ceremony that allows close friends and family to say their final good-byes to the

deceased. If chosen, a committal ceremony usually takes place at a gravesite or crematorium chapel.

ALTERNATIVES TO THE HIGH COST OF FUNERALS

A loving disposition and commemoration service need not be expensive or elaborate. Memorial societies and direct disposition firms help consumers reduce the high cost of funerals, cremation, and services.

Memorial Societies

Memorial societies, sometimes called funeral societies, are nonprofit, democratically run consumer organizations dedicated to providing members with dignified, economical alternatives for disposition and services. Generally these organizations contract with local funeral homes to offer lower prices for their members or advise consumers on how to arrange for reasonably priced disposition and commemoration services, which can range from a simple burial or cremation to a complete traditional funeral. Cost savings through membership in memorial societies can be substantial. Ideally membership should be bought before death, but if your loved one was not a member of a memorial society, you may be able to make him or her a member at the time of death. Usually, membership is available for a small, one-time fee. Even nonmembers may be able to receive recommendations to funeral homes in their area at time of need. Friends of FAMSA, sponsored by the Funeral and Memorial Societies of America, serves those with no memorial society in their state. When choosing a memorial society, be aware that some organizations use the word "society" in their name but are not in fact nonprofit memorial societies. They may be direct disposition firms or other enterprises.

Direct Disposition

Direct or immediate disposition refers to burial without embalming, visitation, or a funeral, or cremation without prior ceremony. A direct disposition agency or funeral home that provides direct disposition services will transport your loved one's body directly to the place of burial or cremation. Generally these arrangements, particularly direct cremation, afford families considerable savings if price comparisons are done first. Although direct disposition firms are not to be confused with memorial societies, they often offer lower

FUNERAL AND MEMORIAL SOCIETIES OF AMERICA (FAMSA)

1-800-458-5563

FAMSA can provide inquirers with general information about planning an economical funeral, referrals to local memorial societies, or membership in Friends of FAMSA for those without a memorial society in their area.

Embalming involves the removal of blood from the deceased's body and replacing it with an injectable solution that delays the process of decomposition. The embalmer may perform cosmetic and/or restorative work, if necessary, and dress the deceased in order to prepare the body for viewing, if desired. Most funeral directors require embalming when the body is to be viewed in an open casket. However, if the casket is to be closed and there is to be no viewing or visitation, embalming is not necessary when refrigeration is available and no state or local law requires embalming. Embalming is not required for immediate burial or direct cremation.[4] State law does not usually mandate embalming unless: a body is to be transported by common carrier, such as rail or airway, or taken across state lines; death occurs from a communicable or contagious disease; or if there is a certain interval between death and disposition. A funeral director or memorial society representative should be able to tell you what the law in your state mandates. It is a violation of the Funeral Rule (see below) for a funeral director to tell you that state or local law requires embalming when it does not.[5]

Unless the circumstances of your loved one's death make embalming necessary, funeral directors must have the family's permission before going ahead with the procedure. If you don't want embalming, however, you should immediately make this clear to the funeral director.

rates to their members. When contemplating low-cost direct disposition services, it's important to ask for information about everything that may be included in the total price. For example, ask about any fees that will be charged in addition to the actual disposition (cremation or burial), including a basic service fee, the cost of a burial container for the body or an urn, transportation, and the use of facilities or equipment if you choose to have a memorial or committal service on the premises.

You do not have to purchase a casket for direct cremation. This makes sense when you consider that a casket, which can cost hundreds to thousands of dollars, will be destroyed in the cremation process. Under the federal Funeral Rule, a funeral director providing direct disposition services must allow you to select some type of rigid container in lieu of a casket or allow you to provide your own casket.

Direct cremation firms can be found in the yellow pages of your local telephone directory. The Neptune Society and Telophase are examples of direct disposition firms operating in some states.

BURIAL, CREMATION, AND OTHER OPTIONS FOR DISPOSITION

Interment (burial in the ground) is the most common form of disposition in the United States. Generally, interment must take place in a cemetery. But many people want to be buried on their own land or in another special place. State or local law may permit burial outside a cemetery in some areas, but some research and preplanning is usually necessary to accomplish this. Lisa Carlson's *Caring for Your Own Dead*, listed in the Recommended Reading section at the end of this book, describes measures you can take to personally provide for a loved one. If you have lost a very young child, you may be able to put your child to rest on private property or in a churchyard without much difficulty.

When burial is chosen for an adult, a casket, cemetery plot, and headstone or marker must be selected. A vault or grave-liner may be included among necessary purchases, and there will be a fee for opening and closing the grave and for maintenance.

Cremation, an age-old practice customary in England and Japan, involves placing a body in a special furnace called a retort, thus reducing it to fragments of bone over a period of hours. The cremated remains, which consist largely of bone fragments, may be pulverized for scattering and can be fairly heavy. Cremation may be done through a funeral home,

crematory, or through a direct disposition firm. Once cremation has taken place, the crematory will return the cremated
remains in a plain container to you or the funeral director
unless you have made other arrangements. You may want to
buy an urn or use a vessel that has special significance for
you, unless you plan to scatter the remains, in which case
this may be an extraneous expense.

Most people associate cremation with the scattering of
cremated remains in nature, for example, along a stream or
at the base of a hill. There are also other options. You may
bury the cremated remains in a cemetery, keep the cremated
remains at home, or house them in a purchased niche or
room in a columbarium, a building designed to house cremated remains. Some cemeteries and churches have designated areas, often referred to as "gardens," where the cremated remains can be buried or scattered.

Cremation does not necessarily preclude a visitation and
funeral. When a funeral is conducted, a casket, which can
be rented, must generally be used and embalming may be
required by the funeral director when a casket is open for
viewing. However, the Funeral Rule forbids a funeral director to tell you that a casket is required for cremation. If
a funeral director offers direct cremation, she or he must
make an alternative container, such as a container made of
fiberboard or an unfinished wood box, available to you for
cremation.

Some religious groups forbid or disapprove of cremation.
Those who wish to obey the proscriptions of their faith
should consult with their clergyperson. On the other hand,
your religious beliefs may require family members to participate in cremation. You should then make certain that the
funeral home or crematory will allow and welcome family
involvement. Be aware, however, that you may be charged an
extra fee to witness the cremation.

Entombment. Mausoleums are above-ground structures
that house the dead. Usually located in cemeteries, they may
be built especially for families or may house people who are
unrelated. Generally, a casket is placed inside the tomb or
niche and sealed with a marker. Entombment can be very
expensive, but you may want to compare prices for entombment to the total cost of burial in your area.

Body and organ donation. Medical and dental schools use
bodies for research and teaching purposes. This charitable
alternative to traditional forms of disposition must usually be
arranged in advance rather than at the time of death. Some
schools may have a surplus of bodies, and some schools may
not accept bodies from which organs have been removed.

Nor will medical schools generally accept autopsied bodies, bodies that have been badly damaged, or the bodies of those who died from a contagious disease or under other conditions specified by the receiving institution, even if prearrangements have been made. If any of these circumstances are present, other arrangements may have to be made, and the school should be contacted immediately.

Organ donation is an outstanding way to perpetuate the values of the one who has died and to extend a gift of life to the many who are waiting for transplants. Generally, organs must be taken quickly, which may preclude donation from those who die at home.[6] Likewise, if someone has died of AIDS or cancer, most organs may not be accepted. Otherwise, if organs are harvested, funeral or cremation can take place as scheduled.

The Uniform Anatomical Gift Act permits an individual to authorize organ donation before death by filling out the requisite forms, such as a form on the back of a driver's license in some states or a Uniform Donor Card.

REVIEW YOUR CONTRACT WITH THE FUNERAL DIRECTOR

The funeral director will discuss your options for disposition and services at a meeting called the "arrangements conference." At the end of the conference, you should be given an itemized list of all purchases that you want to make with your price total. Review this list very carefully. Ask the funeral director any questions you have and make any changes you want before signing the contract for services. Do not sign if you feel pressured. You may or may not be asked to make a down payment or to pay for goods and services in full at the time you sign.

WHEN A PROBLEM ARISES WITH THE FUNERAL DIRECTOR

If you have encountered a problem with a provider or wish to register a complaint, it's best to talk it over with the funeral director first, as many problems are the result of misunderstanding. If talking to the provider doesn't produce results, the following organizations may prove helpful:

- Most states have a board that licenses funeral directors. To locate the organization, you may want to call the state capitol, your local political representative's office, the state consumer protection agency, or ask a funeral director for the telephone number. These organizations investigate complaints and discipline members of the profession.

- ◆ The Funeral Service Consumer Assistance Program (FSCAP) at 1-800-662-7666, available 9 A.M. to 4 P.M. Monday through Friday Central Standard Time, is a nonprofit organization funded by the National Funeral Directors Association that can help mediate disputes between consumers and funeral providers.
- ◆ The Cemetery Consumer Service Council at 1-800-645-7700 is a nonprofit, industry-sponsored organization providing informal means of resolving complaints regarding cemeteries and memorial parks. Participation is voluntary for both consumers and providers.
- ◆ You can also contact the state attorney general's office for information and assistance.
- ◆ The Federal Trade Commission does not investigate individual complaints, but registering your complaint with the FTC may reveal a pattern of practice by a funeral home warranting action against the provider in the future. (Check the United States government section in your local white pages for the number of the regional office or the Resource Directory for the federal office.)

Paying for the Funeral

If you have discussed preparations for disposition with your loved one or if you have a document describing the deceased's instructions after death, you may know of any arrangements the deceased made to pay for funeral expenses, such as a bank account or trust created for this purpose. You can also:

- ◆ contact the deceased's employer, bank, union, or fraternal organization to find out whether there are any death benefits/accounts to be paid to survivors
- ◆ If death occurred while the deceased was acting in the scope of his or her employment, you may be eligible for death benefits and reasonable burial expenses under workers' compensation laws.
- ◆ If your loved one died as the result of a violent crime, you may be eligible for reimbursements for funeral expenses through your state's Victim Compensation Program.

Families of Veterans

A modest allowance for burial and funeral expenses may be available for certain veterans who were, at the time of death, entitled to receive a pension or compensation, or would have been eligible to receive compensation but for the receipt of military pay, and for certain veterans who die in a Department of Veterans Affairs (VA) facility or contract nursing home. A headstone or grave marker may also be available to veterans at no charge, except for the cost of placing the headstone or marker on the grave.[7] Veterans and armed forces members who died on active duty may also be eligible for burial at no charge in any of the national cemeteries in which space is available. Many of these cemeteries have columbaria on the premises. Spouses of veterans and veterans' minor children may also be eligible. However, spaces cannot be reserved. Applications must be made at the time of death.[8] Unfortunately, many of these cemeteries are full and there may not be space in the national cemetery nearest you.

A funeral director should be able to help you apply for VA death benefits and other continuing benefits for which you may be eligible, or you can call or write the Superintendent of Documents, P.O. Box 371954, Pittsburgh, PA 15250-7954; (202) 512-1800; to order copies of the current edition of *Federal Benefits for Veterans and Dependents*. Allow two to four weeks for delivery.

Social Security Death Benefits

A one-time lump-sum death benefit, currently set at $255, may be available to the surviving spouse or dependent children of a worker who has been employed long enough to be covered by the program. You must apply directly for benefits. You can do this by contacting the Social Security Administration at 1-800-772-1213 or 1-800-325-0778 (TTY, for people with speech or hearing impairments) Monday through Friday 7 A.M. to 7 P.M. You can also visit the nearest Social Security office to file for benefits or ask a funeral director to file on your behalf. In addition, you and/or your children may be eligible for continuing survivor's benefits. Contact the Social Security Administration for information.

If You Have a Very Low Income

The county or state government may pay for very simple burials or cremation for poor families, but may not include funeral or memorial service expenses. A memorial society, a hospital social worker, or the Department of Social (Human) Services may be able to advise you.

After the Funeral: Important Things to Do

After the funeral, when grief is often the most acute, you and/or the executor of your loved one's will (also called personal representative) may need to attend to the following. These are very basic suggestions. If you have utilized a trust or other complex estate planning device, consult with your attorney or accountant.

- Locate the original will. If you don't know where the will or other important papers are, contact the deceased's attorney and check the deceased's safe-deposit boxes. If unsuccessful, check your loved one's drawers and files, and inquire of friends, employers, or anyone else who may know whether or not your loved one left a will.
- Contact the executor, if someone other than yourself. If you are the executrix, you will be responsible for filing the will in probate court, petitioning to begin the probate process, locating witnesses, if necessary, and seeing that the deceased's debts, taxes, and other costs are paid and that his or her assets are distributed to beneficiaries. Even when there is no will or other estate planning device, such as a trust, an estate with assets must go through probate under the laws of intestate succession in the state where the deceased lived. Many people hire an attorney for advice and assistance, particularly if the estate is large or at all complicated. Remember that you do not have to use the attorney who drew up the will to settle the estate. You are free to retrieve the will (if there is one) and use another lawyer, if you choose. If the deceased's probate estate is small or not very complex, you may be able to proceed without a lawyer's involvement. Contact the local probate court (also called surrogate's court) for information.
- Order several to a dozen certified copies of the death certificate, if you have not done so already.
- Locate and gather all important documents, such as a letter of instruction, checkbooks, passbooks, deeds, titles, insurance policies, military discharge papers, recent tax returns, marriage and divorce certificates, birth certificates, and any other documents you may need to

inventory the estate, transfer and receive funds, or apply for benefits.

- Contact the deceased's bank and other financial institutions to find out whether there are accounts payable on death. In order to collect accounts, you will probably need evidence of the deceased's ownership, such as a checkbook or passbook, and a copy of the death certificate. Call ahead to find out what you must bring. In some states, joint accounts may be frozen until the account can be inspected by a tax official. The contents of solely owned safe-deposit boxes must go through probate before you can gain access.

- Contact your insurance agent or companies for information on procedures to file claims for any benefits that may be payable to you. If you have an attorney, an accountant, or other professional adviser, discuss the ways in which you may elect to receive your benefits.

- Contact the deceased's employer(s) (if applicable) for information about pension and retirement benefits, unpaid wages, and insurance benefits that may be payable upon death.

- Check with the Department of Veterans Affairs and the Social Security Administration and unions or fraternal organizations of which the deceased was a member to find out whether you are eligible for survivors' benefits.

- Contact credit card companies to have any credit cards held jointly with the deceased transferred to your name. Credit cards owned solely by the deceased should be canceled.

- In addition to income and other taxes, if federal or state estate taxes are due, it will be the executor's responsibility to file them. At present, federal estate taxes are not due on estates valued at under $600,000, although legislation has been introduced to increase this amount. Some states levy inheritance taxes on the property beneficiaries' receive. To find out whether your state imposes an inheritance tax, you can call your state legislator's local office or the state tax department, or consult your attorney.

- If you were married or partnered to the deceased, create a budget so that you can determine how much you have to live on and whether you will need to make adjustments or changes to address your financial situation in the future.

- Review and update your will, if necessary.

- You may have to gather the deceased's belongings. This is often a very sad and exhausting job. If you and other relatives are contemplating dividing property, and your loved one made no specific designations, think about meeting beforehand to decide how you will settle disagreements. Grief may manifest itself in arguments about who will get what, and compromises made ahead of time may reduce the possibility of conflict.

• Take your time making decisions, especially decisions about major life changes, such as selling your home. Grief can sometimes cloud one's judgment and you may regret decisions made too quickly.

For more information about things to do after the death of a loved one, you may want to get a copy of AARP's brochure *Final Details*. (See the Recommended Reading section at the end of the book.)

GRIEF AND MOURNING

Grief is the word that describes the intense pain felt when someone you love has died or has been diagnosed with a terminal illness. Death is the most profound loss one can experience. Only you can really understand the depth of your pain. The grief you are feeling is unique because your relationship to the person who died is unique.

The flood of emotion that can accompany the loss of someone loved may surprise and confuse you. Many of us feel inadequately prepared for the experience of grief. In Western society in particular, death, dying, and grief are subjects seldom discussed in families or even in religious settings. We are often uninformed about what to expect and are sometimes made to feel weak or out of control when we respond to death and loss naturally.

Because we are often unprepared for the range of feelings that accompany loss, it's understandable that we may try to distance ourselves from these emotions. You may search for any activity, any thought, any substance that might end or at least dull your suffering. Although it can be extremely painful, it is natural and necessary to grieve. Powerful emotions don't disappear when ignored, and grief that is suppressed is destructive. Grief submerged may reappear in the form of various disturbances, such as illnesses and emotional pain that are seemingly unrelated to the loss. Others who have not yet suffered similarly or who do not want to see you in pain may try to push you through the grieving process to ease their own discomfort. But it is important to care for yourself at this time, to summon all the support that is available to

EXTEND YOUR HEALTH INSURANCE

If you or your children were covered by your loved one's employee health insurance policy, you may want to consider extending it. Under the Consolidated Omnibus Budget Reconciliation Act of 1986, better known as COBRA, spouses and dependent children of deceased employees have the right to continue the core benefits of their health coverage plans for at least thirty-six months by paying the premiums. COBRA generally applies to companies with twenty or more employees, excluding plans sponsored by the federal government and certain church related groups.[9] COBRA coverage is expensive — you will usually pay 102 percent of the premium. But it may be worthwhile to extend your coverage until you can find and qualify for another plan. Within a certain period after notice of your loved one's death, the plan's administrator must provide you with notice of your right to elect coverage. You will then have sixty days to elect coverage. The first premium payment will be due in forty-five days.

Another federal law, the Health Insurance Reform Act, allows employees and their dependents who were eligible for health insurance through their place of employment, but declined it because they were enrolled in another group plan and then lost it due to a qualifying event, such as death, to enroll in the plan within thirty days of the qualifying event. This is another option for continued insurance that may be available to you.

you, and to allow yourself to express your feelings. In time, the pain will lessen, although your relationship with your loved one will never end.

Grief researchers have identified feelings common to mourners and developed various theories about the stages or phases through which many grieving people pass. Having a sense of the various emotions of grief can help you to understand that there is a wide spectrum of feeling and behavior that is natural to the grieving process. This section will describe some of these feelings. But you shouldn't be expected to feel all of these emotions or to go through them one by one until you have neatly concluded your grieving process. Grief is unpredictable. There may be days when you think that you have gone through the worst of it and then find yourself suddenly hit by a wave of intense emotion. You may also find yourself going from one emotion to the next with no warning, or you may even experience these diverse feelings all at once.

Keeping in mind that every person and every loss is unique, here are some of the identified emotions of grief:

Shock. When you first hear the news of a terminal diagnosis or death, you may not believe it. You may be numb. You may have the sensation of moving through the world on "automatic." Others may remark on how well you're handling your loss. Shock and a period of denial are nature's way of helping you to cope with pain and to function for a while.

Anger. You may feel searing anger or rage at the injustice of your loss. Your anger may be turned against yourself, at the person who is ill or who has died, at God, at doctors and nurses, at others who are going about their lives as usual, and certainly, if someone you love died by suicide or was murdered, at the criminal justice system, which can be intrusive and unfeeling.

Guilt. For many reasons, survivors often feel guilt when someone dies. The fragility of human life and the little control that we have over the events within it can be very difficult to accept. You may blame yourself, feeling as though you could have prevented the death or illness. Family members may blame each other. An argument or sour exchange with the person you love prior to death can lead to feelings of guilt, as can having been absent when your loved one died. Anger at the ill person or the deceased is very natural and common. Yet when we are uncomfortable with anger, we often turn the feeling inward where it manifests as guilt.

Searching. When someone dies, you may find yourself feeling restless, actively searching for your loved one, pacing, going from room to room, driving, calling out to the person who is gone. It's not uncommon to have an experience in which you hear or see your loved one. For example, parents may hear their babies' cries; wives or partners may see their loved one in a crowd; someone who has died may reappear in a vision. These experiences can be very disturbing or greatly comforting.

Depression can be the most difficult aspect of grief. You may feel tremendous lethargy. It may be hard to get out of bed or to concentrate on anything. You may feel deep sorrow and hopelessness and cry all the time. You may not feel like eating or you may overeat. You may have trouble sleeping. It may be difficult to find interest in formerly pleasurable activities or to want to visit with anyone. You may feel empty and alone. It's not unusual to want to kill yourself, although these feelings should be addressed with professional help if they persist or become concrete.

Physical Symptoms of Grief

Grief can produce unsettling physical symptoms. Stomach problems, difficulty breathing, dizziness, asthma, and nausea are common complaints. You may feel pressure or heaviness in your chest or tightness in your throat and find yourself sighing frequently. It's not unusual for parents who have lost a child to feel an aching in their arms.

Resolution. For most, the pain will lessen over time. Some hopeful feeling will peek through the despair. It will be easier to think about the person who has died, and eventually it will be possible to rebuild a life. Integrating your loss into the whole of your life's experience and approaching a resolution is not the same as forgetting the person who died or ending your relationship with the deceased. It does not mean that you will feel indifferent to the death. It just means that you will be able to go on living, accepting what has happened, in less pain. Resolution doesn't always come without effort. Professional help may be needed to achieve a sense of resolution.

WE GRIEVE DIFFERENTLY

This section will briefly discuss differences in the way we grieve. There are differences caused by the circumstances of death and differences that may be the result of the way we deal with pain as individuals. These are very important issues, which a book of this nature cannot thoroughly address. Fortunately, there are many good books available in libraries and bookstores that can help you further understand and cope with the unique circumstances of your loss. The reading resource list at the end of the book offers some suggestions.

How Your Loved One Died

We are all influenced by our past experiences and previous losses. Your personality and relationship to the deceased, your age, and your religious and cultural background will shape your experience and your expression of grief, as may the circumstances of death.

If your loved one died after a prolonged illness, you may have begun to mourn prior to the actual death, but this is not always the case. Death may seem sudden and shocking to survivors even when the deceased battled a long illness. You may also find that, although you have experienced some initial relief that the person you love is no longer suffering, renewed and intense feelings of grief have surfaced. It's not at all unusual for caregivers who devoted tremendous time and energy to nursing the ill person to feel that they have somehow failed their loved one. If you were not able or didn't want to provide care for your loved one, you may also feel guilty. Yet there are many times when caregiving is not possible or appropriate.

When death is sudden, there is no time to say good-bye, no time to address problems that may have existed in your relationship, no time to tell the deceased what she or he meant to you. The person you love is simply gone. The shock is pronounced, and the grief can be overwhelming.

When a loved one is murdered, survivors often feel rage at the human being who could have committed the act and horror when left to wonder what their loved one might have endured. Fear and the desire for retribution and justice may be consuming. The support system that might have been available in other crises may vanish. It may be hard for others to deal with what has happened or with the survivor's anger. Often the only people who really understand are other survivors of homicide victims.

Likewise, survivors of suicide victims may find that fellow survivors are most capable of understanding the intense hurt, anger, shame, guilt, and stigma felt in the aftermath of suicide, feelings which may be vivid for years. Sometimes, survivors feel relief, particularly when the relationship with the deceased was very problematic. Left unspoken, this natural feeling can lead to increased guilt. In addition to terrible self-blame, survivors are often laden with blame by others.

Family members may accuse one another of causing or provoking the death. Suicide is a complex phenomenon, difficult to understand and prevent. Families may never know why the person they loved chose suicide. Professionals trained in helping survivors of suicide victims and support groups for this purpose can help families and individuals vent feelings in a safe environment. Professional intervention is often recommended for survivors, who are at a very high risk for suicide themselves. If you are thinking about killing yourself, it's essential to seek professional help immediately.

Your Relationships

We are often unaware of just how much relationships contribute to our lives until someone dies. When someone you love dies, a part of you also dies. A wife or partner may feel abandoned by the deceased, and her sense of identity may be challenged. Many years may have been spent making decisions and planning a life together, and when the person loved is gone, there may be a struggle to redefine oneself, to create a new role for oneself in the world. A parent who loses a child may feel intense pain unimaginable to others who have not had a similar experience. Not only has she lost her irreplaceable child, but all the hopes and dreams that grew with that child. A grandparent may not only grieve the loss of a special grandchild but may suffer as she endures her own child's pain. When a parent dies, a child may lose the one person who knew her thoroughly and loved her unconditionally. Part of your history is lost when a parent dies: there are perhaps few other people who have had such intimate knowledge of your life as a child and as a growing, evolving person. But if the relationship with the deceased was strained or adversarial, grief can be complicated by unresolved feelings.

Communication is often difficult for family members when someone dies. Spouses and partners, for example, may not express grief in the same way. Some people are very comfortable expressing pain and seeking support; others are not. Men and women often grieve differently. Many of our cultures encourage men to appear unemotional when in pain, giving them little permission to mourn. When a child dies, for example, the father's feelings may go unaddressed, as relatives and friends often focus their concern largely on the mother's experience. Men may not verbalize their emotions and may respond to grief by taking action — involving themselves in work, creating, building, or exercising, for example. Women, on the other hand, are often, but not always, more comfortable expressing pain, for example, by crying, wailing, screaming, talking, and seeking comfort from others. When differences in styles of mourning are not acknowledged and respected, misunderstandings can develop. One partner may feel that the other's response suggests lack of feeling or, conversely, too great an intensity of feeling. It's important to tell your partner what you need, but at the same time to understand that your partner may not be capable of providing you with all the support that you must have at this time. As difficult and disappointing as this may be, you can still help yourself by seeking out others who can listen — a friend, a clergyperson, counselor, or therapist, or a support group. Couples counseling may also be beneficial.

Friends and family members can provide an almost unending source of love and hope. Yet, they may also find it difficult to see you in pain. Often those closest to you are anxious for your mourning to end. You may be expected to be "over" your loss in rapid time. When you talk about the deceased, the subject may change. Conversely, people may want to listen but may be afraid of upsetting you by bringing up the topic. Some people in your life may not be prepared to help you at all. Those who stay away may feel awkward or inept in the presence of your grief. Your loss may touch too much on their own sense of fragility and mortality or remind them of a previous loss too painful to revive. The possible reasons are many, but it is likely that those who cannot be with you now don't mean to hurt or neglect you. It's not easy to dull the disappointment or resentment that others' lack of response may cause, but it may help to remember that we all have shortcomings. It may be that you have felt the same way in the past or will someday in the future. Forgiveness may be the best course. Meanwhile, you may find the profound and ready kindness of others unforgettable.

What Helps

- Talk about how you are feeling. Let people know that you want to talk. Seek out those who will listen without judgment and who will respond sincerely.
- Writing about your feelings in a journal can be a very effective outlet for grief. You may find this especially helpful if you cannot find someone who will listen.
- Take care of your health. Grief can be physically exhausting and challenging to your immune system. To

prevent illness, it's important to eat nutritious foods, to avoid alcohol and caffeine, to rest as much as possible, and to exercise.

- Accept help from others. If someone asks, "How can I help?" tell her. If you can, make a list of things that friends and family can do. They don't have to be significant things, just little things that will help you get through a day. For example, your neighbor may be able to watch your children for an afternoon, make telephone calls, or go to the market for you.
- Be patient with yourself. Grieving can take a long time, much longer than you expect.
- Put off making major decisions.
- Explore resources for support. You may not be a "group person" or you may have other reservations about attending a support group, but when you're in pain, others who have had similar experiences can help you a great deal.

How to Help Someone Who Is Grieving

When someone dies, friends and family members often want to help, but don't know how. It's not unusual to feel uncomfortable with someone who is grieving. But your friend or relative needs you now, and it won't be too hard to help. You don't have to spend a great deal of time searching for the right words to say. No philosophical statement or illumined phrase can put an end to grief. You cannot and should not try to take away someone else's pain. There are, however, some things that you can do to help.

- Visit, if you can. Holding a hand, touching a shoulder, and hugging can help.
- Bring nutritious food when you visit.
- Express your sorrow. You have only to say "I'm sorry."
- Listen.
- Don't be afraid to talk about the deceased.
- Refrain from judgment. Your friend or relative may not express pain as you might, but everyone grieves differently. Differences must be respected.
- Offer practical help. Tell your friend or relative what you can do — take the dog for a walk, cook a meal, baby-sit, write thank-you notes — and then do it.
- Once the funeral is over, the real mourning begins. Don't stop visiting, phoning, or extending invitations. Be patient with the person who is grieving. If she

doesn't want to talk or go out when you call, try again. Stay available to listen.

Some things that can hurt:

* Don't assume or say that you know how the grieving person feels. No one can experience another's pain.
* Don't tell the grieving person that the loss of his or her loved one was "for the best" or "God's will." These sort of statements usually serve only to reduce our own discomfort with pain and grief. They can wound much more than they soothe.
* Don't espouse your philosophy of life and death.
* Be patient with yourself. We all make mistakes. If you've said or done something that you regret, you can always apologize. Allowing that the apology is accepted, you can begin again, perhaps with one of the helpful gestures mentioned above.

CHILDREN AND GRIEF

Children grieve and experience many of the same feelings as adults, but do not always express them in ways adults expect. Grief may manifest itself in angry behavior, depression, or withdrawal. Alternatively, a child who does not fully understand death or who has not yet accepted the death may seem relatively unaffected. Surviving siblings may feel ignored in favor of a child who has died. Because it can be hard for parents to know how to talk to their children about death and grief, the following general suggestions are given. However, you may want to consult books written specifically to help parents cope with a child's grief. They often cover many circumstances of death and discuss children's reactions according to developmental level.

* Children are likely to have many questions about death. It's important to answer them gently and honestly in language they can understand. You may have to answer the same question or types of questions many times before children understand.
* Avoid euphemisms such as, "Grandma is sleeping." Such statements can confuse a young child, who may fear, for example, that if she goes to sleep she will die too.
* Young children pass through a stage of "magical thinking" wherein they believe that their thoughts and actions can cause bad things to happen. They must be

assured that neither their thoughts, words, or actions caused your loved one to die.

- Children may fear for their own safety and security after someone close dies. Stress to them that they will be cared for and kept safe. Plenty of hugs and kisses can help to provide reassurance.
- Share your beliefs about death with your child. You may want to read a good children's book about death together to make it easier to talk.
- If at all possible, don't send your child away to live with another person while you mourn. Children need to feel secure within the family and included in the family's experience.
- A child should be allowed to participate in the funeral or memorial service if he wants, but should never be forced. Tell him what he will see and what to expect before going to the service together. Let your child know in advance that people will be crying and expressing emotion.
- Teenagers may not want to reach out to you for help in their grief, but may still need someone to talk to. A relative, friend, clergyperson, or counselor whom your child likes and trusts may help.
- You may be concerned about your child's reactions. If feelings of grief, such as denial, anger, withdrawal, or depression are persistent, or if you notice major changes in behavior, you may want to seek bereavement counseling for your child. A school counselor, pediatrician, a hospice program with which you're involved, a family service agency, hospital social worker, or funeral director may be able to refer you to a grief specialist or group bereavement program for children. It's important to look for someone who is trained and experienced in both child/adolescent psychology and bereavement issues. (Also see the Dougy Center for Grieving Children in the Resource Directory.)

WHEN IS IT WISE TO SEEK PROFESSIONAL HELP FOR YOURSELF?

Help from a grief specialist may be very beneficial in certain situations, such as when you experience:

- suicidal thoughts or behaviors
- prolonged or incapacitating depression
- excessive guilt
- persistent, intense anger

- health problems related to grief
- an inability to move on from or through grief
- lack of any feeling
- self-destructive behavior, such as consistent overeating, or alcohol or other drug use
- a feeling that the death has just occurred even though a significant amount of time has passed
- a need or desire for help

Grief is a complex life experience. Getting help doesn't mean that you are inadequate or incapable of addressing life's difficulties. Recognizing the need for assistance is in fact a way of coping, a sign of strength and courage.

When seeking assistance, look for a counselor or therapist who specializes in grief and bereavement issues, someone who has training and experience in helping people who have suffered a loss similar to yours. It's important to note that bereavement counseling is a growing specialty and that not all mental health professionals are experienced in bereavement issues.

Members or offices of local support groups or a friend who has suffered a similar loss may be able to recommend a therapist, counselor, or clergyperson who specializes in helping bereaved people. The Association for Death Education and Counseling, listed in the Resource Directory, does not make referrals but can provide you with the names of grief specialists in your area. With any recommendation, whether it comes from a friend or organization, you must assess the value of the services you receive yourself. If medication is suggested to you, you might want to read the section on medication in Chapter Seven for questions to ask before accepting a drug.

❖

Resource
Directory

❖

This resource directory was developed using questionnaires mailed to national helping organizations. The description of services for each agency was taken directly from material returned by the solicited agencies.

Entries in this directory are not recommendations or representations of the author's views. The information is provided to you in order to make locating and contacting resources as simple as possible. Only you can determine whether the services or publications offered by a particular organization are valuable and relevant to your needs.

How to use this directory

This directory is designed to be used with the book. There is a Resource Directory chapter for every book chapter. For example, if you want to find resources mentioned in Chapter One, you can refer to the directory chapter on work. You can also use the Resource Directory separately. Simply turn to the section in your area of interest.

Listings are generally arranged by subject matter and listed alphabetically. The following section will tell you more about locating resources in your community.

Finding resources in your community

National Self-Help Clearinghouses

There are many national and local self-help and mutual support groups throughout the country. If you can't find the information you are seeking in the Resource Directory, the following clearinghouses may help you find a support group that meets your needs:

American Self-Help Clearinghouse
Northwest Covenant Medical Center
25 Pocono Rd.
Denville, NJ 07834
Information/helpline: (201) 625-7101
    or (201) 625-9053 (TDD), 9 A.M. to
    5 P.M. EST.

Provides information on national and model one-of-a-kind support groups dealing with a wide range of situations, such as addictions, bereavement, parenting, disabilities, mental health, and rare disorders. Also provides information on other self-help clearinghouses nationwide. Publishes *The Self-Help Sourcebook,* a directory of more than seven hundred national self-help groups.

National Self-Help Clearinghouse
25 West 43rd St., Suite 620
New York, NY 10036
Information/helpline: (212) 354-8525
    (9 A.M. to 5 P.M.; 24-hour machine)

Provides information and referral to self-help groups and regional self-help clearinghouses. Conducts training for self-help group leaders, helps people start self-help groups, holds conferences, carries out research activities, and publishes manuals, training materials, and a newsletter.

LOCAL INFORMATION AND REFERRAL SERVICES

In many urban and other communities, there are information and referral telephone services to link callers with organizations providing appropriate assistance. Information and referral services that are approved by or part of the United Way may be named "First Call for Help." "INFO-Line," "Information and Referral line" and "I & R line" are other names of such services. Area Agencies on Aging, discussed in Chapter Nine, and other information services targeted to older people are also great community resources.

To find out if there is an information and referral line in your community, look in the front pages or your local telephone directory (usually the yellow pages) or call your local reference librarian for information. Many public libraries maintain information about community services.

YOUR LOCAL TELEPHONE DIRECTORY

Often, the information you need is nearby in the telephone directory. Check the front pages to find out if there is a community resource section. The government section also contains information about local, state, and federal agencies providing a variety of services.

UPDATING TELEPHONE NUMBERS

Telephone numbers go out of date quickly. To update a federal government number or to locate addresses and telephone numbers of other federal government organizations not listed in the Resource Directory, contact the Federal Information Center at 1-800-688-9889. If you've dialed a 1-800 number that is out of date, try calling 1-800-555-1212 for the new number. If the organization you are calling is a self-help or support and advocacy group, you can also try the clearinghouses listed above for new information.

ORGANIZE YOUR SEARCH BEFORE YOU DIAL

Although the telephone can be a great source of information, assistance, and comfort, it can also be a source of frustration in times of distress. If you must make more than one call for help — as is often the case — this section will help you get organized and get results.

FOCUS ON THE PROBLEM

Before you pick up the phone, sit down and write a brief description of your problem and the type of assistance you need. If you have more than one problem, separate and clarify each issue. Then, write down all the questions you want to ask of the people you call. This will help you focus your search further and better prepare you to get the information you need from service providers.

ORGANIZE A NOTEBOOK

Nothing is more irritating than being referred back to an organization you've already contacted or to be told one thing by one person and another by another person with no way to document who said what. It is necessary to record the date and time of each telephone call you make, the name of the organization and the person to whom you spoke, and the substance of your conversation. When you make calls, use your prepared list of questions and write down the answer to each question as you receive it.

Documenting your calls may seem excessive at first. But the information you gather now may be needed later. If you don't write it down, it will be impossible to remember details accurately. This is particularly true when you need extensive services, for example, if you are organizing rehabilitative or health care services or dealing with government agencies, or if you are searching for a missing child.

WHO CAN HELP YOU?

Once you've isolated your problem, the next step is to determine who can best meet your needs. Some organizations provide comprehensive services. For example, an AIDS service organization may help people with HIV infection or AIDS gain access to health care, transportation, legal assistance, and other services. Other organizations provide a single service to the general public. For example, educationally oriented AIDS organizations may provide the public with pamphlets on HIV/AIDS. Read the descriptions of the organizations listed in the Resource Directory carefully to determine whether or not they will meet your needs.

COMMUNICATE YOUR NEEDS DIRECTLY

A receptionist or secretary may answer your call. She or he can help route your call to the most appropriate staff member and will be able to serve you best if you can articulate your needs clearly. Try to be brief and direct. For example, "I'm calling to ask whether your organization can refer me to hospitality houses or other programs serving families of seriously ill children who must travel out of town for hospitalization." It's best to write down your question before you call.

Go to the top

Often, the information you need can only be had by talking to a staff member with a significant amount of responsibility in the organization, for example, a supervisor, executive director, or other person at the head of the organization. Don't hesitate to ask to speak to the person in charge, especially if you are dissatisfied with the information or services you receive.

Be prepared to wait

Voice mail and answering machines are modern necessities. But in a crisis, they are less a convenience than a source of intense frustration. If you must leave a message on someone's voice mail, clearly and slowly state and spell your name, state the reason you're calling, and leave your telephone number with the area code. If the matter is urgent, ask the operator to put you in touch with someone else who can help you. The receptionist may tell you, "I'll have someone call you back." If so, get the name of the person who will be calling you so that you'll recognize it and so that you can call back again if you get no response. It's not unusual to have to wait one or two days for a return telephone call.

If you can't help me, who can?

If the organization you reach can't serve your needs, ask for a referral to another organization that can. Emphasize your need for assistance. If the person on the other line can't provide you with a referral, ask to speak to the person in the organization most able to do so.

Be polite and persistent

It's not always easy to get the help that you need, and when you are under stress, it may not be easy to keep your cool. But remember that the person on the other line may answer dozens, if not hundreds, of calls a day. You are most likely to get a response if you are polite and professional. Remember that being assertive does not mean being abusive. Treat the people you call with respect and you will probably receive the same treatment in return.

Not every person or organization to whom you speak will be able to help you. Don't give up! Keep searching for help. Contact as many people and agencies as possible. There are people who care, but if you give up early in your search you'll never find them.

I. CRISES AT WORK

CHILDCARE

Child Care Aware
2116 Campus Drive S.E.
Rochester, MN 55904
Info/helpline: 1-800-424-2246 (9 A.M. TO 5 P.M.). Office: (507) 287-2220.
English/Spanish.

This service is available to parents who are looking for childcare. Parents are referred to the childcare resource and referral agency in their community.

ENVIRONMENTAL HEALTH

CHEMTREC Non-Emergency
    Services
1300 Wilson Blvd.
Arlington, VA 22209
Information/helpline: 1-800-262-8200.
    Office: (703) 741-5000. AT&T
    language line capabilities. Web site:
    http.//www.cmahg.com.

Hotline assists the general public with nonemergency health, safety, and environmental questions about chemical products and the chemical industry. Staff can provide product and technical information, and company and manufacturer, health and safety and regulatory referrals. Provides access to CMA library of over 1 million Material Safety Data Sheets, which provide health and safety information about hazardous materials and chemicals.

Citizens Clearinghouse for Hazardous
    Waste
P.O. Box 7010
Falls Church, VA 22040-9839
(703) 237-2249
Web site:
    http://www.essential.org/cchw.

A membership-based organization founded and led by grass-roots leaders organizing for environmental justice. Responds to questions on chemical hazards and other issues. Produces guidebooks on issues ranging from hazardous waste incineration to environmental racism. Quarterly and monthly magazine.

Clearinghouse on Environmental
    Health Effects
2605 Meridan Parkway, Suite 115
Durham, NC 27713
Information/helpline: 1-800-643-4794
    (8 A.M. to 8 P.M. EST).
    English/Spanish.

Provides information on environmental health effects, including articles and brochures related to women's health. The service is free and open to all callers.

Office of Equal Employment
　Opportunity
EEOC
1801 L St. NW
Washington, D.C. 20507
1-800-669-EEOC or (202) 663-4494
　(TDD)
Washington, D.C., area: (202) 275-7377

See Chapter One for more information. Brochures about the EEOC and workplace discrimination are available in print, Braille, or on tape.

Office of Special Counsel for
　Immigration-Related Unfair
　Employment Practices
1-800-255-7688 (voice) or
　1-800-237-2515 (TDD)

Information about the Immigration Reform and Control Act and document abuse.

President's Committee on
　Employment of People with
　Disabilities
1331 F St. NW, Ste. 300
Washington, D.C. 20004
Information/helpline: (202) 376-6200
　or (202) 376-6205 (TDD).
　Job Accommodation Network:
　1-800-526-7234

Provides information, training, and technical assistance to business leaders, organized labor, rehabilitation and service providers, advocacy organizations, and people with disabilities and their families. Also supervises the Job Accommodation Network.

United States Department of Justice
Civil Rights Division, Disability Rights
　Section
P.O. Box 66738
Washington, D.C. 20035
ADA information line: 1-800-514-0301
　(voice) or 1-800-514-0383 (TDD).
　English/Spanish.

Provides information about the Americans with Disabilities Act (ADA). An automated service provides recorded information and through it you can order publications. It operates twenty-four hours a day, seven days a week. ADA specialists are available on Monday, Tuesday, Wednesday, and Friday from 10 A.M. to 6 P.M. and on Thursday from 1 P.M. to 6 P.M. EST to provide technical assistance or answer questions about filing a complaint. Offers many publications about ADA law including *ADA Questions and Answers,* which provides basic information in a simple question-and-answer format. Available in English and Spanish.

U.S. Department of Labor
Women's Bureau
200 Constitution Ave. NW,
    Room S3002
Washington, D.C. 20210
Information/helpline: 1-800-827-5335,
    11 A.M. to 4 P.M. EST. Office: (202)
    219-4486. Fair Pay Clearinghouse:
    1-800-347-3741 Web site:
    http://www.dol.gov/dol/wb/
    welcome.html.

This is a resource center responsive to dependent care and women's issues. Provides information on policies which can help working parents balance their work and family responsibilities, such as flexible work schedules, family leave, emergency childcare, and parent seminars. Also has information regarding the rights of working women, pregnancy discrimination, sexual harassment, and family and medical leave. Provides database searches and information kits.

U.S. Office of Personnel Management
Office of Diversity
1900 E St. NW, Room 6332
Washington, D.C. 20415
Information/helpline: (202) 606-1016
    (8:15 A.M. to 4:45 P.M. EST)

Provides general information for federal employment and a list of federal women's program managers in federal agencies.

JOB RESOURCES FOR WOMEN WITH DISABILITIES

American Council of the Blind
1155 15th St. NW, Suite 720
Washington, D.C. 20005
Information/helpline: 1-800-424-8666
    (9 A.M. to 5:30 P.M. EST)
    Office: (202) 467-5081 (9 A.M. to
    5:30 P.M. EST)

Provides qualified blind people with scholarships, legal assistance, crisis support, a free monthly Braille magazine, and referrals to education, rehabilitation, jobs, recreation, and adaptive aid services.

Job Accommodation Network
918 Chestnut Ridge Rd., Suite 1
Morgantown, WV 26506
Information/helpline: 1-800-526-7234
    (voice/TDD), Monday through
    Thursday 8 A.M. to 8 P.M., Friday
    8 A.M. to 5 P.M.
    English/French/Spanish.

Offers free consulting about job accommodation strategies and the employability of people with disabilities showing ways to change surroundings so that a person with functional limitations can be hired or promoted to a new position. Produces information in English, French, and Spanish, as well as in Braille and large print and on tape or disk.

Job Opportunities for the Blind
1800 Johnson St.
Baltimore, MD 21230
Information/helpline: 1-800-638-7518
    (12:30 A.M. to 5 P.M. EST). Can
    arrange for Spanish interpreter and
    interpreters of certain other
    languages.
Office: (410) 659-9314.

Offers U.S. residents who are blind free services, including a nationwide reference and job referral program, a job hunter's magazine on cassette, recorded job information, materials for employer education, local and national career-planning seminars, consultation on low-vision aids and appliances, and introductions to blind peers employed in the types of jobs that are of interest to job seekers. Publications available on tape.

Mainstream, Inc.
3 Bethesda Metro Center, Suite 830
Bethesda, MD 20814
Information/helpline: (301) 654-2400
    (voice/TDD), 9 A.M. to 5 P.M. EST

Mainstream works with employers, rehabilitation professionals, and people with disabilities to improve employment opportunities for people with disabilities. For individuals seeking employment in the Washington, D.C., or Dallas areas, Mainstream provides placement assistance at no charge. However, applicants must be "job-ready," based on criteria established by Mainstream's employment counselors. For persons seeking employment elsewhere, Mainstream refers job-seekers with disabilities to appropriate community and government organizations.

National Leadership Coalition on
    AIDS
1400 I Street NW, Suite 1220
Washington, D.C. 20005
Information/helpline: (202) 408-4848
    (9 A.M. to 6 P.M. EST).
    English/Spanish.

This national agency focuses exclusively on AIDS as a workplace issue. Provides information and technical assistance to employers, managers, labor representatives and employees. Assists callers by answering questions, making referrals and providing publications on managing the impact of HIV/AIDS. Materials include case studies on reasonable accommodation, sample policies designed to prevent discrimination, and guides for employees and managers for use in education sessions.

Rochester Institute of Technology
National Technical Institute for the
Deaf/Center on Employment
52 Lomb Memorial Dr.
Rochester, NY 14623
Information/helpline: (716) 475-6834
    (voice/TTY), 8:30 A.M. to 4:30 P.M.
    EST

Promotes the successful employment of Rochester Institute of Technology's deaf students and graduates from across the U.S. RIT is the world's largest technological college for deaf students. The Center on Employment also offers resources and training for employers and deaf professionals. A catalog of captioned/signed videotapes is available.

Sensory Access Foundation
385 Sherman Ave., Suite Two
Palo Alto, CA 94306-1804
Information/helpline: (415) 329-0430 or
    (415) 329-0433 (TDD), 9 A.M. to 5 P.M.
    Fax: (415) 323-1062.

Assists individuals who are blind or visually impaired to achieve competitive employment and helps individuals whose jobs are at risk because of their vision loss. Services include job preparation, access-technology evaluation, employee/employer education, an on-the-job loan program, a work incentives program, and technology training.

Legal resources

Equal Rights Advocates
1663 Mission St., Suite 550
San Francisco, CA 94103
(415) 621-0672; hotline: (415) 621-0505.
    Spanish/English.

Priority is given to cases regarding employment and labor policy, which includes affirmative action, pay equity, pregnancy discrimination, and sexual harassment. Other central issues are education and health and immigration policy as they impact women. The advice and counseling hotline offers legal counseling and referrals free of charge. "Know Your Rights" pamphlets are published on sex discrimination in the workplace, pregnancy discrimination in the workplace, and domestic workers' rights. This organization represents both individual and class action litigants and will make referrals for those people whom they cannot represent. Cases are selected mainly on the basis of their precedential value in expanding the scope of women's rights under the law.

Federally Employed Women — Legal and Education Fund
P.O. Box 4830
Washington, D.C. 20008
(202) 462-5235

Specializes in cases of employment discrimination against federal employees. Has a nationwide lawyer referral service featuring attorneys willing to take federal sector cases. Conducts a national training program and makes a variety of publications available for sale. Does not represent litigants but on occasion will file amicus briefs on issues of importance to a large number of federal workers.

Immigrant Workers Resource Center (IWRC)
25 West St.
Boston, MA 02111
Information/helpline: (617) 542-3342 (9 A.M. to 5 P.M. EST). Many languages spoken.

Provides immigrant workers with information about their rights in the workplace. Offers ESL classes and workshops typically focusing on overtime wages, health and safety, discrimination, workers' compensation, and immigration laws. Casework includes direct assistance to immigrants who are experiencing denial of rights and other workplace abuses.

National Center for Lesbian Rights
870 Market St., Suite 570
San Francisco, CA 94102
Office: (415) 392-6257; (415) 431-8821(TDD); youth line: 1-800-246-7743 (9 A.M. to 5 P.M. PST). English/Spanish.

NCLR is a lesbian, feminist, multicultural, legal resource center committed to creating a world where all lesbians can live fully without fear of discrimination. Founded in 1977, NCLR works to change discriminatory laws and create new laws benefiting lesbians in the areas of civil rights, employment, housing, immigration, partner benefits, child custody, donor insemination, adoption, foster parenting, lesbian health and youth rights, with special focus on issues affecting lesbians of color, lesbian families, lesbian and gay youth, and gay immigrants. Clients are not charged attorney fees. Also offers workshops, videos, and publications.

NOW Legal Defense and Education Fund
99 Hudson St.
New York, N.Y. 10013-2871
(212) 925-6635 (9:30 A.M. to 5:30 P.M. EST)

Legal advocacy organization for women and girls with groundbreaking legal and legislative work devoted to securing equality in the workplace, home, courts, and schools. The following legal resource kits are available to the public: child custody, child support, divorce and separation, employment — sexual harassment and discrimination, immigrant women's rights, incest and child sexual abuse, insurance rights, policies and procedures on sexual harassment in schools, pregnancy and parental leave, sexual harassment policies manual, teen parents, education and employment, and violence against women. Many other publications are also available.

9 to 5 National Association of Working
   Women
238 W. Wisconsin, Suite 700
Milwaukee, WI 53203
Information/helpline: 1-800-522-0925
   (10 A.M. to 4 P.M.)
   Office: (414) 274-0925

This organization fights for rights and respect for women in the paid workforce. Provides information, support, and advice to women on work-related problems through its national hotline.

Wider Opportunities for Women
815 15th St. NW, Suite 916
Washington, D.C. 20005
Information/helpline: (202) 638-3143
   (9 A.M. to 5 P.M. EST)

Helps women learn to earn, with programs emphasizing literacy, technical and nontraditional skills and career development. Leads the *Women's Work Force Network* comprised of more than five hundred independent women's employment programs and advocates in every state.

Women's Action Alliance
370 Lexington Avenue, Suite 603
New York, NY 10017
Information/helpline: (212) 532-8330
   (9:30 A.M. to 5:30 P.M. EST)

Dedicated to realizing the vision of self-determination for all women. Creates, tests, and implements innovative program models to effect positive change in the lives of women and girls, predominantly those from underserved populations. Multicultural programs address issues of self-esteem, equity in education and in the workplace, health, and safety.

Women Work! The National Network
   for Women's Employment
1625 K St. NW, Suite 300
Washington, D.C. 20006
Information/helpline: 1-800-235-2732
   (24-hour referral line)
   Office: (202) 467-6346 (9 A.M. to
   5 P.M. EST)

This organization is dedicated to empowering women from diverse backgrounds and assisting them to achieve economic self-sufficiency through job readiness, education, training, and employment. More than 1,300 programs nationwide provide career and personal counseling, job readiness, job search, life planning, childcare and transportation assistance. Eligibility and services vary but most programs serve single parents and displaced homemakers. Call for a list of programs in your state, as well as for information on such topics as child support enforcement and student financial aid.

---

2. CHILDREN IN CRISIS

AT-RISK YOUTH/YOUTH DEVELOPMENT

Big Brothers/Big Sisters of America
230 North 13th St.
Philadelphia, PA 19170
Information/helpline: (215) 567-7000

This is a national youth service organization with chapters throughout the United States. BB/BSA makes a positive difference in the lives of children and youth, primarily through a supportive one-to-one relationship with a caring adult to assist them in achieving their greatest potential.

Camp Fire Boys and Girls
4601 Madison Ave.
Kansas City, MO 64112
Information/helpline: (816) 756-1950
   (8:30 A.M. to 5 P.M. CST)

Serves over 700,000 youth nationwide through school-age childcare, clubs, camping opportunities, self-reliance courses, and youth leadership. Seeks to improve conditions in society that affect youth and to help youth become self-directed and responsible to themselves and others. Contact your local council office.

Girl Scouts of the U.S.A.
420 Fifth Ave.
New York, NY 10018
Information/helpline:
   1-800-GSUSA4U (478-7248).
   Web site: http://www.gsusa.com.

Mission is to inspire girls with the highest ideals of character, conduct, patriotism, and service that they may become happy and resourceful citizens. Girl Scouts seeks to accomplish this by providing girls opportunities to develop their potential and have fun with their peers in a supportive, all-girl setting.

MAD DADS, Inc.
3030 Sprague St.
Omaha, NE 68111
(402) 451-3500

MAD DADS is an acronym for Men Against Destruction Defending Against Drugs and Social-Disorder. The organization was founded in 1989 by a group of concerned Nebraskan African-American men fed up with gang violence and the steady flow of drugs into their community. With chapters in twelve states, the organization provides role models of concerned and loving parents. As a model for other chapters, the Omaha chapter provides street patrols to report crime and other destructive activities, positive community activities for youth, chaperoned events, and visits to local jails and prisons to counsel and encourage. There is also a division of mothers and children.

Midnight Basketball League, Inc.
P.O. Box 2982
Landover Hills Branch
Hyattsville, MD 20784
Information/helpline: (301) 772-1711

Founded in 1986 as an alternative for young adults to drugs, crime, and other problem activities, MBL gets kids off the streets by offering late night basketball and mandatory education, counseling, mentoring, and personal development workshops in a safe environment. Recognized locally as well as nationally for its unique approach and success in improving communities across America, MBL is open to all young adults sixteen to twenty-one years of age residing in Prince George's County, Maryland.

National Resource Center for Youth Services
202 West 8th
Tulsa, OK 74119
Information/helpline: (918) 585-2986
   (8 A.M. to 5 P.M.)

This is a training program of the national arm of the University of Oklahoma College for professionals with a focus on children and families. Its mission is to enhance the quality of life for at-risk youth. Offers information and referral services and publications.

Boys Town National Hotline
Father Flanagan's Boys' Home
13940 Gutowski Rd.
Boys Town, NE 68010
Information/helpline: 1-800-448-3000
　　or 1-800-448-1833 (TTY); operates
　　24 hours. Office: 1-800-842-1488.
　　English and Spanish spoken.

National Hotline provides short-term crisis counseling, referral to local resources, and emergency intervention as needed. Highly trained, skilled and professional counselors deal with family conflicts, suicide, pregnancy, abuse, running away, alcohol/drug addictions, and other crisis situations.

Childhelp USA
P.O. Box 630
Hollywood, CA 90028
Information/helpline:
　　1-800-4-A-CHILD and
　　1-800-2-A-CHILD (TDD); operates
　　24 hours. Office: (213) 465-4016.
　　Many languages spoken.

Twenty-four-hour hotline provides crisis intervention, information and referral to anyone who has concerns about child abuse.

Children of the Night
P.O. Box 4343
Hollywood, CA 90078
Information/helpline: 1-800-551-1300.
　　Operates 24 hours.
　　English/Spanish. Office:
　　(818) 908-4474.

Provides a nationwide toll-free hotline, a twenty-four-bed shelter home, and Southern California street program for children ages eleven to seventeen who are sexually abused and forced to prostitute for food and a place to sleep. The shelter features unique placement services, counseling, life planning, recreation, and an in-house school. All services are free to clients.

Covenant House Nineline
346 West 17th St.
New York, NY 10011
Crisis line: 1-800-999-9999; operates
　　24 hours. English/Spanish. Office:
　　212-727-4021.

Provides crisis intervention, referral and information to homeless, runaway and other troubled youth and their families throughout the U.S. Problems range from child abuse, mental health, suicide, and drugs to family and peer problems. With a database of more than 25,000 agencies, trained crisis counselors are able to refer callers to help in their own communities. Also arranges transportation home or to a safe shelter and provides a message relay service to inform families that their child is safe.

American Humane Association,
    Children's Division
63 Inverness Drive East
Englewood, CO 80112
Information/helpline: 1-800-227-4645
    (8 A.M. to 5 P.M. MT).
    Web site:
    http://www.amerhumane.org/aha.

Provides information and referrals on child maltreatment issues to researchers, child welfare professionals, legislatures, other advocacy organizations, and the public at large.

ARCH National Resource Center for
    Respite and Crisis Care Services
800 Eastowne Dr., Suite 105
Chapel Hill, NC 27514
Information/helpline: 1-800-473-1727
    or 1-800-7 RELIEF for the National
    Respite Locator Service (8:30 A.M.
    to 5 P.M.).
    Office: (919) 490-5577.

Respite means temporary relief for families and caregivers. It is a service provided to children with disabilities, chronic or terminal illnesses, and to children at risk of abuse and neglect. The National Respite Locator Service can provide the name of respite programs in your area that may be able to provide help. (See the Resource Directory under "Disabilities" for more information.)

Child Welfare League of America
440 First St. NW, Suite 310
Washington, D.C. 20001
Information/helpline: (202) 638-2952.
    Web site: http://www.cwla.org.

This is a national membership organization made up of eight hundred public and private voluntary child welfare agencies that are expert in child welfare, including adoption, child daycare, child protection from abuse and neglect, family foster care, chemical dependency, housing, and homelessness. Many publications are available for children, parents, and professionals.

National Clearinghouse on Child
    Abuse and Neglect Information
U.S. Department of Health and
    Human Services
P.O. Box 1182
Washington, D.C. 20013
Information/helpline: 1-800-FYI-3366
    (8:30 A.M. to 5:30 P.M.).
    Office: (703) 385-7565

Automated bibliographies and custom searches are developed from the Clearinghouse's database of child abuse and neglect documents. Provides information about state child abuse and neglect statutes. A catalog of services and publications is available.

National Court Appointed Special
   Advocates Association (CASA)
100 W. Harrison, North Tower
   Suite 500
Seattle, WA 98119
Information/helpline: 1-800-628-3233
   (8 A.M. to 5 P.M.) Office:
   (206) 270-0072. Web site:
   http://www.nationalcasa.org.

An organization of 641 programs across the U.S. that trains volunteers to speak up for the best interests of abused and neglected children in court. With information provided by CASA volunteers, judges are able to make informed decisions as to what is best for the child — foster care, reunification, or adoption. Referrals to programs closest to you.

National Committee to Prevent Child
   Abuse
332 South Michigan Ave., Suite 1600
Chicago, IL 60604
Information/helpline: (312) 663-3520
   (9 A.M. to 5 P.M.). English and
   Spanish spoken. Web site:
   http://www.childabuse.org.

Dedicated to preventing child abuse in all its forms. NCPCA publishes materials, conducts research, and maintains a fifty-state network of chapters.

Parents Anonymous
675 West Foothill Blvd., Suite 220
Claremont, CA 91711
Information/helpline: (909) 621-6184
   (8 A.M. to 4:30 P.M.)

This national organization provides support for parents who would like to learn more effective ways of raising their children and avoid abusive behavior. Nationwide, there are more than 2,100 support groups, which are confidential, professionally facilitated, and peer led. Groups meet weekly and are free of charge.

Voices in Action
P.O. Box 148309
Chicago, IL 60614
Information/helpline:
   1-800-7VOICES; operates 24 hours.
   Office: (312) 327-1500.

An international organization that provides assistance to victims of incest and child sexual abuse. Provides members with referrals to self-help groups, therapists, and puts survivors in touch with others who have experienced similar types of abuse. Publishes an informational "survival kit," a newsletter, and offers national and regional conferences.

JUVENILE JUSTICE RESEARCH

Juvenile Justice Clearinghouse
P.O. Box 6000
Rockville, MD 20849-6000
1-800-688-4252 or (301) 251-5500. Call
   for BBS or Internet information.

The Juvenile Justice Clearinghouse is the Office of Juvenile Justice and Delinquency Prevention's link to juvenile justice practitioners, policymakers, and the public. Services of the clearinghouse include disseminating publications, fact sheets, and other types of information. Information specialists can provide custom searches, referrals, and videotapes. Some publications are available at no charge. There is a fee for database searches.

American Civil Liberties Union
   (ACLU)
Children's Rights Project
404 Park Ave. South, 11th Floor
New York, NY 10016
(212) 683-2210

This is a national program of litigation, advocacy, and education designed to ensure that when government intervenes in the lives of children, appropriate services and treatment are provided in a nondiscriminatory manner and that families are not needlessly broken up by the state. It also seeks to ensure that when the state must remove children from their biological parents, alternative, permanent placements are arranged as soon as possible. The Project focuses its efforts on representing children in class-action litigation with the goal of reforming foster care systems. Although the Children's Rights Project lacks the resources to take on individual cases, it does provide referrals and general information on foster care issues.

ℒESBIAN, GAY, AND BISEXUAL YOUTH

Parents FLAG/Los Angeles
1101 14th St. NW, Suite 1030
Washington, D.C. 20005
Information/helpline: (202) 638-4200.
   English/Spanish. Web site:
   http://www.pflag.org.

National organization that promotes the health and well-being of gay, lesbian, and bisexual persons, their families and friends through support, education, and advocacy. Helps families understand their gay family member, operates hotlines to help distressed people and their families, publishes and distributes educational materials, monitors and appears on the media, testifies at legislative hearings, and has an active speaker's bureau. There are chapters in 365 communities in the U.S. and eleven other countries.

Hetrick-Martin Institute
2 Astor Pl.
New York, NY 10003
Information/helpline: (212) 674-2400
   or (212) 674-8695 (TTY), 9 A.M. to
   6 P.M. EST.

The Hetrick-Martin Institute was founded in 1979 to address the need for sensitive, accessible, and professional service, support, education, and advocacy for lesbian, gay, and bisexual youth. Over the years, HMI has provided counseling, social/recreational programs, and support to thousands of youth and their families. Each year, HMI's educators and trainers reach more than five thousand youth and professional adult audiences with information on sexuality and HIV risk reduction. In addition, the Harvey Milk High School lets lesbian and gay youth continue their education if they are unable to attend their home schools due to harassment. Project First Step was established in 1988 to meet the growing needs of a special group of homeless and runaway youth — those who are lesbian, gay, bisexual, or transgendered. All services are free for those younger than twenty-two.

Child Find of America
P.O. Box 277
New Paltz, NY 12561
Information/helpline:
    1-800-I-AM-LOST and
    1-800-A-WAY-OUT.
    Office: (914) 255-1848

Locates missing children, prevents and resolves parental abduction through mediation, and provides public information about the missing children issue at no fee. Services include in-house investigation of missing children, national networking with local law enforcement, FBI, state clearinghouses, and schools, and dissemination of photos of missing children. Nationwide network of fifty volunteer professional mediators are part of the program to return parentally abducted children through confidential dispute resolution.

Children's Rights of America
8735 Dunwoody Pl., Suite 6
Atlanta, GA 30350
Information/helpline:
    1-800-442-HOPE; operates 24 hours.
    Office: (770) 998-6698

In cases where children have been kidnapped, resources such as private investigation, technical assistance to professionals, coordination with authorities and the media, and family support are available free of charge. In cases of child abuse, this organization offers direct case intervention, which includes coordination of documentation, independent investigations, and interrogation of witnesses. Information is disseminated to court personnel, child protective services, law enforcement agencies, and high-ranking government officials. Emergency hotlines are answered twenty-four hours every day by trained staff. Callers use hotline to report possible location of a missing child and to report suspected child abuse situations. The hotline is also available for youth who are abused, suicidal, chemically dependent, depressed, abandoned, or who have run away.

The National Center for Missing and
    Exploited Children
2101 Wilson Boulevard, Suite 550
Arlington, VA 22201
Information/helpline: 1-800-843-5678
    (THE LOST), 1-800-826-7653
    (TDD); operates 24 hours.
    Office: 703-235-3900

Assists in finding missing children and in preventing child abduction, abuse, and exploitation through community education and awareness to children, adults, and professionals. Contact by phone is the intake procedure.

National Center for Missing and
    Exploited Children
Florida Branch
9176 Alternate A-1-A, Suite 100
Lake Park, FL 33403
Information/helpline: 407-848-1900;
    operates 24 hours.

Assists in finding missing children and in preventing child abduction, abuse, and exploitation through community education and awareness to children, adults, and professionals.

Operation Lookout National Center
for Missing Youth
2725 Wetmore Ave.
Everett, WA 98201
Information/helplines:
   1-800-782-SEEK (7335); operates
   24 hours; 1-800-LOOKOUT,
   ext. 1234. Office: (206) 771-SEEK.
   Fax: (206) 388-0130. Web site:
   http://www.premier1.net/~lookout/.

Assists families with missing children who disappear prior to age eighteen, including noncustodial parental kidnappings, stranger abductions, runaways, and unexplained disappearances. Conducts searches, displays pictures nationwide, serves as a victim advocate and law enforcement liaison, makes community and legal referrals, and provides emotional support and reunification planning. No charge for services. Contact is by phone, Web site, fax, or mail.

Vanished Children's Alliance
2095 Park Ave.
San Jose, CA 95126
Information/helpline:
   1-800-VANISHED, 24-hour sighting
   line. Office: (408) 296-1113.

Provides assistance to families in all categories of missing children — nonfamily abductions, family abductions, and runaways. Free, extensive services include abduction prevention, liaison between parents/guardians of missing children and law enforcement, counseling and technical assistance, active case management and distribution of children's posters and photos, computerized database, referral list of professionals, translation services, legal assistance, and involvement in family reunification. In the case of family abduction, the registering parent must have legal custody.

Missing children, international

Office of Children's Issues
Department of State
2201 C Street NW, Room 4811
Washington, D.C. 20520-4800
Information/helpline: (202) 736-7000
   (8:15 A.M. to 5 P.M. EST).
English/Spanish. Fax: (202) 647-2835.
   Web site: http://www.travel.state.gov.

Has taken action in more than eight thousand cases of international parental child abduction. Where the Hague Convention applies, assists parent in filing applications with foreign authorities for return of the child. In other cases, attempts to locate, visit, and report on the child's general welfare. Provides the left-behind parent with information on the country to which the child was abducted, including its legal system, family laws, and a list of attorneys there who are willing to accept American clients; provides a point of contact for the left-behind parent at a difficult time; monitors judicial or administrative proceedings overseas; assists parents in contacting local officials in foreign countries or contacts them on the parent's behalf; provides information on domestic remedies, such as warrants, extradition, and passport revocation; alerts foreign authorities to any evidence of child abuse or neglect.

International Social Service, American Branch
390 Park Ave. South
New York, NY 10016
Information/helpline: (212) 532-6350, ext. 400 (8:30 A.M. to 5 P.M. EST). English/Greek/Spanish/French.

Dedicated to providing intercountry casework assistance consultation, including permanency planning for children, child custody assistance, child protection, placement of children, search for missing parents, intercountry adoption. Interprets unfamiliar rules, cultures, customs, translations; liaison with governmental and social agencies worldwide.

RELIGIOUS ORGANIZATIONS SERVING LESBIAN, GAY, AND BISEXUAL PEOPLE AND THEIR FAMILIES

Dignity/USA
1500 Massachusetts Avenue NW, Suite 11
Washington, D.C. 20005
Information/helpline: 1-800-877-8797 (9 A.M. to 5 P.M. EST).
Office: (202) 861-0017.

National organization of gay, lesbian and bisexual Catholics, their families and friends who recognize the inherent dignity of all people regardless of gender or sexual orientation. They work to promote spiritual development, social interaction, educational outreach, social reform, and feminist issues.

Reconciling Congregation Program
3801 N. Keeler Avenue
Chicago, IL 60641
Information/helpline: (773) 736-5526, 9 A.M. to 5 P.M. CST Monday through Friday. Fax: (773) 736-5475.

National network of United Methodist churches that publicly welcome all persons, regardless of sexual orientation. Provide resources on Christianity and homosexuality, including an ecumenical quarterly magazine. Makes referrals to churches and pastoral services (primarily United Methodist) for lesbian, gay, and bisexual persons and their families.

RUNAWAY HOTLINES AND SERVICES

National Runaway Switchboard
3080 N. Lincoln Avenue
Chicago, IL 60657
Crisis line: 1-800-621-4000 or 1-800-621-0394 (TDD); operates 24 hours. Office: (312) 880-9860.

Provides crisis intervention and referrals for youth through a national switchboard, as well as advocacy and educational services on the problems of youth. Switchboard services include conference calls to parents, message delivery from runaways to their parents or guardians, and conference calls to shelters or other agencies to locate available services.

INFORMATION ABOUT RUNAWAYS AND HOMELESS YOUTH

National Network of Runaway and Youth Services
1319 F Street NW, Suite 401
Washington, D.C. 20004
Office: (202) 783-7949 (9 A.M. to 6 P.M. EST). English/Spanish.

Represents a network of community-based, youth-serving agencies, but does not offer direct services to the public. Offers training and technical assistance for the professional development of youth workers. Publishes fact sheets on runaway and homeless youth, alcohol and other drug use, and HIV/AIDS prevention.

Parents as Teachers National Center
10176 Corporate Square Drive
    Suite 230
St. Louis, MO 63132
Information/helpline: (314) 432-4330
    (8 A.M. to 5 P.M.)

This model program is designed to offer developmental information to all parents, from single teenage mothers to two-parent, well-educated families. Includes home visits by PAT-certified parent educators trained in child development, group meetings with other parents, periodic screening of development, language, hearing, and vision, and resource network of special services.

3. DIVORCE

ALTERNATIVE DISPUTE RESOLUTION

Academy of Family Mediators
1500 S. Hwy. 100 #355
Golden Valley, MN 55416
(612) 525-8670

For further information, call the Academy of Family Mediators.

American Arbitration Association
140 West 51 St.
New York, NY 10020-1230
(212) 484-4000

For further information, call the American Arbitration Association.

ATTORNEYS

American Academy of Matrimonial
    Lawyers
150 N. Michigan Ave., Suite 2040
Chicago, IL 60601
(312) 263-6477 (8:30 A.M. to 4:30 P.M.
    CST)

Membership association of matrimonial attorneys across the United States who specialize in marriage, divorce, annulment, unmarried cohabitants, child custody, alimony, property distribution, and support. Develops informational programs, books, and videos for matrimonial attorneys and the public.

Legal Services Corporation
750 First St. NE, Tenth Floor
Washington, D.C. 20002-4250
Information/helpline: (202) 336-8800
    (9 A.M. to 5:30 P.M. EST)

Established by Congress to help provide equal access to justice under the law for all Americans, the Legal Services Corp. operates more than 1,200 neighborhood law offices throughout the U.S. and benefits 5 million individuals — the majority of them children living in poverty. Typical cases are domestic violence, child abuse or neglect, evictions, foreclosures, divorces, child custody, wage claims, access to health care, and unemployment or disability claims. Special programs serve the needs of migrant workers, Native Americans, older people, and small-family farmers. Call for the number of the office nearest you.

CHILD CUSTODY

Custody Action for Lesbian Mothers, Inc.
P.O. Box 281
Narberth, PA 19072
Information/helpline: (610) 667-7508
(9 A.M. to 5 P.M. EST)

CALM, Inc., is a free legal counseling service that provides volunteer lawyers who will represent the mother. A volunteer counselor, usually a lesbian mother, advises the woman as to her options, offers psychological support throughout the process, and accompanies her to attorney visits and to the courtroom. Referrals are made nationwide to lesbian mothers' groups and attorneys who provide a similar service.

Through the Looking Glass
2198 Sixth St.
Berkeley, CA 94710-2204
Information/helpline: 1-800-644-2666
(9 A.M. to 12 P.M. and 1 A.M. to
5 P.M. PST)
Office: (510) 848-1112.

National information and referral source for parents with disabilities, their family members, and service providers.

National Center for Lesbian Rights
870 Market St., Suite 570
San Francisco, CA 94102
Office: (415) 392-6257. Youth line:
1-528-NCLR (6257) or (415) 431-8821
(TDD), 9 A.M. to 5 P.M. PST.
English/Spanish.

NCLR is a lesbian, feminist, multicultural, legal resource center committed to creating a world where all lesbians can live without fear of discrimination. Founded in 1977, NCLR works to change discriminatory laws and create new laws benefiting lesbians in the areas of civil rights, employment, housing, immigration, partner benefits, child custody, donor insemination, adoption, foster parenting, and lesbian health and youth rights. There is special focus on issues affecting lesbians of color, lesbian families, lesbian and gay youth, and gay immigrants. Clients are not charged attorney fees. Also offers workshops, videos, and publications.

CHILDREN'S GRIEF

Rainbows
1111 Tower Rd.
Schaumburg, IL 60173
Information/helpline: (847) 310-1880
(8:30 A.M. to 4:30 P.M. CST)

Offers peer support groups for children, adolescents, and adults who are grieving a loss due to death, divorce, or other painful transitions in the family. Assists people who are grieving in expressing and understanding their feelings, in accepting what has happened, and in feeling a sense of belonging and love.

The Association for Children for
    Enforcement of Support
(ACES)
2260 Upton Ave.
Toledo, OH 43606
Information/helpline: 1-800-537-7072
    (8 A.M. to 5 P.M. EST). Office:
    (419) 472-6609.

ACES provides educational information about child support
and visitation, including your legal rights and remedies, information about agencies to contact for assistance, local and
out-of-state methods available under current law to collect
current and back child support, and methods to resolve visitation problems. Free booklet available. ACES has a national
office and chapters in forty-nine states.

The Children's Foundation
725 15th Street NW, Suite 505
Washington, D.C. 20005-2109
Information/helpline: (202) 347-3300
    (9 A.M. to 5 P.M. EST)

This national organization, established in 1969, offers training to childcare providers and information to parents looking
for childcare and those wishing to improve their parenting
skills. Helps custodial parents get the court-ordered child
support due their children. Books and other publications are
available.

OFFICE OF CHILD SUPPORT ENFORCEMENT REGIONAL OFFICES

The federal Office of Child Support
Enforcement helps develop, manage,
and operate child support enforcement programs according to federal
law. Write or call for a general informational booklet about the child
support enforcement program.

Office of Child Support Enforcement, Headquarters
U.S. Department of Health and Human Services
Administration for Children and Families
Office of Child Support Enforcement
370 L'Enfant Promenade SW
Washington, D.C. 20447
Office: (202) 401-9373 (8:30 A.M. to 5 P.M. EST)

Region I (Connecticut, Maine,
    Massachusetts, New Hampshire,
    Rhode Island, Vermont)

OCSE Program Manager
Administration for Children and Families
John F. Kennedy Federal Building
20th Floor, Room 2000
Boston, MA 02203
(617) 565-2440

Region II (New York, New Jersey,
    Puerto Rico, Virgin Islands)

OCSE Program Manager
Administration for Children and Families
Federal Building, Room 4048
26 Federal Plaza
New York, NY 10278
(212) 264-2890

Region III (Delaware, Maryland, Pennsylvania, Virginia, West Virginia, District of Columbia)

OCSE Program Manager
Administration for Children and Families
P.O. Box 8436
3535 Market St., Room 4119 MS/15
Philadelphia, PA 19104
(215) 596-4136

Region IV (Alabama, Florida, Georgia, Kentucky, Mississippi, North Carolina, South Carolina, Tennessee)

OCSE Program Manager
Administration for Children and Families
101 Marietta Tower, Suite 821
Atlanta, GA 30323
(404) 331-2180

Region V (Illinois, Indiana, Michigan, Minnesota, Ohio, Wisconsin)

OCSE Program Manager
Administration for Children and Families
105 W. Adams St., 20th Floor
Chicago, IL 60603
(312) 353-4237

Region VI (Arkansas, Louisiana, New Mexico, Oklahoma, Texas)

OCSE Program Manager
Administration for Children and Families
1200 Main Tower Building, Suite 1050
Mail Stop A2
Dallas, TX 75202
(214) 767-3749

Region VII (Iowa, Kansas, Missouri, Nebraska)

OCSE Program Manager
Administration for Children and Families
601 East 12th St.
Federal Building, Room 276
Kansas City, MO 64106
(816) 426-3584

Region VIII (Colorado, Montana, North Dakota, South Dakota, Utah, Wyoming)

OCSE Program Manager
Administration for Children and Families
Federal Office Building, Room 325
1961 Stout St.
Denver, CO 80294
(303) 844-3100 (8 A.M. to 4:30 P.M. MT)

Region IX (Arizona, California, Hawaii, Nevada, Guam)

OCSE Program Manager
Administration for Children and Families
50 United Nations Plaza, Mail Stop 351
San Francisco, CA 94102
(415) 437-8463

Region X (Alaska, Idaho, Oregon, Washington)

OCSE Program Manager
Administration for Children and Families
2201 Sixth Ave., Ste. 600, Mail Stop RX-70
Seattle, WA 98121
(206) 615-2547

Parents' Organizations

Gay and Lesbian Parents Coalition International
P.O. Box 50360
Washington, D.C. 20091
Information/helpline: (202) 583-8029

Provides advocacy, education, and support in child-nurturing roles for gay and lesbian persons and their families worldwide. Membership organization with local chapters in the U.S. and eight other countries. Publications available.

Mothers at Home
8310A Old Courthouse Road
Vienna, VA 22182
Information/helpline: 1-800-783-4666
   (9 A.M. to 3 P.M. EST).
Office: (703) 827-5903.

Offers support to mothers across the country who choose, or would like to choose, to devote their exceptional skills and good minds to nurturing their families. The organization's purpose is to help mothers excel, to provide practical information, and to correct society's many misconceptions about mothering today. Offers a monthly journal and other publications.

Parents Without Partners
401 N. Michigan Avenue
Chicago, IL 60611
Information/helpline: 1-800-637-7974
   (9 A.M. to 5 P.M. CST). Office:
   (312) 644-6610

Makes referrals to local chapters throughout North America that have ongoing activities for the single parent and her/his family. Programs include discussion groups on parent-child relationships, effective communication, dating, self-improvement, recreational activities for parents and children, and adult social activities. Publishes *The Single Parent* magazine.

National Organization of Single Mothers
P.O. Box 68
Midland, NC 28107
Information/helpline: (704) 888-KIDS

Committed to helping the country's 12 million single parents meet the challenges of daily life by uniting them in a network of mutual support and action through its publication *Single Mother* and by establishing nationwide support groups.

Stepfamily Association of America
215 Centennial Mall South, #212
Lincoln, NE 68508
Information/helpline: (402) 477-7837

Provides education and support through local chapters and national advocacy. Offers an eight-step success program, books, and a quarterly publication.

Straight Spouse Support Network
8215 Terrace Dr.
El Cerrito, CA 94530-3058
Information/helpline: (510) 525-0200
(10 A.M. to 10 P.M. PST).
English/French.

International support network of heterosexual women and men who are married or were married to gay, lesbian, or bisexual partners. Provides confidential personal support and resource information about spousal and children's issues. The network includes individual spouses, support groups, and professionals who are experienced in issues of mixed marriages and relationships.

PENSION ISSUES

National Pension Rights Center
918 16th St. NW
Washington, D.C. 20006
Information/helpline: (202) 296-3776
(Thursdays and Fridays, 2 P.M. to 4 P.M. EST)

Provides direct legal assistance to women going through divorce and to their lawyers who contact the center with pension problems. Also makes lawyer referrals free of charge. Publishes the book *Your Pension Rights at Divorce: What Women Need to Know.* Also has a fact sheet that explains pension problems for working women, widows, and divorced women.

WELFARE SYSTEM

Center on Social Welfare Policy and Law
275 Seventh Ave., Suite 1205
New York, NY 10001
(212) 633-6967

Works with and on behalf of poor people to ensure that adequate income support is available whenever and to the extent necessary to meet basic needs and foster healthy human and family development. Serves as direct counsel or cocounsel in welfare litigation across the country; works with and represents client/underprivileged people's organizations; and is expanding its capability as the primary reference on federal, state, and local welfare programs. Outreach to the broader community through dissemination of materials, a periodic newsletter on welfare reform issues, and media contacts.

Welfare Warriors
2711 W. Michigan
Milwaukee, WI 53208
Information: (414) 342-6662 (1 P.M. to 9 P.M. CST). English/Spanish.
Office: (414) 342-6662.
Fax: (414) 342-MOMS.

A group of low-income mothers who staff a daily "Mom's Line" to teach mothers how to survive poverty and/or government abuse. Also fights for guaranteed public support for all minors. Publishes *Welfare Mothers Voice,* a twenty-four-page national quarterly written by mothers who have depended on government child support when private support was unavailable or inadequate.

FAMILY COUNSELING

Family Service America
11700 W. Lake Park Dr.
Milwaukee, WI 53224
Information/helpline: 1-800-221-2681
   (9 A.M. to 5 P.M. CST)

This is a network of three hundred agencies that assist individuals and families to solve problems associated with parent-child tensions, marital difficulties, drug and alcohol dependency, teenage pregnancy, eldercare, child abuse and neglect, family violence, and work-related problems.

HOTLINES

Emergency Contraception Hotline
P.O. Box 33344
Washington, D.C. 20033
Information/helpline: 1-800-584-9911
   (24 hours). English/Spanish.

The Reproductive Health Technologies Project operates the Emergency Contraceptive Hotline, a nationwide toll-free service enabling women to access information about emergency contraception and to obtain referrals to clinicians who provide emergency contraceptives. The hotline is completely confidential, fully automated, and available twenty-four hours a day in English and Spanish. Callers receive information about emergency contraceptive methods available in the U.S. as well as the names, telephone numbers, and locations (city and state) of three providers nearest them.

National Domestic Violence Hotline
3616 Far West Blvd., Suite 101-297
Austin, TX 78731
Hotline: 1-800-799-SAFE (7233);
   TDD: 1-800-787-3224 (24 hours).
   English/Spanish with access to
   translators for 139 languages.
   Office: (512) 453-8117.

The National Domestic Violence Hotline links individuals to services through a nationwide database. The system stores up-to-date information on domestic violence and other emergency shelters, legal advocacy and assistance programs, and social service programs. One call summons immediate help, including crisis intervention to assist the caller in identifying problems and possible solutions, and making plans for safety in an emergency. The hotline can be accessed in all fifty states, the District of Columbia, Puerto Rico, and the U.S. Virgin Islands. Information materials are published in a variety of formats and languages.

National Organization for Victim
   Assistance
1757 Park Rd. NW
Washington, D.C. 20010
Information/helpline: 1-800-879-6682,
   24 hours, English/Spanish.
   Office: (202) 232-6682.

Information and referral for victims of violent crime and disaster. Services are available for victims, survivors, and their loved ones.

Rape, Abuse and Incest National
   Network (RAINN)
252 Tenth St. NE
Washington, D.C. 20002
Hotline: 1-800-656-HOPE
   (24 hours)

Provides survivors of sexual assault access to counseling twenty-four hours a day from anywhere in the country. Computer identifies caller's location by area code and the call is instantaneously routed to the rape crisis center nearest the caller, which handles the call as if it had come in directly. RAINN is toll-free and confidential.

NATIONAL DOMESTIC VIOLENCE COALITION

National Coalition Against Domestic
   Violence
P.O. Box 18749
Denver, CO 80218
Information/helpline: 1-800-799-7233;
   Office: (303) 839-1852.

This organization serves primarily as an advocate and national communications network for community-based programs that provide services, and often shelters, to battered women and their children. They can refer you to local programs and state coalitions and also send you a general information packet on request. They do *not* provide legal services.

PLASTIC SURGERY FOR VICTIMS OF VIOLENCE

Educational and Research Foundation
   for the American Academy of Facial
   Plastic and Reconstructive Surgery
Information/helpline: 1-800-842-4546
   (9 A.M. to 5 P.M.)

AAFPRS recognizes that many victims of domestic violence receive severe facial injuries and for many reasons, including financial, are not able to receive adequate care. In partnership with the National Coalition Against Domestic Violence (NCADV), AAFPRS will provide free facial plastic and reconstructive surgery to victims of domestic violence. The toll-free helpline will refer the caller to a shelter to meet with a counselor. The counselor will call AAFPRS and offer a professional opinion as to whether or not the individual is a good candidate for the program. After receiving permission from the shelter, AAFPRS will call the individual with the name of a participating surgeon who will provide free consultation and perform surgery if appropriate.

RESEARCH RESOURCES/PUBLICATIONS

Family Violence Prevention Fund
383 Rhode Island St., Ste. 304
San Francisco, CA 94103-5133
Information/helpline:
   1-800-END-ABUSE. Spanish
   spoken. Office: (415) 252-8900.
   Fax: (415) 252-8991. Web site:
   http://www.fvpf.org/.

Focuses on domestic violence education, prevention, and public policy reform. The Fund's publications and model programs have been distributed to and replicated in every state and several foreign countries. Publications include *Take Action* and *You Have the Right to Be Free from Violence in Your Home: Questions and Answers for Immigrant and Refugee Women.* They are available in English, Spanish, Chinese, Tagalog, and Korean.

Family Violence and Sexual Assault
    Institute
1121 East Southeast Loop 323, Ste. 130
Tyler, TX 75701
Information/helpline: (903) 534-5100

This is a national resource center of information concerning family violence and sexual abuse. Its overall purpose is to improve networking among researchers, practitioners, and agencies and to disseminate information and develop treatment programs and educational training. They answer all inquiries regarding family violence and sexual abuse.

---

5. CRISES IN CONCEPTION AND SEXUALITY

EMERGENCY CONTRACEPTION

Emergency Contraception Hotline
P.O. Box 33344
Washington, D.C. 20033
Information/helpline: 1-800-584-9911
    (24 hours). English/Spanish.

The Reproductive Health Technologies Project operates the Emergency Contraceptive Hotline, a nationwide, toll-free service that offers women information about emergency contraception and referrals to clinicians who provide emergency contraceptives. The hotline is completely confidential, fully automated, and available twenty-four hours a day in English and Spanish. Callers receive information about emergency contraceptive methods available in the United States as well as the names, telephone numbers, and locations (city and state) of the three closest providers.

ABORTION INFORMATION/REPRODUCTIVE RIGHTS

American Civil Liberties Union
203 North LaSalle St., Suite 1405
Chicago, IL 60601
(312) 201-9740

The ACLU initiates/defends court actions protecting a person's constitutional rights and civil liberties against governmental actions, including women's reproductive rights. Represents individual litigants and classes of litigation. They select cases based on whether they are within ACLU policy. Provides public information by telephone.

The Center for Reproductive Law &
    Policy
120 Wall Street
New York, NY 10005
(212) 514-5534

Through litigation and public education, the Center's mission is to ensure that all women have access to freely chosen reproductive health care. There is special focus on young women, low-income women, rural women, and women of color. Responds to both phone and written requests for information. Offers a biweekly newsletter and publications to the general public, most of which are free. The Center represents both individual litigants and groups of litigants, such as prochoice coalitions, clinics, and physicians and the women they serve. This organization provides technical assistance on legislative proposals to policymakers across the country.

Catholics for a Free Choice
1436 U Street NW, Suite 301
Washington, D.C. 20009
Information/helpline: (202) 986-6093
(9 A.M. to 5 P.M. EST).
English/Spanish.

This educational organization shapes and advances sexual and reproductive ethics that are based on justice, that reflect a commitment to women's well-being and respect, and that affirm the moral capacity of women and men to make sound and responsible decisions about their lives. Works to infuse these values into public policy, community life, feminist analysis, and Catholic social thinking and teaching.

National Abortion Federation
1436 U Street NW, Suite 103
Washington, D.C. 20009
Information/helpline: 1-800-772-9100;
1-800-424-2280 (TDD), 9:30 A.M. to
12:30 P.M. and 1:30 P.M. to 5:30 P.M.
EST. English/Spanish. Office:
(202) 667-5881.

The hotline answers urgent questions about abortion, pregnancy, and restrictive laws, and helps women find the nearest medical facilities for the care they need. Distributes educational materials such as fact sheets and a printed English/Spanish guide to recognizing a safe facility.

National Network of Abortion Funds
c/o Hampshire College
Amherst, MA 01002
Information/helpline: (413)582-5645

This is an umbrella organization comprised of thirty-five abortion funds across the country. While NNAF does not provide direct financial aid, the member organizations all provide direct aid in the form of loans and/or grants to low-income women seeking to terminate an unwanted pregnancy.

Planned Parenthood Federation of America
810 Seventh Avenue
New York, NY 10019
Information/helpline: 1-800-230-PLAN
(24 hours). Connects
callers to nearest Planned
Parenthood Health Center.
English/Spanish spoken, depending
on the region. Office: (212) 541-7800.

PPFA is a federation of 159 affiliate organizations operating nearly 1,000 health centers nationwide. Centers provide family planning counseling, contraception, pregnancy testing, prenatal care, adoption, referrals, abortion services, Pap tests and other cancer screening, testing, and treatment for sexually transmitted infections and sex education to nearly 4 million women and men each year. Fees are on a sliding scale.

Reproductive Health Technologies Project
1818 N Street NW, Suite 450
Washington, D.C. 20036
Office: (202) 328-2200

The Reproductive Health Technologies Project brings together leaders from a wide range of constituencies and disciplines for the purpose of dialogue and consensus building on issues of reproductive health. Its mission is to advance the right of every woman to achieve full reproductive freedom through increased information and access to a wide range of safe and effective means for controlling fertility and protecting her health. The project is a nonprofit organization supported by grants from private foundations and individual contributions.

The ALMA Society (Adoptees' Liberty Movement Association)
P.O. Box 727, Radio City Station
New York, NY 10101
Information/helpline: (212) 581-1568
  (9 A.M. to 5 P.M. EST)

Search and support organization for adult adoptees, natural parents of adoptees over eighteen, foster children over eighteen, unwed mothers, adoptive parents, and siblings who have been separated from families. Registry is a computerized, multilevel, cross-reference file system. Also has newsletter, rap groups, search workshops, and an extensive library.

The American Adoption Congress
1000 Connecticut Avenue NW #9
Washington, D.C. 20036
Information/helpline: (202) 483-3399

An advocacy organization open to all who are interested in achieving changes in attitudes, policies, and legislation that will guarantee access to identifying information for all adoptees and their birth and adoptive families.

Child Welfare League of America
440 First Street NW, #310
Washington, D.C. 20001
Information/helpline: (202) 638-2952
  Web site: http://www.cwla.org.

This is a national membership organization made up of eight hundred public and private voluntary child welfare agencies that are expert in child welfare, including adoption, child daycare, child protection from abuse and neglect, family foster care, chemical dependency, and housing and homelessness. Many publications available for children, parents, and professionals.

Concerned United Birthparents
2000 Walker Street
Des Moines, IA 50317
Information/helpline: 1-800-822-2777;
  operates 24 hours
  Office: (515) 263-9558.

Provides mutual support for birth parents, men and women who have surrendered children to adoption; also includes adoptees, adoptive parents, other adoption-affected persons, and professionals. Purposes are to prevent unnecessary family separations, assist adoption-separated relatives in searching for family members and educating the public about adoption issues. Monthly meetings, monthly newsletter, reunion registry, search workshops, correspondence, and phone calls provide mutual support to members. Many booklets are available.

Council for Equal Rights in Adoption
356 East 74th St.
New York, NY 10021
Information/helpline: (212) 988-0110
  (Monday, Tuesday, and Wednesday
  from 10 A.M. to 4 P.M. EST).
  English/French.

This organization helps birth mothers locate their children who were adopted and helps adoptees search for their mothers. Also offers free counseling to pregnant women. Support for all involved in adoption.

Family Service America
11700 W. Lake Park Dr.
Milwaukee, WI 53224
Information/helpline: 1-800-221-2681
  (9 A.M. to 5 P.M. CST)

This is a network of three hundred agencies that assist individuals and families to solve problems associated with parent-child tensions, marital difficulties, drug and alcohol dependency, teenage pregnancy, eldercare, child abuse and neglect, family violence, and work-related problems.

International Soundex Reunion Registry
P.O. Box 2312
Carson City, NV 89702
Information/helpline: (702) 882-7755
(9 A.M. to 4 P.M. PST)

Provides a reunion registry service for people who wish to contact or reunite with their next of kin-by-birth. Serves the needs of people who have been separated from their families due to divorce, adoption, foster care, or war. Available to any child/adoptee who is eighteen or older, to birth parents, and to adoptive parents of adoptees who are under eighteen. Does not perform a search but notifies registrants if there is a match in the reunion registry.

National Adoption Information Clearinghouse
P.O. Box 1182
Washington, D.C. 20013-1182
Toll-free: 1-888-251-0075;
(703) 352-3488 (8:30 A.M. to 5:30 P.M. EST). Fax: (703) 385-3206.
E-mail: naic@calib.com.
Web site: http://www.calib.com/naic.

Responds to all questions about adoption. Library of Adoption Materials is open to the public, or you may request a search and receive a printout. Publishes fact sheets on adoption. Directory lists crisis pregnancy centers, adoption agencies, and support groups. Maintains copies of every state's adoption laws and all federal laws and will provide copies. Does not place children for adoption or provide counseling but does make referrals to such services and to adoption experts.

The National Council for Adoption
1930 Seventeenth Street NW
Washington, D.C. 20009
Information/helpline: (202) 328-1200
(9 A.M. to 5:30 P.M. EST).
English/Spanish. Web site:
http://www.ncfa-usa.org.

This is a national association of licensed, nonprofit agencies that provide adoption services and counseling to people considering adoption. Its purpose is to promote sound, ethical adoption practices for all types of adoption. Also works to promote adoption through federal and state legislation, provides general information about the adoption process, and has a social worker available to give crisis pregnancy counseling. Has an extensive publication list.

National Council for Single Adoptive Parents
P.O. Box 15084
Chevy Chase, MD 20825
Information/helpline: (202) 966-6367
(9 A.M. to 6 P.M. EST)

National information service for single women and men interested in adoption that provides advice on the process. Publishes a handbook on how to adopt and how to cope once you become a parent.

INFERTILITY AND REPRODUCTIVE HEALTH

The American Society for Reproductive Medicine
1209 Montgomery Highway
Birmingham, AL 35216-2809
Information/helpline: (205) 978-5000
(8:30 A.M. to 5 P.M. CST)

Membership organization of physicians, scientists, and allied health professionals from every state devoted to advancing knowledge and expertise in all phases of reproductive medicine and biology. Services include patient education brochures, recommended readings and a monthly medical journal, and ethical guidelines covering reproductive technologies. Requests are forwarded to an automatic voicemail message system and are then answered by mail only, in about four to six weeks.

RESOLVE
1310 Broadway
Somerville, MA 02144
Information/helpline: (617) 623-0744
(9 A.M. to 12 P.M. and 1 to 4 P.M.
EST) Office: (617) 623-1156.
Web site: http://www.resolve.org.

Mission is to provide timely, compassionate support and information to people who are experiencing infertility and to increase awareness of infertility issues through advocacy and public education. Services include a national telephone helpline, national newsletter, more than sixty RESOLVE publications, physician referral service, medical call-in hours, a member-to-member contact system, and support service through fifty-seven local chapters.

Postpartum depression

Depression After Delivery
P.O. Box 1282
Morrisville, PA 19067
Information/helpline: 1-800-944-4773.
Office: (215) 295-3994.

This national organization provides support for women with postpartum depression. Offers education, information, and referrals for women and families coping with mental health issues associated with childbearing, promotes awareness of such issues to all sectors of the community, and advocates for the well-being of families.

Postpartum Support International
927 North Kellogg Avenue
Santa Barbara, CA 93111
Information/helpline: (805) 967-7636
(8 A.M. to 5 P.M. daily)
E-mail address:
74442.3467@CompuServe.com.

This worldwide network of support groups, institutions, and individuals is dedicated to eliminating denial and ignorance pertaining to maternal mood and anxiety disorders. Provides support to women and their families experiencing emotional difficulties related to childbearing and technical assistance on establishing support groups. Members receive a quarterly newsletter.

National Association of Postpartum
Care Services
P.O. Box 284
Glen Oaks, NY 11004
Information/helpline:
1-800-45-DOULA; operates
24 hours. Office: (512) 371-0782.

Association of national and international professionals concerned with the practical responsibilities and personal needs of families during the postdelivery period. A "doula" educates and helps the new mother, typically working on an hourly basis.

The Twins Foundation
P.O. Box 6043
Providence, RI 02940
Information/helpline: (401) 729-1000
(10 A.M. to 4 P.M. Monday through
Thursday).

A research information center that focuses on twins and other multiples. Serves twins, their families, the media, medical and social scientists, and the public through its publications, its National Twin Registry, and its multimedia resource center.

Twin Services, Inc.
P.O. Box 10066
Berkeley, CA 94709
Information/helpline: (510) 524-0863
(9 A.M. to 4:30 P.M. PST)

This organization is dedicated to reducing increased health and psychological risks associated with multiple births. The agency's TWINLINE staff provides health and parenting education, psychosocial services, and referrals. For educators and health and family services professionals, the agency offers technical assistance, training, and resources. Alameda and Contra Costa county residents may call the line to speak with a multiple-birth counselor for free. There is a fee for this service for those calling from outside these counties. Sliding scale fees are available. You can also call the TWIN-LINE to request a brochure describing available handouts and publications.

Visiting Nurse Association
National Headquarters
520 South Lafayette Park Pl. Suite 500
Los Angeles, CA 90057
(213) 386-7200. Refer to your phone
   directory for the office nearest you.

VNA home care is a comprehensive program offering a complete array of specialized services and support, including skilled care and private duty, nursing speciality services, infusion therapy, physical, occupational, speech, and respiratory therapy, medical social work, home health aide services, homemaking and companionship, maternal childcare, supportive care, telephone reassurance, durable medical equipment, respite care, and hospital home care coordination.

PREGNANCY AND INFANT LOSS

Abiding Hearts
P.O. Box 5245
Bozeman, MT 59717
e-mail: hearts@imt.net.

A support network for parents continuing pregnancy after an adverse prenatal diagnosis. Provides literature, information on how to best support parents, and a contact parent program for parents who wish to talk with other parents who have survived taking a fatally diagnosed baby to term.

A.M.E.N.D. (Aiding a Mother &
   Father Experiencing Neonatal
   Death)
4324 Berrywick Terr.
St. Louis, MO 63128
Information/helpline: (314) 487-7582

Offers a one-on-one peer contact for bereaved parents who have experienced the loss of an infant through miscarriage, stillbirth, or neonatal death.

American Sudden Infant Death
   Syndrome Institute
6065 Roswell Rd., Suite 876
Atlanta, GA 30328
Information/helpline: 1-800-232-7437
   (outside Georgia), 1-800-847-7437
   (Georgia), operates 24 hours. Office
   telephone: (404) 843-1030.

The institute's mission is to prevent and conquer SIDS and promote infant health through research, clinical services, professional and community education. Clinical services are provided for infants at increased risk for SIDS after referral by the infant's physician regardless of the family's ability to pay. Crisis phone counseling, bereavement literature, and referrals are available.

Association for the Care of Children's Health
7910 Woodmont Ave., Suite 300
Bethesda, MD 20814-3015
Information/helpline: (301) 654-6549.
  Fax: (301) 986-4553.

A multidisciplinary membership organization of health care providers, family members, facility designers, teachers, hospitals, childlife specialists, and others committed to improving the quality of care for children and their families through education, dissemination of resources, research, and advocacy. Publications of interest to families and professionals involved with neonatal care are available.

Bereavement Services/RTS
Gundersen Lutheran Medical Center
1910 South Ave.
La Crosse, WI 54601
Information/helpline: 1-800-362-9567, ext. 4747 (8 A.M. to 4:30 P.M. CST)
  Office: (608) 791-4747

Provides training and support materials to professionals working with parents who have lost a baby through miscarriage, ectopic pregnancy, stillbirth, or newborn death. Parents will find a compassionate staff who listen, provide written resources, and/or offer referrals to local support groups or RTS-trained health professionals. A catalog of resources is available on request.

Center for Loss in Multiple Birth (CLIMB)
P.O. Box 1064
Palmer, AK 99645-1064
Information/helpline: (907) 746-6123
  (10 A.M. to 10 P.M. PST)

Support by and for parents who have experienced the death of one or both twins or higher multiples during pregnancy or birth, in infancy, or in childhood. Provides a packet of information and support articles, a quarterly newsletter, a parent contact list throughout the U.S. and Canada, and information on local networks.

High Risk Moms, Inc.
P.O. Box 389165
Chicago, IL 60638-9165
Information/helpline: (630) 515-5453

A peer support group available to all women and their families who have had, anticipate, or are experiencing a high-risk pregnancy. A telephone support network, a newsletter, information sheets, and Lamaze tapes are available.

The March of Dimes
Birth Defects Foundation
1275 Mamaroneck Ave.
White Plains, NY 10605
Information line: 1-800-MO DIMES;
  (914) 997-4764 (TTY). Helpline:
  (914) 428-7100 (9 A.M. to 5 P.M. EST). English/Spanish.

Mission is to improve the health of babies by preventing birth defects and infant mortality. Campaign for Healthy Babies funds research, community services, education, and advocacy. Although this organization does not offer direct services, single copies of public health education brochures are available. Offers information about prenatal care, pre-pregnancy planning, and birth defects. Referrals to support groups are available.

National Society of Genetic Counselors
233 Canterbury Dr.
Wellingford, PA 19086
Inquire by mail.

Professional membership organization serving the educational needs of its members. Provides referrals to genetic counselors. Does not provide information about specific genetic disorders.

National Sudden Infant Death Syndrome Resource Center
2070 Chain Bridge Road, Suite 450
Vienna, VA 22182
Information/Helpline: (703) 821-8955 or (703) 902-1249 ext. 249 (8:30 A.M. to 5:30 P.M. EST)

Provides information services and technical assistance on SIDS and related topics. Develops bibliographies, information sheets, the Information Exchange newsletter, conducts customized searches of databases on SIDS, and provides referrals to state SIDS services and other national and local organizations.

Pen Parents, Inc.
P.O. Box 8738
Reno, NV 89507-8738
Phone and Fax: (707) 322-4773 or (702) 323-2489. E-mail: penparents@prodigy.com.

Provides addresses and telephone numbers of organizations serving bereaved parents.

Pregnancy and Infant Loss Center
1421 East Wayzata Blvd. #30
Wayzata, MN 55391
Information/helpline: (612) 473-9372 (9 A.M. to 4 P.M., CST)

Provides information, comfort, understanding, resources, and perspective to individuals and families who have experienced the death of their baby. Referrals to national and international support groups. Publishes a newsletter and distributes literature.

Pregnancy Loss Support Program
9 East 69 St.
New York, NY 10021
Information/helpline: (212) 535-5900, ext.10 (9 A.M. to 5 P.M. EST)

A nonsectarian counseling program funded by the National Council of Jewish Women to aid grieving couples who have experienced a pregnancy loss. Free phone counseling is provided by trained volunteers. Following telephone counseling, participants may join peer support groups. Support services are also available for couples who are pregnant after a loss. Referral information is available on physicians and psychotherapists who specialize in pregnancy loss.

SHARE-Pregnancy and Infant Loss Support
St. Joseph Health Center
300 First Capitol Dr.
St. Charles, MO 63301
Information/helpline: 1-800-821-6819 or (314) 947-6164 (9 A.M. to 5 P.M. CST). Answering machine after hours. Fax: (314) 947-7486. Web site: http://nationalshareoffice.com.

Through its network of more than one hundred groups nationwide, SHARE offers support and understanding to those who have been touched by the death of a baby through miscarriage, stillbirth, ectopic pregnancy, or newborn death. This support encompasses emotional, physical, spiritual, and social healing, as well as sustaining the family unit through mutual-help groups. Publishes bimonthly newsletter and other bereavement resources. Makes referrals to local groups.

Southwest SIDS Research Institute
100 Medical Drive
Lake Jackson, TX 77566
Information/helpline: 1-800-245-7437 (7 A.M. to 5 P.M. CST). Office: (409) 299-2814. English/Spanish.

Provides research, educational, and counseling services to families of SIDS and high-risk infants nationwide. Medical services are provided to Texas residents who can attend regularly scheduled clinic appointments.

Sudden Infant Death Syndrome
  Alliance
1314 Bedford Ave., Suite 210
Baltimore, MD 21208
Information/helpline: 1-800-221-SIDS
  (24 hours). Office:
  (410) 653-8226.

National support network with fifty-five affiliates whose primary users are new and expectant parents and grandparents and SIDS parents. Provides information and referrals to peer parent support and professional counseling groups. A counselor on staff is available to respond to emergency calls.

Sexually transmitted diseases

American Social Health Association
P.O. Box 13827
Research Triangle Park, NC 27709
National STD Hotline: 1-800-227-8922
  (8 A.M. to 11 P.M.)
National Herpes Hotline:
  (919) 361-8488 (9 A.M. to 7 P.M.)
Herpes Resource Center 1-800-230-6039
  (9 A.M. to 7 P.M.) to order materials
  about herpes.
ASHA Healthline (to order
  publications about sexual health
  communication): 1-800-972-8500,
  24 hours every day.

ASHA is dedicated to the prevention and control of all sexually transmitted diseases, and its Women's Health Program is designed to raise awareness of the disproportionate impact that STDs have on women. Hotline services provide information, counseling, and referrals. The National STD Hotline provides information on herpes, HPV, chlamydia, pelvic inflammatory disease, syphilis, and gonorrhea. The National Herpes Hotline answers questions and offers referrals to local support groups including extended service in French to Canadians. Many publications are available.

6. DISABILITIES

General information and referral

Direct Link for the Disabled
P.O. Box 1036
Solvang, CA 93464
Information/helpline: (805) 688-1603
  (8 A.M. to 1 P.M. PST). Web site:
  http://www.directlinkup.com.

Direct Link for the Disabled, Inc., offers help and hope to people who have run out of answers by linking them to resources nationwide that can make a meaningful difference. Provides local, state, and national referrals. Information and referral by phone is available free of charge. Informational packets, fact sheets, and research services are available for a charge. No direct services or financial assistance is available from Direct Link.

Family Caregiver Alliance
425 Bush St., Suite 500
San Francisco, CA 94108
Information/helpline: 1-800-445-8106
   (California only, 9 A.M. to 5 P.M.
   CST). English, Spanish, Tagalog,
   and Chinese. Office: (415) 434-3388.

Assists families of adults with brain impairments such as Alzheimer's disease, stroke, head injury, Parkinson's, and AIDS dementia. Services include information, educational programs, publications, emotional support and counseling, respite assistance, research, and advocacy. Direct services are available to California residents; information about diagnosis and care options is available to anyone who calls or writes.

Well Spouse Foundation
P.O. Box 801
New York, NY 10023
Information/helpline: 1-800-838-0879;
   operates 24 hours. Office:
   (212) 644-1241 (10 A.M. to 4 P.M.
   EST).

This is a national organization that provides support to husbands, wives, and partners of the chronically ill and/or disabled people through a bimonthly newsletter, local support groups, letter-writing groups, and weekend conferences. Most members are women.

CHILDREN AND STUDENTS WITH DISABILITIES

American Council on Rural Special
   Education
221 Milton Bennion Hall
University of Utah
Salt Lake City, UT 84112
Information/helpline: (801) 585-5659
   (8 A.M. to 5 P.M.)

ACRES is a national organization that brings together special educators, related services staff, administrators, teacher trainers, and parents who are committed to the enhancement of services to students and individuals with disabilities living in rural areas. Publishes a bimonthly newsletter, a quarterly journal, and other publications.

ARCH National Resource Center for
   Respite and Crisis Care Services
800 Eastowne Dr., Suite 105
Chapel Hill, NC 27514
Information/helpline: 1-800-473-1727
   or 1-800-7 RELIEF for the National
   Respite Locator Service (8:30 A.M.
   to 5 P.M. EST). Office:
   (919) 490-5577

Respite means temporary relief for families and caregivers. It is a service provided to children with disabilities, chronic or terminal illnesses, and to children at risk of abuse and neglect. The National Respite Locator Service can provide the name of respite programs in your area which may be able to provide help. ARCH also has a National Resource Center with a lending library of relevant publications and audiovisual material, access to national electronic bulletin boards, and a national registry of consultants.

Association of Birth Defect Children
827 Irma St.
Orlando, FL 32803
Information/helpline: 1-800-313-2232;
   operates 24 hours. Office:
   (407) 245-7035 (9 A.M. to 4 P.M.
   EST).

Provides parents and professionals with information about birth defects and services for children with disabilities. Sponsors the National Birth Defects Register, which collects data and explores links between birth defects and environmental exposures. Matches families of children with similar birth defects for mutual support.

The Council for Exceptional Children
1920 Association Dr.
Reston, VA 22091
Office: (703) 620-3660 (9 A.M. to 5 P.M.)

International professional membership organization dedicated to improving educational outcomes for students with disabilities and/or the gifted. Maintains a clearinghouse for information on children with disabilities. Education Resource Information Center phone is 1-800-328-0272. Some publications may be purchased by nonmembers.

The Eric Clearinghouse on
   Disabilities and Gifted Education
1920 Association Dr.
Reston, VA 22091
Information/helpline: 1-800-328-0272
   (voice/TDD)

Gathers and disseminates educational information on disabilities and giftedness across all age levels. Develops publications, including digests, research summaries, books, and reports that summarize information on current and emerging topics. Provides information users with references and referrals.

Federation for Children with Special
   Needs
95 Berkeley St., Suite 104
Boston, MA 02116
(617) 482-2915

Information and referral services on issues covering special education legislation, respite care, recreation, and health. Current statewide projects to develop self-help groups include Parent Training and Information, Agent Orange Parent Network for Vietnam Veteran families, and the Parent Advocacy League. Works with other parent centers across the country in Technical Assistance for Parent Programs, National Parent Resource Center, and National Early Childhood Technical Assistance System.

Heartspring
240 Jardine Dr.
Wichita, KS 67219
Information/helpline: 1-800-835-1043
   (ext. 315 for TDD), 8 A.M. to 5 P.M.
   CST.

Serves students with multiple disabilities such as autism, cerebral palsy, hearing and visual impairments, behavioral disorders, and mental retardation. Available to young people aged five through twenty-one from anywhere in the U.S. Also offers an intensive seven-week behavioral program and extended comprehensive assessment program during the summer.

HEATH Resource Center of the
   American Council on Education
One Dupont Circle
Washington, D.C. 20036
Information/helpline: 1-800-544-3284
   (voice/TTY), 9 A.M. to 5 P.M. EST;
   Office: (202) 939-9322.

HEATH operates a national clearinghouse on postsecondary education for people with disabilities and disseminates information to students, their families, advisers, and advocates. A HEATH Resource Directory, which lists more than 150 disability organizations, *How to Choose a College: A Guide for the Student with a Disability*, and other publications are available in print or on cassette or computer disk. Single copies are free.

National Center for Youth with Disabilities
University of Minnesota, Box 721
420 Delaware St., S.E.
Minneapolis, MN 55455
Information/helpline: (612) 626-2825;
 (612) 624-3939 (TDD), 8 A.M. to
 4:30 P.M. CST.

This is an information, policy, and resource center focusing on adolescents with chronic illness and disabilities and the issues surrounding their transition to adult life. The library collects current information to assist researchers, service providers, parents, and youth, and is accessible through the toll-free number. Publications are available at nominal cost.

National Information Center for Children and Youth with Disabilities (NICHCY)
P.O. Box 1492
Washington, D.C. 20013-1492
Information/helpline: 1-800-695-0285
 (9 A.M. to 5 P.M. EST).
 English/Spanish. Office:
 (202) 884-8200 (voice/TTY).

Information clearinghouse that provides free information on disabilities and disability-related issues. Children and youth with disabilities, birth to age twenty-two, are this national organization's special focus.

National Information Clearinghouse (NIC) for Infants with Disabilities and Life-Threatening Conditions
Center for Developmental Disabilities, School of Medicine, Dept. of Pediatrics
University of South Carolina
Columbia, SC 29208
Information/helpline: 1-800-922-9234, ext. 201 (voice/TTD), 9 A.M. to 5 P.M. EST.

Information specialists respond to individual requests and assist families in accessing services such as parent support and training, advocacy, health care, financial resources, assistive technology, and early intervention. They also refer callers to local and national resources. NIC produces bibliographies, fact sheets and articles related to the care of and services available to families of infants with disabilities. These are available in English, Spanish, and alternative formats.

National Parent Network on Disabilities
1727 King St., Suite 305
Alexandria, VA 22314
Information/helpline: (703) 684-6763
 (9 A.M. to 5 P.M. EST)

Reports on government policy and planning affecting services for people with disabilities and acts as an advocate. Serves as a link between parent organizations and publishes a newsletter addressing concerns of parents across the United States. Provides information and referrals to parent-training and support groups.

Pediatric Projects
P.O. Box 571555
Tarzana, CA 91357
Information/helpline: 1-800-947-0947

This organization is dedicated to helping children and their families understand health care. Services include toll-free phone consultation for parents of ill, disabled, or hospitalized children, a directory of over four hundred parent support groups, a database of books and articles, medical toys and books that prepare children for medical treatment, as well as a newsletter and professional seminars.

Very Special Arts
1300 Connecticut Ave. NW, Suite 700
Washington, D.C. 20036
Information/helpline: 1-800-933-8721
or (202) 737-0645 (TDD), 9 A.M. to
5 P.M. EST. Web site:
http://www.vsarts.org.

Mission is to promote arts education and creative expression involving children and adults with disabilities. Programs include creative writing, dance, drama, music, and visual arts. Affiliations in fifty states and eighty-five countries.

DISCRIMINATION/LEGAL HELP AND INFORMATION

For information about workplace discrimination and job resources, see the Resource Directory chapter Work.

ACLU Lesbian & Gay Rights/AIDS
Project
132 West 43rd St.
New York, NY 10036
(212) 944-9800, ext. 545 (9 A.M. to
5:30 P.M. EST)

Undertakes precedent-setting litigation, public policy advocacy, and public education on civil liberties issues raised by the AIDS crisis. The Project's work covers issues of discrimination, confidentiality, public health policy, and access to care. Also acts as a backup center for the more than fifty ACLU affiliates around the nation as they work on AIDS issues.

Bazelon Center for Mental Health Law
1101 15th St. NW, Suite 1212
Washington, D.C. 20005
Information/helpline: (202) 467-5730
or (202) 467-4232 (TDD)

Bazelon Center is the pre-eminent national legal advocate for children and adults with mental disabilities. In addition to pursuing test-case litigation and federal policy reform, it provides training and technical assistance to legal services offices, protection and advocacy agencies, state ombudsman programs, and other advocates for low-income individuals and families. It also publishes issue papers, booklets, and manuals explaining and interpreting major federal laws and regulations that protect the rights of children and adults with disabilities. Makes resources available to children and adults with disabilities.

GENERAL INFORMATION AND REFERRAL

Department of Health and Human
Services
Office for Civil Rights
330 Independence Ave. SW
Washington, D.C. 20201
Hotlines: (202) 863-0100 (voice, Metro
area)
(202) 863-0101 (TDD, Metro area)
1-800-368-1019 (voice, outside
Washington)
1-800-863-0101 (TDD, outside
Washington)

The Office for Civil Rights is responsible for enforcing federal laws that protect against discrimination on the basis of race, color, national origin, age, disability, and sex by health and human service providers. OCR will conduct a prompt investigation whenever a complaint indicates a failure to comply with the applicable regulations under their jurisdiction. Any individual, or class of individuals, who believes herself to be subjected to discrimination may file a written complaint with the office.

Department of Housing and Urban
   Development
Office of Fair Housing and Equal
   Opportunity
451 Seventh St. SW
Room 5204
Washington, D.C. 20410-2000
1-800-669-9777 or 1-800-927-9275
   (TDD)

Request information about housing discrimination. The Washington HUD office can also refer you to your regional HUD office for more information.

National Association of Protection and
   Advocacy Systems
(NAPAS)
900 Second St. NE, Suite 211
Washington, D.C. 20002
Information/helpline: (202) 408-9514
   (TDD) or (202) 408-9521,
   8 A.M. to 5 P.M. EST.
English/French.

Provides training and technical assistance to federally mandated protection and advocacy systems (P&As), which operate in every state and territory. Also provides information and referral to eligible clients. Eligibility includes persons with developmental disabilities, mental illnesses, or people who meet the disability definition in the Americans with Disabilities Act. Provides referrals to state protection and advocacy agencies.

National Fair Housing Alliance
1212 New York Ave. NW, Suite 525
Washington, D.C. 20005
(202) 898-1661

To find out if there is a fair housing organization in your area, contact the number at left, check your telephone directory, or look at the listings below for information.

United States Architectural and
   Transportation Barriers
   Compliance Board
1331 F St. NW, Suite 1000
Washington, D.C. 20004
Information/helpline: 1-800-872-2253
   (voice/TTY), 9 A.M. to 5:30 P.M.
   Office: (202) 272-5434 ext. 38.

Responsible for ensuring accessibility in all facilities owned, rented, or funded by the federal government. Offers training and technical assistance to individuals and organizations throughout the country on removing architectural, transportation, and communication barriers.

United States Department of Justice
Civil Rights Division, Disability Rights
   Section
P.O. Box 66738
Washington, D.C. 20035
Information/helpline: 1-800-514-0301
   (voice) and 1-800-514-0383 (TDD)
English/Spanish.

Provides information about the Americans with Disabilities Act (ADA). An automated service to listen to recorded information and to order publications is available twenty-four hours a day seven days a week. ADA specialists are available on Monday, Tuesday, Wednesday, and Friday from 10 A.M. to 6 P.M. and on Thursday from 1 P.M. to 6 P.M. EST to provide technical assistance or answer questions about filing a complaint. Offers many publications about ADA law including *ADA Questions and Answers,* which provides basic information in a simple question and answer format. Available in English and Spanish.

Home adaptation

Adaptive Environments Center
374 Congress St., Suite 301
Boston, MA 02210
Schools Hotline: 1-800-893-1225
    (voice/TDD), 9 A.M. to 5 P.M. EST.
    Office: (617) 695-1225 (voice/TDD).

The Center's goal is to eliminate barriers that limit education, employment and recreational and cultural life to people who have disabilities. Staff answers questions regarding the rights and responsibilities of schools for students, as well as others with disabilities. *The Consumer's Guide to Home Adaptation* includes information about products, financial assistance, and outside help for the alterations process. It is available on audiotape.

Independent living

National Council on Independent
    Living
2111 Wilson Blvd., Suite 405
Arlington, VA 22201
Information/helpline: (703) 525-3406
    (voice) or (703) 525-3407 (TTY),
    8:30 A.M. to 5 P.M.

NCIL is the national membership association of local Independent Living Centers. It is the only cross-disability grassroots national organization run by and for people with disabilities. Provides technical assistance and leadership to its membership in many areas of concern to the disability community.

Library program

National Library Service for the Blind
    and Physically Handicapped
The Library of Congress
Washington, D.C. 20542
Information/helpline: (202) 707-0744
    (voice/TDD), 8 A.M. to 4:30 P.M.
    EST Monday through Friday

This is a free national library program for blind people and people with physical disabilities that selects and produces full-length books and magazines in Braille and on recorded disk and cassette. Materials are circulated through a network of cooperating libraries. Playback equipment is loaned free to readers as long as recorded materials provided by NLS are being borrowed.

Publications

It's Okay! magazine
1 Springbank Drive
St. Catharines, Ontario, Canada
    L2S 2K1

It's Okay! is the only consumer-written quarterly magazine on sex, sexuality, self-esteem, and disability in North America. A great resource for women who are disabled and are experiencing loss of self-esteem and sexual identity. Sample copies $2.

Resources for Rehabilitation
33 Bedford St., Suite 19A
Lexington, MA 02173
(617) 862-6455

Publications provide crucial information to women who have experienced a disability or chronic health condition. Resource guides enable women to find out about organizations, publications, and assistive devices that promote independence. Of special interest is *A Woman's Guide to Coping with Disabilities*, which includes information about sexual functioning, pregnancy, and child rearing.

ABLEDATA
8455 Colesville Rd., Suite 935
Silver Spring, MD 20910
Information line: 1-800-227-0216,
    (301) 608-8998, or (301) 608-8912
    (TTY). Fax: (301) 608-8958.
    Web site: www.abledata.com.

ABLEDATA is a national database of information on assistive technology available from national and international sources. Information specialists, database searches, and fact sheets are available. Most publications and search results are available in large print, cassette, Braille, and on PC-compatible diskettes. For a brochure packet, call the ABLEDATA office.

American Academy of Physical
    Medicine and Rehabilitation
Number One IBM Plaza, Suite 2500
Chicago, IL 60611
(312) 464-9700

The national medical society of physical medicine and rehabilitation physicians (physiatrists). Physiatrists treat acute and chronic pain and musculoskeletal disorders, arthritis, tendonitis, back pain, and work- or sports-related injuries. AAPM&R's mission is to maximize the quality of life while minimizing the incidence, severity, and prevalence of impairments, disabilities, and handicaps. Provides educational brochures and referral lists of physiatrists by geographic area.

The American Occupational Therapy
    Association
4720 Montgomery Ln.
Bethesda, MD 20824
Information/helpline: 1-800-377-8555
    (TDD only). Office: (301) 652-2682.

Offers materials on how occupational therapists help people with disabilities achieve the greatest possible functional independence.

American Rehabilitation Association
1910 Association Drive
Reston, VA 20191
Information/helpline: 1-800-368-3513.
    Office: (703) 648-9300.
    Fax: (703) 648-0346.

The largest not-for-profit organization serving vocational, medical, and community support rehabilitation providers. Serves its members by affecting changes in public policy, developing educational and training programs, and promoting research. In addition, it provides networking and communications opportunities, all of which help to ensure quality care and access to services to more than 4 million persons with disabilities.

American Speech-Language-Hearing
    Association (ASHA)
10801 Rockville Pike
Rockville, MD 20852
Information/helpline: 1-800-638-8255
    (9 A.M. to 4:30 P.M. EST). Office:
    (301) 897-5700.

National professional association of speech-language pathologists and audiologists. Provides information about speech and hearing disorders and referrals to speech-language pathologists and audiologists. Information brochures are available on speech, language, or hearing problems.

Breaking New Ground
1146 ABE Building, Purdue University
West Lafayette, IN 47907
Information/helpline: 1-800-825-4264
(voice/TDD) or (317) 494-5088
(voice/TDD), 8 A.M. to 5 P.M. EST.

Internationally recognized as a primary source of information on rehabilitation technology relating to agricultural work sites. Services that are available to residents of Indiana include a resource center concerned with work-site modifications, adaptive tools, and rural independent living skills.

National Rehabilitation Information Center (NARIC)
8455 Colesville Rd., Suite 935
Silver Spring, MD 20910
Information/helpline: 1-800-346-2742
(voice), 8 A.M. to 6 P.M. EST.
(301) 495-5626 (TTY). English,
American Sign Language. Web site:
http://www.naric.com/naric.

This library and information center has more than 40,000 documents on all aspects of disability and rehabilitation, including physical disabilities, mental retardation, psychiatric disabilities, independent living, medical rehabilitation, special education, employment, assistive technology, law, and public policy. Information specialists provide individualized assistance to patrons and tailor the information to the needs of the user. Quick reference and referrals are provided at no cost to the user; extensive searches for a nominal fee. Publications and searches are available in large print, cassette, or Braille on-line on NARIC's home page and on PC compatible diskette. Also has many fact sheets and resource guides.

Office of Special Education and Rehabilitative Services (OSERS)
U.S. Department of Education
330 C St. SW, Room 3132
Washington, D.C. 20202-2524
Information/helpline: (202) 205-8241
(voice/TTY)

OSERS mission is to provide leadership to help people with disabilities achieve full integration and participation in society. OSERS is divided into three program areas: the Office of Special Education Programs, the Rehabilitation Services Administration, which administers programs to support employment and independence for people with disabilities, such as vocational rehabilitation programs, and the National Institute on Disability and Rehabilitation Research. Also provides information about federal legislation and programs for people with disabilities.

PRIDE (Promote Real Independence for the Disabled or Elderly)
391 Long Hill Rd., Box 1293
Groton, CT 06340-1293
Information line: (860) 445-1448

Rehabilitation assistance in the areas of home management and personal grooming. Resources are available for adaptation and modifications of garments so that everyone can wear fashionable, well-fitted clothes. Sewing assistance, special patterns, books, and informational sheets are available at varying prices. Consultation about a particular problem in dressing, grooming, and home management is available by telephone or letter.

SOCIAL SECURITY

Social Security Administration
1-800-772-1213, 1-800-325-0778 (TTY).
Web site: http://www.ssa.gov.

Information about Social Security and Medicare is available twenty-four hours a day. Call for an appointment or speak to a service representative 7 A.M. to 7 P.M. on business days. Lines are busiest early in the week and early in the month.

The Center for Research on Women with Disabilities, Department of Physical Medicine and Rehabilitation, Baylor College of Medicine
3440 Richmond Ave.
Houston, TX 77046
Information/helpline: (713) 960-0505.
 Fax: (713) 961-3555.

Focuses on the independence, health, and educational needs of women with disabilities. Provides research, training, and technical assistance for independent living centers nationwide.

The Center on Human Policy
Syracuse University
805 South Crouse Ave.
Syracuse, NY 13244
Information/helpline: (315) 443-3851
 (8 A.M. to 5 P.M. EST).

Policy, research, and advocacy organization involved in the national movement to ensure the rights of people with disabilities. Offers referrals and disseminates information. Publications are geared toward women with disabilities.

Deafpride
Chapel Hill
800 Florida Ave. NE
Washington, D.C. 20002
Information/helpline: (202) 675-6700
 (voice/TDD), 8:30 A.M. to 4:30 P.M.
 EST

Advocates to achieve complete access to health services for the deaf community, related to maternal and child health, HIV/AIDS, and drug addiction. Project Access offers advocacy classes to deaf women in Washington, D.C., to enhance their ability to care for their own health and the health of their families. This organization was instrumental in the establishment of both the Black Deaf Advocates, a nationwide organization with many state chapters, and Deaf Women United, a nationwide organization for deaf women.

Health Resource Center for Women with Disabilities
Rehabilitation Institute of Chicago
345 East Superior St.
Chicago, IL 60611
Information/helpline: (312) 908-7997
 (Monday, Tuesday, and Thursday
 from 9:30 A.M. to 4:30 P.M. CST)

This is a program in which disabled women work in collaboration with hospital staff to design and deliver health services for women with disabilities. The Center provides accessible medical services, conducts research in disabled women's health issues, and offers educational resources for women with disabilities and health care professionals. Free newsletter to disabled women nationwide and free quarterly seminars.

The National Clearinghouse on Women and Girls with Disabilities
Educational Equity Concepts
114 E. 32 St., Suite 701
New York, NY 10016
Information/helpline: (212) 725-1803
 (voice/TTY), 9:30 A.M. to 5:30 P.M.
 EST. English and Spanish spoken.
 Fax: (212) 725-0947. e-mail:
 75507.1306@Compuserve.com.

Publishes a national directory of services for women and girls with disabilities. Goals are to increase public awareness of issues faced by women and girls with disabilities. Other EEC programs increase the integration of adults and children with disabilities into all aspects of education, work, and social and family life.

Through the Looking Glass
2198 Sixth St.
Berkeley, CA 94710-2204
Information/helpline: 1-800-644-2666
(9 A.M. to 12 P.M. and 1 P.M. to 5 P.M.
weekdays). Office: (510) 848-1112.

National information and referral source for parents with disabilities, family members, and service providers. It is staffed primarily by people with personal disability experience.

VETERANS AND THEIR FAMILIES

Disabled American Veterans (DAV)
Women Veterans Task Force
807 Maine Ave., SW
Washington, D.C. 20024
Information/helpline: (202) 554-3501
(8:30 A.M. to 4:30 P.M. EST)

DAV works to ensure appropriate medical services for hospitalized women veterans and to assure the availability of treatment for gender-related conditions, gynecological care, and treatment and counseling for posttraumatic stress disorder and related physical conditions for women who were victims of rape and assault in the service. DAV represents individual veterans, their dependents, and survivors in obtaining monetary benefits. Experts on veterans' benefits are available through the regional VA office. Services include counseling, a thorough case review, and representation. Some of the benefits which may be available to you are disability compensation, pension, outpatient treatment, hospitalization at a VA medical facility, educational assistance program, readjustment counseling, and employment assistance.

Swords to Plowshares
995 Market St., Third Floor
San Francisco, CA 94103
Information/helpline: (415) 247-8777

Specializes in veterans rights and provides a full range of direct services to veterans. Provides free referrals, information, and counseling in the areas of human services, employment assistance, and housing. Swords' legal department represents litigants in claims before the Department of Veterans Affairs and the Court of Veterans Appeals. Eligible clients are veterans or dependents of veterans. Cases are accepted on the particular facts at issue.

DISABILITY-SPECIFIC ORGANIZATIONS

ADDISON'S DISEASE AND OTHER ADRENAL GLAND DISEASES

The National Adrenal Diseases
Foundation
505 Northern Blvd., Suite 200
Great Neck, NY 11021
Information/helpline: (516) 487-4992

Dedicated to providing support, information, and research for individuals with Addison's disease as well as other diseases of the adrenal glands. Sponsors support groups across the U.S. Members receive quarterly newsletters, educational materials, and responses to their general physical and mental health questions.

AIDS

See the Directory chapter "Life-Threatening Illness" under "HIV Infection and AIDS."

Alzheimer's Association

Alzheimer's Association
919 North Michigan Ave., Tenth Floor
Chicago, IL 60611
Information/helpline: 1-800-272-3900;
 operates 24 hours. English/Spanish.
 Office: (312) 335-5776.

Services include support groups, adult daycare programs, respite care programs and helplines through its national chapter and volunteer network. Aids families in making the decision to confirm the diagnosis of Alzheimer's disease. Provides information and local chapter referrals. Publishes a quarterly newsletter and distributes many brochures, books, and fact sheets, some of which are free.

Alzheimer's Disease Education and
 Referral Center
P.O. Box 8250
Silver Spring, MD 20907-8250
Information/helpline: 1-800-438-4380
 (8:30 A.M. to 5 P.M. EST).
 English/Spanish.
 Office: (312) 335-8700. Web site:
 http://www.alzheimers.org/adr.

This is a service of the National Institute on Aging, which is funded by the federal government. There are twenty-eight Alzheimer's Disease Centers at major medical institutions across the nation, many of which offer diagnosis and medical management. Provides referrals, information, free publications, and an opportunity to talk with an information specialist and to participate in drug trials and other clinical research.

AMPUTATION

The American Amputee Foundation
P.O. Box 250218
Little Rock, AR 72225
Information/helpline: (501) 666-2523
 (8 A.M. to 5 P.M. CST)

Serves amputees and their families by providing product information, services, and self-help publications. Offers both direct and indirect assistance, such as help with insurance claims, life care planning, direct financial aid for prosthetic devices and home modifications, technical assistance in developing self-help programs, hospital visitations, counseling services, and referrals. Publishes a newsletter and many self-help guides.

National Amputation Foundation
38-40 Church St.
Malverne, NY 11565
Information/helpline: (516) 887-3600
 (10 A.M. to 4 P.M. EST)

Services include legal counsel, vocational guidance and placement, social activities, liaison with outside groups, psychological aid, and training in the use of prosthetic devices. Offers an extensive list of publications, many of which are free.

ARTHRITIS

Arthritis Foundation
P.O. Box 7669
Atlanta, GA 30357
Information/helpline: 1-800-283-7800;
 operates 24 hours

Provides information concerning arthritis through brochures; most are free. Provides services through chapters across the country, many of which offer arthritis education classes, aquatics programs, exercise classes, and physician referrals. American Juvenile Arthritis Organization serves children and offers workshops for parents.

Autism

Autism Services Center
P.O. Box 507
Huntington, WV 25710-0507
Information/helpline: (304) 525-8014
  (9 A.M. to 5 P.M. EST)

Serves people with autism and other developmental disabilities and the people who care for them. Operates a National Autism Hotline for information, referral, and advocacy relating to needs of people with autism. Provides direct personal services to those living in West Virginia, including case management, personal care nursing, residential services, family support, job training and placement, and respite services for caregivers.

Autism Society of America
7910 Woodmont Ave., Suite 650
Bethesda, MD 20814
Information/helpline: 1-800-3AUTISM
  (328-8476), 9 A.M. to 5 P.M. EST.
Office: (301) 657-0881.

Operates a network of more than two hundred chapters in forty-eight states. Works with parents, professionals, and the general public to educate them about autism. Publishes a newsletter and distributes free information packages on autism topics.

Blindness

Look under "Vision" in this chapter.

Brain injury

Brain Injury Association
1776 Massachusetts Ave. NW, Suite 100
Washington, D.C. 20036
Information/helpline: 1-800-444-6443
  (9 A.M. to 5 P.M. EST). Office:
  (202) 296-6443.

Through its Family Helpline, it provides information concerning every aspect of brain injury, including rehabilitation facilities and state associations. Maintains an extensive library of books, brochures, tapes, and videos. Also spearheads a network of information exchange through its Defense and Veterans Head Injury Program and numerous advisory groups and Brain Injury Resource Centers. Direct financial assistance to people with brain injury is available through the foundation and through its scholarship program.

The Perspectives Network
P.O. Box 1859
Cummings, GA 30128
Information/helpline: 1-800-685-6302
  (9 A.M. to 5 P.M. EST). Office:
  (770) 844-6898.

This organization, which serves brain injury survivors, provides peer communication networks, brain injury empathy workshops, a quarterly magazine, computer forums, fact brochures, and a lending library.

Cancer

See the Directory chapter "Life-Threatening Illness."

CEREBRAL PALSY

United Cerebral Palsy Associations, Inc.
1660 L St. NW, Suite 700
Washington, D.C. 20036
Information/helpline:
1-800-USA-5UCP (voice/TDD).
   (202) 776-0406 (voice/TDD).

For further information, contact the United Cerebral Palsy Associations.

CFIDS — CHRONIC FATIGUE SYNDROME

The CFIDS Association of America
P.O. Box 220398
Charlotte, NC 28222
Information/helpline: 1-800-442-3437;
   operates 24 hours. Office:
   (704) 364-0016.

Maintains extensive referral network of more than two thousand support organizations, physicians, and disability attorneys familiar with the disease. Provides free information packets to inquirers on the toll-free 1-800 number. To meet the needs for immediate information, a pay-per-call number (900-896-2343) provides instant access to the most-asked-about topics.

CLEFT PALATE/CRANIOFACIAL DISFIGUREMENT

Children's Craniofacial Association
P.O. Box 280297
Dallas, TX 75228
Information/helpline: 1-800-535-3643;
   operates 24 hours. English/Spanish.
   Office: (214) 994-9902.

Services are geared to craniofacially disfigured individuals and their families. Free patient clinics provide medical consultation, evaluation, opinions, and referrals. Offers a networking list of people with similar conditions and experiences. Publishes a quarterly newsletter, provides financial aid for food, lodging, and travel for eligible patients undergoing treatment. Hosts an annual family retreat.

Cleft Palate Foundation
1218 Grandview Ave.
Pittsburgh, PA 15211
Information/helpline:
1-800-24-CLEFT; operates 24 hours.
   English/Spanish.
   Office: (412) 481-1376.

Activities include providing information and referral to parents of newborns with clefts and other craniofacial anomalies and to adults with such defects. Referrals are made to professional teams and to parent support groups. Brochures and fact sheets are provided at no cost.

FACES: National Association for the Craniofacially Handicapped
P.O. Box 11082
Chattanooga, TN 37401
Information/helpline: 1-800-332-2373
   (9 A.M. to 5 P.M. EST).
   Office: (423) 266-1632.

FACES serves people with severe craniofacial deformities resulting from birth defects, injuries, or disease. Provides financial assistance for expenses incurred while traveling away from home to a craniofacial medical center for reconstructive surgery and/or evaluation. Also publishes a newsletter, provides referrals to other resources, and offers support networks and a national speaker's bureau. There is no charge for any of the services.

Crohn's & Colitis Foundation of America
386 Park Ave. South
New York, NY 10016
Information/helpline: 1-800-932-2423
(9 A.M. to 5 P.M. EST).
Office: (212) 685-3440.

Offers an array of educational and support services. Call for free brochures, information on chapter support groups, or to talk with a public education coordinator.

CYSTIC FIBROSIS

Cystic Fibrosis Foundation
6931 Arlington Rd.
Bethesda, MD 20814
Information/helpline: 1-800-FIGHT-CF (8:30 A.M. to 5:30 P.M. EST).
Office: (301) 951-4422.

Supports cutting-edge research that develops new treatments to improve the quality of life for people with cystic fibrosis and that will ultimately provide a cure. Provides support for a nationwide network of 115 specialized care centers dedicated to treating people with CF and funds twelve CFF research centers. Publications, fact sheets, and videotapes are available on request. A newsletter is published twice a year.

DEVELOPMENTAL DISABILITIES

TASH
29 West Susquehanna, Suite 210
Baltimore, MD 21204
Information/helpline:
1-800-482-TASH; (410) 828-1306
(TDD), 9 A.M. to 5 P.M. EST.
Fax: (410) 828-6706.

An international organization that affirms that quality of life, respect, and dignity are basic human values that apply to all people. TASH serves people who are developmentally or intellectually disabled, including those with mobility and communication problems. Current TASH priorities include working together to achieve inclusion of people with disabilities in the schools, the workplace, and the community; health care reform measures; support for independent living, and more equitable access to lifelong personal assistance service. Information referral department maintains a database of professional contacts who are available to assist with specific problems such as accessibility, advocacy, challenging behaviors and nonaversive solutions, early childhood education, communication and language development, legal issues, multicultural issues, and community living. Publishes a scholarly journal and the monthly TASH newsletter.

Diabetes

American Diabetes Association
1660 Duke St.
Alexandria, VA 22314
Information/helpline: 1-800-232-3472
    (8:30 A.M. to 5 P.M. EST).
    English/Spanish. Office:
    (703) 549-1500, ext. 290.

Patient assistance is offered in many different areas, including general information about diabetes, nutrition, exercise, and treatment. Offers referrals to diabetes medical professionals. Maintains a nationwide network of attorneys and can give referrals to people with diabetes who are facing discrimination. Also conducts educational seminars, culturally diverse programs, support groups, and youth programs. Membership, monthly magazine, and an extensive library providing educational information are available.

National Diabetes Information
    Clearinghouse
National Institute of Diabetes and
    Digestive and Kidney Disease
1 Information Way
Bethesda, MD 20892
Information/helpline: (301) 654-3327
    (9 A.M. to 5 P.M. EST)

The clearinghouse answers inquiries, develops, reviews, and distributes publications and works closely with professional and patient organizations and government agencies to coordinate informational resources about diabetes. Publications include patient booklets about insulin-dependent and non-insulin-dependent diabetes.

Digestive diseases

National Digestive Diseases
    Information Clearinghouse
2 Information Way
Bethesda, MD 20892-3570
Information/helpline: (301) 654-3810
    (9 A.M. to 5 P.M. EST). Web site:
    http://www.niddk.nih.gov.

NDDIC is an inquiry and organization referral service that responds to professional and public requests. The clearinghouse provides fact sheets about specific digestive diseases and information about research developments and organizational and governmental activities related to digestive diseases.

Down syndrome

National Down Syndrome Society
666 Broadway, 8th Floor
New York, NY 10012
Information/helpline: 1-800-221-4602
    (9 A.M. to 5 P.M. EST). English,
    Spanish, French. Office:
    (212) 460-9330.

A professionally staffed hotline provides information and gives referrals to parent support groups, early intervention programs, and state and local resources. A newsletter and information packet containing fact sheets, an information booklet for new parents, and bibliography are given to parents and professionals. Videos, books, and manuals are also available.

EPILEPSY

Epilepsy Foundation of America
4351 Garden City Dr.
Landover, MD 20785
Information/helpline: 1-800-332-1000;
   1-800-332-2070 (TDD), 9 A.M. to
   5 P.M. English/Spanish. Office:
   (301) 459-3700 (voice/TDD).

Specially trained people will answer questions about diagnosis, treatment, medications, first aid, EFA affiliates, community services, parent support groups, self-help groups, employment, and basic information about the medical and social aspects of epilepsy. Local programs often provide needed services in the community, such as recreational and educational programs for youngsters, counseling, advocacy, job education and placement, and help with experience of discrimination.

FETAL ALCOHOL SYNDROME

Family Empowerment Network:
   Supporting families affected by
   FAS/FAE
610 Langdon St., Room 521
Madison, WI 53703
Information/helpline: 1-800-462-5254.
   Office: (608) 262-6590.

National support network for families affected by fetal alcohol syndrome and other alcohol-related birth defects provides support, education, and training. Parents may use the toll-free line to contact FEN or to be put in touch with other families. Offered are monthly sharing meetings over the educational teleconference network, an annual national conference, an annual family retreat, outreach to family support groups nationwide, resource materials, and a quarterly newsletter.

National Organization on Fetal
   Alcohol Syndrome
1819 H St. NW, Suite 750
Washington, D.C. 20006
Information/helpline: 1-800-66-
   NOFAS (9 A.M. to 5 P.M. EST).
   Office: (202) 785-4585.

This is a national clearinghouse that provides information, resources, and referrals. A directory lists prevention programs, support groups, and substance abuse programs for pregnant women nationwide. Newsletter and other publications are offered.

HEADACHE

National Headache Foundation
428 West St. James Place, 2nd Floor
Chicago, IL 60614
Information/helpline: 1-800-843-2256
   (9 A.M. to 5 P.M. CST). Office:
   (773) 388-6394.

Disseminates free information on headache causes and treatments and sponsors educational seminars nationwide. Audio- and videotapes and brochures are available for purchase. A nationwide network of local support groups has been organized.

American Society for Deaf Children
2848 Arden Way, Suite 210
Sacramento, CA 95825
Information/helpline: 1-800-942-2732
(24-hour answering machine).
Office: (916) 482-0121 (9 A.M. to
5 P.M. PST).

Provides support, encouragement, and information about deafness to families with deaf children. Supports sign language for the fullest possible participation of deaf children at home, in school, and in the community. Publishes many brochures.

American Speech-Language-Hearing
Association (ASHA)
10801 Rockville Pike
Rockville, MD 20852
Information/helpline: 1-800-638-8255
(9 A.M. to 4:30 P.M. EST). Office:
(301) 897-5700.

National professional association of speech-language pathologists and audiologists. Provides information about speech and hearing disorders and referrals to speech-language pathologists and audiologists. Information brochures are available on speech, language, and hearing problems.

Better Hearing Institute
5021-B Backlick Rd.
Annadale, VA 22003
Information/helpline:
1-800-EAR-WELL (9 A.M. to 5 P.M.
EST). Office: (703) 642-0580.

A national education organization that implements national public information programs on hearing loss and available medical, surgical, hearing aid, and rehabilitation assistance. Maintains a "Hearing Helpline" that provides information on hearing loss and hearing help to callers from anywhere in the U.S. and Canada. Educational brochures are available.

The Caption Center
125 Western Ave.
Boston, MA 02134
Office: (617) 492-9225 (voice/TTY)

A service of the WGBH Educational Foundation, the Caption Center is the oldest and most experienced captioning agency in the world, with offices in Boston, New York, and Los Angeles. Captions enable deaf and hard-of-hearing people to watch TV and can also benefit adults and children learning to read as well as people learning English as a second language. The Caption Center offers clients an array of services, including off-line captions, real-time captions, and subtitling. Actively advocates for increased media accessibility through captioning and other access innovations.

Hereditary Hearing Impairment
Resource Directory
555 North 30th St.
Omaha, NE 68131
Information/helpline: 1-800-320-1171
(voice/TDD), 8 A.M. to 5 P.M. CST.
Internet address:
htttp://www.boystown.org/hhirr/.

Established to become a resource to the biomedical community in the area of hereditary hearing impairment research, the HHIRR disseminates free information via a newsletter, bulletin, and informational fact sheets on their World Wide Web site. Also collects information from hearing-impaired adults to match families with scientists for appropriate research projects.

International Hearing Society
20361 Middlebelt Rd.
Livonia, MI 48152
Information/helpline: 1-800-521-5247
    (9 A.M. to 4:30 P.M. EST). Office:
    (810) 478-2610

The Hearing Aid Helpline is the professional organization that represents Hearing Instrument Specialists in the U.S. and Canada. Offers general information on hearing aids and hearing loss and referrals to local hearing-instrument specialists.

Helen Keller National Center
111 Middle Neck Rd.
Sands Point, NY 11050
Information/helpline: 1-800-255-0411
    ext. 275; (516) 944-8637 (TTY),
    8:30 A.M. to 4:30 P.M. EST. Office:
    (516) 944-8900 ext. 325.

This is a residential rehabilitation training/job preparation facility offering job preparation and placement for deaf-blind adults who are eighteen years and older at headquarters in Sands Point; counseling, information, and referral for families with children who are deaf-blind; services for older adults and youth in transition. Established the National Family Association for Deaf-Blind (NFADB), supporting people who are deaf-blind and their families. Consultation and resource information are free; fee for training. Publishes a news magazine and other materials.

The National Information Center on
    Deafness
Gallaudet University
800 Florida Ave. NE
Washington, D.C. 20002
Information/helpline: (202) 651-5051 or
    (202) 651-5052 (TTY), 8:30 A.M. to
    4:30 P.M. EST.

Collects, develops, and disseminates information on deafness, hearing loss, and services and programs related to people with hearing loss. The Center maintains contacts with a multitude of resources and experts at the university and across the country. Responds to questions from the general public and deaf and hard-of-hearing people, their families, and professionals who work with them.

National Institute on Deafness and
    Other Communication Disorders
    Information Clearinghouse
1 Communication Ave.
Bethesda, MD 20892-3456
Helpline: 1-800-241-1055 (TTY),
    8:30 A.M. to 5 P.M. EST.
    Office: 1-800-241-1044.

This is a national resource center for information about hearing, balance, smell, taste, voice, speech, and language for health professionals, patients, industry, and the public. Provides fact sheets, bibliographies, information packets, directories of information sources, and a biannual newsletter.

Occupational Hearing Services
P.O. Box 1880
Media, PA 19063
Information/helpline:
    1-800-222-EARS; operates 24 hours.
    Office: (610) 544-7700 (9 A.M. to
    5 P.M. EST).

Provides preliminary hearing screening tests over the telephone. If the service is available in your area, you will be provided with the local test number and instructions. There is no charge. The service is supported by medical providers and hearing help centers, to which referrals may be made. The hearing screening test is not recommended for children.

SEE Center for the Advancement of
  Deaf Children
10443 Los Alamitos Blvd., P.O. Box 1181
Los Alamitos, CA 90720
Information/helpline: (310) 430-1467
  (voice/TDD), 9:30 A.M. to 5 P.M.
  PST

Nationwide telephone information service answers questions about communication and deafness and makes referrals to appropriate sources. In California, conducts workshops on the use of Signing Exact English (SEE), educational interpreting, and education-related communication topics.

Self Help for Hard of Hearing People
7910 Woodmont Ave., Suite 1200
Bethesda, MD 20814
Information/helpline: (301) 657-2248
  (voice), (301) 657-2249 (TDD),
  9 A.M. to 5 P.M. EST.
  Office: (301) 657-2248.

This organization's primary purpose is to educate hard-of-hearing people and their families and friends about the causes, nature, and complications of hearing loss and solutions for it. Services include local chapters and support groups, referral and advocacy activities and annual conventions. Offers an extensive publications list.

Tripod
2901 N. Keystone St.
Burbank, CA 91504
Nationwide hotline: 1-800-352-8888
  (voice/TDD). In California:
  1-800-2TRIPOD (voice/TDD).
  Office: (818) 972-2080 (voice/TDD),
  7:30 A.M. to 6 P.M. PST.

This is a nationwide hotline that provides information on raising and educating hearing-impaired children. Offers summaries of available resources and customized searches if further information is needed. Locally, they offer many educational programs for children.

HEART DISEASE

See Life-Threatening Illness.

HIV/AIDS

See Life-Threatening Illness.

HUMAN GROWTH

Human Growth Foundation
7777 Leesburg Pike, Suite 202 South
Falls Church, VA 22043
Information/helpline: 1-800-451-6434
  (10 A.M. to 5 P.M. EST). English and
  German spoken.
  Office: (703) 883-1773

Helps individuals with growth-related disorders, their families and health care professionals through education, research and advocacy. Provides information and free booklets and has 42 support chapters.

Little People of America Inc.
P.O. Box 9897
Washington, D.C. 20016
Information/helpline: 1-888-LPA-2001
  or (301) 589-0730 (9 A.M. to 5 P.M.
  EST)

Offers information on employment, education, disability rights, adoption of short-statured children, medical issues, adaptive devices, educational scholarships, medical assistance grants, and guidance to teenagers. Annual conference provides social and learning activities and free medical clinic examinations by world-renowned specialists in dwarfism. There are fifty local chapters.

HUNTINGTON'S DISEASE

Huntington's Disease Society
140 W. 22nd St.
New York, NY 10011
Information/helpline: 1-800-345-4372;
  operates 24 hours.
  Office: (212) 242-1968

Has a network of support chapters across the U.S. Disseminates information to patients, the general public, and the professional health community. Call for more information.

INCONTINENCE

National Association for Continence
P.O. Box 8310
Spartanburg, SC 29305
Information/helpline:
  1-800-BLADDER (8 A.M. to 5 P.M.
  EST). Office: (864) 579-7900.

Dedicated to improving the quality of life for people with incontinence through education, advocacy and support to the public and health professionals about causes, prevention, diagnosis, treatment and management alternatives. Has a quarterly newsletter, resource guide, audio/visual programs, books, and a continence referral service.

The Simon Foundation for Continence
P.O. Box 835
Wilmette, IL 60091
Information/helpline: 1-800-23-
  SIMON. Office: (847) 864-3913.

Educates the public through lectures and presentations and through books, videotapes, newsletters, and topic-specific reprints. Free information packet. There are support groups nationwide.

INTERSTITIAL CYSTITIS

Interstitial Cystitis Association
P.O. Box 1553, Madison Square Station
New York, NY 10159
Information/helpline:
  1-800-HELP-ICA; operates 24 hours

This national nonprofit organization works on behalf of all IC patients, 90 percent of whom are women. Goals are to provide IC patients with the most up-to-date information on IC; to provide IC patients, their families, and friends with a support network in their communities; to educate the medical community about the disease and its treatments, and to support research to find effective treatment and cure. ICA quarterly newsletter and other information on IC is available for an annual contribution.

American Association of Kidney
    Patients
100 South Ashley Drive, Suite 280
Tampa, FL 33602
Information/helpline: 1-800-749-2257
    (8:30 A.M. to 5 P.M. EST).
    Office: (813) 223-7099.
Web site: http://cybermart.com/
    aakpaz/aakp.html.

For more than twenty-five years, this organization has been dedicated to helping renal patients and their families deal with the physical, emotional, and social impact of kidney disease. Produces literature of interest to kidney patients and serves as a resource for national news media. Membership offers patients a subscription to a magazine and bulletin, various booklets, and an opportunity to attend the annual convention.

American Kidney Fund
6110 Executive Blvd.
Rockville, MD 20852
Information/helpline: 1-800-638-8299
    (8 A.M. to 5 P.M. EST). English and
    German spoken.
    Office: (301) 881-3052.

Provides direct financial aid to needy dialysis patients, transplant recipients and donors to help cover the cost of treatment-related expenses. Grants are available to help patients afford medication, transportation, transient dialysis, special diet, and other needs. Publishes many brochures in English and Spanish.

National Kidney Foundation
30 E. 33rd St.
New York, NY 10016
Information/helpline: 1-800-622-9010
    (8:30 A.M. to 5:30 P.M. EST).
    Office: (212) 889-2210.
Web site: http://www.kidney.org.

With fifty-two U.S. affiliates, the National Kidney Foundation is dedicated to the prevention and treatment of kidney and urologic diseases. Educational materials available to the public include brochures, fact sheets, newsletters, and videos for children and adults. Many publications are available in Spanish.

LEARNING DISABILITIES

Learning Disabilities Association of
    America
4156 Library Rd.
Pittsburgh, PA 15234
Information/helpline: (412) 341-1515
    (9 A.M. to 4:30 P.M. EST).
    Web site: http://www.ldanatl.org.

A membership organization comprised of parents, professionals, and individuals with learning disabilities who are striving to educate the public about LD. Serves as an information and referral center, and provides a packet of material free of charge to any inquirer. Also publishes a newsmagazine. There are 500 local chapters which offer support meetings. Will act as advocates and provide listings of professionals in a particular area.

National Center for Learning
    Disabilities
381 Park Ave. South, Suite 1420
New York, NY 10016
Information/helpline: (212) 545-7510
    (9 A.M. to 5 P.M. EST Monday
    through Thursday; 9 A.M. to
    3:30 P.M. EST Fridays)

Committed to improving the lives of the estimated one in ten children and adults with learning disabilities. Services include national computerized information and referrals (offered free of charge), educational programs to raise public awareness and understanding, and legislative advocacy. Supports seminars and workshops, the development of new projects, and the replication of successful model programs. Educational tools include a newsletter and video kit.

LEUKEMIA

See Life-Threatening Illness, section on Cancer.

LEUKODYSTROPHY

United Leukodystrophy Foundation
2304 Highland Dr.
Sycamore, IL 60178
Information/helpline: 1-800-728-5483
(8 A.M. to 8 P.M. CST). Web site:
http://www.ceet.niv.edu/ulf.html.

Provides patients and their families with information about leukodystrophy and assists them in identifying sources of medical care, social services, and genetic counseling. Also coordinates a communication network among families and publishes a newsletter.

LIVER DISEASE

American Liver Foundation
1425 Pompton Ave.
Cedar Grove, NJ 07009
Information/helpline: 1-800-223-0179;
operates 24 hours.
Office: (201) 256-2550 (8:30 A.M. to
5 P.M. EST). Web site:
http://www.liverfoundation.org.

Provides information to the public, the medical community, and schools. There are twenty-four chapters. Publishes many brochures and information sheets on cirrhosis, gallstones, hepatitis, hemochromatosis, and liver transplant.

LUNG/RESPIRATORY DISEASE

National Jewish Center for
Immunology & Respiratory
Medicine
Lung Line Information Service
1400 Jackson St.
Denver, CO 80206
Information/helpline:
1-800-222-LUNG (8 A.M. to 5 P.M.
MT). Office: (303) 388-4461

Lung Line is an educational service staffed by specially trained registered nurses who provide information on the latest treatment and research on respiratory diseases and immune disorders, including asthma, emphysema, chronic bronchitis, tuberculosis, occupational or environmental lung diseases, juvenile rheumatoid arthritis, food allergies and other lung/respiratory diseases. This is *not* a crisis line, but it can provide information.

LUPUS

Lupus Foundation of America
260 Maple Court, Suite 123
Ventura, CA 93003
Information/helpline: 1-800-331-1802;
operates 24 hours.
Office: (805) 339-0443 (8 A.M. to
4 P.M. PST).

Assists lupus patients and their families by providing updated literature about lupus, directing them to appropriate resource centers and holding local meetings that feature doctors, nurses, and nutritionists as speakers.

LYMPHEDEMA

See Life-Threatening Illness, section on Cancer.

Marfan syndrome

National Marfan Foundation
382 Main St.
Port Washington, NY 11050
Information/helpline:
   1-800-8-MARFAN (8 A.M. to
   3:30 P.M. EST).
   Office: (516) 883-8712.

This foundation disseminates information to patients, family members, and health care providers through a quarterly newsletter and produces booklets and other materials. Provides support through seventy-five chapters and phone contacts.

Mental retardation

The ARC
500 E Border St., Suite 300
Arlington, TX 76010
Information/helpline: (817) 261-6003 or
   (817) 277-0553 (TDD), 8:30 A.M. to
   5:30 P.M. CST. English/Spanish.

Helps people with mental retardation and related disabilities. Services include education, job training, assistance in seeking employment, developing independent living skills, and protecting rights under the Americans with Disabilities Act. There are 1,200 state and local chapters nationwide. Offers a wide variety of publications.

Muscular dystrophy

Muscular Dystrophy Association
3300 E. Sunrise Dr.
Tucson, AZ 85718
Information/helpline: (520) 529-2000
   (8:30 A.M. to 5 P.M. MT). English
   and Spanish spoken. Web site:
   http://www.mdausa.org.

A voluntary health agency fighting forty neuromuscular diseases through worldwide research and a nationwide network of clinics providing comprehensive medical and support services and through far-reaching professional and public health education. There are 160 chapters that provide direct services including the provision of wheelchairs, recreation at MDA summer camps, and selected transportation assistance. Free brochures available.

Multiple sclerosis

National Multiple Sclerosis Society
733 Third Ave.
New York, NY 10017
Information/helpline: 1-800-FIGHT-
   MS (1-800-344-4867), 11 A.M. to
   5 P.M. EST. English/Spanish.
   Office: (212) 986-3240

Through many of the 140 local chapters, support groups, referral and counseling services, medical equipment loans, educational seminars, and other special programs for those with MS and their families and friends are available. Call the national headquarters for literature or for answers to special questions.

MYASTHENIA GRAVIS

The Myasthenia Gravis Foundation of America
222 South Riverside Plaza, Suite 1540
Chicago, IL 60606
Information/helpline: 1-800-541-5454
(8:45 A.M. to 4:45 P.M. CST).
Office: (312) 258-0522.

A network of 54 chapters and 100 support groups that provides patients and family members with encouragement, emphasizing the management of MG. An extensive referral system offers help through chapter offices and hotlines; a nationwide patient information and registry system is being instituted. MG Foundation supports a low cost medication program, and eight chapters offer diagnostic and treatment services. Publishes many brochures.

OSTEOPOROSIS

National Osteoporosis Foundation
1150 12th St. NW, Suite 500
Washington, D.C. 20036
Information/helpline: 1-800-223-9994.
Office: (202) 223-2226.

The NOF is the nation's leading resource for health care professionals, patients, and organizations seeking up-to-date, medically sound information and program materials on the causes, prevention, and treatment of osteoporosis.

PAIN

American Chronic Pain Association
P.O. Box 850
Rocklin, CA 95677
Information/helpline: (916) 632-0922
(9 A.M. to 5 P.M. PST)

This is a self-help organization with eight hundred chapters all over the world. All support groups must be led by people with chronic pain rather than professionals. Members are helped to cope with pain on a day-to-day basis. Distributes manuals and tapes on pain management and materials for leaders to develop support groups.

National Chronic Pain Outreach
Association
P.O. Box 274
Millboro, VA 24460
Information/helpline: (540) 997-5004

Operates an information clearinghouse that offers a wide range of publications and audiotapes for both pain sufferers and health care professionals. Publishes a quarterly newsletter, maintains a computerized registry of chronic pain support groups in U.S. and Canada, and provides referrals to NCPOA-member health care professionals and medical facilities nationwide.

PARKINSON'S DISEASE

National Parkinson Foundation
1501 N.W. 9th Ave.
Miami, FL 33136
Information/helpline: 1-800-327-4545
outside Florida; 1-800-433-7033 in
Florida (8 A.M. to 5 P.M. EST).
Office: (305) 547-6666. English,
Spanish, and French spoken.

The National Parkinson Foundation supports and is affiliated with twenty-seven centers of excellence both in the U.S. and internationally that perform research and provide clinical services and therapy including physical, occupational, speech, and psychological therapy. They are also involved in testing new drugs prior to approval by the FDA for general use.

United Parkinson Foundation
833 West Washington Blvd.
Chicago, IL 60607
Information/helpline: (312) 733-1893
(9:45 A.M. to 6 P.M. CST)

Services include background literature, exercise materials, and newsletters. Members may call or write for a personal response to specific questions and for referrals to proper diagnosis and clinical care. Works complementarily with the International Tremor Foundation, with which it shares offices.

Plastic surgery

American Society of Plastic and
Reconstructive Surgeons
444 East Algonquin Rd.
Arlington Heights, IL 60005
Information/helpline: 1-800-635-0635
(8:30 A.M. to 4:30 P.M.).
Office: (708) 228-9900.

Assists the public in locating qualified plastic surgeons in their area, including a verification of a physician's certification in plastic surgery. Callers may also request free brochures on general plastic surgery procedures.

National Foundation for Facial
Reconstruction
317 E. 34 St.
New York, NY 10016
(212) 263-6656

The NFFR's main purpose is to aid the rehabilitation of individuals suffering from facial disfigurement by providing facilities for the treatment and assistance of individuals who are unable to afford private reconstructive surgical care; also to train personnel, encourage research, and carry on a public education program. Cannot offer direct financial assistance to individual patients, but will endeavor to refer inquirers to plastic surgery clinics or private plastic surgeons in their own area.

Rubinstein-taybi

Rubinstein-Taybi Parent Group
P.O. Box 146
Smith Center, KS 66967
Information/helpline: (913) 697-2984

Provides contact between families who have children diagnosed with Rubinstein-Taybi syndrome and information and assistance in caring for a child with RTS. Groups throughout North America.

Scleroderma

United Scleroderma Foundation
P.O. Box 399
Watsonville, CA 95077
Information/helpline:
1-800-722-HOPE (8 A.M. to 5 P.M.
PST). Office: 408-728-2202.

Committed to increasing awareness of this devastating disease and raising essential research dollars to determine the cause, enhance treatment, and find a cure. Chapters throughout the U.S. and one in Canada provide personal contact and workshops. Offers many publications to members.

SICKLE CELL ANEMIA

Sickle Cell Disease Association of
    America
200 Corporate Pointe, Suite 495
Culver City, CA 90230
Information/helpline: 1-800-421-8453
    (8:30 A.M. to 5 P.M. PST).
    Office: (310) 216-6363.

Educational materials, referrals, and research support. The organization's 74 member chapters offer programs and supportive services to more than 300 communities nationwide and in Canada. There is no fee for services.

SPINA BIFIDA

Spina Bifida Association of America
4590 MacArthur Blvd. NW
Washington, D.C. 20007
Information/helpline: 1-800-621-3141
    (9 A.M. to 5 P.M. EST).
    Office: (202) 944-3285.

Purposes are to provide information related to spina bifida, including progress in the areas of medicine, education, legislation, and financial support, to help fund research into the causes, effects, and treatment of spina bifida, and to encourage the training of professionals involved in treatment. Services include a toll-free information and referral service, a newsletter and extensive publications list, a liaison to other organizations sharing similar goals, a Professional Advisory Council on education, medicine, and legislation, and a national conference.

SPINAL CORD INJURY

National Spinal Cord Injury
    Association
8300 Colesville Rd., Suite 551
Silver Spring, MD 20910
Information/helpline: 1-800-962-9629
    (11:30 A.M. to 5:30 P.M. EST).
    Office: (301) 588-6959.
    E-mail: nscia2@aol.com.

Dedicated to helping the person living with spinal cord injury, family members, and health care professionals. Chapters provide educational meetings, advocacy services, information, and referrals, among other services. Publishes a quarterly magazine and maintains a resource center with information on many aspects of living with spinal cord injury, including home accessibility, recreation, and personal care.

National Spinal Cord Injury Hotline
2200 Kernan Dr.
Baltimore, MD 21207
Information/helpline: 1-800-526-3456
    (9 A.M. to 5 P.M. EST)

Serves individuals who have sustained a traumatic spinal cord injury resulting in paralysis. The hotline is an information and referral service with questions answered by medical professionals and health administrators. "The Connection" is comprised of individuals who have had similar experiences and who volunteer for the Hotline as peer contacts to give support and assistance to others in their geographic area. There are chapters in twenty-seven states that provide educational meetings, advocacy services, visitation, and referral.

STROKE

See Life-Threatening Illness section on Heart Disease and Stroke.

TAY-SACHS AND ALLIED DISEASES

National Tay-Sachs & Allied Diseases
   Association
2001 Beacon St.
Brookline, MA 02146
Information/helpline: (617) 277-4463
   (9 A.M. to 5 P.M. EST)

Committed to the eradication of Tay-Sachs and the allied diseases, provides programs including public and professional education, carrier screening, laboratory quality control, research, family services, parent peer group, a support network, and referrals.

TOURETTE SYNDROME

Tourette Syndrome Association
42-40 Bell Blvd., Suite 205
Bayside, NY 11361
Information/helpline: (718) 224-2999
   (9 A.M. to 5 P.M. EST)

Offers direct help to TS families in crisis situations, develops state-by-state lists of doctors who can diagnose and treat TS, organizes and assists local chapters and support groups, funds research, represents the interests of its members to the government on critical policy issues, and distributes educational materials.

TUBEROUS SCLEROSIS

National Tuberous Sclerosis
   Association
8181 Professional Pl., Ste. 110
Landover, MD 20785
Information/helpline: 1-800-225-6872
   (8:30 A.M. to 5 P.M. EST).
   Office: (301) 459-9888.

Services include information, referrals, support groups, a volunteer area representative system, video rentals, a quarterly newsletter, pen pal network, and a grandparents network.

VISION

American Council of the Blind
1155 15th St. NW, Suite 720
Washington, D.C. 20005
Information/helpline: 1-800-424-8666
   (9 A.M. to 5:30 P.M. EST).
Office: (202) 467-5081
   (9 A.M. to 5:30 P.M. EST).

Provides qualified blind people with scholarships, legal assistance, crisis support, a free monthly Braille magazine, and referrals to education, rehabilitation, jobs, recreation and adaptive aid service.

American Foundation for the Blind
11 Penn Plaza, Suite 300
New York, NY 10001
Information/helpline: 1-800-232-5463
   or (212) 502-7600 (TDD), 10 A.M. to
   12:00 P.M. or 2 P.M. to 4 P.M. EST,
   weekdays).
Office: (212) 502-7674.

Responds to people who are blind or visually impaired, their families and friends, and professionals in the field who request information about AFB's programs, services, and related topics. Publishes books, pamphlets, videos. Maintains the Careers and Technology Information Bank, which is a network of individuals who are blind who use assistive technology at home, at work, or school and are able and willing to serve as mentors to others.

American Printing House for the Blind, Inc.
1839 Frankfort Ave.
Louisville, KY 40206
Information/helpline: 1-800-223-1839
   (8 A.M. to 4:30 P.M. CST).
Office: (502) 895-2405.

Manufactures books and magazines in Braille, large type, recorded and computer disk form, plus talking book equipment and synthetic speech computer products. Offers an electronic database that lists Braille, large type, and recorded textbooks available from companies, agencies, and volunteers across the United States.

Associated Services for the Blind
919 Walnut St.
Philadelphia, PA 19107
Office: (215) 627-0600
   (8:30 A.M. to 4:30 P.M. EST).
   English and Spanish spoken.

Associated Services for the Blind is Philadelphia's largest nonprofit organization providing services and programs to promote the independence of people who are blind or visually impaired. ASB's Braille Center is one of five in the United States. Also records magazines for subscribers around the world. Catalog of assistive devices available. Provides rehabilitative and social services to local clients.

Association for Macular Diseases
210 East 64th St.
New York, NY 10021
   Information/helpline: (212) 605-3719
   (9 A.M. to 5 P.M. EST)

Maintains a members' hotline to answer questions and provide information and support. Also publishes a quarterly newsletter with updates on research and optical aids available.

The Foundation Fighting Blindness
11350 McCormick Rd.
Hunt Valley, MD 21031-1014
Information/helpline: 1-800-683-5555
   (voice), 1-800-683-5551 (TDD).
Office: (410) 785-1414 (voice) or
   410-785-9687 (TDD).

Provides information and referral services and support networks. Main focus is to fund research on causes, cures, and prevention of all retinal degenerative diseases, including retinitis pigmentosa, macular degeneration, and Usher syndrome. Affiliates throughout the United States.

Guide Dog Foundation for the Blind
371 East Jericho Turnpike
Smithtown, NY 11787
Information/helpline: 1-800-548-4337
   (8 A.M. to 5:15 P.M. EST).
Office: (516) 265-2121

Provides rehabilitation for the blind by breeding and training guide dogs that are given to blind applicants from all over the U.S. at no cost. Recipient and dog train together as a team for twenty-five days on campus. A comprehensive aftercare program is also provided. Funded by donations, the Foundation pays for transportation within the continental United States.

Helen Keller National Center (Refer to listing under "Hearing-Related Organizations.")

The Lighthouse
111 E. 59th St.
New York, NY 10022
Information/helpline: 1-800-334-5497
(9 A.M. to 5 P.M. EST).
English/Spanish. Office:
(212) 821-9489.

Special areas of expertise are age-related vision and vision and child development. Provides information and resource service regarding vision rehabilitation options, vision clinics, and training for independent living, and self-help groups throughout the U.S. Direct services for people in the New York area include vocational training and employment services and a preschool.

National Association for Parents of
the Visually Impaired
P.O. Box 317
Watertown, MA 02272
Information/helpline: 1-800-562-6265
(8 A.M. to 4 P.M. EST).
Office: (617) 972-7441

Enables parents of visually impaired children to find information and resources. Provides leadership, support, and training to assist parents in helping their children to reach their potential through outreach programs, networking, and advocating for the educational needs and welfare of blind and visually impaired children.

National Association for Visually
Handicapped
22 West 21st St.
New York, NY 10010
Information/helpline: (212) 889-3141
(9 A.M. to 5 P.M. EST)

Serves the partially seeing exclusively. Services include visual aids, large print, loan library, emotional support, educational outreach, and referrals worldwide. Free consultations by phone through New York and San Francisco offices only.

National Braille Association
3 Townline Circle
Rochester, NY 14623
Information/helpline: (716) 427-8260
(8:30 A.M. to 5 P.M. EST)

Direct services to blind people include Braille transcription of educational, vocational, and recreational materials. Maintains the Braille Book Bank, which houses and duplicates materials from its Braille collection of textbooks, foreign language, mathematics, music, and general interest materials. Catalogs are available on request. The Reader-Transcriber Registry links visually impaired individuals with Braillists who are able to transcribe material necessary for that person's work, recreation, and daily living.

National Eye Care Project
P.O. Box 429098
San Francisco, CA 94142
Information/helpline: 800-222-3937
(8 A.M. to 4 P.M. PT)

This nationwide outreach program provides medical eye care to disadvantaged senior citizens. Callers who are sixty-five or older and meet the eligibility requirements are mailed the name of a volunteer ophthalmologist in their community who will give an examination and treatment. Doctors accept insurance reimbursement as full payment; uninsured patients are provided care at no cost.

National Federation of the Blind
1800 Johnson St.
Baltimore, MD 21230
Information/helpline: (410) 659-9314

Services include advocacy and protection of civil rights, information and referral, literature about blindness, scholarships, hearing aids, and appliances. Has affiliates in all states. Publications in Braille, print, and on record or cassette available at no cost.

For suicide prevention hotlines in your area, dial 411 or 0 for the telephone number or look in the front section of your local yellow pages under Community Services or a similar heading.

ALCOHOL AND DRUG INFORMATION

American Council on Alcoholism
2522 St. Paul St.
Baltimore, MD 21218
Information/helpline: 1-800-527-5344
    (9 A.M. to 5 P.M. EST).
    Office: (410) 889-0100.

ACA advances the concept that alcoholism is an identifiable, treatable illness. Provides information, counseling referral, a resource library, a monthly newsletter, fact sheets, and alcohol education for drivers.

National Clearinghouse for Alcohol
    and Drug Information
P.O. Box 2345
Rockville, MD 20847
Information/helpline: 1-800-729-6686
    or 1-800-487-4889 (TDD only),
    8 A.M. to 7 P.M. EST. English and
    Spanish spoken.

Collects, classifies, and distributes information about alcohol, tobacco, and other drugs. Prevention strategies and materials, research, treatment approaches and resources, and training programs are available to all interested persons. Provides booklets, directories, reference services, and the use of the library.

National Council on Alcoholism &
    Drug Dependence, Inc.
12 West 21 St.
New York, NY 10010
Information/helpline:
    1-800-NCA-CALL or
    1-800-475-4673; operates 24 hours.
    Office: (212) 206-6770.

Provides education, help, and hope in the fight against alcoholism and other drug addictions. Offers a referral service. NCADD affiliates provide objective information and referrals to appropriate services for individuals and family members who are seeking treatment.

National Drug Information and
    Treatment Referral Hotline
1-800-662-HELP; 1-800-66-AYUDA;
    1-800-228-0427 (TDD).

Provides information on alcoholism and drug dependence through brochures, fact sheets, and posters and services, including assessments, counseling, and treatment through many of its more than 130 affiliates throughout the country. Some affiliates have programs tailored specifically to women.

National Families in Action
2296 Henderson Mill Rd. #300
Atlanta, GA 30345
Information/helpline: (770) 934-6364
  (9 A.M. to 5 P.M.)

Drug prevention agency with a clearinghouse library of more than 510,000 documents in all areas relating to substance abuse. Publishes *Drug Abuse Update Quarterly* and other brochures on specific drugs.

National Organization on Fetal Alcohol Syndrome
1819 H St. NW, Suite 750
Washington, D.C. 20006
  Information/helpline: 1-800-66
NOFAS (9 A.M. to 5 P.M. EST).
Office: (202) 785-4585.

This is a national clearinghouse that provides information, resources, and referrals. A directory lists prevention programs, support groups, and substance abuse programs for pregnant women nationwide. Newsletter and other publications are offered.
(For support for families affected by fetal alcohol syndrome and other alcohol-related birth defects, see the Family Empowerment Network under Disability-Specific Organizations.)

ADDICTIONS/RECOVERY GROUPS

Adult Children of Alcoholics
P.O. Box 3216
Torrance, CA 90510
Information/helpline: (310) 534-1815

A twelve-step, twelve-tradition support group focused on understanding the specific behavior and attitude patterns developed while growing up in an alcoholic or other dysfunctional environment in order to better understand the past and recover.

Al-Anon/Alateen Family Groups
1600 Corporate Landing Parkway
Virginia Beach, VA 23454
Information/helpline: 1-800-356-9996
  (9 A.M. to 4:30 P.M. EST).
  Office: (757) 563-1600.

Al-Anon is a mutual support program that offers help to individuals whether the alcoholic is still drinking or not. It is a fellowship of people whose lives have been affected by the problem drinking of a family member or friend. Anonymity creates a safe place for individuals to share their experience, strength, and hope with each other in order to solve their common problems.

Alcoholics Anonymous
P.O. Box 459, Grand Central Station
New York, NY 10163
Information/helpline: (212) 870-3400
  (9 A.M. to 4:45 P.M. EST).
English/Spanish. Listed under A.A. in all local phone books.

This is a fellowship of men and women who have found a solution to their drinking problem. The only requirement for membership is a desire to stop drinking. Members observe personal anonymity at the public level.

Calix Society
7601 Wayzata Blvd.
Minneapolis, MN 55426
Information/helpline: 1-800-398-0524.
  Office: (612) 546-0544 (9 A.M. to 2 P.M. CST).

Support group for Catholics who are in AA, Alanon or other 12-step groups. Units in U.S., Canada, and Great Britain. Books and newsletter are available.

Cocaine Anonymous World Service
    Office
3740 Overland, Suite C
Los Angeles, CA 90034
Information/helpline: 1-800-347-8998;
    24-hour referral line.
    Office: (310) 559-5833.

Fellowship of men and women who share their experience, strength, and hope with each other that they may solve their common problem and help others to recover from addiction. The only requirement is a desire to stop using cocaine and all other mind-altering substances.

Families Anonymous
P.O. Box 3475
Culver City, CA 90231
Information/helpline: 1-800-736-9805
    (10 A.M. to 4 P.M. PST).
    Office: (310) 313-5800.

An international twelve-step fellowship of support groups. Focus is on the recovery of family members who have been affected by a loved one's use of mind-altering substances, including drugs and alcohol.

800-COCAINE/Phoenix House
164 W. 74th St.
New York, NY 10023
Information/helpline:
    1-800-COCAINE (24 hours)
    Office: (212) 595-5810

Confidential substance abuse information and referral service. This is not a counseling service or crisis line, but it does try to provide access to those services for callers. Available to callers anywhere in the U.S.

Marijuana Anonymous World Services
P.O. Box 2912
Van Nuys, CA 91404
Information/helpline: 1-800-766-6779,
    24 hours.
Web site: http://www.
    marijuanaanonymous.org.

A twelve-step program for recovery from marijuana addiction.

Narcotics Anonymous
World Service Office
P.O. Box 9999
Van Nuys, CA 91409
Information/helpline: (818) 997-3822
    and (818) 376-8600 (TDD), 8 A.M. to
    5 P.M. PST.
    English/Spanish/French/German.

This is an international fellowship of men and women who meet regularly to help each other recover from their addiction to drugs, legal or illegal, including alcohol. There are no fees and anyone who wants to stop using may attend the meetings. Free literature is available. Call the office listed in the white pages of your phone book or call the number at left for information about meetings near you.

National Alliance of Methadone Advocates
435 Second Ave.
New York, NY 10010
Information/helpline: (212) 595-NAMA

The primary objective of NAMA is to advocate for the patient in treatment by destigmatizing and empowering methadone patients and to make treatment available on demand to every person who needs it. Provides education, training, and information about methadone; offers many publications. Seven thousand members represent all states and nine other countries.

Nicotine Anonymous World Services
P.O. Box 591777
San Francisco, CA 94159
Information/helpline: (415) 750-0328
 (24-hour answering machine)

A fellowship of men and women who join together in groups to help each other lead nicotine-free lives. This is a twelve-step program with groups in the U.S. and Canada.

SOS — Secular Organization for Sobriety/Save Our Selves
5521 Grosvenor Blvd.
Los Angeles, CA 90066
Information/helpline: (310) 821-8430;
 operates 24 hours

An alternative recovery method for those alcoholics or drug addicts who are uncomfortable with the spiritual content of twelve-step programs. Local groups dedicated solely to helping individuals achieve and maintain sobriety meet in many cities throughout the country. Publishes a quarterly newsletter.

Women for Sobriety, Inc.
P.O. Box 618
Quakertown, PA 18951
Information/helpline: (215) 536-8026
 (9 A.M. to 4:30 P.M. EST).
 Web site:
 http://www.mediapulse.com/wfs/.

This program for women alcoholics is administered in self-help groups all over the country. Books, booklets, and cassettes tailored specifically to the needs of women alcoholics are also available.

CONSUMER AND FAMILY ORGANIZATIONS

Compeer
259 Monroe Ave., Suite B-1
Rochester, NY 14607
Information/helpline: 1-800-836-0475
 (9 A.M. to 5 P.M. EST).
 Office: (716) 546-8280.

Compeer matches trained volunteers in one-on-one friendship relationships with children and adults receiving mental health treatment. Compeer clients, who are of all ages and come from all walks of life, are referred by their primary therapist. Volunteers meet an average of four hours per month with the client at mutually convenient times for a minimum of one year. Compeer *group* volunteers interact with clients in supervised settings. Compeer's *Project Homeless* meets the needs of local shelters and their residents. Compeer *Calling* addresses the needs of homebound, and the *youth program* provides role models for young clients, helps prevent antisocial behavior, builds self-esteem, and enhances the possibility of avoiding placement in residential treatment facilities.

Lithium Information Center/
  Obsessive Compulsive
  Information Center
Dean Foundation
2711 Allen Blvd.
Middleton, WI 53562
Information/helpline: (608) 827-2390
  (8:30 A.M. to 5 P.M. CST)

Disseminates information about the biomedical uses of lithium and other treatments for bipolar (manic-depressive) disorder. Also maintains physician and support group referral lists and publishes patient information booklets. The staff will answer questions.

National Mental Health Association
1021 Prince St.
Alexandria, VA 22314
Information/helpline: 1-800-969-6642
  (9 A.M. to 5 P.M. EST)
Web site: http://www.nmha.com.

Information Center has referral information on more than four thousand mental health organizations and maintains fact sheets on 130 mental health topics, all provided free.

National Alliance for the Mentally Ill
  (NAMI)
200 N. Glebe Rd., Suite 1015
Arlington, VA 22203
Information/helpline: 1-800-950-NAMI
  (9 A.M. to 5 P.M. EST).
  Office: (703) 524-7600

A family and consumer grassroots, self-help, support, and advocacy organization, NAMI is dedicated to improving the lives of people with severe mental illnesses, including schizophrenia, manic-depressive illness, major depression, panic and obsessive-compulsive disorders, as well as severe disorders in children. Services include a multicultural network, a children's issues network, a sibling network, and a religious network. Helpline callers receive free science-based information about specific mental illnesses and treatments as well as sources of consumer and family support in the caller's own community. There are 1,100 affiliate groups throughout all 50 states.

National Foundation for Depressive
  Illness
P.O. Box 2257
New York, NY 10116
Information/helpline: 1-800-248-4344;
  operates 24 hours

Provides information packets on depression which consist of articles, a bibliography, a referral list of doctors who specialize in treating depression, and a list of local patient support groups.

National Association for the Dually
  Diagnosed
132 Fair St.
Kingston, NY 12401
Information/helpline: 1-800-331-5362
  (8 A.M. to 4 P.M.).
  Office: (914) 331-4336.

Association designed to promote interest of professional and parental development with resources for individuals who have the coexistence of mental illness and mental retardation. Offers parent and professional consulting, centralized computer database for resources and referrals, networking, and accessing industry's leading professionals. Regional chapters allow for local advocacy, networking, newsletters, system development, and conferences. Many publications are available, including a membership directory.

National Empowerment Center
20 Ballard Rd.
Lawrence, MA 01843
Information/helpline:
   1-800-POWER-2-U or
   1-800-TTY-POWER.
   Office: (508) 685-1518.
   English/Spanish.

An organization of people who are mental health consumers and psychiatric survivors, who have come together to build a national voice for consumer/survivors and to offer information and technical assistance to individuals and groups. Offers a national directory of mutual support groups, drop-in centers, and statewide organizations; audiotapes; national, topic-based telephone conferences; database with hundreds of topics.

National Mental Health Consumers'
   Self-Help Clearinghouse
1211 Chestnut St., Suite 1000
Philadelphia, PA 19107
Information/helpline: 1-800-553-4539
   (9 A.M. to 5 P.M. EST).
   English/Spanish.
   Office: (215) 751-1810.

This consumer-run organization provides free technical assistance and information-and-referral services to people diagnosed with mental illnesses who want to develop mental health self-help groups and consumer-run services. The Clearinghouse also promotes the participation of consumers in planning, providing, and evaluating mental health and community support services. Sponsors national training events and conducts consultations on-site and by telephone across the country. It has provided networking and information/referral services, collaborated with research efforts, and developed and distributed technical assistance materials, including its quarterly newsletter, *The Key.*

Through the Looking Glass
2198 Sixth St.
Berkeley, CA 94710-2204
1-800-644-2666; (510) 848-1112
(9 A.M. to 12 P.M. and 1 P.M. to
   5 P.M. PST)

National information and referral source for parents with disabilities, family members, and service providers. Staffed primarily by people with personal disability experience.

FAMILY SERVICE AGENCIES

Association of Jewish Family and
   Children's Agencies
3086 State Highway 27, Suite 11
Kendall Park, NJ 08824
Information/helpline: 1-800-634-7346

Membership organization of over 143 Jewish Family and Children's Agencies in the U.S. and Canada dedicated to enhancing the quality of Jewish family life. Publishes directories and acts as a national clearinghouse for information on addictions and cult and missionary activities in the American Jewish Community. Operates the Schroeder Awardwinning Elder Support Network. Special programming is offered through member agencies to adults and children experiencing divorce, intermarried families, single-parent families and families in the adoption network, as well as services to immigrant Jews, the developmentally disabled, the elderly, and people with AIDS. Call for a referral to a local office.

Child Welfare League of America
440 First St. NW, Suite 310
Washington, D.C. 20001
Information/helpline: (202) 638-2952.
  Web site: http://www.cwla.org.

This is a national membership organization made up of eight hundred public and private voluntary child welfare agencies that are expert in child welfare, including adoption, child daycare, child protection from abuse and neglect, family foster care, chemical dependency, and housing and homelessness. Many publications are available for children, parents, and professionals.

Family Service America
11700 W. Lake Park Dr.
Milwaukee, WI 53224
Information/helpline: 1-800-221-2681
  (9 A.M. to 5 P.M.)

This is a network of three hundred agencies that assist individuals and families to solve problems associated with parent-child tensions, marital difficulties, drug and alcohol dependency, teenage pregnancy, eldercare, child abuse and neglect, family violence, and work-related problems.

GOVERNMENT AGENCIES

Depression Awareness Recognition
  and Treatment (D/ART) Program
National Institute of Mental Health
5600 Fishers Lane, Room 10-85
Rockville, MD 20657
(301) 443-4140. For publications:
  1-800-421-4211. English/Spanish.
  Office: (301) 443-4140.
  Web site: http://www.nimh.n.h.gov/
  publicat/eduprogs/.dart.htm.

A national program to provide information about depressive illnesses — their symptoms, diagnosis, and treatment. Produces educational materials in several languages for professionals, community groups, worksite programs, and directly to the public.

Health Care Financing Administration
200 Independence Ave. SW
Room 314G
Washington, D.C. 20201
(202) 690-6726

The federal agency charged with overseeing Medicare and the federal portion of the Medicaid program. Medicare and Medicaid patients can register complaints about the quality of care with their regional HCFA office. Call for a referral to the regional branch.

National Institute of Mental Health
Information Resources and Inquiries
    Branch
5600 Fishers Lane
Rockville, MD 20857

For information and publications:

Mental disorders and their treatment:
    (301) 443-4513
Panic Disorder Education Program:
    1-800-64-PANIC
Aging research: (301) 443-1185
Child/adolescent research:
    (301) 443-5944
Schizophrenia research: (301) 443-3683
Violence and traumatic stress
    research: (301) 443-3728
Patient referral to research projects:
    (301) 496-1337
AIDS research: (301) 443-7281
Minority/women's mental health
    issues: (301) 443-2847
Rural mental health: (301) 443-9001

Dedicated to improving mental health and preventing mental illness through fostering better understanding, diagnosis, treatment, and rehabilitation of mental and brain disorders. Responds to requests for information from the public. Areas of research include schizophrenia, depression and manic-depressive illness, anxiety disorders, eating disorders, Alzheimer's disease, mental disorders and learning disabilities of children and adolescents, special mental health issues involving minorities, suicidal youths, perpetrators and victims of violence, and homeless people.

U.S. Department of Health and
    Human Services
Inspector General's Hotline
1-800-368-5779
In Maryland, call 1-800-638-3986.
    Fraud hotline: 1-800-HHS-TIPS.

Collects complaints from Medicaid and Medicare patients and will refer to the office of appropriate jurisdiction.

Joint Commission on Accreditation of
    Healthcare Organizations
One Renaissance Blvd.
Oakbrook Terrace, IL 60181
Customer service
    information/helpline: (630) 792-5800
    Office: (630) 792-5000

Mission is to improve the quality of care provided to the public through the provision of health care accreditation and related services that support performance improvement in health care organizations. Accreditation is available for general, psychiatric, children's and rehabilitation hospitals, health care networks, home care agencies, nursing homes, mental health services, ambulatory care providers, and clinical laboratories. Publications are available to help you choose quality care.

PROFESSIONAL ASSOCIATIONS

Association for Ambulatory Behavioral
    Healthcare
301 N. Fairfax St., #109
Alexandria, VA 22314
Information/helpline: (703) 836-2274
    (9 A.M. to 5 P.M. EST)

A membership association of providers who give day treatment for people with mental health and substance abuse problems. Provides names of day treatment clinics across the United States.

American Association for Marriage
    and Family Therapy
1133 15th St. NW, Suite 300
Washington, D.C. 20005
(202) 452-0109

Professional association for the field of marriage and family therapy. Facilitates research, theory development and education. Publishes brochures that inform the public about the field of marriage and family therapy.

American Psychiatric Association
1400 K St.
Washington, D.C. 20005
(202) 682-6325; Fax: (202) 682-6255

This is a professional membership organization which, among its many other activities, informs and educates the public about help available to people with mental illnesses.

American Psychiatric Nurses
    Association
1200 19th St. NW, Suite 300
Washington, D.C. 20036
Information/helpline: (202) 857-1133
    (9 A.M. to 5 P.M.)

This national professional organization's mission is to advance psychiatric-mental health nursing practice, improve mental health care for individuals, families, groups, and communities, and to shape health policy for the delivery of mental health services. For mental health service consumers, it offers a free referral service to advanced practice nurse therapists. A free brochure, *Mental Health Care: A Consumer's Guide,* is also available.

American Psychological
   Association/Women's Programs
   Office
750 First St., NE
Washington, D.C. 20002
Information/helpline: (202) 336-6044

Coordinates APA's effort to ensure equal opportunities for women psychologists and monitors the welfare of women as consumers of psychological services, analyzes the impact of governmental initiatives on women, and promotes the development and application of psychological knowledge to address public policy issues affecting women. Serves as an information and referral resource on women's issues and develops and disseminates reports, pamphlets, and other written materials on professional and consumer issues. Office of Ethnic Minority Affairs works to increase scientific understanding of how culture and ethnicity influence behavior and works to increase and enhance the delivery of appropriate psychological services to minority communities. Other responsibilities of the Public Interest Directorate of the APA include providing staff and support for the Committee on Children, Youth and Families, Committee on Disability Issues in Psychology, Committee on Lesbian and Gay Concerns, Commission on Youth and Violence, special studies on aging, and AIDS-related activities.

Association for Death Education and
   Counseling
638 Prospect Ave.
Hartford, CT 06105
Information/helpline: (860) 586-7503
   (8:30 A.M. to 5:30 P.M. EST)

Works to promote and share research, theories and practice in dying, death, and bereavement for professionals and lay people who work in death education and grief counseling. Offers a certification program, conferences, newsletter, and networking with other bereavement professionals. Provides referrals for grief support and bereavement education.

Association of Black Psychologists
P.O. Box 55999
Washington D.C 20040
Information/helpline: (202) 722-0808
   (9 A.M. to 5 P.M. EST)

Referral service to African-American psychologists is available to the general public.

American Mental Health Counselors
   Association
801 No. Fairfax St., Suite 304
Alexandria, VA 22314
Information/helpline: 1-800-326-2642.
   Office: (703) 548-6002 (8 A.M. to
   5 P.M. EST)

A national professional association representing mental health counselors who help people with a wide variety of problems, such as family conflict, divorce, drug and alcohol abuse, child and spouse abuse, depression, anxiety, and job and career issues. Free brochure and referrals to counselors and/or the community mental health center in your area.

National Academy of Child and
   Adolescent Psychiatry
3615 Wisconsin Ave. NW
Washington, D.C. 20016
Information/helpline: (202) 966-7300
   (8:30 A.M. to 5:30 P.M. EST)

Professional organization of child and adolescent psychiatrists. Academy members actively research, diagnose, and treat psychiatric disorders affecting children, adolescents, and their families.

National Asian Pacific American
    Families Against Substance Abuse
1887 Maplegate St.
Monterey Park, CA 91755-6536
(213) 278-0031 (9 A.M. to 5 P.M. PST)

Dedicated to strengthening families and promoting culturally competent substance abuse and related services, including health care, gang and domestic violence, mental health,
and poverty through research, education, and advocacy. Produces informational materials and a newsletter to assist
members in applying for federal and other funds to improve
local programs.

National Association of Rehabilitation
    Professionals in the Private Sector
    (NARPPS)
313 Washington St.
Newton, MA 02158
(617) 692-2035 (9 A.M. to 5 P.M. EST)

National association that represents the interests of rehabilitation professionals who work in the private sector.

National Association of Social Workers
750 First St. NE
Washington, D.C. 20002
Information/helpline: 1-800-638-8799,
    ext. 291. Office: (202) 408-8600
    (8:30 A.M. to 5:30 P.M. EST).

Professional association that advocates on behalf of social
workers. It also fosters the improvement of society by striving for sound social policies and by elevating the standards
for social work practice. Publishes a newspaper, professional
journals, books, and reference works and maintains the National Social Work Library. Offers free referral to clinical
social workers (who provide services for a fee) through its
Register of Clinical Social Workers. Also provides basic information on mental health and other social work practice
areas through various publications.

SURVIVORS OF ABUSE AND INCEST

Incest Survivors Resource Network
    International
P.O. Box 7375
Las Cruces, NM 88006
Information/helpline: (505) 521-4260
    (2 P.M. to 4 P.M. and 11 P.M. to
    12 P.M. Monday through Saturday
    EST). e-mail: ISRNI@zianet.com.
    Web site:
    http://www.zianet.com/ISRNI.

This is a survivor-run, Quaker witness educational resource.
It operates a helpline for both survivors and professionals.
Calls are answered by incest survivors. Information about
forming self-help groups is available. Since its inception,
ISRNI has encouraged inquiries from adult survivors of
mother-son incest.

One Voice: The National Alliance for
    Abuse Awareness
P.O. Box 27958
Washington, D.C. 20038
Information/helpline: (202) 667-1160
    (9 A.M. to 5 P.M.)

Offers a national resource line where callers are referred to
local and national organizations or attorneys regarding child
sexual, physical, and emotional abuse. Has brochures on
violence and trauma, a newsletter, and a video.

Survivors of Incest Anonymous
P.O. Box 21817
Baltimore, MD 21222
Information/helpline: (410) 282-3400

A twelve-step, self-help recovery program started in 1982. There are no dues or fees, and incest is defined very broadly. Survivors are learning that we are not to blame and that healing is possible. International support groups, literature, bimonthly bulletins, pen pals, and speakers. Send a business-size self-addressed envelope for more information.

Voices in Action
P.O. Box 148309
Chicago, IL 60014
Information/helpline: 1-800-7-VOICE8
  (24 hours). Office: (312) 327-1500.

An international organization that provides assistance to victims of incest and child sexual abuse. Provides members with referrals to self-help groups, therapists, and puts survivors in touch with others who have experienced similar types of abuse. Publishes an informational "survival kit" and a newsletter and offers national and regional conferences.

8. LIFE-THREATENING ILLNESS

GENERAL RESOURCES

For information about support for families and caregivers, see the aging and disabilities sections.

Living/Dying Project
P.O. Box 357
Fairfax, CA 94978
Information/helpline: (415) 456-3915
  (1 P.M. to 5 P.M. PST)

Spiritual support for people with life-threatening illnesses and for those who care for them. One-on-one support for those who are ill. Workshops and training programs for the general public and for health care professionals.

St. Francis Center
4880A MacArthur Blvd. NW
Washington, D.C. 20007
Information/helpline: (202) 333-4880
  (9 A.M. to 5 P.M. EST).
  Fax: (202) 333-4540.

Offers guidance, information and support for people living with illness, loss, and bereavement. Offers pro bono psychotherapy for persons with HIV infection in Maryland, northern Virginia, and the District of Columbia for individuals without insurance coverage or the ability to pay. Other services include children's programs, support groups, publications, and referrals.

Medic Alert Foundation
2323 Colorado Ave.
Turlock, CA 95382
1-800-432-5378; operates 24 hours.
  Office: (209) 668-3333. Spanish,
  French translators available.

Wearing an engraved ID bracelet or necklace can save the lives of those with chronic medical conditions. Emblems produced by Medic Alert Foundation provide key medical facts for emergency personnel, plus the number of a twenty-four-hour hotline that is called collect from anywhere in the world to receive the patient's vital medical facts. Initial subscription cost is $35, which includes a bracelet or necklace, followed by a $15 annual fee. Members can update records as often as necessary at no charge. Persons with special needs are eligible for free memberships.

National Latina Health Organization/Organizacion Nacional de la Salud de la Mujer Latina
P.O. Box 7567
Oakland, CA 94601
Information/helpline: (510) 534-1362 (9 A.M. to 5 P.M. PST). English and Spanish spoken.

Formed to raise Latina consciousness about health. Promotes self-help methods and self-empowerment processes as a vehicle for greater control of our health practices and lifestyles. Committed to work toward bilingual access to quality health care and the empowerment of Latinas through culturally sensitive education programs, health advocacy, outreach, research, and the development of public policy. Services include self-help groups, health advocacy and referral, and health education. Services are free.

National Women's Health Network
514 10th St. NW, Suite 400
Washington, D.C. 20004
Information/helpline: (202) 628-7814 (9 A.M. to 5 P.M. EST).
Office: (202) 347-1140.

Offers a long list of publications on women's health issues, including cancer, AIDS, reproductive health, heart disease, osteoporosis, and many others.

National Women's Health Resource Center
2425 L St. NW, 3rd Floor
Washington, D.C. 20037
Information/helpline: (202) 293-6045, 8 A.M. to 4 P.M. EST.

National clearinghouse for women's health information. This organization does not provide counseling or hotline services. It does provide information to consumers and health professionals in several ways. Publishes *The National Women's Health Report,* which provides comprehensive health information as well as resources on a wide variety of issues. The database can direct women to centers and services near them. Searches on any women's health topic are available for a nominal fee for nonmembers and are free to members.

People's Medical Society
462 Walnut St.
Allentown, PA 18102
Information/helpline: (610) 770-1670 (8:30 A.M. to 5 P.M. EST)

This medical consumer advocacy organization is founded on the premise that the existing health care system is too expensive, impersonal, and unwilling to focus on preventive medicine and foster a partnership between consumer and physician. Provides consumer information, publications, and referrals to other organizations.

GOVERNMENT RESOURCES

Office of Alternative Medicine
National Institutes of Health
P.O. Box 8281
Silver Spring, MD 20907
Information line: 1-888-644-6226.
Office: (301) 402-2466.
Fax: (301)-402-4741.

Sponsors conferences and research into alternative treatments and serves as a public information clearinghouse on alternative medical practices. HIV/AIDS, cancer, research, and general information packets are available. Does not refer to practitioners or recommend treatments.

U.S. Department of Health and
   Human Services
Inspector General's Hotline
1-800-368-5779
In Maryland call 1-800-638-3986.
   Fraud hotline: 1-800-HHS-TIPS.

Collects complaints from Medicaid and Medicare patients and will refer to the office of appropriate jurisdiction.

Health Care Financing Administration
200 Independence Ave. SW
Room 314G
Washington, D.C. 20201
(202) 690-6726

This is the federal agency charged with overseeing Medicare and the federal portion of the Medicaid program. Medicare and Medicaid patients can register complaints about the quality of care with their regional HCFA office. Call for a referral to the regional branch.

The Medicare Hotline
1-800-638-6833; 1-800-820-1202 (TTY)

Operating 8 A.M. to 8 P.M. Eastern Standard Time, the hotline offers callers information on mammograms, insurance to supplement Medicare, and HMOs. You can also report suspected Medicare fraud or order a copy of the latest Medicare handbook using this number.

National Health Information Center
P.O. Box 1133
Washington, D.C. 20013
Information/helpline: 1-800-336-4797
   (1 P.M. to 5 P.M. EST).
   English/Spanish. In Maryland call
   (301) 468-1273.

Links consumers and health professionals who have health questions to organizations best able to provide answers. Maintains an on-line directory of 1,100 health-related organizations. Offers many publications and also an Internet health information service.

Office of Minority Health Resource
   Center
P.O. Box 37337
Washington, D.C. 20013-7337
Information/helpline:
   1-800-444-MHRC (6472) or
   (301) 589-0951 (TDD)

A nationwide service providing information related to the concerns of people with diverse heritages. Spanish and English operators available.

U.S. Public Health Service Office on
   Women's Health
U.S. Department of Health and
   Human Services
200 Independence Ave. SW
Washington, D.C. 20201
Information/helpline: (202) 690-7650

A major priority is the development and implementation of effective women's health programs and policies coordinated with other federal departments, and public and private organizations at the national, state, and local levels. Other critical goals are strengthening a broad range of research on the diseases and conditions that affect women; promoting comprehensive and culturally appropriate health promotion/disease prevention, diagnostic and treatment services for women; supporting public and health care professional education; and training and information dissemination on women's health issues.

AIDS Clinical Trials Information Service
1-800-TRIALS-A

The Public Health Service makes information about AIDS clinical trials available through this service.

AIDS Education/Services for the Deaf
2222 Laverna Ave.
Los Angeles, CA 90041
Office: (213) 550-4250 (voice/TDD),
8:30 A.M. to 5 P.M. PST

National hotline assists callers with their concerns or questions. For residents of southern California provides case management, peer counseling, information, and referrals. Sign language interpreter on duty; free except when not related to program.

American Red Cross
8111 Gate House Rd.
Falls Church, VA 22042
Information/helpline: Contact your local Red Cross chapter (check your telephone directory or ask your local operator for the number).

American Red Cross provides nonjudgmental, culturally appropriate HIV/AIDS educational programs and materials throughout the United States.

Centers for Disease Control and Prevention
National AIDS Hotline
1600 Clifton Rd., Mail Stop E-25
Atlanta, GA 30333
CDC National AIDS Hotline; operates 24 hours. English: 1-800-342-AIDS. Spanish: (8 A.M. to 2 A.M. EST): 1-800-344-7432. TTY (Monday through Friday 10 A.M. to 10 P.M.): 1-800-243-7889.

Provides current, accurate, anonymous, and confidential information about HIV infection and AIDS. Call to find out about taking a test for HIV, talking to children about HIV/AIDS, and for referrals in your local area and nationally for legal, financial, and treatment information, to receive publications, or to ask questions.

Center for Women Policy Studies
1211 Connecticut Ave. NW, Suite 312
Washington, D.C. 20036
Office: (202) 872-1770 (9 A.M. to 5 P.M. EST)

An independent feminist policy research and advocacy institution founded in 1972, the Center focuses on a variety of issues of concern to women. Among its many publications are *The Guide to Resources on Women and AIDS: Third Edition, WomenCare Action Kit,* and *More Harm Than Help: The Ramification for Rape Survivors of Mandatory HIV Testing of Rapists.* Prices vary.

National AIDS Information
  Clearinghouse
Centers for Disease Control and
  Prevention
P.O. Box 6003
Rockville, MD 20849
Information/helpline: 1-800-458-5231,
  1-800-243-7012 (TDD), 9 A.M. to
  7 P.M.). English/Spanish.

This information and referral service provides access to a number of AIDS-related databases through its reference service and bulletin board service. Distributes a number of publications.

National Association of People with
  AIDS
1413 K St. NW, 7th Floor
Washington, D.C. 20005
Information/helpline: (202) 898-0414
  (9 A.M. to 6 P.M.)
English, Spanish, French, Chinese
  spoken.

Serves through education by providing information about prevention, treatment, and medical and psychosocial resources for people affected by HIV. The National Speaker's Bureau employs speakers from across the U.S. and especially targets women, adolescents, communities of color, and people in the workplace. *Medical Alert,* a bimonthly publication addresses the latest in treatments and alternative therapies. NAPWA-FAX provides latest information on legal issues, service providers, nutrition, opportunistic infections, and treatment. Fax is free by calling (202) 789-2222.

National Native American AIDS
  Prevention Center
2100 Lakeshore Ave.
Oakland, CA 94606
Information/helpline: 1-800-283-2437
  (8:30 A.M. to 1 P.M. and 2 P.M. to
  5 P.M.)
  Office: (510) 444-2051.

Operates the toll-free Native American AIDS information line and a national clearinghouse for Native American–specific HIV/AIDS information. Trains community-based HIV educators, provides technical assistance in community organizing, and publishes a newsmagazine. Offers case management in the Oklahoma City office and the National Indian AIDS Media Consortium in Minneapolis.

National Pediatric and Family HIV
  Resource Center
15 South 9 St. North
Newark, NJ 07107
1-800-362-0071 or (201) 268-8251

Project Inform
1965 Market St., #220
San Francisco, CA 94103
HIV/AIDS Treatment hotline:
  1-800-822-7422 (national); local and
  international: (415) 558-9051 (10 A.M.
  to 4 P.M. PST).
  Office: (415) 558-8669.

The Project Inform HIV/AIDS Treatment Hotline is a nationwide service devoted exclusively to updating people on the latest in a broad range of treatment issues and debunking the latest in treatment hype. Also produces a journal, newsletter, and fact sheets.

American Silicone Implant Survivors, Inc.
1288 Cork Elm Dr.
Kirkwood, MO 63122
Information/helpline: (314) 821-0115
(9 A.M. to 5 P.M. CST)

A patient activist group that provides support, physician referrals, and a newsletter. The group's work concerns any silicone implantable device, silicone, and saline breast implants. Services are available to women, men, and children born to women with silicone implants.

U.S. Food and Drug Administration
Office of Consumer Affairs
5600 Fishers Lane, Rm. 75
Rockville, MD 20857
Information Line: 1-800-532-4440 or
(301) 443-3170 (10 A.M. to 4 P.M. EST
Monday through Friday).
Office: (301) 827-4420.

Provides general information about breast cancer and an information package on breast implants.

Cancer

African-American Breast Cancer Alliance
P.O. Box 8981
Minneapolis, MN 55408
Information/helpline: (612) 825-3675

Services include distribution of educational pamphlets, information workshops, and monthly meetings. Produces a brochure and videocassette to provide a realistic message of education, hope, and self-advocacy for African-American women.

American Cancer Society
1599 Clifton Rd. NE
Atlanta, GA 30329
Information/helpline: 1-800-ACS-2345
(8:30 A.M. to 5 P.M. EST)

Nationwide community-based health organization dedicated to eliminating cancer as a major health problem. Patient service programs are available throughout the country. Some of the following may be offered in your area: "I Can Cope" consists of educational classes for cancer patients and their families; "Look Good . . . Feel Better" helps women learn to overcome the appearance-related side effects of cancer treatment; "Reach to Recovery" offers one-on-one visitation for women who have concerns about breast cancer; "Road to Recovery" provides cancer patients with transportation to and from treatment; "Group Support Programs" serve patients and their families. In addition, many patient education materials are available from the American Cancer Society.

Breast Cancer Action
55 New Montgomery, Suite 624
San Francisco, CA 94105
Information/helpline: (415) 243-9301
(9 A.M. to 5 P.M. PST)

A grassroots breast cancer activist group dedicated to making breast cancer a national priority through education and advocacy, promoting and refocusing research into the causes, prevention, treatment and cure, and empowering women and men so they can fully participate in decisions relating to breast cancer. Publishes a nationwide newsletter. Membership is open to all people.

Cancer Care
1180 Avenue of the Americas
New York, NY 10036
Information/helpline:
1-800-813-HOPE (9 A.M. to 5 P.M.
 EST). English/Spanish.
 Office: (212) 221-3300.

Centers in New York, New Jersey, and Connecticut provide counseling, financial assistance, outreach programs to meet the special needs of children and older adults, referral to home and childcare services, hospices, hospitals and community resources, and educational workshops. Many services are also available in Delaware and Florida.

Cancer Information Service
National Cancer Institute
Building 31, Room 10A16
Bethesda, MD 20892
Information/helpline:
 1-800-4-CANCER (9 A.M. to
 4:30 P.M. EST). Spanish/English.

This nationwide network of nineteen regional field offices provides specific information about particular types of cancer, as well as information on how to obtain second opinions and availability of clinical trials. Callers are automatically routed to the office in their region.

Cancer Research Center
1600 Pierce St.
Denver, CO 80214
Information/helpline: 1-800-525-3777
 (8:30 A.M. to 5 P.M. MT).
 Office: (303) 233-6501.

Through this nationwide telephone line, callers have access to the latest information on cancer prevention, detection, diagnosis, treatment and rehabilitation, including the Physicians' Data Query, a database of research studies and treatment protocols from the nation's cancer centers. Counselors also help with coping with the side effects of therapy, the emotional effects of cancer, communicating with doctor and family members, and in seeking a second opinion.

Candlelighters® Childhood Cancer
 Foundation
7910 Woodmont Ave. — 460
Bethesda, MD 20814
Information/helpline: 1-800-366-2223
 (9 A.M. to 5 P.M. EST)

Services include education, advocacy, and support for families of children with cancer and adult survivors of childhood cancer. Provides computerized searches of protocols, treatment options, and literature, acts as a clearinghouse to match families with sources of help, has a worldwide network of peer support groups for parents, and publishes newsletters and other materials. Local chapters often provide emergency funding, summer camps, and transportation.

Leukemia Society of America
600 Third Ave., Fourth Floor
New York, NY 10016
Information/helpline: 1-800-955-4572;
 operates 24 hours.
 Office: (212) 573-8484.
 Web site: http://www.leukemia.org.

Provides supplementary financial assistance to patients with leukemia, the lymphomas, and multiple myeloma. Gives referrals to other services in local communities. Chapters are located throughout the U.S. Alerts the public to disease danger, treatment, and therapy through written and audiovisual materials. Many publications are free of charge.

National Alliance of Breast Cancer
Organizations
9 East 37 St., Tenth Floor
New York, NY 10016
Information/helpline: (212) 719-0154
(9:30 A.M. to 5:30 P.M. EST)

This is a network of breast cancer organizations that provides information, assistance, and referrals to anyone with questions about breast cancer and acts as a voice for the interests and concerns of breast cancer survivors and women at risk.

National Coalition for Cancer
Survivorship
1010 Wayne Ave., Fifth Floor
Silver Spring, MD 20910
(301) 650-8868 (9 A.M. to 5 P.M. EST).
English/Spanish.

NCCS is a coalition of individuals, cancer support organizations, and treatment centers that advocates on behalf of the cancer survivorship community. NCCS defines cancer survivorship from the moment of diagnosis and for the balance of life. It serves as a clearinghouse for information on a wide range of quality-of-life issues and specifically addresses the issues of cancer-based employment discrimination and access to health insurance. It maintains a database of cancer support services nationwide and publishes a *Networking Directory of National Cancer Support Programs* as well as many other publications.

The National Lymphedema Network
2211 Post St., Suite 404
San Francisco, CA 95115
Information/helpline: 1-800-541-3259
(message line; can ring through in
emergency). English/German.
Web site: http://www.hooked.net/
users/lymphnet.

Gives emotional support, provides education and offers referrals to health care professionals, local support groups, and exercise programs, publishes newsletters and a resource guide that lists treatment centers, health care professionals, support groups, pen pals, and conferences.

National Marrow Donor Program
3433 Broadway St. NE, Suite 500
Minneapolis, MN 55413
Information/helpline:
1-800-MARROW-2 (8 A.M. to 6 P.M.
CST). Office: 1-800-526-7809. AT&T
Languageline accepts 141 different
languages.

This program is a computerized registry of unrelated potential volunteer marrow donors. NMDP provides information on how to be listed as a potential donor along with providing transplant information for patients with leukemia, aplastic anemia, and other life-threatening diseases. The need for minority donors is especially great. The office can give resource information on bone marrow transplants and transplant centers in their network.

Susan C. Komen Breast Cancer
Foundation
5005 LBJ Freeway, Suite 370
Dallas, TX 75244
Information/helpline: 1-800-462-9273
(9 A.M. to 5 P.M. CST).
English/Spanish.
Office: (214) 233-0351.

A volunteer-driven national organization raises money to fund breast cancer research and offers education programs and low-cost screening programs. Sponsors "Race for the Cure" events, staffs a helpline for cancer patients and their families to call for information about breast cancer issues.

United Ostomy Association
36 Executive Park, Suite 120
Irvine, CA 92614
Information/helpline: 1-800-826-0826
 (7 A.M. to 4 P.M. PST).
 Office: (714) 660-8624.

Provides free educational and support group information, including packets of reading material. Chapters are located throughout the U.S., Canada, and foreign countries to assist patients, nurses, and doctors with support. Publishes a quarterly magazine.

Y-ME National Breast Cancer
 Organization
212 W. Van Buren St., 5th Floor
Chicago, IL 60607-3908
Information/hotline: 1-800-221-2141;
 operates 24 hours, 7 days a week.
 Spanish hotline:
 1-800-986-9505.
 Web site: http://www.y-me.org.

Y-ME is a nonprofit consumer-driven organization that provides information, referral, and emotional support to individuals concerned about or diagnosed with breast cancer. Its national toll-free hotline is staffed by trained counselors and volunteers who have experienced breast cancer. Several men whose partners have breast cancer are also available. Y-ME national and its chapters conduct support and educational meetings in many states. Y-ME provides free written materials and publishes a bimonthly award-winning newsletter. A wig and prosthesis bank is available for those in need.

YWCA of the U.S.A. ENCORE Plus
 Program
624 Ninth St. NW, 3rd Floor
Washington, D.C. 20001
Information/helpline: (202) 628-3636
 (9 A.M. to 5 P.M. EST). English,
 Spanish, French spoken.

The community-based programs target women older than the age of fifty in need of early detection education and breast and cervical cancer screening and support services. Also helps women suffering from breast cancer with a combined peer support group and exercise program. There are fifty-three ENCORE program sites at YWCAs in twenty-five states. The YWCA will implement a national training program that will assist with the implementation and monitoring of local ENCORE programs.

Women's Cancer Resource Center
3023 Shattuck Ave.
Berkeley, CA 94705
Information/helpline: (510) 548-9272 or
 (510) 548-9288 (TDD/TTY),
 Tuesdays 2 P.M. to 5 P.M.,
 Wednesday and Thursday 4 P.M. to
 7 P.M., Saturday 12 P.M. to 4 P.M.
 PST. Spanish/English.
 Office: (510) 548-9288.

Reaches out to all women, including poor women, the elderly, women of color, lesbians and women exploring nontraditional approaches to care with an information and referral hotline, library, and a newsletter. Volunteer lawyers offer workshops, free consultations, and referrals. Offers a wide range of support groups and one-to-one practical and emotional support, including assisting with housekeeping, respite care, and shopping. Referrals to licensed massage therapists who donate their services.

The Mended Hearts
7272 Greenville Ave.
Dallas, TX 75231
Information/helpline: (214) 706-1442
  (9 A.M. to 5 P.M. CST)

The purpose of Mended Hearts is to offer encouragement to heart disease patients and their families, especially through hospital visits. Most of the members have been affected by heart disease and can empathize with those who are undergoing treatment. There are 240 chapters throughout the United States.

The National Heart, Lung and Blood
  Institute
P.O. Box 30105
Bethesda, MD 20824-0105
Information/helpline: (301) 251-1222
  (8:30 A.M. to 5 P.M. EST). Web site:
  http://www.nilbi.nih.gov/nhlbi/
  nhlbi.htm.

Supports research and provides information to the public and professionals on disorders of the heart, blood vessels, lungs and blood. Free fact sheets, pamphlets, and other informational material are available.

National Institute of Neurological
  Disorders and Stroke
National Institutes of Health
P.O. Box 5801
Bethesda, MD 20892
Information/helpline: 1-800-352-9424
  (8:30 A.M. to 5 P.M. EST).
  Office: (301) 496-5751.

By supporting and conducting research, the NINDS seeks better understanding, diagnosis, treatment, and prevention of neurological disorders. Its public information program provides physicians, patients, and the public with educational materials and research highlights. Materials provided by the information office include brochures, fact sheets, information packets, reports, and professional interest publications on many neurological disorders and diseases. All publications are free.

National Stroke Association
96 Inverness Dr. East
Suite I
Englewood, CO 80112
Information/helpline:
  1-800-STROKES (8 A.M. to 4:30 P.M.
  MT Monday through Thursday).
  Office: (303) 649-9299.

Committed to stroke prevention, treatment, rehabilitation, and support for stroke survivors and their families. Services include National Information and Referral Center on Stroke, *Directory of Stroke Support Groups* (provides guidance for stroke survivors), local NSA chapters, a national clearinghouse on stroke-related publications, references, videos and other resources, advocacy, and public awareness campaigns. Offers many booklets at a nominal cost.

Stroke Connection
American Heart Association
7272 Greenville Ave.
Dallas, TX 75231
Information/helpline: 1-800-553-6321

Goal is to provide a forum for stroke survivors, their family members, and professionals to share information and experiences related to living with stroke. There are more than 830 stroke groups nationwide and some in foreign countries. Stroke Connection also assists members in finding information and referrals. Many clubs are associated with AHA affiliates. Publishes a magazine, newsletter, and book.

American Academy of Pediatrics
P.O. Box 927
Elk Grove Village, IL 60009
Information/helpline: (847) 981-6757

This is an organization of 50,000 pediatricians dedicated to the health, safety, and well-being of infants, children, and adolescents. Will provide the names of pediatricians or pediatric subspecialists if you send a self-addressed, stamped envelope specifying your geographic area to the above address, Attention: Pediatric Referral Service. For a complete listing of available literature, write to the above address, Attention: Department C:PRG.

American Academy of Nurse
  Practitioners
P.O. Box 12846
Austin, TX 78711
Information/helpline: (512) 442-4262
  (8 A.M. to 5 P.M. CST)

A professional organization of nurse practitioners who have advanced education to provide primary care in specialized areas such as adult, family, elder, and child health, mental health, school health, and women's OB-GYN. Services to the public include locating a nurse practitioner in their area. Brochures that explain the nurse practitioner role are available in English and Spanish.

American Association of Oriental
  Medicine
433 Front St.
Catasauqua, PA 18032
Information/Helpline: (610) 266-1433
  (9 A.M. to 5 P.M. EST)

National association for the development of Oriental medicine as a complementary field of health care in America. National referral network for qualified practitioners (licensed acupuncturists, Chinese herbologists, doctors of Oriental medicine) nearest to the inquirer. Also has a library of articles pertaining to Oriental medicine treatments.

The American Board of Medical
  Specialties
1007 Church St., Suite 404
Evanston, IL 60201-5913
(847) 491-9091
Specialties certification line:
  1-800-776-2378

You can find out whether a physician is board certified and learn the year of his or her certification by calling the American Board of Medical Specialties certification line.

American College of Radiology
1891 Preston White Dr.
Reston, VA 22091
Information/helpline: 1-800-227-5463
  (9 A.M. to 5:30 P.M. EST).
  Office: (703) 648-8910.

This national medical specialty association offers a number of booklets for the general public that educate patients about their diagnostic and treatment options including mammography and breast cancer.

American Holistic Medical Association
4101 Lake Boone Trail, Suite 201
Raleigh, NC 27607
Information/helpline: (919) 787-5181
  (8:45 A.M. to 4:45 P.M. EST)

Membership organization for M.D.s, D.O.s, and medical students who practice alternative therapies. Publishes a national directory of holistic practitioners and a quarterly journal.

Joint Commission on Accreditation of
Healthcare Organizations
One Renaissance Blvd.
Oakbrook Terrace, IL 60181
Customer service
information/helpline: (630) 792-5800
Office: (630) 792-5000.

The Joint Commission's mission is to improve the quality of care provided to the public through the provision of health care accreditation and related services. Accreditation is available for general, psychiatric, children's, and rehabilitation hospitals, health care networks, home care agencies, nursing homes, mental health services, ambulatory care providers, and clinical laboratories. Publications are available to help you choose quality care.

The National League for Nursing
350 Hudson St.
New York, NY 10014
(212) 645-9685 (9 A.M. to 5 P.M. EST)

Professional membership organization that is the sole accrediting body for all types of nursing education programs in the U.S. Publishes scholarly as well as consumer-oriented paperback books and fifty health-related videos.

9. CRISES IN AGING

GENERAL INFORMATION AND REFERRAL SERVICES

The Eldercare Locator
1-800-677-1116 (9 A.M. to 11 P.M. EST
    Monday through Friday)

Can put you in touch with local Area Agencies on Aging and other resources for information about a range of services, including home-delivered meals, legal assistance, housing options, adult daycare, senior center programs, home health services, nursing home ombudsman services, transportation, and elder abuse prevention services. Be prepared to give the zip code of the person for whom you are calling, your own zip code, and a brief description of your problem or question.

Association of Jewish Family and
    Children's Agencies
3086 State Highway 27, Suite 11
Kendall Park, NJ 08824
Information/helpline: 1-800-634-7346

Membership organization of over 143 Jewish Family and Children's Agencies in the U.S. and Canada dedicated to enhancing the quality of Jewish family life. Publishes directories and acts as a national clearinghouse for information on addictions and operates the Schroeder Award–winning Elder Support Network. Special programming is offered through member agencies to adults and children experiencing divorce, intermarried families, single-parent families, families in the adoption network, as well as services to immigrant Jews, the developmentally disabled, the elderly, and people with AIDS. Call for a referral to a local office.

AGING ORGANIZATIONS

AARP Women's Initiative
601 E St. NW
Washington, D.C. 20049
Information/helpline: (202) 434-2400

Works to insure that the economic, social, health, and long-term needs of midlife and older women are met. The Women's Initiative advocates and supports policies, programs, and legislation that improve the status of women.

Offers the publication *Divorce After 50* and others on personal money management, pensions, social security, credit, employment, and housing.

American Geriatrics Society
770 Lexington Ave., Suite 300
New York, NY 10021
Information/helpline: (212) 308-1414

The AGS has a long history of promoting high quality health care for older adults. Since 1942, AGS has provided leadership for health care professionals and policymakers by developing, implementing, and advocating innovative programs in patient care, research, professional education, and public policy. Has become a pivotal force in shaping attitudes, policies, and practices in geriatrics health care. Publishes *The American Geriatrics Society Complete Guide to Aging and Health,* a practical resource that covers a broad array of medical and health care topics relevant to older adults and their caregivers.

Gray Panthers
P.O. Box 21477
Washington, D.C. 20009
Information/helpline: (202) 466-3132

Founded in 1970 by the late Maggie Kuhn, this is a national organization of intergenerational activists dedicated to social change, including peace, jobs for all, housing, antidiscrimination (ageism, sexism, racism), family security, the environment, and campaign reform. There are fifty local networks.

National Adult Day Services
    Association
c/o National Council on the Aging
409 Third St. SW
Washington, D.C. 20024
(202) 479-6682

National organization that serves professionals and providers of adult day service centers. Research and development, public policy, and advocacy. Offers some publications for caregivers and consumers.

National Asian Pacific Center on Aging
1511 Third Ave., Suite 914
Seattle, WA 98101
Information/helpline: (206) 624-1221
    (8:30 A.M. to 5 P.M. PST). English,
    Chinese, Japanese, Ilocano,
    Tagalog, Indonesian, and Dutch
    spoken.

Develops programs for Asians and Pacific Island elders; provides free information and referrals; and sponsors Senior Community Service Employment Programs, employing hundreds of elders across the country. Publishes *Demographic and Socioeconomic Characteristics of Elder Asian and Pacific Island Americans, Guide to Supplemental Security Income,* the *Asian Pacific Affairs* newsletter, *Pacific/Asian Elderly Bibliography,* and disseminates brochures on health, employment, and social services in a dozen A/PI languages.

National Association of Professional
    Geriatric Care Managers
1604 N. Country Club Rd.
Tucson, AZ 85716
Information/helpline: (520) 881-8008

A geriatric care manager specializes in assisting older people and their families with long-term-care arrangements, including financial, legal, or medical issues. In addition, case managers offer counseling and support, provide crisis intervention, act as liaisons to families at a distance, and assist in other ways. Send a stamped, self-addressed envelope for names of geriatric care managers in your state.

National Center on Elder Abuse
810 First St. NE, Suite 500
Washington, D.C. 20002
Information/helpline: (202) 682-2470

The NCEA manages a Clearinghouse on Abuse and Neglect of the Elderly, the nation's only automated, elder abuse literature search and retrieval system. It also publishes a quarterly newsletter, compiles and disseminates "best practice" information, provides agencies with assistance in improving their elder abuse information systems, and responds to inquiries about elder abuse from the public.

OWL (The Older Women's League)
666 Eleventh St. W., Suite 700
Washington, D.C. 20001
Information/helpline: 1-800-825-3695.
    Office: (202) 783-6686.

Advocates for economic and social equity for midlife and older women. Issues include employer-sponsored pensions, Social Security, universal health care, violence against women, discrimination, housing, advanced directives, and caregiving. Offers many publications. Membership is open to peoples of any age and gender.

CAREGIVERS

Children of Aging Parents
1609 Woodbourne Rd., Suite 302A
Levittown, PA 19057
Information/helpline: 1-800-227-7294
    (9 A.M. to 3 P.M. EST).
    Office: (215) 945-6900.

National mission is to assist the caregivers of the elderly with reliable information, referrals, and support. CAPS has phone numbers and names for nursing homes, retirement communities, elder law attorneys, daycare centers, medical insurance providers, respite care, assisted living centers, state and county agencies, and support groups across the United States. Also has fact sheets, a newsletter, and workshops.

National Family Caregivers Association
9621 East Bexhill Dr.
Kensington, MD 20895
Information/helpline: 1-800-896-3650.
    Office: (301) 942-6430.

Mission is to improve the overall quality of life for family caregivers. A person-to-person linkage helps caregivers build supporting relationships with other caregivers. A twenty-four-hour helpline is planned to provide assistance to caregivers no matter where they live. Publishes a quarterly newsletter and educational materials.

Well Spouse Foundation
P.O. Box 801
New York, NY 10023
Information/helpline: 1-800-838-0879
    (24 hours). Office: (212) 644-1241
    (10 A.M. to 4 P.M. EST).

This is a national organization that provides support to husbands, wives, and partners of the chronically ill and/or disabled through a bimonthly newsletter, support groups in many parts of the country, letter-writing support groups, an annual weekend conference, and other weekend meetings across the country. Also offers a publications program. Membership dues are $20, but if that is a hardship, well spouses pay whatever they can afford. No one will be turned away.

Consumer Information Center
P.O. Box 100
Pueblo, Colorado 81002

Free and low-cost information from the federal government. Publications include *Guide to Choosing a Nursing Home* (647 B, 1993) and *Some Things You Should Know About Prescription Drugs* (607 B, 1984 FDA).

Council of Better Business Bureaus
4200 Wilson Blvd., #800
Arlington, VA 22203
Information/helpline: (703) 276-0100
(8:30 A.M. to 5:30 P.M. EST)

Promotes the highest ethical relationship between business and the public through voluntary self-regulation, consumer and business education, and service excellence. Serves consumers nationwide by providing informational materials and through alternative dispute resolution services.

National Consumers League
1701 K Street NW, Suite 1200
Washington, D.C. 20006
Office number: (202) 835-3323. Fraud helpline: 1-800-876-7060 (9 A.M. to 5:30 P.M. EST). English/Spanish.

Publishes brochures, handbooks, and manuals on a range of subjects, including credit, fraud, health insurance, and food and drug safety. Many are available in Spanish. Also publishes material to serve low-literacy populations. Sponsors conferences and workshops on health care, medication, safety, and consumer fraud. The National Fraud Information Center is a project of National Consumers League, which gives advice to consumers who have received suspicious telemarketing solicitations. Also files reports of telemarketing fraud for victims, which are forwarded to appropriate authorities. Consumer fraud publications are available.

National Fire Protection Association
11 Tracy Dr.
Avon, MA 02322
1-800-344-3555 (to order products), 8:30 A.M. to 8:30 P.M. Monday through Friday

This private nonprofit membership organization is dedicated to reducing the burden of fire on the quality of life. Offers a variety of fire safety educational products and audiovisual materials.

National Shared Housing Resource Center
321 East 25th St.
Baltimore, MD 21218
Information/helpline: (410) 235-4454
(9 A.M. to 5 P.M.)

Makes referrals to 350 shared housing programs across the country. Publishes *A Consumer's Guide to Homesharing* and other information about shared housing. For people of all ages, but particular emphasis is on serving elders, students, displaced homemakers, and single parents. Services are free of charge and available to people of all ages.

National Association of State Units on
   Aging
1225 I St. NW, Suite 725
Washington, D.C. 20005
Information/helpline: (202) 898-2578
   (8:30 A.M. to 5:30 P.M. EST)

Operates a National Resource Center on Long Term Care and the National Information and Referral Support Center. Collaborates with other organizations in providing resources: Eldercare Locator (1-800-677-1116), a nationwide directory assistance service designed to help older persons and caregivers link to local aging services; National Resource Center on Elder Abuse; and National Long Term Care Ombudsman Resource Center Programs for nursing home reform. Develops publications on topics such as older worker issues, elder abuse, state long-term care, and nutrition programs.

National Institute on Aging
   Information Center
P.O. Box 8057
Gaithersburg, MD 20898
Information/helpline: 1-800-222-2225;
   1-800-222-4225 (TTY), 8:30 A.M. to
   5 P.M., EST. Office: (301) 496-1752.

Provides publications and fact sheets on health issues affecting the aging population. Also provides referrals to other agencies and national organizations for topics not covered by the National Institute on Aging.

The Medicare Hotline
1-800-638-6833; 1-800-820-1202 (TTY)

Operating 8 A.M. to 8 P.M. EST, the hotline offers callers information on mammograms, insurance to supplement Medicare, and HMOs. You can also report suspected Medicare fraud or order a copy of the latest Medicare handbook using this number.

HOME CARE AND VISITING NURSES

Foundation for Hospice and Homecare
513 C St. NE
Washington, D.C. 20002-5809
(202) 547-6586

For further information, call the Foundation for Hospice and Homecare.

Visiting Nurse Association
National Headquarters
520 South Lafayette Park Pl., Suite 500
Los Angeles, CA 90057
(213) 386-7200. Refer to your local
   phone directory for the office
   nearest you.

VNA home care is a comprehensive program offering a complete array of specialized services and support, which includes skilled care and private duty, nursing speciality services, infusion therapy, physical, occupational, speech, and respiratory therapy, medical social work, home health aide services, homemaking and companionship, maternal childcare, supportive care, telephone reassurance, durable medical equipment, respite care, and hospital home care coordination.

LEGAL PROFESSIONALS

Legal Services for the Elderly
130 West 42nd St., 17th Floor
New York, NY 10036
Office: (212) 391-0120 (9 A.M. to
    5 P.M. EST)

This is an advisory center for lawyers specializing in problems affecting the elderly. It does not service clients directly. Offers some publications.

National Academy of Elder
Law Attorneys
1604 N. Country Club Dr.
Tucson, AZ 85716
Information/helpline: (520) 881-4005

Dedicated to improving the quality of legal services provided to the elderly, this organization examines and advocates on public policy issues. Provides information on how to select an elder law attorney and publishes brochures on elder law topics. Many attorneys have developed practices specifically designed to serve the elderly client.

NURSING HOMES AND ASSISTED-LIVING FACILITIES

American Association of Homes and
    Services for the Aging
901 E St. NW, Suite 500
Washington, D.C. 20004
Information/helpline: (202) 783-2242
    (8:30 A.M. to 5:30 P.M. EST)

National association of not-for-profit organizations dedicated to providing high-quality health care, housing, and home- and community-based services to the elderly through advocacy, education, and information. Offers guidebooks and directories to help consumers find care for older people.

Assisted Living Facilities Association
    of America
10300 Eaton Pl., Suite 400
Fairfax, VA 22030
Information/helpline: (703) 691-8100
    (8:30 A.M. to 5 P.M. EST)

Provides information about assisted-living facilities as a long-term option for people who need help with activities of daily living but do not need the skilled medical care of a nursing home. Send a business-sized self-addressed stamped envelope for a free brochure or call the Eldercare Locator at 1-800-677-1116.

California Advocates for Nursing
    Home Reform
1610 Bush St.
San Francisco, CA 94109
Information/helpline: 1-800-474-1116.
    Office: (415) 474-5171.

Provides counseling on choosing a nursing home, alternatives to nursing home care, financial considerations, Medi-Cal eligibility requirements, legal concerns, and admission issues. Provides a database on all 1,400 nursing homes in California, a lawyer referral service, pension rights counseling, and many consumer publications.

The National Citizens' Coalition for
Nursing Home Re-
form (NCCNHR)
1424 16th St. NW, Suite 202
Washington, D.C. 20036-2211
Information/helpline: (202) 332-2275.
Fax: (202) 332-2949. Web site:
http://www.aginet.com/nccnhr.

NCCNHR is a consumer organization whose membership includes several hundred grassroots nursing home advocacy groups and ombudsman programs working to protect and improve the quality of life for nursing home residents throughout the United States. In addition to advocacy, NCCNHR offers the public and professionals reasonably priced publications, including *Nursing Homes: Getting Good Care There*, *Avoiding Physical Restraint Use: New Standards in Care*, and *Avoiding Drugs Used as Chemical Restraints: New Standards in Care*.

---

10. DEATH AND DYING

NATIONAL ORGANIZATIONS

American Association of Suicidology
4201 Connecticut Ave. NW, Suite 310
Washington, D.C. 20008
Information/helpline: (202) 237-2280
(9 A.M. to 5 P.M. EST)

Serves as a clearinghouse for information on suicide. Promotes research, education, and training for professionals and volunteers. Sponsors workshops and Suicide Prevention Week; produces a newsletter and journal and directory of support groups in the U.S. and Canada. Open to everyone.

Association for Death Education and
Counseling
638 Prospect Ave.
Hartford, CT 06105
Information/helpline: (860) 586-7503
(8:30 A.M. to 5:30 P.M. EST)

Works to promote and share research, theories, and practice in dying, death, and bereavement for professionals and laypeople who work in death education and grief counseling. Offers a certification program, conferences, newsletter, and networking with other bereavement professionals. Provides referrals for grief support and bereavement education.

Choice in Dying
200 Varick St.
New York, NY 10014
Information/helpline: 1-800-989-WILL
(9455); operates 24 hours.
Office: (212) 366-5540.
Web site: http://www.choices.org.

A national, not-for-profit organization dedicated to fostering communication about complex end-of-life decisions among individuals, their loved ones, and health care professionals. Advocates for the right of patients to participate fully in decisions about their medical treatment at the end of life. Deals practically with end-of-life issues and provides substantial public and professional education, advance directives, and counseling about the preparation and use of advance directives. Pioneered the living will twenty-five years ago and provides reasonably priced state-specific advance directives to individuals who contact them. Offers several publications and phone counseling to answer questions about end-of-life issues.

Funeral Service Consumer Assistance
   Program
National Research and Information
   Center
2250 E. Devon Ave., Suite 250
Des Plaines, IL 60018
1-800-662-7666 (9 A.M. to 4 P.M. CST
   Monday through Friday)

For information, see Chapter Ten.

U.S. Federal Trade Commission
Sixth and Pennsylvania Ave. NW
Washington, D.C. 20580
(202) 326-2222 or (202) 326-2502 (TDD)

Information about the Funeral Rule. Also publishes the pamphlets *Funerals: A Consumer's Guide* and *Caskets and Burial Vaults.*

Cemetery Consumer Service Council
P.O. Box 2028
Reston, VA 20195
Information/helpline: 1-800-645-7700.
   Office: (703) 391-8407 (9 A.M. to
   5 P.M. EST)

Assists consumers, without charge, in resolving complaints, such as improper maintenance, deceptive sales practices, truth in lending, and other contractual deficiencies. Also answers inquiries regarding cemetery services and policies involving private cemeteries and memorial parks.

GRIEF/EMOTIONAL SUPPORT

AARP's Widowed Persons Service
601 E St. NW
Washington, D.C. 20049
(202) 434-2260 (8 A.M. to 6 P.M. EST)

Trained widowed volunteers offer support to newly widowed persons in 235 communities nationwide. Services include visits to the newly bereaved, telephone services that newly widowed persons can call for referral information and assistance, group sessions to discuss mutual problems, a directory of local services, and many publications.

Compassionate Friends
P.O. Box 3696
Oak Brook, IL 60522
Information/helpline: (708) 990-0010
   (9 A.M. to 4 P.M. CST)

A national mutual assistance and self-help organization that offers support and understanding to bereaved parents and siblings through more than six hundred chapters. Aids parents in the positive resolution of the grief experienced upon the death of their child. Publishes a newsletter and resource catalog and makes referrals to local chapters.

The Dougy Center for Grieving
   Children
3909 SE 52nd Ave.
P.O. Box 86852
Portland, OR 97286
Information/helpline: (503) 775-5683
   (9 A.M. to 5 P.M. PST)

Provides grief support services to children and youth aged three to nineteen and their adult family members who have experienced a death through accident, illness, suicide, or homicide. The Center has a national directory of children's grief support programs and provides a crisis information and referral line.

The Grief Recovery Institute
Educational Foundation
8306 Wilshire Blvd., #21A
Beverly Hills, CA 90211
Information/helpline: 1-800-445-4808
(9 A.M. to 5 P.M. PST).
Office: (213) 650-1234.

The helpline is a national telephone service available for the bereaved which offers safe, noncritical counseling to help reduce the griever's sense of isolation. Weekly support groups throughout North America focus on recovery from loss, death, or divorce. Also offers a handbook, seminars, and certification program for professionals.

International THEOS Foundation
322 Boulevard of the Allies, Suite 105
Pittsburgh, PA 15222
Information/helpline: (412) 471-7779
(9 A.M. to 3 P.M. EST Monday
through Thursday; a 24-hour
answering machine operates)

This nondenominational organization provides a mutual support system for newly widowed men and women. There are 144 chapters in the U.S. and Canada. Publishes *Survivors Outreach* magazine.

Living/Dying Project
P.O. Box 357
Fairfax, CA 94978
Information/helpline: (415) 884-2343

Spiritual support for people with life-threatening illnesses and for those who care for them. One-to-one support for those who are ill. Workshops and training programs for the general public and for health care professionals.

Mothers Against Drunk Driving
511 E. John Carpenter Freeway,
Suite 700
Irving, TX 75062
Information/helpline: 1-800-GET
MADD; operates 24 hours.
Office: (214) 744-6233.

Mission is to stop drunk driving and to support the victims of this violent crime. MADD has more than 550 chapters throughout the country. Offers victim services such as emotional support, guidance through the criminal justice system, court accompaniment, and victim support groups. Open to any concerned citizen, including victims and families of those killed or injured, law enforcement and traffic officials, and health care workers.

National Organization for Victim
Assistance (NOVA)
1757 Park Rd. NW
Washington, D.C. 20010
Information/helpline: 1-800-879-6682;
operates 24 hours. English/Spanish.
Office: (202) 232-6682.

Information and referral for victims of violent crime and disaster. Services available for victim/survivors and their loved ones.

Parents of Murdered Children
100 E. Eighth St., B-41
Cincinnati, OH 45202
Information/helpline: (513) 721-5683;
operates 24 hours

Provides emotional support to families and friends of homicide victims with a nationwide network of chapters and contact persons. Its goals are education, prevention, advocacy, and awareness, including a program to keep murderers behind bars and to raise public awareness regarding the insensitivity of murder as entertainment in media.

Rainbows
1111 Tower Rd.
Schaumburg, IL 60173
Information/helpline: (847) 310-1880
 (8:30 A.M. to 4:30 P.M. CST)

Offers peer support groups for children, adolescents, and adults who are grieving a loss due to death, divorce, or other painful transitions in the family. Assists people who are grieving in expressing and understanding their feelings, in accepting what has happened, and in feeling a sense of belonging and love.

RID-USA Victim Center
P.O. Box 520
Schenectady, NY 12301
Information/helpline: (518) 393-HELP

Provides long-term emotional support to the victims of drunk driving crashes and their families, counsels and accompanies victims throughout all phases of the criminal case against the offender, helps victims obtain compensation, refers victims to various appropriate supportive agencies, operates 150 victim support chapters in 41 states. Also monitors drunk driving cases and advocates for legislative change.

St. Francis Center
4880A MacArthur Blvd. NW
Washington, D.C. 20007
Information/helpline: (202) 363-8500
 (9 A.M. to 5 P.M. EST).
 Fax: (202) 333-4540.

Offers guidance, information, and support for people living with illness, loss, and bereavement. Offers pro bono psychotherapy for individuals with HIV infection in Maryland, northern Virginia, and the District of Columbia who don't have insurance coverage or the ability to pay. Other services include a children's program, support groups, publications, and referrals.

Hospice organizations

Children's Hospice International
1850 M St. NW, #900
Washington, D.C. 20036
(703) 684-0330; 1-800-24-CHILD
 (9 A.M. to 5 P.M. EST);
 Fax: (703) 684-0226.

Provides information and referrals to families of children with life-threatening conditions and to the health care professionals who treat them. Works to further incorporate the hospice perspective in pediatric health care.

Foundation for Hospice and Homecare
513 C St. NE
Washington, D.C. 20002-5809
(202) 547-6586

For further information, call the Hospice and Homecare.

Hospice Association of America
228 7th St. SE
Washington, D.C. 20003
Information/helpline: (202) 546-4759
 (9 A.M. to 6 P.M. EST)

Serves as a voice in Congress for more than two thousand hospices to improve the quality of hospice care. Publishes a newsletter and magazine for members.

National Hospice Organization
1901 N. Moore St., Suite 901
Arlington, VA 22209
Information/helpline: 1-800-658-8898
    (8:30 A.M. to 5:30 P.M. EST).
    Office: (703) 243-5900.

Devoted to hospice in the United States to meet the needs of the terminally ill and promote the philosophy of hospice care. Helpline is available for the public as a resource for finding information about hospice care and referrals to hospices in their area. Brochures are available.

Recommended Reading

---

1. CRISES AT WORK

HANDLING DEBT

Leonard, Robin. *Money Troubles: Legal Strategies to Cope with Your Debts.* Fourth Edition. Berkeley, CA: Nolo Press, 1995.

JOB LOSS

Beyer, Cathy, Doris Pike, and Loretta McGovern. *Surviving Unemployment: A Family Handbook for Weathering Hard Times.* New York: Henry Holt and Company, 1993.

Riehle, Kathleen A. *What Smart People Do When Losing Their Jobs.* New York: John Wiley and Sons, Inc., 1991.

Schuyler, Nina. *The Unemployment Survival Handbook.* New York: Allworth Press, 1993.

JOB SEARCHING

Allen, Jeffrey G. *Successful Job Search Strategies for the Disabled: Understanding the ADA.* New York: John Wiley and Sons, Inc., 1994.

Arden, Lynie. *The Work-at-Home Sourcebook: Over 1,000 Job Opportunities Plus Home Business Opportunities and Other Options, Fourth Edition.* Boulder, CO: Live Oak Publications, 1992.

Bolles, Richard Nelson. *The (1996) What Color Is Your Parachute.* Berkeley, CA: Ten Speed Press, 1996.

Goldman, Katherine Wyse. *If You Can Raise Kids, You Can Get a Good Job.* New York: HarperCollins Publishers, 1996.

Harty, Terry, and Karen Kerkstra Harty. *Finding a Job After Fifty.* Hawthorne, NJ: Career Press, 1994.

King, Julie Adair, and Betsy Sheldon. *The Smart Woman's Guide to Resumes and Job Hunting, Second Edition.* Hawthorne, NJ: Career Press, 1993.

Schmidt, Peggy. *The Job Hunter's Catalog.* New York: John Wiley and Sons, Inc., 1996.

SEXUAL HARASSMENT

Bravo, Ellen, and Ellen Cassedy. *The 9 to 5 Guide to Combating Sexual Harassment.* New York: John Wiley and Sons, Inc., 1992.

Langelan, Martha J. *Back Off! How to Confront and Stop Sexual Harassment and Harassers.* New York: Fireside, Simon and Schuster, 1993.

Petrocelli, William, and Barbara Kate Repa. *Sexual Harassment on the Job.* Berkeley, CA: Nolo Press, 1995.

WORKERS' RIGHTS

McWhirter, Darien A. *Your Rights at Work, Second Edition.* New York: John Wiley and Sons, Inc. 1989, 1993.

Repa, Barbara Kate. *Your Rights in the Workplace: A Complete Guide for Employees, Third National Edition.* Berkeley, CA: Nolo Press, 1997.

Ross, Susan Deller, Isabelle Katz Pinzler, Deborah A. Ellis, and Kary L. Moss. *The Rights of Women: The Basic ACLU Guide to Women's Rights, Third Edition.* Carbondale, IL: Southern Illinois University Press, 1993.

2. CHILDREN IN CRISIS

CHILD ABUSE

Byerly, Carolyn M. *The Mother's Book: How to Survive the Molestation of Your Child, Second Edition.* Dubuque, IA: Kendall/Hunt Publishing Company, 1992.

Engel, Beverly. *Families in Recovery: Working Together to Heal the Damage of Childhood Sexual Abuse.* Los Angeles: Lowell House, 1995.

Hillman, Donald, and Janice Solek-Tefft. *Spiders and Flies: Help for Parents and Teachers of Sexually Abused Children.* Lexington, MA: Lexington Books, 1988.

Mach, Kathleen Flynn. *The Sexually Abused Child: A Parent's Guide to Coping and Understanding.* Williamsburg, MI: Family Insight Books, 1994.

Schaefer, Karen. *What Only a Mother Can Tell You About Child Sexual Abuse.* Washington, D.C.: Child Welfare League of America, 1993.

FOR SURVIVORS

Bass, Ellen, and Laura Davis. *The Courage to Heal: A Guide for Women Survivors of Child Sexual Abuse, Third Edition.* New York: HarperPerennial, 1994.

FOR YOUNG PEOPLE AND ADULTS

Bass, Ellen, and Kate Kaufman. *Free Your Mind: The Book for Gay, Lesbian, and Bisexual Youth — and Their Allies.* New York: HarperPerennial, 1996

Due, Linnea. *Joining the Tribe.* New York: Anchor Books, 1995.

Heron, Ann; ed. *Two Teenagers in Twenty: Writings by Gay and Lesbian Youth.* Boston: Alyson Publications, 1994.

IF YOUR CHILD IS ARRESTED

Homes, Edward. *No Matter How Loud I Shout: A Year in the Life of Juvenile Court.* New York: Simon and Schuster, 1996.

Reaves, John, and James B. Austin. *How to Find Help for a Troubled Kid: A Parent's Guide to Programs and Services for Adolescents.* New York: Henry Holt and Co., 1990.

LOVING YOUR GAY, LESBIAN, OR BISEXUAL TEEN

Bernstein, Robert A. *Straight Parents, Gay Children: Keeping Families Together.* New York: Thunder's Mouth Press, 1995.

Borhek, Mary V. *Coming Out to Parents: A Two-Way Survival Guide for Lesbians and Gay Men and Their Parents.* Cleveland: The Pilgrim Press, 1983.

Fairchild, Betty, and Nancy Hayward. *Now That You Know: What Every Parent Should Know About Homosexuality.* New York: Harcourt Brace Jovanovich, 1979.

Muller, Ann. *Parents Matter: Parents' Relationships with Lesbian Daughters and Gay Sons.* Tallahassee, FL: Naiad Press, 1987.

Rafkin, Louise, ed. *Different Daughters: A Book by Mothers of Lesbians.* Pittsburgh: Cleis Press, 1987.

TEEN PREGNANCY

Beyer, Kay. *Coping With Teen Pregnancy.* New York: The Rosen Publishing Group, 1992.

Lindsay, Jeanne Warren. *Teen Dads: Rights, Responsibilities and Joys.* Buena Park, CA: Morning Glory Press, 1994.

Roles, Patricia. *Facing Pregnancy: A Handbook for the Pregnant Teen.* Washington, D.C.: Child Welfare League of America, 1990.

Simpson, Carolyn. *Coping with an Unplanned Pregnancy.* New York: The Rosen Publishing Group, 1994.

———. *Everything You Need to Know About Living with Your Baby and Your Parents Under One Roof.* New York: The Rosen Publishing Group, 1996.

3. DIVORCE

Ahrons, Constance. *The Good Divorce: Keeping Your Family Together When Your Marriage Comes Apart.* New York: HarperPerennial, 1994.

Berger, Esther M. *Money Smart Divorce: What Women Need to Know About Money and Divorce.* New York: Simon and Schuster, 1996.

Cane, Michael Allan. *The Five-Minute Lawyer's Guide to Divorce.* New York: Dell Publishing, 1995.

Cohen, Harriett Newman, and Ralph Gardner, Jr. *The Divorce Book: For Men And Women: A Step-by-Step Guide to Gaining Your Freedom without Losing Everything Else.* New York: Avon Books, 1994.

Collins, Victoria F., and Ginita Wall. *Smart Ways to Save Money During and After Divorce.* Berkeley, CA: Nolo Press, 1994.

Hoffman, C. J. *Dead-Beat Dads: How to Find Them and Make Them Pay.* New York: Pocket Books, 1996.

Jensen, Geraldine, with Katina Z. Jones. *How to Collect Child Support.* Stamford, CT: Longmeadow Press, 1991. To order a copy, call ACES at 1-800-537-7072 or (416) 472-6609.

Lansky, Vicki. *Vicki Lansky's Divorce Book for Parents: Helping Your Children Cope with Divorce and Its Aftermath.* Deephaven, MN: The Book Peddlers, 1996.

Neumann, Diane. *Divorce Mediation: How to Cut the Cost and Stress of Divorce.* New York: Henry Holt and Company, 1989.

BOOKS FOR CHILDREN

The Centering Corporation, a nonprofit corporation, at 1531 N. Saddle Creek Road, Omaha, Nebraska, 68104-5064, (402) 553-1200, carries a number of books and booklets for children of divorcing parents, among other titles on loss and grieving. A range of low- to reasonably priced books and booklets includes *I Have Two Dads* (for blended families), *Two Homes to Live In, My Daddy Is a Stranger, When Mom and Dad Separate,* and for older children, *How It Feels When Parents Divorce.*

4. VIOLENCE AGAINST WOMEN

DOMESTIC VIOLENCE

Agtuca, Jacqueline R., in collaboration with the Asian Women's Shelter. *A Community Secret: For the Filipina in an Abusive Relationship.* Seattle: Seal Press, 1992, 1994.

Evans, Patricia. *The Verbally Abusive Relationship; How to Recognize It and Respond, Expanded Second Edition.* Holbrook, Mass.: Adams Media Corporation, 1996.

Grass, Linden. *To Have or To Harm: True Stories of Stalkers and Their Victims.* New York: Warner Books, 1994.

Jones, Ann, and Susan Schechter. *When Love Goes Wrong: What to Do When You Can't Do Anything Right — Strategies for Women with Controlling Partners.* New York: HarperPerennial, 1992.

Levy, Barrie, ed. *In Love and In Danger: A Teen's Guide to Breaking Free of Abusive Relationships*. Seattle: Seal Press, 1992.

Lobel, Kerry, ed. *Naming the Violence: Speaking Out About Lesbian Battering*. Seattle: Seal Press, 1986.

Rouse, Linda P. *You Are Not Alone: A Guide for Battered Women*. Holmes Beach, Fla.: Learning Publications, Inc. 1986.

Walker, Lenore E. *The Battered Woman*. New York: Harper-Perennial, 1979.

White, Evelyn C. *Chain Chain Change: For Black Women Dealing with Physical and Emotional Abuse*. Seattle: Seal Press, 1985.

Zambrano, Myrna M. *Mejor Sola Que Mal Acompanada: Para la Mujer Golpeada/For the Latina in an Abusive Relationship, Bilingual Edition*. Seattle: Seal Press, 1985.

LOW-COST AND FREE INFORMATION

Finding Low-Cost Information About Rape and Domestic Violence

Many rape crisis centers and women's shelters offer free or low-cost information to survivors of rape or domestic violence. You can locate your nearest rape crisis center or women's shelter by using the hotline numbers provided in the chapter Violence Against Women. Your state or local women's commission (often called commission on the status of women), listed in the government section of your local telephone directory, may offer free booklets and pamphlets to the public.

✤ If it would endanger you to have materials sent to your house, have them sent to a trusted friend unknown to the abuser or to another place where it will be safe for you to receive them.

Bowker, Lee. *Considering Marriage: Avoiding Marital Violence*. Santa Cruz, CA: ETR Associates, 1987. Available at no charge by calling ETR Associates at 1-800-321-4407.

Cantrell, Leslie. *Into the Light: A Guide for Battered Women*. Charlotte, NC: Kidrights, 1996. Available from Kidsrights at 1-800-892-KIDS or (704) 541-0100.

Domestic Violence and the Law (1996), which contains basic information about protection orders, and *Suggested Safety Plan Guidelines* are available at no charge from the National Victim Center Infolink at 1-800-FYI-CALL.

Escape! A Handbook for Battered Women Who Have Disabilities, is written by volunteers of Finex House primarily for women in Massachusetts. Available for $3 from Finex House at P.O. Box 1154, Jamaica Plain, MA 02130. Attn: Chris Womendez.

Helpful Guide for Stalking Victims. Arlington, VA: National Victim Center, 1994. This, and other publications, are available at no charge from the National Victim Center at (703) 276-2880.

RAPE

Benedict, Helen. *Recovery: How to Survive Sexual Assault: For Women, Men, Teenagers and Their Families, Revised and Expanded Edition.* New York: Columbia University Press, 1994.

Brownmiller, Susan. *Against Our Will.* New York: Simon and Schuster, 1975.

Estrich, Susan. *Real Rape: How the Legal System Victimizes Women Who Say No.* Cambridge, MA: Harvard University Press, 1987.

Johnson, Kathryn M. *If You Are Raped: What Every Woman Needs to Know.* Holmes Beach, FL: Learning Publications, Inc., 1985. To order, call 1-800-222-1525, ext. Q.

Ledray, Linda E. *Recovering from Rape.* New York: Henry Holt and Company, 1994.

McEvoy, Alan, and Jeff Brookings. *If She Is Raped: A Book for Husbands, Fathers, and Male Friends.* Holmes Beach, FL.: Learning Publications, Inc., 1991. To order, call 1-800-222-1525.

Warshaw, Robin. *I Never Called It Rape: The Ms. Report on Recognizing, Fighting, and Surviving Date and Acquaintance Rape.* New York: HarperPerenniel, 1988.

Wiehe, Vernon R., and Ann L. Richards. *Intimate Betrayal: Understanding and Responding to the Trauma of Acquaintance Rape.* Thousand Oaks, CA: Sage Publications, Inc., 1995.

5. CRISES IN CONCEPTION

ABORTION

Bonavoglia, Angela, ed. *The Choices We Made: Twenty-five Women and Men Speak Out About Abortion.* New York: Random House, 1991.

The Boston Women's Health Book Collective, *The New Our Bodies, Ourselves: A Book By and For Women.* New York: Touchstone, 1992.

Chalker, Rebecca, and Carol Downer. *A Woman's Book of Choices: Abortion, Menstrual Extraction, RU-486.* New York: Four Walls, Eight Windows, 1992.

ADOPTION

Jones, Merry Bloch. *Birthmothers: Women Who Have Relinquished Babies for Adoption Tell Their Stories.* Chicago: Chicago Review Press, Inc., 1993.

Harsin, Rebecca. *Wanted: First Child: A Birth Mother's Story.* Santa Barbara, CA: Fithian Press, 1991.

Hauser, Barbara R., ed., with Julie A. Tigges. *Women's Legal Guide: A Comprehensive Guide to Legal Issues Affecting Every Woman.* Golden, CO: Fulcrum Publishing, 1996.

Lifton, Betty Jean. *Journey of the Adopted Self: A Quest for Wholeness.* New York: Basic Books, 1994.

———. *Lost and Found: The Adoption Experience.* New York: The Dial Press, 1979.

Schaefer, Carol. *The Other Mother: A True Story.* New York: Soho Press, Inc., 1991.

Sorosky, Arthur D., Annette Baran, and Reuben Pannor. *The Adoption Triangle.* New York: Anchor Press, 1978.

BOOKS ON PREGNANCY AND INFANT LOSS FOR CHILDREN

Cohn, Janice. *Molly's Rosebush.* Morton Grove, Ill.: Albert Whitman and Company, 1994.

A helpful and sensitive book about a young girl whose family suffers when her mother has a miscarriage.

The Adoption Home-Study Process
Are You Pregnant and Thinking About Adoption?
The Impact of Adoption on Birth Parents
Issues Facing Adult Adoptees
Searching for Birth Relatives

The Centering Corporation also publishes several other books: *No New Baby* for youngsters whose mothers miscarry (also ask about the Spanish translation *No Bebe Nuevo*), *Where's Jess?* about newborn death, and *Katie's Premature Brother,* for siblings of NICU babies.

EMERGENCY CONTRACEPTION

Hatcher, Robert A., M.D., James Trussell, Felicia Stewart, Susan Howells, Caroline R. Russell, and Deborah Kowal. *Emergency Contraception: The Nation's Best-Kept Secret.* Atlanta, GA: Bridging the Gap Communications, 1995. Available through the Emergency Contraception Hotline; 1-800-584-9911.

Where to Find Low-Cost Information About Adoption

Free single copies of the following informational reports are available from the National Adoption Information Clearinghouse at (888) 251-0075 in Washington, D.C.

Many other reports are available to prospective adoptive parents. Call for information.

LOW-COST BOOKLETS

The Centering Corporation publishes a wide range of books and low-cost booklets to help people who have experienced loss, including bereaved parents. The following are some examples of low-cost resources. To order or request a catalog, contact the Centering Corporation, 1531 N. Saddle Creek Road, Omaha, NE 68104, (402) 553-1200; Fax: (402) 553-0507.

Johnson, Marvin, Joy Mohnson, et al. *Miscarriage: A Book for Persons Experiencing Fetal Death.* 1992.
———. *Newborn Death: A Book for Parents Experiencing the Death of a Very Small Infant.* 1992.
Wheat, Rick. *Miscarriage: A Man's Book.* 1995.

The Centering Corporation offers low-cost information on deciding whether to continue or interrupt a pregnancy because of a prenatal diagnosis, emotional support after an abortion, a booklet for grieving grandparents, and many more helpful resources.

The Centering Corporation also will provide this book:
Ilse, Sherokee. *Unsupported Losses: Ectopic Pregnancy, Molar Pregnancy and Blighted Ovum.* St. Paul, MN: DeRuyter-Nelson Publications, 1994.

In addition to offering direct assistance, organizations dedicated to helping bereaved parents may offer low-cost books and pamphlets, or they can refer you to sources of additional information. Check the Resource Directory for names, addresses, and telephone numbers.

THE POSTPARTUM PERIOD AND POSTPARTUM REACTIONS

Dix, Carol. *The New Mother Syndrome: Coping with Postpartum Stress and Depression.* New York: Pocket Books, 1985.
Dunnewold, Ann, and Diane G. Sanford. *Postpartum Survival Guide.* Oakland, CA: New Harbinger Publications, Inc., 1994.
Kleiman, Karen R., and Valerie D. Raskin. *This Isn't What I Expected: Recognizing and Recovering From Depression and Anxiety After Childbirth.* New York: Bantam Books, 1994.
Placksin, Sally. *Mothering the New Mother: Your Postpartum Resource Companion.* New York: Newmarket Press, 1994.

PREGNANCY AND INFANT LOSS

Davis, Deborah L. *Empty Cradle, Broken Heart: Surviving the Death of Your Baby, Revised and Expanded Edition.* Golden, CO: Fulcrum Publishing, 1996.
Horchler, Joani Nelson, and Robin Rice Morris. *The SIDS*

Survival Guide: Information and Comfort for Grieving
Families and Friends and Professionals Who Seek To Help
Them. Hyattsville, MD: SIDS Educational Services, Inc.,
1994.

Ilse, Sherokee. Empty Arms: Coping with Miscarriage, Stillbirth and Infant Death. Maple Plain, MN: Wintergreen
Press, 1990.

———. Precious Lives, Painful Choices: A Prenatal Decision-
Making Guide. Long Lake, MN: Wintergreen Press, 1993.

Kohn, Ingrid, Perry-Lynn Moffitt, with Isabelle A. Wilkins,
M.D. A Silent Sorrow: Pregnancy Loss: Guidance and Support for You and Your Family. New York: Dell Publishing,
1992.

Limbo Rana K., and Sara Rich Wheeler. When a Baby Dies:
A Handbook for Healing and Helping. La Crosse, WI: RTS
Bereavement Services, 1995.

Luebbermann, Mimi. Coping with Miscarriage: A Simple,
Reassuring Guide to Emotional and Physical Healing.
Rocklin, CA: Prima Publishing, 1995.

Minnick, Molly A., Kathleen J. Delp, and Mary C. Ciotti. A
Time to Decide, A Time to Heal: For Parents Making Difficult Decisions About Babies They Love, Fourth Edition. St.
Johns, MI: Pinneaple Press, 1994. This booklet can be ordered by calling or writing Pinneaple Press at P.O. Box
312, St. Johns, MI 48879 (517) 224-1881.

Sears, William, M.D. SIDS: A Parent's Guide to Understanding and Preventing Sudden Infant Death Syndrome.
Boston: Little, Brown and Company, 1995.

Simons, Harriet Fishman. Wanting Another Child: Coping
with Secondary Infertility. New York: Lexington Books,
1995.

SEXUALLY TRANSMITTED
DISEASES

Ebel, Charles. Managing Herpes: How to Live and Love with
a Chronic STD. Research Triangle Park, NC: American
Social Health Association, 1994. Available through the
Herpes Resource Center at 1-800-230-6039 or the National
Herpes Hotline at (919) 361-8488.

Rosenthal, Sara M. The Gynecological Sourcebook. Los Angeles, Calif.: Lowell House, 1994.

Public libraries, university libraries, and feminist and general interest bookstores are good places to start a search for books and publications. Support and advocacy groups may also offer bibliographies or make titles available at a cost to consumers. Many public libraries offer home delivery through the mail, book mobiles, or personal delivery using volunteers. If you cannot travel to the library, find out if any of these services are available. You can also order books and journals directly from the publisher and from bookstores. The following is only a partial list of publications. By networking with other women with disabilities, you can gather and share more information and advocate for changes in health care and social service systems that are often inaccessible and unresponsive to the needs of women with disabilities.

BARRIER-FREE HOUSING

Branson, Gary D. *The Complete Guide to Barrier-Free Housing: Convenient Living for the Elderly and Physically Handicapped.* White Hall, VA: Betterway Publications, Inc., 1991.

A Consumer's Guide to Home Adaptation from the Adaptive Environments Center. Available from Adaptive Environments Center, 374 Congress Street, Suite 301, Boston, MA 02210, (617) 695-1225, ext. 0 (voice/TDD).

LEGAL AND FINANCIAL MATTERS

DuBow, Sy, Sarah Geer, and Karen Peltz Strauss. *Legal Rights: The Guide for Deaf and Hard-of-Hearing People, Fourth Edition.* Washington, DC: Gallaudet University Press, 1992.

Johnson, Mary, ed., and the editors of the Disability Rag. *People with Disabilities Explain It All for You.* Louisville, KY: The Advocado Press, 1992. Discusses the public accommodations section of the Americans with Disabilities Act.

Parry, John. *Mental Disability Law: A Primer, Fifth Edition.* Washington, D.C.: American Bar Association, 1995.

Schlachter, Gail A., and R. David Weber. *Financial Aid for The Disabled and Their Families, 1996–1998.* San Carlos, Calif.: Reference Service Press, 1996.

Summary of Existing Legislation Affecting People with Disabilities. U.S. Department of Education. Washington, D.C.: USGPO. Free from the Office of Special Education and Rehabilitative Services (OSERS) in the U.S. Department of Education, 330 C Street SW, Room 3132, Washington, D.C. 20202 (202) 205-8241 (voice/TTY).

DISABILITY CIVIL RIGHTS
MOVEMENT

Shapiro, Joseph. *No Pity: People with Disabilities Forging a New Civil Rights Movement, Second Edition.* New York: Times Books, Random House, 1993.

EXPERIENCES OF WOMEN WITH
DISABILITIES

Browne, Susan E., Debra Connors, and Nanci Stern, eds. *With the Power of Each Breath: A Disabled Women's Anthology.* Pittsburgh: Cleis Press, 1985.

Fine, Michelle, and Adrienne Asch, eds. *Women with Disabilities: Essays in Psychology, Culture and Politics.* Philadelphia: Temple University Press, 1988.

Keith, Lois, ed. *What Happened to You? Writing by Disabled Women.* New York: The New Press, 1996.

Matthews, Gwyneth Ferguson. *Voices from the Shadows: Women with Disabilities Speak Out.* Toronto: Women's Education Press, 1983.

Panzarino, Connie. *The Me in the Mirror.* Seattle: Seal Press, 1994.

Rousso, Harilyn. *Disabled, Female, and Proud: Stories of Ten Women with Disabilities.* Boston: Exceptional Parent Press, 1993.

Saxton, Marsha, and Florence Howe. *With Wings: An Anthology of Literature By and About Women with Disabilities.* New York: The Feminist Press at The City University of New York, 1987.

Zola, Irving Kenneth, ed. *Ordinary Lives: Voices of Disability and Disease.* Cambridge, MA: Apple-wood Books, 1982.

FOR CHILDREN

The following are examples of available books for children. The National Information Center for Children and Youth with Disabilities (NICHCY), (1-800-695-0285 voice/TTY) or (202) 884-8200, offers a bibliography of books for children that includes topics such as attention deficit disorder, blindness, cerebral palsy, deafness, Down syndrome, learning disabilities, and other disabilities.

Burns, Kay. *Our Mom.* New York: Franklin Watts, 1989.

Howe, James. *The Hospital Book.* New York: A Morrow Junior Book, 1994.

Krementz, Jill. *How It Feels to Live with A Physical Disability.* New York: Simon & Schuster, 1992.

Roy, Ron. *Move Over, Wheelchairs Coming Through!* New York: Clarion Books, 1985.

**FOR OLDER CHILDREN
AND TEENS**

Cherry, Glenn Alan. *Teens with Physical Disabilities: Real-Life Stories of Meeting the Challenge.* Springfield, New Jersey: Enslow Publishers, 1995.

Ratto, Linda Lee. *Coping With a Physically Challenged Brother or Sister.* New York: The Rosen Publishing Group, Inc., 1992.

MAGAZINES AND NEWSLETTERS

Ability Magazine. 16892 Langley Avenue, Irvine, CA 92714. (714) 854-8700 or TDD (714) 251-7011.

Abled! Abled Publications, 12211 Fondren, Suite 703, Houston, TX 77035 (703) 726-1132.

Accent on Living. P.O. Box 700, Bloomington, IL 61702. (309) 378-2961.

It's Okay! An international consumer written quarterly on sexuality, sex, and disability. 1 Springbank Drive, St. Catharines, Ontario, Canada, L2S 2K1.

The Ragged Edge Magazine. P.O. Box 145, Louisville, KY 40201-0145.

Resourceful Women: Women with Disabilities Striving Toward Health and Self-Determination. To be placed on the mailing list, call or write the Health Resource Center for Women with Disabilities, Rehabilitation Institute of Chicago, 345 East Superior St., Room 106, Chicago, IL 60611, (312) 908-7997.

**MAGAZINES FOR PARENTS OF
CHILDREN WITH DISABILITIES**

Connections: The Newsletter of the National Center for Youth with Disabilities. Available in alternative formats on request. For more information contact the National Center for Youth with Disabilities, Center for Children with Chronic Illness and Disability, University of Minnesota, Box 721, 420 Delaware St. SE, Minneapolis, MN 55455. (612) 626-2825 or (612) 624-3939 (TDD).

The Exceptional Parent. P.O. Box 3000, Dept. EP, Denville, NJ 07834. 1-800-562-1973.

PERSONAL ASSISTANTS

Susik, D. Helen. *Hiring Home Caregivers: The Family Guide to In-Home Eldercare.* San Luis Obispo, CA: American Source Books, 1995.

The following low-cost booklets by Mary Ann Board, Jean A. Cole, Lex Frieden, and Jane C. Sperry are available from Independent Living Research Utilization (ILRU), 2323 S. Shepherd, Suite 1000, Houston, TX 77019, (713) 520-0232 and (713) 520-5136 (TTY):

Independent Living with Attendant Care: A Guide for the Personal Care Attendant (1980).

Independent Living with Attendant Care: A Guide for the Person with a Disability (1980).

Independent Living with Attendant Care: A Message to Parents of Handicapped Youth (1980).

PREGNANCY AND PARENTING

Campion, Mukti Jain. *The Baby Challenge: A Handbook on Pregnancy for Women with a Physical Disability.* New York: Routledge, 1990. (This book is expensive. University and public libraries may carry it.)

Preston, Paul. *Mother Father Deaf (Living Between Sound and Silence).* Cambridge, Mass.: Harvard University Press, 1994.

Rogers, Judi, and Molleen Matsumara. *Mother to Be: A Guide to Pregnancy and Birth for Women with Disabilities.* New York: Demos Publications, 1991.

PRODUCTS AND RESOURCES

Backstrom, Gayle. *The Resource Guide for the Disabled.* Dallas, TX: Taylor Publishing Co., 1994.

HEATH Resource Center. National Clearinghouse on Postsecondary Education for Individuals with Disabilities. *Resource Directory.* Washington, D.C.: HEATH Resource Center. This free booklet is not limited to educational organizations. Contact: HEATH Resource Center, American Council on Education, One Dupont Circle, Suite 800, Washington, D.C. 20036-1193. 1-800-544-3284 (voice/TTY) or (202) 939-9320 (voice/TTY).

Kalles, June Isaacson. *Resource List: Wellness, Self-Care, Exercise and Aging with Disability.* Downey, CA: Los Amigos Research and Education Institute, 1995.

Resources for Rehabilitation. *Living with Low Vision: A Guide for People with Sight Loss, Third Edition.* Lexington, MA: Resources for Rehabilitation, 1993.

REPRODUCTIVE HEALTH

Ferreyra, Susan, and Katrine Hughes. *Table Manners: A Guide to the Pelvic Exam for Disabled Women and Health Care Providers.* San Francisco, CA: Sex Education for Disabled People, 1984. Available from Planned Parenthood Alameda, 815 Eddy Street, San Francisco, CA (415) 441-7858. The cost is $1.50, although the minimum shipping charge is $3.25 for individual booklets. There is a 15 percent shipping charge for orders of ten or more.

SEXUALITY

Griffith, Ernest R., and Sally Lemberg. *Sexuality and the Person with Traumatic Brain Injury: A Guide for Families.* Philadelphia: F.A. Davis, 1992. Available through the National Brain Injury Association, 1776 Massachusetts Ave.

NW, Suite 100, Washington, D.C. 20036. 1-800-444-6443 or (202) 296-6443.

Kroll, Ken, and Erica Levy Klein. *Enabling Romance: A Guide to Love, Sex, and Relationships for the Disabled (and the People Who Care About Them)*. New York: Harmony Books, 1992.

7. CRISES IN MENTAL HEALTH

Ammer, Christine, with Nathan T. Sidley, M.D. *Getting Help: A Consumer's Guide to Therapy*. New York: Paragon House, 1991.

Ehrenberg, Otto, and Miriam Ehrenberg. *The Psychotherapy Maze: A Consumer's Guide to Getting In and Out of Therapy, Revised and Updated*. New York: Simon & Schuster, Inc., 1986.

Finney, Lynne D. *Reach for Joy: How to Find the Right Therapist and Therapy for You*. Freedom, CA: The Crossing Press, 1995.

White, Barbara J., and Edward J. Madara, eds. *The Self-Help Sourcebook: The Comprehensive Reference of Self-Help Resources, Fifth Edition*. Denville, NJ: Northwest Covenant Medical Center, 1995.

ALCOHOL AND DRUGS

Greenleaf, Vicki D. *Women and Cocaine: Personal Stories of Addiction and Recovery*. Los Angeles, Calif.: Lowell House, 1989.

Kirkpatrick, Jean. *Goodbye Hangovers, Hello Life*. New York: Atheneum, 1986. Available through Women For Sobriety, Inc. at (215) 536-8026

Knapp, Caroline. *Drinking: A Love Story*. New York: The Dial Press, 1996.

BIOGRAPHIES

Duke, Patty. *A Brilliant Madness: Living with Manic Depressive Illness*. New York: Bantam Books, 1992.

Millet, Kate. *The Loony-Bin Trip*. New York: Simon & Schuster, 1990.

North, Carol. *Welcome Silence*. New York: Simon & Schuster, 1987.

Schiller, Lori. *The Quiet Room: A Journey Out of the Torment of Madness*. New York: Warner Books, 1994.

Thompson, Tracy. *The Beast: A Reckoning with Depression*. New York: G. P. Putnam's Sons, 1995.

Depression	McCoy, Kathleen. *Understanding Your Teenager's Depression: Issues, Insights and Practical Guidance for Parents.* New York: Perigee, 1994. McGrath, Ellen. *When Feeling Bad Is Good.* New York: Henry Holt and Company, 1992.
Low-cost resources	The following organizations offer a range of low-cost informational brochures and pamphlets: National Institute of Mental Health Information Resources and Inquiries Branch 5600 Fishers Lane, Room 7C-02 Rockville, MD 20857 (301) 443-4513 (301) 443-8431 (TDD) 1-800-64-PANIC (panic disorder information) 1-800-421-4211 (depression information) (301) 443-3266 (schizophrenia) (301) 443-4513 (aging research) The National Mental Health Association 1021 Prince St. Alexandria, VA 22314 (703) 684-7722; Fax: (703) 684-5968 National Information Center for Children and Youth with Disabilities (NICHCY) P.O. Box 1492 Washington, D.C. 20013-1492 1-800-695-0285 (voice/TTY)
Mental health professions	Caplan, Paula J. *They Say You're Crazy: How the World's Most Powerful Psychiatrists Decide Who's Normal.* Reading, Mass.: Addison-Wesley Publishing, 1995.
Suicide	Long, Robert Emmet. *Suicide.* New York: The H.W. Wilson Company, 1995. Marcus, Eric. *Why Suicide? Answers to 200 of the Most Frequently Asked Questions About Suicide, Attempted Suicide, and Assisted Suicide.* San Francisco, CA: Harper San Francisco, 1996.
Survivors of childhood sexual abuse	Bass, Ellen, and Laura Davis. *The Courage to Heal: A Guide for Women Survivors of Child Sexual Abuse, Third Edition.* New York: HarperPerennial, 1994. Engel, Beverly. *Families in Recovery: Working Together to*

Heal The Damage of Childhood Sexual Abuse. Los Angeles: Lowell House, 1995.

---

8. LIFE-THREATENING ILLNESS

*B*REAST CANCER

Brinker, Nancy G., with Catherine McEvily Harris. *The Race Is Run One Step at a Time: Every Woman's Guide to Taking Charge of Breast Cancer and My Personal Story*. Arlington, TX: The Summit Publishing Group, 1995.

Faust, Rita Baron, with the physicians of the New York University Medical Center Women's Health Service and the Kaplan Comprehensive Cancer Center. *Breast Cancer: What Every Woman Should Know*. New York: William Morrow and Company, 1995.

Komarnicky, Lydia, M.D., and Anne Rosenberg, M.D., with Marian Betancourt. *What To Do If You Get Breast Cancer: Two Breast Cancer Specialists Help You Take Charge and Make Informed Choices*. Boston: Little, Brown and Company, 1995.

Love, Susan M., M.D., with Karen Lindsey, Second Edition, Fully Revised. *Dr. Susan Love's Breast Book*. Reading, MA: Addison-Wesley Publishing Company, 1995.

Runowicz, Carolyn, M.D., and Donna Haupt. *To Be Alive: A Woman's Guide to a Full Life After Cancer*. New York: Henry Holt and Company, 1995.

Bimonthly Newsletter

The Breast Cancer Action newsletter provides solid, clear information on new developments in prevention, detection, and treatment. For information, write to Breast Cancer Action, 55 New Montgomery Street, Number 624, San Francisco, CA 94105, or call (415) 243-9301.

*B*REAST IMPLANT INFORMATION

Bruning, Nancy. *Breast Implants: Everything You Need to Know, Second Revised Edition*. Alameda, CA: Hunter House, Inc., 1995.

U.S. Food and Drug Administration. *Breast Implants: An Information Update*. Rockville, MD: U.S. Food and Drug Administration, 1996. Available free from the U.S. Food and Drug Administration, 5600 Fishers Lane, Rockville, MD 20857; 1-800-532-4440.

CANCER

Blain, Lisa J. *A Parent's Guide to Childhood Cancer*. New York: Dell Publishing, 1995.

Bruning, Nancy. *Coping with Chemotherapy: Up-to-Date Authoritative Information You Can Trust — from Experts*

---

and from Someone Who's Been There. New York: Ballantine Books, 1993.

Cook, Alan R., and Peter D. Dresser, eds. *Cancer Sourcebook for Women, Health Reference Series, Volume Ten*. Detroit: Omnigraphics, Inc., 1996.

Dollinger, Malin, M.D., Ernest H. Rosenbaum, M.D., and Greg Cable. *Everyone's Guide to Therapy: How Cancer Is Diagnosed, Treated, and Managed Day to Day, Revised Second Edition*. Kansas City: Andrews and McMeel, 1994.

Sherry, Michael M., M.D. *Confronting Cancer: How to Care For Today and Tomorrow*. New York: Plenum Press, 1994.

Zakarian, Beverly. *The Activist Cancer Patient: How to Take Charge of Your Treatment*. New York: John Wiley and Sons, 1996.

DOCTOR-PATIENT
COMMUNICATION

The following booklets provide lists of questions to ask your doctor following a cancer diagnosis. Please see the Resource Directory for the addresses and telephone numbers of organizations providing these resources.

Questions to Ask Your Doctor About Breast Cancer. Available from the National Cancer Institute at 1-800-4-CANCER.

Teamwork: The Cancer Patient's Guide to Talking with Your Doctor. Available from the National Coalition for Cancer Survivorship at (301) 650-8868.

EXPERIENCES OF WOMEN WITH
CANCER

Kahane, Deborah Hobler. *No Less A Woman: Femininity, Sexuality and Breast Cancer, Revised Second Edition*. Alameda, CA: Hunter House, 1995.

Lorde, Audre. *The Cancer Journals*. San Francisco: Aunt Lute Books, 1980.

Free and Low-Cost Information About Cancer

The National Cancer Institute, the American Cancer Society, and other national support and advocacy groups offer many free and low-cost publications for people with cancer and their families. Issues covered include diagnosis and treatment, breast reconstruction, clinical trials, nutrition, emotional support, financial and legal assistance, and more. For the addresses and telephone numbers of these organizations, see the Resource Directory.

HEART DISEASE

Diethrich, Edward B., M.D., and Carol Cohan. *Women and Heart Disease*. New York: Ballantine Books, 1992.

Kra, Siegfried J., M.D. *What Every Woman Must Know About Heart Disease: A No-Nonsense Approach to Diagnosing, Treating, and Preventing the Number One Killer of Women*. New York: Warner Books, 1996.

Notelovitz, Morris, M.D., and Diana Tonnessen. *The Essen-*

tial Heart Book for Women. New York: St. Martin's Press, 1996.

Pashkow, Frederic J., M.D., and Charlotte Libov. *The Woman's Heart Book: The Complete Guide to Keeping Your Heart Healthy and What to Do If Things Go Wrong.* New York: Penguin Books, 1993.

People's Medical Society. *Your Heart: Questions You Have . . . Answers You Need.* Allentown, PA: People's Medical Society, 1996.

Ross, Elizabeth, M.D., and Judith Sachs. *Healing the Female Heart: A Holistic Approach to Prevention and Recovery from Heart Disease.* New York: Pocket Books, 1996.

Texas Heart Institute Heart Owner's Handbook (foreword by Denton A. Cooley, M.D.). New York: John Wiley and Sons, 1996.

𝓗IV/AIDS

Note: Many of the following books were written before the introduction of new drugs, viral load tests, home testing kits, and changes in federal law that affect welfare benefits. However, the information they contain is still very valuable. Watch for new books on the market.

Bartlett, John G., M.D., and Ann K. Finkbeiner. *The Guide to Living with HIV Infection, Third Edition.* Baltimore, MD: The John Hopkins University Press, 1996.

Crockett, Paul Hampton. *HIV Law: A Survival Guide to the Legal System for People Living with HIV.* New York: Three Rivers Press, 1997.

Greif, Judith, and Beth Ann Golden. *AIDS Care at Home: A Guide for Caregivers, Loved Ones, and People with AIDS.* New York: John Wiley and Sons, 1994.

Huber, Jeffrey T., ed. *How to Find Information About AIDS, Second Edition.* New York: The Haworth Press, 1992.

Kloser, Patricia, M.D., and Jane Maclean Craig. *The Woman's HIV Sourcebook: A Guide to Better Health and Well-Being.* Dallas: Taylor Publishing Company, 1994.

Martelli, L. J., F. D. Peltz, W. Messina, and S. Petrow. *When Someone You Know Has AIDS.* New York: Crown Publishers, Inc., 1993.

McCormack, Thomas P. *The AIDS Benefits Handbook: Everything You Need to Know to Get Social Security, Welfare, Medicaid, Medicare, Food Stamps, Housing, Drugs, and Other Benefits.* New Haven: Yale University Press, 1990.

O'Sullivan, Sue, and Kate Thomson, eds. *Positively Women: Living with AIDS.* San Francisco, CA: Pandora, 1996.

Petrow, Steven, ed. *The HIV Drug Book.* New York: Pocket Books, 1995.

Pinsky, Laura, and Paul Harding Douglas with Craig Metroka, M.D. *The Essential HIV Treatment Fact Book.* New York: Pocket Books, 1992.

Free or Low-Cost ($5 and Under) Booklets and Brochures

Gay Men's Health Crisis publishes the following materials: *Facing the Future: A Legal Handbook for Parents with HIV Disease; Positive Options* (a handbook for people recently diagnosed); and *Legal Answers About AIDS.* Contact Gay Men's Health Crisis, 129 West 20th Street, New York, NY 10011. Videos are also available. Call for a publications catalog: (212) 337-1950.

Impact AIDS publishes the following materials: *The AIDS Medical Guide* (available in English and Spanish); *Living with HIV: A Guide for Women; Taking Charge: The HIV Planning Guide; Caring for Children with HIV Infection; The HIV Drug Book;* and *HIV1 : Working the System.* Contact Impact AIDS, 440 Cerrillos Road, Suite F, Santa Fe, NM 87501. San Francisco number: (415) 861-3397. Prices vary.

TPA Network publishes *Early Intervention Kit.* Contact TPA Network, Inc., 1258 W. Belmont Avenue, Chicago, IL 60657. (312) 404-8726.

HIV/AIDS Information for Parents

HIV and Your Child. A booklet about the way HIV affects children. Spanish/English. Available for free from the National AIDS Hotline at 1-800-342-AIDS or 1-800-243-7889 (TDD) or write to AHCPR HIV Guideline, CDC National AIDS Clearinghouse, P.O. Box 6003, Rockville, MD 20849-6003.

Merkel-Holguin, Lisa. *Because You Love Them: A Parent's Planning Guide.* Washington, D.C.: Child Welfare League of America, 1994. For copies, call the CDC National AIDS Clearinghouse at 1-800-458-5231.

Parent Information Booklets. Easy-to-read information booklets include *Your Family and HIV/AIDS, My Child Is HIV Infected; What Do I Do Next? How Can I Take Care of Myself? What Should I Tell My Child About HIV?* and *What About How I'm Feeling?* (English/Spanish). Available from the National Pediatric and Family HIV Resource Center at (201) 268-8251. Also ask for a list of other available publications.

Rave, A. S. *Children at Risk: HIV Infection and AIDS: Training for Foster Parents.* Available for $7.70 from the CDC National AIDS Clearinghouse Document Delivery Services, P.O. Box 6003, Rockville, MD 20849-6003; 1-800-458-5231.

Tasker, Mary. *How Can I Tell You? Secrecy and Disclosure*

with Children When a Family Member Has AIDS, Second Edition. Bethesda, MD: Institute for Family-Centered Care, 1995.

Available free of charge from the National Maternal and Child Clearinghouse, 2070 Chain Bridge Rd., Ste. 450, Vienna, VA 22182; (703) 356-1964.

Newsletters and Journals

News about AIDS and HIV infection treatment changes quickly. Newsletters offer a means of keeping up to date. Although prices for subscriptions vary, costs are often reduced for people with HIV infection and AIDS. Call the offices of the publication in which you are interested for more information:

AIDS Treatment News. ATN Publications. P.O. Box 411256, San Francisco, CA 94141. 1-800-TREAT-1-2 or (415) 255-0588. Internet: aidsnews@aidsnews.org.

GMHC: Treatment Issues: Newsletter of Experimental AIDS Therapies. Monthly. Gay Men's Health Crisis (GHMC) Treatment Education and Advocacy, 129 West 20th St., New York, NY 10011. (212) 337-3656. Also ask about Lesbian AIDS Project (LAP) — LAP Notes, a newsletter for lesbians living with HIV and AIDS.

Medical Alert. National Association of People with AIDS. 1413 K St. NW, 7th Floor, Washington, D.C. 20005. (202) 898-0414.

PI Perspective. Project Inform. 1965 Market St., Suite 220, San Francisco, CA 94103. (415) 558-8669. National hotline: 1-800-822-7422.

WORLD (Women Organized to Respond to Life-Threatening Diseases). P.O. Box 11535, Oakland, CA 94611. (510) 658-6930; Fax: (510) 601-9746. English (monthly); Spanish (quarterly).

Testing

Voluntary HIV Counseling and Testing: Facts, Issues, and Answers. Centers for Disease Control, U.S. Public Health Service, 1993. Free. Contact the CDC National AIDS Clearinghouse at 1-800-458-5231.

STROKE

Caplan, Louis R., M.D., Mark L. Dyken, M.D., and J. Donald Easton, M.D. *The American Heart Association Family Guide to Stroke: Treatment, Recovery and Prevention.* New York: Times Books, 1994.

Senelick, Richard C., and Peter W. Rossi, M.D., with Karla Dougherty. *Living with Stroke: A Guide for Families.* Chicago: Contemporary Books, 1994.

Shimberg, Elaine Fantle. *Strokes: What Families Should Know.* New York: Ballantine Books, 1990.

Singleton, LaFayette, M.D., with Kirk A. Johnson. *The Black Health Library Guide to Stroke.* New York: Henry Holt and Company, 1993.

Free and Low-Cost Information About Stroke and Heart Disease

The National Stroke Association and your local chapter of the American Heart Association offer many free and low-cost pamphlets and brochures. You can also order booklets about high blood pressure and stroke and fact sheets about angina, arrhythmia/rhythm disorders, coronary heart disease, heart failure, and mitral valve prolapse from the National Heart, Lung, and Blood Institute at (301) 251-1222.

---

9. CRISES IN AGING

CAREGIVERS

Adams, Tom, and Kathryn Armstrong. *When Parents Age: What Children Can Do: A Practical and Loving Guide to Giving Them the Help, Support and Independence They Need.* New York: The Berkeley Publishing Company, 1993.

Berman, Claire. *Caring for Yourself While Caring for Your Aging Parents: How to Help, How to Survive.* New York: Henry Holt and Company, 1996.

Buckingham, Robert W., ed. *When Living Alone Means Living at Risk: A Guide for Caregivers and Families.* Buffalo, NY: Prometheus Books, 1994.

Carter, Rosalynn, with Susan K. Golant. *Helping Yourself Help Others: A Book for Caregivers.* New York: Random House, 1994.

Heath, Angela. *Long Distance Caregiving: A Survival Guide for Far Away Caregivers.* Lakewood, Colo.: American Source Books, 1993.

Mace, Nancy L., and Peter V. Rabins, M.D. *The 36-Hour Day: A Family Guide to Caring for Persons with Alzheimer's Disease, Related Dementing Illness and Memory Loss in Later Life.* New York: Warner Books, 1991.

DRUGS AND RESTRAINTS

The National Citizens' Coalition for Nursing Home Reform and Sarah Greene Burger. *Avoiding Physical Restraint Use: New Standards in Care* (1993) and *Avoiding Drugs Used as Chemical Restraints: New Standards in Care* (1994). For information call the National Citizens' Coalition for Nursing Home Reform at (202) 332-2275.

Free and Low-Cost Booklets

Nursing Home Life: A Guide for Residents and Families Staying at Home. A Guide to Long-Term Care and Housing

---

Product Report. PERS (Personal Emergency Response System), Vol. 1. No. 1. For a free copy of this or other publications or for a catalog of publications, write to: American Association of Retired Persons, 601 E Street NW, Washington, D.C. 20049.

Also remember that nursing home advocacy organizations and ombudsmen programs often provide free or low-cost publications on choosing a nursing home and alternative housing options. See Chapter Nine.

HIRING HOME HEALTH AIDES

Susik, Helen D. *Hiring Home Caregivers: The Family Guide to In-Home Eldercare*. San Luis Obispo, CA: American Source Books, 1995.

HOME ADAPTATION AND SAFETY

Branson, Gary D. *The Complete Guide to Barrier-Free Housing: Convenient Living for the Elderly and the Physically Handicapped*. White Hall, VA: Betterway Publications, 1991.

A Consumer's Guide to Home Adaptation from the Adaptive Environments Center. Available from Adaptive Environments Center, 374 Congress Street, Suite 301, Boston, MA 02210, (617) 695-1225, ext. 0 (voice/TDD). Current price: $12.00.

U.S. Consumer Product Safety Commission. *Safety for Older Consumers*. Free booklet available by writing the U.S. Consumer Product Safety Commission, Washington, D.C. 20207.

NURSING HOMES

Burger, Sarah Greene, Virginia Fraser, Sara Hunt, and Barbara Frank. *Nursing Homes: Getting Good Care There*. Washington, D.C.: National Citizens' Coalition for Nursing Home Reform (NCCNHR). For information, write or call NCCNHR at 1424 16th St. NW, Suite 202, Washington, D.C. 20036. (202) 332-2275.

Matthews, Joseph. *Beat the Nursing Home Trap: A Consumer's Guide to Choosing and Financing Long-Term Care, Second Edition*. Berkeley, CA: Nolo Press, 1995. Nolo Press often updates its publications. Call 1-800-992-6656 for information about recent editions.

Rollins, Mary Richard. *Patients, Pain and Politics: A Nursing Home Inspector's Shocking True Story and Expert Advice for You and Your Family* Garden Grove, CA: New Century Publishing, 1994.

CAREGIVERS

Beresford, Larry. *The Hospice Handbook*. Boston: Little, Brown and Company, 1993.

Buckingham, Robert W., M.D. *The Handbook of Hospice Care*. New York: Prometheus Books, 1996.

Duda, Deborah. *Coming Home: A Guide to Dying at Home With Dignity*. New York: Aurora Press, 1987.

Greif, Judith, and Beth Ann Golden. *AIDS Care at Home: A Guide for Caregivers, Loved Ones, and People with AIDS*. New York: John Wiley and Sons, 1994.

Sankar, Andrea. *Dying at Home: A Family Guide for Caregiving*. New York: Bantam Books, 1995.

ESTATE PLANNING

Clifford, Denis, and Cora Jordan. *Plan Your Estate, Third Edition*. Berkeley, CA: Nolo Press, 1995.

Curry, Hayden, Denis Clifford, and Robin Leonard. *A Legal Guide for Lesbian and Gay Couples, Eighth Edition*. Berkeley, CA: Nolo Press, 1994.

FUNERALS

Carlson, Lisa. *Caring for Your Own Dead, Second Edition*. Hinesburg, Vermont: Upper Access Publishers, 1997.

Morgan, Ernest. *Dealing Creatively with Death: A Manual of Death Education and Simple Burial*. Bayside, NY: Zinn Communication, 1994.

Sublette, Kathleen, and Martin Flagg. *Final Celebrations: A Guide for Personal and Family Funeral Planning*. Ventura, CA: Pathfinder Publishing of California, 1992.

Young, Gregory W. *The High Cost of Dying: A Guide to Funeral Planning*. Buffalo, New York: Prometheus Books, 1994.

GENERAL RESOURCES ABOUT PRACTICAL MATTERS

Anderson, Patricia. *Affairs in Order: A Complete Resource Guide to Death and Dying*. New York: Macmillan Publishing Company, 1991.

Burnell, George M., M.D. *Final Choices: To Live or to Die in an Age of Medical Technology*. New York: Insight Books, 1993.

GRIEF

Bode, Janet. *Death is Hard to Live with: Teenagers Talk About How They Cope with Loss*. New York: Bantam Doubleday Dell Publishing Group, 1993.

Caine, Lynn. *Being a Widow*. New York: William Morrow, 1988.

Donnelly, Katherine Fair. *Recovering from the Loss of a Loved One to AIDS*. New York: Ballantine Books, 1994.

Finkbeiner, Ann K. *After the Death of a Child: Living with Loss Through the Years.* New York: The Free Press, 1996.

Fitzgerald, Helen. *The Grieving Child: A Parent's Guide.* New York: Simon and Schuster, 1992.

———. *The Mourning Handbook: A Complete Guide for the Bereaved.* New York: Simon and Schuster, 1994.

Grollman, Earl, ed. *Bereaved Children and Teens: A Support Guide for Parents and Professionals.* Boston: Beacon Press, 1995.

Lightner, Candy, and Nancy Hathaway. *Giving Sorrow Words: How to Cope with Grief and Get on with Your Life.* New York: Warner Books, Inc., 1990.

Rosof, Barbara D. *The Worst Loss: How Families Heal from the Death of a Child.* New York: Henry Holt and Company, 1994.

Staudacher, Carol. *Men and Grief: A Guide for Men Surviving the Death of a Loved One.* Oakland, Calif.: New Harbinger Publications, Inc., 1991.

ILLNESS AND DYING

Aronheim, Judith, M.D., and Doron Weber. *Final Passages: Positive Choices for the Dying and Their Loved Ones.* New York, Simon and Schuster, 1992.

Kübler-Ross, Elisabeth, M.D. *On Death and Dying: What the Dying Have to Teach Doctors, Nurses, Clergy and Their Own Families.* New York: Macmillan Publishing Company, 1969.

Nolsen, Patricia Wee. *The Art of Dying: How to Leave This World with Dignity and Grace, at Peace with Yourself and Your Loved Ones.* New York: St. Martin's Press, 1996.

Notes on Living Until We Say Goodbye: A Personal Guide. Nungusser, Lon G., with William David Bullock. New York: St. Martin's Press, 1988.

Low-Cost Information

Many of the organizations listed in the Resource Directory offer free or low-cost information. In addition, you may find the following fact sheets, brochures, and booklets helpful:

The American Association of Retired Persons (AARP), 601 E Street NW, Washington, D.C. 20049, publishes *On Being Alone: A Guide for Widowed Persons* (#D150); *Final Details: A Guide for Survivors When Death Occurs* (#D14168); *A Consumer's Guide to Probate* (#D13822); *"So Many of My Friends Have Moved Away or Died. . ." — Reflections and Suggestions on Making New Friends* (#D13831), *Knowing the Facts: Spousal Bereavement and Primary Health Care* (#D13503), *Pre-Planning Your Funeral?* (D13188) and *Shape Your Health Care Future with Health Care Advance Directives* (D15803). Single copies are free; write to the

AARP. It's a good idea to order early, as delivery may take six to eight weeks.

Because You Love Them: A Parent's Planning Guide. Washington, D.C.: Child Welfare League of America, 1994. This reasonably priced workbook can help parents make decisions about planning for their children's future. For copies, call the CDC National AIDS Clearinghouse at 1-800-458-5231.

The Centering Corporation publishes a wide range of books and booklets to help people who are experiencing loss. Current low-cost titles include: *After Suicide Just Us — Overcoming and Understanding Homicidal Loss and Grief; Who Lives Happily Ever After? For Families Whose Child Has Died Violently;* and *Recovering from the Loss of a Parent.* Contact the Centering Corporation at 1531 N. Saddle Creek Road, Omaha, NE 68104. (402) 553-1200; Fax: (402) 553-0507.

Centering Corporation's children's titles include *AIDS: A Heartbeat Away* (for children whose mothers have died of AIDS); *I Heard Your Mommy Died;* and *I Heard Your Daddy Died.*

The Federal Trade Commission at (202) 326-2222 and (202) 326-2502 (TDD) publishes *Complying with the Funeral Rule* for funeral directors. This guide can help you understand what the Federal Rule requires of funeral directors. The FTC also publishes the pamphlets *Funerals: A Consumer's Guide* and *Caskets and Burial Vaults.*

The Social Security Administration at 1-800-772-1213 or 1-800-325-0778 (TDD) will send you a free copy of the booklet *Survivors,* which explains Social Security benefits.

The National Consumers League at (202) 835-3323 publishes *A Consumer Guide to Hospice Care* and *A Consumer Guide to Home Health Care.*

Notes

1. CRISES AT WORK

1. *EEOC and Castrejon* v. *Tortilleria "La Mejor"* 758 F Supp 585 (ED Cal 1991).
2. *EEOC* v. *Switching Systems Division of Rockwell International Corporation* 783 F Supp 369 (NDIll 1992).
3. 42 U.S.C. sec. 2000e-2(a)(1).
4. 42 U.S.C. sec. 2000e-2(a)(2).
5. *Ida Phillips* v. *Martin Marietta Corporation* 400 US 542, 27 L.Ed.2d 613, 91 S Ct 496 (1971).
6. 42 U.S.C. sec. 2000e-2(e)(1).
7. *Griggs* v. *Duke Power Co.*, 401 US 424 (1971).
8. 29 C.F.R. sec. 1604.11.
9. Martha F. Davis and Alison Wetherfield, "A Primer on Sexual Harassment Law," *Clearinghouse Review* (July 1992): 311.
10. *Teresa Harris* v. *Forklift Systems, Inc.* 126 L.Ed. 2d 295, 510 US — , 114 S Ct 367 (1993).
11. 29 C.F.R. Appx to Part 1604 — Questions and Answers on the Pregnancy Discrimination Act. Public Law 95–555, 92 Stat 2076 (1978), Introduction.
12. 29 C.F.R. Part Appx 1604. Q 22.
13. *International Union, UAW* v. *Johnson Controls* 499 US 1196, 113 L.Ed.2d 158, 11 S Ct 1196 (1991).
14. 42 U.S.C. sec. 2000e-2(e)(1).
15. 42 U.S.C 1981 (b).
16. 29 U.S.C. Section 623 (f)(2)(A).
17. 29 U.S.C. Section 623 (f)(1).
18. 42 U.S.C. 12112 (6).
19. U.S. Equal Employment Opportunity Commission, *A Technical Assistance Manual on the Employment Provisions (Title I) of the Americans with Disabilities Act* (January 1992): II-4.
20. Ibid., III-12.
21. Lambda Legal Defense and Education Fund, Inc. *Summary of States, Cities, and Counties Which Prohibit Discrimination Based on Sexual Orientation as of February 21, 1996.* New York: Lambda Legal Defense and Education Fund, 1996.

2. CHILDREN IN CRISIS

1. Suzanne M. Sgroi, M.D., *Handbook of Clinical Intervention in Child Abuse* (Lexington, Mass., Lexington Books, 1982): 112–114.
2. Debra Whitcomb, *When the Child Is a Victim, Second Edition* (Washington, D.C.: National Institute of Justice, 1992): 128.
3. Community Research Associates for the Office of Juvenile Justice and Delinquency Prevention, *Video Training Guide: Law Enforcement Custody of Juveniles.* Office of Juvenile Justice and Delinquency Prevention, U.S. Department of Justice (March 1992): 10. NCJ #133012.
4. Juvenile Probation Officer Initiative Working Group, *Desktop Guide to Good Juvenile Probation Practice.* Pittsburgh, Penn.: National Center for Juvenile Justice (March 1991): 34–35, 64.
5. Ibid., 35.

6. Alfred C. Kinsey, Wardell B. Pomeroy, Clyde E. Martin, and Paul H. Gebhard, *Sexual Behavior in the Human Female* (Philadelphia: W.B. Saunders Company, 1953): 468–76; Alfred C. Kinsey, Wardell B. Pomeroy, and Clyde E. Martin, *Sexual Behavior in the Human Male* (Philadelphia: W.B. Saunders Company, 1948): 636–59.

7. Emery S. Hetrick and Damien A. Martin. "Developmental Issues and Their Resolution for Gay and Lesbian Adolescents," *Journal of Homosexuality* 14, nos. 1/2 (1987): 35–36; Gerald P. Mallon, "Counseling Strategies with Gay and Lesbian Youth," *Helping Gay and Lesbian Youth: New Policies, New Programs, New Practice,* ed. Teresa DeCrescenzo (New York: The Haworth Press, Inc., 1994): 81.

8. Richard E. Redding, *Due Process Protections for Juveniles in Civil Commitment Proceedings* (Washington, D.C.: American Bar Association, 1991): 4; Marc N. Sperber, "Short-Sheeting the Psychiatric Bed: State-Level Strategies to Curtail the Unnecessary Hospitalization of Adolescents in For-Profit Mental Health Facilities," *American Journal of Law and Medicine* XVIII, no. 3 (1992): 253–254; Holly Metz, "Branding Juveniles Against Their Will: How Wayward Adolescents are Punished for The Crime of Rebellion," *Student Lawyer* 20, no. 6 (February 1992): 22, 26; Mary Keegan Eamon, "Institutionalizing Children and Adolescents in Private Psychiatric Hospitals," *Social Work: Journal of the National Association of Social Workers* 39, no. 5 (September 1994): 590.

3. DIVORCE

1. Mary Pat Treuthart, "In Harm's Way? Family Mediation and the Role of the Attorney Advocate," *Golden Gate University Law Review* 23, no. 3 (summer 1993): 766–73.

2. Marygold S. Melli, "Alimony Trends," *Family Advocate* 19, no. 2 (fall 1996): 21–24.

3. Nancy S. Erickson, "Custody of Non-Marital Children," *The Women's Advocate* 14, no. 3 (May 1993): 6,7.

4. Hayden Curry, Denis Clifford, and Robin Leonard, A *Legal Guide for Lesbian and Gay Couples, Eighth National Edition* (Berkeley, CA: Nolo Press, 1994): 8–12.

5. Sharon A. Drew, "Remedies for Nonpayment," *Family Advocate* 16, no. 2 (1993): 36–37.

6. 18 USC 228.

7. Marianne Takas, "Assisting Young Mothers with Paternity and Child Support Orders," *Children's Legal Rights Journal* 13, no. 1 (Winter 1992): 6.

4. VIOLENCE AGAINST WOMEN

1. Joel Epstein and Stacia Langenbahn. *The Criminal Justice and Community Response to Rape* (Washington, D.C.: U.S. Department of Justice, May 1994): 82.

2. Dean G. Kirkpatrick, Christine N. Edmunds, and Anne K. Seymour, *Rape in America: A Report to the Nation* (Arlington, VA: National Victim Center and Crime Victim's Research and Treatment Center, Medical University of South Carolina, April 23, 1992): 4. See also Ronet Bachman, *Violence Against Women: A National Crime Victimization Survey Report* (Washington, D.C.: U.S. Department of Justice, January 1994): 1. "Over two-thirds of violent victimizations against women were committed by someone known to them . . ."

3. National Victim Center and Crime Victim's Research and Treatment Center, Rape in America: A Report to the Nation: 4.

4. 42 U.S.C. sec. 13891 (b).

5. Craig Perkins and Patsy Klaus. "About 6 out of 10 [Rapes/Sexual Assaults] occurred in the victim's or someone else's home," Bureau of Justice Statistics Bulletin, National Crime Victimization Survey. *Criminal Victimization 1994.* Washington, D.C: U.S. Department of Justice. April 1996, NCJ #158022, p. 8.

6. U.S. Department of Justice, Office of Justice Programs, Bureau of Justice Assistance, *Family Violence: Interventions for the Justice System.* Program Brief, October 1993: 1, citing Antonia C. Novello, "From the Surgeon General U.S.

Public Health Service," *Journal of the American Medical Association* 267, no. 23 (1992): 3,132.

7. Lee Bowker, Michelle Arbitell, and J. Richard McFerron, "On the Relationship Between Wife Beating and Child Abuse," *Feminist Perspectives on Wife Abuse,* eds. Kersti Yllo and Michele Bograd, (Beverly Hills, CA: Sage Publications, 1988): 162–63.

8. Carole Echlin and Larry Marshall, "Child Protection Services for Children of Battered Women: Practice and Controversy," in *Ending the Cycle of Violence: Community Responses to Children of Battered Women,* eds. E. Peled, P. G. Jaffe, and J. L. Edleson (Thousand Oaks, CA: Sage Publications, 1995): 172.

9. Jacqueline R. Agtuca in collaboration with the Asian Women's Shelter, *A Community Secret: For the Filipina in an Abusive Relationship* (Seattle: Seal Press, 1994): 35.

10. National Center on Women and Family Law, *Battered Women's Laws: Mandatory Police Reporting,* item no. 68. New York: NCOWFL, 1990.

11. Casey G. Gwinn, "The Path to Effective Intervention: Trends in the Criminal Prosecution of Domestic Violence," *Prosecutor* 27, no. 5. (November/December 1993): 21.

12. Peter Finn and Sarah Colson. *Civil Protection Orders: Legislation, Current Court Practice, and Enforcement* Washington, D.C.: U.S. Department of Justice, March 1990): 14–15.

13. Ibid., 15, 60–61.

14. Ibid., 61.

15. Linda P. Rouse, *You are Not Alone* (Holmes Beach, FL: Learning Publications, Inc., 1986): 85.

16. National Victim Center, *Helpful Guide for Stalking Victims.* (Arlington, VA: National Victim Center, 1994): 3.

5. *CRISES IN CONCEPTION AND SEXUALITY*

1. Rebecca Chalker and Carol Downer, *A Woman's Book of Choices: Abortion, Menstrual Extraction, and RU-486* (New York: Four Walls, Eight Windows, 1992): 68; See also American College of Obstetricians and Gynecologists, *Induced Abortion: Important Medical Facts* (Washington, D.C.: American College of Obstetricians and Gynecologists, May 1994): 5.

2. The NARAL Foundation and NARAL, *A State-by-State Review of Abortion and Reproductive Rights: Who Decides? Fifth Edition* (Washington, D.C.: The NARAL Foundation and NARAL, 1995): ix.

3. Chalker, *A Woman's Book of Choices: Abortion, Menstrual Extraction, and RU-486,* 209.

4. Annette Baran and Reuben Pannor, *Perspectives on Open Adoption, The Future of Children* 3, no. 1 (Los Altos, CA: The David and Lucile Packard Foundation, Center for the Future of Children, spring 1993): 123.

5. Department of Health and Human Services, Office for Civil Rights, Administration for Children and Families, *Policy Guidance on the Use of Race, Color or National Origin as Consideration in Adoption and Foster Care Placement,* 6.

6. Ibid., 7, 10.

7. Department of Health and Human Services, Office for Civil Rights, Administration for Children and Families, *The Multiethnic Placement Act (MEPA) Fact Sheet,* 1.

8. Department of Health and Human Services et al., *Policy Guidance on the Use of Race, Color or National Origin as Consideration in Adoption and Foster Care Placement,* 7.

9. 25 U.S.C.S. 1913 (a).

10. 25 U.S.C.S. 1912 (b).

11. Carole Anderson, "Placing Your Child for Adoption," *Women's Legal Guide,* ed. Barbara R. Hauser (Golden, CO: Fulcrum Publishing, 1996): 169.

12. Neville F. Hacker and J. George Moore, M.D., *Essentials of Obstetrics and Gynecology* (Philadelphia: W. B. Saunders Company, 1986): 217.

13. M. Willinger, L. S. James, and C. Catz, "Defining the Sudden Infant Death Syndrome (SIDS): Deliberations of an Expert Panel Convened by the National Institute of

Child Health and Human Development," *Pediatric Pathology* 11 (1991): 677–84.

14. U.S. Department of Health and Human Services, Public Health Service, Health Resources and Services Administration, Maternal and Child Health Bureau, *Sudden Infant Death Syndrome: Trying to Understand the Mystery* (McLean, VA: National Sudden Infant Death Syndrome Resource Center, February 1994): iv.

15. Thomas G., Keens, M.D., Sudden Infant Death Syndrome: Insights From the Fourth SIDS International Conference, 16th Annual California SIDS Conference, California SIDS Program, Palm Springs, California, October 17, 1996.

16. The American Fertility Society Guideline for Practice, *Recurrent Pregnancy Loss* (Birmingham, AL: American Fertility Society, June 15, 1993): 1; Robert G. Wells, M.D., "Managing Miscarriage: The Need for More Than Medical Mechanics," *Postgraduate Medicine* 89, no. 2 (February 1, 1991): 207.

17. Ron Maymon, M.D., et al., "Ectopic Pregnancy: The New Gynecological Epidemic Disease; Review of the Modern Work-up and the Nonsurgical Treatment Options," *International Journal of Fertility* 37, no. 3 (May–June 1992): 147; Jaque L. Slaughter and David A. Grimes, "Methotrexate Therapy: Nonsurgical Management of Ectopic Pregnancy," *Western Journal of Medicine* 162, no. 3 (March 1995): 225.

18. The American Fertility Society, *Early Diagnosis and Management of Ectopic Pregnancy* (Birmingham, AL: The American Fertility Society, 1992): 2.

19. Maymon et al., *Ectopic Pregnancy*, 147; Slaughter, *Methotrexate Therapy*, 225. See also Jane Thorburn, "Advancing Conservative Treatment of Ectopic Pregnancy — Laparoscopic and 'Non-Surgical' Management," *Annals of Medicine* 24, no. 1 (February 1992): 44; Sjarlot Kooi, M.D., and Hans C. L. V. Kock, M.D., "Surgical Treatment for Tubal Pregnancies," *Surgery, Gynecology and Obstetrics* 176 (May 1993): 521; American Fertility Society, *Guideline for Practice, Early Diagnosis*

and Management of Ectopic Pregnancy (1992): 2.

20. American Social Health Association, *STD(VD): Questions, Answers* (Research Triangle Park, NC: American Social Health Association, 1994). Pamphlet.

21. American Social Health Association, *Women and Sexually Transmitted Diseases* (Research Triangle Park, NC: American Social Health Association, n.d.):1.

22. Centers for Disease Control and Prevention, *1993 Sexually Transmitted Diseases Treatment Guidelines*. MMWR 1993; 42 (no. RR-14):[83].

23. Alan E., Nourse, M.D., *Sexually Transmitted Diseases* (New York: Franklin Watts, 1992): 94.

24. Miriam J. Alter and Eric E. Mast, M.D., "The Epidemiology of Viral Hepatitis in the United States," *Gastroenterology Clinics of North America* 23, no. 3 (September 1994): 443.

25. *1993 Sexually Transmitted Diseases Treatment Guidelines*: 91.

26. See "ACIP Recommends Hep B Shots for Pre-Teens," *Needle Tips and the Hepatitis B Coalition News* 5, no. 1 (May 1995): 1–6 and "Nation Expands Hepatitis B strategy: Adolescents and Immigrant Children Need hepatitis B shots," *Needle Tips and the Hepatitis B Coalition News* 6, no. 1 (January 1996): 1.

27. John T. Daugirdas, M.D., *S.T.D.: Sexually Transmitted Diseases, Including HIV/AIDS*. Hinsdale, IL: Medtext, Inc., 1992: 20.

28. Jean L. Goens, M.D., Camila K. Janniger, M.D., and Kathleen De Wolf, M.D., "Dermatologic and Systemic Manifestations of Syphilis," *American Family Physician* (October 1994): 1016.

29. "Drugs for Sexually Transmitted Diseases," *Medical Letter on Drugs and Therapeutics* 36, issue 913 (January 7, 1994):1.

---

6. RESOURCES FOR ADULTS AND CHILDREN WITH DISABILITIES

1. Patricia Bussen Smith, "Providing Rehabilitation Services to Blind People: 'All Plus

More,'" *American Rehabilitation* 18, no. 2 (summer 1992): 20.

2. American Hospital Association, Section for Rehabilitation Hospitals and Programs, *A Guide to Choosing a Comprehensive Inpatient Medical Rehabilitation Facility*, ed. Christie Enman. (Chicago: The American Hospital Association, 1987): 6.

3. Andrew I. Batavia, *The Payment of Medical Rehabilitation Services: Current Mechanisms and Potential Models* (Chicago: American Hospital Association, 1988): 26–27.

4. 42 C.F.R. 482.43; See also Alfred J. Chiplin, Jr., "Medicare Discharge-Planning Regulations: An Advocacy Tool," *Clearinghouse Review* (June 1995): 152–61.

5. Waring Rorden, Judith Taft, and Elizabeth Taft, *Discharge Planning Guide for Nurses* (Philadelphia: W. B. Saunders Company, 1990): 220–22.

6. Lawrence A. Frolik and Richard L. Kaplan, *Elder Law (in a Nutshell)* (St. Paul, MN): West Publishing Company, 1995): 72.

7. Lawrence A. Frolik and Melissa C. Brown, *Advising the Elderly or Disabled Client* (Englewood Cliffs, NJ: Rosenfeld Launer Publications, 1992): sections 9.5 and 9.6, pp. 9–18.

8. Ibid., section 10.4, pp. 10–29.

9. Margaret A. Nosek, *The Effect of Personal Assistance on the Long-Term Health of a Rehabilitation Hospital Population* (Houston: Independent Living Research Utilization, October 1991): 1, 2.

10. 60 F.R. 39222, no. 147, Tuesday, August 1, 1995.

11. Ibid.

12. 29 U.S.C.S. 723(a) (2) and (15).

13. 29 U.S.C.S. 723 (a) (16).

14. See 29 U.S.C.S. 723 (a); 34 C.F.R. 361.42.

15. 29 U.S.C.S. 722(4)(A).

16. 34 C.F.R. 361.31; 61 F.R. 24402. Tuesday, May 14, 1996.

17. 34 C.F.R. 361.47.

18. 29 U.S.C.S. 722 (d)(2)(A); 34 C.F.R. 361.48 (c) (2)(i).

19. 29 U.S.C.S. 706 8(B).

20. 29 U.S.C.S. 794(a).

21. 24 C.F.R. 100.202 (c).

22. *Cason v. Rochester Housing Authority* WDNY 748 F Supp 1002 (1990).

23. John Parry, *Mental Disability Law: A Primer. Fifth Edition* (Washington, D.C.: American Bar Association, 1995): 38.

24. 24 C.F.R. 100. 203 Example (2).

25. NAPAS Annual Report, 1994–1995. Washington, D.C.: National Association of Protection and Advocacy Systems, p. 9.

26. Social Security Administration, *Social Security: Working While Disabled*. SSA publication no. 05-10095 (January 1996): 7, 11.

27. Lawrence A. Frolik and Melissa C. Brown, *Advising the Elderly or Disabled Client: Legal, Health Care, Financial and Estate Planning* (Englewood Cliffs, NJ: Rosenfeld Launer Publications, 1992.) 1995 Cumulative Supplement, no. 2. Boston: Warren, Gorham and Lamont, sec. 5.2., pp. S5–3.

28. 20 C.F.R. 416.933.

29. 20 C.F.R. 416.934.

30. 34 C.F.R. 303.16 Note 2.

31. 34 C.F.R. 303.344.

32. 34 C.F.R. 303.12; 24 C.F.R. 303.13.

33. 34 C.F.R. 303.12 (b)(2).

34. 34 C.F.R. 303.402, 303.403.

35. 20 U.S.C. 1480(2), 34 C.F.R. 303.460.

36. 34 C.F.R. 300.532 (f).

37. 34 C.F.R. 300.572; 34 C.F.R. 300.502.

38. 34 C.F.R. 300.7(a)(1).

39. 34 C.F.R. 300.346.

40. 34 C.F.R. 300.16.

41. 34 C.F.R. 104.3 (k) (2); National Center for Law and Deafness, *Legal Rights: The Guide for Deaf and Hard of Hearing People, Fourth Edition* (Washington, D.C.: Gallaudet University Press, 1992): 53; Office for Civil Rights, *The Rights of Individuals with Handicaps Under Federal Law* (Washington, D.C.: U.S. Department of Education, February 1989): 4.

7. CRISES IN MENTAL HEALTH

1. American Psychiatric Association, *Diagnostic and Statistical Manual of Mental Disorders*,

Fourth Edition (Washington, D.C.: American Psychiatric Association): 327.

2. John L. McIntosh, *The Suicide of Older Men and Women: How You Can Help Prevent a Tragedy* (Washington, D.C.: American Association of Retired Persons, 1993): 2.

3. Beth A. Stroul, *Psychiatric Crisis Response Systems: A Descriptive Study* (Rockville, MD: Community Support Program/Center for Mental Health Services, Substance Abuse and Mental Health Services Administration, September 1993): 1, 11.

4. Ibid., 71.

5. A. Anthony Arce and Miles C. Ladenheim, "Forensic Issues in Rehabilitation and Mental Health," *Psychiatric Rehabilitation in Practice*, eds. Robert W. Flexer and Phyllis L. Solomon (Boston: Andover Medical Publishers, 1993):233.

6. Sherry Glied and Sharon Kofman, *Women and Mental Health: Issues for Health Reform* (New York: The Commonwealth Fund, Commission on Women's Health, March 1995): 83; Frederick M. Jacobsen, "Psychopharmacology," *Women of Color: Integrating Ethnic and Gender Identities in Psychotherapy*, eds. Lillian Comas-Diaz and Beverly Greene (New York: The Guilford Press, 1994): 326–27.

7. Jacobsen, "Psychopharmacology," 323.

8. Joint Commission on Accreditation of Health Organizations, "Standards for Restraint and Seclusion," *Joint Commission Perspectives* (January/February 1996): RS-1.

9. E. Fuller Torrey, M.D., *Surviving Schizophrenia: A Manual for Families, Consumers and Providers, Third Edition* (New York: Harper-Perennial, 1995): 181; Matthew P. Dumont, M.D., "The World Economy, Privatization and Mental Health," *The Disability Rag and Resource* (March/April 1995):15; Charles G. Ray and James K. Finley, "Did CMHCs Fail or Succeed? Analysis of the Expectations and Outcomes of the Community Mental Health Movement," *Administration and Policy in Mental Health* 21, no.4 (March 1994):289.

10. Michael G. MacDonald, Robert M. Kaufman, Alexander M. Capron, Irwin M. Birnbaum, eds. *Treatise on Health Care Law, Volume Four* (New York: Matthew Bender & Co., Inc., 1995): 20–278, sec. 20.09[4]; Cumulative Supplement to Volume 4 (May 1995): 38.

11. Robert I. Simon, M.D., *Clinical Psychiatry and the Law, Second Edition* (Washington, D.C.: American Psychiatric Press, Inc., 1992): 115; Francine Cournos, M.D., and John Petrila, "Legal and Ethical Issues," *The Columbia University College of Physicians and Surgeons Complete Home Guide to Mental Health* (New York: Henry Holt and Company, 1992): 423.

12. See MacDonald et al., *Treatise on Health Care Law, Volume 4*, sec. 20.11.[3] (c), pp. 20–289, Cumulative Supplement to Volume 4 (May 1995): 48. See also Paul S. Sherman, Advance Directives for Involuntary Psychiatric Care. *Proceedings of the 1994 National Symposium on Involuntary Interventions: The Call for a National Legal and Medical Response* (Houston: University of Texas, 1995): 5–6.

13. Excerpted from the pamphlet "Healthy Women/Healthy Lifestyles: Here's What You Should Know About Alcohol or Other Drugs." Available from the U.S. Department of Health and Human Services Public Health Service, Substance Abuse and Mental Health Services Administration. DHHS publication no. PHD691 (1995).

8. LIFE-THREATENING ILLNESS

1. Mark J. Alberts, M.D., Larry B. Goldstein, M.D., and Tony Smith, M.D., "Guidelines on the Use of Thrombolytic Agents in Stroke" (letter to the editor), *Journal of the American Medical Association* 274, no. 3 (July 19, 1995): 218.

2. American College of Cardiology/American Heart Association Ad Hoc Task Force on Cardiac Catheterization, *ACC/AHA Guidelines for Cardiac Catheterization and Cardiac Catheterization Laboratories*, JACC 18, no. 5 (November 1, 1991): 1,164–167.

3. Gail McBride and Jamie Spencer, *Harvard*

Health Publications Special Report: Post-menopausal Hormone-Replacement Therapy. *Harvard Women's Health Watch* (Boston: Harvard Medical School Health Publications Groups, 1996): 29.

4. American Cancer Society, *Cancer Facts for Women: What You Can Do to Protect Yourself Against Cancer*. American Cancer Society, Inc., 1992. This is the current listing of warning signs. Contact the American Cancer Society for future revisions.

5. The Office of Alternative Medicine, National Institutes of Health, *General Information* (October 4, 1994): 1.

9. *CRISES IN AGING*

1. National Institute on Adult Daycare, *Adult Day Care Fact Sheet* (Washington, D.C.: NIAD, June 1995): 1.

2. Ibid., 2.

3. Teresa A. Coughlin, Leighton Ku, and John Holahan, *Medicaid Since 1980: Costs, Coverage and the Shifting Alliance between the Federal Government and the States* (Washington, D.C.: The Urban Institute Press, 1994): 116.

4. Older Women's League 1993 Mother's Day Report, *Room for Improvement: The Lack of Affordable, Adaptable and Accessible Housing for Midlife and Older Women* (Washington, D.C.: Older Women's League, 1993): 7.

5. Richard L. Douglass, *Domestic Mistreatment of the Elderly: Towards Prevention* (Washington, D.C.: American Association of Retired Persons): 7.

6. Health Care Financing Administration, *Your Medicare Handbook 1996* (Washington, D.C.: U.S. Government Printing Office, 1996): 9.

7. 42 U.S.C.S. 1395i-3(c)(6)(B)(i); 42 U.S.C.S. 1396r(c)(6)(B) (i).

8. Toshio Tatara, *Elder Abuse: Questions and Answers: An Information Guide for Professionals and Concerned Citizens* (Washington, D.C.: National Center on Elder Abuse, July 1995): 5.

10. *DEATH AND DYING*

1. For more information about the Uniform Transfers to Minors Act, see Denis Clifford and Cora Jordan, *Plan Your Estate, Third Edition* (Berkeley, CA: Nolo Press, 1995): 6–11.

2. Kathleen Sublette and Martin Flagg, *Final Celebrations: A Guide for Personal and Family Funeral Planning* (Ventura, CA: Pathfinder Publishing of California, 1992): 36–37.

3. 16 C.F.R. 453.2 (b)(1).

4. 59 F.R. 1613 Tuesday, January 11, 1994; 16 C.F.R. 453.3 (2)(i)(A)(B)(C).

5. 16 C.F.R. 453.3 (a)(1)(i).

6. Deborah Duda, *Coming Home: A Guide to Dying at Home with Dignity* (New York: Aurora Press, 1987): 67.

7. Department of Veterans Affairs, *A Summary of Department of Veterans Affairs Benefits*. (VA pamphlet 27-82-2) Washington, D.C.: Department of Veterans Affairs, March 1991: 20–21; Department of Veterans Affairs, *Federal Benefits for Veterans and Dependents*, 1996 Edition (Washington, D.C.: Office of Public Affairs, Department of Veterans Affairs, 1996):30–32.

8. DVA, *Federal Benefits for Veterans and Dependents* 1996, 30–32.

9. PWBA's Division of Public Affairs, *Health Benefits Under the Consolidated Omnibus Budget Reconciliation Act (COBRA)* (Washington, D.C. U.S. Department of Labor, Pension and Welfare Benefits Administration, 1994): 2.

Index

For organizations and government agencies, look under the appropriate subject headings rather than the name of the organization.

AA, 357–58, 580

AAA. *See* Area Agencies on Aging (AAA)

AARP, 409, 415, 603, 606, 637–38

Abduction of children, 67, 120–22, 125, 531–33

Abiding Hearts, 236, 548

ABLEDATA, 267, 558

Abortion: alternatives to surgical abortion, 200–201; anti-abortion protesters, 192; complications, 196–97; cost, 197–98; definition, 190; dilatation and evacuation (D&E), 195, 197–98; emotions after, 197; finding abortion provider, 191–92; first-trimester abortions, 190, 193–95, 197; health insurance coverage, 27; hotline, 190; hysterotomy, 196; impact on later pregnancies, 191; induction abortion, 195–96; Medicaid coverage, 190, 198, 406; methotrexate and misoprostol, 201; mifepristone, 200; for minors, 190–91, 198–99; obstacles to safe and legal abortion, 198; organizations, 190, 198, 543–44; paying for, 190, 197–98, 406; after prenatal diagnosis of genetic or fetal abnormality, 235; procedures, 193–96, 198; questions to ask about abortion procedure and clinic, 198; reading materials, 619; scheduling of, 190; second-trimester abortions, 192, 195–96; and teenage pregnancy, 89–91; unsafe methods, 191

Abuse of children. *See* Child abuse and neglect; Child sexual abuse; Elder abuse and neglect

Accelerated life insurance benefits payments, 473

Access to Care and Help (ARCH), 313

Accessibility, 290, 418–20, 556, 635

Accessory apartments for elderly, 441–42

ACES, 132, 133

ACLU, 530–31, 542, 555

Acquired Immunodeficiency Syndrome. *See* AIDS

Activities of daily living (ADLs), 268, 269

ADA, 32–35, 37–40, 289–90, 343, 359, 522, 556, 574

Adapting home environments. *See* Home adaptation

Addictions. *See* Alcohol and drug abuse

Addison's disease, 561

ADEA, 8, 30–32, 35, 37, 40

Adjudicatory hearing for juvenile offenders, 77–78

ADLs, 268, 269

Adolescents. *See* Teenagers

Adoption: adoptee's access to information about birth parents, 217–19, 545–46; adoption plan, 208; after mother's death, 484; agency adoption process and questions, 207–212, 219–21; birth mother's ability to see child afer adoption, 217–19; birth mother's time with baby in hospital, 217; choice of adoptive parents by birth parents, 209–10, 214–15; consent or relinquishment form, 215–16; counseling and support for birth mothers, 205; decision to place child for adoption, 201–203; definition, 203; due to

Adoption, *cont.*
child abuse and neglect, 64; and father's rights, 216–17; finding adoption agencies, 211–12; finding adoption attorney, 214; finding information on, 201, 205, 210, 545–46, 620; foster care before adoption placement, 211; home study, 208–209, 213; identified adoption, 208; independent (attorney-facilitated) adoption, 212–15; information clearinghouses, 201, 205, 210; multiservice family agencies, 202, 207, 208; mutual consent registries, 218; of Native American children, 210–11; open adoptions, 204–206; organizations, 545–46; placement after baby's birth, 211, 215; questions for agencies of attorneys, 219–22; racial and ethnic issues, 210–11; reading materials, 620; relative adoption, 206; reunion registries, 218; sealing of adoption records, 217–18; single adoptive parents, 545–46; and teen pregnancy, 90–91; traditional (or confidential) adoptions, 203, 204; types, 204–206
Adoption agencies, 202, 207–12, 219–21
Adoption Assistance and Child Welfare Act, 64
Adrenal gland diseases, 561
Adult Children of Alcoholics, 358, 582
Adult daycare, 419, 604
Adult protective services (APS), 138, 180–81, 467–69
Adult survivors of childhood sexual abuse, 591–92 628–29
Adults with disabilities: assis-tive devices, 267, 279, 557, 626; and child custody, 118–19; Client Assistance Programs (CAPs), 283–84, 287, 288, 293; at colleges and universities, 288; discrimination against, 32–35, 288–93, 555–56, 624–25; employment, 32–35, 288–90, 289, 522; filing for benefits, 297–98; finding information on services, 265–67; home adaptation, 281, 291–92, 557, 619; housing, 290–93, 623; income, 294–300; independent living centers, 279–82, 298, 557; legal and financial matters, 623–24; legal definition, 33; library program, 557; medical rehabilitation, 267–79; national organizations, 266–67; organizations, 266–67, 523–24, 552–80; personal care attendants, 281, 625–26; pregnancy and parenting, 626; protection and advocacy organizations (P&As), 293–94, 298, 555–56; reading materials, 623–24; reasonable accommodation in workplace, 33–34; reproductive health, 626; sexuality, 626–27; Social Security disability insurance (SSDI), 7, 294–95; specific disabilities, 561–80; supplemental security income (SSI), 295–97; support and advocacy groups, 266; vocational rehabilitation, 283–88; women's experiences, 624; workers' compensation, 298–300
Advance directives, 345–46, 347, 460, 485–88, 609
AFDC. *See* Welfare assistance
Affirmation action, 21
African Americans: breast can-cer, 594; professional associations, 327, 587; stroke, 370
Age discrimination, 30–32
Age Discrimination in Employment Act (ADEA), 8, 30–32, 35, 37, 40
Aging: adult daycare, 419; alternative housing, 440–42, 445–49, 608; Area Agencies on Aging (AAA), 266, 298, 329, 412, 417, 425–26, 431, 469; assessment of amount of care needed, 445; assistive devices for everyday living, 420–21; consumer information, 606; cost for in-home and community services, 418; counseling and other community services, 417; discrimination against older people, 30–32; elder abuse and neglect, 138, 427, 464–70, 605; finding information on, 411–14, 585, 603–609, 634–35; Friendly Visitors, 415, 423, 427, 469; geriatric care managers, 417, 436, 445, 470, 604; government agencies, 608; home adaptation for safety and accessibility, 418–20, 635; home health care, 420, 422–35; insurance counseling, 417; legal assistance, 416–17, 608; long-term care defined, 410; Long-Term-Care Ombudsman, 413, 443–44; maintaining independence at home, 414–22; Meals on Wheels, 415–16, 423, 469; medical equipment purchases, 421–22; medications and older women, 340–41; moving in with children, 440; notebook for information on, 414; nursing homes, 64, 442–45, 449, 608–609; organizations and government agencies, 559,

Aging *cont.*

585, 603–609; personal care attendants, 427; preparation before crisis, 410–11; reading materials, 630–32; respite care, 417–18; senior centers, 414; services for, to maintain independence at home, 415–18; state units, 414, 607; telephone reassurance and personal emergency response (PERS), 415; transportation, 416

AIDS: AIDS service organizations (ASOs), 395–98; alternative therapies, 399; Clinical Trials Information Service, 397, 595; covered under Americans with Disabilities Act, 33; definition, 385–86; discrimination due to, 404; doctor-patient relationship, 399–400; finding information on illness and treatment, 385, 398–99, 409, 524, 554, 585, 595–96, 631–33; and gay, lesbian, and bisexual teens, 88; HIV antibody test, 387; hotlines, 248, 255, 385, 396, 397, 398, 595–96; medical care, 393, 394, 396–402, 404–405; medical tests for monitoring health, 400–402; newsletters and journals on, 633; organizations and government agencies, 524, 554, 588, 595–96; reading materials, 631–33; reporting of AIDS cases, 403; safer sex, 402, 405; signs and symptoms of medical problems, 402; telling others about diagnosis, 402–404. *See also* HIV infection

AIDS service organizations (ASOs), 282, 298, 332–33, 385, 387–88, 393, 394, 395–98, 404–405, 409, 426, 473

Airlines: people with disabilities, 290; relatives' airfares after death in family, 496–97

Al-Anon/Alateen, 358, 582

Alcohol and drug abuse: addictions/recovery groups, 357–58, 579–81; detoxification, 355–356; drug-free outpatient programs, 356; family twelve-step programs, 358; finding information on, 581–84, 627; finding treatment programs, 354–55, 358–60; health risks associated with, 351–54; as heart attack risk factor, 375; HIV infection, 394; hotlines for treatment programs, 355, 361, 581; inpatient programs, 356; methadone programs, 356; organizations, 361, 581–84; overview of issues, 349–51; of parents and child abuse, 59–60; paying for substance abuse treatment, 360–61; pregnancy, 352–54, 358–59; reading materials, 627; recovery options for, 62; rehabilitation for, covered under Americans with Disabilities Act, 33; residential therapeutic communities (TCs), 356–57; self-assessment questions on, 351; as stroke risk factor, 370–71; testing, 34; treatment programs, 354–61, 581–84; twelve-step programs, 357–58, 581–84; and women with disabilities, 359

Alcoholics Anonymous (AA), 357–58, 582

Alimony: change in amount, 114; cohabitation, 113; collection, 114; definition, 112; determination of, 112–13; fault considered in, 100, 113;

length of payment, 113–14; past-due alimony, 114; rehabilitative alimony, 113

Alliances for the Mentally Ill (AMI), 322–23, 344

ALMA Society, 545

Alternative therapies: AIDS/HIV, 399; cancer, 384; government agency, 384, 593

Alzheimer's disease, 419, 444, 449, 456–57, 473, 486, 562

American Association for Retired Persons (AARP), 409, 415, 603, 610, 637–38

American Civil Liberties Union (ACLU), 531, 543, 555

American Heart Association, 367, 372, 376, 634

American Psychiatric Association, 85, 87, 327, 589

American Psychological Association, 87, 327, 590

American Social Health Association (ASHA), 247–48, 249, 551

American Speech-Language-Hearing Association (ASHA), 270, 421, 558, 568

Americans with Disabilities Act (ADA), 32–35, 37–40, 289–90, 343, 359, 522, 556, 574

Amputation, 562

Aneurysm, 364, 366

Angina, 371, 373

Angioplasty, 375–76

Annulment, 99–100

Anonymous HIV testing, 388, 392–93

Anticoagulants (blood thinner), 365–66

Antidepressants, 368, 490

APA. *See* American Psychiatric Association; American Psychological Association

Aphasia, 367

APS, 138, 180–81, 467–69

ARC, 574

ARCH National Resource Center for Respite and Crisis Care Services, 62, 313, 529, 552

Architectural barriers. *See* Accessibility; Home adaptation

Area Agencies on Aging (AAA), 266, 298, 329, 412, 417, 425–26, 431, 469

Arraignment of juvenile offenders, 77

Arrests. *See* Criminal justice system; Juvenile justice system

Arrhythmias, 373

Arteriography, 364–65

Arteriovenous malformation (AVM), 364, 366

Arthritis, 562

ASHA. *See* American Social Health Association (ASHA); American Speech-Language-Hearing Association (ASHA)

Asian Pacific Americans, 587, 604

ASOs. *See* AIDS service organizations (ASOs)

Aspirin therapy, 366, 375

Assault, definition, 162. *See also* Domestic violence; Rape

Assets. *See* Family finances

Assisted living facilities, 446–47, 608–609

Assistive devices, 267, 279, 420–21, 557, 626

Association for Children for Enforcement of Support (ACES), 132, 133, 537

"At will" employer-employee relationship, 12

Atherectomy, 377

Atherosclerosis, 373–74

Attendants, 281, 427, 625–26

Attorneys: court orders for protection, 175; "discovery" on income and assets, 112; divorce, 98, 101–104, 535; durable power of attorney drafted by, 483; family lawyers, 102; fees for handling divorce, 103; finding, 101, 102; independent adoption, 212–15, 221–22; juvenile offenders, 73–74, 80; and mediation, 105; Medicaid law and nursing homes, 454–55; medical rehabilitation services, 275; Miranda attorneys, 73–74; nonpayment of child support, 133; organizations, 535; questions for, in divorce case, 104; representing parents in child abuse and neglect investigation, 65; wills, 477; workplace discrimination, 41–43. *See also* headings beginning with Legal

Autism, 563

Autopsy, 226, 233, 497

AVM. *See* Arteriovenous malformation (AVM)

Bankruptcy Act, 13

Banks, and death of loved one, 506

Baseline test for toxoplasmosis, 401

Battered spouse waiver, 177

Battery, definition, 162. *See also* Domestic violence

Behavior therapy, 325–26

Benzodiazepines, 354

Bereavement. *See* Grief and mourning

Better Business Bureau, 17, 413, 606

BFOQ, 20, 28, 31

Birth. *See* Childbirth; Pregnancy

Birth control pills, 187. *See also* Contraception

Birth defects, 552

Bisexuals: discrimination against, 35–36; misinformation on, 84–85; organizations, 533–34, 554; parents' reactions, 82–88; reading materials, 611–12; religious organizations, 533–34; teenagers as, 88–97; women's shelters, 181

Blacks. *See* African Americans

Blighted ovum, 239

Blindness. *See* Visual disabilities

Blood platelet antiaggregants, 366

Blood thinner (anticoagulants), 365–66

Body donation to medical school, 498, 501–502

Bona fide occupational qualification (BFOQ), 20, 28, 31

Brain injury, 563

Breast cancer, 597–600, 629

Breast implants, 597, 629

Brown bag test for medications, 340–41

Budgeting. *See* Family finances

Burial, 498–500, 500

Bypass surgery, 377

CABG. *See* Coronary artery bypass graft (CABG)

CAD. *See* Coronary artery disease (CAD)

Cancellation of removal, 177

Cancer: breast cancer, 597–600, 629; cervical cancer and HPV, 260; complementary (alternative) medical practices, 384; definition, 380–81; finding information on, 361, 382–84, 597–600, 629–30; metastasis, 381; organizations, 597–600; Pap smear as screen for cervical cancer, 401; reading materials, 629–30; response to diagnosis, 381; risk associated with

Cancer *cont.*
hormone replacement therapy (HRT), 379–80; symptoms, 381
Candlelighters Childhood Cancer Foundation, 472, 473, 598
CAPs, 283–84, 287, 288, 293
Cardiac catheterization, 375–76
Cardiac enzyme panel, 372
Cardiac rehabilitation, 378
Cardiology, 376. *See also* Heart disease; Stroke
Cardiopulmonary resuscitation (CPR), 372
Career counseling, 7, 18
Caregivers: elder abuse and neglect by, 427, 466; guidelines, 435, 437–40; and hospice care, 491–95; organizations, 552, 605; reading materials, 634–36; respite care services, 62, 312–13, 408, 417–18; support groups, 438–49, 472
Carotid endartectomy, 365, 366
CASA, 53, 530
Case management services: geriatric care managers, 417, 436, 445, 470, 605; medical case management, 275; mental health care, 341
Caskets, 500, 501
CAT scan, after stroke, 364
Catholic Charities, 61, 62, 93, 96, 180, 413, 426, 467
CCU, 372
CD₄ cell count, 400

Cemetery Consumer Service Council, 503, 610
Centering Corporation, 617, 620, 621, 638
Centers for independent living (CIL). *See* Independent living centers
Cerebral infarction, 363
Cerebral palsy, 564
Certified occupational therapy assistants (COTAs), 269–70

Certified Rehabilitation Registered Nurses (C.R.R.N.), 270
Certified Respiratory Therapy Technicians (CRTT), 270
Cervical cancer, and HPV, 260
CFIDS (chronic fatigue syndrome), 564
Chemical restraints in nursing homes, 458–60, 635
Child abuse and neglect: adoption of child, 64; and child custody decision, 120; child neglect defined, 57–58; and corporal punishment, 59; divorce in cases of, 106; and domestic violence, 161–62; dynamics of, 58–60; educational neglect, 57–58; emotional neglect, 58; emotional/psychological abuse defined, 57; and family services, 64; and foster care placement of child, 64; help for new mothers, 60; hotlines, 45, 60–61, 319, 528–29; investigation, 63–65; medical neglect, 57; organizations, 62, 529–30; parental alcohol and drug abuse, 59–60, 353; and parental stress, 58–59; parents at risk for physically abusing child, 54–56; physical abuse defined, 56–57; physical and emotional consequences, 58; physical neglect, 57; prevention of, 59–63; reading materials, 615; reporting, 63, 337; self-assessment questions, 55; shaken baby syndrome (SBS), 56; and temporary removal of child from home, 64; and termination of parental rights, 64; and unrealistic expectations of child's behavior, 59; and visitation rights, 125, 132

Child advocacy centers, 52
Child custody: changing custody order, 124–25; and child abuse or neglect, 120; custody orders, 120, 123–25; decisions on, 118–19, 122; and documentation of mother's caregiving role, 119; and domestic violence, 119, 120–21, 178; factors affecting custody decisions, 118–19, 122; joint custody, 117–18; legal custody, 117, 136; lesbian mothers, 123–24, 536; and moral issues or marital misconduct, 122; organizations, 536; and parental kidnapping, 120–22, 125; parents' income affecting, 122; and parents with physical disability or chronic illness, 118–19; partial custody, 125; physical custody, 117; and protection orders, 171–72; and relocation, 122; in separation agreement, 117; sole custody, 117; split custody, 118; temporary custody orders, 120, 122–123, 171–72; tender years doctrine, 119; types of custody arrangements, 117–118; unmarried mothers' need for custody order, 123, 136; and visitation, 124, 125, 131–32, 172; and women with psychiatric disabilities, 345
Child in need of supervision (CHINS), 81–82
Child neglect. *See* Child abuse and neglect
Child Protective Services (CPS) agency, 50, 51, 52–53, 62, 63–65, 71
Child sexual abuse: arrest of offender, 53; behavioral indicators of, 47; as crime, 44–45; definition, 44; difficulty in de-

tecting, 46–47; disclosure of, by children, 46; and domestic violence, 162; guidelines on parental responses, 48–50; hotlines, 45; indicators, 46–48; intrafamilial sexual sexual abuse, 44–45, 51–52; investigation, 52–53; medical attention for child, 50; parent's emotional reactions on first learning about, 48; physical force not necessarily used by offenders, 45–46; physical indicators, 47–48; reporting, 51–52; therapy for child and family members, 53–54; trial, 53; videotaped interview of child, 52–53

Child sexual abuse survivors, 588, 615, 624–25

Child support: changes in, 130–31; collection, 130, 132–35; considerations for getting best support for child, 129; crime of nonpayment, 133; and death of ex-spouse, 130; decisions about, 127–28; definition, 127; ex-husband's leaving state and collection of, 134–35; failure to pay, 132–35; hotline, 132; length of time for paying, 130; medical support for children, 128–29; organizations, 537–39; past-due child support, 132–35; paternity establishment, 135–36; unmarried mothers, 135–36; and visitation, 131–32, 536; and welfare assistance, 133–34, 135

Child Support Amendments of 1984, 128

Child Support Enforcement (CSE) office, 114, 127, 130–35, 537–39

Child Support Recovery Act of 1992, 133

Child Welfare League of America, 207, 211–12, 529, 544, 587

Childbirth: emotions following, 242–43; health insurance coverage, 27; postpartum disorders after, 243–48, 621; stillbirth, 231; support for mothers following, 242–44. See also Newborns; Pregnancy loss

Childcare, 521

Childhelp USA, 45, 51, 528

Children in crisis: abduction of children, 67, 120–22, 125, 532–33; arrest of child, 72–82, 528, 612; child abuse and neglect, 54–65, 528–30, 611; child sexual abuse, 44–54; divorce, 125–26; domestic violence, 161–62, 178; finding information on, 45, 65, 526–35, 615–16; gay, lesbian, or bisexual teens, 82–88, 533–34, 611–12; grief and mourning, 228–29, 514–15, 536, 610–12; HIV infection in children, 406–408; hotlines, 45; organizations, 45, 65, 526–35; parental kidnapping, 120–22, 125; parent's HIV/AIDS diagnosis, 403–404; play therapy, 326; reading materials, 611–12; runaways, 65–71, 532–34; teenage pregnancy, 88–97, 612

Children with disabilities: assessment of, for early intervention, 302; early intervention for newborns and toddlers, 301–306, 408; eligibility for early intervention, 302–303; EPSDT program, 312, 408; evaluation of, for early intervention, 302; finding services for, 300–301; Head Start, 311; Individualized Family Service Plan

(IFSP), 302, 303–304; organizations, 552–55; parents' reading materials, 625; reading materials, 624–25; residential schools, 306; respite care, 312–13; special education, 306–11, 552; special needs trust, 480

CHINS, 81–82

Chlamydia, 257, 264

Choice in Dying, 485, 486, 487, 609

Chronic fatigue syndrome, 564

Chronic pain. See Headache; Pain control

Cigarette smoking, 352–54, 361, 375

Civil Rights Act of 1866, 19, 29–30, 37

Civil Rights Act of 1964, 13, 18–20, 21, 26, 29, 35–40

Civil Rights Act of 1991, 37, 39–40

Cleft palate/craniofacial disfigurement, 564

Client Assistance Programs (CAPs), 283–84, 287, 288, 293

Clot busters (thrombolytics), 362, 365, 372

Clubhouses, 342

CMHC. See Community mental health centers (CMHC)

CMV, 401–402

COBRA, 5–6, 111, 507

Cocaine, 357, 361, 583. See also Alcohol and drug abuse

Cognitive-behavioral therapy, 326

Cognitive therapy, 326

Cohabitation, and alimony, 113

Colitis, 564

Colleges and universities: career counseling at, 18; Disabled Student Services (DSS), 288; geriatric center of, 413; HEATH Resource Center on people with

Colleges and universities *cont.*
disabilities, 553; law schools
providing low-cost legal assistance, 11; mental health clinics at, 329; teen parents, 96
Committal service, 498–99
Communication: with community agencies about needs,
519–521; doctor-patient relationship, 399–400
Community colleges. *See* Colleges and universities
Community mental health centers (CMHC), 61, 330, 417
Community property states, 108
Community resources: communication with community
agencies about needs, 519–
521; finding, 517–21; information and referral services, 62,
518; notebook for organizing,
414, 519; self-help clearinghouses, 517–18; telephone directory, 267, 518; updating
telephone numbers, 518
Compeer, 584
Complementary medical practices. *See* Alternative therapies
Comprehensive rehabilitation
facilities, 273
Comprehensive rehabilitation
outpatient facilities
(CORFs), 274, 276
Conception, timing of, 189. *See
also* Pregnancy
Conception crises: abortion,
190–201, 543–44, 619; adoption, 201–22, 543–46, 620;
emergency contraception,
186–89, 541, 543, 620; infertility and reproductive health,
546; organizations, 543–51;
postpartum disorders, 242–
47, 546–47, 621; pregnancy
and infant loss, 222–42, 548–
50, 621–22; reading materials,

619–22; sexually transmitted
diseases, 247–64, 551, 620;
unexpected pregnancy, 189–
90
Conditional ("traditional") vol-
untary commitment in psy-
chiatric hospital, 347
Condoms, for protection from
STDs, 253–55
Confidentiality: adoptions, 203,
204; AIDS/HIV patients, 404;
counseling and therapy, 336–
37; HIV testing, 388–89, 403
Congestive heart failure, 373
Congregate housing, 447
Congressional Accountability
Act, 35, 290
Consolidated Omnibus Budget
Reconciliation Act (CO-
BRA), 5–6, 111, 507
Consumer Credit Protection
Act, 13
Consumer protection: aging,
606; debt collection, 11; evic-
tion, 11; funeral homes, 503;
organizations, 413, 606, 638;
work-at-home ad frauds,
17
Consumer/survivor movement
in mental health, 323, 335–
37, 347, 584–86
Continence, 571
Contingent employment, 17
Continuing Care Retirement
Communities, 447
Contraception: emergency con-
traception, 91, 146, 186–89,
540, 620; emergency contra-
ception following rape, 146;
failures of, 186
Copper-T IUD insertion, 188–
89
CORFs, 274, 276
Coronary artery bypass graft
(CABG), 375, 376, 377–78
Coronary artery disease (CAD),
373–74

Coronary artery stents, 377
Coronary care unit (CCU), 372
Corporal punishment, 59
Correctional facilities for juvenile offenders, 79–80
COTAs, 269–70
Counseling and therapy: to
avoid divorce, 99; behavior
therapy, 325–26; birth mothers in adoption process, 205,
213–14; child sexual abuse,
53–54; cognitive-behavioral
therapy, 326; cognitive therapy, 326; confidentiality, 336–
37; costs of, 326; after diagnosis of sexually transmitted
diseases, 252; elderly, 417;
family and couples (or marital) therapy, 99, 326, 540;
finding and choosing therapist, 328–29, 333–37; forms of
therapy, 325–26; gay, lesbian,
and bisexual teens, 87, 88;
grief and mourning, 515–16;
group therapy, 326; HIV antibody test, 389–91; incorrigible children, 81; individual
therapy, 326; interpersonal
therapy, 326; parents, 54, 62;
parents after infant death,
227–28; play therapy for children, 326; postpartum disorders, 247; pregnant teens and
their families, 93; psychodynamic psychotherapy, 325;
psychotherapy, 324–29; questions to ask therapist, 335;
rape survivors, 147; runaways
and family members, 71; sexual misconduct of therapist,
336; supportive psychotherapy, 325; terminally ill and
their families, 472; types of
mental health professionals,
327–28. *See also* Mental
health care; Mental health
crises

Court appointed special advocate (CASA), 53, 530
Court cases. *See* Legal action
Court orders of protection: behaviors prohibited by, 171; definition, 169–70; delivery of, to law enforcement agency, 176; eligibility, 174; emergency orders of protection, 170–71; filing, 175; permanent orders of protection, 171; procedures for getting, 174–76; risks and benefits of, 173; service of process, 170; stalking, 185; and temporary child custody, 171–72; violation of, by abuser, 172–73
CPR (cardiopulmonary resuscitation), 372
CPS. *See* Child protective services (CPS) agency
Craniofacial disfigurement/cleft palate, 564
Creatine kinase, 372
Credit card companies, and death of loved one, 506
Creditors, harassment by, 11
Cremation, 498, 500–501
Criminal justice system: child sexual abuse offenders, 53; domestic violence, 163–66, 168–69; rape, 149–50, 152–54. *See also* Juvenile justice system
Crisis hotlines. *See* Hotlines
Crisis intervention, 318–21. *See also* Mental health crises
Crisis pregnancy centers, 89–90, 189–90
Crohn's disease, 565
CRTT, 270
CSE office. *See* Child Support Enforcement (CSE) office
CT scan, after stroke, 364
Custody. *See* Child custody
Custody orders, 120, 123–25
Cystic fibrosis, 565

Cytomegalovirus (CMV), 401–402

D&E, 195, 197–98, 239
Deafness. *See* Hearing disabilities
Death and dying: advance directives, 485–88, 609; alternatives to dying in hospital, 490–95; alternatives to high cost of funerals, 499–500; arrangements following death of loved one, 495–97; autopsy following death, 497, 502; burial, cremation, and other disposition options, 498, 500–502; choice in dying organizations, 485; contacting close relatives and friends after death of loved one, 496; death certificate, 497, 505; do-not-resuscitate (DNR) orders, 488; durable power of attorney, 482–83, 486–87; embalming, 500; financial details tasks following funeral, 505–507; financial help for terminally ill, 473–74; funeral arrangements, 482, 497–99, 503–505, 610; funeral instructions prepared by person ahead of time, 482; guardianship or adoption for children, 483–85; hospice care, 422, 491–95, 608, 612–13; and insurance counseling programs, 472–73; letter of instruction, 480–82, 495; life support decisions with no advance directive, 488; living will, 486; murder, 510; and organization of paperwork, 474–75; organizations, 485, 609–13; pain control for dying person, 488–90; paying for funerals, 503–505; probate avoidance techniques,

479–80; prolonged illness, 510; reading materials, 474, 636–38; relatives' transportation after death in family, 496–97; right to die movement, 485, 609; sudden death, 510; support for terminally ill and their families, 471–74; wills and property, 475–79, 495. *See also* Grief and mourning; Suicide
Death certificate, 497, 505
Death of infants: autopsy, 226, 233; death scene investigation by law enforcement, 233–34; decisions after, 224–26; family's and friends' reactions, 229–30; funeral arrangements after, 226–27; grandparents' and caregivers' reactions, 230–31; grief over, 223–31; guidelines for helping someone whose child has died, 230; in hospitals, 224–26; marital relationship following, 228; newborn's death, 231; organizations, 548–51; parental support following, 227–28; photographs of infant, 225; reading materials, 620, 621, 622; sibling reactions, 228–29; stillbirth, 231; sudden infant death syndrome (SIDS), 232–35, 353, 548, 549, 550, 551. *See also* Pregnancy loss
Debt collection agencies, 11
Debts: Fair Debt Collection Practices Act, 11; harassment by creditors, 11; information and records on, in divorce cases, 110–11; reading materials, 614; wage garnishment, 13
Delinquency. *See* Juvenile delinquency

Dementias, 419. *See also* Alzheimer's disease

Dental dam, for protection from STDs, 253

Dental schools, body donation to, 501–502

Dentists, for people with AIDS/HIV, 404–405

Dependency tax deduction, 129

Depositions in divorce cases, 112

Depression: alcohol and drug abuse, 350; caregivers, 440; finding information on, 587; grief, 509; heart attack survivors, 378; postpartum depression, 243–247, 323, 547–48, 617; reading materials, 624; stroke survivors, 367–68; suicide risk factor, 315–16, 318

Detention hearing for juvenile offenders, 77

Detoxification, 355–356

Developmental disabilities, 565

Diabetes, 370, 375, 566

Dietitians, 424

Digestive disorders, 566

Dilatation and evacuation (D&E), 195, 197–98, 239

Direct disposition, 499–500

Disabilities: discrimination against people with disabilities, 32–35; finding information on, 265–67; information lines on disability laws, 290; legal definition of, under Americans with Disabilities Act, 33; library program for blind and physically handicapped, 557; magazines and newsletters, 557, 621; organizations and government agencies, 34, 266–67, 551–580; reading materials, 557, 623–27, 625; reasonable accommodation in workplace, 33–34; specific disabilities, 561–80. *See also* Adults with disabilities; Children with disabilities

Disability insurance, 6, 7

Disability leave, for pregnant women, 26

Disabled Student Services (DSS), 288

Discharge planning units in hospitals, 274

Discipline of children, 59

Discovery, and hidden assets in divorce cases, 112

Discrimination: adults with AIDS/HIV infection, 404; adults with disabilities, 32–35, 288–93, 555–56, 623–24; adults with psychiatric disabilities, 343; citizenship or national origin, 30; compensatory and punitive damages, 39–40; EEOC process for filing charges, 37–40; Executive Order 11246, on 21; Executive Order 11375, on 21; federal discrimination laws, 18–21; housing discrimination against adults with disabilities, 290–93; information from state or local human rights commission, 14; legal action for workplace discrimination, 37–43; mediation, 42; nursing homes and Medicaid recipients, 452–54; older people, 30–32; organizations and government agencies combating, 522–25, 552–57; pregnancy discrimination, 26–29; pregnant teens, 95–96; pros and cons of legal action, 41–43; sex- or race-plus discrimination, 19; sexual orientation, 35–36; state discrimination laws, 35; wage discrimination, 13, 20, 37

Diseases. *See* Illnesses; Medical care; and specific illnesses

Disparate impact, 20

Displaced homemaker programs, 18

Disposition (sentencing) for juvenile offenders, 78–79

Diversion programs for juvenile offenders, 74–75

Divorce: alimony, 100, 112–114; attorney for, 98, 101–104, 535; attorney's fees, 103; avoidance of, 99; budget for future expenses, 111–12; cautions on signing documents, 111; child custody, 117–25, 536; child support and visitation, 127–36, 537–39; children's coping with, 125–26, 536; cost, 103, 105; definition, 99; domestic violence causing, 176; fault-based grounds, 100; finding information on, 535–40, 616–17; grounds for, 100; health insurance after, 111–12; hidden assets, 112; independent legal counsel versus using husband's attorney, 102; marriage and family therapy to avoid, 99; mediation, 101, 104–107, 535; need for information, 98; negotiations for, 101, 117, 127–28; no-fault divorce, 100; organizations, 535–40; parental kidnapping after, 120–22, 125; property division, 107–111; questions to ask lawyer, 104; reading materials, 616–17; Social Security benefits, 114–116; temporary orders, 101; trial, 101; uncontested divorce, 101; welfare after, 116–17

DNR orders, 488

Doctors: advance directives, 488; home health care for elderly, 420, 424, 431; patient-doctor relationship, 399–400; patient's need for nursing home care, 452; pediatricians, 602; professional associations, 602–603. *See also* Medical care

Documents and documentation: to bring to women's shelter, 182; child custody decision, 119; employment discrimination lawsuits, 42, 43; locating important documents after funeral, 505–506; organization of, for end-of-life decisions, 474–75; safe place for vital records, 475; sexual harassment, 23; vital records, 182, 474–75, 505–506

Domestic violence: abusers' blame of partner, 160; abusers' excuses, 160–61; and child abuse, 161–62; and child custody, 119, 120–21, 178; and child sexual abuse, 162; court orders of protection, 169–76; as crime, 162–63; criminal complaint against abuser, 168–69; decision to leave relationship, 177; decision to stay in relationship, 178–79; definition and description, 158–62; and divorce or legal separation, 106, 176; finding information on, 138, 541–42, 617–19; guidelines for helping someone being abused, 162; hotlines, 158, 178, 181, 541–42; impact on children, 161–62; lawsuits against abuser, 176–77; leaving with children, 178; local laws and policies, 164–65; medical treatment for injuries, 166–67; not caused by woman being abused, 160; and older women, 467; organizations, 138, 541–43; photographs of

injuries, 167; plastic surgery for victims, 542; police intervention, 163–66; questions indicating abuse, 159–60; questions on criminal justice procedures, 165, 168; reading materials, 617–19; state coalitions against, 138; statistics, 158; and visitation rights, 125, 172; women's shelters, 52, 62, 138, 162, 164–65, 168, 174, 179–83; worsening of early abuse, 161

Do-not-resuscitate (DNR) orders, 488

Douching, and STDs, 254

Down syndrome, 566

Drop-in centers, 342–43

Drug abuse. *See* Alcohol and drug abuse

Drug-free outpatient programs, 356

DSS. *See* Disabled Student Services (DSS)

Due process in special education, 310

Durable power of attorney, 460, 482–83, 486–87

Dying. *See* Death and dying

EAPs, 355, 418, 438

Early intervention for newborns and toddlers, 301–306, 408

Early retirement incentives, 8, 31–32

ECG, 364, 372

ECHO (Elder Cottage Housing Opportunity) housing, 440–41

Echocardiogram, 364

Ectopic pregnancy, 187, 188, 241–42

Education: for pregnant teens, 94–95. *See also* Colleges and universities; Special education

Education Amendments of 1972, 94–95

Educational neglect, 57–58

EEOC, 21, 24, 25–26, 30, 32, 35, 37–40, 522

EKG, 364, 372

Elder abuse and neglect: Adult Protective Services (APS), 138, 467–69; by caregivers, 427, 466; domestic violence and older women, 467; emotions of elderly caused by, 466–67; and isolation, 427, 469–70; nursing homes, 463; organization, 601; signs, 464–65; types, 464; what to do, 469

Eldercare Locator, 411–12, 414, 603

Elderly. *See* Aging

Electrocardiogram (ECG), 364, 372

ELISA, 387, 389, 391

Embalming, 500, 501

Emergency contraception: consequences or serious side-effects of, 187, 188; consideration of, 91, 146, 186–87; copper-T IUD insertion, 188–89; estrogen-progestin pills, 187; hotline on, 186, 187, 541, 542; progestin-only minipills, 187; after rape, 146; reading materials, 616; Reproductive Health Technologies Project, 187; timing, 187; types, 187–89

Emergency orders of protection, 170–71

Emotional neglect, 58. *See also* Child abuse and neglect

Emotional problems. *See* Counseling and therapy; Mental health care; Mental health crises

Emotions: after abortion, 197; after childbirth, 242–43;

Emotions *cont.*
diagnosis of STDs, 251–52; after firings and layoffs, 15–16; grief and mourning, 507–509; new mothers, 60; parents of gays and lesbians, 83–84; parents' response to child sexual abuse, 48; physically abused children, 58; after sexual harassment, 22; sexually abused children, 54. *See also* Grief and mourning

Employee Assistance Programs (EAPs), 355, 418, 438

Employee Retirement Income Security Act (ERISA), 7, 13

Employment. *See* Firings and layoffs; Job search; Work crises

Employment agencies, 17

Employment Non-Discrimination Act (ENDA), 35

ENCORE, 600

ENDA, 35

Endometriosis, 241

Entombment, 498, 501

Environmental health, 27–28, 521

EPA, 13, 20, 37

Epilepsy, 567

EPSDT program, 312, 408

Equal Employment Opportunity Commission (EEOC), 21, 24, 25–26, 30, 32, 35, 37–40, 522

Equal Pay Act (EPA), 13, 20, 37

Equitable distribution states, 108–109

ERISA, 7, 13

Estate planning, 479–82, 632

Estate taxes, 506

Estrogen-progestin pills, 187

Ethnic groups. *See* Racial and ethnic groups

Eviction, 11

Evidentiary examination after rape, 143–47

Executive Order 11246 on discrimination, 21

Executive Order 11375 on discrimination, 21

Failure to thrive (FTT), 58

Fair Debt Collection Practices Act, 11

Fair Housing Act of 1968, 290–92, 343

Fair Labor Standards Act (FLSA), 13

Fairweather Lodges, 342

Families Anonymous, 358, 583

Family and couples therapy, 99, 326, 328, 540, 587

Family and Medical Leave Act (FMLA), 29, 35, 438

Family finances: budgeting following death of loved one, 506; budgeting following divorce, 111–12; and child support, 127–28, 129; hidden assets, 112; income and child custody, 122; income and child support, 129; information and records on, in divorce cases, 109–11

Family planning clinics, 89, 94, 189, 192, 212, 387–88, 397, 543–44

Family service agencies, 189, 212, 319, 330, 413, 417, 426, 467, 541, 545, 586–87. *See also* Social service agencies

Family Service America, 189, 212, 413, 541, 545, 587

Family support programs, 96

Family violence. *See* Domestic violence

FAS, 353, 567, 582

Fathers: and adoption, 216–17; establishment of paternity, 135–36, 217; organizations, 527; teen fathers, 97; visitation rights, 125, 131–32, 172. *See also* Child support

Fault-based grounds for divorce, 100

FECA, 298

Federal employees, 35, 39, 290, 298, 525

Federal Employees' Compensation Act (FECA), 298

Federal Trade Commission: debt collection, 11; Funeral Rule, 496, 500, 503, 610, 638; work-at-home ad frauds, 17

Felonies, definition, 173, 183

Female condom, for protection from STDs, 253

Fetal abnormality, prenatal diagnosis of, 235–36

Fetal alcohol syndrome (FAS), 353, 567, 582

Finances. *See* Family finances

Firings and layoffs: "at will" employer-employee relationship, 12; disability insurance, 7; early retirement incentives, 8, 31–32; emotional recovery following, 15–16; and finding new job, 14–15, 16–18, 42; health insurance, 5–6; illegal firing, 12–15, 38; legal advice, 4; pensions, 7; reading materials, 610; severance pay, 4–7; unemployment compensation, 8–10; willful misconduct, 9

FLSA, 13

FMLA, 29, 35, 438

Food stamps, 297

Forensic accountants, 112

Foster care, 134, 211, 313, 484–85

Friendly Visitors, 415, 423, 427, 469

FTT, 58

Full Faith and Credit for Child Support Orders Act, 135

Funeral homes and funeral directors: ceremony choices, 498–99; contacting after death of loved one, 495–96;

contract with, 502; direct disposition, 500; disposition options, 498, 500–502; embalming, 500, 501; Federal Trade Commission Rule on, 496, 500, 503, 610, 638; making funeral arrangements, 497–99; problem resolution with, 502–503, 610; transportation of body to, 496

Funerals: alternatives to high cost of, 499–500; definition, 498; for infants, 226–27; instructions for prepared by person ahead of time, 482, 495; paying for, 503–505; planning and arranging, 497–99; purpose, 498; reading materials, 636

GAL, 53
Gang parent law, 80
Gay and Lesbian Parents Coalition International, 539
Gay men, 35–36, 82–97, 534, 616, 632
Genetic abnormalities, prenatal diagnosis of, 235–36
Genetic counseling, 236, 237–38, 549
Genital warts, 253, 258–60, 264
Geriatric care managers, 417, 436, 445, 470, 604
Gift tax, 479
Gift-giving, 479
Gonorrhea, 257–58, 264
Gray Panthers, 604
Green card, and domestic violence, 177
Grief and mourning: and children, 228–29, 514–15, 536, 610–12; at death after prolonged illness, 510; at death of infant, 223–31, 234; definition, 507; differences in, 509–11; at ectopic pregnancy, 242; emotions of, 507–509; of fam-

ily and friends at death of infant, 229–30; finding information on, 536, 549, 610–12, 636–38; of grandparents and caregivers at death of infant, 230–31; guidelines for what helps, 512–14; help for someone who is grieving, 512–14; at miscarriage, 240–41; at multifetal reduction, 238; at murder of loved one, 510; organizations, 536, 549, 610–612; physical symptoms, 509; at prenatal diagnosis of genetic or fetal abnormality, 235; professional help, 515–16; reading materials, 636–38; sibling reactions to infant death, 228–29; at sudden death, 510; at suicide, 510–11; support groups, 231, 234, 511
Griggs v. *Duke Power Co.*, 20
Group homes for juvenile offenders, 79–80
Group therapy, 326
Guardian ad litem (GAL), 53
Guardianship, 484–85

Handicaps. *See* Adults with disabilities; Children with disabilities; Disabilities
Harassment: by creditors, 11; racial harassment, 29–30; sexual harassment, 21–26
Hatch Acts, 36
HCB waivers, 277–78, 426, 445
Head Start, 311
Headache, 567. *See also* Pain control
Health care. *See* Hospitals; Medical care; Mental health care
Health Care Financing Administration (HCFA), 349, 588, 594
Health insurance: abortion, 27, 198; in child support order,

128; counseling for terminally ill, 472–73; counseling programs on, 417, 473; after divorce, 111–12; extension of, after death of partner, 507; HIV testing, 388, 392; HIV/AIDS, 394, 399; home health care, 430; hospital costs following rape, 147; after job loss, 5–6; medical equipment and supply purchases, 421–22; medical rehabilitation, 276; mental health care, 348–49; occupational therapy, 421–22; pregnancy and childbirth, 27; sex discrimination prohibited in, 27; spouses, 27; waiting periods for preexisting conditions, 6. *See also* Medicaid; Medicare
Health Insurance Reform Act, 6, 111–12, 507
Hearing aids, 568
Hearing and speech therapists, 270, 424, 558
Hearing disabilities, 524, 560, 568–70
Heart attacks, 371–75. *See also* Heart disease
Heart disease: angina, 371, 373; angioplasty, 375–76; arrhythmias, 373; aspirin therapy, 375; atherectomy, 377; atherosclerosis, 373–74; bypass surgery, 377; cardiac catheterization, 375–76; cardiac rehabilitation, 378; complications after heart attack, 373; congestive heart failure, 373; coronary artery bypass graft (CABG), 377; coronary artery disease (CAD), 373–74; CPR for heart attacks, 372; depression following, 378; emergency room care of heart attacks, 372–73; heart

Heart disease *cont.*
attacks, 371–75; hormone replacement therapy, 378–80; hospital care, 372–73; laser angioplasty, 377; long-term-treatment options, 375–78; medications for heart attack, 372, 373, 375; myth on women not having heart disease, 374; organizations, 367, 372, 376, 601, 633; reading materials, 633–34; risk factors for atherosclerosis, 374; risk factors for heart attack, 375; statistics, 374; what to do in case of heart attack, 371–73

Hepatitis B, 260–61, 264, 401

Hepatitis B test, 401

Herpes, 243, 248, 252, 253, 261–262, 264, 551

Hidden assets, and divorce, 112

Higher education. *See* Colleges and universities

HIV antibody test, 146, 251, 257, 386–93, 405, 633

HIV infection: accuracy of HIV antibody test, 391–92; AIDS service organizations (ASOs), 395–98; alternative therapies, 399; anonymous testing, 388, 392–93; anonymous testing of newborns, 392–93; children with, 406–408; confidential testing, 388–89, 403; cost of HIV antibody test, 392; counseling before and after HIV antibody test, 389–91; covered under Americans with Disabilities Act, 33; definition, 384–85; diagnosis, 264; discrimination based on, 404; doctor-patient relationship, 399–400; finding information on, 385, 398–99, 595–96, 631–33; and gay, lesbian, and bisexual

teens, 88; home testing kits, 390–91; hotlines, 248, 255, 385, 396, 397, 398, 595–96; living with, 393–94; mandatory HIV testing, 392–93; medical care, 393, 394, 396–402, 404–405; medical tests for monitoring health, 400–402; medication, 396; newsletters and journals, 633; organizations and government agencies, 524, 595–96; partner notification, 252–53; during pregnancy, 251, 405–406; and rape, 146; reading materials, 631–33; reporting, 403; results of HIV antibody test, 391; risk factors, 386–87; safer sex, 402, 405; signs and symptoms of medical problems, 402; telling children about diagnosis, 403–404; telling others about diagnosis, 402–404; telling partner about diagnosis, 402–403; testing for, 146, 251, 257, 386–93, 633; timing of HIV antibody test, 391. *See also* AIDS

HMOs, 276, 430

Holistic medicine, 602

Home adaptation, 281, 291–92, 418–420, 557, 623, 635

Home and community-based (HCB) waivers, 277–78, 426, 445

Home health aides, 423, 424, 427, 635

Home health care: agencies providing, 423–26; certification and accreditation, 432–33; combination of options to tailor plan of service, 426, 428; definition, 422; family service agencies and other social service organizations, 426; geriatric care managers,

417, 436, 445, 470; home health care agencies, 423, 425; hospice care, 422, 491–95, 607–608, 612–13; housekeeping and chore services, 423; Medicaid coverage, 425, 429–30, 432, 445; medical rehabilitation, 274, 277–78; Medicare coverage, 420, 428–29, 432, 435; need for, 423; organizations, 607; Patient's Bill of Rights, 435; paying for, 420, 428–31; personal care, 422–23, 425; private insurance and HMOs, 430; professionals providing, 424; questions for choosing, 433–35; search for, 431–33; services provided, 422–23; veterans' benefits, 431

Home health care agencies, 423, 425

Home pregnancy kits, 189

Home study for adoption, 208–209, 213

Home testing kits for HIV infection, 390–91

Home visiting programs: child abuse prevention, 61–62; elderly, 415–16; Friendly Visitors, 415, 423, 427, 469; home health care, 420, 422–35; homemaker services to new mothers, 243–44; Meals on Wheels, 415–16, 423, 469; mothers and children with HIV/AIDS, 408; pregnant and parenting teens, 96; visiting nurse programs, 96, 243–44, 408, 423, 425, 607

Homeless youth. *See* Runaways

Homemaker services, 243–44, 423, 424

Homosexuals. *See* Bisexuals; Gay men; Lesbians

Hormone replacement therapy (HRT), 370, 378–80

Hospice care, 422, 491–95, 607–608, 612–13

Hospitals: accreditation, 589, 599; advance directives, 345–46; aftercare following discharge, 274; alcohol/drug abuse treatment programs, 356; coronary care unit (CCU), 372; death of infant, 224–26; discharge planning units, 274; general hospitals with psychiatric units/beds, 345; geriatric center, 413; heart attack patients, 372–73; HIV antibody testing, 387, 389; intensive care unit (ICU), 372; medical case management, 275; medical rehabilitation, 273; medical social workers, 270, 275, 298, 319, 329–30; for mental health crises, 344–47; nursing home referrals, 444–45; private psychiatric hospitals, 345; public hospitals, 345; rape exam, 142–48; stroke patients, 362–66; teaching hospitals, 345; Veteran's Administration (VA) hospitals, 345. See also Medical care

Hostile environment harassment, 25

Hotlines: abortion, 190; AIDS/HIV, 248, 255, 385, 396, 397, 398, 595, 596; alcohol and drug abuse, 355, 361, 581–84; child abuse and neglect, 45, 60–61, 319, 528–29; child support, 132; domestic violence, 158, 178, 181, 541–42; elder abuse, 138; emergency contraception, 186, 187, 541; INFO-line (or I&R line), 62; Medicare, 594, 607; parent stress- or information lines, 61; runaways, 65, 67, 68, 534; sexually transmitted diseases (STDs), 247–48, 251–52, 551; spinal cord injury, 577; substance abuse treatment programs, 355, 361, 581–84; suicide, 581; women's shelters, 62

Housekeeping and chore services. See Homemaker services

Housing: accessory apartments for elderly, 441–42; adults with disabilities, 290–93, 623; adults with psychiatric disabilities, 343; assisted living facilities, 446–47, 608; congregate housing, 447; Continuing Care Retirement Communities, 447; ECHO housing, 440–41; elderly, 440–42, 445–49; Life Care Communities, 447; organizations, 555–56; shared housing, 441, 606

HPV, 258–60, 264, 401

HRT, 370, 378–80

Human growth, 570

Human Immunodeficiency Virus. See HIV infection

Human papillomavirus (HPV), 258–60, 264, 401

Huntington's disease, 571

Hysterotomy, 196

I-9 Form, 30

IC. See Interstitial cystitis (IC)

ICU, 372

IDEA, 300, 301, 305, 306–10

Identified adoption, 208

IEE, 307

IEP, 307–309

Illegal firing, 12–15, 38

Illnesses: angina pectoris, 373; breast implants, 625–26; cancer, 380–84, 597–600, 629–34; coronary artery disease, 373–74; government agencies, 590–91; heart attack, 371–73, 371–75; heart disease, 371–80, 601, 633; HIV infection and AIDS, 384–408, 631–33; opportunistic infections, 384–85, 396, 400–402; organizations, 382, 383, 385, 398, 561–80, 592–603; paying for prescription drugs, 408–409; reading materials, 629–34; specific illnesses, 561–80; stroke, 362–71, 601, 633; support for terminally ill and their families, 471–74. See also AIDS; HIV infection; Hospitals; Medical care; Sexually transmitted diseases (STDs)

Immigrants, 177, 522, 525

Immigration Reform and Control Act of 1986 (IRCA), 30, 522

Incentives for early retirement, 8, 31–32

Incest, 44–45, 51–52, 54, 139, 541. See also Child sexual abuse

Incest survivors, 591–92, 615, 628–29

Income. See Family finances

Income taxes. See Taxes

Incomplete miscarriage, 239

Incontinence, 571

Incorrigibles, 72, 81–82

Independent adoption, 212–15

Independent contractors, 9, 19

Independent educational evaluation (IEE), 307

Independent home health aides, 427

Independent living centers: adults with psychiatric disabilities, 343; AIDS service organizations, 282; assistance from, in applying for benefits, 298; assistive devices information from, 421; cost, 282; definition and

Independent living centers *cont.*
description, 279–80; elderly,
413; eligibility criteria, 282;
finding information on, 267,
281–82, 557; services, 280–81,
343
Indian Child Welfare Act, 210–
11
Indians. *See* Native Americans
Individualized Education Pro-
gram (IEP), 307–309
Individualized Family Service
Plan (IFSP), 302, 303–304
Individualized written rehabilitation program (IWRP), 286–
87
Individuals with Disabilities
Education Act (IDEA), 300,
301, 305, 306–10
Induction abortion, 195–96
Inevitable miscarriage, 239
Infant death. *See* Death of in-
fants
Infertility and reproductive
health, 546–47
"Informal" voluntary commit-
ment in psychiatric hospital,
347
Information and referral serv-
ices, 62, 518
Inheritance taxes, 506
Inpatient programs for drug/al-
cohol abuse, 356
Insurance. *See* Disability insur-
ance; Health insurance; Life
insurance; Long-term-care
insurance
Insurance counseling pro-
grams, 417, 473
Intensive care unit (ICU), 372
Inter vivos trust, 479
Interment (burial in ground),
498, 500
Interpersonal therapy, 326
Interstitial cystitis (IC), 571
Intravenous drug use, and
STDs, 255

Involuntary commitment in psy-
chiatric hospital, 346–47
IRCA, 30, 522
Ischemic stroke, 363
ISFP, 302, 303–304
IT. *See* Interpersonal therapy
(IT)
IUD, 188–89, 241
IV drug use. *See* Intravenous
drug use
IWRP, 286–87

Jewish Family and Children's
Services, 61, 62, 93, 96, 180,
413, 426, 467, 586, 603
Job Accommodation Network
(JAN), 289, 290, 523
Job/career counseling, 7, 18
Job crises. *See* Work crises
Job loss. *See* Firings and layoffs
Job search, 14–18, 610
Joint Commission on Accreditation of Healthcare Organizations, 273, 344, 433, 589,
603
Joint custody, 117–18
Juvenile correctional facilities,
79–80
Juvenile court, 77–78, 80
Juvenile delinquency: arrest of
child, 72–82, 616; definition,
72; prevention of, 81; services
for at-risk children, 82
Juvenile Justice and Delinquency Prevention Act, 73
Juvenile justice system: adjudicatory hearing, 77–78; arraignment of juvenile offenders, 77; arrest of child, 72–82,
612; attorney for juvenile offenders, 73–74, 80; and children tried as adults, 80; correctional facilities, 79–80;
detention hearing, 77; disposition (sentencing), 78–79; diversion programs, 74–75; formal probation, 79; guidelines

for parents, 80–82; juvenile
court, 77–78; juvenile court
intake interview, 75–76; legal
protections for juvenile offenders, 73; options for placement of incorrigible children, 81–82; organization,
528; parental responsibility
for children's actions, 80; and
parents, 72–77, 80–81; parents' response to child's arrest, 72–73; plea bargaining,
78; police contact of parent
after child's arrest, 72; police
station, 75; prevention of juvenile delinquency, 81; probable cause hearing, 77; release of juvenile offender
to parents or guardians, 77;
services for at-risk children,
82

Kidnapping, 67, 120–22, 125
Kidney disease, 572
Kinship foster care, 484

Landlords, eviction by, 11
Laser angioplasty, 377
Latinas, 370, 593
Law clinics, 11
Law enforcement: abduction of
children, 67; child sexual
abuse, 50, 51, 52–53; court orders of protection, 176; death
scene investigation of infant
death, 233–34; domestic violence, 163–66; information
on laws on violence against
women, 138; juvenile justice
system, 72–82; rape reporting, 140, 142–43, 148–52; runaways, 66–69. *See also* Criminal justice system; Juvenile
justice system
Law schools, low-cost legal assistance from, 11
Lawsuits. *See* Legal action

Lawyers. *See* Attorneys; and headings beginning with Legal

Layoffs. *See* Firings and layoffs

Learning disabilities, 33, 572

Legal action: child sexual abuse, 52–53; EEOC process for filing charges and complaints, 37–40; lawsuits against domestic violence perpetrators, 176–77; lawsuits against rapists, 154–55; mediation of workplace discrimination, 42; pros and cons of, for workplace discrimination, 41–43; tort law, 40; workplace discrimination, 37–43. *See also* Trials

Legal aid organizations. *See* Legal assistance

Legal assistance: adults with disabilities, 298; adults with psychiatric disabilities, 343; court orders for protection, 175; divorce cases, 103; elderly, 416–17, 485, 486, 487; low-cost options, 11, 535; professional organizations, 608. *See also* Attorneys

Legal custody, 117, 136

Lesbians: child custody, 124–25, 535–36; court orders of protection for lesbian relationships, 174; discrimination against, 35–36; misinformation on, 84–85; organizations, 124, 525, 533–36, 555; parents' reactions, 82–88; reading materials, 615–16; religious organizations, 533–34; teenagers as, 88–97, 615–16; visitation and lesbian mothers, 124; and women's shelters, 181

Letter of instruction, 480–82, 495

Leukemia, 472, 595

Leukodystrophy, 573

Libraries, 382–83, 398, 557

Licensed practical nurses (LPNs), 424

Licensing of adoption agencies, 212

Life insurance: accelerated life insurance benefits payments to terminally ill, 473; and alimony, 113; and child support, 130; filing claims after death of loved one, 506; viatical settlements, 473

Life-threatening illnesses. *See* Illnesses; and specific illnesses

Lithium, 585

Liver disease, 573

Living wills, 486

Long-term care for elderly *See* Nursing homes

Long-term-care insurance, 455, 473

Long-Term-Care Ombudsman, 413, 443–44

LPNs, 424

Lung/respiratory disease, 573

Lupus, 573

Lymphedema, 596

MAD DADS, Inc., 527

MADD, 511, 611

Magnetic resonance angiography (MRA), 365

Magnetic resonance imaging (MRI), 364

Marfan syndrome, 574

Marijuana, 357, 583. *See also* Alcohol and drug abuse

Marital property, 107, 109

Marital rape, 141, 169

Marital therapy, 99, 326, 328, 540, 589–90

Marriage. *See* Divorce; and headings beginning with Marital

Marrow donor program, 599

Material Safety Data Sheet (MSDS), 27–28

Maternity leave, 26–27, 28, 29

Meals on Wheels, 415–16, 423, 469

Mediation: abuse or violence in relationship, 106; cost, 105; disadvantages of, for divorce, 105–106; for divorce, 101, 104–107, 534–35; finding mediator, 106–107; organizations, 534–35; questions to ask for finding mediator, 107; workplace discrimination, 42

Medic Alert Foundation, 592

Medicaid: abortion coverage, 190, 198, 406; adoption process, 208; application, 116; child support enforcement, 133–34; complaints, 588, 594; elderly in-home and community services, 418; EPSDT program, 312, 408; HIV/AIDS, 397, 408; home health care, 425, 429–30, 432, 445; hospice care, 492–93; medical rehabilitation, 275, 277–78; mental health services, 330, 349; nursing homes, 450, 451–54, 460; rape exam, 147; SSI, 296; substance abuse treatment, 360; transportation to medical appointments through cab vouchers, 416

Medi-Cal. *See* Medicaid

Medical advance directives, 345–46, 347, 460, 485–88

Medical care: advance directives, 345–46, 347, 460, 485–88, 605–606; cancer, 384, 625–27; children with HIV infection, 407–408; doctor-patient relationship, 399–400, 626; domestic violence, 166–67; do-not-resuscitate (DNR) orders, 488; durable power of

Medical care *cont.*
attorney for decisions on, 486–87; EPSDT program, 312, 408; government agencies, 590–91; heart disease, 372–73, 375–78, 630–31; HIV/AIDS, 393, 394, 396–402, 404–405; holistic medicine, 602; home health care, 420, 422–35; Oriental medicine, 602; pain control for dying, 488–90; prenatal care, 93–94; professional associations, 598–99; rape exam, 142–48; stroke, 364–66, 630; for terminally ill, 485–90. *See also* Hospitals; Illnesses; Medications; and specific illnesses

Medical case management, 275
Medical child support, 128–29
Medical equipment, purchase of, 421–22
Medical examination: before seeking psychotherapy, 335; before taking psychotropic medication, 338–39; child sexual abuse, 50; pregnancy determination, 189; pregnant teens, 90
Medical leave, 29
Medical neglect, 57
Medical rehabilitation: acute care settings, 273; appropriateness and effectiveness, 268–69; assistance on return home following, 278–79; attorney's role in finding services, 275; case manager, 275; comprehensive rehabilitation facilities, 273; comprehensive rehabilitation outpatient facilities (CORFs), 274, 276; definition, 267–68; finding services, 274–76; home health care, 274; inpatient rehabilitation programs, 273;

medical social workers, 270, 275, 329–30; Medicare coverage, 276–77; outpatient services, 273–74; paying for, 276–78; private insurance and HMOs, 276; professionals and services provided, 269–72; settings for delivery of, 272–74; skilled nursing facilities, 274, 277; stroke survivors, 369–70; timing for beginning of, 268; workers' compensation coverage, 275, 278, 299

Medical rights, 148, 435
Medical schools, body donation to, 501–502
Medical social workers, 270, 275, 298, 319, 329–30, 424
Medicare: complaints, 584, 594; discharge planning, 274; home health care, 420, 425, 428–29, 432, 435; hospice care, 492–93; hospital costs following rape, 147; hotline, 594, 607; medical equipment and supply purchases, 421–22; medical rehabilitation, 276–77; mental health care, 330, 349; nursing homes, 450–51; occupational therapy, 421–22; Patient's Bill of Rights, 435; SSDI, 295

Medications: anticoagulants (blood thinner), 365–66; antidepressants, 368, 490; "brown bag test" for, 340–41; chemical restraints in nursing homes, 458–60, 631; heart attack, 372, 373, 375; heart disease, 375; HIV/AIDS, 396, 409; mail-order prescription or buyers clubs, 409; older women, 340–41; pain control for dying, 488–90; paying for, 408–409; psychotropic medica-

tions for psychiatric disorders, 337–41; stroke, 362, 365–66; thrombolytics (clotbusters), 362, 365, 372

Memorial services, 498
Memorial societies, 495–96, 499
Menopause, HRT for, 378–80
Mental health association, 321–22

Mental health care: case management services, 341; circumstances warranting, 324; clinical mental health counselors, 328; clinical psychologists, 327; clinical social workers, 327; in clinics, 330–33; clubhouses, 342; community mental health centers (CMHC), 330; confidentiality, 336–37; consumer/survivor movement, 323, 335–36, 347, 581–83; costs, 326; discrimination against adults with psychiatric disabilities, 343; drop-in centers, 342–43; Fairweather Lodges, 342; family services agencies, 330; finding and choosing therapist, 328–29, 333–37; finding information on, 321–23, 361, 523–25, 578–88; after firings and layoffs, 15–16; government agencies, 587–88; grief and mourning, 515–16; hospitalization, 344–47; housing options for adults with psychiatric disabilities, 343; income for adults with psychiatric disabilities, 343; information centers, 321–23; involuntary commitment in psychiatric hospital, 346–47; legal assistance for adults psychiatric disabilities, 343; marriage and family therapists or counselors, 328; medication, 337–41; mental health professionals, 327–29; older women and medications, 340–41; organizations, 321–23, 361, 581–91; outpatient settings, 329–37; partial hospitalization (day treatment), 344; pastoral counselors, 328; paying for, 347–49; professional associations, 589–91; psychiatric nurses, 328, 348; psychiatrists, 327, 347–48; psychosocial rehabilitation, 341–42; psychotherapy, 324–29; questions on psychotropic medications, 339–40; questions to ask therapist, 335; reluctance concerning, 324–25; rights of mental health consumers, 335–37, 347; rural areas, 588; sexual misconduct of therapist, 336; support groups, 332; vocational rehabilitation, 342; voluntary commitment in psychiatric hospital, 347. *See also* Counseling and therapy; Mental health crises

Mental health centers/clinics, 319, 320–21, 330–33

Mental health crises: alcohol and drug abuse, 349–61, 581–84, 627; biographies, 627; clubhouses, 342; covered under Americans with Disabilities Act, 33; crisis intervention, 318–21; drop-in centers, 342–43; Fairweather Lodges, 342; finding and choosing therapist, 328–29, 333–37; finding information on, 321–23, 361, 523–25, 581–92; government agencies, 587–88; hospitalization for, 344–47; involuntary commitment in psychiatric hospital, 346–47; and medication, 337–41; mental health professionals

for, 327–29; organizations, 321–23, 361, 581–91; outpatient settings for treatment, 329–37; paying for mental health care, 347–49; psychosocial rehabilitation, 341–42; psychotherapy for, 324–29; reading materials, 627–29; suicide prevention, 314–18, 624; and vocational rehabilitation, 342; voluntary commitment in psychiatric hospital, 347

Mental illness. *See* Mental health care; Mental health crises

Mental retardation, 574

MEPA, 210, 211

Merit system, 20

Metastasis, 381

Methadone programs, 356, 584

Methotrexate and misoprostol, for abortion, 201

MG, 575

Mifepristone, 200

Minipills, 187

Minor in need of supervision (MINS), 81–82

Minority groups. *See* Racial and ethnic groups

Minors: and abortion, 190–91, 198–99; inheritance, 480; minor in need of supervision (MINS), 81–82; and placement of child for adoption, 216; and rape, 148; and sexually transmitted diseases (STDs), 250. *See also* Children in crisis; Teenagers

MINS, 81–82

Miranda attorneys, 73–74

Miscarriage, 239–41

Misconduct, firing for, 9

Misdemeanors, definition, 172, 183

Misoprostol and methotrexate, for abortion, 201

Missed miscarriage, 239

Missing children. *See* Abduction of children; Runaways

Mitigation of damages, 15, 42

"Morning after pill". *See* Emergency contraception

Mothers. *See* Lesbians; Parents; Pregnancy; Unmarried mothers; and headings beginning with Child and Children

Mothers Against Drunk Driving (MADD), 511, 611

Mourning. *See* Grief and mourning

MRA, 365

MRI, 364

MS, 574

MSDS, 27–28

Multiethnic Placement Act (MEPA), 210, 211

Multifetal pregnancy reduction (selective reduction), 237–38

Multiple sclerosis (MS), 574

Multiservice family agencies, 202, 207, 208

Murder victims and families, 479, 511, 610–12

Muscular dystrophy, 574

Mutual consent registries, 218

Myasthenia gravis (MG), 575

NAMI, 322, 323, 585

Narcotics Anonymous, 357, 583

NARIC, 267, 290, 420, 559

National Alliance for the Mentally Ill (NAMI), 322, 323, 585

National Center for Missing and Exploited Children (NCMEC), 67, 68, 120, 532

National Child Search Assistance Act, 66

National Court Appointed Special Advocates Association, 53, 530

National Information Center for Children and Youth with Disabilities (NICHCY), 301–

National Information Center for Children and Youth with Disabilities (NICHCY) *cont.* 302, 309, 310, 311, 480, 554, 624, 628

National Labor Relations Act (NLRA), 14

National Rehabilitation Information Center (NARIC), 267, 290, 420, 559

Native Americans, 210–11, 370, 596

NCMEC, 67, 68, 120, 531–32

Neglect of children. *See* Child abuse and neglect

Neonatal death. *See* Death of infants; Newborns

Newborns: death of, 231, 548; early intervention for newborns with disabilities, 301–306, 408; HIV testing, 392–93. *See also* Death of infants

NICHCY, 301–302, 309, 310, 311, 480, 553, 624, 628

Nicotine Anonymous, 357, 584

NLRA, 14

No-fault divorce, 100

Nonorganic failure to thrive (FTT), 58

Notice for production of documents, in divorce cases, 112

Nurses: home health care, 420, 422–35; licensed practical nurses (LPNs), 424; professional associations, 328, 589, 602–603; psychiatric nurses, 328, 348, 589; registered nurse and home health care, 424; rehabilitation nurses, 270; visiting nurse programs, 96, 243–44, 408, 423, 425, 607

Nursing Home Reform Act, 461

Nursing homes: abuse and neglect in, 463; advance directives, 460; assessment of need for care, 452; bed-hold policies, transfers and dis-

charges, 459; chemical and physical restraints in, 458–60, 635; consumer/advocacy organizations, 442–43; contract, 461; cost, 450; discrimination against Medicaid recipients, 452–54; financial issues and services, 460–61; finding information on, 442–45, 608–609, 635; geriatric care managers' recommendations, 445; hospital referrals to, 444–45; legal advice, 454–55; long-term-care insurance, 455, 473; Long-Term-Care Ombudsman, 413, 443–44; Medicaid coverage, 450, 451–54, 460; medical rehabilitation, 274, 277; Medicare coverage, 450–51; organizations, 608–609; paying for, 450–52, 455; planning ahead, 449–55; problem resolution, 462–64; questions to ask over the telephone, 456–57; reading materials, 635–36; residents' participation in care plan, 461–62; search for, 455–58; standard surveys (inspection reports), 458; support and advocacy groups' referrals to, 444; touring facilities, 457–58; transition to, 449–50; veterans' benefits, 452

O&M instructors, 271–72

OAA, 413, 418, 425–46, 443

OBRA, 128, 461

Obsessive compulsive disorders, 585

Occupational Safety and Health Act (OSHA), 14

Occupational therapists, 269–70, 420, 422, 424, 558

Older Americans Act (OAA), 413, 418, 425–46, 443

Older women. *See* Aging

Older Workers Benefit Protection Act (OWBPA), 8

Ombudsman for long-term care, 413, 443–44

Omnibus Budget Reconciliation Act of 1993 (OBRA), 128, 461

Open adoptions, 204–206

Opportunistic infections, 384–85, 396, 400–402

Options counseling, 189

Options House, 65

Organ donation, 498, 502

Oriental medicine, 602

Orientation and mobility (O&M) instructors, 271–72

OSHA, 14

Osteoporosis, 379, 575

Ostomy, 600

Outpatient mental health settings, 329–37

Outpatient programs for alcohol/drug abuse, 356

Outplacement services in severance package, 7

OWBPA, 8

P&As, 293–94, 298, 301, 345, 346, 347, 555

PAIMI, 347

Pain control, 488–90, 575. *See also* Headache

PAIR, 293, 347

Panic disorder, 588

Pap smear, 260, 264, 401

Parent education and support groups, 61, 96, 301, 306, 313, 534

Parent Training and Information Centers (PTI), 301, 306, 313

Parenting leave, 28, 29

Parents: abortion consent for minors, 198–99; adults with disabilities as, 626; alcohol and drug abuse by, and child abuse, 59–60, 353; child abuse or neglect report made against, 63–65; child custody, 117–25; counseling and therapy, 54, 62; of gay, lesbian, and bisexual teens, 82–88, 533, 538; HIV/AIDS information, 632–33; home visiting programs, 61–62, 243–44; incorrigible children, 81–82; investigation of child abuse and neglect, 63–65; as legally responsible for children's actions, 80; new mothers, 60; organizations, 533, 538–39; prevention of child abuse and neglect, 59–63; respite services, 62; runaway children, 65–71; sexually abused children, 48–54; stepfamilies, 539; support and services, 60–63; teen parents, 91–97; and teenage pregnancy, 88–97; termination of parental rights, 64. *See also* Adoption; Childbirth; Children in crisis; Children with disabilities; Death of infants; Divorce; Pregnancy

Parents Anonymous, 45, 61, 530

Parents, Families and Friends of Lesbians and Gays (PFLAG), 82, 88, 531

Parents Without Partners, 539

Parkinson's disease, 449, 575–76

Partial custody, 125

Partial hospitalization (day treatment), 344

Part-time employment, 17

PASS program, 297

Pastoral counselors, 328

Paternity establishment, 135–36, 217. *See also* Fathers

Patient Self-Determination Act, 487

PCP, 384, 396

PDA, 26–29

PDQ database, 382

Pediatricians, 602

Pelvic examination, after rape, 145

Pelvic inflammatory disease (PID), 188, 241, 258, 264

Pensions, 7, 109, 540

Percutaneous transluminal coronary angioplasty (PTCA), 376

Permanent orders of protection, 171

PERS, 415

Personal care, 422–23, 425

Personal care attendants, 281, 427, 625–26

Personal emergency response system (PERS), 415

Physiatrists, 272

Physical abuse. *See* Child abuse and neglect; Elder abuse and neglect

Physical custody, 117

Physical medicine and rehabilitation (PM&R), 268, 272, 557. *See also* Medical rehabilitation

Physical neglect, 57

Physical restraints in nursing homes, 458–60, 635

Physical therapists, 269, 424

Physician Data Query (PDQ) database, 382

Physicians. *See* Doctors; Medical care

PID, 188, 241, 258, 264

Piercing of body, 255

PIH, 94

Planned Parenthood, 89, 94, 189, 192, 212, 397, 544

Plastic surgery, 542, 576

Play therapy, 326

Plea bargaining for juvenile offenders, 78

PM&R, 268, 272, 557

Pneumocystis carinii pneumonia (PCP), 384, 396

Police. *See* Law enforcement

Polygraphs, 14

Postpartum care services, 243–44

Postpartum depression, 243–44, 245, 247, 323, 547–48, 621

Postpartum disorders, 60, 244–48, 547–48, 621

Postpartum psychosis, 246

Preeclampsia, 94

Preexisting conditions, 6

Pregnancy: adults with disabilities, 626; alcohol/drug use during, 352–54, 358–59; bona fide occupational qualification (BFOQ), 28; cigarette smoking during, 352–354; community resources for pregnant or parenting teens, 96; crisis pregnancy centers, 89–90, 189–90; diagnosis of genetic or fetal abnormality during, 235–36; discrimination due to, 26–29; early pregnancy detection for teens, 89–90; education for pregnant teens, 94–95; fetal alcohol syndrome (FAS), 353, 567, 582; and genital warts, 260; health insurance coverage, 27; and herpes, 262; and HIV antibody test, 405; and HIV infection, 405–406; home pregnancy kits, 189; loss of child during, 222–42; medical exam to determine, 189; not covered under Americans with Disabilities Act, 33; options counseling, 189; prenatal care for teens, 93–94; problem pregnancy centers, 89–90; signs of early pregnancy, 89, 189; stages, 189; teen fathers, 97; teenage pregnancy, 88–97, 616; teens' decision about, 90–91; timing of conception, 189; and toxic

Pregnancy *cont.*
substances in workplace, 27; unexpected pregnancy, 189–90. *See also* Abortion; Adoption; Childbirth; Contraception

Pregnancy counseling, 189

Pregnancy Discrimination Act (PDA), 26–29

Pregnancy-induced hypertension (PIH), 94

Pregnancy loss: diagnosis of genetic or fetal abnormality, 235–36; ectopic pregnancy, 187, 188, 241–42; miscarriage, 239–41; multifetal pregnancy reduction (selective reduction), 237–38, 549; organizations, 547–50; reading materials, 620–22

Prenatal care for teens, 94–95

Prescription drugs. *See* Medications

Private adoption agencies, 207–208

Private psychiatric hospitals, 345

Probable cause hearing for juvenile offenders, 77

Probate of wills, 478–80

Probation for juvenile offenders, 79

Problem pregnancy centers, 89–90

Progestin-only minipills, 187

Property agreement in divorce, 101

Property division: in divorce, 107–111; in wills, 475–79

Protection and Advocacy for Individual Rights (PAIR), 293, 347

Protection and Advocacy for Individuals with Mental Illness (PAIMI), 347

Protection and advocacy organi-

zations (P&As), 293–94, 298, 301, 345, 346, 347, 556

Protection orders, 169–76

Psychiatric crisis intervention, 319–21

Psychiatric disabilities. *See* Mental health crises

Psychiatric hospitals, 345

Psychiatric nurses, 328, 348

Psychiatrists, 327, 347–48, 589, 590

Psychodynamic psychotherapy, 325

Psychological abuse of children. *See* Child abuse and neglect

Psychological problems. *See* Counseling and therapy; Mental health care; Mental health crises

Psychologists: clinical psychologists, 327, 348; fees, 348; professional associations, 327, 587, 589–91; rehabilitation psychologists, 270–71

Psychosocial rehabilitation, 341–42

Psychotherapy. *See* Counseling and therapy

Psychotropic drugs, 337–41

PTCA, 376

Public adoption agencies, 207–208

Public employees, 35, 36, 39, 290, 298, 525

QMB, 295

QMCSO, 128–29

Qualified medical child support orders (QMCSO), 128–29

Qualified Medicare Beneficiaries (QMB), 295

Quid pro quo harassment, 25

Racial and ethnic groups: adoption, 210–11; AIDS prevention, 595; breast cancer, 597;

health organizations, 593–94; mental health issues, 586; professional associations, 327, 589; stroke, 370; substance abuse prevention, 581–84

Racial harassment, 29–30

Radiology, 602

Rape: civil action against rapist, 154; cost for hospital visit following, 147–48; counseling following, 147; criminal justice system procedures, 149–50, 153–54; definition and description of, 139–141; evidentiary examination, 143–47; finding information on, 138, 139, 154, 542, 619; guidelines for helping rape survivors, 157; guidelines on what to do and what not to do following, 140; lawsuits concerning, 154–55; legal definition, 141; location of, 157; medical attention following, 142–48; medical rights following, 148; of minor, 148; myths, 141; organizations, 139, 154, 542; photographs of injuries, 144; reactions to, 155–58; reading materials, 619; reporting to law enforcement, 140, 142–43, 148–52; spousal rape, 141, 169; workplace rapes, 40–41

Rape crisis centers, 41, 54, 137–39, 156–58, 319

Rape shield laws, 153–54

Reconciling Congregation Program, 534

Recovery groups, 357–58, 582–84. *See also* Alcohol and drug abuse

Registered nurses, and home health care, 424

Registered Respiratory Therapists (RRT), 270

Rehabilitation: cardiac rehabilitation, 378; elderly, 424; medical rehabilitation, 267–79, 369–70; professional association, 558–59, 587; psychosocial rehabilitation, 341–42; stroke survivors, 369–70; vocational rehabilitation, 283–88

Rehabilitation Act of 1973, 32, 282, 288–89, 310–11, 343

Rehabilitation nurses, 270

Rehabilitation psychologists, 270–71

Rehabilitative alimony, 113

Relative adoption, 206

Reproductive medicine, 546

Reproductive rights, 543–44. *See also* Abortion

Residential schools for children with disabilities, 306

Residential therapeutic communities (TCs), 356–57

Resignation from job, and unemployment compensation, 9–10

Respiratory disease, 573

Respiratory therapists, 270

Respite care services: child abuse prevention, 62; children with disabilities, 312–13; elderly, 417–18; organization on, 62, 313, 529, 552; persons with HIV infection/AIDS, 408

Restraining order. *See* Court orders of protection

Restraints in nursing homes, 458–60, 635

Retirement, 8, 31–32

Reunion registries, and adoption, 218

Revised Uniform Reciprocal Enforcement of Support Act (RURESA), 134

Revocable living trusts, 479–80

Right to die movement, 485, 609

Roe v. *Wade,* 191

RRT, 270

RU-486, 200

Rubinstein-Taybi syndrome, 576

Runaways: counseling or therapy, 71; first time for running away, 66–67; flyers for locating, 68–69; guidelines for parents, 66–69; hotlines, 65, 67, 68, 534; information/helplines, 531–33; organizations, 534; pattern of running away, 67–69; phone calls to parents, 67, 69–70; reasons for running away, 70–71; returning home, 71; shelters, 68–69, 71

Rural areas: mental health care, 588; special education, 551

RURESA, 134–35

Safer sex, 255–56, 402, 405

Safety: environmental health, 521; fire protection association, 606; home safety for elderly, 418–20, 635; toxic substances, 27–28; women's shelters, 182–83; workplace safety, 14, 27–28, 521

SBS, 56

Schizophrenia, 588

Scleroderma, 576

Section 504, Rehabilitation Act, 310–11

Selective reduction (multifetal pregnancy reduction), 237–38

Self-employed, unemployment compensation for, 9

Self-help clearinghouses, 517–18

Self-petition for legal permanent residency (green card), 177

Self-proving wills, 477

Senior centers, 414

Seniority system, 20, 31

Separate property, 108

Separation, 99, 176

Separation agreement in divorce, 101, 117, 127–28

Service of process, 170

Settlement agreement in divorce, 101

Severance pay, 4–7

Sex discrimination. *See* Discrimination

Sexual abuse of children. *See* Child sexual abuse

Sexual assault. *See* Rape

Sexual harassment: company's grievance procedure, 23–24; definition, 21; fears about reporting, 24; hostile environment harassment, 25; identification, 21–22; law, 25–26; lawsuit against employer, 25; policy, 24; quid pro quo harassment, 25; reading materials, 611; steps to combat, 23–24

Sexual misconduct of therapist, 336

Sexual orientation: causes, 85; definition, 84; discrimination due to, 35–36; gay, lesbian, or bisexual teens, 88–97, 533–34, 615–16; guidelines for parents, 82–88; misinformation on, 84–85. *See also* Bisexuals; Gay men; Lesbians

Sexuality: adults with disabilities, 624, 625, 626–27; discussion of safer sex, 255–56; practicing safer sex for those with HIV/AIDS, 402, 405

Sexually transmitted diseases (STDs): chlamydia, 257, 264; consequences, 250, 252; description, 257–64; diagnosis, 264; discussion of safer sex with partner, 255–56; emotions following diagnosis, 251–52; genital warts, 253, 258–60, 264; gonorrhea,

Sexually transmitted diseases (STDs) *cont.*
257–58, 264; hepatitis B, 260–61, 264; herpes, 243, 252, 253, 261–262, 264, 550; hotlines, 248, 251–52, 551; HPV (human papillomavirus), 258–60, 264, 401; and intravenous drug use, 255; organizations, 550; partner notification, 252–53; pelvic inflammatory disease (PID), 188, 258, 264; during pregnancy, 250–51; protection from and prevention, 253–57; and rape, 145–46; reading materials, 622; reporting of, to health department, 253; risk factors, 248–49; statistics, 249; symptoms, 249–50, 254; syphilis, 263–64; and teenagers, 94; testing, 145–46, 250, 256–57; treatment, 250, 264. *See also* AIDS; HIV infection
Shaken baby syndrome (SBS), 56
Shared housing, 441, 606
Sickle cell anemia, 370, 577
SIDS, 232–35, 353, 548–51
Silicone implants. *See* Breast implants
Situational crisis intervention, 318–19
Skilled nursing facilities. *See* Nursing homes
SLMB, 295
Smoking. *See* Cigarette smoking
Social Security Administration, 7, 115, 294, 504, 506, 559, 638
Social Security benefits, 114–16, 504
Social Security disability insurance (SSDI), 6, 7, 294–95, 343, 408
Social service agencies, 202–

203, 207, 208, 329. *See also* Family service agencies
Social Service Block Grants, 418, 426
Social workers: alcohol and drug abuse treatment programs, 355; clinical social workers, 327; fees, 348; financial help for terminally ill, 473; medical social workers, 270, 275, 298, 319, 329–30, 424; professional association, 327, 588
Sole custody, 117
Spanking, 59
Special education, 267, 306–11, 551, 559
Special needs trust, 480
Specified Low-Income Medicare Beneficiaries (SLMB), 295
Speech and hearing therapists, 270, 424, 558
Spermicides, for protection from STDs, 254
Spina bifida, 577
Spinal cord injury, 577
Split custody, 118
Spontaneous abortions, 239
Spousal abuse. *See* Domestic violence
Spousal rape, 141, 169
SSDI, 6, 7, 294–95, 343, 408
SSI, 295–97, 343, 408
Stalking, 183–85
Standby guardianships, 484
Status offenders, 72, 73
STDs. *See* Sexually transmitted diseases (STDs)
Stepfamilies, 539
Stillbirth, 231
Straight Spouse Support Network, 540
Stroke: causes, 363–64; complications, 368–69; consequences for survivor, 366–68; definition, 363; depression

following, 367–68; early warning signs, 363; emergency room treatment, 362–63; hemorrhagic stroke, 363–64; and hormone replacement therapy, 370; hospital care for, 362–66; ischemic stroke or cerebral infarction, 363; and living will, 486; medications, 362, 365–66; organizations, 601; reading materials, 630; rehabilitation for stroke survivors, 369–70; risk factors, 370–71; surgery following, 366; tests following, 364–65; thrombolytics (clot-busters), 362, 365; transient ischemic attacks (TIAs), 364, 375; treatment, 364–66; warning signs, 363; what to do, 362–63
Subpoenas, in divorce cases, 112
Substance abuse. *See* Alcohol and drug abuse
Substituted judgment standard, 347
Sudden infant death syndrome (SIDS), 232–35, 353, 548, 549, 550, 551
Suicide: cluster suicides, 316; grief of family members and friends following, 510–11; guidelines for helping at-risk persons, 316–17; hotlines, 581; organization, 511, 609; prevention, 314–18; reading materials, 628; risk factors, 314–16, 318; and teenagers, 316; warning signs, 316
Supplemental security income (SSI), 295–97, 343, 408
Support groups: addictions/recovery groups, 357–58, 579–81; adults with disabilities, 266; bereavement support groups, 231, 234, 511; caregivers, 438–49, 472;

death of infants, 231, 234; description, 332; elderly, 413; finding, 332–33; gay, lesbian, and bisexual teens, 87–88, 333; parents, 61, 71, 96; stroke survivors, 368; teen parents, 96; terminally ill and their families, 471–72; work crises, 15–16, 42

Surgery: angioplasty, 375–77; atherectomy, 377; bypass surgery, 377; choice of cardiac surgeons, 377–78; coronary artery bypass graft (CABG), 377–78; plastic surgery, 541, 576; after stroke, 366

Syphilis, 263–64, 400

TASH, 565

Tattooing, 255

Taxes: alimony, 114; child support, 129; dependency tax deduction, 129; and divorce, 109; estate taxes, 506; gift taxes, 479; inheritance taxes, 506; unemployment benefits, 10

Tay-Sachs and allied diseases, 578

TB skin test, 401

TCs, 356–57

TDD, 290, 421

Teaching hospitals, 345

Teenagers: and abortion, 190–91, 198–99; arrest of, 72–82, 612; community resources for pregnant or parenting teens, 96; with disabilities, 624–25; education for pregnant teens, 94–95; as fathers, 97; finding information on, 587; gay, lesbian, or bisexual teens, 82–88, 533–34, 611–12; as parents, 91–93, 96; pregnant teens, 88–97, 612; prenatal care for pregnant teens, 94–95; runaways, 65–71; and

sexually transmitted diseases, 94; suicide risk factors, 316. See also Minors

Telecommunication devices for the deaf (TDD), 290, 421

Telephone directory, 267, 518

Telephone reassurance, 415

Temporary custody orders, 120, 122–23, 171–72

Temporary orders in divorce, 101

Temporary orders of protection, 170–71

Tenants' rights, 11

Tender years doctrine, 119

Terminal illness. See Death and dying

Terminations. See Firings and layoffs

Therapeutic communities (TCs), 356–57

Therapy. See Counseling and therapy

Threatened miscarriage, 239

Thrombolytics (clotbusters), 362, 365, 372

Through the Looking Glass, 119, 345, 536, 560, 583

TIAs, 364, 375

Ticlid, 366

Ticlopidine, 366

Tissue plasminogen activator (t-PA), 372

Title IX of Education Amendments of 1972, 94–95

Title VII of Civil Rights Act of 1964, 13, 18–20

Tourette syndrome (TS), 578

Toxic substances in workplace, 27–28, 521

Toxoplasmosis, 401

T-PA (tissue plasminogen activator), 372

"Traditional" (conditional) voluntary commitment in psychiatric hospital, 347

Traditional (or confidential) adoptions, 203, 204

Transient ischemic attacks (TIAs), 364, 375

Transportation: accessibility of air carriers, 290; of body to funeral home, 496; for elderly, 416; relatives' transportation following death in family, 496–97

Traumatic stress, 585

Trials: criminal versus civil trials, 149–50; divorce, 101; rape trials, 149–50, 153–54. See also Legal action

Tripod, 570

Trusts, 479–80, 481

TS, 578

Tuberculosis, 396, 400–401

Tuberculosis skin test, 401

Tuberous sclerosis, 578

Twelve-step programs, 357–58, 581–84

Twins, 547–48

UIFSA, 135

Ulcerative colitis, 564

Ultrasound techniques, after stroke, 364

Uncontested divorce, 101

Undocumented workers, 24, 164–65, 177

Unemployment. See Firings and layoffs

Unemployment comp., 8–10

Uniform Anatomical Gift Act, 502

Uniform Interstate Family Support Act (UIFSA), 134–35

Uniform Reciprocal Enforcement of Support Act (URESA), 134

Uniform Transfer to Minors Act, 480

United Way, 61, 62, 96, 189, 266, 413, 431

Universities. See Colleges and universities

Unmarried mothers: child support, 135–36; custody order, 123, 136

Unstable angina, 373

URESA, 134–35

VA hospitals, 345

Valium, 354

VAWA, 143, 154, 163, 175, 176, 185

Veterans: assistance in filing for benefits, 298; burial and funeral expenses, 504; home adaptation for veterans with disabilities, 281; home health care, 431; nursing homes, 452; organizations, 298, 561; survivors' benefits, 506; VA hospitals, 345

Viatical settlements, 473

Victim compensation programs, 147, 278, 503

Victim/witness assistance programs, 138, 154, 168

Violence against women. *See* Domestic violence; Rape; Stalking

Violence Against Women Act (VAWA), 143, 154, 163, 175, 176, 185

Vision: organizations, 578–80

Visitation rights, 124, 125, 131–32, 172, 536. *See also* Child custody

Visiting Nurse Association (VNA), 96, 243–44, 408, 423, 425, 548, 607

Visual disabilities, 421, 523, 557, 578–80

Vital records. *See* Documents and documentation

Vocational rehabilitation: for adults with psychiatric disabilities, 342; Client Assistance Programs (CAPs), 283–84, 287, 288; cost, 287; definition, 283; eligibility criteria, 285–86; eligibility decisions, 286; evaluation period,

286; finding vocational rehabilitation agencies, 283–84; individualized written rehabilitation program (IWRP), 286–87; length of time needed, 287; review procedures for denials and complaints, 288; services of vocational rehabilitation agencies, 284–85; SSDI/SSI beneficiaries, 285–86

Vocational rehabilitation agencies (state), 278, 283–86. *See also* Vocational rehabilitation

Wage discrimination, 13, 20, 37

Wage garnishment, 13

Waiver of right to sue employer, 8

Want ads, 17

Welfare assistance, 94, 116–17, 133–36, 408, 540

Western blot test, 387, 389, 391

Whistle-blower statutes, 13

WIC program, 408

Wife battering. *See* Domestic violence

Wills: changes to, 478; executor, 476, 505; funeral instruction, 495; information needed to write will, 476; locating, after death of loved one, 505; need for attorney in writing, 477; probate, 478–79; reasons for, 475; review of, at end of life, 476; safe place for, 477–78; self-proving wills, 477; valid will as typed, signed, and witnessed, 477

Withholding, for unemployment benefits, 10

Women's shelters: accommodations, 179–80; children at, 178; crisis intervention, 62, 319; documents to bring to, 182; filing criminal complaint

against abuser, 168; finding, 181–82; items to bring to, 182; lesbians and bisexuals at, 181; local laws and policies, 164–65; older women at, 180–81, 467; order of protection, 168, 174; safety precautions, 182–83; services, 52, 62, 138, 162, 179, 319; and women with disabilities, 180–81, 560

Work crises: age discrimination, 30–32; and disability insurance, 7; discrimination against adults with disabilities, 32–35, 288–90; discrimination based on citizenship or national origin, 30; discrimination related to sexual orientation, 35–36; early retirement incentives, 8, 31–32; and eviction from home, 11; federal discrimination laws, 18–21; finding information on, 521–26, 614–15; finding new job, 14–15, 16–18, 42; firings and layoffs, 4–18; and harassment by creditors, 11; and health insurance, 5–6; illegal firing, 12–15, 38; legal action for workplace discrimination, 37–43; legal advice, 4, 7, 10; organizations, 521–26; pensions, 7; pregnancy discrimination, 26–28; racial harassment, 29–30; reading materials, 614–15; severance pay, 4–7; sexual harassment, 21–26, 615; unemployment compensation, 8–10; waiver of right to sue employer, 8

Workers' compensation, 275, 278, 298–300

Wrongful firing, 12–15

Xanax, 354

YWCA, 18, 61, 88, 96, 600